Wings Over the Fleet
British Naval Aircraft Since 1945

Wings Over the Fleet

British Naval Aircraft Since 1945

James Jackson

First published 2025 by Crécy Publishing Ltd

© James Jackson 2025

ISBN 978 180035 3343

All rights reserved. No part of this book may be reproduced or transmitted in any form or by any means, electronic or mechanical, including photocopying, recording, scanning or by any information storage without permission from the Publisher in writing. All enquiries should be directed to the Publisher.

A CIP record for this book is available from the British Library

Publisher's Note: Every effort has been made to identify and correctly attribute photographic credits. Any error that may have occurred is entirely unintentional.

Printed in Turkey by Pelikan

Crécy Publishing Limited
1a Ringway Trading Estate
Shadowmoss Road
Manchester M22 5LH

www.crecy.co.uk

FRONT COVER UPPER Vickers-Supermarine Scimitar F.1 XD236 during its time with the Fleet Requirements Unit during 1966-68. Designed as a day fighter, the Scimitar successfully filled the role of a fighter-bomber and became the Fleet Air Arm's first operational aircraft capable of carrying nuclear weapons. *Tony Buttler Collection*

FRONT COVER LOWER The British Aircraft Corporation EAG.8469 design study of 1971 was a navalised version of a developed Super-STOL SEPECAT Jaguar fitted with radar, two Rolls-Royce XJ.99 lift engines and two Turbo-Union/Rolls-Royce RB.199-42R turbojets fitted with thrust-diverting cascades. *Luca Landino*

REAR COVER UPPER A Vickers-Supermarine Scimitar F.1 proudly proclaims its operator under its wings. Two AGM-12 Bullpup air-to-surface missiles are mounted on the outer hardpoints. *Tony Buttler Collection*

REAR COVER MIDDLE LEFT McDonnell Douglas F-4K Phantom FG.1 XV567 of 892 Naval Air Squadron at full thrust about to be launched from HMS Eagle's during flight trials in 1969. *Gerald H. Balzer via Tony Buttler*

REAR COVER MIDDLE RIGHT To celebrate 25 years of Sea Harrier operations, in July 2004 Sea Harrier FA.2 ZH809 of 899 Naval Air Squadron received a gloss blue finish reminiscent of the original pre-Falklands conflict FRS.1 colour scheme. *Terry Panopalis Collection*

REAR COVER LOWER Blackburn Buccaneer S.2 XV357 of 809 Naval Air Squadron aboard HMS Ark Royal during the early 1970s along with an array of weaponry: two practice bomb carriers, an AIM-9 Sidewinder air-to-air missile, an AGM-12 Bullpup air-to-surface missile and a SNEB rocket launcher pod. *Terry Panopalis Collection*

FRONT FLAP A mixed formation of five de Havilland Sea Vixen FAW.1 all-weather fighters and four Vicker-Supermarine Scimitar F.1 fighter-bombers during an aerial display in the early 1960s. *Blue Envoy Collection*

HALF-TITLE PAGE A Westland Sea King HAS.1 patrolling over the commando carrier HMS *Bulwark* in the 1970s. On *Bulwark*'s flight deck can be seen Westland Wessex HU.5 transport helicopters. *Blue Envoy Collection*

TITLE PAGE TOP Leonardo AW159 Wildcat HMA.2 ZZ518, 'Miss Aisle' of 815 Naval Air Squadron conducting the first Martlet missile launch in the Bay of Bengal on 16 October 2021. *MOD via Terry Panopalis*

TITLE PAGE BOTTOM The BAe Sea Harrier FRS.1 maintained the Royal Navy's fixed-wing aircraft capability for over 20 years. This 'Shar' is XZ454 of 800 Naval Air Squadron. *Terry Panopalis*

Contents

Acknowledgements 6
Introduction 8

1 Transition to the Jet Age 12
2 Rubber Decks and Angled Decks 36
3 Strike fighter 51
4 Defending the Fleet 82
5 Buccaneer – Not just a weapon 110
6 Missile generation 142
7 Anti-submarine warfare 158
8 Anti-submarine helicopters 179
9 Airborne Early Warning 214
10 CVA generation 239
11 Fly vertical 271
12 New generation helicopters 297
13 Assault from the air 324
14 Carrier Strike Group 344

Appendix One Royal Navy Aircraft Carriers & Helicopter Ships 370
Appendix Two Production Lists 383
Appendix Three Requirements & Specifications 388
Glossary 393
Bibliography and Sources 394
Index 395

Acknowledgements

The creation of a book relies on the work and support of many people beyond that of the author. The research has relied on primary sources to a large extent. Thanks must go to the staff of The National Archives at Kew, London. The National Archives is a treasure trove of official information and a fantastic resource. I would like to give special thanks to Tony Buttler for all his kind assistance in the supply of information and images for this book, including some hitherto unpublished materials and for access to the late Philip Butler's photographic archive. I would also like to give special thanks to Chris Gibson for his invaluable information and our discussions on a variety of technical topics. He was also very generous in the supply of images and line drawings. Thanks are also due to Jeremy Graham at the Leonardo archives at Yeovil, who is always a pleasure to work with. Bruce Sellers kindly gave permission to use some material available from his father's collection, who worked at Bristol's helicopter department at Weston-super-Mare. Thanks must go to Chris Budgen for all his assistance.

As ever with a book this broad, support from subject experts has been vital for fact checking and material. It has been a pleasure to work with Les Whitehouse again, this time on the topic of vertical lift fan jets on which Boulton Paul was working during the late 1950s. Prof. Michael Pryce and Steve Richardson both provided very useful clarifications on ASTOVL aircraft. I also wish to thank Dave Forster for his avionics knowledge. Thanks also goes to Peter Marland for his valuable knowledge and insight regarding naval combat control systems. The late Chris Farara will be greatly missed. I would like to give a special mention for the Secret Projects Forum (*www.secretprojects.co.uk*) run by Paul Martell-Mead, which is an invaluable resource on an eclectic mix of aviation and defence projects and which is a productive meeting place for aviation researchers from around the world. Paul's strong interest in the Saro P.177 led to us to pooling our research, including some interesting material from the National of Archives of Australia. Paul was also very generous in giving me permission to use the late Barrie Hygate's redrawn plans of the Hawker P.1121 naval development.

The book would be incomplete without images. Luciano Alviani deserves special mention for his excellent commissioned paintings of several of the drawing board projects described in this book – he has brought them to life magnificently (the eagled-eyed reader will spot one or two naval projects in the backgrounds). Luca Landino's wonderful 3D artworks are no less impressive. Special thanks goes to Terry Panopalis for providing so many interesting and previously unseen images from his seemingly inexhaustible archive. Jens Baganz and Joe Cherrie also deserve mention for their contributions.

I would like to thank my family, friends and work colleagues for all their support and encouragement throughout this project.

I must also thank those involved in the production of the book. It has been a pleasure to work with Jeremy Pratt, Jordan Bradley and Alistair Plumb at Crécy Publishing in bringing *Wings Over the Fleet* to life.

James Jackson
Morecambe, 2025

LEFT A Westland Sea King HAS.1 anti-submarine helicopter pulls its Type 195 dipping sonar transducer out of the water before moving to another location to triangulate a bearing on a submerged sonar contact. *Leonardo UK via Terry Panopalis Collection*

RIGHT 'Simon's Sircus' of 892 Naval Air Squadron in their Sea Vixens lead the Buccaneers of the 'Phoenix 5' of 809 NAS during the 1968 Farnborough Show. *Terry Panopalis Collection*

WINGS OVER THE FLEET

Introduction

The Royal Navy began its association with aviation as far back as 1908, when Captain Reginald Bacon submitted a proposal to build a rigid airship based on the German Zeppelin design for aerial reconnaissance. Although the resulting His Majesty's Airship No. 1 was destroyed by an errant gust of wind before the airship could be fully withdrawn from its hangar, the RN enthusiastically adopted both lighter-than-air and heavier-than-air aviation.

The Second World War saw naval aviation come of age and the Naval Air Branch – commonly referred to as the Fleet Air Arm (FAA) – was involved in every area of maritime combat operations. From 1941 the RN had the second-largest fleet of aircraft carriers in the world and maintained this status until the late-1970s. The end of the war came just as the aircraft development and carrier construction programmes were getting into their stride; work was then slowed or, even, halted. The onset of the Cold War and the rise of the threat from the Soviet Union – especially following the outbreak of the Korean War in June 1950 – led to increased funding for naval aviation and until the 1990s the focus was on countering the expanding Soviet Navy.

The RN has been involved in many of Britain's post-war trouble spots and wars: performing strike operations during the Korean War and the Suez Crisis; supporting anti-insurgency actions in Arabia and East Africa; deploying Royal Marines via helicopter during the 'Confrontation' with Indonesia over the incorporation of North Borneo into Malaysia; enforcing the oil blockade against the unilaterally independent Southern Rhodesia; a string of operations in the Arabian Gulf over a period of sixty years; the Falklands/Malvinas Conflict of 1982; and supporting peacekeeping operations in the aftermath of the breakup of Yugoslavia during the 1990s. This book does not offer in-depth narratives of operational campaigns or unit histories which have been amply covered in other works, but rather focuses on the naval aircraft that have been used since 1945; how and why they were selected for production; and the numerous unbuilt projects that never left the drawing board. The important technical developments in missiles and carrier equipment are also examined.

The Admiralty's aviation staff officers – the Naval Air Warfare Division between 1951 and 1962, becoming the Naval Air Division in 1963/64, then the Directorate of Naval Air Warfare – had plenty of problems to solve. The pressures of defence spending and national economics would affect how many carriers they could afford to build and operate and what types of aircraft could equip them. Aircraft carriers had consigned the battleship to history but they were just as expensive to build, operate and man.

Technological advances in jet propulsion offered new possibilities. The FAA was an early adopter of jet technology, Lieutenant Commander Eric 'Winkle' Brown conducting the world's first jet-powered aircraft landing and take-off on HMS Ocean on 3

A typically busy scene on the flight deck of HMS *Victorious* circa early 1959. The parked aircraft include Supermarine Scimitar F.1 day fighters of 803 Naval Air Squadron, de Havilland Sea Venom FAW.21 all-weather fighters of 893 NAS and Douglas Skyraider AEW.1 airborne early warning aircraft of 849 NAS 'B' Flight. *Tony Buttler Collection*

December 1945 in a de Havilland Sea Vampire. The early jet fighters – the Supermarine Attacker and Hawker Sea Hawk – were day fighters, which soon gained a ground attack fighter-bomber role. Jet power also brought practical problems that needed to be overcome. The solutions would be innovations such as the steam catapult, the angled landing deck and the mirror landing sight which would be widely adopted by other navies across the world, including the United States. Other innovations like the inflatable rubber flexible deck for aircraft without wheeled undercarriages were extensively tested but bypassed by less complicated developments.

The use of offensive airpower from carriers was a cornerstone of the Admiralty's doctrine. Jet fighters soon became more than fighter bombers, the Supermarine Scimitar which entered service in 1957 gained tactical nuclear strike role. Numerous other strike fighter concepts existed on the drawing boards of Britain's aviation companies. The requirement for a nuclear-armed, carrier-based strike aircraft, capable of low-altitude penetration of enemy air defences, resulted in the Blackburn Buccaneer, which was among the most sophisticated tactical strike aircraft in the world on its introduction to service in 1962. The Buccaneer's operational service was to span over twenty years; ironically, half of that time would be with the RAF as the carrier force was drawn down during the late 1960s and early 1970s.

The advent of airborne interception radar enabled all-weather fighter operations. Following a convoluted development phase over many cycles of design and cancellation, the de Havilland DH.110 Sea Vixen FAW.1 entered service in 1959, becoming the FAA's first fighter with air-to-air guided missiles as its primary armament.

Development of the supersonic second generation, the Saro P.177N interceptor, Hawker Siddeley P.1154 V/STOL fighter and a new multi-role interceptor/strike aircraft to Operational Requirements OR.346 and OR.356 was a story of failure. These technically ambitious programmes were cancelled for a variety of economic and technical reasons. The RN decided to opt for improved variants of the Sea Vixen and Buccaneer alongside McDonnell F-4 Phantom II fighters purchased from the USA. No bespoke fixed-wing aircraft would ever be ordered again for the FAA.

The Defence Review of February 1966 controversially cancelled the CVA-01 aircraft carrier programme and the resulting retirement of the carrier fleet by the late 1970s was seen as the death of naval fixed-wing aviation. However, the Escort Cruiser programme to provide a dedicated anti-submarine warfare (ASW) helicopter carrier emerged as the *Invincible*-class in the late 1970s which formed the carrier fleet until 2014. The three ships were paired with the innovative Hawker Siddeley Harrier V/STOL fighter, which following modification as the Sea Harrier FRS.1, entered service in 1980 and famously made its combat debut two years later over the Falklands. The upgraded Sea Harrier FA.2 was regarded as one of the most capable fighters in the world before its early retirement in 2006. From 2000, the two Sea Harrier units – 800 and 801 Naval Air Squadrons (NAS) – became part of the Joint Force Harrier. Following the Sea Harrier's retirement, they switched to Harrier GR.9 until the 2010 Strategic Defence and Security Review prematurely retired the Harriers, leaving the RN without any fixed-wing aviation capability for the first time since 1915.

Following a relatively brief continuation with carrier-based ASW aircraft like the Fairey Gannet

McDonnell Douglas Phantom FG.1 XV592 of 892 NAS is hurled airborne from the waist steam catapult aboard HMS *Ark Royal* in October 1970. In the background is a Westland Wessex HAS.1 plane guard hovering in case of an accident and ditching. *Terry Panopalis Collection*

WINGS OVER THE FLEET

The Cold War at sea was more visceral than the static lines of the barbed wire and minefields running from along the East German and Czechoslovakian borders. A Westland Lynx HAS.2 equipped with Helitele imaging equipment gets a close look at the Soviet Project 1134A Berkut-A (NATO reporting name *Kresta II*) class cruiser *Admiral Nakhimov* in 1984. The Kresta-IIs were primarily anti-submarine ships, the large box launcher containing four Metel (SS-N-14 *Silex*) missiles, which were similar to the RN's Ikara. Note that one of the 30mm cannon mounts appears to be trained on the Lynx. *Crown Copyright*

and the aborted Short Seamew, the ASW task passed to more effective helicopters. The Westland Whirlwind, Wessex and Sea King carried dipping sonars to detect submerged submarines. These were joined by Westland Wasp HAS.1 helicopters aboard anti-submarine frigates as part of the Manned Torpedo-Carrying Helicopter (MATCH) weapons system. During the 1970s the Westland Lynx was developed to replace the Wasp and was equipped with Ferranti Seaspray radar and Sea Skua air-to-surface missiles to combat Soviet small fast attack craft. The Sea Skua and Lynx combination achieved an enviable combat record with seven hits out of eight launches during the Falklands/Malvinas Conflict and sinking ten Iraqi vessels and damaging three more during Operation Granby in 1990. The Sea King Replacement occupied most of the 1970s and 1980s, Westland developing the WG.34 which in 1979 became a collaborative venture with Italy that resulted in the EH101 Merlin, entering service in 1997, following a lengthy development. The Lynx has also been replaced; it was developed into the Leonardo AW159 Wildcat, which offers an equally potent anti-ship strike capability.

Helicopters also transformed the RN's amphibious warfare capabilities, being able to transport troops ashore rapidly with greater operational flexibility. Proven in many counter-insurgency operations and during the Falklands/Malvinas Conflict, the commando carriers saw extensive use. After some delay they were replaced by a dedicated ship in the late 1990s – HMS *Ocean* – and although the FAA still operates the Merlin in the Commando role, the RN currently lacks a dedicated helicopter amphibious warfare ship.

The Navy has also operated Airborne Early Warning (AEW) aircraft equipped with long-range search radars. Douglas Skyraiders were provided under US defence aid until a variant of the Gannet could be developed. The Gannet AEW.3 served until 1978 – several interesting replacements during the 1960s remaining on the drawing board. The subsequent

INTRODUCTION

reliance during the 1970s on RAF AEW assets seemed logical given the focus on Northern Atlantic and European waters to meet NATO defence tasks. The warship losses to Argentine aerial attacks during the Falklands Conflict exposed this weakness and the Sea King was pressed into the role, equipped with the Thorn EMI Searchwater radar. Upgraded several times over the following years, the replacement was a converted Merlin – the Crowsnest programme aiming for full operational capability by 2025. Looking into the future it is likely that unmanned aerial vehicles will play an increasing role as force multipliers as sensor and logistics platforms.

Planning for replacing the Sea Harrier and the *Invincible*-class occupied most of the 1980s and 1990s. The Advanced Short Take-Off Vertical Landing (ASTOVL) fighter design studies led to collaboration with the USA which resulted in the UK becoming a Tier 1 partner in the Joint Strike Fighter. The Lockheed Martin F-35B Lightnings are operated as a joint RAF/FAA force, with No. 617 Squadron 'The Dambusters' and 809 NAS being the two frontline squadrons. The need for a 'floating airbase' able to project military power in an increasingly unstable post-Cold War world led to the construction of the two *Queen Elizabeth*-class carriers which will operate well into the 2060s, continuing the RN's enduring legacy of aviation operations.

Note on units

By the 1970s the British aviation industry had adopted metric measurements but for consistency imperial units will be given alongside metric conversions, these are rounded for figures over 1,000. Statute miles were often used in range calculations until the 1960s and where these are quoted from original documents a conversion is given to nautical miles (nm) and kilometres (km) for consistency. Speeds are given in knots (kt), weights in pounds (lb) and kilograms (kg). Where possible aircraft weights quoted in the main text will be the all-up weight (AUW) which includes the weight of the aircraft's structure, engines, fuel, oil, crew and payload.

Note on designations

Until very recently all aircraft serving with the British armed forces were given an official designation outlining their role and a Mark number denoting any differences between variants. For example naval fighter-bombers were given an 'FB' prefix, e.g. as FB.Mk.2. In the main text the designations are presented in a shortened form, e.g. FB.2. Royal Navy vessels are prefixed His/Her Majesty's Ship, this is abbreviated to HMS. Unarmed Royal Fleet Auxiliary support vessels are prefixed RFA. The Royal Navy has a tradition of naming its shore establishments ('Stone Frigates') as ships, I have not included these for Naval Air Stations and refer only to the geographical placename for reasons of brevity.

A Lockheed Martin F-35B Lightning of No. 617 'Dambusters' Squadron aboard HMS *Queen Elizabeth* with the lift fan door open. *MOD/Open Government Licence*

1 Transition to the Jet Age

The Royal Navy entered the jet age on 3 December 1945 when the Chief Naval Test Pilot at the Royal Aircraft Establishment (RAE), Lieutenant Commander (Lt Cdr) Eric 'Winkle' Brown landed a de Havilland Sea Vampire F.1 aboard the *Colossus*-class light fleet carrier HMS *Ocean*. In fact, the Admiralty had begun to closely examine the Royal Air Force's new jet powered aircraft – the Gloster Meteor and the Vampire – in early 1944. A year earlier, Fairey Aviation had submitted a dual piston and turbojet-powered design (with a Rolls-Royce Merlin in the nose and a Whittle turbojet in the rear fuselage) to meet Specification N.7/43 for a fleet interceptor that could equal the performance of land-based fighters. The Vampire was selected as the first jet-powered aircraft for carrier deck trials. Within a year, both Hawker and Supermarine were penning jet-powered developments, picking up where the Fury/Sea Fury and Spiteful/Seafang left off. These would materialise as the Sea Hawk and Attacker.

> "Whilst we realise that it is part of Boscombe's job to criticise, we feel that they have gone out of their way in this case – even to the extent of making incorrect statements."
>
> JOE SMITH, CHIEF DESIGNER AT VICKERS-ARMSTRONGS (SUPERMARINE), AUGUST 1948

Turbojet aircraft required new techniques for take-off and landing; they lacked the propeller slipstream blowing over the control surfaces and usually had tricycle undercarriages. Jets took longer to respond to throttle movements; had higher landing speeds and greater fuel consumption. Operating limits were critical aboard an aircraft carrier, from the speed the ship had to obtain to achieve the required wind speed over the deck for aircraft take-offs; better arrester gear to handle faster and heavier aircraft; and even more mundane items such as stowage of paraffin and later AVTAG and AVCAT (Aviation Carrier Turbine) jet fuels. Carrier design would have to alter to accommodate the new breed of aircraft. Research led to innovations such as the steam catapult, angled landing deck and mirror landing sights. There was also a concerted effort to develop a flexible rubber-decked ship that could operate jets lacking a wheeled undercarriage so that the aircraft could carry more fuel. Remarkably, within a decade all these items were in place.

The transition from props to jets. de Havilland Sea Vampire F.20 VV150 of 702 Naval Air Squadron is being manhandled off the forward lift aboard the light fleet carrier HMS *Theseus* on 29 June 1950 while sailing in the English Channel. Also aboard *Theseus* for training exercises were 30 officers and 70 ratings of 1832 Royal Naval Reserve Squadron with 20 Supermarine Seafire F.XVs, some of which can be seen parked forward. *Tony Buttler Collection*

Floating airfields

The technical performance and parameters of naval aircraft have an impact on the ships they can operate from, and *vice versa*. (For additional technical data on the carriers, please see Appendix 1.) Larger and heavier aircraft required larger carriers and this growth had been apparent during the Second World War. All carriers at this time had axial flight decks aligned fore and aft along the ship's centreline with one or two hydraulic accelerators/catapults forward and wire arrester gear aft. In 1946 most British carriers had a BH.III hydraulic accelerator, capable of launching a 16,000lb (7,255kg) aircraft at 66kt, being upgraded to 20,000lb (9,070kg) at 56kt by 1949.

In 1946 the RN had six *Illustrious* and *Implacable*-class ships, these were fleet carriers designed in the late 1930s which featured an armoured flight deck and enclosed hangar, the later ships having a small additional lower hangar to increase aircraft capacity. These ships had a flight deck 740 to 750ft (225.5–228.6m) long and 80ft (24.3m) wide but all had seen extensive wartime service, suffering serious combat damage in some cases. Reconstructions were planned for several of these ships, but most were later dropped for financial and materiel reasons. HMS *Illustrious* was assigned as trials carrier for the aircraft testing programme.

The wartime Building Programmes included ten *Colossus*, six *Majestic* and eight *Centaur*-class light fleet carriers along with three *Eagle* and four *Malta*-class fleet carriers. The *Colossus*-class vessels were designed to operate aircraft weighing 15,000lb (6,800kg); the *Majestics* of the 1942 Building Programme were upgraded to handle 20,000lb (9,070kg) aircraft. The flight deck was 680ft (207.2m) long and 80ft (24.3m) wide. Nine of the *Colossus* class were completed by 1947 (two as aircraft maintenance tenders), but several were loaned to Commonwealth nations, plus one to France. The RN converted two as *ad hoc* commando carriers for helicopter amphibious assault but all of them were sold by the mid-1950s as they were unsuited to jet operations, None of the *Majestics* was completed for the RN, being destined for Australia, Canada and India instead during 1947–61.

The *Centaur* class was designed in 1943 to operate 30,000lb (13,605kg) aircraft with a 17ft 6in (5.33m) high hangar to accommodate the latest aircraft. They had armoured spaces and improved compartmentalisation for torpedo defence. The flight deck was 710ft (216.4m) long and 100ft (30.4m) wide. Eight ships were planned but only four were completed during the 1950s: *Centaur* to the original design but with the new BH.V hydraulic catapults rated at 20,000lb (9,070kg) at 56kt; *Bulwark* and *Albion* with interim angled decks (123ft (37.5m) wide) and upgraded BH.V catapults capable of launching a 30,000lb (13,605kg) aircraft at 75kt; and *Hermes* commissioned in November 1959 with a full angled deck (144ft [43.9m] width) and steam catapults.

The *Ark Royal*-class fleet carriers were designed from 1942, originally as successors to the *Implacable* class, but evolving with double-decker hangars 17ft 6in (5.33m) high, able to stow up to 80 aircraft, four abreast. The ships would have a flight deck 775ft (236.2m) long and 105ft (32m) wide. With the end of the war, the building programme was reshuffled: *Eagle* was scrapped, her name being reassigned to the incomplete *Audacious* which was

The harbour at Gibraltar in 1955 holds an example of each of the three main early postwar RN carrier classes: At top left HMS *Ocean* of the Colossus-class, at top right HMS *Ark Royal* and at the bottom HMS *Albion* of the Centaur-class. In the background is an Essex-class carrier of the US Navy. *Terry Panopalis Collection*

HMS *Implacable* is drawing the crowds at Klampenborg in Denmark in 1950. On the flight deck are Hawker Sea Furies and de Havilland Sea Hornets. With her propeller-driven air wing *Implacable* looks little different from how she did during the Second World War. At this time she was a training carrier. *Terry Panopalis Collection*

commissioned in October 1951. *Ark Royal* was not completed until early 1955 with an angled deck (800 × 112ft ft [243.8 × 34.1m]) and BS.4 steam catapults. The succeeding *Malta* class was to be a larger development with a flight deck 900ft (274.3m) long, but all four ships were cancelled by January 1946 before any had been laid down. As later events unfolded, no new aircraft carrier would be built from the keel up until HMS *Invincible* was laid down in July 1973.

The introduction of jet engines also required changes of fuel. Early turbojets were thirsty so more

The Batsman looks on as DH Sea Vampire F.20 VV144 is about to catch the arrester wire aboard HMS *Implacable* on 8 September 1949. The FAA had to learn how to safely operate the heavier and faster jet aircraft aboard the confined deck space that the carriers provided. *Tony Buttler Collection*

The pilot of DH Sea Vampire F.20 VV144 goes around to attempt another landing on *Implacable*. The Sea Vampire was essentially identical to its land-based brethren apart from the modifications to the undercarriage, flaps and the provision of catapult attachments and arrester hook. *Tony Buttler Collection*

fuel was required, but the protected tanks low in the ship's hull were of finite capacity. The first jet engines ran on paraffin and it seemed likely that this less volatile fuel could be stowed as part of the ship's main oil fuel bunkerage in the double-bottom keel tanks. In 1950 the US armed forces standardised on petrol, NATO members soon followed suit, including the UK. Paraffin was replaced by AVTAG, a wide-cut petrol (called AVGAS in the USA). The other solution was to use paraffin at sea and AVTAG ashore, but this would require engine adjustments each time the aircraft embarked and disembarked. Instead, the RN followed the US Navy (USN) in mixing paraffin and AVTAG to create a high-flashpoint fuel called AVCAT. This change of fuels would force the retirement of piston-engined aircraft, which could not use jet fuels.

Enter the Jet: Vampire & Meteor

In early 1944 the RAE's Aerodynamics Flight ('A' Squadron) at Farnborough was asked by the Admiralty to recommend a suitable jet-powered fighter for deck trials. The choice was between the Meteor F.1 and the Vampire F.1. Although the Vampire's twin-boom rear fuselage was potentially a complication for arrested deck landings, the Flight considered it to be the more suitable aircraft.

The second Vampire prototype, serial LZ551/G (the 'G' suffix denoting a top secret aircraft that required a guard when parked out on an airfield), was modified during the summer of 1945 with extended chord-and-span flaps, to provide 40% more area, and enlarged dive brakes, which lowered the stalling speed and eliminated the 'float' from the ground effect caused by the low wing and short undercarriage. Flying in its navalised form for the first time on 23 August 1945, LZ551/G was delivered to Farnborough a couple of weeks later and Lt Cdr 'Winkle' Brown was satisfied that the handling was satisfactory for deck landings.

Following the fitting of a DH-designed V-frame arrester hook, Brown began arrester gear trials on the dummy carrier deck runway at Farnborough, the wing root frame attachments unfortunately breaking away. Returned for repairs, the opportunity was taken to install a higher thrust 3,300lbf (14.6kN) DH Goblin 2 engine and a teardrop canopy, as well as relocating the pitot tube to the port wing to avoid position errors at high angles of attack.

Brown began Airfield Dummy Deck Landings (ADDLs) at Royal Naval Air Station (RNAS) Ford on 26 November. Following the success of these, Brown touched down on *Ocean* on 3 December. Brown took off from the ship and made another two successful landings, but on the fourth, the port wing dipped and the flaps struck the deck. The flaps were then trimmed by 4ft² (0.37m²) to increase the deck clearance. Further periods of trials were undertaken aboard *Ocean's* sistership *Triumph* at the end of June 1946 (the seven-month hiatus was due to indecision at the Ministry of Supply (MoS) whether to proceed using the Vampire) by the RAE's Naval Test Squadron ('C' Squadron). Landing trials then took place aboard *Illustrious* in November by 778 Naval Air Squadron (NAS), the Service Trials and Carrier Trials Unit based at Ford, LZ551/G being damaged in the process.

TRANSITION TO THE JET AGE

Vampire F.1 TG314 was fitted with an arrester hook and interconnected throttle and flap for variable lift control trials to lower the landing approach speed for evaluation by 'A' Squadron in July 1946 and then trialled an interconnected throttle and air brake in March 1947. These tests continued into late 1950. TG326 was converted with larger flaps – whose operation was interconnected with the throttle – dive brakes and arrester hook for the RAE in May 1946, being assigned to flexible landing trials in January 1948.

The initial trials convinced the Admiralty that the Vampire was not suitable as a frontline fighter due to its slow throttle response and insufficient fuel capacity, but it was ideal as a training platform and acquisition of navalised aircraft went ahead. Specification 45/46/P was issued on 14 January 1947 to meet Operational Requirement OR.240. Two Vampire F.3 fighters were to be converted as the Sea Vampire F.20 and F.21 prototypes to full naval standards. VF315 was converted as the F.20, flying on 6 October 1947 and VG701 became the F.21 for flexible deck experiments. A production order was placed on 21 March 1947 for 30 Sea Vampire F.20 – reduced to 18 in January 1948 – converted from Vampire FB.5 fighter-bombers. These aircraft were covered by Specification 46/46/P. The aircraft were taken from the English Electric production line at Preston and modified at DH's Hatfield factory. Changes to the airframe included the V-frame arrester hook, longer-stroke undercarriage legs to absorb a descent of 16ft/min (4.8m/min), enlarged air brakes (36% more area) and longer chord flaps (31% larger) with an additional flap section joining the inboard and outboard sections.

Prototype VF315 arrived at Boscombe Down for catapult and arrester trials in January 1948, then joining a highly successful tour of Canada and the USA aboard the Canadian carrier HMCS *Magnificent* along with three DH Sea Hornets of 806 NAS. The first production aircraft, VV136, began its trials programme at the Aeroplane and Armament Experimental Establishment (A&AEE) in September 1948. The A&AEE noted that the enlarged air brakes were highly effective. The RAE's 'C' Squadron was also busy with trials, operating VV137 and VV138 aboard *Illustrious* in November, also involving pilots from 703 NAS, the Naval Air Warfare Development Unit. The programme totalled around 60 landings. The RAE reported that the Sea Vampire had poor take-off performance due to insufficient engine thrust. Even so, visibility on landing was excellent and the landing performance was very good.

In April 1949 702 NAS was reformed at RNAS Culdrose as the Naval Jet Evaluation and Training Unit under the command of Lt ABB Clark with six Sea Vampires (VV144-148 and VV150) and two Meteor T.7 two-seat trainers. The unit operated aboard *Implacable* between 21 September and 11 November. The axial deck layout and lack of a crash barrier caused some difficulties. A deployment was made aboard *Theseus* between 2 May and 30 June 1950. The ship was too slow to obtain enough wind speed over the deck for unassisted take-offs, the BH.III catapult having to be used each time. During this deployment, Lts Clark and Peter Perrett achieved another notable first on 19 June – the first nighttime landing aboard a carrier. No major problems were encountered, Clark and Perrett completing five take-offs and landings between them.

702 NAS evolved into an operational conversion unit with eight Sea Vampire F.20s and four Meteor T.7s. Lt Perrett revised the training programme and wrote a training syllabus covering 120 flying hours of familiarisation flights, battle flying and formation drills, fighter tactics, carrier descents, ADDLs, deck qualification, navigation and cross-country flying. By 1952 the unit's students were going on to form the initial cadre of Supermarine Attacker pilots.

787 NAS at RAF West Raynham was the Naval Air Fighting Development Unit and received two Vampire F.1 aircraft (VF268 and VF269), carrying out an evaluation against the Sea Fury, Sea Hornet and Supermarine Seafire in February 1949. It later received Sea Vampire F.20s and 10 Vampire FB.5s from the RAF during 1949-51 for training. Vampire F.1 TG285 was transferred to the Fleet Air Arm (FAA) in December 1947 for crash barrier trials.

Even though the Vampire was selected as the RN's initial jet fighter for trials work, the Meteor was also trialled. The first Meteor prototype, DG202/G, was craned aboard the escort carrier HMS *Pretoria Castle* for static deck handling trials in the Firth of Clyde during 11–26 August 1945. Gloster converted two Meteor F.3 airframes, fitting them with the A-frame arrester hook from the Sea Hornet, uprated Rolls-Royce Derwent V turbojets, some fuselage and

A large flame shoots out the back of Vampire F.20 VV137 as the Goblin fires up aboard HMS *Illustrious*. Beneath the canopy is the title 'Carrier Trials Unit'. VV137 was the second F.20 completed. *Terry Panopalis Collection*

The first Supermarine Type 392 Attacker prototype TS409, lacked folding wings or any naval features except for catapulting spools. It also differed in having split trailing edge flaps. Mainly used for handling flight tests, TS409 also tested the ventral drop tank in 1948. *Author's Collection*

undercarriage strengthening and an improved brake system. EE337 arrived at Farnborough for deck trials on 10 February 1948 and made the first British landing of a twin-jet aircraft aboard *Implacable* on 8 June 1948 with Lt Cdr Brown at the controls. EE387 followed on 15 June, before performing deck trials aboard *Illustrious* during late October and high-speed approach trials on *Glory* a year later. Catapult, arrester gear and Rocket Assisted Take-Off Gear (RATOG) trials were conducted with both aircraft until 1950. Lt Cdr DG Parker made 36 touch-and-go landings with EE387 aboard *Triumph* during 12–13 February 1951, following that feat with 13 landings on *Illustrious* on 3 March 1952. Retired the following day, EE387 was recalled for further trials aboard *Illustrious* the following July.

Attacker

In July 1944, Supermarine's Chief Designer Joe Smith and his team drew up the Type 392, marrying the laminar-flow wings of the ultimate development of the Spitfire – the Spiteful – to a new fuselage containing a 4,200lbf (18.7kN) Rolls-Royce B.41 centrifugal-flow turbojet (later to be named Nene) – at that time the most powerful turbojet in the world. The estimated maximum speed was 490kt with a sea level rate of climb of 6,000ft/min (1,830m/min). The Air Staff and the RAE were enthusiastic and Supermarine proposed a navalised 'Jet Seafang'. At the Mock-Up Conference on 23 November, the Central Fighter Establishment called for a tricycle undercarriage and for the four 20mm Hispano Mk.V cannon to be moved to the nose, but neither change was made.

Specification E.10/44 was issued on 6 February 1945 to cover development and three prototypes (TS409, TS413 and TS416) and 24 pre-production aircraft were ordered in July; six for the RAF and 18 navalised aircraft. Specification E.1/45 was issued on 17 July to meet OR.195 for the navalised variant with a thrust spoiler to enable a take-off run within 880ft (268m) with a 27kt wind over the deck (interestingly Specification N.5/45 for the Seafang was issued on 26 February, for comparison its take-off run requirement was 430ft [131m]). The decision to convert 18 Sea Vampire F.20s resulted in the cancellation of the 18 'Jet Seafangs' in February 1946.

The prototype, the Type 392 TS409, had no wing folding, navalised undercarriage or provision for RATOG, but it did receive provision for catapulting and differed from the subsequent aircraft in having split flaps. TS409 made its maiden flight at Boscombe Down on 27 July 1946 with Chief Test Pilot Jeffery Quill at the controls. It underwent manufacturer's handling trials and ventral drop tank jettison tests before going to the A&AEE, which conducted level speed, climb performance and fuel consumption tests during 6 February to 11 March 1948. At combat power, a maximum speed of 508kt was recorded at sea level and 456kt at 35,000ft (10,670m) with a sea level rate of climb of 6,350ft/min (1,935m/min).

The second and third prototypes were completed with a V-frame arrester hook, becoming Type 398 'Hooked Jet Spitefuls'. In addition to the arrester hook, TS413 had a long-stroke undercarriage and lift spoilers with plain landing flaps. Supermarine test pilot Lt Cdr Mike Lithgow made the first flight on 17 June 1947. Preliminary deck landing trials took place during September–October, first with ADDLs and then aboard *Illustrious*. These were flown by Mike Lithgow, Lt Cdr Eric Brown and A&AEE pilot Lt Orr. The approach speed was limited to 98kt due to the 60kt limit of the ship's Mk.6 arrester gear. The pilots found the visibility in the approach poorer than expected and the lift spoilers proved to be ineffective. Only three carrier landings and take-offs were made – insufficient to decide at that stage if the Attacker was a practicable deck landing aircraft.

In late 1948 Supermarine proposed fitting jet exhaust deflection to increase the lift coefficient and lower the approach and take-off speeds. A ventral flap would deflect the exhaust stream 77° downwards, the thrust being aligned through the centre-of-gravity (CG) – although the RAE raised concerns about controlling the resulting change of trim. Supermarine was especially interested in applying this to the swept wing Type 510 Swift, along with reheat to counteract any thrust loss. Converting a Type 398 Attacker to Type 519 standard would require a new rear fuselage. Rolls-Royce was interested in the concept and had already tested a balanced spherical valve (which proved to be impractical) and believed that further development could lead to a workable solution. The MoS argued that Supermarine and Rolls-Royce were overloaded with work and that it would take up to three years to complete the project. Rolls-Royce suggested that the National Gas Turbine Establishment should lead the development; they assessed the proposal, but firmly believed that industry should carry out the work. No further work was undertaken.

TRANSITION TO THE JET AGE

The third Type 392 Attacker prototype was TS416. This aircraft differed from other Attackers in having larger intakes and the wing was positioned 13.5in (34cm) farther aft. It was used for RATOG trials at the RAE, the triple rocket booster packs can be seen mounted above and below the port wing root. Maximum weight take-offs required eight boosters. *Tony Buttler Collection*

By early 1948 the early formation and training of embarked jet fighter squadrons was of primary concern to the Admiralty. The Sea Vampire lacked the range to be operationally useful, the Type 598 Attacker had performance comparable with Hawker's N.7/46 Sea Hawk and would be an interim solution, planned to be in service 18–24 months sooner. The Spiteful wings were already fully tooled and many parts had been made. Initial plans were to order 50–75 aircraft for two squadrons, for operation from *Ark Royal* and *Hermes*-class carriers. In May it was agreed to order 60 Attackers for the 1949 Programme. The A&AEE felt that the deck landing trials conducted up to that time were insufficient, the Admiralty agreed but decreed that nothing was to hold up the entry into service. The MoS was advised to commence production without waiting for further trials or evaluation.

At the Mock-Up Conference on 13 August it was noted that the draft Staff Requirements did not call for external stores; Supermarine had already provided basic provision for a pair of 1,000lb (454kg) bombs under the wings or eight 3in (76mm) rocket projectiles (RPs), but the MoS advised the Admiralty to accept the aircraft without bomb racks to avoid the risk of any production delays that might arise following armament clearance trials.

Naval Staff Requirement NR/A.27 for an interceptor and long-range strike support day fighter called for a maximum speed of 465kt at 30,000ft (9,145m), a service ceiling of at least 45,000ft (13,715m) and a 75kt maximum landing speed (assuming a 28kt wind over the deck). Take-offs would use a catapult or RATOG, but a rolling take-off should be within 350ft (106m) (without external stores). Endurance covered a 2hr 30min combat air patrol at 30,000ft or a 400nm (740km) support strike radius of action, plus five minutes of combat and 20 minutes loitering before landing. The requirement to limit fuel loss to 20% capacity from a single hit required a major redesign of the fuel system and so was dropped. An ejection seat, cockpit pressurisation and airbrakes were required features. The carriage of reconnaissance cameras was deleted as there was no space for them.

With the requirements formalised, on 12 August 1948 the Treasury sanctioned £1,132,500 for 63 Attackers plus jigging and tooling for 100–120 aircraft for a peak production rate of eight per month. Deliveries were to be completed by 31 March 1951. The Admiralty wanted to ensure it was in production 18 months sooner than the Hawker P.1040 and advised the MoS to commence production without waiting for further trials evaluation. The Treasury and the MoS expected Vickers-Armstrong (Aircraft) Ltd – Supermarine's parent – to foot the bill for extending South Marston's runway for jet aircraft. On 18 November the designation Attacker F.1 was approved. But production problems soon arose at South Marston and on 23 June 1950 MoS official F Holroyd (AD/RDN) wrote to Joe Smith commenting that, "You will appreciate that you have fallen down rather badly on the programme previously agreed with you for the Attacker." During September 1950, the Naval Staff called for the carriage of external stores due to 'new strategical considerations' – the outbreak of the Korean War three months earlier.

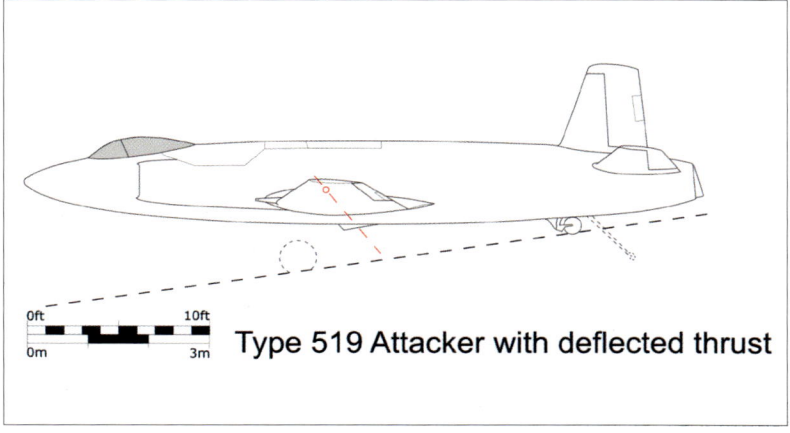

A side view of the proposed Type 519 with the ventral deflected thrust nozzle, the thrust line (shown in red) going through the aircraft's centre of gravity to minimise any change of pitch. *Author*

Supermarine Attacker

	Type 392 Design	Type 392 E.10/44 TS409	Type 398 Attacker F.1 & FB.2	Type 527 Attacker Mk.2
Span	36ft 11in (11.25m)	36ft 11in (11.25m)	36ft 11in (11.25m)	36ft 11in (11.25m)
Length	37ft 2in (11.3m)	37ft 6in (11.43m)	37ft 6in (11.43m)	37ft 6in (11.43m)
Wing area	226ft² (21.02m²)	226ft² (21.02m²)	226ft² (21.02m²)	226ft² (21.02m²)
All-up weight	11,000lb (4,990kg) RAF; 13,080lb (5,932kg) RN	?	11,500lb (5,215kg)	12,975lb (5,885kg) with Avon; 13,025lb (5,910kg) with Tay
Powerplant	1x B.41 Nene, 4,200lbf (18.7kN)	1x Nene, 4,300lbf (19.1kN)	1x Nene Mk.3, 5,100lbf (22.7kN)	1x Avon, 6,500lbf (28.9kN); or 1x Tay, 6,250lbf (27.8kN)
Max speed	512kt at SL; and 540kt at 30,000ft (9,145m) RAF	508kt (940km/h) at SL; 456kt (844km/h) at 35,000ft (10,670m)	512kt (949km/h) at SL; 487kt (902km/h) at 20,000ft (6,095m); 467kt (865km/h) at 30,000ft (9,145m)	520kt (964km/h) at SL with Avon; 519kt (962km/h) at SL with Tay; 479kt (887km/h) at 30,000ft (9,145m) with either engine
Rate of climb	6,100ft/min (1,860m/min) at SL	6,350ft/min (1,935m/min) at SL	6,350ft/min (1,935m/min) at SL	9,250ft/min (2,820m/min) at SL with Avon; 7,900ft/min (2,410m/min) at SL with Tay
Service ceiling	51,000ft (15,545m)	45,000ft (13,715m)	45,000ft (13,715m)	?
Armament	4x 20mm Hispano, 2x 1,000lb (454kg) bombs, 8x 60lb (27kg) RPs	4x 20mm Hispano	4x 20mm Hispano; FB.2, 2x 1,000lb (454kg) bombs, 8x 60lb (27kg) RPs	4x 20mm Hispano; FB.2, 2x 1,000lb (454kg) bombs, 8x 60lb (27kg) RPs

Compatibility with the USN's universal tow bar was added to most British naval aircraft then under development, including the Attacker, for easier cross-decking between each nations' carriers.

The flight testing programme was delayed by an accident to one of the prototypes. TS413 went to the A&AEE at Boscombe Down for a brief handling assessment in June 1948. The assessment was critical of the cockpit layout, ground handling, the airbrakes, the control column forces at low and medium speeds and argued that the limiting Mach number of 0.82 was too low for a fighter. Joe Smith was not happy and the Director of Military Aircraft Research and Development (DMARD) agreed that the A&AEE had been unduly critical and had not appreciated the Attacker was intended to be a stopgap. It was planned to begin catapult trials at the RAE on 29 June 1948 but the aircraft was lost in an accident seven days earlier. During a test flight to assess the stability, climb stalling speed and stick forces per g at 30,000ft with the 270gal (1,227L) ventral drop tank fitted, the A&AEE pilot Lt. Tobias King-Joyce encountered rudder overbalance. The aircraft immediately bunted on jettisoning the ventral tank and King-Joyce's head hit the canopy, breaking his neck.

The prototype, TS409, was drafted into the programme to cover the loss. The planned installation of a DH Ghost engine was cancelled in June 1948 and it was intended to fit the dive brake-equipped wing intended for TS416 to get the programme back on track. In the event, this did not happen. TS409 was used for further handling trials with the ventral drop tank in early 1950. The tank's effect on longitudinal handling and control was very slight, but the elevators were heavy and the A&AEE advised a limiting Mach number of 0.78. The tank was later redesigned to improve ground clearance, reducing its capacity to 250gal (1,136L).

TS416 was of similar standard to TS413 but had larger intakes and the wing was positioned 13.5in (34cm) further aft, so was not entirely representative of the production Attacker. It was used for arrester gear, catapulting and RATOG trials at the RAE before going to the A&AEE for armament trials (Seafang VB895 had done most of this work).

Further deck landing trials took place during September–October 1949 (halted when TS409's tailwheel collapsed) and January–February 1950 with TS416 aboard *Illustrious*. TS409 completed 11 landings and TS416, 22. The Attacker proved satisfactory for normal service operation. Approach speeds were 115–106kt with arrester wire entry speeds up to 66kt; it was warned that excessive tailwheel loads would occur unless a slightly sinking approach was made. The heavy elevators were again criticised; the lift spoilers were unused, but their retention was recommended. TS416 suffered skin wrinkling on the edge of port main wheel well and near the root fillet but no serious damage was incurred.

TS409 tested lighter ailerons in February 1951, which provided a much better rate of roll, as well as a tail fin fillet to overcome rudder locking in a sideslip. This was followed by tests of a modified, flat-sided elevator, which gave lighter control loads – though still heavy for a fighter. Following all these revisions, 30 trial deck landings were made aboard *Illustrious* on 17–18 May. Lateral and directional stability was improved, longitudinal stability was still poor due to the elevator response, however, but was acceptable for service use. These modifications were assessed again on production Attacker F.1 WA535 in April 1952 with comparable results. TS416 received a steerable tailwheel, which markedly improved deck handling.

Handling check trials of the first production aircraft, WA469, took place in August 1950 and again during November and December following airbrake modifications. The A&AEE concluded that the Attacker was not suitable for combat as a gun platform above 35,000ft. An A&AEE night flying assessment using WA471 in April 1951 highlighted no issues for deck landing at night.

Service release was delayed by the remaining trials and updating of the early production aircraft. There were also cockpit pressurisation issues in the first ten aircraft. Interim clearance for shore use was achieved in December 1950 but with no gun firing, no RATOG and a Mach 0.78 restriction. The first frontline squadron to receive its Attackers was 800 NAS at Ford in August 1951.

Of the 63 Attacker F.1s ordered, only 50 were completed to that standard. The last 11 were completed with provision for bomb racks as the FB.1 and two further aircraft were cancelled (an additional FB.1 was ordered on 2 March 1950 to replace an aircraft lost during a production test flight.) The following 84 Attacker FB.2s received the Nene 102 engine. Always intended as an interim type, the Attacker's career was brief and was replaced by the Sea Hawk and Sea Venom during 1954. Several Royal Naval Volunteer Reserve (RNVR) squadrons flew Attackers until the defence cuts of 1957 disbanded them on 10 March.

Attacker F.1 WA469 was the first production aircraft. Note the folding wing tip sections; the wing was essentially that of the earlier piston-powered Seafang. WA469's flying career of 214 hours was devoted to A&AEE flying trials until 1954, when it became a ground instruction airframe. *Author's Collection*

Supermarine attempted to market the Attacker for export. In January 1950 TS409 was demonstrated to Air Marshal Iver Law-Chapman, the Commander-in-Chief (Designate) of the Royal Indian Air Force. The same aircraft was then loaned to the

The pilot of Attacker FB.1 WA530 of 800 NAS tucks up the undercarriage on take-off. It is easy to see why the ventral drop tank was redesigned to improve ground clearance, reducing its capacity to 250gal (1,136L). WA530 suffered an emergency belly landing at RAF Valley on 7 September 1952 when one undercarriage leg refused to extend. Retired in 1954, WA530 was used for ground instruction until 1957. *Author's Collection*

WINGS OVER THE FLEET

Supermarine Attacker F.1 WA484 on the deck of HMS *Eagle* on 28 March 1952. Given the reception committee the pilot must have been a senior officer! A month later the aircraft was transferred from 800 to 890 NAS. *Tony Buttler Collection*

manufacturer in May for a Middle East sales tour. The only success was an order for 36 Type 538 Attackers for the Royal Pakistan Air Force. The Type 538 was de-navalised but otherwise similar to the Type 398 FB.2. The first production aircraft were received during 1951, equipping No. 11 Squadron until they were replaced by North American F-86F Sabres in 1956.

Supermarine began design work on an improved Type 527 Attacker Mk.2 during the summer of 1949. The Nene was replaced by a 6,500lbf (28.9kN) Avon or the older centrifugal 6,250lbf (27.8kN) Tay along with some additional fuel in the rear fuselage – 33gal (150L) for the Avon and 63gal (286L) for the Tay. A new all-moving tailplane with power assistance to raise the limiting Mach number and drooped, powered ailerons would be fitted. The aim was not to disrupt production, so a tricycle undercarriage was not added, although larger intakes were required and in turn the wing was moved backwards by 13.5in (3.43cm), which enabled a reduction in nose ballast. These changes had already been tested on prototype TS416 (which in effect was a prototype Mk.2) and the all-moving

Attacker FB.2 WK338 fitted with eight RATOG boosters and two 1,000lb (454kg) bombs. Completed in October 1952, it was issued to 800 NAS at RNAS Ford. A heavy landing on 9 May 1956 following a stall fractured the wing spar and wrinkled the fuselage skinning, resulting in a write-off. *Tony Buttler Collection*

This Type 538 Attacker was a land-based version for the Pakistan Air Force seen on display at the SBAC Farnborough Show. The array of bomb and rocket ordnance was equal to that of the Attacker FB.1 and FB.2. *Author's Collection*

tail was already in development for the Type 510 Swift. With the Avon the AUW was 12,975lb (5,885kg) with an estimated maximum speed of 479kt at 30,000ft, a limiting Mach number of Mach 0.86 and 9,250ft/min (2,820m/min) sea level rate of climb. The Tay offered nearly identical performance apart from a reduced rate of climb of 7,900ft/min (2,410m/min). The MoS and the Admiralty were disappointed, however, that the Type 510's swept wings were not being considered and the proposal went no further.

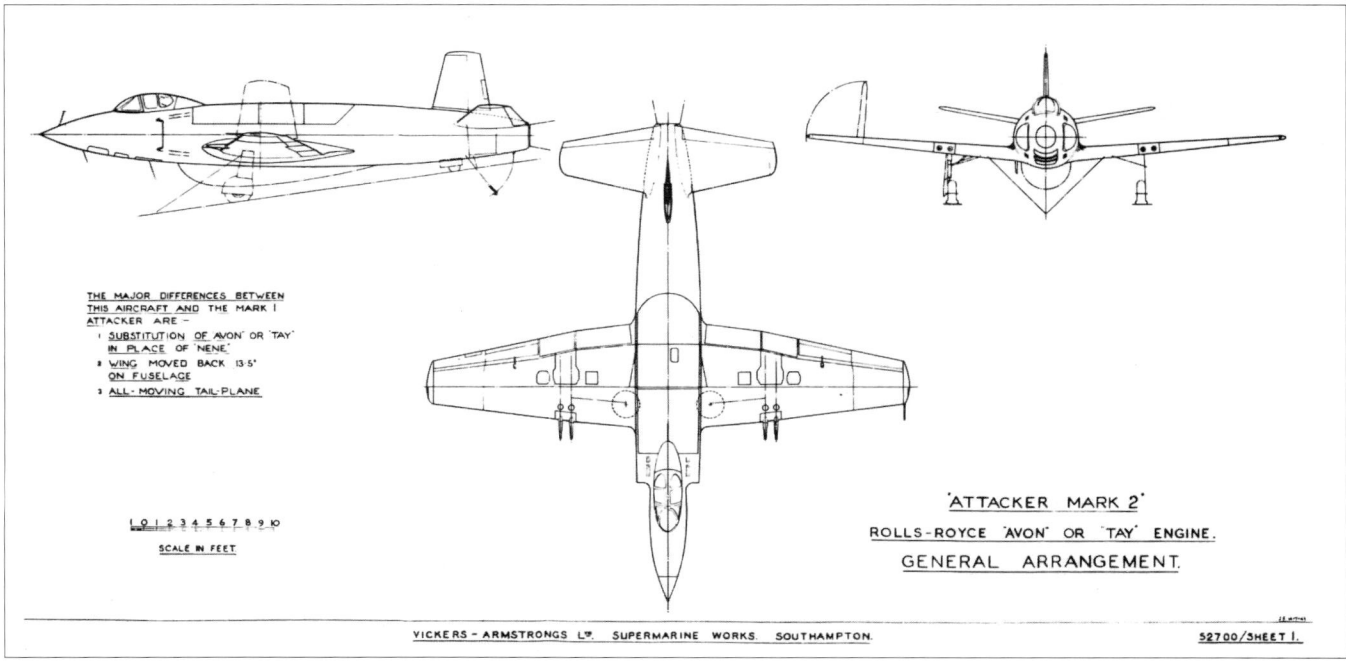

A general arrangement drawing of the Attacker Mk.2 which could be powered by either a Rolls-Royce Tay or Avon turbojet. This private venture did not achieve any orders. *BAE Systems*

Sea Hawk

Hawker Aircraft's wartime design team based at Claremont House in Esher, Surrey, sketched out a jet-powered development of the piston-powered Fury in 1944 as the P.1035. A Rolls-Royce B.41 centrifugal-flow turbojet was fitted behind the cockpit, with wing root intakes and a bifurcated jet pipe exiting on both sides of the fuselage, a feature drawn up by Development Engineer JV Stanbury. The Ministry of Aircraft Production's (MAP) Director of Operational Requirements Mr Wardle and Director of Technical Development NE Rowe visited Claremont House in November, where they examined the P.1035 project. A few days later, Rowe supplied the latest data on the B.41 (soon to be named the Nene) and Hawker requested Rolls-Royce's comments on their proposed bifurcated jet pipe; the engine manufacturer having some reservations, but the short intake and exhaust reduced thrust losses, a vital factor for the low-powered first generation turbojets.

The refined P.1040 design emerged on 22 December with a new unswept but tapered wing and retaining little visible Fury heritage. There was ample space within the fuselage ahead and behind the engine for fuel tanks totalling 450gal (2,045L). At this stage wingspan was 36ft 6in (11.1m) and fuselage length 37ft 2in (11.3m).

On 16 February 1945, Rowe sent a letter to Hawker's Chief Designer Sydney Camm suggesting, "you might take on a fighter-bomber design based on a jet propulsion fighter (F.2/43 replacement)." The aircraft had to have high performance, good endurance at all heights and be suitably armed for the low attack role. Camm wasted no time, submitting a full tender 11 days later. Camm's team also looked at potential naval versions, including the P.1043 lacking an undercarriage for use with a rubber flexible deck (see Chapter 2).

Rowe had been enthusiastic, but by June he felt that Gloster's E.1/44 Ace would be sufficiently advanced for the RAF's needs and preferred Supermarine's undercarriageless design to meet the RN's needs. He argued that the P.1040 and DH's planned 'thin wing' Vampire were 'not worth proceeding with'. Indeed, the Air Staff had already declared no interest in a general purpose jet fighter, they wanted an interceptor. One of the Ministry's technical experts, Handel Davies, suggested adding auxiliary rockets to jet interceptors enable them to reach 45,000ft (13,715m) in three minutes. Rowe sent Davies to Hawker and Supermarine to discuss the idea and on 20 September Camm sent Rowe his resulting thoughts.

Camm concluded that using a Nene with rocket augmentation would equal, or even exceed, the rate of climb possible from using Rolls-Royce's planned 6,500lbf (28.9kN) AJ.65 axial-flow turbojet and be able to serve as a general purpose fighter and a carrier-based fighter. The P.1040's bifurcated jet pipe layout allowed easy installation of a rocket and its fuel tanks. Camm suggested reducing the area wing and removing the undercarriage to increase structural strength and reduce weight and 'extreme sweepback' – a swept wing. He outlined four stages of development:

- **Stage 1** – a Nene-powered 'General Purpose Medium Range Fighter' to replace the Fury and Sea Fury with possible exploration of swept wings using the same airframe.

- **Stage 2** – an interceptor with an additional 2,000lbf (8.89kN) rocket in the tail.

- **Stage 3** – final interceptor development with a smaller wing and no undercarriage for an optimum rate of climb and very high maximum speed.

- **Stage 4** – new centre and forward fuselage for the AJ.65, either as a general purpose fighter with Stage 1 wings or an interceptor with Stage 3 wings.

Future armament needs were changing too. Davies visited Camm again to discuss armament developments. It was generally felt that the increased altitudes and closing speeds in future air combat would make 20mm calibre cannon obsolete, new cannon would have to be at least 30mm (perhaps even as large as 50mm), based on the latest German designs, such as the Mauser 213 revolver cannon, which were now undergoing evaluation by the Allies. The RAE conducted bomb and RP release tests with Hawker Tempests at speeds over 400kt. These revealed unstable bomb trajectories and a nose-down effect on RPs, but these were thought not to be insurmountable problems with refinements to bomb and RP design.

Hawker submitted another brochure on 4 October, including the rocket engine and provision for 30mm cannon and 3in (76mm) RPs. In Rowe's opinion this had "removed the chief criticism of the original design, viz. that it was no more than another version of the E.1/44." He gave the go ahead as an interceptor the following day.

Wingspan of the basic P.1040 was now 36ft 6in (11.12m) with an area of 256ft² (23.7m²). The armament remained 4x 20mm Hispano Mk.V cannon until newer cannon were developed. The AUW with 370gal (1,682L) of internal fuel was estimated at 11,000lb (4,990kg). The estimated maximum speed at sea level was 564kt with 512kt at 30,000ft (9,145m). Maximum rate of climb was 8,000ft/min (2,240m/min), taking five minutes to reach 30,000ft and eight minutes to 40,000ft, with a service ceiling of 53,000ft (16,155m). Estimated range was 712nm (1,320km) at 30,000ft, increasing to 930nm (1,720km) with 450gal (2,045L) of fuel and 1,216nm (2,250km) with the addition of two 50gal (227L) underwing drop tanks.

The naval version with a rocket added aft (plus 2,700lb (1,225kg) of rocket fuel) had an AUW of

The second prototype Hawker P.1040 was VP413. It was used for intensive deck landing trials aboard HMS *Illustrious* between 17 October and 5 November 1949 and 6–17 February 1950. *Author's Collection*

13,080lb (5,932kg). The estimated maximum speed at sea level was 512kt and 540kt at 30,000ft, the maximum rate of climb at sea level would be 11,400ft/min (3,475m/min), reaching 35,000ft (10,670m) in 3.5min. The take-off run with into a 27kt headwind would be 720ft (219m).

The brochure refined the four stages:

- **Stage 1** – same as the original proposal.

- **Stage 2** – addition of the rocket in the tail in both the land and carrier-based versions and installation of 2x 30mm cannon (100 rounds per gun). Performance included 30 minutes' endurance at 40,000ft plus 10 minutes of combat, maximum rate of climb 13,000ft/min (3,960m/min) and time of 3.75min to 40,000ft.

- **Stage 3** – removal of the undercarriage and reduced area wings – possibly with 45° leading-edge sweep. The estimated maximum speed was over 565kt with a climb of three minutes to 40,000ft. Camm acknowledged that a swept wing would cause issues for naval operations from aircraft carriers; at that time there had been no serious attempt to design an optimum wing, but it was clear that leading-edge slots would be required.
- **Stage 4** – replacement of the Nene with AJ.65 at some point in the future.

A meeting in December at the new Ministry of Supply (MoS) – the successor to MAP – saw the RAF's Director of Operational Requirements, Air Commodore AR Wardle, declaring that the RAF was still not interested, it did not want a rocket-powered interceptor and was thinking in terms of a Meteor development with two AJ.65s as the likely future fighter.

The Deputy Chief Naval Representative at the MoS, Captain ACG Ermen, commented that interception from the deck at sea was not yet considered practical and standing patrols seemed the only solution to counter enemy high-speed jet aircraft. The Admiralty preferred a general purpose fighter omitting the rocket to replace the Sea Fury within three years, but provision for a rocket would be retained to avoid early obsolescence and it was suggested that Hawker should study an AJ.65-powered version. Rowe thought it was a 'well founded project' and recommended an order for three prototypes (VP401, VP413 and VP433) and a structural test specimen – a fourth prototype with a rocket engine was not approved.

The AUW had been reduced to 11,500lb (5,215kg) by January 1946 and Camm was hoping to avoid the need to provide wing folding to save another 300lb (136kg). The take-off run was now 700ft (213m) and the landing approach speed was 100kt. Estimated range 550nm (1,020km) at 30,000ft, increasing to 860nm (1,590km) with 450gal (2,045L) of fuel and 1,160nm (2,150km) with drop tanks. Maximum speed was 520kt at 20,000ft (6,100m) and the rate of climb at sea level was 7,700ft/min (2,350m/min), taking 5.5min to reach 30,000ft.

By this time switching to the AJ.65 had been ruled out, both Hawker and Supermarine argued that the longer axial-flow engine would require swept wings to obtain the desired short tail arm loading for balance. The Stability and Control Sub-Committee of the Aeronautical Research Council backed up this opinion, also advising that more data on swept wing design was required. The swept wing version became the P.1052, developed under Specification E/38.46, issued on 18 March 1947, the first of two prototypes (VX272 and VX279) flying on 19 November 1948.

Approval to order the three P.1040 prototypes was given on 17 February and work began on drafting Specification N.7/46 and Operational Requirement

OR.218. The MoS's chief technical evaluator, Captain RN Liptrot, considered the P.1040 to be an 'orthodox design' that was similar in performance to Supermarine's Type 392 and a proposed navalised Gloster E.1/44. Liptrot's weight estimates were a little higher than Hawker's and the climb performance estimates a little lower. There was uncertainty over the speed estimates due to the imperfect knowledge of compressibility effects at that time and the results extrapolated from diving aerodynamic tests had been shown to be unreliable. Though it was theoretically capable of attaining Mach 0.88 at 40,000ft, Liptrot felt that trim change and compressibility effects might reduce that in practice (similar effects limited the Vampire to Mach 0.78). Liptrot concluded that the "Project promises to give us very little more, if any, than the Supermarine E.1/45 [Type 392] and the Gloster E.1/44, but the point which perturbs me most is that the whole project centres on the Nene engine, which is at the limit of its development and which really will be obsolescent by the time the aircraft is ready." Liptrot would have preferred using the AJ.65, estimating that it would be available before the P.1040 reached production.

A draft Specification N.7/46 appeared in April (it would not be finalised until October). It called for an aircraft capable of fulfilling the roles of long-range, strike-support day fighter; land assault (including ground attack, visual and photographic tactical reconnaissance, artillery spotting and supply dropping); and day interceptor fighter. Interestingly, an additional night fighter intruder role was deleted from the draft. The dimensions were not to exceed 40ft (12.2m) length, 15ft 9in (4.8m) height with the wings folded (originally 13ft 9in [4.1m]) and wingspan of 18ft (5.48m) folded and 40ft (12.2m) spread. The weight should not exceed 14,000lb (6,350kg) fully loaded. The undercarriage had to withstand a descent of 14ft/sec (4.2m/sec), but Hawker argued that this would be difficult to accommodate (especially for the nose wheel) and preferred 12ft/sec (3.6m/sec). Combat radius for a support sortie was to be 400nm (740km) with 440gal (2,000L) of internal fuel. The armament remained a quartet of 20mm Hispano cannon with a pair of 30mm cannon to be fitted later. Armour protection against 30mm cannon shell fragments was to be provided for the pilot. An ejection seat was required (Hawker wanted to design the seat itself using Martin-Baker mechanicals), as was cockpit pressurisation (this was soon deferred to the 100th aircraft onwards). A request for powered controls was rejected by Camm, who preferred using spring trimming tabs, as on the Sea Fury.

The high stalling speed of 97kt was worrying given that the current Mk.6 and Mk.7 arrester gear was only rated at 60kt, although the *Eagle*-class carriers would have the higher-rated Mk.10 capable of arresting a 12,500lb (5,670kg) aircraft at 75kt. Take-offs using the BH.III accelerator were ruled out, only the more powerful BH.V was suitable which limited the number of carriers that the P.1040 could operate from. There were also worries about pilot safety on impacting safety barriers given that jet aircraft had their cockpits mounted in the nose. There was no obvious solution to this.

Camm consulted DMARD, JE Serby, in May 1946 regarding landing devices suitable for laminar flow wings and proposed reducing the weight of armour plating required – 307lb (139kg) – to shave 1.5kt off the stalling speed. The MoS and the Naval Staff agreed, the armour being reduced to splinter protection. The camera fit for the land assault role was reduced by one camera to one F24 vertical and one oblique camera to save weight and space.

The following September Serby visited Hawker's Kingston upon Thames design office to discuss the approach speed problem in more detail. At a landing weight of 8,980lb (4,075kg) the approach speed was 106kt with the arrester hook catching the wire at 76kt, just within the limit of the newer 75kt rated gear. A&AEE Vampire trials had shown that a lift control device, such as dive-recovery flaps or split flaps was vital during the approach. Hawker resisted copying Supermarine's jet deflection method as this was harder to incorporate with the bifurcated jet pipe. Lift spoilers were ruled out as impractical given the size required. Instead, it was agreed to increase the wing area by 5% to 268ft² (24.8m²) to reduce the stalling speed by 4kt. The second and third prototypes were completed with the larger wing. The span was increased by 2ft 6in (76cm) to increase the aspect ratio from 5.0 to 5.5. The chord of the brake flaps was also increased and slots added on the advice of the RAE to avoid buffeting.

Vampire F.1 TG314, modified with an interconnected throttle and flap, had conducted successful landing trials and Serby and Camm agreed that this was an ideal solution. The MoS proposed a landing approach with the brake flaps and landing flaps deflected by 13° with adjustment using the landing flap interconnected to the throttle. For a baulked landing, the pilot would open the throttle to lower the flaps, the brake flaps retracting to climb away, causing a nose-down change of trim with a significant drag increase. Hawker proposed a better method of approaching with the brake flaps and landing flaps deflected by 80° with descent adjustment using the elevator and slight throttle; a baulked landing would simply require the pilot to open the throttle and use elevator to climb. By July 1949 Hawker had abandoned the interconnected throttle and flap on the advice of its Chief Test Pilot Trevor 'Wimpy' Wade. In tests with the third prototype VP413, Wade found that using the air brakes on approach reduced feel in lateral control, plus the buffeting caused by the air brakes concealed what little stall warning there was. Instead, Wade applied full flap (53.5°), approaching at 102kt. The air brake was fixed closed and the air brake button was altered to give a further 33° flap deflection (86.5° total). Wade was able to fly ADDLs with slightly reduced stalling speed and applying more power could easily maintain a constant rate of descent.

Sea Hawk F.2 WF240 fresh from the Armstrong Whitworth Bitteswell factory in February 1954. This was the first production F.2 and was used by A&AEE's 'C' Squadron for decking landing practice and target towing trials. It was finally retired in July 1959. *Tony Buttler Collection*

Development Engineer JV Stanbury revisited the jet spoiler idea in July 1947, envisioning a single flap spoiler for each bifurcated jet pipe exhaust, recessed into the wing root fillet to deflect a substantial proportion of the jet stream outboard. Hawker proposed modifying the rear fuselage of the static fatigue test airframe and fitting it to one of the prototypes. In the event, no further progress was made.

Another problem was the incidence of the aircraft (the angle of the aircraft as it sat on the deck). With 0° incidence, a 12,950lb (5,875kg) overload take-off with full flaps into a 30kt wind was predicted to lead to an unacceptable drop on leaving the bows – risking striking the surface of the sea. Limiting the drop to 5ft (1.2m) required an incidence of 10.6°. The MoS suggested either lengthening the nose wheel leg by 2ft (60cm) or increasing the wing area. Hawker argued that a longer nose leg would require a larger – and heavier – nose section to accommodate and proposed using a take-off trolley instead. By using standard RATOG kit at 11,900lb (5,400kg) a rolling take-off into a 20kt wind could be accomplished in 270ft (82m) or 450ft (137m) at an overload weight of 13,510lb (6,130kg).

By the winter of 1947, the need for more thrust saw proposals to fit a water-methanol boost system for the Nene offering 115% thrust for 30 seconds, enabling a 602ft (183m) take-off run at 11,900lb. An improved 128% thrust version would cost 360lb (163kg) in weight but shorten the take-off to just 396ft (120m). The Admiralty was interested in providing 'exhaust reheat' – afterburners – to avoid storing large amounts of methanol aboard the carriers. At this time reheat was a technical unknown and the bifurcated tail pipe did not easily lend itself to fitting afterburners.

Range worries were exacerbated as the estimates continued to fall, the radius of action at 30,000ft reducing from 257nm to 233nm (475-430km) compared to the required 550nm (1,020km). Adding two 100gal (454L) drop tanks only achieved 400nm (740km). The Assistant Chief Naval Representative worried that dropping the 100gal tanks in combat would be unadvisable due to the low supply available aboard the carriers and he called for Hawker to study alternative wing tip tanks. A smaller 88gal (400L) drop tank was designed instead. (Camm did revisit the idea of tip-tanks in June 1948 to reduce the Mach limiting number.) In October 1949, Hawker reported on removing wing folding to save between 95lb and 230lb (43–104kg) weight, depending on the extent of the redesign of the wing structure. The Admiralty, however, refused to delete the wing folding given the hangarage requirements.

Hawker Sea Hawk

	P.1040 Design (October 1945)	P.1040 Design (January 1946)	Sea Hawk F.1	Sea Hawk FGA.6
Span	36ft 6in (11.12m)	36ft 6in (11.12m)	39ft 0in (11.89m); 13ft 3in (4.03m) folded	39ft 0in (11.89m); 13ft 3in (4.03m) folded
Length	38ft 0in (11.58m)	38ft 0in (11.58m)	40ft 0in (12.19m)	40ft 0in (12.19m)
Wing area	256ft² (23.7m²)	256ft² (23.7m²)	278ft² (25.83m²)	278ft² (25.83m²)
All-up weight	12,500lb (5,670kg)	11,500lb (5,216kg)	13,200lb (5,990kg)	Max take-off 16,200lb (7,350kg)
Powerplant	1x B.41 Nene, 4,200lbf (18.7kN); plus 2,000lbf (8.89kN) rocket motor for RN	1x B.41 Nene, 4,200lbf (18.7kN)	1x Nene Mk.101, 5,000lbf (22.2kN)	1x Nene Mk.103, 5,400lbf (24.0kN)
Max speed	577kt (1,070km/h) at SL; 517kt (957km/h) at 40,000ft (12,190m)	520kt at 20,000ft (6,100m)	513kt (951km/h) at SL	520kt (964km/h) at SL
Rate of climb	8,000ft/min (2,240m/min) at SL, RAF; 11,400ft/min (3,475m/min) at SL, RN	7,700ft/min (2,350m/min) at SL	?	5,700ft/min (1,735m/min) at SL
Service ceiling	53,000ft (16,155m) RAF	?	44,500ft (13,565m)	44,500ft (13,565m)
Range	712nm (1,320km) at 30,000ft (9,145m); 930nm (1,720km) with 450gal (2,045L) of fuel; 1,216nm (2,250km) with 2x 50gal (227L) drop tanks	550nm (1,020km) at 30,000ft (9,145m); 860nm (1,590km) with 450gal (2,045L) of fuel; 1,160nm (2,150km) with 2x 50gal (227L) drop tanks.	695nm (1,787km)	420nm (777km); 1,216nm (2,253km) with 2x 50gal (227L) drop tanks.
Armament	4x 20mm Hispano	4x 20mm Hispano	4x 20mm Hispano	4x 20mm Hispano; 4x 500lb (227kg) bombs, 16x 60lb (27kg) RPs

In late 1949 the Chief Naval Representative, Rear Admiral LD Mackintosh of Mackintosh, had been interested in using the higher-thrust Rolls-Royce RB.44 Tay rather than the AJ.65 Avon to further develop the Sea Hawk. Hawker studied the idea but found no speed advantage with a straight wing due to the compressibility limits. The resulting P.1081 research aircraft received the P.1052's swept wing and a new rear fuselage and tail with a single jet pipe for reheat. Given the changes needed, Camm advocated a naval F.3/48 (to become the P.1083 Hunter) instead. The Admiralty lost interest, seeing duplication with the Supermarine N.9/47 (see Chapter 3) and in November 1950 the DMARD, AE Woodward Nutt, rejected the aircraft for naval use due to aerodynamic flow problems around the empennage and the tail jet pipe shifting the CG too far aft.

The first P.1040 prototype, VP401, made its maiden flight at Boscombe Down on 2 September 1947 (Hawker's Langley factory in Surrey only had a grass runway). The first of the two fully navalised prototypes, VP413, flew at Boscombe Down on 3 September 1948 and the third prototype, VP422 took to the air on 17 October 1949.

Lt Cdr Eric Brown flew a handling test in VP401 at the A&AEE on 3 November 1947. The flight was to investigate the airframe vibrations noted by Hawker's Chief Test Pilot William Humble. Brown encountered slight vibration in normal flight, which became severe when diving, Brown worrying the aircraft might break-up. Even so, he appraised the Sea Hawk as providing, "Promise of being a very fine aircraft and particularly in respect to its deck-landing role." This preview was followed by further A&AEE tests in May and June 1948. Good handling characteristics were noted, Mach 0.85 was attained with 3g turns without compressibility effects. The report noted, however, that the take-off performance was inadequate for carriers, even in clean condition. Following this feedback, Sydney Camm undertook to fit an aileron trimmer and reduce the stick force required at high Mach numbers. In December, a trial engine change with the wings folded went very well, a complete change would take 40 manhours in production aircraft, although in practice serviceability was hampered by poor access to most components on the airframe.

Treasury sanction to order 150 Sea Hawk F.1s was given in November 1948, with delivery to be completed by March 1952 at a production rate of 20 per month. The cost was £3.37 million, including jigs and tooling.

Changes to meet production Specification 25/48/P included: a revised canopy installation, new curved glass windscreen, Martin Baker ejection seat, retractable gun sight, revised instrument panel layout, improved rudder bar adjustment, a long-travel nose wheel leg to withstand 5g acceleration on catapulting and a strengthened arrester hook which was moved forwards to reduce adverse CG effects. The strike sortie radius was reduced to 285nm (527km) plus 20 minutes loitering before landing. The engine would be the 5,000lbf (22.2kN) Nene Mk.101. Until the carriage and release of bombs and RPs from high-speed jet aircraft was fully researched and cleared, the armament was restricted to just the Hispano cannon.

The constant design changes and unsettled specifications – as well as disagreements over Hawker's tenure at Langley – delayed the issuing of the Instruction to Proceed until November 1949, the cost having risen slightly to £3.39 million. The first production aircraft, WF143, made its first flight on 14 November 1951. In January 1951 Armstrong Whitworth Aircraft (AWA, another company within the Hawker Siddeley group) was brought into the production programme to free Hawker's Kingston works for the RAF's P.1081 Hunter and AWA took over all Sea Hawk design and production responsibility in 1952. Only 30 of the 95 Sea Hawk F.1s would be completed at Kingston. By May 1951, the total requirement stood at 336 Sea Hawks and by June 1953 the Sea Hawk programme had cost £7.54 million with 148 Sea Hawks on order. Under the Mutual Defense Assistance Program (MDAP), the USA had offered 100 ex-USN Vought F4U-4 Corsairs, soon changed to 50 of the improved F4U-7 or 50 UK-built fighters funded by an off-shore purchase. The final MDAP agreement for the UK, the Low Countries, France and Italy funded $281.54 million of fighters, which included 107 Sea Hawks worth $12.81 million.

By the end of 1949, the prototype, VP401, was of little further use to the trials programme as it was non-standard with the smaller non-folding wing, lacking air brakes, arrester hook and any provision for armament. The aircraft was converted into the P.1072 with a 2,000lbf (8.89kN) Armstrong Siddeley Snarler rocket engine in the rear fuselage (fuelled by liquid oxygen and water-methanol), flying in this form on 20 November 1950. The second and third prototypes, VP413 and VP422, were completed to the N.7/46 specification (although VP413 lacked provision for drop tanks or RATOG). VP413 undertook A&AEE clean handling trials, deck trials and RAE preliminary catapulting tests before arrester gear and mat landing development.

Hawker used VP422 for its contractor's trials, then it went to the A&AEE for gun firing trials and then drop tank, RATOG and radio clearance trials. Six production aircraft were used for service clearance flying: three for short-term trials, two for intensive deck handling and intensive flying and another for tropical trials.

Initial flight testing had resulted in some improvements. New 'pen-nib' heat shield fairings were fitted to the exhausts to improve handling and production aircraft gained a bullet fairing at the tailplane intersection with the tail fin. Hawker entered and won the Society of British Aircraft Constructors Challenge Cup on 1 August 1949, with VP401 clocking an average speed of 443kt.

Initial A&AEE deck landing trials in February 1949 took place aboard *Illustrious*. Some modifications were made to increase the speed limit of the arrester gear to 65–70kt, but a landing at those speeds would require 40kt wind over the deck to sufficiently reduce the contact speed. Hawker also sent its test pilots Trevor Wade and Neville Duke on deck landing courses.

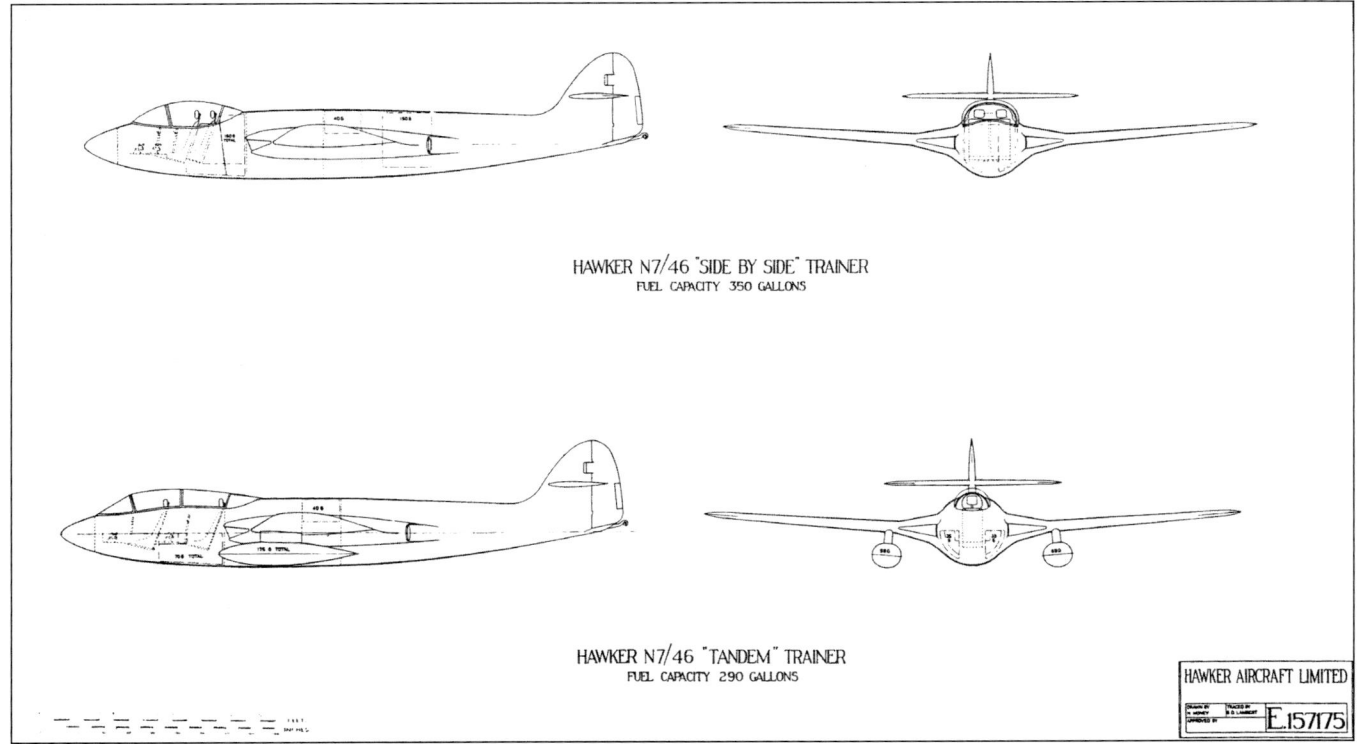

Hawker proposed the P.1040-20 two-seat conversion trainer variant, studying both side-by-side and tandem seating for the student and instructor. The FAA did not proceed with this idea. *Chris Farara*

Sea Hawk FGA.4 WV836 of 801 NAS starting its Rolls-Royce Nene aboard HMS *Bulwark* in 1957 or 1958. The puff of smoke is from the engine's Coffman cartridge starter (an explosive charge like an oversized shotgun cartridge) to get the Nene's impeller spinning to begin the combustion cycle. *Tony Kilner via Tony Buttler*

The Director of Naval Air Warfare, Captain Ernest Shattock, studied the first 10 landings aboard *Illustrious* by the A&AEE pilots. Entry into the arresting gear was at 117.2–98.9kt, which was beyond the capacity of the latest Mk.10 arrester gear. A tendency to float over the arrester wires saw a longer tail hook being fitted. The Sea Hawk was judged unsuitable for the older *Illustrious*-class ships, whose planned modernisation was in the future. This restricted the Sea Hawk to the *Eagle* and *Hermes*-classes and any future modernised fleet carriers.

Intensive deck landing trials by the RAE took place aboard *Illustrious* between 17 October and 5 November 1949 and 6–17 February 1950 using VP413 flown by Lt Cdr Richmond and Lt Reynolds. The trials were hampered because of a lack of suitable weather, with high wind speeds over the deck only occurring for short periods. 42 landings were made (100 were planned), recording deceleration up to 2.05*g* and 14.7ft/sec (4.48m/sec) undercarriage impact velocities. The aircraft was damaged on the third landing when the arrester hook hit the coaming of the round-down on the stern, rebounding and damaging the rudder. This was a hazard of using a tail down attitude to check the rate of descent.

A&AEE deck landing assessment and low-speed handling tests took place in June 1952 using production Sea Hawk F.1 WF145. The low-speed handling was generally good and the ADDL characteristics were excellent but there were negative points; insufficient stall warning in the approach configuration and notable roll with sideslip (a Dutch Roll). On take-off the aircraft became airborne at 92–95kt, the approach speed was 110kt to avoid excessive sink when making power adjustments. It was advised that when no ammunition was carried that ballast should be added to improve longitudinal stability at low speeds.

The intensive flying trials by Service Trials Unit, 703 NAS, at RNAS Ford took place during 22 September 1952 to 2 March 1953 using Sea Hawks WF151, 152, 153, 155, 156 and 158. A total of 376 flying hours was achieved in 540 sorties (only two hours were flown at night in WF152). These sorties included engine-proving flights, target towing tests, armament clearance and cold weather trials at the Central Experimental Proving Establishment in Namao, Alberta, Canada. Poor serviceability, such as wing lock and folding issues, hampered the trials.

Four aircraft aboard *Eagle* in January conducted 62 deck landings, 12 rolling take-offs and 50 catapult launches. With catapult launching the aircraft could be airborne within 40sec but rolling take-offs needed the entire flight deck. In mock combat it was found that the Sea Hawk could out-manoeuvre the Meteor with ease at 30,000ft but the Meteor was superior below 20,000ft. Initial service release was obtained on 1 January 1953 (the armament was still not cleared for use). Trials by 703

1 TRANSITION TO THE JET AGE

ABOVE The officers aboard HMS *Albion* have a grandstand view as Sea Hawk FGA.6 XE334 emerges from the hangar in 1960. *Terry Panopalis Collection*

LEFT Sea Hawk FGA.6 XE456 fully laden with two 500lb (227kg) bombs and eight 60lb (27kg) rocket projectiles. *Tony Buttler Collection*

29

WINGS OVER THE FLEET

On 27 May 1957 Her Majesty Queen Elizabeth II made a Royal visit to HMS *Ark Royal* in the Firth of Clyde. The ship's air group of Hawker Sea Hawks, Westland Wyvern AS.4s and Douglas Skyraider AEW.1s was parked on deck for inspection. *Blue Envoy Collection*

The Royal visit also included a mass start-up of 806 NAS's Sea Hawks, the Coffman cartridge starters providing plenty of noise and smoke! *Blue Envoy Collection*

NAS continued into 1955, the unit merging into 700 NAS in August.

Powered ailerons were trialled on WF147 in late 1953, they provided a marked improvement in manoeuvrability and increased the rate of roll. They were introduced on the 40 Sea Hawk F.2 aircraft, the first to be completed being WF241 on 5 January 1954 with deliveries to 802 NAS beginning in April. These were followed by 116 Sea Hawk FB.3 fighter-bombers with strengthened wings and modified underwing racks for a 500lb (227kg) bomb or a mine each. The FB.3 entered service in July 1954, 77 of them paid for by MDAP funds. The Sea Hawk FGA.4 received an extra pair of underwing hardpoints to double the bombload or allow up to sixteen 3in (76mm) RPs to be carried. The first FGA.4, WV792, was flown on 26 August 1954 – nearly a decade after the P.1040 had been penned at Claremont House. A total of 97 were supplied, the remaining 86 being completed to FGA.6 standard (another 54 were cancelled.)

The first frontline squadron to receive the Sea Hawk was 806 NAS at RNAS Brawdy on 10 March 1953. The squadron participated in the Coronation Review at Spithead and on 23 June 1953 the commanding officer, Lt Cdr PCS Chilton, made the first landing onto an angled carrier deck by a British aircraft when he touched down aboard USS *Antietam* (for more details see Chapter 2.) 806 NAS made its first sea deployment aboard HMS *Eagle* in February 1954.

The Sea Hawk had its baptism of fire with the FAA during the Suez Crisis (Operation MUSKETEER) of November 1956. *Albion* had embarked 800 and 802 NAS, while her sistership *Bulwark* carried 804, 895 and 899 NAS and *Eagle* had 810 and 897 NAS. The Sea Hawk was used for attacks on airfields and military installations in the Canal Zone and two aircraft were lost.

During 1954 the 5,400lbf (24kN) Nene Mk.103 became available and the RN Aircraft Yard at RNAS Fleetlands converted 50 FB.3 and 40 FGA.4 with the new engine as the FB.5 and FGA.6. The FGA.6 also received the ARI.18048 *Green Salad* UHF radio homer for navigational assistance. The frontline service was relatively brief, 806 NAS giving up its FGA.6s on 15 December 1960 when it returned from the Far East aboard HMS *Albion*. The RNVR received several Sea Hawks in 1956, but the defence cuts of 1957 saw the RNVR squadrons being disbanded on 10 March. The civilian operated Fleet Requirements

1 TRANSITION TO THE JET AGE

Sea Hawk FGA.6 XE340 at the Aircraft Holding Unit at RNAS Brawdy in July 1962, retaining its 801 NAS markings. By the end of the year the aircraft was Brawdy's gate guard. Today it is in outdoor storage at the Fleet Air Arm Museum (sadly in deteriorating condition). *Terry Panopalis Collection*

Unit at Hurn used several Sea Hawks for radar calibration and target duties until February 1969.

Trials were conducted with two modified drop tanks; one containing an inflight-refuelling probe in an attempt to extend the range; the other with a forward-facing F.94 camera to augment the reconnaissance role. Neither idea was taken further. In the summer of 1954, AWA was awarded a contract to investigate the use of blown flaps to reduce the approach and landing speeds; some research was carried out, but no trials conversion materialised.

Export interest was shown by the Royal Australian Air Force, which was looking for a new fighter (interest soon centred on the Tay-powered P.1081) – but neither Australia nor Canada ordered Sea Hawks for their carriers. Prototype VP401 was flown by Captain Rasmissen of the Royal Danish Air Force in late 1949 and AWA demonstrated the Sea Hawk to the French Aéronavale at Lann-Bihoué on 12 April 1954, but no interest was received. The Dutch Marine Luchtvaartdienst obtained 22 Sea Hawk Mk.50 aircraft via MDAP funding, with deliveries

The Sea Hawk had a successful second life as a training aircraft for fighter pilots. A pair of Sea Hawk FB.3s – WV921 in the foreground and WV834 behind – of 700 NAS up on a sortie from RNAS Yeovilton sometime during 1959–61. *Tony Kilner via Tony Buttler*

The first aircraft completed at Baginton as an FGA.6 was XE339. From September 1965 it was on the strength of the Fleet Requirements Unit operated by Airwork Limited acting as a fast target for ship gunners. *Terry Panopalis Collection*

Sea Hawk FGA.6 XE456 was used by AWA as the prototype for the German Mk.100/101 and is seen here with the Hawker Siddeley Group logo on the nose. Displayed at Farnborough in September 1956 it was sold to AWA in 1958. *Tony Buttler Collection*

from the re-opened production line commencing in July 1957. The Mk.50 was essentially an FGA.6 with US-supplied UHF radios. They were operated aboard the *Colossus*-class carrier *Karel Doorman* (ex-HMS *Venerable*) until October 1964. The Federal Republic of Germany's Marineflieger (the air arm of the German Navy) ordered 34 Sea Hawk Mk.100 and 34 Mk.101, again based on the FGA.6, but with taller tail fins and rudders and UHF radios. The Mk.101 was equipped with Ekco Type 34 search radar mounted in a pod replacing the drop tank on the starboard wing. Deliveries began in February 1958; they were replaced by Lockheed F-104G Starfighters during 1964–65. The Indian Navy decided to order the Sea Hawk when it acquired INS *Vikrant* (ex-HMS *Majestic*). AWA had to re-open the production line again, building 14 FGA.6s and converting 16 ex-FAA FB.3s to FGA.6 standard. Short Brothers & Harland converted another 16 and the Indian Navy acquired 28 ex-German Mk.100 and Mk.101 aircraft during the late 1960s. Seeing action during the Indo-Pakistan War in November 1971, they were finally replaced by the British Aerospace Sea Harrier FRS.51 in 1982.

Westland competitors

Westland's Technical Director, Arthur Davenport (who had recently taken over from WEW 'Teddy' Petter) submitted a design brochure to the MAP in March 1945 for an undercarriageless fighter for

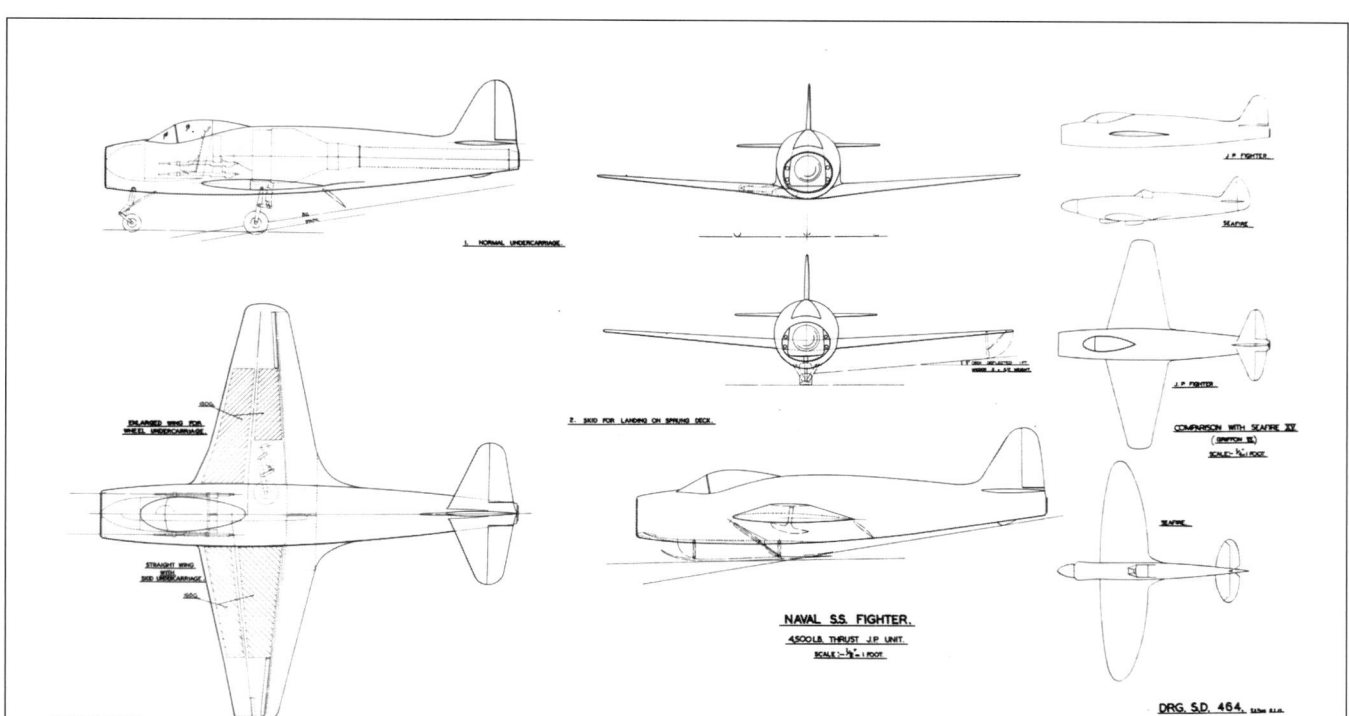

Westland's attempt to equal the Supermarine Attacker was this handsome design, offered with either a wheeled undercarriage or a skid for use on a flexible deck. Note the comparison against the Seafire on the right-hand side of the drawing. *Leonardo UK via Jeremy Graham*

Westland's next naval fighter with a swept wing was advanced for mid-1945. Note the four cannon blast tubes inside the nose intake – in reality, this would likely have caused engine surging issues. The conventional unswept wing shown on the top view was for comparison. *Leonardo UK via Jeremy Graham*

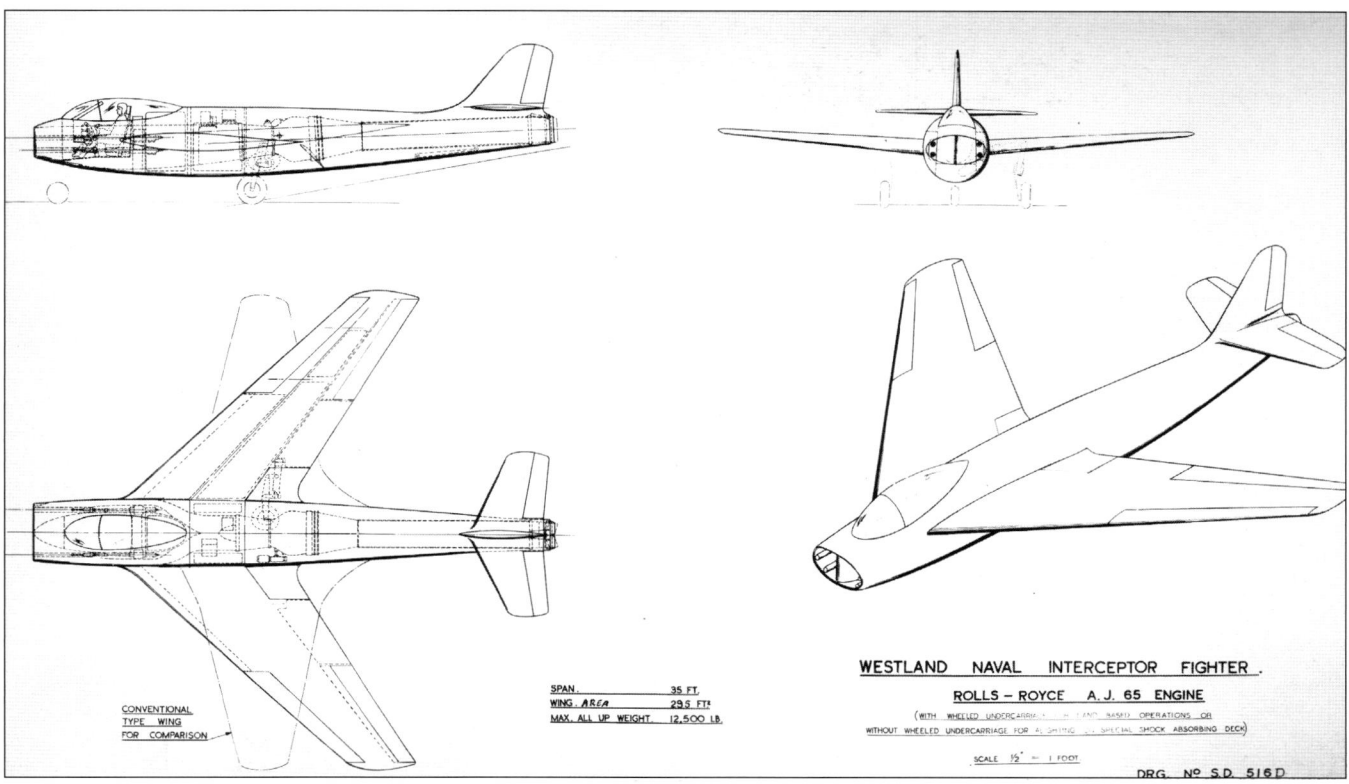

WINGS OVER THE FLEET

Westland private venture F.11/45 Naval interceptor fighter

	Jet-powered	Jet & rocket-powered
Span	35ft 0in (10.67m)	35ft 0in (10.67m)
Length	38ft 0in (11.58m)	38ft 0in (11.58m)
Wing area	295ft² (27.43m²)	290ft² (26.94m²)
t/c ratio	12%	12%
Gross weight	12,500lb (5,670kg)	12,500lb (5,670kg)
Powerplant	1x AJ.65 Avon, 6,500lbf (28.9kN)	1x AJ.65 Avon, 6,500lbf (28.9kN); 1x 3,750lbf (16.7kN) rocket motor
Max speed	577kt (1,070km/h) at SL; 517kt (957km/h) at 40,000ft (12,190m)	?
Rate of climb	9,000ft/min (2,745m/min) at SL	23,500ft/min (7,165m/min) at SL
Service ceiling	48,250ft (14,705m)	?
Armament	4x 20mm Hispano or 2x 30mm ADEN	4x 20mm Hispano or 2x 30mm ADEN

operation from a flexible runway, which seems to have been a private-venture competitor against Joe Smith's proposed Type 392 Jet Spiteful. It had a single belly skid, plus wing tip skids and was powered by the AJ.65. A wheeled version with a tricycle undercarriage was powered by an RB.41 Nene and featured a nose intake.

A naval interceptor version was submitted in March 1946 with a mid-mounted swept wing, a refined skid layout, an AJ.65 plus a rocket motor with 120sec of fuel to reach 35,000ft (10,670m) in 1min 43sec. Again, a conventional undercarriage version was also offered. This design seems to have been a direct competitor to the Hawker P.1040. Westland must have gotten wind of the work going on at South Marston and Claremont House and offered two innovative designs off its own bat, but neither proposal was taken up.

Swept wing tests

The Admiralty was keen to evaluate examples of swept wing fighters aboard the carriers to gain experience. Specification E.41/46 had been issued on 26 April 1947 for a swept wing development of the Attacker. Two Type 510 prototypes were ordered, VV106 and VV119. Chief Test Pilot Lt Cdr Mike Lithgow made VV106's maiden flight at Boscombe Down on 29 December 1948. The wing was swept by 44° on the leading edge, had a thickness-to-chord ratio (t/c) of 10% and was mounted on the same pick-up points as the Attacker's wing. The tailplane was swept by 45°. The tailwheel undercarriage was retained. The Type 510 suffered from poor handling at high and low speeds, with tip stalling evident at low speed.

During the summer of 1950 VV106 was modified in readiness for carrier deck landing trials. It received an A-frame arrester hook, provision for RATOG, a heavily-framed cockpit canopy and – because the AUW had increased by 613lb (278kg) – the main undercarriage doors were removed. Mike Lithgow flew VV106 in its new condition on 14 September; it was delivered to the RAE three days later.

The trials lasted three months and included ADDLs and RATOG take-offs. *Illustrious* was used for the deck landing trials, Lt J Elliott making the world's first swept wing carrier deck landing on 8 November. Elliott, Lithgow and A&AEE pilot Lt Cdr DG Parker made a dozen landings and take-offs that day. Only two RATOG rockets were required, fixed to the wing roots. On the following day, Parker encountered severe asymmetric thrust when one of the rockets failed to ignite on take-off. The aircraft swung, the wingtip hitting one of the ship's gun turrets, but Parker was able to get airborne without further mishap. No further deck handling trials were made with the Type 510, Hawker's P.1052 taking up the research baton.

The second Supermarine Type 510 VV106 carried out deck landing trials aboard HMS *Illustrious*, making history when Lt J Elliott made the world's first swept wing carrier deck landing on 8 November 1950. This photograph shows one of that day's intensive trials of 12 landings. Only two RATOG rockets were required for take-off, which can be seen affixed to the wing root. *Author's Collection*

LEFT The Hawker P.1052 VX272 received FAA fighter paintwork and Royal Navy titles for the duration of the brief carrier trials programme. *Tony Buttler Collection*

BELOW P.1052 VX272 descending to catch the arrester wire aboard HMS *Eagle* on 27 or 28 May 1952. *Crown Copyright via Tony Buttler Collection*

By the end of 1948, DMARD JE Serby wanted one of the two P.1052 prototypes to undertake carrier landing trials. The first prototype, VX272, undertook a preliminary deck landing assessment at Farnborough and nearby Chilbolton on 10, 14 and 15 January 1952. The pilot was Lt TG Innes.

VX272 had been modified with an arrester hook, a long-stroke undercarriage (which could only be retracted in an emergency) and had received VX279's strengthened rear fuselage. The wing sweep was 35° at quarter-chord. The variable incidence tailplane was fixed in position and the dive-recovery flaps were made inoperable. The AUW was 10,595lb (4,805kg).

Innes flew ADDLs at Farnborough; using full flap deflection the normal approach speed was 120kt, reducing to 112-115kt before touchdown. The controls were effective and well harmonised, but similar longitudinal trim issues to those of the Sea Hawk were noted, especially if the rear fuel tanks contained more than the forward ones. Worries about the hook striking the carrier round-down or catching the No.1 wire while still airborne, echoed similar fears on the Sea Hawk. The P.1052's poor Dutch Roll characteristics were judged to be problematic if the air was turbulent astern of the carrier, or if the pilot made a poor skidding turn on approach. On take-off, the aircraft had to be held down for the whole deck run. In summary, a high degree of accurate flying was required and Innes judged that the P.1052 was only satisfactory for deck operations for experimental purposes. A programme of deck trials aboard *Eagle* followed on 27–28 May, the aircraft being painted in FAA colours and markings, but the results were of academic interest by this time given the new prototypes that were already taking to the air.

Swept wing research aircraft

	Supermarine Type 510 Swift	Hawker P.1052
Span	31ft 8½in (9.65m)	31ft 6in (11.12m)
Length	39ft 6in (12.0m)	37ft 7in (11.44m)
Wing area	272.9ft² (25.36m²)	278ft² (25.83m²)
t/c ratio	10%	10%
All-up weight	12,177lb (5,522kg); 12,790lb (5,800kg) with RATO	13,488lb (6,120kg)
Powerplant	1x Nene RN.2, 5,000lbf (22.2kN)	1x Nene RN.2, 5,000lbf (22.2kN)
Max speed	569kt (1,054km/h)	514kt (952km/h) at 25,000ft (7,620m)
Rate of climb	?	3,864ft/min (1,177m/min)
Service ceiling	30,000ft (9,145m)	44,500ft (13,565m)
Armament	None	None

2 Rubber Decks and Angled Decks

The advent of jet propulsion not only changed the science of aeronautical engineering, but also naval architecture. Deck trials using de Haviland Sea Vampires, Hawker Sea Hawks, Supermarine Attackers and the swept wing Hawker P.1052 and Supermarine Type 510 Swift prototypes, had revealed that jet aircraft had high approach speeds, which resulted in longer landing runs for safety in case an arrester wire (or all of them) was missed. Heavier aircraft required more propulsive force from catapults to produce the acceleration necessary to get airborne safely. The design of the aircraft carrier's flight deck would have to be modified to enable safe simultaneous take-off and landing operations by jets. As early as 1944, the Royal Aircraft Establishment (RAE) and aircraft designers were proposing to remove the undercarriage from naval aircraft to enable them to carry more fuel to overcome the thirst of the early turbojets.

How then, would you land aboard a ship without an undercarriage? Vertical take-off and landing (VTOL) for fixed-wing aircraft was still science-fiction. The unlikely solution was to land on an air-filled rubber mattress. This effort has often been remembered as a rather silly idea cooked up by gin-addled Admirals, but in fact both aircraft designers and naval architects took the idea seriously and made practical experiments and the US Navy (USN) also became very interested in the project.

Longer landing runs and longer catapults meant that the available deck space was rapidly shrinking. The ideal solution was to remove the necessity for a

HMS *Hermes* shows the three main technological developments necessary to allow carriers to operate jet aircraft. Forward are two BS.4 steam catapults, the angled landing deck and the mirror landing sight amidships on the portside. *Netherlands Ministry of Defence/Wikimedia*

This is the Stage 1 Flexible Deck used for drop tests to check if the inflated mattress could withstand the impact without deflating. The crane is holding aloft a weighted dummy lower fuselage. The crane looks to be newly acquired war booty, being mounted on a German 8-tonne Krauss-Maffei Zgkw 8t halftrack. *Crown Copyright*

crash barrier – a rope net which 'captured' an aircraft if it missed the wires or suffered another mishap like the arrester hook breaking off. Jet-powered fighters had the cockpit in the nose, risking pilot injury on impact – impacts which were now faster and harder. Removing the barrier would make it unsafe to park aircraft on the deck. Ultimately, in a 'eureka moment' a simple yet brilliant solution was hit upon: offset the end of the landing deck to port of the ship's centreline. The angled deck thus created also enabled standard wheeled undercarriage aircraft to operate as usual. The Royal Navy and the USN worked together to bring it to fruition and this solution has been adopted worldwide in many carrier designs.

In August 1948, 778 Naval Air Squadron, the Service Trials Unit at Royal Naval Air Station Lee-on-Solent, was disbanded and reformed as 703 NAS. Moving to RNAS Ford in April 1950, the squadron found itself busy with arrester gear trials ('wire pulling' to test installations aboard the carriers), angled deck trials and tests with the mirror landing system. They were assessing the cutting edge innovations of carrier aviation.

The Flexible Deck

The RAE began its investigations into undercarriageless aircraft and how to operate them aboard carriers during 1944. Removing the undercarriage was calculated to save at least 6% of the aircraft's all-up weight (AUW), which could then be devoted to additional fuel or payload. Major Fred M Green of the RAE proposed an inflated air-cushioned rubber deck, fitted with a single arrester wire. The idea was rapidly approved for trials and during February 1945 the Ministry of Aircraft Production's Director of Technical Development (DTD), NE Rowe asked Supermarine's Chief Designer Joe Smith to draw up an undercarriageless interceptor.

In March 1945, RAE test pilot Lieutenant Commander (Lt Cdr) Eric 'Winkle' Brown was tasked with devising a suitable landing approach. He undertook the first Airfield Dummy Deck Landings (ADDLs) at Farnborough, flying at a horizontal attitude of 3° in a Bell P-39 Airacobra (due to its ability to fly accurately at low altitude) and then aboard the trials carrier HMS *Pretoria Castle*, including test landings using a Grumman F6F Hellcat.

Suitable jet-powered aircraft were required for the trials. As related in the previous Chapter, two Vampire F.3 fighters were converted as the Sea Vampire F.20 and F.21 prototypes to full naval standards. The F.21 prototype, serial VG701, for the flexible deck trials was followed by an order placed on 13 December 1946 for another five Vampire F.3 conversions (VT795, VT802–805) with reinforced engine access doors, a reinforced tailpipe fairing and squared-off wing tips. The undercarriage was retained. During the trials the arrester hook was fitted with a microswitch which retracted the dive brakes and flaps when the arrester wire was caught. The flaps were set at 45° for landing instead of the normal 78° and the dive brakes were only extended to 60° instead of the normal 90°. An inertia cut-out was also fitted to switch off the engine following landing to prevent the hot exhaust from damaging the rubberised deck. Until the F.21s were ready, two Vampire F.1s were assigned (TG286 and TG426); Brown beginning to fly ADDLs at Farnborough with TG426 in August 1947.

Farnborough's Naval Aviation Department (NAD) drew up a four-stage development plan:

- **Stage I:** one-eighth scale model tests to determine the flexible material required and suitable methods of tensioning the rubberised deck surface. These took place during early 1945.

- **Stage II:** construction of a 34 × 30ft (10.3 × 9m) deck section at Farnborough from January 1946. This was used in static test drops of weighted cylinders and a ballasted General

How not to do it. Lt Cdr Eric Brown in de Havilland Sea Vampire TG426 hits the flexible deck having accidently caught the arrester hook on the edge of the deck. Part of the port tail cone has detached due to the impact. The aircraft would bounce the remaining length of the deck, ending up on the ground with a split fuselage. The spray is the lubricant which was used to reduce skin friction to prevent abrasive damage to the wooden fuselage nacelle. *Phil Butler Collection via Chris Gibson*

Aviation GAL.48 Hotspur glider fuselage. In March 1947 a new 200ft (61m) by 60ft (18.2m) section was constructed with four layers of traverse inflatable tubes (surplus 7¼in (185mm) diameter fire hoses) beneath a top surface of rubberised cord fabric and with a single arrester wire mounted 30in (76cm) above the deck. Three ballasted Hotspurs (weight 12,000lb [5,440kg]) fitted with arrester hooks were launched from a rocket-powered trolley onto the deck; making 34 successful landings.

- **Stage III:** a full-scale mattress with five layers of substrate tubes laid alongside Runway 04/22 for use with the Sea Vampires. The first landing by Lt Cdr Eric Brown on 29 December 1947 ended with Vampire F.1 TG426 being wrecked when the tail impacted the ground short of the deck, causing the aircraft to nose over and the arrester hook to retract, bouncing across the flexible deck and ending up nose-first on the ground; luckily, Brown escaped injury. A total of 52 successful landings were made using Vampire F.1 TG286. Use was also made of loaned Gloster Meteor F.8 VZ438 in March 1951.

- **Stage IV:** trials aboard an aircraft carrier to determine the feasibility of landing an aircraft onto the flexible deck at sea.

The following stages were subsequently added:

- **Stage V:** a full-scale mattress of a modified design laid alongside Runway 07/25, 400 × 80ft (122 × 24.3m), codenamed *Red Rufus* by the Ministry of Supply (MoS). The flexible deck was in two sections with new single-layer substrate of 30in (760mm) diameter tubes inflated at lower air pressure. Two American Mk.4 arrester units were connected to form a tandem unit. Four low-pressure air blowers taken from submarines were provided to inflate the substrate.

- **Stage VI:** Demonstration of a complete launching and landing cycle using a cordite-powered slotted tube catapult and the flexible deck. The flexible deck was a mix of equipment from Stages IV and V.

Serious planning for Stage IV began in June 1947. The Director of Naval Construction was also involved in the design of the ship installation. The *Colossus*-class light fleet carrier HMS *Warrior* was selected for conversion, the design of the installation being finalised in December. The flexible deck was fitted over the aft portion of the flight deck during the following summer at Portsmouth Dockyard; it ran from the after end of the island to within 150ft (45.7m) of the round-down at the stern.

The Sea Vampire would take off normally using the BH.III hydraulic catapult before landing on the flexible deck with the undercarriage retracted, then being lifted off the deck by the ship's crane and the undercarriage lowered to enable the aircraft to taxi to the catapult for another flight. The 80ft (24.3m) width of the deck reduced the arrester wire run-out and this limited the wire engagement speed to 87kt.

Four Sea Vampire F.21s were embarked aboard *Warrior* in November 1948. The trials lasted until May 1949 (excessive ship movement in the rough winter seas having interrupted the trials several times), a total of 271 landings being made. One outcome was that the friction forces on landing doubled the arresting effect of the wire gear, therefore doubling the deceleration g load that the fuselage – and the pilot – had to withstand. Experiments followed to find a suitable lubricant to avoid friction damage to the aircraft, a diglycol distearate graphite mix being the most effective. Following the trials, the deck was removed from *Warrior*.

A total of 250 landings both at Boscombe Down and on *Warrior* had been achieved by January 1950 during Stages III and IV. Ten pilots had been involved: four Fleet Air Arm (FAA) test pilots, three RAF test pilots and three FAA squadron pilots, one – Lt Cdr Thomas – being a USN exchange pilot. The wire engagement speed was 92kt on land and 103kt aboard *Warrior* with 20–37kt winds over the deck. The vertical velocity on touchdown was around 11ft/sec (3.3m/sec) – higher than for wheeled aircraft but not unduly problematic for the airframe or the pilot. Crosswind landings in low wind conditions were attempted, with some loss of height and wing dropping experienced at the low landing speed.

The pilots were generally satisfied with the flexible deck but advised that it should be located farther forward on the ship to give the pilot additional time to adjust the aircraft's height before catching the wire, ideally with a longer arrester hook. While landing on the flexible deck was within the scope of

This series of photographs shows Lt Cdr Eric Brown making a successful landing aboard HMS *Warrior's* flexible deck, catching the single arrester wire. The aircraft is Sea Vampire F.21 VT803. VT803 went on to serve with 771 and 764 NAS as a training aircraft until mid-1956. *Eric Morgan Collection via Tony Buttler*

Hawker P.1040 VP413 sits on the specially developed handling trolley following a flexible deck landing trial in November 1953. *Phil Butler Collection via Chris Gibson*

the average pilot, the need to maintain the correct height and attitude on approach called for very precise flying and concentration (the arrester wire was missed 63 times out of 266 landing attempts). Indeed some mishaps did occur; VT802 was caught by a wind eddy and impacted the ground, suffering serious – but not irreparable – damage on 2 June 1948 with Flt Lt Genders at the controls. VT795 lost its arrester hook aboard *Warrior* on 25 January 1949 and Lt Cdr Ellis flying the same aircraft suffered porpoising on the Farnborough carpet on 17 June 1953 and ended up making a wheels-up landing on the ground. VT795 was again involved when Lt Checketts approached too low, missed the wire, bouncing off the carpet and coming to rest in the overshoot area on 1 May 1954.

Preliminary trials of towing the landed aircraft along the deck using a winch to place it onto a wheeled trolley were carried out, the process taking around 60 seconds. The RAE also studied a Universal deck – the flexible carpet being laid inside a trench to make it flush with the main landing deck – and a collapsible deck to allow use by wheeled aircraft, being inflated for undercarriageless use. The plan was to develop a deck suitable for aircraft weighing up to 30,000lb (13,600kg) with landing speeds of 150kt. A sign of the growing interest in the system was the issuing of Specification ER.110T in February 1951 for a supersonic fighter equipped with variable-geometry wings as an experimental design – the design tenders were allowed to offer undercarriageless designs to work with flexible carpets as a solution to save weight given the complex wing mechanisms required.

The Stage V trials at Farnborough lasted between April 1952 and January 1955. A total of 23 pilots flying the Sea Vampires achieved 302 landings. The modified second prototype Hawker P.1040, VP413, was also used. To solve the problem of deck manoeuvring with an undercarriageless aircraft, a special trolley was devised and rapid-handling trials with three Sea Vampires on 20 November 1952 achieved 44 seconds between each landing.

Stage VI did not take place until 12 November 1953, some five years after the *Warrior* trials. Lt WH Noble made a take-off and landing using P.1040 VP413. The slotted catapult launched the aircraft at 104kt at a weight of 11,960lb (5,425kg), Noble cruised for 20 minutes to reach the landing weight of 10,800lb (4,900kg) for a wheels up landing on the flexible deck. Just one flight took place – the catapult was required for static trials at Bedford – before the project was wound up.

It was estimated that removing the undercarriage from existing aircraft could reduce the AUW by 7%, increasing endurance by up to 54% or military load by 37%. A purpose-designed aircraft might achieve a 32% AUW reduction to increase endurance by 70% or military load by 47%, the rate of climb by 40% and reduce the approach speed by 23kt. Purpose-built undercarriageless aircraft would need to be of mid or high-wing layout to ensure adequate flap clearance, a flat belly with large radius curvature of the lower fuselage, low-mounted tailplanes had to be avoided and carriage of wingtip or underwing stores was problematic. A slightly nose-up wing incidence setting was advised to achieve a smooth horizontal attitude once the arrester wire was engaged.

By late 1951 the Admiralty was looking towards a future jet bomber weighing over 100,000lb (45,360kg) for its future aircraft carriers. In October, work began on a proposal to convert an English Electric Canberra PR.3 photo-reconnaissance aircraft for flexible deck trials as a preliminary step in assessing how heavier aircraft behaved on the novel surface. The layout of the Canberra with its wing-mounted engines and smooth underfuselage leant itself well to belly landings. The PR.3 was chosen over the bomber variant of the Canberra as the bomb bay section was shorter and therefore it was easier to strengthen the ventral structure to withstand the impact of landing. The Stage V flexible deck would be upgraded with two Mk.10 arrester gear units to handle the Canberra's 24,500lb (11,110kg) landing weight. A steam catapult would be required for take-off.

The RAE carried out an investigation into the idea, reporting back to the MoS in May 1952. Removing the undercarriage would save around 700lb (317kg) AUW (despite the additions of an arrester hook and fuselage strengthening), which if it were put into fuel would increase range by 110nm (203km) – which the RAE thought was insufficient return on the investment in the specialist deck handling gear required. They also highlighted the lack of funding and that carrying out experimental work with the Canberra might delay an operational naval bomber by up to three years. The RAF's Assistant Chief of the Air Staff (Operational Requirements), Air Vice-Marshall Geoffrey Tuttle pointed out that a new aircraft would not be ready until 1960 and queried whether the flexible deck would remain viable during that time. For Tuttle, the flexible deck was only useful in that it reduced airfield vulnerability, rather than any performance improvement that might be attained. The consensus was that further experimental work was not justified and the Canberra proposal was shelved.

The Admiralty recognised the shortcomings of the flexible deck: the inability of undercarriageless aircraft to operate ashore without some kind of auxiliary landing gear; the inability of propeller-driven anti-submarine and airborne early warning (AEW) aircraft to use the flexible deck (which implied that jet-powered or helicopter replacements would be required); a slower landing rate; deck handling problems; and the need to refit all existing carriers. In addition, the trials aboard *Warrior* did not indicate any increase in safety when landing in heavy seas due to the motion of the flexible deck. (Increasing the number of arrester wires was proposed as a remedy.) Even so, they also saw the advantages in terms of removing deck landing performance constraints and increased aircraft performance. Efforts to develop a universal barrier able to arrest both undercarriageless and wheeled aircraft were unsatisfactory – another factor which made the angled deck more attractive.

Talks with the USN began in May 1952 on flexible and angled landing decks. By October plans had been put in place to obtain a flexible deck – either from the RAE or American manufacturers – for the Naval Air Test Center at Patuxent River, Maryland, along with $2.75 million funding for a two-year programme. This would also cover the conversion of two Grumman F9F-6 Panther jet fighters for undercarriageless operation and provision of a steam catapult. Future plans saw the possibility of a carrier conversion and the use of the Convair F2Y Sea Dart delta-winged hydro-ski fighter. The United States Marine Corps (USMC) also became interested in the flexible deck as a mobile airstrip for amphibious assault operations. The United States Air Force was also interested.

The *Essex*-class fleet carrier USS *Antietam* was earmarked for the trial flexible deck, but this was soon overtaken by the greater interest in the angled deck, which was fitted to *Antietam* instead. The flexible deck was built at Patuxent River for tests with modified F9F-7 Cougars and trials went on into early 1955.

The system had worked but was a blind alley in terms of aircraft carrier and aircraft development, it was too complicated and expensive compared with more practical solutions like the angled deck and beginnings of serious practical VTOL aircraft development. Thoughts that it might still be useful as an interim solution were swept aside by the adoption of the angled deck.

Look, no wheels!

Following the request by DTD NE Rowe, Supermarine's Chief Designer Joe Smith hoped to get his team working once the war in Europe ended. Work soon began on the Type 505 in late 1945 and the transonic wing was tested in the wind tunnel at University College, Southampton during May and June 1946; in August model spinning tests were carried out at the National Physical Laboratory. The Admiralty's Director Aircraft Carrier Research decided to limit the aircraft to an overall length of 47ft 6in (14.4m), a folded width of 27ft (8.2m) and a weight of 20,000lb (9,070kg) to enable it to fit onto most of the available carriers – up to 54 on the *Eagle*-class or a dozen on the *Colossus* and *Majestic*-classes.

The design emphasis was on rate of climb and Smith selected the new Rolls-Royce 6,500lbf (28.9kN) AJ.65 axial-flow turbojet (to become the Avon). Initial plans to use a single jet with a rocket booster in the tail were dropped when it became clear that it would require a swept wing to make the most of the power available, which at that time was untested. An MoS meeting on 8 July selected the twin AJ.65-powered design, which gave a broad fuselage and provided ample space for 405gal

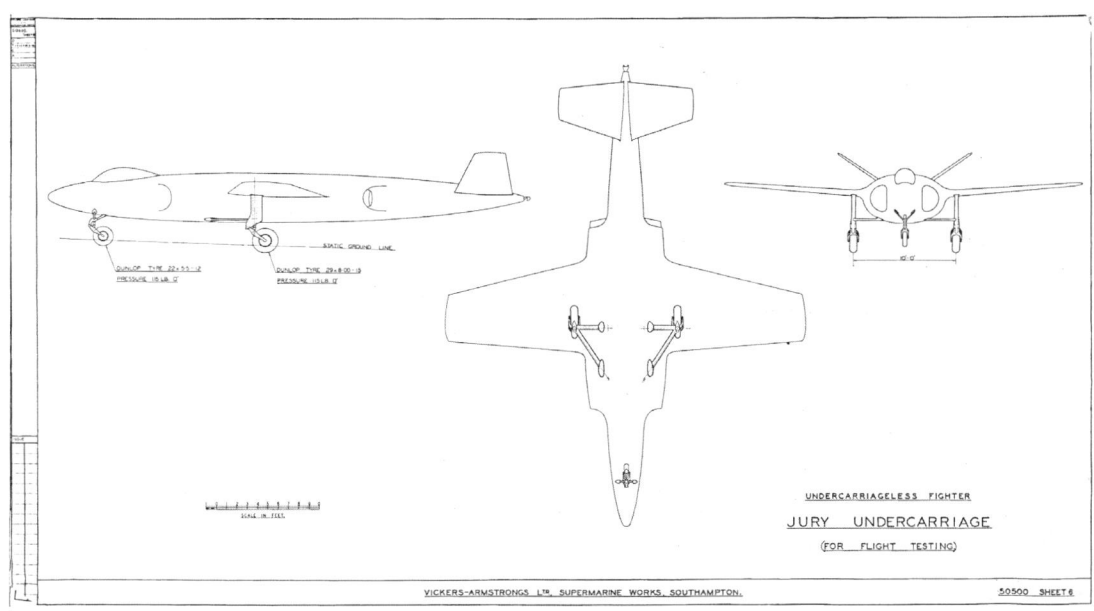

A general arrangement drawing of the Supermarine Type 505 shows the temporary fixed undercarriage that would have been used for the initial flight trials. *RAF Museum Hendon via Ralph Pegram*

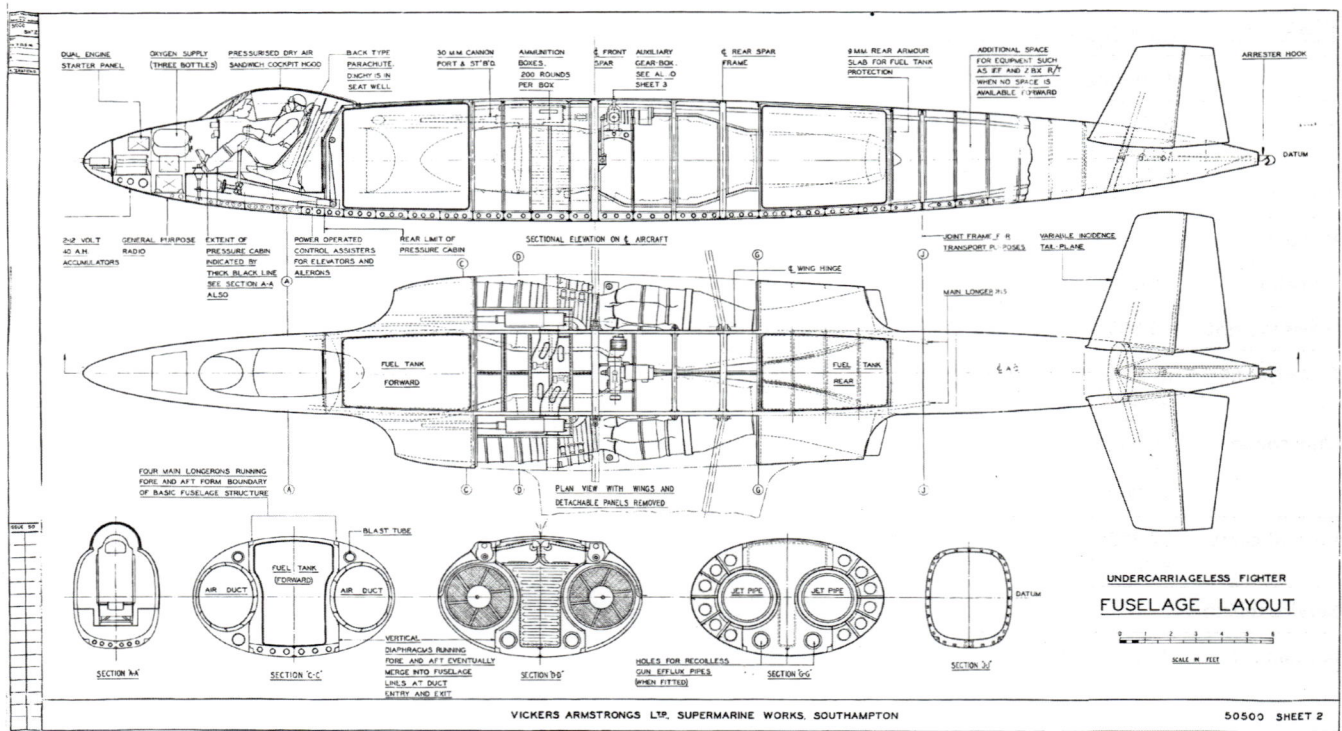

This technical drawing from April 1946 illustrates the Type 505's internal layout. Note the broad low curvature lower fuselage on the cross-sections, a design feature to ensure stability when landing on the flexible deck. *RAF Museum Hendon via Ralph Pegram*

(1,840L) of fuel and an armament of four 30mm ADEN cannon or a 5.9in (150mm) calibre rocket gun or a 4.5in (114mm) recoilless gun (the latter two weapons never reached the hardware stage). The straight mid-mounted wing with 8° leading edge sweep and low 7% thickness-to-chord (t/c) ratio had power-operated wide-chord ailerons, spoilers for use in the approach, 25% chord plain flaps, dive recovery flaps under the wings and a full span leading edge nose flap for additional lift. The nose flaps could be replaced by boundary layer control later. A V-tail was provided, the incidence being altered to steer the aircraft and using traditional elevators during landing. The cockpit layout was almost identical to the Attacker's. Drop tanks would be fitted inboard under the wings.

The estimated maximum speed at sea level was 595kt and 512kt at 45,000ft (13,715m), when loaded to 13,500lb (6,120kg) the sea level rate of climb was estimated at 27,250ft/min (8,305m/min), reaching 45,000ft within three minutes. The naval version was estimated to weigh 15,500lb (7,030kg) loaded.

Supermarine's tender for the Type 505 stated that an unarmed prototype could be delivered within 15 months of the Instruction to Proceed. A fixed tricycle undercarriage would be fitted for the early test flying programme to prove the handling. At the MoS, a meeting on 9 August 1946 to discuss the aircraft agreed not to proceed with the project as no flexible deck trials had begun and converting a trials carrier was some time away. The Principal Director of Technical Development, Stuart Scott Hall, felt that Supermarine was avoiding facing up to the development of swept wings by claiming that the thin wing and lighter undercarriageless fuselage would achieve the same performance, calling it "a cowardly approach" (Joe Smith was present at the meeting!) In the interim, the Vice-Controller (Air) and Chief Naval Representative (CNR), MS Slattery, wanted Supermarine to work on a naval strike aircraft and thought that a conventional Type 505 would be suitable. There was also a need for an insurance in case the Hawker Sea Hawk design failed or that swept wing fighters proved difficult to operate from carriers. Supermarine added an undercarriage and increased the wing area by 13% to reduce the approach speed, creating the Type 508, the prototype of which, VX133, flew in August 1951. Ultimately, the Type 508 would lead to the Type 544 Scimitar F.1 day strike fighter which entered service rather belatedly in 1958 – 13 years after Rowe's request – becoming the most enduring legacy of the flexible deck programme.

Supermarine issued a brochure in 1951 outlining its ideas for the next generation of undercarriageless fighters. The Type 543 was designed to be supersonic and reach 45,000ft (13,715m) within three minutes. The designers argued that not having an undercarriage reduced the size and weight of the airframe by 35%. The design followed the RAE's recommendations following the Sea Vampire trials; a broad flat fuselage, a mid-mounted wing and a T-tail. The swept wings had a t/c ratio of 5% to 7% from root to tip and were equipped with drooping high-lift leading edge slats and double-slotted flaps. Wing folding was provided, as was a short arrester hook. The armament was either four 30mm ADEN cannon in the fuselage sides or two ADEN and twenty 50mm recoilless guns in the wing roots, each firing a spin-stabilised rocket.

Flexible Deck capable designs

	Supermarine Type 505	**Supermarine Type 543**	**Saro P.121/1**	**Saro P.121/2 (hydro-ski)**
Span	35ft 0in (10.67m); 25ft 0in (7.62m) folded	32ft 6in (9.91m); 20ft (6.10m) folded	41ft 6in (12.65m)	39ft 9in (12.12m)
Length	46ft 9in (14.25m)	58ft 6in (17.83m)	49ft 6in (15.09m)	51ft 6in (15.70m)
Wing area	270ft² (25.11m²)	450ft² (41.95m²)	315ft² (29.29m²)	490ft² (45.57m²)
t/c ratio	7%	5-7%	?	?
Gross weight	15,500lb (7,030kg)	30,300lb (13,745kg)	11,750lb (5,550kg)	22,000lb (9,980kg)
Powerplant	2x AJ.65 Avon, 6,500lbf (28.9kN)	2x BE.15, 9,000lbf (40.0kN)	1x Sapphire with reheat	1x Sapphire Sa.4, 12,500lbf (55.6kN) reheat
Max speed	590kt (1,094km/h) at SL; 547kt (1,013km/h) at 45,000ft (13,715m)	766kt (1,420km/h) at SL; 880kt (1,630km/h) at 36,000ft (10,975m)	576kt (1,067km/h) at SL; 563kt (1,044km/h) at 10,000ft (3,050m)	612kt (1,134km/h) at SL; 534kt (998km/h) at 45,000ft (13,715m)
Rate of climb	27,250ft/min (8,305m/min) at SL	37,000ft/min (11,280m/min) at SL	9,800ft/min (2,985m/min) at SL	16,200ft/min (4,940m/min) at SL
Service ceiling	?	45,000ft (13,715m)	53,300ft (16,305m)	55,000ft (16,765m)
Armament	2x 30mm ADEN	4x 30mm ADEN or 2x 30mm ADEN & 20x 2in (50mm) recoilless gun-fired rockets	2x 30mm ADEN	4x 30mm ADEN

The Type 543 was powered by a pair of 9,000lbf (40kN) Bristol BE.15 with reheat or developments of the Rolls-Royce Avon, Armstrong Siddeley Sa.50 Sapphire or the Napier E.143 (the BE.15 was destined to remain on the drawing board and does not appear to have appeared on any other design). Each engine was fed via a nose intake. The estimated maximum speed was Mach 1.53 at 36,000ft (10,970ft). The endurance was 60 minutes, plus 10 minutes of combat at 45,000ft. Ground handling would be via an eight-wheel trolley towed by a tractor and the brochure outlined the necessary land and ship carpets required – including a novel double-decker carrier concept with the fore end of the upper hangar opening onto a catapult-equipped lower flight deck. The Type 543 was offered to the RN and the RAF but no official interest resulted.

Two of the Specification N.114T all-weather fighter contenders (see Chapter 4) also spawned undercarriageless versions in late 1951. Blackburn Aircraft modified their B.87 swept wing design as the B.94 with a reduced wing area of 575ft² (53.4m²) and Short Brothers proposed a version of their PD.5 design.

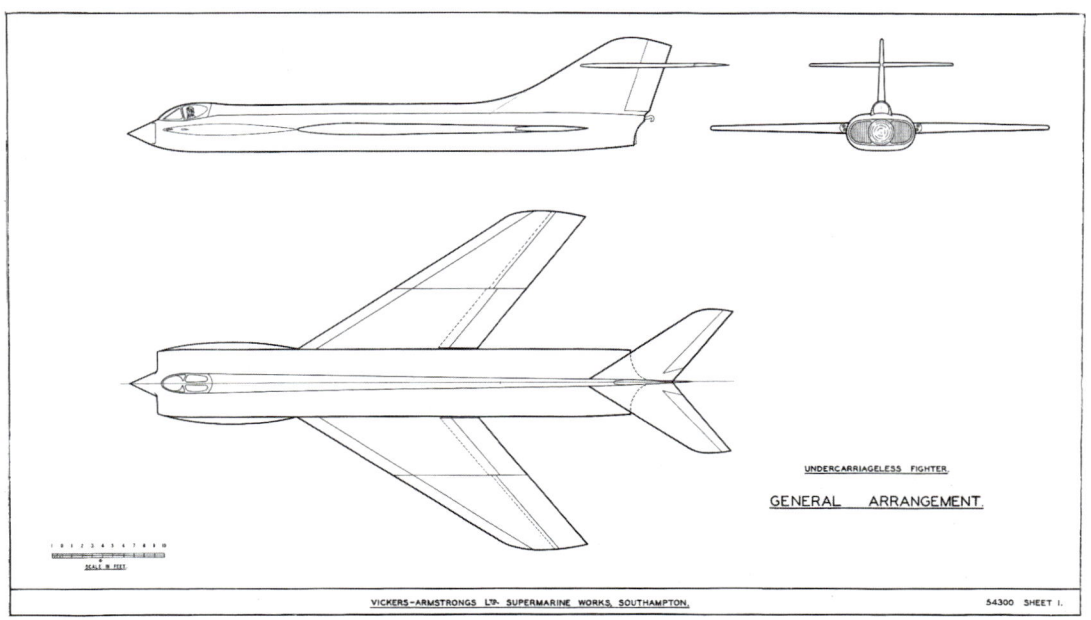

The Supermarine Type 543 was one of the few purpose designed flexible deck aircraft. The fuselage was as broad as possible to prevent the aircraft rolling on touchdown. *RAF Museum Hendon via Ralph Pegram*

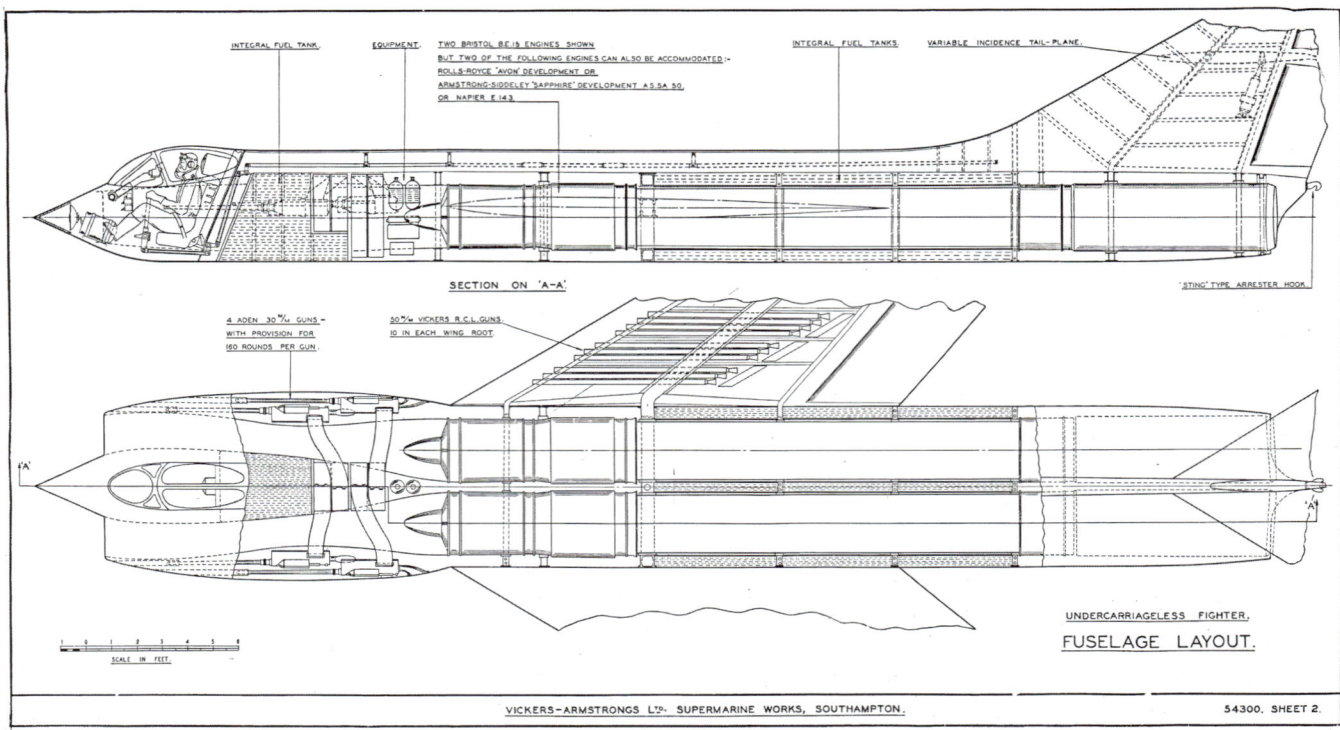

This internal diagram shows how the majority of the fuselage was taken up by the twin turbojets and their jet pipes. Also of note are the batteries of ten single-round 2in (50mm) calibre recoilless guns in the wing roots, the discharge gases venting from ports in the lower wing skin. *RAF Museum Hendon via Ralph Pegram*

Should aircraft designers be trusted to become naval architects? While this flexible deck carrier with its separate take-off and landing decks looks like something out of the *Dan Dare* comic strip in *Eagle*, the Director of Naval Construction did assess similar layouts. The danger of an aircraft missing the arrester wire or crashing through the safety barrier to topple onto the deck below makes this proposition a non-starter. *RAF Museum Hendon via Ralph Pegram*

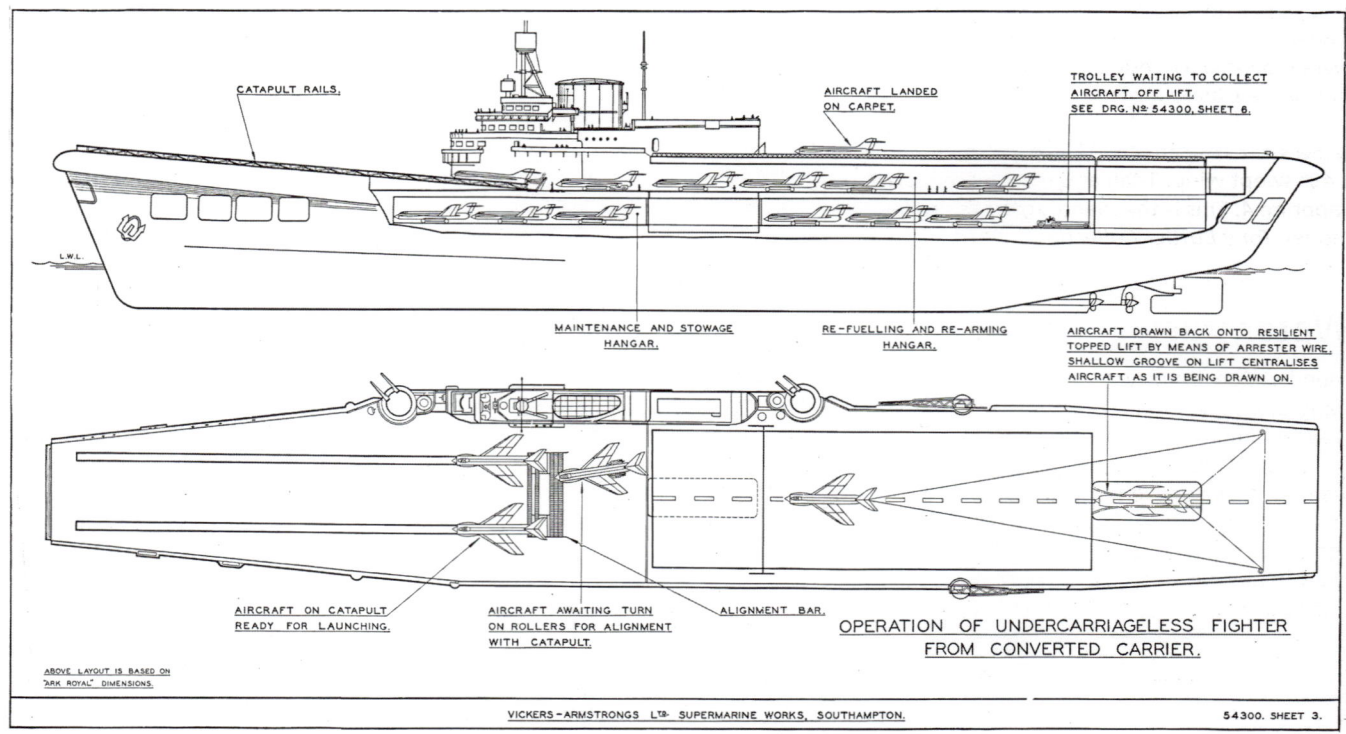

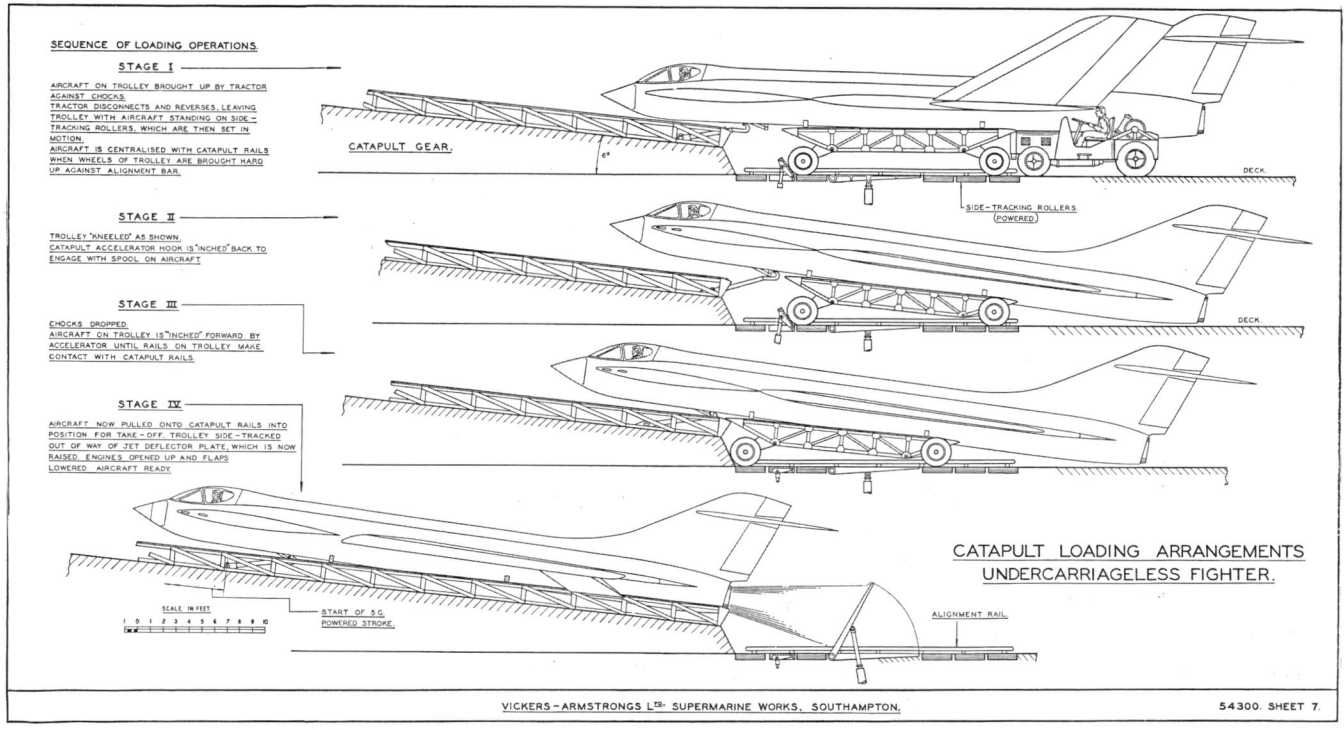

ABOVE A detailed diagram of the launching sequence from the fixed catapult. *RAF Museum Hendon via Ralph Pegram*

RIGHT The Saro P.121 was unusual in being one of a handful of jet-propelled seaplane fighters, which could have also operated from flexible decks. A development from the SR/A.1, it had a traditional flying boat hull and a 35° swept wing, V-tail and a dorsally-mounted reheated Armstrong Siddeley Sapphire. The two 30mm ADEN cannon were mounted alongside the cockpit. *National Aerospace Library via Tony Buttler*

BELOW RIGHT The Saro P.121/2 had a single hydro-ski, a 40° swept wing, T-tail and a dorsal reheated Sapphire 4. This is the manufacturer's display model. *Tony Buttler Collection*

Water-skis

Saunders-Roe (Saro) was a noted manufacturer of flying boats and in July 1947 had flown the first jet-powered fighter flying boat, the SR/A.1 designed to meet Specification E.6/44. By late 1950 the design team was working on the P.121 hydro-ski fighter which could operate from water and the flexible deck. The hydro-ski was a retractable planing surface which when retracted into the lower fuselage gave comparable drag figures to conventional fighters.

A brochure in December 1950 outlined three design studies. The P.121/1 was a development from the SR/A.1 and lacked the hydro-ski. It had a 35° swept wing, V-tail and a dorsally mounted single Armstrong

WINGS OVER THE FLEET

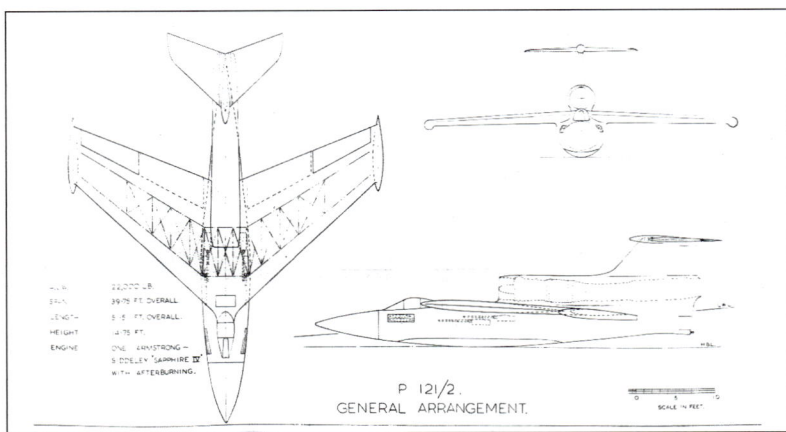

The Saro P.121/2's armament of four 30mm ADEN cannon was fitted on each side of the fuselage, the blast ports being below the cockpit canopy. This general arrangement drawing shows the internal structure of the wings. *Leonardo UK via Tony Buttler*

Artwork of August 1953 shows the P.121-2's hydro-ski and wing tip skis deployed for landing. *Tony Buttler Collection*

Siddeley Sapphire with reheat. The P.121/2 had a single hydro-ski, a 40° swept wing, T-tail and a dorsal 12,530lbf (55.7kN) reheated Sapphire Sa.4 and an armament of four 30mm ADEN cannon. The estimated AUW was 22,000lb (9,980kg). The P.121/3 had a refined hydro-ski and two wing tip skis. It was estimated to reach Mach 1.1 in a dive with the Sa.4; the AUW remained 22,000lb.

Designer J Cohen argued that removing an aircraft's undercarriage and adding fuselage strengthening would save 2.5% of the AUW, which would equate to 15% more military load. Although the MoS rated the designs favourably, more experimentation was required on the hydro-skis and the need for a water-based fighter was unclear and no further development took place.

The Angled Deck

The advent of jet-powered aircraft with higher approach speeds required more powerful arrester gear, which meant a longer pull-out of wire to safely slow the aircraft to a standstill without overstressing the airframe. The carrier also needed room for a safety barrier in case the aircraft missed a wire or the arrester hook failed, to prevent them crashing into aircraft parked on the deck (deck parks being important, as the internal hangars could not accommodate the entire air group). Efforts to develop improved barriers proved troublesome. Jet-powered aircraft were also getting heavier and required longer-stroke catapults to get them airborne. Within the finite limits of available deck length, a means had to be found to safely combine all these features.

Lengthening the flight deck was impractical for most ships, removing the deck park meant reducing the capacity of the carriers and the flexible deck was still in the experimental stages with constraints of its own. Removing the safety barrier seemed the only solution – but how to do so safely?

In August 1951 the head of the NAD at Farnborough, Lewis Boddington, looked at a plan of HMS *Ark Royal* and came up with the idea of a

RIGHT This photo of an 801 NAS Hawker Sea Hawk making a wheels-up landing aboard HMS *Centaur* in December 1959 illustrates why a crash barrier was necessary aboard axial flightdeck carriers to prevent aircraft careering into machines parked forward. *Tony Buttler Collection*

ABOVE A pilot's eye view of the landing approach to an angled deck. There was now no obstruction ahead; a go-around could be safely made if the arrester wires were missed or the approach misjudged. *Crown Copyright*

LEFT The NAD's painted model of HMS *Illustrious* to illustrate the angled deck concept. It was just the deck markings which were skewed to port. The V-tailed aircraft on deck were generic future swept wing jets. *Crown Copyright*

BELOW Supermarine Attacker FB.2 WP295 flies off USS *Antietam*'s angled deck in 1953. *Tony Buttler Collection*

'skewed deck'; offsetting the landing by 7° or 8° to port from the centreline. If the pilot missed the arrester wires – a situation informally known as a 'bolter' – he could simply open the throttle and go around again for another attempt. Boddington even proposed a slight ramp at the end of the angled portion of the landing deck to help the aircraft get airborne. Up to 25% of the air group could be safely parked on the inboard and forward deck areas. Boddington's idea was at once called "most ingenious" by Captain Dennis RF Cambell, the Deputy CNR (Cambell had consulted Boddington about the deck problem a year earlier) and the Director of Naval Air Warfare, Captain Charles LG Evans, was equally enthusiastic. Cambell also issued a report which came to the same conclusions. Boddington also offered a double-decker carrier with separate decks for take-off as a potential solution. The NAD painted angled deck markings on a scale model of HMS *Illustrious* to illustrate the concept. Later comparative deck layout studies by the NAD in June 1953 included having the island superstructure located either to starboard or port as well as new two-deck layouts.

A practical demonstration was required and a programme was quickly prepared. HMS *Triumph* had her centreline markings repainted at an angle of 10°, sufficient for touch-and-go landings with the unaltered arrester gear being unrigged. This demonstration was carried out in February 1952. A similar batch of tests, also including use of the new mirror-landing sight, was conducted aboard *Albion* during August and September 1954 using de Havilland Sea Venom FAW.20 WM510. *Warrior* was used to evaluate a landing approach method in which the pilot did not spool down the engine before touchdown; Sea Vampire F.20 VV142 made 15 successful landings in May 1953.

The idea was shared – along with the flexible deck – with the USN, which moved rapidly ahead with an experimental modification to USS *Antietam* with a 10.5° angled deck, the preliminary trial landings taking place during 11–15 January 1953. The results were highly positive from the beginning. An RN team of observers was present aboard *Antietam* in March, along with a pair of Hawker Sea Furies and two Attackers for flight tests. A visit to the UK in June saw Sea Vampire F.21s VT795 and VT804 making landings aboard the *Antietam*.

HMS *Centaur* was completed in September 1953; her angled deck was achieved by simply painting the deck markings at a slant of 5.5°, with the arrester gear realigned to match. *Crown Copyright via Tony Buttler Collection*

In March 1953 the Admiralty began to plan its own 'quick fix' conversion ahead of the completion of the redesigned *Centaur*-class *Hermes* which would receive a 6.5° angled deck and the completion of *Ark Royal* with a 5.5° angled deck and a deck-edge lift (her flight deck was 800ft [243.8m] long and 112ft [34.1m] wide). The RAE was asked to provide a study into what the minimum requirements were and which cheap options were feasible for the *Centaurs*; for example, a 4° angled deck that did not require a portside hull extension to be built. *Centaur* completed in September 1953 with her deck markings angled by 5.5° to improvise an angled deck, with the arrester gear realigned. *Albion* and *Bulwark* completed the following year with 5¾° angled decks with a small deck overhang on the port side. The *Illustrious*-class fleet carrier *Victorious* completed her reconstruction in January 1958 and was the first carrier to combine the steam catapult, an 8¾° angled deck and the mirror landing sight (the flight deck was 775ft [236.2m] long and 157ft [47.8m] wide) and could operate 35 aircraft weighing up to 40,000lb (18,145kg).

Other innovations

The hydraulic catapult was insufficiently powerful to cope with the increasing weights of aircraft. By 1949 the upgraded BH.V catapult could launch a 30,000lb (13,605kg) aircraft at 75kt. By the early 1950s the next generation of fighters was approaching 40,000lb (18,140kg) in normal loaded condition and new strike aircraft would be even heavier.

The RN's supplier of catapults, MacTaggart, Scott & Company Limited's designer, Colin Mitchell, had conceived the idea of a steam-propelled catapult as early as 1936, obtaining a patent in 1938 but no funding to put his ideas into reality. During the Second World War, Mitchell served with the Engineer-in-Chief's department at the Admiralty, inspecting captured German slotted-cylinder catapults used for launching V-1 flying bombs. He constructed an experimental cordite-powered ventral slotted-cylinder catapult at the Shoeburyness gunnery ranges in late 1944 and tests continued at Farnborough into 1952 in connection with the flexible deck experiments. In a similar experiment, during the summer of 1950 the RAE investigated a rocket-powered trolley running on a fixed rail. In 1946 the Admiralty approved the slotted-cylinder catapult, to be powered by steam taken directly from the ship's boilers.

Design work on the BXS-1 prototype began in 1948, being fitted aboard the *Colossus*-class maintenance tender HMS *Perseus* in 1951. A test programme of 1,560 launches followed. The BXS-1 could launch a 40,000lb aircraft at 78kt. This led to production BS.4 catapults, varying in length from 199ft (60.6m) in the waist position aboard *Eagle* and *Ark Royal* to 139ft (42.3m) aboard the refitted *Centaur*, depending on the length of deck available. The steam catapult's acceleration is reasonably constant throughout its length; a longer catapult achieves a higher end speed. The BS.4 could launch a 50,000lb (22,680kg) aircraft at 94–105kt depending on its length. In her modernisation during 1959–64, *Eagle* received a pair of improved BS.5 catapults, 199ft (60.6m) long and rated at 50,000lb (22,680kg) at 105kt.

Pilots approaching the carrier deck at over 100kt had to react very quickly to signals from the Deck Landing Control Officer – commonly known as the 'batsman'. Reacting to visual signals using the bats was increasingly inadequate and aircraft touchdown was occurring further along the deck. Radio telephone (R/T) talk-down had been trialled during the flexible deck tests in an attempt to overcome this issue. As early as 1936 lights were trialled for night landings aboard *Glorious* and in 1945 an automated radar-controlled approach was proposed. The technology of the day did not allow this to become a reality. An RAE paper of November 1951 by R Duddy and D Lean proposed a system of azimuth control by radar, height control by the aircraft's radio altimeter and the carrier transmitting a 'cut' signal when the pilot should begin his touchdown.

The following month, Captain Cambell and Lt Cdr HCN Goodhart proposed replacing the batsman with a stabilised mirror, onto which a powerful beam of light was shone to indicate the horizontal datum to the pilot. Back at Farnborough, Lean had come to similar conclusions, building an improvised experiment beside Runway 04/22 using polished tinplate and sodium lamps, which proved remarkably successful with 60 landings made during the following three months. The temporary rig was installed aboard *Illustrious* in July 1952 to enable Sea Vampire F.20 VV151 to clear the round-down by 8ft (2.4m) with a vertical velocity on touchdown of 8ft/sec (2.4m/sec).

A purpose-built mirror sight using a concave metal mirror was then built at Farnborough, being fitted to *Illustrious* in October. The reflected light was in the centre of the mirror if the pilot was on the correct glidepath, if it was higher or lower, the approach flightpath had to be corrected accordingly. The sight was mounted aft on the starboard side but was moved to port following pilot feedback. In 1953 further engineering input came from John Curran Limited and GEC Research Laboratories and the first production set was fitted aboard *Illustrious*, Sea Vampire VT802 making six landings using the new sight on 25 November 1953.

The USN was an enthusiastic adopter, fitting its first mirror sight to the *Essex*-class USS *Bennington* in September 1955. Development continued with GEC and the RAE developing the Deck Landing Projector Sight using Fresnel lenses, which replaced the mirror; a multi-coloured array would show the pilot whether he was above or below the glidepath. An audio feed to indicate the airspeed was also developed. *Bulwark* was used for trials during 1955. The first Mk.3 projector sight was fitted to the rebuilt *Victorious* in 1958. By the time the Mk.4 sight appeared in 1965 the batsman was abolished as redundant and the sight became standard equipment in aircraft carriers around the world.

With the angled deck, steam catapult and mirror sight in development to solve most of the practical problems, planning began to determine the carrier modernisation schedule. Of the *Illustrious*-class, *Illustrious* would continue as the training and trials carrier until 1957 when she would be replaced by the refitted *Indomitable*; *Formidable* (in reserve since 1947) and *Victorious* were earmarked for modernisation (*Victorious* entered dock to begin her reconstruction on 23 October 1950) with *Implacable* and *Indefatigable* scheduled to follow in 1953-55 and 1954-57. The new HMS *Eagle* would complete in 1951 and receive her steam catapults in 1956, her sister *Ark Royal* completing in 1954. This would give a force of five fleet carriers and one training carrier. The light fleet carriers *Warrior* and *Vengeance* would receive a limited modernisation to allow them to operate Sea Venoms and Fairey Gannets on trade protection duties (*Vengeance* would go into reserve on completion of her refit). The first three *Centaur*-class carriers would replace four of the remaining *Colossus*-class ships, with *Hermes* completing to a modified design with angled deck and steam catapults in 1955 (in reality November 1959; her design was upgraded in 1957 with a 6.5° angled deck, two 151ft BS.4 steam catapults, deck-edge lift, mirror sight and Type 984 3-D air-search radar).

In early 1952, with Korean War rearmament funds in full flow, the Admiralty began planning for at least one large fleet carrier able to operate aircraft

The mirror landing sight was a simple device. If the pilot was on the correct glidepath and rate of descent, the reflected light was in the centre of the mirror, the lights on the two arms indicated if the pilot was straying from the centreline to port or starboard. *Crown Copyright*

HMS *Eagle* in 1956, fresh from her refit with two BS.4 steam catapults and interim 5.5° angled deck. (Note that the second gun turret to port had its weapons removed due to the angled deck.) The air group comprised de Havilland Sea Venom all-weather fighters forward; Hawker Sea Hawks and Westland Wyvern strike fighters aft. *Crown Copyright*

WINGS OVER THE FLEET

HMS *Victorious* completed her reconstruction in January 1958 and was the first RN carrier to combine steam catapults, a full 8¾° angled deck and the mirror landing sight. The ship also received the new Type 984 3-D air search radar. The lengthy and expensive work led to her sistership never receiving their planned reconstructions. *Crown Copyright*

weighing 60,000lb (27,215kg) with take-off and landing speeds of 120–135kt with a range of 1,000nm (1,852km). This would require a flight deck 1,000ft (305m) long and a displacement of at least 55,000 tons. The carrier design was then uprated to match the 70,000lb (31,750kg) maximum weight limit of the USN's new *Forrestal*-class – the first to be dubbed 'supercarriers' – and for take-off and landing speeds of 140—150kt. The ship would have an angled landing deck 690ft (210m) long, two deck-edge lifts, two islands and two Type 984 search radars. The hangar would be much the same size that of the *Eagle*-class, the air group would be 82 aircraft. The size of the ship was limited by the available dry docks as the Admiralty could not afford to fund major infrastructure projects.

Reality hit hard. In June 1953 design work on the new carrier was stopped, the money to build it was unavailable. Smaller 30–35,000 ton designs in 1954 fared no better. The reconstruction of *Victorious* was proving more complicated and expensive than estimated and the remaining fleet carrier modernisations were cancelled (instead of completing in 1954, it was January 1958 before *Victorious* returned to service.) These ships were then decommissioned following the Radical Review of 1953–54, as they could never operate modern aircraft. The four remaining *Colossus*-class entered the reserve, being kept available for wartime mobilisation. *Indomitable* was sold for scrapping in 1953 and *Illustrious* was instead replaced by *Warrior*, which was cheaper to operate (*Warrior* was sold to Argentina in 1957). The planned force was now just three fleet and three light fleet carriers (*Hermes* would replace her sister *Bulwark*.) The 1957 Defence White Paper by Minister of Defence Duncan Sandys reduced the force to just five ships (*Victorious*, *Eagle*, *Ark Royal*, *Centaur*, *Hermes*), with four in service at any one time. *Albion* and *Bulwark*, lacking steam catapults, became helicopter carriers for the amphibious assault role.

In October 1956 the Admiralty defined the standards for carrier capability with six tiers:

- **A:** fully angled deck (8–10°), steam catapults, Mk.13 arrester gear, Type 984 3-D air-search radar with 32 or 48-track Comprehensive Display System (CDS) and Digital Plot Transmission datalink (*Eagle* following 1959–64 refit, *Hermes* as completed, *Victorious* following reconstruction, *Ark Royal*'s planned refit was cancelled).

  A(H): addition of High Test Peroxide (HTP) fuel for rocket-powered interceptors.

  B*: as 'A' but with older Type 982, 983 and 960 search and height-finding radars and a lower-standard 32-track CDS (*Eagle* as refitted).

- **B:** as B* but without CDS (planned refits for *Centaur*, *Albion* and *Bulwark* were cancelled).

- **C:** interim angled deck (5°) (*Ark Royal* as completed).

  C(H): addition of High Test Peroxide (HTP) fuel for rocket-powered interceptors.

- **D:** as 'C' but with BH.V hydraulic catapults, Mk.10 or 11 arrester gear, limited to Sea Hawk, Sea Venom and Gannet, Type 982/983/960 or earlier radars (*Eagle* following 1954–55 refit, *Centaur*, *Albion* and *Bulwark* as completed).

- **E:** axial deck, Mk.10 or 11 arrester gear, earlier radars (*Warrior* as refitted 1952-53).

- **F:** interim angled deck, earlier radar, training or trials role only (*Warrior* as refitted 1955–56).

HMS *Eagle* was rebuilt to A Standard during 1959 to 1964 with the angled deck realigned to 8.5°, one 199ft (60.6m) and one 151ft (46m) BS.4 steam catapult, Type 984 and 48-track CDS. The time and cost of *Eagle*'s refit meant that her sistership *Ark Royal* never received her A Standard refit (she would not receive an 8.5° angled deck until her 1967–70 refit to operate the McDonnell Douglas Phantom). As an interim solution to maintain hull numbers, *Centaur* received two 139ft (42.3m) BS.4 catapults to enable her to operate 12 de Havilland Sea Vixens, eight Gannets and four Douglas Skyraider AEW aircraft for defensive roles.

Following a decade of experimentation the RN had developed most of the innovations that it required to operate jet-powered aircraft from carriers. Within another decade most of its carrier fleet had been refitted to incorporate them in various forms. The FAA would now rapidly become an operator of jet fighters and strike aircraft.

3 Strike fighter

The predecessor of the Fleet Air Arm, the Royal Naval Air Service, soon grasped that it was capable of projecting striking power over long distances. On Christmas Day 1914, the RNAS bombed the Zeppelin bases at Cuxhaven, Nordholz and Wilhelmshaven; during 1915 the RNAS led the development of Britain's first strategic bomber, the Handley Page O/100, and on 19 July 1918, undertook the first bombing mission against a land target from an aircraft carrier, attacking the Zeppelin base at Tondern. The Admiralty never lost sight of the aircraft carrier's ability to project long-range strikes against shore targets, this ability being proven many times during the Second World War.

As the war ended the RN had a multitude of strike aircraft in development: the Short Sturgeon to meet Specification S.11/43 for a reconnaissance bomber (originally a torpedo-bomber); the Fairey Spearfish torpedo-bomber to Specification O.5/43; de Havilland DH.98 Sea Mosquito TR.33 torpedo-bomber version of the versatile Mosquito; the DH.103 Sea Hornet F.20 long-range fighter-bomber; Blackburn B.46 Firebrand and B.48 Firecrest torpedo/strike fighters;

"The three present types of Naval fighters are considerably outmatched by the MiG-15, and their value against light and medium bombers is doubtful. The N.113 is the only Naval aircraft with the Naval Staff requirement of being able to intercept from the deck."

MEMORANDUM BY THE ADMIRALTY, 25 FEBRUARY 1952

The pugnacious Supermarine Scimitar F.1 was designed as a day fighter but found itself better suited to being a fighter-bomber. The provision of AGM-12 Bullpup ASMs and AIM-9 Sidewinder AAMs brought the FAA into the 'Missile Age'. *Tony Buttler Collection*

The starboard underwing pod on Fairey Firefly FR.4 VG985 houses a AN/APS-4 ASH surface search radar. The FR.4 was a fighter-reconnaissance variant but the ASH radar meant that the Firefly could also operate in the night fighter and anti-ship/submarine strike roles. VG985 was converted as a TT.4 target tug in 1958 for the Indian Navy, becoming INS117. *Author's Collection*

Fairey's Strike Fighter based on its earlier Specification O.21/44 torpedo-bomber designs (successors to the Spearfish); Westland W.34 Wyvern torpedo-fighter to Specifications N.11/44 and N.12/45 with piston and turboprop engine options. Of these, only the Sea Hornet, Firebrand and Wyvern would enter service in numbers, production of the remainder being cancelled at the war's end. In addition to this plethora of options, several aircraft companies had tendered private-venture designs which were not taken up. The FAA also operated fighter-bomber Fairey Fireflies and Hawker Sea Furies and (as related in Chapter 1) the Supermarine Attacker and Hawker Sea Hawk jet-powered interceptors were recast as fighter-bombers before their prototypes had even flown.

In this chapter we examine the development of the post-war generation of fighter-bombers and day fighters, a type often referred to as strike fighters – single-seat fighters that were capable of high performance while carrying heavy offensive payloads.

Versatile Firefly

The Fairey Firefly had been designed in 1940 by a team led by Herbert Eugene Chaplin as a two-seat fighter to meet Specification N.5/40 for a successor to the Fairey Fulmar. It was powered by a Rolls-Royce Griffon 12-cylinder inline V-12 piston engine and was armed with four 20mm Hispano Mk.V cannon in the wings. The first production examples were delivered in March 1943 and were found to be versatile aircraft, being fitted with radar and operated as night-fighters and long-range fighter-reconnaissance aircraft.

The fighter-reconnaissance Firefly FR.4 was a late-war development powered by the 2,100hp (894kW) Griffon 74 with a two-speed two-stage supercharger. The airframe received a revised wing with radiators in the inner wing section, clipped tips, powered wing-folding and outer wing underwing nacelles for additional fuel, the starboard pod often being modified to fit an American-supplied AN/APS-4 ASH (Air-Surface, Model H) radar. The first of 160 production aircraft, serial TW687, was delivered in July 1946, with production ending in February 1948 (another 133 were cancelled). Some were later converted as TT.4 target tugs and 29 were transferred to the Royal Canadian Navy, including seven converted to AS.5 anti-submarine standard before delivery.

The Mk.5 was a multi-role variant capable of easy conversion for the fighter-reece, night-fighter and anti-submarine warfare (ASW) roles, being designated FR.5, NF.5 or AS.5 depending on the equipment fit. Armament comprised four 20mm Hispano Mk.V cannon plus underwing loads of eight 3in (76mm) rocket projectiles (RPs) or two 1,000lb (454kg) bombs. A total of 352 were built (another 92 were cancelled), with the first aircraft, VT362, making its maiden flight on 9 January 1948. The FR.5 entered service with 778 and 782 Naval Air Squadrons (NAS) in May for service trials before 812 NAS began re-equipping in July. Five were transferred to the Royal Australian Navy (RAN), together with 12 dual-control T.5 trainers. The Firefly was increasingly seen as an ASW platform (a more detailed history of the ASW variants can be found in Chapter 7) but events in the Far East cemented its position as one of the FAA's most potent fighter-bombers.

The *Colossus*-class carrier HMS *Triumph* was just about to return home to the UK following a trip to Japan when North Korean forces invaded South Korea on 25 June 1950. The carrier joined the US Navy's Carrier Task Force 77 at Okinawa. TF 77 flew its first sortie over Korea on 3 July when nine Firefly FR.Is and 12 Supermarine Seafires attacked Haeju airfield. *Triumph's* second and third patrols (18–21 July and 24–30 July) saw the Fireflies undertaking anti-submarine sorties; the fourth patrol (14–15 August) involved armed reconnaissance sorties along the western coast as part of the naval blockade of North Korea. During September the Fireflies were part of the force covering the amphibious landing at Inchon.

Triumph was replaced by sistership *Theseus*, whose air group included 810 NAS with Firefly FR.5s, conducting several ground attack strikes. On 27 April 1951 *Glory* arrived to relieve *Triumph*, staying for two tours of duty until May 1952. During these tours, 812 NAS with Fireflies and 804 NAS with Sea Furies accomplished 4,834 sorties, losing 27 aircraft. In between *Glory's* tours, 817 NAS of the RAN filled the gap, operating Firefly FR.5s from HMAS *Sydney*.

HMS *Ocean* replaced *Glory* in May 1952 with the Fireflies of 825 NAS aboard. Operating in consort with 802 NAS's Sea Furies, they shared the Boyd Trophy for their joint efforts, including 123 attacks in a single day and expending 6,000 RPs and 4,000 bombs. *Ocean's* tour lasted until October when *Glory* returned. In May 1953 *Ocean* and 810 NAS arrived, conducting four patrols with the last ending on 23 July, just four days before the ceasefire.

Concurrent with the Korean War was the Malayan Emergency, a guerrilla war fought by the communist pro-independence Malayan National Liberation Army and the Malaysian Communist Party against British, Malayan and Commonwealth forces from 1948 until 1960. The RN lent much support to the land forces and the RAF during the campaign. 827 NAS disembarked from *Triumph* to conduct ground attack strikes with its Fireflies on 21 and 23 October 1947, before re-embarking and transiting to Singapore, from where the squadron was operated on ground attack sorties until the end of January 1950. As the carriers rotated to and from Korea, they often provided ground attack support as they staged through Singapore. The Korean-bound *Ocean* flew sorties with 825 NAS's Firefly FR.5s on 25 April 1951 and the same squadron launched 16 attacks on targets in Central Johore on 27 May 1952. While *Glory* was enroute to Korea, 821 NAS conducted 18 sorties on 27 October 1952. 825 NAS would reprise its role in 1954 while embarked aboard *Warrior*.

Wyvern: pistons and turboprops

Westland's Technical Director, William Edward Willoughby 'Teddy' Petter, in early 1944 proposed a single-seat naval fighter designed around the new Rolls-Royce RH.2SM Eagle 24-cylinder H-24 layout piston engine, initially rated at 3,230hp (2,409kW) but planned to ultimately attain 4,500hp (3,356kW). Among the early studies was also a turboprop-powered version. Petter's layout for the W.34 had the large engine in the centre fuselage, leaving the nose clear for the cockpit which provided excellent visibility, but at the cost of 800lb (363kg) extra

This view of the second production Firefly Mk.4 TW688 in 1946 illustrates the wing leading edge radiators for the Rolls-Royce Griffon 74 V-12 piston engine. TW688 was operated by 727 NAS, the Air Experience Unit, from October 1949 as that unit's only Firefly giving non-FAA naval officers flying experience until it disbanded on 17 January 1951, TW688 then becoming a ground instruction airframe. *Author's Collection*

A wind tunnel model of the original Westland W.34 design with the mid-mounted Rolls-Royce Eagle 24-cylinder piston engine with a chin radiator. *Leonardo UK via Jeremy Graham*

weight and 435nm (805km) less range. Therefore, in April – while Petter was absent from the Yeovil works – the engine was moved to the nose and cockpit raised slightly to maintain a 10° downward view over the nose. The Ministry of Aircraft Production (MAP) agreed that the W.34 would be an asset. The official tender was submitted on 23 June for short-range fleet fighter, torpedo-fighter and RAF short-range fighter versions.

By early July the RAF was concerned that despite the engine power on offer, the estimated 417kt maximum speed, service ceiling and rate of climb were inferior to the Fury and Hornet already under development and it quickly abandoned the W.34. Despite this, the Admiralty was becoming interested and drafted Specification N.11/44, ordering six prototypes in August. N.11/44 was drawn up alongside Operational Requirement OR.174, primarily for a fighter with a secondary attack role.

As a fighter it had to reach 15,000ft (4,570m) in five minutes with a radius of 240nm (445km) or 400nm (740km) with drop tanks, or 373nm (690km) when loaded with 2,000lb (907kg) of bombs. The

The prototype W.34 Wyvern TF.1 TS371 with its eight-blade Rotol contra-rotating propeller powered by the 24-cylinder Rolls-Royce Eagle. This was the pinnacle and twilight of the piston age. A propeller pitch mechanism bearing failure resulted in a wheels-up landing which killed Westland's test pilot Peter Garner on 15 October 1947. Blue Envoy Collection

armament options included an 18in (457mm) diameter Mk.XVII torpedo, one 1,820lb (825kg) Mk.VI mine, a 2,000lb armour-piercing bomb or three 1,000lb (454kg) or 500lb (227kg) bombs, or eight 3in (76mm) RPs with 60lb (27kg) warheads. Four 20mm Hispano Mk.V cannon were fitted in the wings. The dimensional constraints were an overall length of 40ft (12.19m), 18ft (5.48m) folded width and 15ft 9in (4.79m) height with the wings folded.

Petter's turboprop-powered version evolved into the W.35 with a new fuselage containing a Rolls-Royce RB.39 Clyde rated at 2,300shp (1,715kW) plus 1,040lbf (4.6kN) residual exhaust thrust at sea level. Specification N.12/45 was issued on 14 February 1945 to cover development to meet Operational Requirement OR.213/ Naval Staff Requirement NR/A.7 and three prototypes were ordered.

During 1945 several events conspired to reshape the aircraft. Petter left Westland to join English Electric, being replaced by Arthur Davenport, with John Digby becoming Chief Designer. Rolls-Royce's Director and General Manager, Ernest Hives, admitted that his company lacked the resources to develop the Eagle and the Clyde concurrently. The Eagle would need two years' development to attain its full potential and the company was already heavily invested into jet technology and felt that the Clyde was the future. The Royal Aircraft Establishment (RAE) concurred, judging that the lighter Clyde would reduce the wing loading and provide a modest speed increase at sea level. At this stage, the idea of fitting the Napier Sabre H-24 piston engine as a fall-back option was dropped. Davenport estimated that the Eagle-powered W.34 would have an all-up weight (AUW) of 19,194lb (8,705kg) as a fighter and 21,879lb (9,925kg) when armed with a torpedo. Fitting the Clyde would reduce these weights to 16,300lb (7,395kg) and 19,045lb (8,640kg). The estimated speed of 386kt at 20,000ft (6,100m) was not impressive, but the combat range of 550nm (1,020km) was respectable for a fighter.

In May 1946 the Armstrong Siddeley Python turboprop was selected as a back-up choice. This was a wise move as the Clyde's development was already behind schedule. The W.35 needed some redesign to accommodate the larger Python, requiring an increase in fuselage length by 21in (53cm) and greater fuselage depth to fit the bifurcated exhaust. The engine fitted was the 3,670shp (2,736kW) and 1,180lbf (5.2kN) exhaust thrust-rated ASP.3 Python.

In May 1946 the prototype programme was altered to six Eagle-powered W.34s, 20 pre-production W.34, two Python-powered W.35 prototypes and three Clyde-powered W.35s. Up to 500 production W.35s were wanted. Post-war economic cutbacks saw the W.35 prototypes rearranged to just four, a pair with each engine. In 1947 the official name Wyvern was bestowed.

Six W.34 prototypes were built, the first, TS371, making its maiden flight on 12 December 1946. The first two TF.1 prototypes lacked folding wings and arrester gear to speed their construction. TS371 was lost on 15 October 1947 when the propeller bearing failed, killing Westland test pilot Peter Garner. Of the pre-production Wyvern TF.1s, only 10 were built and only four delivered for flight trials. Of the W.35 prototypes, the Python-powered VP109 and VP113 flew on 22 March 1949 and 20 August respectively; VP113 crashed on 31 October following an engine flame-out, killing test pilot Squadron Leader Mike Graves. VP120 with the Clyde flew on 18 January 1949 and was the only aircraft to ever receive the Clyde, Rolls-Royce having cancelled its development in favour of concentrating on the Avon axial-flow turbojet (VP120 only amassed 50 flying hours). The fourth prototype, VR159, was cancelled. They were followed by 20 Python-powered TF.2 pre-production aircraft and a single T.3 two-seat trainer which had been ordered in September 1948 to meet Specification T.12/48.

Specification T.12/48 had called for a Python-powered Wyvern TF.2 modified with a tandem cockpit for an instructor and student with fully duplicated flying and engine controls. The T.3 was to have a weapons training capability consisting of two 20mm cannon and the usual array of underwing ordnance. Endurance was to be 360nm (666km) with drop tanks and in addition to the usual naval radio equipment an ASV.16N surface-search radar was also required. Westland began work on the W.38, deepening the rear fuselage for the instructor's cockpit. The prototype

VZ739 first flew on 11 February 1950. Its test flying career was short, it force-landing in the Axe estuary following a turbine blade failure of the Python. On 22 December 1950 the Admiralty cancelled the T.3, citing the lack of need.

Carrier deck landing trials used the third prototype TS378, which had a six-blade de Havilland contra-rotating propeller and smaller elevator horn balances, with TS380 held in reserve. Airfield Dummy Deck Landings (ADDLs) took place at Boscombe Down in May 1948 with TS378 making the first ship landing aboard HMS *Implacable* on 9 June. Progress was interrupted by a grounding order following a propeller failure on TS380. Trials resumed on 13 July, TS378 making 15 take-offs and landings and TS380 making seven the next day.

Prototype Wyvern T.3 VZ139 had a short flying career. During a test flight on 3 November 1950, a turbine blade failure forced Squadron Leader Derek Colvin to land on the marshland of the Axe estuary in Devon. A successful recovery from the mud proved impossible and the Admiralty had already decided not to proceed with the T.3. *Leonardo UK via Jeremy Graham*

The sole Clyde-powered Wyvern TF.2 prototype VP120 on the engine thrust measuring rig at Yeovil in 1949. *Leonardo UK via Jeremy Graham*

The third W.34 prototype TS378 was used for carrier landing trials aboard *Implacable* and *Illustrious* during 1948 and 1949. The deck crew swarming around the Wyvern give scale to how large it was for a single-seat aircraft. TS378 ended its days at the Shoeburyness target range. *Blue Envoy Collection*

Wyvern S.4 VW872, probably at RNAS Merryfield. Note the original tailplane without dihedral. Rotol modified the propeller to match it to the Armstrong Siddeley Python's power. The engine/propeller control took some time to perfect, leading to delays in the Wyvern entering service. *Leonardo UK via Jeremy Graham*

Wyvern S.4 WN334 carrying a full load of 24 60lb (27kg) rocket projectiles under the wings. These 3in (76mm) calibre rockets were an improved version of the wartime RPs that had been widely used for anti-ship and ground attacks. *Author's Collection*

TS378 undertook another round of deck trials aboard *Illustrious* during May and June 1949.

The first pre-production TF.2, VW867 flew on 16 February 1950, undertaking deck landing trials on *Illustrious* during May and June 1950. Progress was not swift; Armstrong Siddeley and Rotol struggled with perfecting the engine/propeller speed control, with lagging or surging being experienced in response to throttle movements. These issues were exacerbated by the decision to use the propeller as a dive brake (the Ministry of Supply [MoS] had no idea if this would be successful but decided to try the idea anyway.) VW867 spent three years on engine development and was joined by four other TF.2s at Armstrong Siddeley. Safety issues with the constant speed unit led to a restriction on anyone but Westland test pilots flying them for a period during early 1952.

The airframe underwent several modifications: small air brakes were fitted, which led to small boundary layer fences being required to prevent aileron twitch; a taller tail fin; a stronger cockpit canopy; a cutback engine intake cowling to improve access to the cartridge starter. Then, as Controller Air release to service neared in August 1952, an Aeroplane & Armament Experimental Establishment (A&AEE) pilot experienced rudder lock-on which led to a prolonged sideslip. Westland spent four months until a workable solution of adding finlets on the tailplane was cleared. The Wyvern received a new 'Strike' designation – S.4 – replacing the torpedo-fighter terminology. In all, 84 production S.4 aircraft were built.

The first Wyvern unit was scheduled to be formed on 1 February 1953 to replace the Blackburn Firebrand. In fact, 813 NAS at Royal Navy Air Station (RNAS) Ford only received its first aircraft on 20 May, although by October 1954 it had 20. 703W Flight was also formed in May at Ford as a training unit. The second frontline squadron, 827 NAS, began converting the following month. In September 1954 813 NAS took its Wyverns to sea aboard *Albion* but suffered from fuel-starvation and flameouts during catapult launches – Lt BO Macfarlane making history with the first underwater ejection using the Martin-Baker 1B seat when VZ783 fell into the sea. The Wyverns were landed ashore in Malta, remaining there until hitching a lift back to the UK aboard *Albion* the following March. In November 1955 813 and 827 NAS disbanded, handing their aircraft to 830 and 831 NAS which operated aboard *Eagle* and *Ark Royal*. Trials with 200gal (909L) drop tanks and 100gal (455L) wing tip tanks from the DH Venom to increase range did

STRIKE FIGHTER

The first production Wyvern S.4 was VW867 (originally ordered as a TF.2) and was the first to be fitted with the dihedral tailplane. It underwent deck trials aboard HMS *Illustrious* on 21 June 1950 and is seen here at the SBAC Show at Farnborough in September 1950. Westland's Chief Test pilot Harald Penrose belly landed VW867 following a hydraulic failure at RNAS Merryfield on 8 January 1952. *Terry Panopalis Collection*

Wyvern S.4 WN336 of 830 NAS at Hal Far, Malta in 1956. *Terry Panopalis Collection*

WINGS OVER THE FLEET

Loading up. Wyverns being armed with RPs aboard HMS *Eagle*; in the background are Hawker Sea Hawks. This photo shows well the Wyvern's wing folding mechanism. *Author's Collection*

not result in operational use.

The Wyvern took part in Operation Musketeer during the Suez Crisis in November 1956. Equipped with nine Wyverns aboard *Eagle*, 830 NAS made 18 sorties on 1 November attacking Dekheila airfield and flying photographic recce sorties. By 6 November the squadron had flown 79 sorties but two aircraft were lost, both pilots safely ejecting into the sea. Both 830 and 831 NAS disbanded in February 1957, but 813 NAS – which had reformed in October 1956 – retained the last operational Wyverns until 29 March 1958. Today, only the Eagle-powered TF.1 VR137 survives in the hands of the Fleet Air Arm Museum at Yeovilton.

Several alternative engine proposals were made. One was the Armstrong Siddeley Double Mamba (as fitted to the Fairey Gannet), which would provide sufficient power to increase the take-off weight by 1,000lb (454kg) and increasing the strike radius to 400nm (740km). Another choice was the Bristol Proteus Series 3 turboprop. In April 1950 the Clyde-powered prototype VP120 was delivered to Napier for the installation of an E.145 Nomad compound engine consisting of a 12-cylinder, two-stroke diesel engine combined with an exhaust-fed turbo-compressor – an engine billed as the most fuel-efficient (and the most complex) ever devised – but it ran into development issues and the conversion was cancelled.

The first jet-powered Wyvern design study was undertaken in June 1946, with a low-power Armstrong Siddeley Cobra turbojet replacing the Python. This went no further as the Cobra was never built. It was followed in April 1947 by the W.36 with a single Rolls-Royce 6,500lbf (28.9kN) AJ.65 or 7,000lbf (31.9kN) Metrovick F.9 axial-flow turbojet in the nose with a nose intake and retaining the bifurcated jet pipe layout of the turboprop W.35. A new tricycle undercarriage would be fitted, along with a new wide-chord inner wing section and 600gal (2,728L) of fuel. Four 30mm ADEN cannon would be fitted in the wings and the external armament included a torpedo, one *Bootleg* high-speed airborne torpedo, two 1,000lb (454kg) bombs, two *Red Angel* anti-ship rockets or 3in (76mm) RPs.

With the AJ.65 in the torpedo-fighter role the maximum sea level speed was 449kt (486kt in the short-range fighter role), with a 5,100ft/min (1,554m/min) sea level rate of climb in dry thrust or 7,820ft/min (2,386m/min) with reheat, the service ceiling being 40,200ft (12,250m). With the F.9 torpedo-fighter could attain 450kt at sea level (500kt as a short-range fighter), 5,300ft/min (1,615m/min) sea level rate of climb dry or 7,160ft/min (2,182m/min) reheated, with a service ceiling of 40,600ft (12,375m).

The Wyvern S.5E was proposed in May 1954 powered by a 6,000shp (4,474kW) Napier E.141 Double Eland turboprop driving an eight-blade, contra-rotating propeller. The Double Eland was a proposed coupled Eland development, paralleling the lower-powered Double Mamba. A new engine

Wyvern VZ792 on a rainy airfield open day. Slung underneath the aircraft is an 18in (457mm) diameter Mk.XVII torpedo – in which a visitor is taking a strong interest in (or merely sheltering from the elements!). *Blue Envoy Collection*

STRIKE FIGHTER

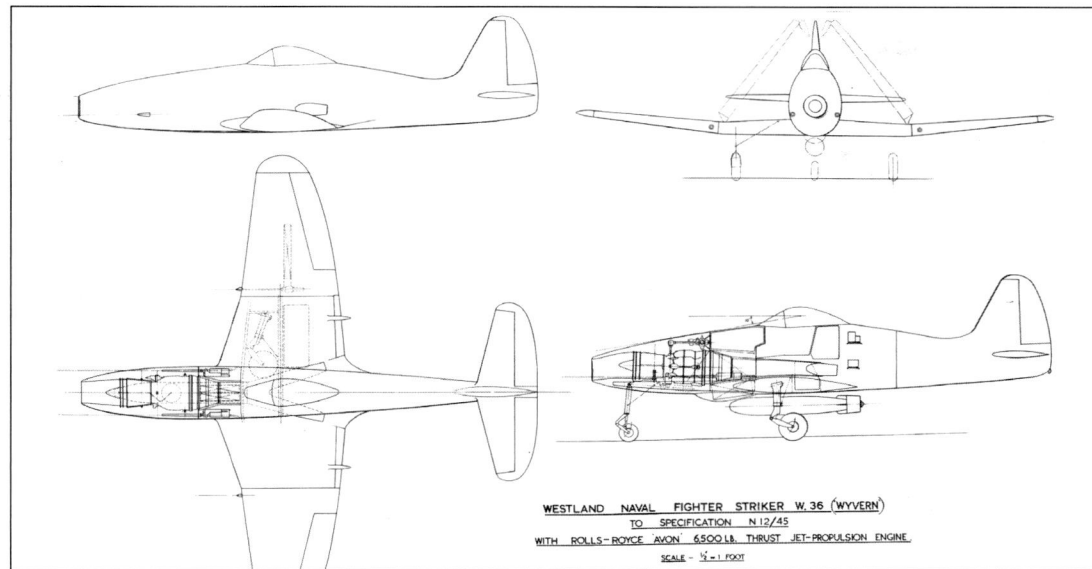

A general arrangement drawing of the jet-powered W.36. This variant has a Rolls-Royce Avon jet in the nose. Note the pairs of 30mm cannon each side of the engine and in the wings. *Leonardo UK via Jeremy Graham*

cowling was required for the wider powerplant and the wing was modified with an increased span centre section and wing tip fuel tanks. The undercarriage would be beefed up to cope with the take-off weight of 20,060lb (11,820kg). A two-seat radar-equipped strike leader version was also offered.

Loaded with a torpedo, the estimated maximum speed was 400kt at 22,000ft (6,705m), 4,500ft/min (1,372m/min) rate of climb and a service ceiling of 30,000ft (9,145m). The low-level attack radius was 580nm (1,074km), or 810nm (1,500km) at high altitude. Westland pitched the S.5E as an interim strike aircraft that could be in service within three years to fill the gap until the NA.39 jet-powered nuclear-capable strike aircraft was ready. No interest was forthcoming from the Admiralty.

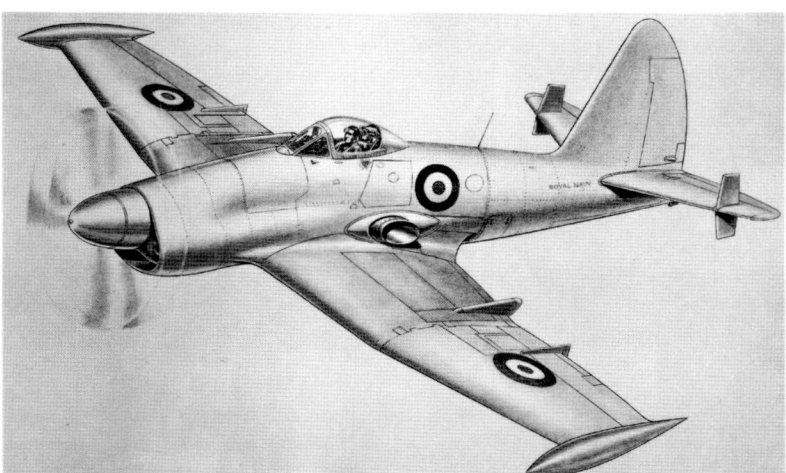

ABOVE The Wyvern S.5E looked chunkier thanks to its larger Napier Double Eland turboprop which required a wider engine nacelle and forward fuselage. *Leonardo UK via Jeremy Graham*

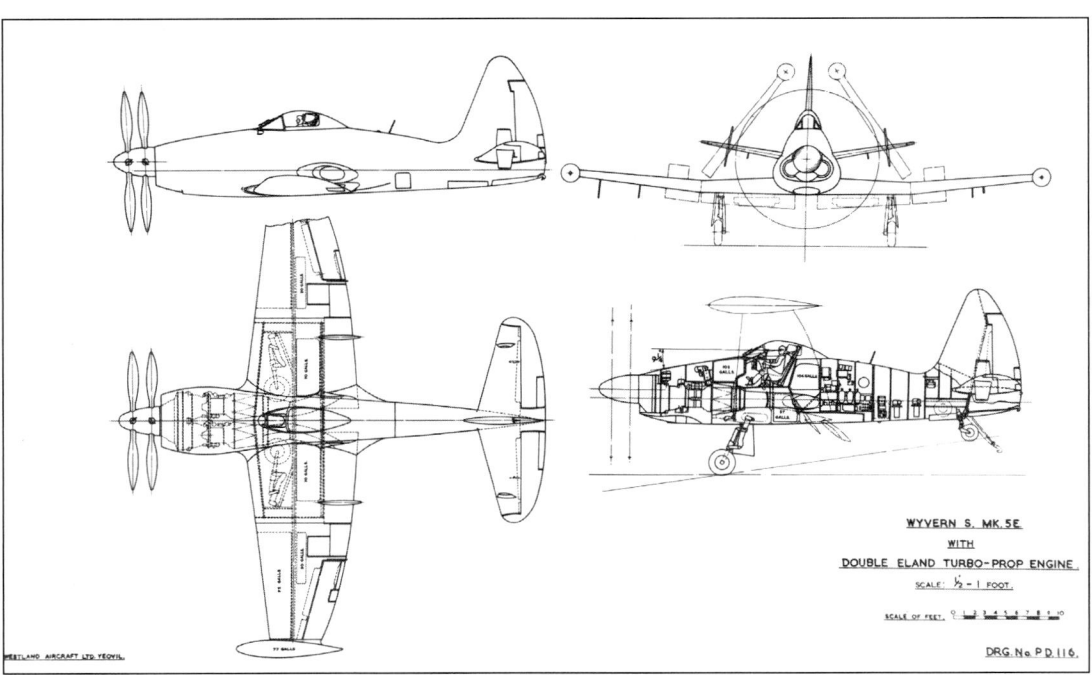

LEFT This general arrangement drawing of the Wyvern S.5E shows the Napier Double Eland turboprop in the nose and the optional tip tanks on the wider span wing. *Leonardo UK via Jeremy Graham*

The prototype Blackburn B.48 Firecrest VF172. Like the Westland W.34, it represented the end of the piston age with its Bristol Centaurus twin-row radial engine. *Author's Collection*

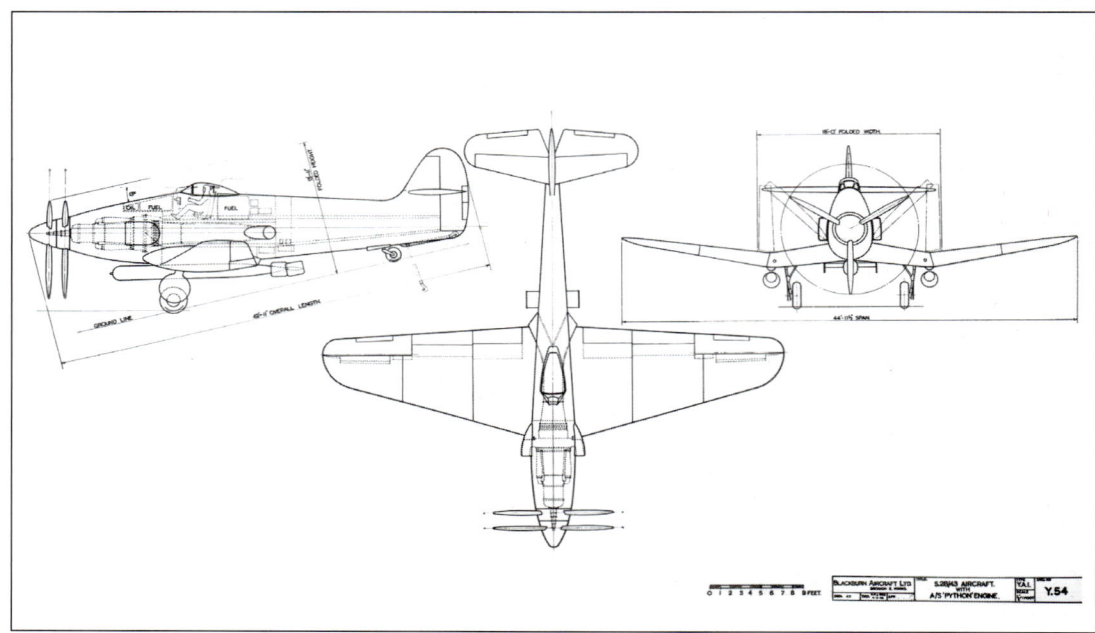

Blackburn drew up the B.62 turboprop-powered Firecrest as a back-up to the Westland W.35 Wyvern. Technical drawing Y-54 featured an Armstrong Siddeley Python with a six-blade co-axial propeller. *Tony Buttler Collection*

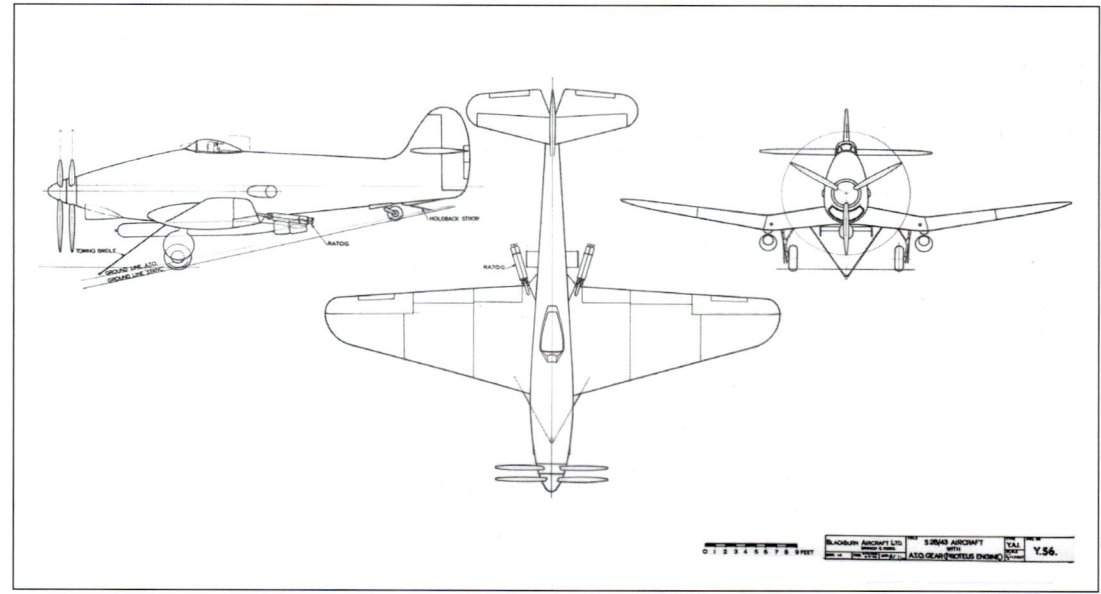

Technical drawing Y-56 was a Bristol Proteus-powered Firecrest. Another engine choice was the Rolls-Royce Clyde. Little is known about the B.62 proposals. *Tony Buttler Collection*

Blackburn's striker-fighter

During the final year of the Second World War, Blackburn's B.46 Firebrand TF.V was just about to enter service following a long development programme dating back to 1941. The laminar flow-winged B.48 Firecrest development had been approved in 1943, but progress was slow and although intended as a back-up to the Wyvern, only three Y.B.1 prototypes were built and only two of them flew during 1947. The Clyde, Python or Proteus-powered B.62 (also known as the Y.A.6) of 1946 was popular with the Admiralty as a back-up to the Westland W.35, but the MoS decided that too much additional design work would be required and only the Bristol Centaurus radial-engined B.48 was sanctioned.

On 17 February 1945 Blackburn submitted three 'fighter-striker' concepts to the MAP as a private-venture. The B.50 designs covered two aircraft with a single RB.41 Nene and one powered by a piston engine (probably a Rolls-Royce Griffon) in the nose and a centrifugal-flow turbojet (possibly a Nene) in the rear fuselage. Armament included a torpedo or underwing bombs and RPs, four 20mm Hispano Mk.V cannon were fitted in the nose. The first was labelled as a 'conventional' layout with a nose intake and an inverted gull wing of 40ft 6in (12.3m) span with marked leading and trailing edge taper. The fuselage was 41ft 10in (12.7m) long. AUW as a 'striker' was 18,700lb (8,480kg) with 800gal (3,638L) of fuel. The second was a more compact design with a length of 39ft 1in (11.9m), using a twin-boom layout.

By July it was clear there was no interest from the MAP or the Admiralty. The Deputy Chief Naval Representative wanted Blackburn to work on a Fairey Barracuda torpedo-bomber replacement instead, but the MAP's Director of Technical Development NE Rowe, felt that Fairey was better suited to that task – pondering a replacement for the Barracuda seems odd considering that Fairey was already working on two torpedo-carrying strike aircraft plus there were the Short Sturgeon and three torpedo-fighter projects (Firebrand, Firecrest and Wyvern) under development at that time.

Blackburn B.50 design

	B.50 (Conventional)	B.50 (Twin Boom)
Span	40ft 6in (12.34m)	40ft 6in (12.34m)
Length	41ft 10in (12.74m)	39ft 1in (11.92m)
Wing area	465ft² (43.24m²)	465ft² (43.24m²)
All-up weight	14,300lb (6,85kg) fighter; 18,700lb (8,480kg) striker	?
Powerplant	1x Nene	1x Nene
Max speed	452kt (837km/h) fighter	?
Armament	4x 20mm Hispano, 1x 18in (457mm) torpedo, 2x 1,000lb (454kg) bombs or mines, 2x 500lb (227kg) bombs, 16x 60lb (27kg) RPs	4x 20mm Hispano, 1x 18in (457mm) torpedo, 2x 1,000lb (454kg) bombs or mines, 2x 500lb (227kg) bombs, 16x 60lb (27kg) RPs

Westland's jet striker

In April 1950 Westland completed the design of its W.37 jet-powered successor to the Wyvern. Westland's effort was a private-venture but was based on the requirements laid down in Specification N.9/47 and Naval Staff Requirement NR/A.19, which had been raised to cover the development of several Vickers-Supermarine designs.

The W.37/1 was powered by a 7,500lbf (33.3kN) reheated Armstrong Siddeley Sapphire turbojet (it could alternatively accommodate an Avon or a larger engine up to 10,000lbf [44.4kN] thrust) and had an internal weapon bay capable of carrying one 18in torpedo, three 1,000lb bombs or mines, three *Red Angel* rockets or 18 RPs. Fixed armament was a

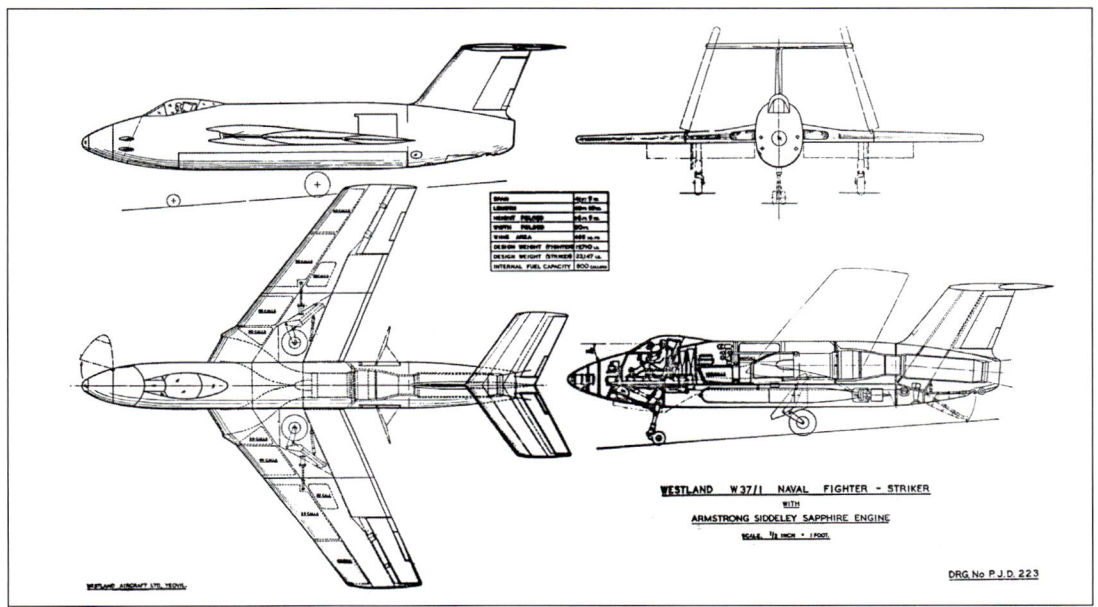

The Westland W.37/1 design was sleek with its large, enclosed bomb bay able to accommodate a torpedo. *Leonardo UK via Jeremy Graham*

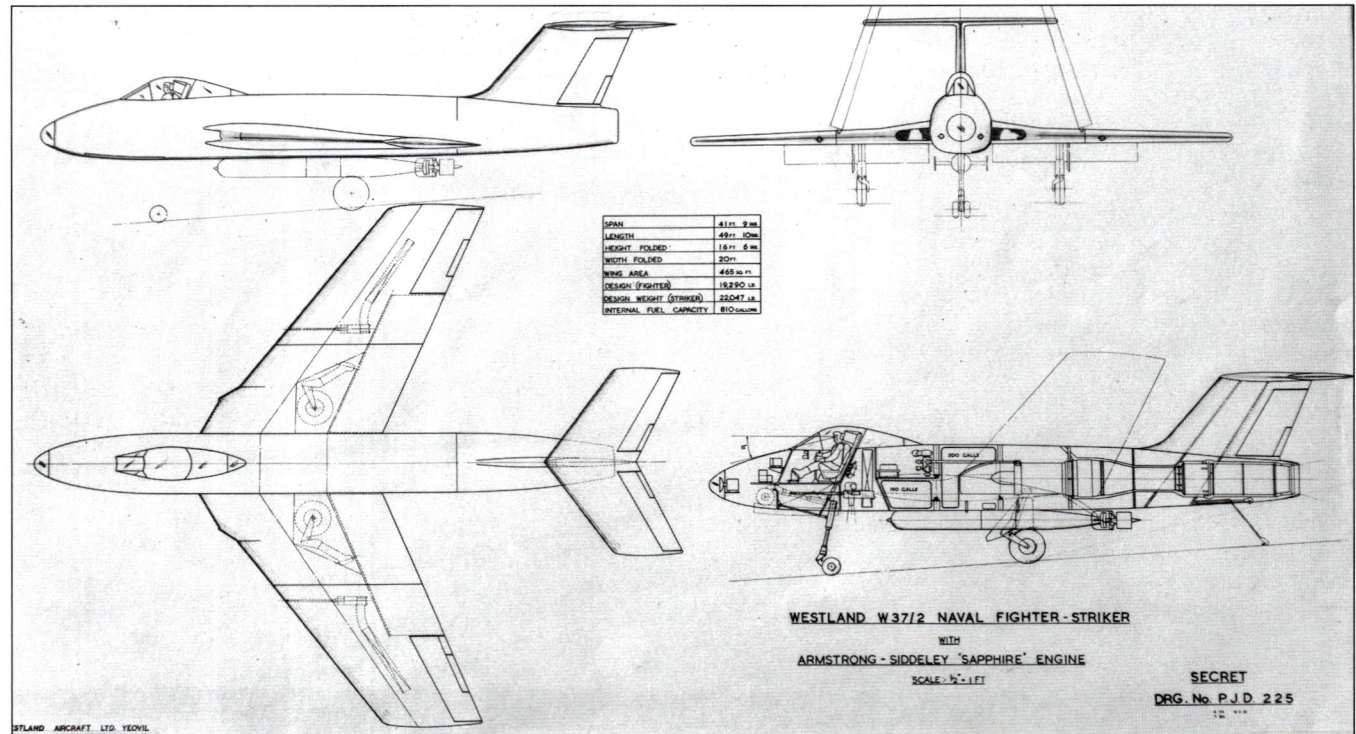

The W.37/2 relied on external weapons carriage to reduce drag in the fighter role. The basic swept wing design with wing root intakes and a T-tail was unchanged. *Leonardo UK via Jeremy Graham*

Westland W.37 Fighter-striker design

	W.37/1	W.37/2
Span	41ft 9in (12.73m); 20ft 0in (6.10m) folded	41ft 9in (12.73m); 20ft 0in (6.10m) folded
Length	49ft 10in (15.18m)	49ft 10in (15.18m)
Wing area	465ft² (43.24m²)	465ft² (43.24m²)
t/c ratio	13-10%	13-10%
Gross weight	19,710lb (8,940kg) fighter; 22,147lb (10,046kg) striker	19,290lb (8,750kg) fighter; 22,067lb (10,010kg) striker
Powerplant	1x Sapphire Sa.2, 7,500lbf (33.3kN)	1x Sapphire Sa.2, 7,500lbf (33.3kN)
Max speed	529kt (980km/h) at SL; 570kt (1,056km/h) at SL with reheat; 487kt (902km/h) at 35,000ft (10,670m)	535kt (991km/h) at SL, fighter; 495kt (917km/h) at SL, striker; 572kt (1,060km/h) at SL with reheat, fighter; 560kt (1,038km/h) at SL with reheat, striker; 487kt (902km/h) at 35,000ft (10,670m), fighter; 477kt (884km/h) at 35,000ft, striker
Rate of climb	5,160ft/min (1,575m/min) at SL, fighter; 4,510ft/min (1,375m/min) at SL, striker	5,340ft/min (1,628m/min) at SL, fighter; 4,100ft/min (1,250m/min) at SL, striker
Service ceiling	40,000ft (12,190m) fighter; 37,500ft (11,430m) striker	40,500ft (12,345m) fighter; 35,400ft (10,790m) striker
Radius of action	460nm (852km) fighter	475nm (880km) fighter
Armament	4x 20mm Hispano or 30mm ADEN, 1x 18in (457mm) torpedo, 1x 2,000lb (907kg) AP bomb, 3x 1,000lb (454kg) bombs or mines, 3x Red Angel, 18x 95lb (43kg) RPs	4x 20mm Hispano or 30mm ADEN, 1x 18in (457mm) torpedo, 1x 2,000lb (907kg) AP bomb, 3x 1,000lb (454kg) bombs or mines, 3x Red Angel, 18x 95lb (43kg) RPs

quartet of 30mm ADEN or 20mm Hispano cannon in the lower nose. The gross weight was 19,710lb (8,940kg) in the long-range fighter role and 22,147lb (10,045kg) in the strike role. The W.37/2 had a slimmer fuselage, carrying its torpedo, bombs and rockets externally (two of the cannon were moved to the outer wing sections too.) Its gross weight was 19,290lb (8,750kg) as a fighter and 22,067lb (10,010kg) as a striker. The W.37 was also offered as a two-seat armed operational trainer.

Both designs had moderately 35° swept wings with Fowler/Youngman-type flaps and a 10% thickness-to-chord (t/c) ratio. The aircraft had wing root intakes and a T-tail; the outer wing sections folded to reduce width to 20ft (6.1m). The estimated performance of the W.37/1 included a top speed of 487kt at 35,000ft (10,670m) in dry thrust, the W.37/2 achieving 487kt as a fighter and 477kt as a striker (due to the extra drag from the external stores). The W.37/1's rate of climb at sea level was 5,160ft/min (1,573m/min) or 4,510ft/min (1,375m/min) as a fighter or striker respectively, the equivalent figures for the W.37/2 being 5,340ft/min (1,628m/sec) and 4,100ft/min (1,250m/min). The fighter radius of action was 460nm (852km) for the W.37/1 and 475nm (880km) for the W.37/2. A mock-up was built but no official interest was forthcoming and the W.37 designation was re-used in 1951 for the all-weather fighter project submitted to Specification N.114T (see Chapter 4).

From 508 to Scimitar

As outlined in Chapter 2, the Supermarine Type 505 undercarriageless day fighter was redesigned in January 1947 as the Type 508 as an insurance in case the Hawker P.1040 (Sea Hawk) design failed to live up to expectations. Joe Smith's design team added an undercarriage and increased the wing area by 13%, to reduce the approach speed to below 105kt, while the t/c ratio was increased to 9% to lighten the structure and improve room for the wing-folding and control surface mechanisms; the leading edge sweep was 8°. Dive recovery flaps were fitted under the wings with spoiler air brakes on the upper surface. The estimated maximum speed at sea level was 566kt, the sea level rate of climb being 15,600ft/min (4,755m/min). The estimated AUW was 18,000lb (8,165kg). At that time, take-off relied on the hydraulic BH.V catapult, it was thought that further development would be required to handle these weights with sufficient velocity to get airborne safely. Thoughts of a jettisonable cabin instead of an ejection seat and a tailwheel undercarriage were dropped during the design process. (The choice of a tailwheel reflected Joe Smith's worries about the force of impact of arrested landings onto the nosewheel and adverse aerodynamic effects of sweeping up the rear fuselage for sufficient deck clearance on take off.) The cannon armament was beefed up from a quartet of 20mm Hispano Mk.V to the 30mm ADEN.

Naval Staff Requirement NR/A.17 was drawn up to cover development, along with Specification N.9/47 issued in April 1947 (the Type 508 was also offered to the RAF to meet Specification F.43/46 for a day fighter). Three prototypes were ordered in August (VX133, XV136 and VX138). The aim was to obtain a design suitable to produce 250 aircraft as a day interceptor and long-range strike support fighter. The mock-up was inspected on 24 September 1948 and in mid-1949 construction began of VX133. The aircraft received a larger wing than the original proposal with an area of 340ft² (31.6m²) and a span of 41ft (12.5m).

It is believed that Hawker submitted the twin Avon-powered P.1063 to both F.43/46 and N.9/47. It had a swept wing and the turbojets were stacked in the rear fuselage, the lower engine being below the cockpit and the upper engine in the rear fuselage. This layout had several drawbacks, however, for the

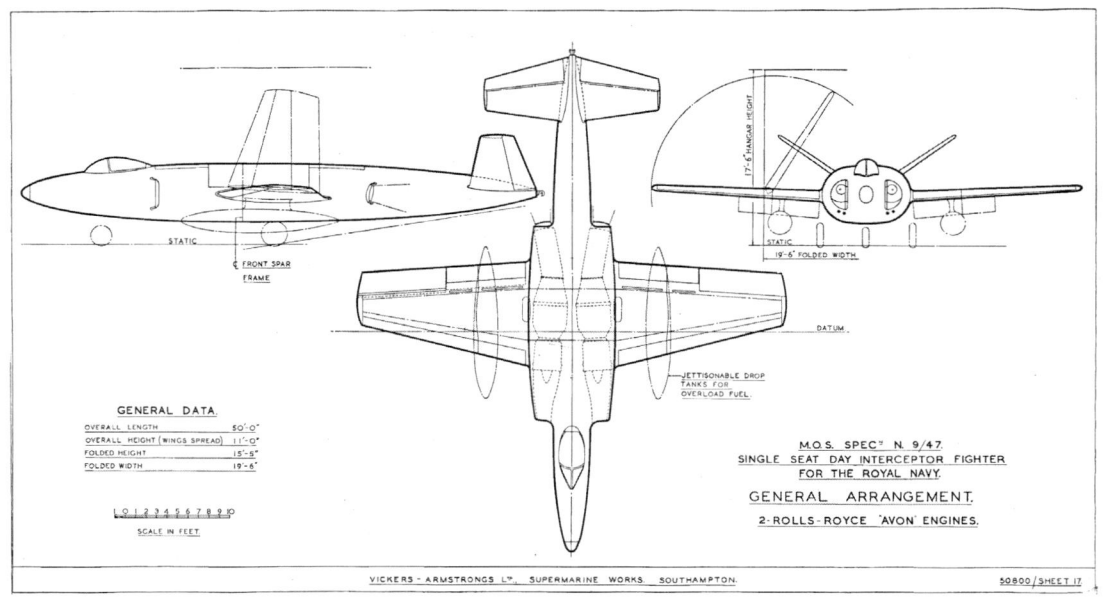

A general arrangement drawing of the Supermarine Type 508. *RAF Museum Hendon via Ralph Pegram*

A fine view of prototype Type 508 VX133. It was a large aircraft for a day fighter, but with swept wings and a conventional tail it would become an adept fighter-bomber. VX133 was used for arresting trials at the RAE (the arrester hook being pulled out!), deck landing trials aboard Eagle and Bulwark and was used to test the strength of Centaur's hangar deck to accommodate heavier jets. Author's Collection

layout of the fuel, armament and undercarriage. Blackburn may have offered its B.74 design; both were probably speculative ventures rather than responses to official interest from the MoS.

While the development of a night-fighter to meet Naval Staff Requirement NR/A.14 and Specification N.40/46 was underway, the Admiralty's flexible thinking included examination of the strike role to replace the Wyvern from 1957 onwards – indeed Fairey's night-fighter submission in 1947 had included a strike derivative with a weapon bay. The Director of Naval Air Warfare (DNAW), Captain EH Shattock, favoured a strike variant of the N.40/46, but refused to relax a requirement to cover 87nm (160km) when cruising on combat power at 5,000ft (1,525m) to deliver a 2,000lb (907kg) armour-piercing bomb. Due to evolving technology, it was not clear whether future fighters and strike aircraft would need one or two crew, so Shattock preferred to develop single and two-seat strikers based on N.40/46 and N.9/47. If N.9/47 failed then he reasoned a single-seat N.40/46 could replace it. When the de Havilland DH.110 was selected for N.40/46, one strike-fighter prototype was ordered to meet Specification N.8/49, alongside the RN's two night-fighter prototypes. Then in November 1949, economic problems forced defence cuts and the naval DH.110 was axed.

Joe Smith's design team had looked at a dedicated strike development of the Type 508, the Type 522 which had the guns removed and the space between the Avons was utilised as two shallow bomb bays, covered by external fairings, for one 2,000lb armour-piercing bomb or two 1,000lb bombs or up to four Mk.VIII mines. Under the wings would be racks for two *Red Angel* anti-ship rockets or eight RPs. Internal fuel would be 600gal (2,727L), which could be doubled with underwing drop tanks and tanks in the bomb bays.

The first Type 508 prototype VX133's maiden flight was made on 31 August 1951 at Boscombe Down with Supermarine's Chief Test Pilot Mike Lithgow at the controls. It was displayed at the Society of British Aircraft Constructors (SBAC) show at Farnborough a couple of weeks later. The Type 508 proved sprightly in the climb, but the maximum level speed was only 523kt at 30,000ft (9,145m). Flight testing revealed lateral and directional issues, some of which were due to the V-tail, the later addition of large strakes ahead of the tailplanes having a positive effect. The second prototype, VX136 received some internal modifications and four 30mm ADEN cannon (the planned ranging radar in the nose, and tail-warning radar were never fitted), becoming the Type 529. The aircraft flew on 29 August 1952 at Boscombe Down. In subsequent trials it reached 527kt (Mach 0.92) at 30,000ft. An emergency landing with only the port undercarriage extended on 2 December 1953 caused considerable damage, VX136 being struck off charge and expended as a gunnery target at Shoeburyness.

Deck landing trials began with VX133 at RAE's Thurleigh site near Bedford in April 1952, returning to Farnborough for arrester gear trials the following month before heading to RNAS Ford and making seven landings and take-offs aboard *Eagle* with success. Arresting load trials were carried out at the RAE on 15 April 1953. On 24 September 1956 VX133 was craned aboard *Centaur* for hangar deck load trials, before heading to Bedford on 28 November for arrester gear development tests.

The RAE's Naval Air Department (NAD) had moved from Farnborough to Thurleigh during 1955-58; Runway 07/25 being converted into the Arrested Landing Deck experimental area which could accommodate up to three arrester systems. A BXS.4 Catapult Site was built in parallel with the runway, with a 2,500ft (760m) paved runway at the end of the

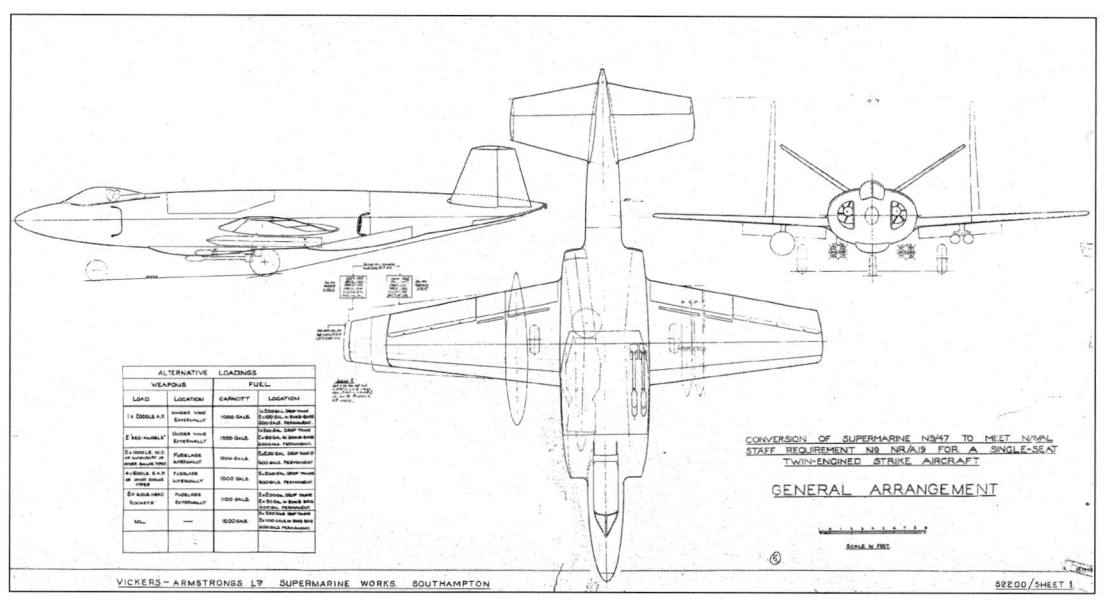

The Type 522 was a strike version of the Type 508 to NR/A.19 with two shallow bomb bays fore and aft of the main undercarriage bays. The underwing armament options included the *Red Angel* RP (shown under the port wing) and smaller 60lb (27kg) RPs under the intakes. Note the revised outer wing planforms shown at the tip of the starboard wing, increased area being required to improve lift at high weights. *RAF Museum Hendon via Ralph Pegram*

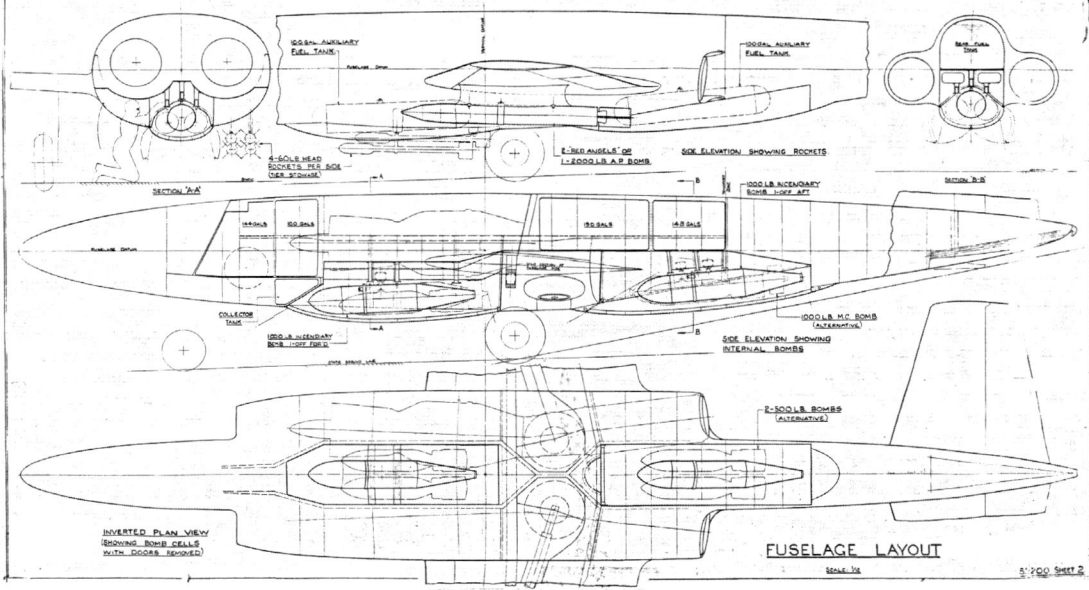

This technical drawing of the fuselage layout shows the two bomb bays squeezed along the centreline as well as the arrangement of the fuel tanks. *RAF Museum Hendon via Ralph Pegram*

The Supermarine Type 529 prototype VX136 gets airborne during the SBAC Show at Farnborough in early September 1952. An emergency landing at Chilbolton on 2 December 1953 ended its flying days and by 1956 it was a ballistic trials target at Shoeburyness. *Tony Buttler Collection*

WINGS OVER THE FLEET

What if? Had the Admiralty not pursued the swept wing it is likely that the Type 529 would have formed the basis of the Scimitar and quite possibly would have been available for Operation MUSKETEER in November 1956 as a fighter-bomber. This Type 529 of 806 NAS is based aboard the newly completed HMS *Malta* while the RN's latest 6in (152mm) gun cruisers give fire support to the amphibious assault on Port Said. *Luciano Alviani*

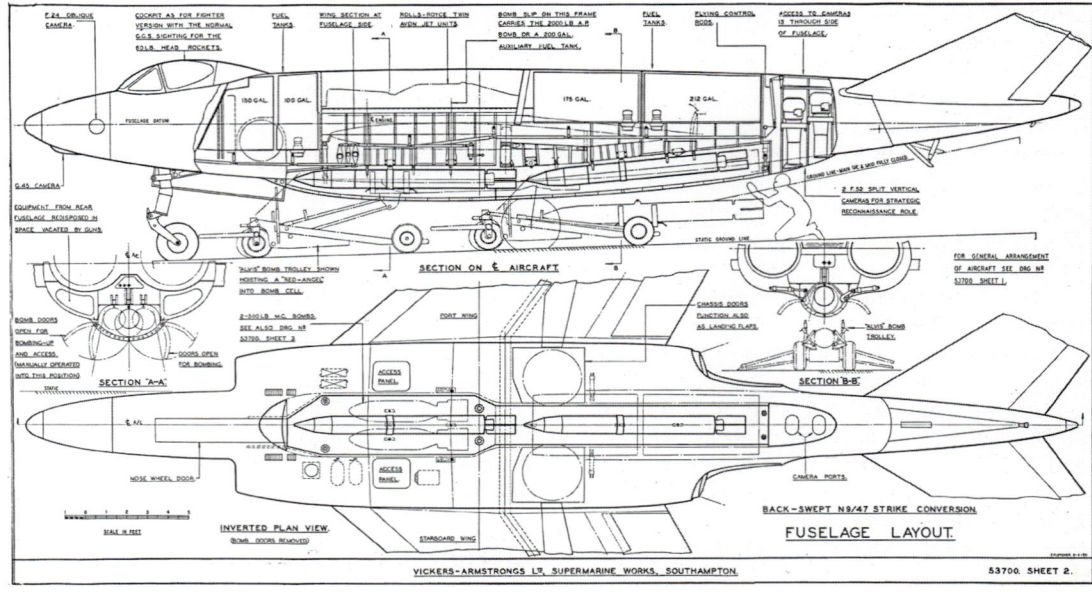

Fitting the Type 525's swept wing to the Type 522 resulted in the Type 537, which had a revised bomb bay layout. This would be the last pre-Scimitar development with an internal bay. *RAF Museum Hendon via Ralph Pegram*

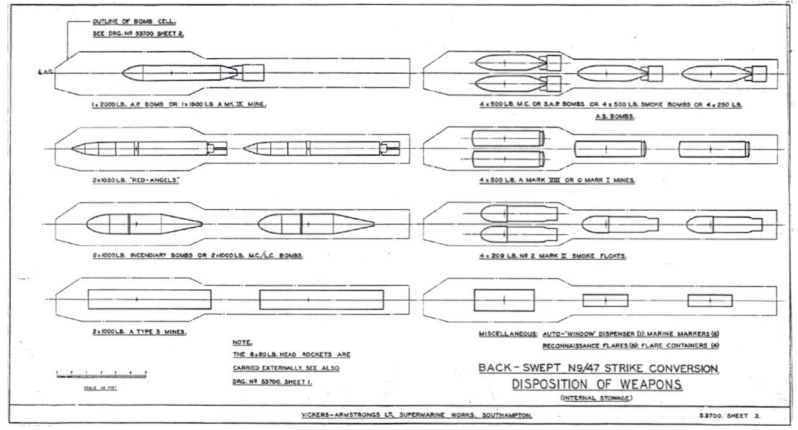

steam catapult and a safety barrier 350ft (107m) from the end of the runway. The BXS.4 steam catapult was mounted 6ft (1.8m) above the ground and used for evaluating aircraft and proof-testing airborne stores and equipment. It was capable of accelerating an aircraft weighing 30,000lb (13,600kg) to 155kt within 203ft (62m) with a maximum force of 6g. A second site completed in 1960 received a BXS.5 steam catapult mounted flush with the ground.

The array of bombs and other payloads that could be accommodated in the Type 537's narrow bomb bay. *RAF Museum Hendon via Ralph Pegram*

The attractive cream-painted Type 525 prototype VX138 at the Farnborough Show in September 1954. *Tony Buttler Collection*

A meeting at the MoS offices at Thames House on 3 April 1950 discussed progress with the RN's jet fighter programmes. The RAE commented that the latest Avon and Sapphire-powered aircraft with reheat would have more than sufficient thrust, so their speed limits would be determined by the aircraft's aerodynamics. They felt that a single-engined design could achieve the N.9/47's capability at less cost with a smaller airframe, at the very least a swept wing was needed to increase the critical Mach speed. The Admiralty could not afford to wait the estimated 30 months for a new design to fly, so the decision was made to re-order the third prototype with swept wings and reheated Avons as the Type 525. NR/A.17 was rewritten around the revised design and the third prototype re-ordered in November.

Naval Requirement NR/A.19 was raised in early 1950 for a strike version of the NR/A.17. The Type 526 was drafted, based on the earlier Type 522 with internal bomb stowage and no cannon. Estimated performance was 574kt (591kt with reheat) at 20,000ft (6,100m), 4min 39sec to reach 45,000ft and a 365nm (676km) radius of action. For the recce role a 200gal (909L) bomb bay tank and 215gal (977L) wing tip drop tanks would be fitted to extend range. The Type 537 design added a swept wing and revised the undercarriage layout to allow a single centreline bomb bay, which improved the trimming of the centre of gravity (CG).

N.9/47 was replaced by Specification N.113D on 16 July 1951, calling for a swept wing day fighter and long-range strike support aircraft. It had to be capable of 640kt at sea level and 560kt at 45,000ft (13,715m) without reheat, armed with four 30mm ADEN, RPs and, later, *Blue Sky* or *Red Dean* air-to-air missiles (AAMs.) (*Blue Sky* was the Fairey Aviation Fireflash beam-riding missile, *Red Dean* at this time was Folland Aircraft's active-homing design, but within a year Vickers would take over this project.) ARI.5820 Radar Ranging Mk.1 was to be fitted (ARI is an Airborne Radio Installation). Endurance covered two hours patrolling at economic speed at 45,000ft, five minutes combat at 20,000ft and 20 minutes loitering at 2,000ft (607m) before landing. The aircraft was to be capable of operating from BS.4 steam catapults without reheat and landing with only one engine operable. Maximum take-off weight was to be 31,000lb (14,060kg).

In December 1949 the CNR confirmed the need for fighters capable of at least 540kt with an AUW up to 30,000lb (13,607kg). The MoS was so confident that a swept wing Type 508 would work, that it ordered Supermarine to begin design work before N.113D was finalised. Supermarine had foreseen the need; a 45° swept wing and swept V-tails had been proposed back in June 1949 (a Type 523 swept wing development of the Type 522 was also studied.) The carrier trials with the Type 510 also gave the company confidence that a swept wing was compatible with carrier operations. A design brochure was completed in August and a full proposal was submitted to the MoS in February 1950, approval being granted in June and construction work begun by November.

The wing would have drooped nose flaps and double-slotted trailing edge flaps. Two sets of airbrakes were fitted on the underside of the

A Supermarine artwork of the original swept wing Type 525 design, which retained the Type 508's V-tail. *Author's Collection*

The Type 525 VX138 gets wet as it rolls along Farnborough's waterlogged runway at speed during the 1954 SBAC Show. *Terry Panopalis Collection*

The Type 525 VX138 making a low-speed landing at Boscombe Down on 2 July 1955 with its blown flaps in operation. Only three days later the aircraft was destroyed when it stalled and spun into the ground during another trial low-speed carrier approach. Sadly, the pilot, Lt Cdr Tony Rickell ejected too late and died of his injuries. *Tony Buttler Collection*

forward fuselage and under the wings (the latter being wire-locked shut). In redesigning VX138 to Type 525 standard – following RAE analysis – Supermarine replaced the V-tail with a conventional swept tail due to the estimated structural stresses and the fuel tanks were modified to suit the altered CG. Performance with reheat was estimated to be 585kt at 20,000ft with a sea level rate of climb of 22,200ft/min (6,770m/min). The AUW had increased to 28,169lb (12,777kg) – then the heaviest British single-seat fighter. The approach speed was estimated at 105–115kt by the RAE.

Mike Lithgow made VX138's first flight on 27 April 1954 from Boscombe Down, flying for 20 minutes. VX138 appeared at the SBAC Show at Farnborough in September that year. The Avon RA.7 never received reheat, so the performance was lower than estimated, reaching Mach 0.954 at 30,000ft (9,145m), but reaching Mach 1.08 in a dive on 1 November. Climb performance was not improved and engine surging and pitch-up problems were encountered. A wooden extended outer section leading edge was fitted to reduce the t/c ratio to improve the Mach number limit and reduce the pitch-up. Handling problems with yaw and oscillations required the tail to be redesigned with increased area and a modified rudder with a friction damping device.

Disappointed, the MoS refused permission for the RAE to get involved in aerodynamic improvements (the RAE's pilots refused to fly it from Supermarine's Chilbolton airfield in any case.) The Type 525 had been surpassed by this time by the Type 544 to meet N.113 and was only suitable for research. On 5 July 1955 the aircraft stalled and spun into the ground during a low speed ADDL sortie at Boscombe Down. The pilot, Lt Cdr Tony Rickell, ejected too late and later died of his injuries. VX138 had only amassed 61hr 20min flying time.

A month before its loss, VX138 had been fitted with blown flaps, showing much improved stability and controllability at low speeds and reducing the approach speed by 10kt. These flaps had been approved on 25 March 1954 to test the concept of 'supercirculation'; high-pressure supersonic air was blown over the extended flaps to re-energise the airflow to prevent it breaking away, which improved the lift and reduced the stalling speed. The air was tapped from the Avons' compressor section.

Type 544 Scimitar prototype WT854 descends into *Ark Royal's* hangar on 5 April 1956. Chief Test Pilot Mike Lithgow is in the cockpit, having made the first ever landing onto an RN carrier by an aircraft weighing over 25,000lb (11,340kg). WT854 conducted flying and ground testing of arrester gear until 1959. By 1967 it was a target at the Shoeburyness ranges – the graveyard of many prototype aircraft. *Tony Buttler Collection*

Supermarine had already embarked on a redesign as the Type 544 in order to fully meet N.113, receiving an order for three prototypes (WT854, WT859 and WW134) in May 1953. The fuselage was waisted (not to be confused with area ruling which smooths out changes in cross-sectional drag). The wings were heavily revised. The wing tips were reshaped to reduce the onset of compressibility drag rise and blown flaps were also incorporated (although the prototype was completed with double-slotted flaps to save time). WT854 took to the air for 15 minutes on 19 January 1956 at Boscombe Down with Lithgow at the controls. Joe Smith died on 20 February, being succeeded by his former deputy, Alan Clifton.

WT854 began conducting ADDLs at Boscombe Down on 24 March to 5 April, making 38 sorties at a landing weight of 29,000lb (13,154kg) into Mk.13 arrester gear. Experience from these and previous Type 525 ADDLs set the ideal approach speeds between 138–135kt and touchdown speeds of 132–130kt. Turbulent air on approach affected the air speed indicator by as much as 5kt, making the audio-approach equipment unusable. Measured take-off runs led to a reduction of the take-off weight to 27,800lb (12,610kg) for the first carrier take-offs for safety.

The day before the ADDL programme began, Mike Lithgow wrote to Clifton's deputy, George Henson. In his letter he described the Type 544 as "just useable at 35,000ft in a fighter role," and he criticised the "deplorable" rudder power, being nearly uncontrollable on take-off with a crosswind. He also doubted whether the blown flaps were worth the additional complication; not altogether positive comments on the new design.

The carrier trials began on 5 April aboard *Eagle*. Lithgow had difficulty seeing the mirror landing sight and the arrester hook struck the round-down, thankfully without causing any damage. (This was traced to a settings error in the mirror sight which could not be corrected aboard ship.) Despite this, Lithgow and the A&AEE pilots Lt Cdr Colin Little (who succeeded in taking off with the parking brake still on!), Lt Cdr Derek Whitehead and Cdr Stan Orr made 29 deck landings. As the aircraft was not yet cleared for catapult launches, all were free rolling take-offs of 650–785ft (198–239m) into a 40kt wind over the deck. Catapult launches on Thurleigh's raised BXS.4 steam catapult were carried out in November, both with, and without flap blowing.

To cure the pitch-up problems, the tailplane with its 10° of dihedral was effectively turned upside down, the resulting 10° anhedral proving sufficient. Inertia cross-coupling worries were intensively studied by the manufacturer and rolls were restricted to 360° with 5*g* pullout at full aileron, or 7.5*g* with partial aileron. Stalling tests were successfully passed and emergency single-engine take offs were proved possible at 135kt.

The second prototype, WT859, carried out its initial test flights with Avon RA.28 engines before receiving the Avon 202 to allow the jet flap system to be used. WT859 suffered structural damage during

Supermarine Scimitar design pathway

	Type 508 VX133	Type 529 VX136	Type 522	Type 523 (for RAF)	Type 525 Design	Type 525 VX138	Type 537	Type 544 & 560 Scimitar F.1
Span	41ft 0in (12.50m); 26ft 0in (7.92m) folded	41ft 0in (12.50m); 26ft 0in (7.92m) folded	41ft 0in (12.50m); 26ft 0in (7.92m) folded	37ft 0in (11.27m)	42ft 0in (12.80m); 20ft 0in (6.10m)	37ft 2in (11.33m); 20ft 6.5in (6.1m) folded	37ft 6in (11.43m)	37ft 2in (11.33m); 20ft 6.5in (6.1m) folded
Length	50ft 0in (15.24m)	50ft 0in (15.24m)	?	52ft 6in (16.0m)	52ft 0in (15.85m)	53ft 0in (16.15m)	54ft 0in (16.46m); 50ft 0in (15.24m) folded	53ft 3in (16.84m)
Wing area	340ft² (31.62m²)	340ft² (31.62m²)	?	?	490ft² (45.57m²)	450ft² (41.85m²)	?	485ft² (45.10m²)
t/c ratio	9%	9%	9%	8%	8%	8%	8%	8%
Gross weight	18,850lb (5,550kg)	22,584lb (10,244kg)	?	Take-off weight 19,100lb (8,665kg) with reheat	21,650lb (9,820kg)	19,910lb (9,030kg)	23,950lb (10,865kg)	Loaded 34,200lb (15,510kg)
Powerplant	2x Avon RA.3, 6,500lbf (28.9kN)	2x Avon RA.3, 6,500lbf (28.9kN)	2x Avon RA.3, 6,500lbf (28.9kN)	2x Avon RA.3, 6,500lbf (28.9kN)	2x Avon RA.3, 6,500lbf (28.9kN)	2x Avon RA.7, 7,500lbf (33.3kN)	2x Avon	2x Avon RA.24 or RA.28, 10,000lbf (44.4kN); later Avon Mk.202, 11,250lbf (50.0kN)
Fuel capacity	510gal (2,318L)	510gal (2,318L)	600gal (2,727L); plus 2x 200gal (909L) drop tanks & 2x 100gal (454L) bomb bay tanks	350gal (1,591L) no reheat, 440gal (2,000L) with reheat	630gal (2,864L); plus 2x 215gal (977L) drop tanks	630gal (2,864L)	637gal (2,895L); plus 200gal (909L) auxiliary bomb bay tank	1,065gal (4,841L); plus 2 or 4x 200gal (909L) or 220gal (1,000L) drop tanks; refuelling probe
Max speed	523kt (970km/h) at 30,000ft (9,145m)	527kt (977km/h) at 30,000ft (9,145m)	?	617kt (1,142km/h) at SL with reheat; 558kt (1,033km/h) at 45,000ft (13,715m) with reheat	610kt (1,130km/h) at SL; 416kt (770km/h) at 45,000ft (13,715m) with reheat	562kt (1,041km/h)/ Mach 0.954 at 30,000ft (9,145m)	589kt (1,090km/h) at SL clean; 495kt (916km/h) at SL with drop tanks	640kt (1,186km/h) at SL; Mach 0.97 at altitude
Rate of climb	18,700ft/min (5,700m/min) at SL	?	?	?	18,500ft/min (5,640m/min) at SL	18,000ft/min (5,485m/min) at SL	?	12,000ft/min (3,655m/min) at SL
Service ceiling	45,000ft (13,715m)	45,000ft (13,715m)	?	?	45,000ft (13,715m)	49,000ft (14,935m)	?	46,000ft (14,020m)
Armament	4x 30mm ADEN (not fitted)	4x 30mm ADEN	1x 2,000lb (907kg) AP, 2x 1,000lb (454kg) or 4x 500lb (227kg) bombs, 2–4x mines, 2x Red Angel RPs, 8x 60lb (27kg) RPs	4x 20mm Hispano (provision for 6x), 1x 2,000lb AP, 2x 1,000lb or 4x 500lb bombs, 2–4x mines, 2x Red Angel RPs, 8x 60lb RPs	4x 20mm Hispano	None fitted	1x 2,000lb AP, 2x 1,000lb or 4x 500lb bombs, 2–4x mines, 2x Red Angel RPs, 8x 60lb RPs	4x 30mm ADEN, 1x Red Beard, bombs, RPs, 4x AIM-9 Sidewinder, 4x AGM-12 Bullpup

STRIKE FIGHTER

Wheels and four-piece flaps down for landing. The provision of 'supercirculation' – blown flaps – was instrumental in allowing heavy jets like the Scimitar to land safely aboard carriers at reasonably slow approach speeds. Seventh production Scimitar F.1 XD218 spent most of its 453hr 30min flying career on armament trials until 1965, briefly returning to the FAA before being sold for scrap in 1967. *Tony Buttler Collection*

resonance tests in supersonic dives on 17 June 1957. In October 1956, the third prototype, WW134, which was built to production standards with Avon RA.24 engines, joined the test programme, carrying out ADDLs and arrester tests at Boscombe Down and Thurleigh at the end of the year.

Carrier trials aboard *Ark Royal* beckoned on 3 January 1957, with A&AEE test pilots Cdr Pat Chilton and Lt Cdr Derek Whitehead along with Lithgow. The five jet flap-assisted landings took place at weights of 28,800–34,000lb (13,060–15,420kg) and catapult launches between 29,600 and 34,400lb (14,425 and 5,600kg). Chilton was satisfied with the performance but criticised the poor view from the cockpit on approach. Production aircraft would receive a revised nose cone to improve the downwards field of view. By the end of 1958 most of the prototype testing was complete, costing £4.3 million, some £1.3 million more than originally estimated, partially due to weight saving and noise-induced fatigue issues that needed rectifying in the final design.

Scimitar

Initial plans to produce 100 aircraft costing £12.5 million were approved in December 1952 (despite a strong campaign against N.113 by the RAF in an attempt to claim Supermarine's production capacity for the Type 541 Swift day fighter.) The following May, Specification N.113P was issued, including fitment of the Avon Mk.202 and a specified combat weight of 28,400lb (12,882kg). Trade protection, especially of the convoy routes to Scandinavia, was the main role envisioned as part of the 1952 Global Strategy but the RN had accepted that the Scimitar was unlikely to be an effective day fighter and during 1953 N.113P was amended to include the carriage of a 4,000lb (1,814kg) bomb as a long-range bomber. This 4,000lb bomb became the 'Bomb, Aircraft, HE 2,000lb, MC', better known by its MoS Rainbow Code *Red Beard*, a 25kT yield tactical nuclear bomb. Bomb delivery was via the Low Altitude Bombing System (LABS), which calculated the 'toss' manoeuvre to lob the bomb onto the target whilst keeping the aircraft out of the range of anti-aircraft defences and the blast of the bomb. LABS trials began in June 1958 using XD218. Final *Red Beard* trials began in September 1963, again using XD218.

The aircraft was added to the MoS's growing list of 'super-priority' programmes during the Korean War rearmament programme in June 1953, following a request from the First Lord of Admiralty, Admiral Sir Rhoderick McGrigor. Although intended to take effect once the production phase began, the 'super-priority' scheme lapsed, having caused bottlenecks across the industry. The name Scimitar was officially bestowed in March 1957. Production costs had soared from the original estimate, totalling £37.3 million by January 1957 and the order was later cut to just 76 aircraft. The Treasury was unimpressed that what started out as a £750,000 project in 1946 (the original Type 508) had ballooned to such figures.

The first production aircraft, XD212, flew from South Marston on 11 January 1957 with Mike Lithgow at the controls. The fuselages were built at Supermarine's original Itchen works in Southampton, the wings at Eastleigh and other sub-components in Trowbridge. Assembly took place at Hursley Park (until its closure), the airframe being transported by road to South Marston for reassembly and test flying by production test pilot Les Colquhoun. The second production aircraft XD213 did not fly until May 1957 but the average rate of production increased to two per month.

WINGS OVER THE FLEET

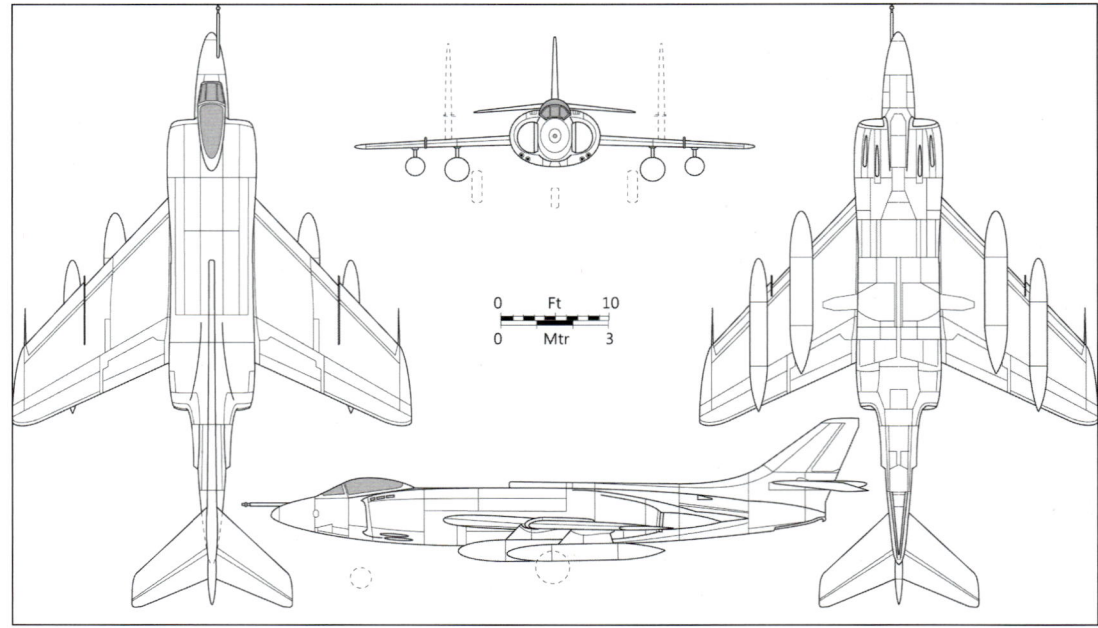

A general arrangement drawing of the definitive Type 560 Scimitar F.1 carrying four drop tanks. *Chris Gibson*

Following the first 50 aircraft, production shifted to the Type 560 which added the ARI.5885 *Blue Silk* Ground Position Indicator Mk.4A Doppler navigation radar in addition to an improved ARI.18107/1 *Green Salad* UHF radio homer plus a Tactical Air Navigation (TACAN) beacon and UHF radio. The 52nd aircraft onwards also received revised artificial feel units, which improved the handling. The initial aircraft were later upgraded, but not to full Type 560 standard and they retained VHF radio. The last production Scimitar was XD333 in December 1960 – its completion had been delayed by two months because an over-zealous storekeeper had already passed several components to the scrap dealer. Appropriately admonished, he had to buy the parts back at suitably inflated prices!

Gunnery acceptance trials were flown by XD212 in May and June 1957, only minor modifications being required. WW134 and XD215 undertook intensive flying trials on *Ark Royal* during 18–25 July. Both had the reprofiled nose, XD215 sporting a dummy in-flight refuelling probe. The pilots were Cdr Pat Chilton, Lt Cdr Derek Whitehead, Mike Lithgow, Lt Cdr HG Julian and Lt Cdr Danny Norman of the A&AEE and Lt Cdr Geoff Higgs of RAE Bedford. A total of 148 landings and catapult launches were accomplished up to weights of 34,400lb (15,603kg), the flap blowing being used for all but 13 landings, and XD215 made 94 dummy landings. The results were very satisfactory, although fuel leaks did cause some concern.

The Scimitar Intensive Flying Trials Unit, 700X NAS, formed at Ford on 27 August 1957, XD221 arriving as its first aircraft on 25 September. Performance trials in November using WT859 and XD216 achieved a maximum speed of 682kt (Mach 1.32) and four

The Scimitar was an attractive aircraft. XD234's wings are folded and on the nose is the inflight refuelling probe. The black radome is for the Ranging Radar. Beneath the intake can be seen the firing ports of the port 30mm ADEN cannon. *Terry Panopalis Collection*

climbs to 45,000ft (13,715m) by WW134 and XD212 recorded a rate of climb of 20,700ft/min (6,310m/min) at 5,000ft (1,524m). Relighting the Avons in the event of a flameout proved problematic above 25,000ft (7,620m) and it took until 1959 for Rolls-Royce to find an effective solution – fitting slotted shroud mini-cage burners to increase the relight altitude limit to 30,000ft (9,145m).

Carriage of large external stores caused some aerodynamic issues that were rectified by fitting new pylons with a swept leading edge, which in turn caused further problems when the wings had to be strengthened to withstand the forces of the explosive release unit they used. Excessive cockpit and avionics bay heat in tropical conditions also required investigation. In total, around £450,000 was spent on modifications to achieve full Service Release clearance. In addition, development and addition of the nose-mounted aerial refuelling probe cost £405,000 in 1958.

The newly recommissioned HMS *Victorious* was tested using Scimitars XD220, 221 and 226 between 29 August and 4 September 1958. The BS.4 catapults were tested by launching the aircraft at weights up to 37,500lb (17,010kg), all 15 launches were achieved at 142kt, 15kt above the minimum launch speed. The Mk.13 arrester gear was tested by landings made at 34,500lb (15,650kg) maximum emergency landing weight. Some issues were found on landing, especially during off-centreline landings, and the risk of potential damage to the aft lift from the arrester hook. Two landing aids were also tested: the Audio Incidence Indicator on XD220 and the Air Speed Sensing Unit fitted to XD221 and XD226. When 700X NAS disbanded on 27 May 1958, the unit had achieved 982 sorties and 935 flying hours.

The first frontline squadron commissioned on the Scimitar, 803 NAS, reformed on 3 June 1958 with a cadre from 700X, replacing its Sea Hawks and

Scimitar F.1 XD236 during its time with the Fleet Requirements Unit operated by Airwork Limited during 1966–68. One of the FRU's tasks included providing high-speed radar targets to train the aerial warfare officers aboard the RN's warships. A radar altimeter failure led to a fatal crash for XD236, flying into high ground at St. Catherine's Point on the Isle of Wight in poor visibility while acting as a target for the radar picket destroyer HMS *Corunna* on 26 June 1968. *Tony Buttler Collection*

Scimitar XD250 of 803 NAS releases four 1,000lb (454kg) HE bombs. On 17 February 1966, while operating with 803 NAS from HMS *Ark Royal* in the Indian Ocean a hydraulic failure led to a fire which caused the starboard flaps and air brakes to deploy; the pilot ejected safely. *Blue Envoy Collection*

embarking aboard *Victorious* on 23 September – the Officer Commanding, Cdr JD Russell sadly being drowned when the arrester wire snapped and his jet ran off the end of the angled deck. More ill luck with jet pipe cracking curtailed 803's trip to the Far East at Malta. Despite these early troubles, 803 NAS went on to deploy to the Far East three times aboard *Victorious*, before embarking onto *Hermes* on 25 May 1962, having spent the previous month on deck trials on the smaller carrier. Deployment aboard

Scimitar XD328 of 803 NAS at RAF Leuchars in 1964 is loaded with a dummy *Red Beard* tactical nuclear bomb, balanced to starboard by a fuel tank and with AIM-9 Sidewinders outboard. *A. Carlaw via Terry Panopalis*

Ark Royal followed in 1965, the ship making a last visit by a British carrier to Aden in May 1966. Returning to the UK in August, on 1 October the squadron was disbanded.

The next squadron to form was 807 NAS at RNAS Lossiemouth on 1 October 1958, having received its first pair of Scimitars two days earlier. The squadron was assigned to *Ark Royal*, followed by the smaller *Centaur* in April 1961. On 15 May 1962, *Centaur* returned from its Far East deployment and the squadron disbanded the same day.

800 NAS reformed at Lossiemouth on 1 July 1959. Its first deployment was on *Ark Royal* along with 807 NAS. The squadron was chosen to be the Royal Navy Display Team, *The Red Blades*, which flew at the Paris Air Show in June 1961, followed by the SBAC Show at Farnborough in September and many other airshows. The squadron remained with *Ark Royal*

Scimitar XD248 of 807 NAS makes a practice RP attack in a shallow dive. During 1966 the aircraft was loaned to RAE West Freugh for trials of the No.907 and No.947 bomb fuzes and 1,000lb (454kg) retarded bombs and 28lb (12.7kg) retarded practice bombs. *Phil Butler Collection via Chris Gibson*

until 31 December 1963, disbanding on 25 February 1964 and passing its aircraft to 807 NAS.

800B NAS was formed on 9 September 1964 specially to develop an aerial refuelling capability to support the Blackburn Buccaneer S.1 fleet. Up to 14 Scimitars were fitted with a Flight Refuelling Limited Mk.20A refuelling pod on the starboard inboard pylon. The pod carried 145gal of fuel (659L), augmenting the full internal fuel load of 1,065gal (4,841L). The unit embarked four aircraft onto Eagle in December 1964 and operated with this ship until 800B was disbanded on 14 August 1966, having become surplus to requirements once the longer-range Buccaneer S.2 entered service.

The third Lossiemouth Scimitar squadron was 804 NAS, formed on 1 March 1960. The assigned carrier was Hermes, the ship nearly being deployed to the Persian Gulf in July 1961 during the period of tension when Iraq threatened to invade its neighbour Kuwait. The squadron only operated Scimitars for 18 months, disbanding on 15 November 1961. (Originally the squadron had been planned to transfer to Ark Royal alongside 800 NAS and not disband until May 1964.)

In March 1960 the Admiralty requested the modernisation of the Scimitar's armament with up to four AGM-12 Bullpup air-to-surface missiles (ASMs) in the strike role or four AIM-9B Sidewinder infrared (IR)-homing AAMs when operated as a fighter to extend the Scimitar's service life until 1965 (500 missiles were ordered from the USA in October 1960.) The provision of missiles required suitable storage and test facilities to be refitted into the carriers. The Bullpup was guided via a radio command link, the pilot having to maintain a steady course while he guided the missile onto the target. The Bullpup had a 250lb (113kg) warhead. When

XD274 sits on *Eagle's* waist catapult awaiting take-off for a tanker sortie in the Mozambique Strait in April 1966 during the Beira Patrol to enforce an oil blockade in response to Rhodesia's self-proclaimed independence. The Mk.20 refuelling pod is under the starboard wing. Within four months XD274 had retired to become a ground instructional airframe. *Terry Panopalis Collection*

The second photograph of Scimitar F.1 XD274 aboard HMS *Eagle*. In September 1964 it was issued to 800B Flight as a refuelling tanker for the carrier's Blackburn Buccaneers. During 1965 it suffered several tanking mishaps: on 20 January the hose separated from the Mk.20A refuelling pod, hitting Buccaneer XN953; another hose defect was encountered on 3 February; on 18 March the port drop tank refused to release and the port aileron hit the arrester gear on landing; the refuelling hose parted again on 20 May; the starboard drop tank fell off on 11 November and on 9 March 1966 yet another hose was lost! *Terry Panopalis Collection*

WINGS OVER THE FLEET

The fifth production Scimitar F.1 XD216 is loaded with an AIM-9 Sidewinder (at the time designated AAM-N-7 by the US Navy) trials round from the USN's Naval Ordnance Test Station at China Lake, California during the Scimitar's Sidewinder clearance trials. *Tony Buttler Collection*

carrying Bullpups the maximum speed was limited to 625kt (Mach 1.1) with a maximum rolling pullout of 5g. The capability to carry Sidewinders was cleared in 1963. The requirement to carry a new napalm bomb to meet Naval Staff Target AW.261 was cancelled in January 1958. Interest in napalm would resurface a couple of years later, but governmental approval to develop such weapons only occurred in December 1964.

Export interest from the Federal Republic of Germany's Marineflieger, Switzerland (a de-navalised Type 560 and the two-seat Type 563 project), Canada and a request from Venezuela received by Vickers in September 1957 to build them an aircraft carrier and supply Scimitars, brought no orders.

One oddity was the Type 539, a two-seat conversion trainer based on the Type 525, but with a modified forward fuselage with a tandem cockpit, the instructor in the rear seat having a periscope for the gunsight. The fixed armament was reduced to two 20mm Hispano cannon, but the ranging-radar in the nose was retained and two F.24 cameras could be fitted in the rear fuselage. Two fuselage fuel tanks were removed to make room for the additional seat and No. 2 fuselage tank was slightly enlarged to compensate. The Type 539 would have been a formidable weapons trainer, but no interest was forthcoming.

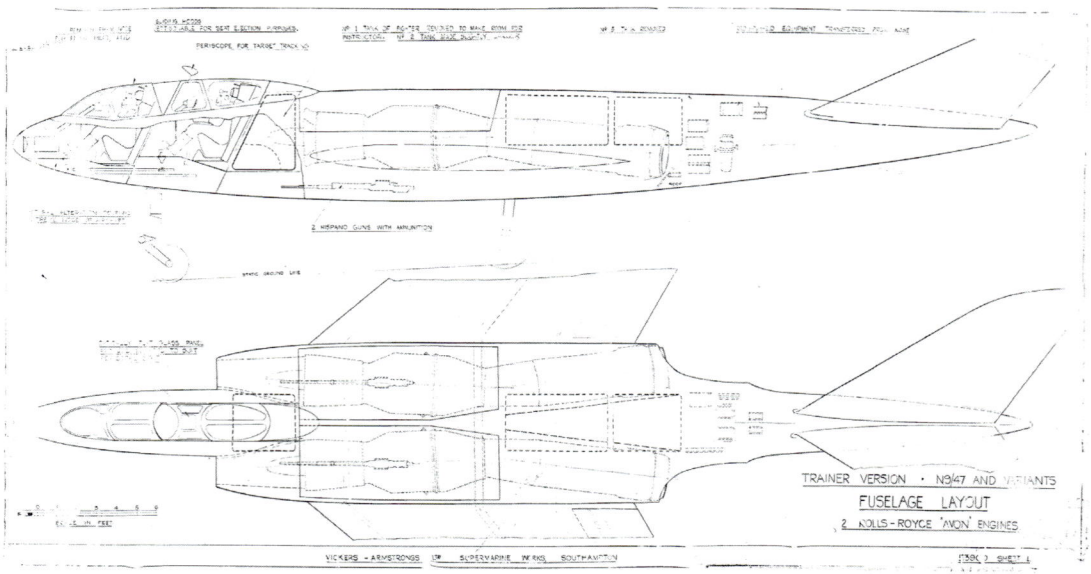

The proposed Type 539 conversion trainer retained a full combat capability. The instructor in the rear cockpit would be provided with a periscope for his reflector gun sight to check the student's aim. *RAF Museum Hendon via Ralph Pegram*

Scimitar developments

There were other unbuilt developments of the Scimitar (the two-seat Type 556 interceptor is covered in Chapter 4.) Revised Specification N.113P2 was connected to NR/A.17 Issue 5 in 1955 for a high-altitude interceptor armed with a pair of *Blue Jay* AAMs, an IR-homing missile developed by de Havilland Propellers, which entered service as the Firestreak. Making a high-altitude aircraft out of the low level load lugger was not easy. At first it was thought that reheat and blown flaps would overcome any weight increase but adding that kit brought its own weight penalty. The designer of the Type 558 decided to strip out the reheat and the blown flaps, increasing the wing area to compensate (the wing fold line was moved outboard) and with a maximum speed limited to 660kt. The service ceiling would be 49,450ft (15,070m); the AUW was 37,200lb (16,873kg). Armament would be two ADEN cannon and two *Blue Jays*, Radar Ranging Mk.3 would be fitted and the engines were two 13,400lbf (56.6kN) dry thrust Avon RA.24. The proposal was presented to DNAW and the Director of Military Aircraft Research and Development (Royal Navy) on 15 April, but the 'Scimitar Mk.2' proposal went no further, although the de-navalised Type 561 was offered to the RAF as a low-altitude tactical nuclear bomber.

The succeeding Type 562 of early 1956 – work began in January and the brochure was submitted to the MoS in mid-July – was another step further

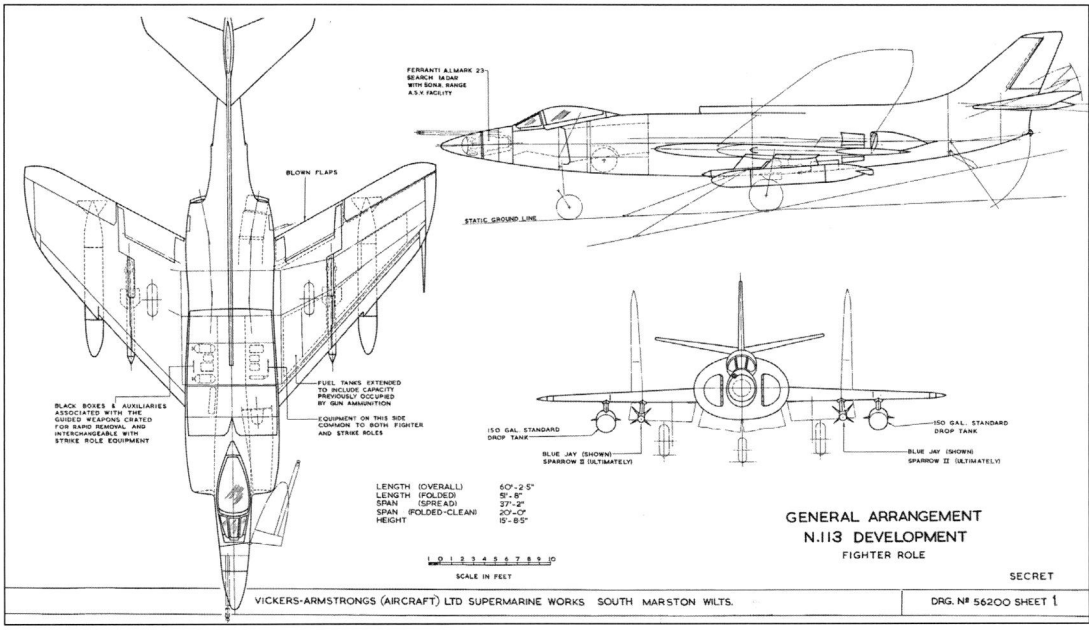

The Type 562 in this general arrangement drawing is fitted for the interceptor role with two *Blue Jays* (the Douglas Sparrow II being Supermarine's preferred ultimate choice) and Ferranti AI.23 radar. The cannon were removed for additional fuel space and the in-flight refuelling probe was retained. *RAF Museum Hendon via Ralph Pegram*

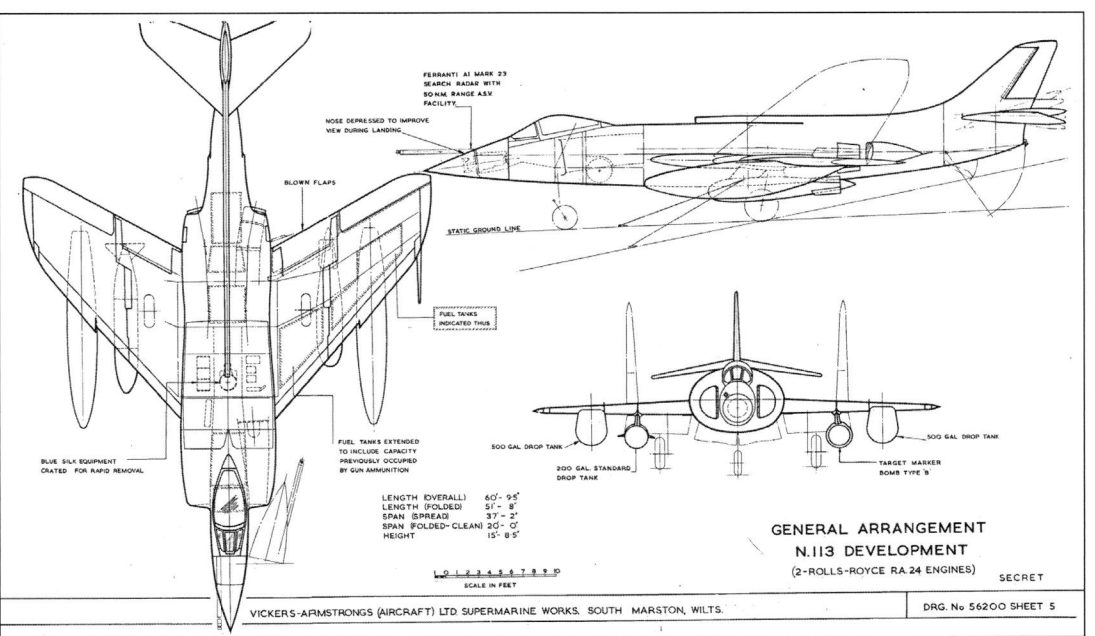

The Type 562 evolved, a new sharper nose cone being designed to improve the view on landing. Shown in the strike role, this drawing shows a single TMB (*Red Beard*) under the port wing and the palletised *Blue Silk* Doppler radar pack behind the cockpit for improved navigational accuracy. A mock-up was built but the design went no further. *RAF Museum Hendon via Ralph Pegram*

WINGS OVER THE FLEET

Supermarine Scimitar Projects

	Type 558 Scimitar Mk.2	Type 560	Type 561	Type 562	Type 563
Intended for	FAA	Switzerland	RAF	FAA	Switzerland
Crew	One	One	One	One	Two
Span	43ft 3in (13.19m); 27ft 5in (8.38m) folded	37ft 2in (11.33m)	43ft 3in (13.19m)	37ft 2in (11.33m); 20ft 0in (6.09m) folded	37ft 2in (11.33m)
Length	56ft 1in (17.06m); 51ft 0in (15.54m) folded	53ft 3in (16.84m)	56ft 1in (17.06m)	60ft 9.5in (18.56m); 51ft 8in (15.74m) folded	?
Wing area	650ft² (60.38m²)	485ft² (45.10m²)	650ft² (60.38m²)	485ft² (45.10m²)	485ft² (45.10m²)
t/c ratio	?	8%	?	8%	8%
Gross weight	37,200lb (16,875kg)	?	?	Take-off weight 40,990lb (18,595kg) with Red Beard	Take-off weight 32,845lb (14,900kg)
Powerplant	2x Avon RA.24, 13,400lbf (59.6kN)	2x Avon Mk.202, 11,250lbf (50.0kN)	2x Avon RA.24, 13,400lbf (59.6kN)	2x Avon RA.24 or RA.29R or Conway 31 or Sapphire 10R; or 1x Gyron Junior PS.38 & 1x rocket, 8,000lbf (35.5kN)	2x Avon RA.24
Fuel capacity	? internal, plus 2 or 4x drop tanks, refuelling probe	1,065gal (4,841L), plus 2 or 4x drop tanks	500gal (2,273L), plus 2x 500gal & 1x 200gal (909L) drop tanks	2,360gal (10,728L), plus 2x 150gal (682L) or 2x 500gal & 1x 200gal drop tanks, refuelling probe	1,142gal (5,191L), \plus 2x 500gal drop tanks
Max speed	635kt (1,175km/h) at SL; 548kt (1,014km/h) at 45,000ft (13,715m)	640kt (1,186km/h) at SL; Mach 0.97 at altitude	635kt (1,175km/h) at SL; 548kt (1,014km/h) at 45,000ft (13,715m)	640kt (1,186km/h) at SL; 562kt (1,041km/h) at 40,000ft (12,190m)	?
Rate of climb	22,750ft/min (6,935m/min) at SL	12,000ft/min (3,655m/min) at SL	22,750ft/min (6,935m/min) at SL	21,200ft/min (6,462m/min) at SL	?
Service ceiling	49,450ft (15,070m)	46,000ft (14,020m)	49,450ft (15,070m)	?	?
Armament	2x 30mm ADEN, 2x Firestreak	4x 30mm ADEN, bombs, RPs	1x Red Beard, 4x 1,000lb (454kg) or 500lb (227kg) bombs, RP pods	4x Firestreak or Sparrow II, 1x Red Beard, 4x 1,000lb (454kg) or 500lb (227kg) bombs, RP pods	4x 30mm ADEN, bombs, RPs

along the evolution to improve the Scimitar's operational efficiency. The range was to be increased by two large 500gal (2,273L) underwing fuel tanks and an increased internal capacity of 2,360gal (10,730L) – the cannon being removed to make space (the inflight refuelling probe was retained.) The strike radius would increase by 350nm (648km) and the interception role would include a Combat Air Patrol 100nm (185km) from the carrier task force. Improved weapons capability would be provided by installing a modified Ferranti AI.23 radar with a 50nm (93km) surface-search mode in the modified nose. Navigation aids for the strike role would include *Blue Silk* or *Yellow Lemon* Doppler navigation radar.

In the strike role the single *Red Beard* on the starboard inner pylon was balanced by a 200gal (909L) drop tank to port. For the interception role it was intended to use the DH Propellers *Red Top* (originally *Blue Jay* Mk.5), an improved Firestreak

Type 564	Type 565	Type 567	Type 572	Type 575	Type 576
FAA	RAF	FAA	RAF	Canada	FAA
One or Two	One or Two	One or Two	One	One	One
37ft 2in (11.33m); 20ft 0in (6.09m) folded	37ft 2in (11.33m)	37ft 2in (11.33m); 20ft 0in (6.09m) folded	37ft 2in (11.33m)	37ft 2in (11.33m)	41ft 2in (12.54m); 43ft 6.8in (13.22m) with wing tip rocket nacelles; 20ft 0in (6.09m) folded
60ft 9.5in (18.56m); 51ft 8in (15.74m) folded	Single-seat 62ft 2in (18.95m); two-seat 61ft 5.5in (18.75m)	Single-seat 61ft 0in (18.59m); two-seat 61ft 10.5in (18.84m); 51ft 8in (15.74m) folded	?	55ft 4in (16.86m)	61ft 0in (18.59m); 51ft 8in (15.74m) folded
485ft² (45.10m²)	485ft² (45.10m²)	485ft² (45.10m²)	485ft² (45.10m²)	485ft² (45.10m²)	?
8%	8%	8%	8%	8%	?
48,764lb (22,119kg)	Take-off weight 48,570lb (22,030kg) with Red Beard	50,578lb (22,941kg) with Red Beard	?	?	50,964lb (21,116kg)
2x Gyron Junior DGJ.1, 7,000lbf (31.1kN)	2x Avon RA.24 Mk.2; optional 1x Spectre rocket pack, 8,000lbf (35.5kN)	2x Avon RA.24	2x Avon RA.24	2x Avon RA.24	2x RB.146, 13,220lbf (58.8kN) dry & 2x Spectre, 10,000lbf (44.4kN); or 2x RB.146, 15,000lbf (69.8kN) reheat
? internal, plus 2 or 4x drop tanks, refuelling probe	? internal, plus 2x 500gal & 1x 200gal drop tanks	? internal, plus 2x 500gal & 1x 200gal drop tanks	?	? internal, plus 2x 150gal (682L) & 1x 200gal (909L) drop tanks, refuelling probe	1,515gal (6,887L) one-seat, 1,995gal (9,070L) two-seat, & HTP, plus 2x 500gal & 2x 200gal drop tanks, refuelling probe
?	Mach 0.93	?	?	?	RB.146 & Spectre, Mach 1.8 at 65,000ft (19,810m)
?	?	?	?	?	?
?	?	?	?	?	?
4x Firestreak or Sparrow II/III, 1x Red Beard, 4x 1,000lb (454kg) or 500lb (227kg) bombs, RPpods	1x Red Beard, 6x 1,000lb (454kg) or 500lb (227kg) bombs, RP pods	1x Red Beard, 4x 1,000lb (454kg) or 500lb (227kg) bombs, RP pods	Internal cameras, RP pods	4x 1,000lb (454kg) or 500lb (227kg) bombs, RP pods	4x Firestreak or Red Top

with all-aspect homing capability against supersonic targets. Alan Clifton and George Henson offered a wide range of upgrade possibilities to tackle Mach 2 targets at 60,000ft (18,290m): IR-homing *Blue Vesta* (*Blue Jay* Mk.4), Vickers *Red Hebe* with continuous wave semi-active homing and from America the radar-guided Douglas AAM-N-3 Sparrow II or semi-active radar homing Raytheon AAM-N-6 Sparrow III (which later become the famous AIM-7 Sparrow) plus the IR-homing Hughes GAR-1A and GAR-1C Falcon. In reality the best achievable capability was engaging a Mach 1.3 target at 50,000ft (15,240m).

The engine choice was equally varied: the Avon RA.24 or RA.29 either without reheat with an 8,000lbf (35.5kN) rocket booster for take-off; with reheat and no rocket; Rolls-Royce Conway 31 without reheat plus a rocket; the Armstrong Siddeley Sapphire 10R with reheat (this was the favoured choice). The Type 564 had a single 7,000lbf

The chunky Scimitar had plenty of engine thrust but preferred cruising at high subsonic speed. The Type 576 was designed to achieve a supersonic capability. This is the single-seat version, with a TMB under the port wing. The enlarged dorsal spine housed additional fuel tanks. *RAF Museum Hendon via Ralph Pegram*

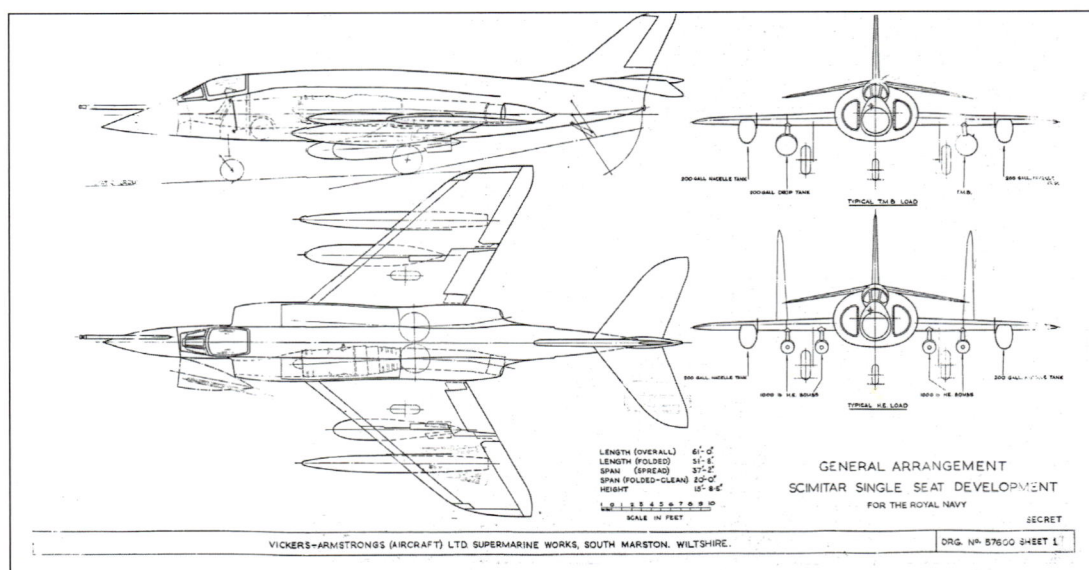

The two-seat version of the Type 576 looks visually better with the 'hunchback' appearance being better faired into the wider cockpit section. *RAF Museum Hendon via Ralph Pegram*

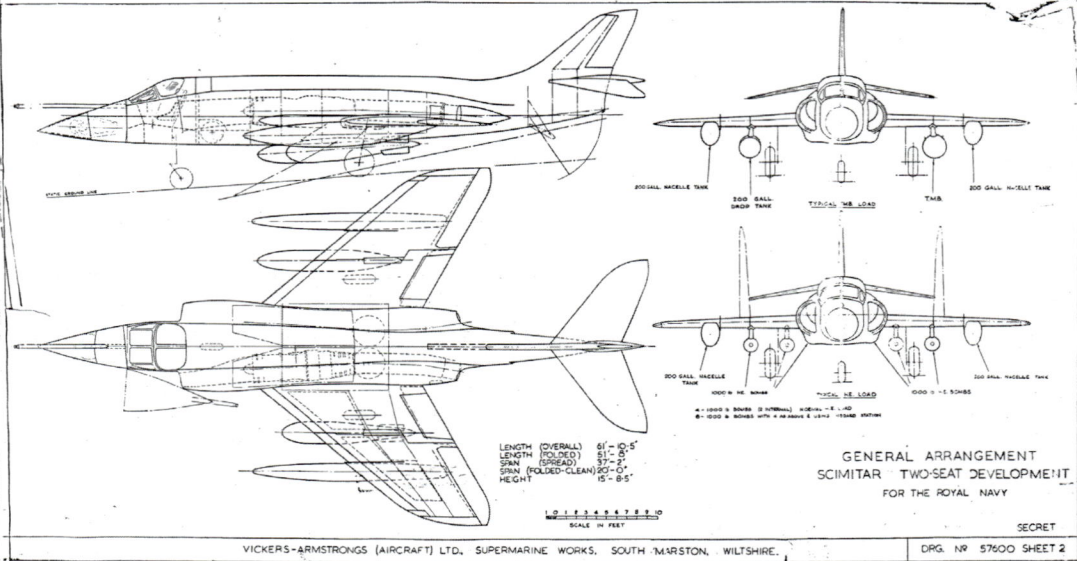

Despite using the new 13,220lbf (58.8kN) Rolls-Royce RB.146 more thrust was required. Two 10,000lbf (44.4kN) DH Spectre rocket motors were installed just beneath the tail jet pipes. Four Firestreaks could be carried in the interceptor role. *RAF Museum Hendon via Ralph Pegram*

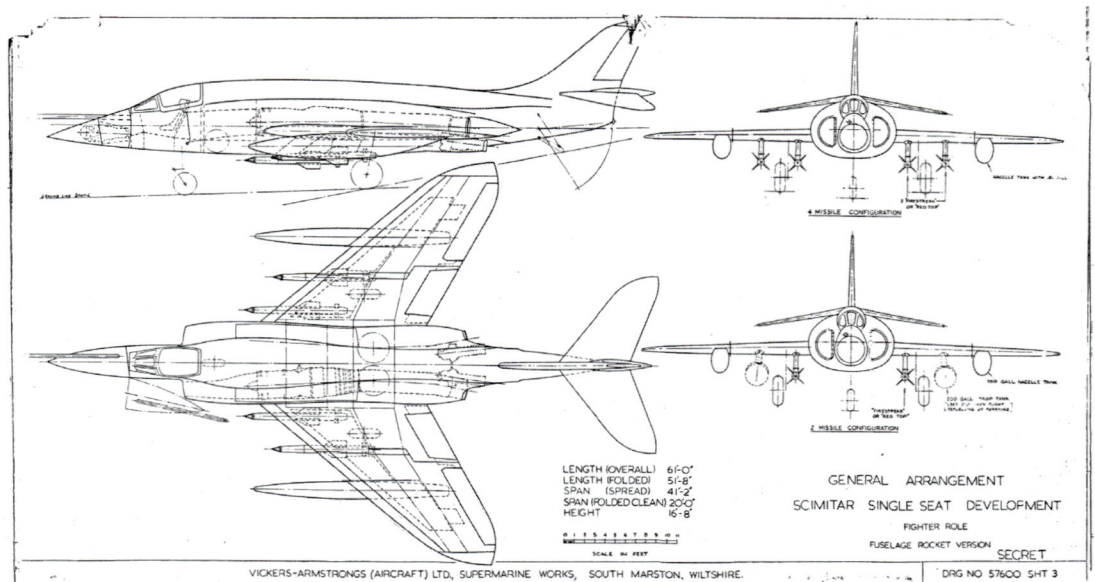

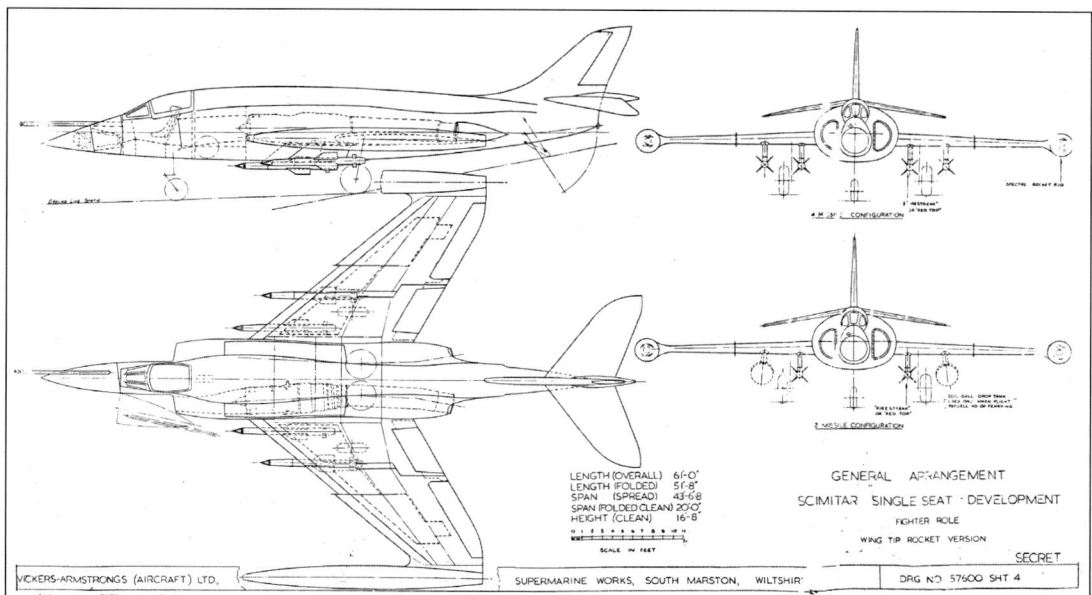

This version placed the DH Spectre rockets in wing tip pods. For some reason Supermarine chose one of the worst places to put a rocket motor. If one of the motors failed on take-off the asymmetric thrust would have resulted in a nasty accident. *RAF Museum Hendon via Ralph Pegram*

(31.1kN) dry thrust de Havilland Gyron Junior PS.78 with reheat plus the rocket, with the landing weight reduced by 2,100lb (952kg). Blown ailerons would be fitted and additional fuel increased the ferry range to 2,540nm (4,705km).

On 18 September 1956 the go ahead was given for a mock-up and Supermarine estimated that the Type 562 could enter service in 1959, following from the 101st Scimitar F.1. Alternatively, the Type 564 could be ready for 1961, receiving the more advanced *Blue Parrot* radar from the Buccaneer and *Yellow Lemon* Doppler navigation. Design work, however, progressed to the Type 567 in September 1957, in either single or two-seat forms, with wing tip tanks and integral wing tanks to extend the range. The AUW with one *Red Beard* was 50,578lb (22,941kg). The two-seater would have a wider forward fuselage for side-by-side seating.

The final development, the Type 576 of December 1958, had dramatic changes to the fuselage. The dorsal spine was fattened for additional High Test Peroxide (HTP) fuel tanks for the rocket engines, maximum AUW increasing to 50,964lb (23,116kg). The engines would be upgraded to the 13,220blf (58.8kN) Rolls-Royce RB.146 (the 300 Series Avon with an additional compressor stage) and two large wing tip nacelles would carry 10,000lbf (44.4kN) de Havilland Spectre rocket motors, later these were moved to the rear fuselage to reduce drag (and the dangers from asymmetric thrust should an engine fail). Extended wing tips were also fitted to enable a speed of Mach 1.8 at 65,000ft (18,910m). Another alternative had reheated 15,000lbf (66.7kN) RB.146s with no rockets and thinner outer wing sections, achieving Mach 1.6 at 45,000ft. A new thinner wing from root to tip would reduce fuel capacity but would improve speed and manoeuvrability, this was the definitive version.

A typical interception sortie would be patrolling at 45,000ft at Mach 0.95, then following detection of a Mach 2 target at 65,000ft, a rocket-boosted climb to 55,000ft (17,765m) at Mach 1.4 would put the aircraft in the position to launch a Firestreak or *Red Top* AAM (four would be carried) which could 'jump up' 15,000ft (4,570m) to make the intercept. Alternatively, a battery of 2in (5cm) diameter RPs would be fitted. Six hardpoints were provided, the outer ones for drop tanks. Avionics included the Ferranti AI.23 AIRPASS I search radar, *Blue Silk* Doppler and a Kelvin-Hughes Roller Map display for the strike role.

Vickers-Supermarine claimed that all the modifications could be retrofitted to existing Scimitar F.1s and that new-build aircraft could be ready to enter service in 1962 (or 1963 with the thinner wing). A two-seat version was submitted to Specification M.148B. The Royal Canadian Air Force was offered a similar version, the Type 575. Despite all these further designs the Scimitar was quickly overtaken by the Buccaneer in the strike role and the DH Sea Vixen in the interceptor role.

4 Defending the Fleet

"The advent of the Russian MiG-15 Fighter has had a profound effect on naval aircraft plans. The performance and fire power of the MiG-15 are superior to those of the Sea Hawk which, as you know, we had been relying for the day fighter role for some time to come. There are therefore now grave doubts of our ability to operate our carriers in the face of strong shore based opposition without ourselves having the benefit of shore based cover. It is thus clearly important that all possible measures should now be taken to expedite the introduction into the Naval Service of a fighter which would be a match for the MiG-15."

LETTER FROM THE HEAD OF THE ADMIRALTY AIR BRANCH TO THE TREASURY, 12 OCTOBER 1951

Defence of the fleet was a vital role for the Fleet Air Arm. The Royal Navy emerged from the Second World War with six years of experience of combatting aerial attack, which included threats from dive-bombers, low flying torpedo-bombers, first-generation guided air-to-surface missiles (ASMs) such as the radio-command guided Ruhrstahl SD 1400 X *Fritz-X* bomb and the Henschel Hs 293 and the terrifyingly determined Japanese Kamikaze suicide pilots. These attacks had taken place in all climatic conditions, from the frozen waters of the Barents Sea to the tropical heat of the southwestern Pacific by day and by night.

The advent of radar was as revolutionary for naval air defence as it was on land. But future aerial threats would be jet-powered aircraft armed with guided missiles and from the late-1950s it was increasingly likely those missiles had nuclear warheads. Although the Soviet Union at this time did not build any aircraft

The large scanner seen atop HMS *Hermes'* bridge is the Type 984 long-range search radar. This sophisticated unit was complex but one of the most advanced search radars in the world at the time it entered service. In the foreground is a Supermarine Scimitar ready for take-off from the starboard steam catapult. *Author's Collection*

carriers, the RN's Mediterranean Fleet could find itself within range of land-based jet fighters and bombers, with long-range bombers being the main threat in the North Atlantic and the Norwegian Sea. As we have seen in Chapter 1, initially it was planned to have rapidly climbing interceptors using combined turbojet and rocket motor propulsion. But this was not considered practical in 1946 and standing Combat Air Patrols (CAP) seemed the only counter to jet aircraft, despite the thirsty turbojets which limited endurance. The development of the Armstrong Whitworth Sea Slug surface-to-air missile (SAM) was under development but was still a decade away from entering service. The deck-launched interception (DLI) concept would have to be revisited and in the 1950s rocket propulsion came to the fore once again. The path to acquiring a modern radar-equipped all-weather fighter took over a decade, marred by indecision and changing threats. This chapter details the efforts required to provide the fleet with 24-hour aerial protection.

Punch and Judy

Exercises during 1948 showed that raids of more than 20 piston-engined aircraft could overwhelm the aircraft carrier's Action Information Organisation (AIO), where up to 60 officers and ratings attempted to make sense of the aerial picture and organise interceptions. The main problem was time lag, it took 20 seconds to transfer (by verbal and manual methods) the radar indication of an incoming target onto the vertical (altitude) plot – a supersonic aircraft could cover 3nm (5.5km) in that time. It took the AIO four minutes to vector the CAP onto an incoming raid. The DLI fighters would take-off and rapidly climb head-on to the target – the incoming bomber covering 20nm (37km) – before manoeuvring into a pursuit course to attack from astern, taking another 2.75nm (5km) (this is why collision-course air-to-air missiles [AAMs] became increasingly important from the mid-1950s).

The stated threat in 1948 was a bomber releasing its ASM 30nm (55km) away from 50,000ft (15,240m) or 20nm (37km) from 35,000ft (10,670m) or 10nm (18.5km) at sea level. A high-altitude intercept had to take place 55nm (100km) from the centre of the fleet, requiring an initial radar detection at 135nm (250km) with precision target tracking from 85nm (157km).

The solution was automation of the AIO's functions and an advanced search radar. Development began on a Comprehensive Display System (CDS), a computer which could maintain data on 40 tracks and compute intercepting vectors (HMS *Hermes* received a more compact 32-track CDS and *County*-class guided missile destroyers had a 24-track version). The Digital Plot Transmission (DPT) was a datalink to the escort ships. The workload limits of verbal intercept instructions to the pilot could be overcome with greater provision of Aerial Interception (AI) radar for the fighters for a 'Punch and Judy' intercept – the

A de Havilland Sea Vixen FAW.1 on approach to land. The Sea Vixen entered frontline service in 1959 – the culmination of 14 years of policy indecision, defence cutbacks and numerous design studies. *Blue Envoy Collection*

controller calling 'Punch' over the radio when the aircraft should be within AI radar range and the observer replying 'Judy' when he acquired the target in his scope, the observer would then guide his pilot to the target for the attack.

The CDS was linked to the advanced Type 984 S-band, three-dimensional radar with five simultaneously scanning beams for height finding (a sixth beam was a long-range low-altitude warning beam), capable of detecting targets 180nm (333km) away at altitudes up to 100,000ft (30,480m) and tracking them within 90nm (166km). HMS *Victorious* was the first carrier to receive the 27-ton Type 984 in 1958, with *Hermes* and *Eagle* following by 1964. Containing 8,912 radio valves, 47,400 resistors and 2,115 relays, it was complicated and demanding to maintain, but its operational debut aboard *Victorious* in Exercise Riptide in 1959 against US Navy (USN) aircraft was impressive. *Eagle* during her 'A' Standard refit during 1959–64 received the digital Action Data Automation Weapon System 1 (ADAWS 1) successor to CDS. There were some development issues but it led to a series of improved combat and weapon control systems.

Radar coverage could be extended by Airborne Early Warning (AEW) aircraft (of which the RN had none at that time, see Chapter 9 for their

WINGS OVER THE FLEET

The second prototype de Havilland Sea Hornet F.21 PX239 was converted by Heston Aircraft from an unfinished Hornet F.1 fuselage and was fully navalised. This view shows the observer's cockpit in the rear fuselage with its bubble canopy and the nose radome of the AN/APS-4 ASH radar (known in British service as AI.15). PX239 also trialled the AN/APS-13 radar. *Tony Buttler Collection*

development) and radar picket ships. In January 1946 this latter concept became the Fleet Aircraft Direction Escort (FADE). The ships would have Type 982 narrow-beam long-range search, Type 983 height-finding and Type 960 broad-beam early warning radars (170nm [314km] range against an aircraft at 40,000ft [12,190m] or 60nm [111km] at 5,000ft [1,525m]), along with an AEW terminal. The ships would conduct fighter direction with dedicated Aircraft Direction and Target Indication Rooms. The FADEs would be conversions, either from *Dido*-class anti-aircraft cruisers (FADE I), *Battle*-class destroyers (FADE II) or a new-build modified *Daring*-class destroyer design (FADE III, IV & V). The United Kingdom's financial straits put an end to this programme and the proposed cheaper conversions of the fast minelayer HMS *Abdiel* (FADE VI) and the *Dido*-class cruiser *Scylla*.

By 1954 fleet commanders were calling for radar picket ships, the minimum requirement was six ships to maintain four pickets on station. A new Marconi search radar to replace the Type 960 entered service as the Type 965M with a single AKE(1) aerial and as the Type 965P with an AKE(2) double-array (which increased the detection range of a bomber from 200nm [370km] at 45,000ft [13,715m] to 280nm (520km) at 100,000ft [30,480m]). It was a P-band broad-beam search set, but lacked any moving-target indication, which prevented it from distinguishing targets flying over land (a serious problem during the Falklands campaign in 1982.) Slower convoy escort forces would receive an Air Direction (A/D) frigate. The Type 61 *Salisbury*-class was a variant of the Type 41 diesel-powered anti-aircraft frigate, sacrificing one of the two 4.5in (115mm) calibre Mk.6 twin-gun turrets for Type 960 air search, Type 277Q height-finding, Type 982M S-band long-range target indication and Type 293Q S-band short-range/low-altitude target indication radars. Other equipment included an American AN/SRR-4A AEW video datalink (a television camera aboard the aircraft filmed the radar scope and transmitted the picture) and radio equipment providing seven UHF ship-to-air radio channels. Later refits saw the Type 960 replaced with Type 965P. Four ships were built during 1952–58; HMS *Salisbury*, *Chichester*, *Lincoln* and *Llandaff*. They were too slow at 23kt for fleet work, however, and three further ships were cancelled. To make up numbers, it was intended to refit five *M*-class destroyers as Type 62 A/D frigates, but these were cancelled in 1955.

The Admiralty's 1955–65 plan covered refitting all four *Weapon*-class destroyers and the first four 1943 *Battle*-class destroyers for service until 1969–72. This order was reversed in the 1957 '80 Plan' (referring to the number of fleet escorts). The *Battle*-class ships *Agincourt*, *Aisne*, *Barossa* and *Corunna* received the double-array Type 965P, Type 277Q or Type 278 height-finding and Type 293Q target indication radar, along with an AEW terminal; this cost £1.75 million per ship. The *Weapons* were refitted as 'third-rate' pickets with only the Type 965 radar and no direction facilities. The *Leander* and Type 81 *Tribal*-class frigates were fitted with Type 965 radars in an attempt to provide enough pickets.

Sea Hornet

In 1946 the FAA's night-fighter (NF) force consisted of just the Fairey Firefly NF.I, equipped with pod-mounted American-supplied AN/APS-4 ASH (Air-Surface, Model H) radar. These were replaced from 1948 by the multi-role, ASH radar-equipped, Firefly Mk.5, capable of easy conversion to fighter-reconnaissance, NF and anti-submarine warfare (ASW) roles (designated FR.5, NF.5 and AS.5 respectively).

Looking for a higher-performance aircraft, during 1945 Operational Requirement OR.226 was drawn up and Specification N.21/45 issued for a two-seat development of the de Havilland DH.103 Sea Hornet. A mock-up was inspected on 22 May 1945 and the Heston Aircraft Company was sub-contracted to convert Hornet F.1 prototype PX230, flying in its new guise on 9 July 1946 (two months before N.21/45 was issued!). The aircraft was modified with a second cockpit with a bubble canopy in the rear fuselage for the observer, who sat facing the tail and operated the APS-4 ASH radar mounted in the nose. The armament was four 20mm Hispano Mk.V cannon with 190 rounds per gun with provision for up to 2,000lb (907kg) of bombs or rocket projectiles (RPs) under the wings. The range requirements were 610nm (1,130km) at mean economical cruising speed at 20,000ft (6,100m), or 1,140nm (2,110km) with drop tanks.

Short Brothers & Harland was asked to prepare a conversion of the S.A.1 Sturgeon torpedo-bomber as a fallback option in case all the required AI equipment could not be fitted into the Hornet's sleek fuselage. Shorts opted to install higher-powered engines and provide wider arcs for the ASH radar. The S.A.3 'Jet Sturgeon' of late 1945/early 1946 was a two-seater powered by two 4,000lbf (17.7kN) Rolls-Royce AJ.40 axial-flow turbojets, with 910gal (4,138L) of fuel and armed with four 20mm cannon. Although sometimes attributed to Specification N.7/46, the S.A.3 could

Piston-engine night-fighters

	Fairey Firefly NF.1	**Fairey Firefly NF.5**	**de Havilland DH.103 Sea Hornet F.21**
Span	44ft 6in (13.56m); 13ft 6in (4.11m) folded	41ft 2in (12.55m) ; 13ft 6in (4.11m) folded	45ft 0in (13.71m); 27ft 6in (8.32m) folded
Length	37ft 7¼in (11.46m)	37ft 11in (11.55m)	39ft 1in (11.9m)
Wing area	328ft² (30.47m²)	330ft² (30.65m²)	361ft² (33.53m²)
Loaded weight	13,284lb (6,025kg)	13,927lb (6,317kg)	19,530lb (8,560kg)
Powerplant	1x Griffon IIB, 1,735hp (1,293kW); or Griffon XII, 1,990hp (1,483kW)	1x Griffon 74, 2,245hp (1,674kW)	2x Merlin 135/135 RM.14SM, 2,030hp (1,513kW) at +25lb/in² boost & 150 octane fuel
Max speed	277kt (513km/h) at 17,000ft (5,180m)	335kt (621km/h) at 14,000ft (4,265m)	317kt (587km/h) at SL; 373kt (692km/h) at 22,000ft (6,705m)
Rate of climb	1,800ft/min (548m/min) at SL	2,050ft/min (625m/min) at SL	16,900ft/min (5,150m/min) at SL
Service ceiling	28,200ft (8,595m)	29,200ft (8,900m)	32,400ft (9,875m)
Max range	945nm (1,750km)	1,130nm (2,090km)	1,300nm (2,415km)
Armament	4x 20mm Hispano, 2x 1,000lb (454kg) bombs, 8x 60lb (27kg) RPs	4x 20mm Hispano, 2x 1,000lb (454kg) bombs, 8x 60lb (27kg) RPs	4x 20mm Hispano, 2x 1,000lb (454kg) or 500lb (227kg) bombs, 8x 60lb (27kg) RPs

have been an attempt to match, or surpass, the Sea Hornet's performance.

Prototype Hornet PX230 was lost on 16 May 1947 when the port Rolls-Royce Merlin engine and its nacelle fell off when pulling out of a high-speed dive at 417kt during Royal Aircraft Establishment (RAE) trials, the pilot Commander (Cdr) Ken Hickson and his observer bailing out successfully. A fully navalised second prototype, PX239, followed. Production Sea Hornet NF.21 VV434 made deck landing assessments aboard *Illustrious* during 25–27 October 1948, discovering that a minimum wind speed of 35kt over the deck was required. Catapulting clearance followed on July 1949. The F.21 with its two 2,030hp (1,513kW) Merlin 134/135 engines was – at 400kt – just 4kt slower than the single-seat F.20. A total of 78 were built, equipping 809 Naval Air Squadron (NAS) which was formed at Royal Naval Air Station (RNAS) Culdrose on 20 January 1949. In addition to NF duties, 809 NAS also acted as navigators for strike forces of single-engined aircraft until the Hornets were retired in May 1954.

A fine view of Sea Hornet F.21 VW946 of 809 NAS. This aircraft suffered two accidents in 1953, its propellers striking the safety barrier aboard HMS *Eagle* on 20 January and a belly landing due to engine failure at RNAS Culdrose on 18 June which effectively ended its flying career. *Tony Buttler Collection*

N.40/46

Although the Sea Hornet was one of the fastest piston-engined fighters in the world, it could not hope to compete with future jet-powered fighters and bombers. In addition it was, like its Firefly counterpart, a conversion job and not purpose-built. In the autumn of 1946, work began on OR.246 for a twin-jet two-seat night-fighter. Specification N.40/46 was issued on 10 February 1947 and called for a maximum speed of 500kt up to 20,000ft (6,100m), the 'highest possible fighting manoeuvrability' and an all-up weight (AUW) not exceeding 30,000lb (13,610kg). Blackburn, Gloster and Westland responded to a request to tender, Hawker declining to submit a proposal.

Blackburn's B.67 design featured a very thick swept wing with a thickness-to-chord (t/c) ratio of 12% – two 30mm ADEN cannon were stacked in each wing root – and a V-tail. The two crew members sat in tandem, the de-rated 5,000lbf (22.2kN) thrust Rolls-Royce AJ.65 (soon to be named Avon) axial-flow turbojets were fitted in the wing roots. The estimated AUW was 29,160lb (13,277kg) and the performance was a maximum speed of 534kt, a sea level rate of climb of 5,200ft/min (1,585m/min) and a practical ceiling of 41,000ft (12,500m).

Gloster submitted the P.231, a derivative of the Meteor with a moderately swept wing of 9% t/c ratio and a V-tail. Three 30mm ADEN cannon were located in the lower fuselage (two to port, one to starboard). The engines were a pair of 7,000lbf (31.1kN) Metrovick F.9 axial-flow turbojets (this engine became the Armstrong Siddeley Sapphire). The estimated AUW was 28,000lb (12,700kg) with a performance of 552kt at sea level, a sea level rate

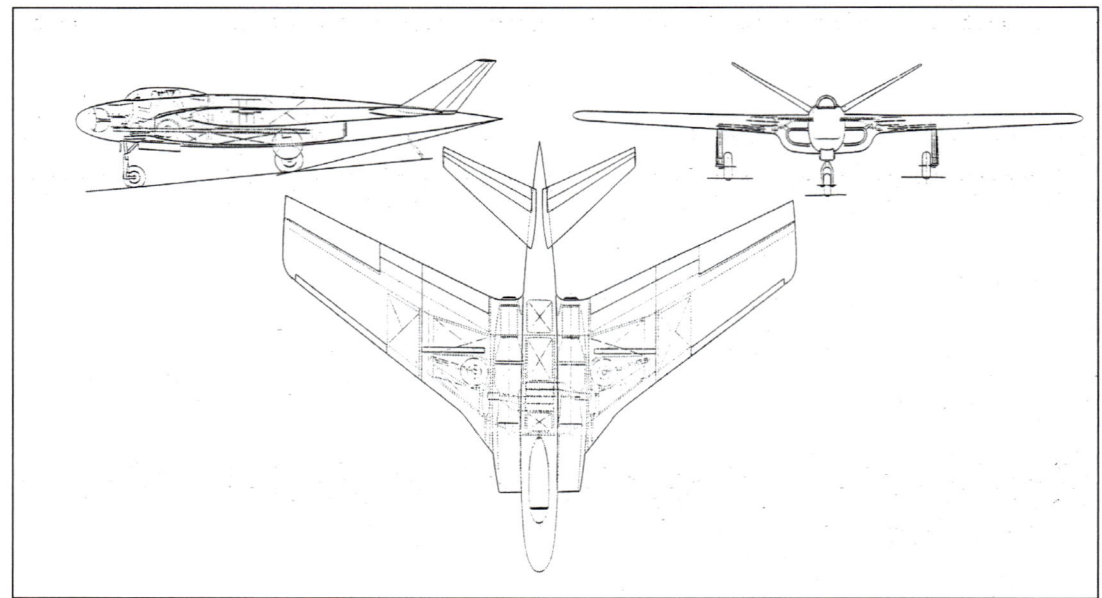

The Blackburn B.67 with its V-tail and swept wings looked futuristic in 1946. Note the stacked cannon in the thick wing roots. *Brough Heritage via Tony Buttler Collection*

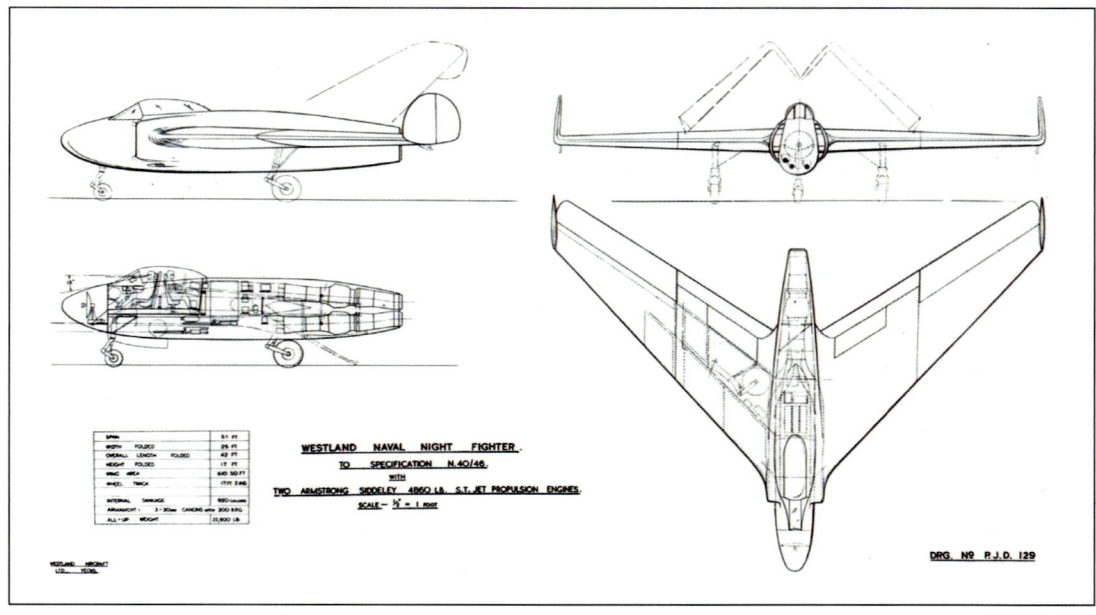

Westland's PD.129 design was cutting-edge, being a tailless swept-wing design with stacked turbojets and wing tip fins. Pilot and observer sat back to back. The internal view shows how the intakes for the upper and lower engines curved around the wing spars. *Leonardo UK via Jeremy Graham*

of climb of 10,700ft/min (3,260m/min) and a ceiling of 45,800ft (13,960m).

Westland studied several designs before submitting the PD.129 (this designation is the number of the technical drawing), the most ambitious designed offered, probably influenced by that firm's pre-war Pterodactyl IV tailless aircraft. The aircraft was a tailless, swept wing design, having a short fuselage with two engines stacked one above the other (these engines were a notional 4,860lbf [21.6kN] Armstrong Siddeley design but Westland also considered a single Avon or Metrovick F.9). The two crew sat in tandem, the observer facing to the rear. The wing had 45° of sweep and a t/c ratio of 15% for a critical Mach number of 0.87. The outer wing sections had elevons for longitudinal and lateral control combined with wing tip rudders on small end fins, slotted flaps of 25-30% chord were fitted inboard and a jet spoiler for landing was planned. The estimated approach speed was 88kt, with Westland considering fitting boundary layer control later in the aircraft's life. The armament was three 30mm ADEN cannon in the lower nose (one to port, two to starboard). The radar was the AI.9 with a 35in (89cm) diameter scanner, developed during the war as a lock-follow set, designed to make interceptions easier. It was overtaken by the US-built SCR-720 (designated AI.10 in British service) and never entered service.

The Tender Design Conference convened at the Ministry of Supply's (MoS) Thames House on 4 March 1947. After studying the proposals, it was clear that the full combat manoeuvrability called for would take up to five years to attain and involve the use of boundary layer control by suction, a major research and development project. The conference advised that the MoS's Chief Naval Representative (CNR) should review the requirements. One major change was the reduction of the AUW limit to 28,000lb (12,700kg) and the cruising endurance was cut from three to two hours. With the review completed in June, a revised specification was issued to a wider distribution of Blackburn, de Havilland (DH), Fairey, Gloster, Hawker and Westland. Again, Hawker declined to tender.

Blackburn revisited the B.67, but still only offered de-rated Avons. The RAE in its assessment substituted full power 6,500lbf (28.9kN) AJ.65s, boosting the maximum speed at sea level to 580kt and the sea level rate of climb to 8,600ft/min (2,620m/min). Blackburn offered to build a scaled-down prototype to prove the aerodynamics.

DH had a new design ready, the DH.110, which it had submitted to meet the RAF's Specification F.44/46 the previous March. The DH.110 was an enlarged development of the Vampire/Venom

These poor quality but rare images show three of the various wind tunnel models tested by Westland with both stacked and side-by-side engine layouts. The bottom model appears to have small wing tip rudders on the upper wing surfaces. *Leonardo UK via Jeremy Graham*

Specification N.40/46 Designs (1st Round)

	Blackburn B.67	Gloster P.231	Westland PJD.129
Span	51ft 6in (15.70m)	48ft 0in (14.63m)	51ft 0in (15.54m)
Length	43ft 0in (13.11m	24ft 0in (12.80m)	42ft 0in (12.80m)
Wing area	590ft² (54.87m²)	605ft² (56.27m²)	610ft² (56.73m²)
t/c ratio	12%	9%	15%
All-up weight	29,160lb (13,230kg)	28,000lb (12,700kg)	25,500lb (11,565kg)
Powerplant	2x scaled AJ.65 Avon, 5,000lbf (22.2kN)	2x Metrovick F.9, 7,000lbf (31.1kN)	2x Armstrong Siddeley, 4,860lbf (21.6kN)
Max speed	534kt (989km/h) at SL	552kt (1,023km/h) at SL	540kt (1,000km/h)/Mach 0.87 at SL
Rate of climb	5,200ft/min (1,585m/min) at SL	10,700ft/min (3,260m/min) at SL	7,600ft/min (2,315m/min) at SL
Service ceiling	41,000ft (12,500m)	45,800ft (13,960m)	51,000ft (15,545m)
Armament	4x 30mm ADEN	3x 30mm ADEN	3x 30mm ADEN

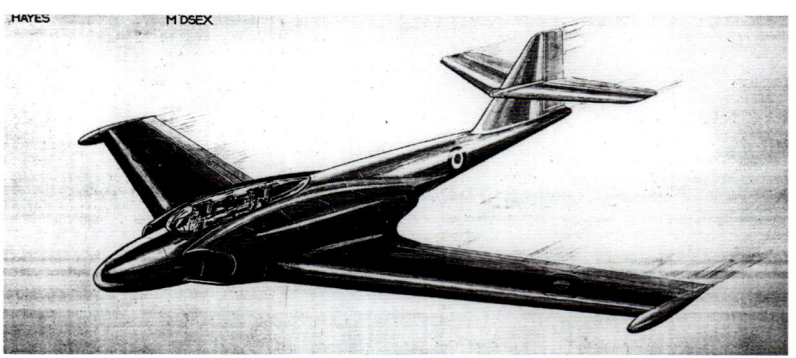

Fairey's Scheme 1A design. One of the wing tip pods housed a ranging radar scanner. The design was aerodynamically clean but its 25° wing sweep was too conservative. *Tony Buttler Collection*

Fairey submitted four designs, Schemes 1A, 1B, 2A and 2B. The baseline design was Scheme 1A, a conservative aircraft with a tandem cockpit and an elliptical cross-section fuselage in which two AJ.65s were mounted side by side with wing root intakes. The wing was swept by 25° with a 12% t/c ratio for a critical Mach number of 0.835 and had high-lift flaps and tip nacelles – one of them housing the AI.16's secondary 10in (25cm) diameter ranging scanner. Internal fuel totalled 1,140gal (5,180L). The armament comprised four 20mm Hispano or 30mm ADEN cannon and Fairey also studied the provision of a 4.5in (114m) recoilless gun in the belly or a semi-recessed Folland *Red Hawk* beam-riding AAM (which was being developed to Naval Staff Requirement AW.121 for an all-aspect homing weapon.) Scheme 2A differed in having two Napier E.131 turbojets.

Schemes 2A and 2B were Avon and E.131-powered versions designed to meet the original three-hour endurance requirement; the overload weight increased from 26,690lb (12,230kg) for the 1A to 30,630b (13,895kg) for the 2A. Scheme 1A's maximum sea level speed was 537kt with a sea level rate of climb of 7,740ft/min (2,360m/min), the 1B having a rate of climb of 11,700ft/min (3,565m/min) with reheat, the 2A and 2B offering 6,470ft/min (1,970m/min) and 9,850ft/min (3,000m/min) respectively.

Fairey also offered two strike versions, the 3A and 3B, with the wing tip nacelles removed and a 'cranked' centre wing spar to allow space for a bomb bay along the centreline capable of housing one 2,000lb (907kg) armour-piercing bomb or two

family, a swept wing, twin-boom design powered by two Avons, the crew sitting side by side in the fuselage nacelle. The 40° swept wing had been designed for Mach 0.87 to meet F.44/46 so it easily met the Mach 0.82 requirement of N.40/46. The wing had had full span leading edge slots and Fowler-type high-lift flaps. Future items could include an all-moving tailplane and boundary layer suction. The compact airframe and power-boosted ailerons were expected to provide excellent manoeuvrability. The radar was the AI.9D with a 28in (71cm) diameter scanner. Under the cockpit there was space for four 20mm Hispano Mk.V or 30mm ADEN cannon. The total internal fuel capacity was 1,050gal (4,770L), optionally plus two 150gal (682L) drop tanks. The estimated AUW was 28,950lb (13,130kg) with a performance of 570kt at sea level, a sea level rate of climb of 8,500ft/min (2,590m/min) and a ceiling of 45,800ft (13,960m).

Specification N.40/46 designs (2nd round)

	Blackburn B.67 (RAE Estimates)	DH.110	Fairey Schemes 1A & 1B	Fairey Schemes 2A & 2B	Westland PJD.144 (RAE Estimates)
Span	51ft 6in (15.70m)	49ft 6in (15.09m)	53ft 0in (16.15m)	55ft 0in (16.76m)	55ft 0in (16.76m)
Length	43ft 0in (13.11m)	52ft 0in (15.85m)	50ft 0in (15.24m)	54ft 0in (16.46m)	43ft 6in (13.26m)
Wing area	590ft² (54.87m²)	640ft² (59.52m²)	520ft² (48.36m²)	520ft² (48.36m²)	745ft² (69.29m²)
t/c ratio	12%	10%	12% root, 10% tip	12% root, 10% tip	15%
All-up weight	29,450lb (13,358kg)	28,950lb (13,130kg)	25,000lb (11,340kg)	25,000lb (11,340kg)	27,260lb (12,365kg)
Powerplant	2x AJ.65 Avon, 6,500lbf (28.9kN)	2x AJ.65 Avon, 6,500lbf (28.9kN)	1A 2x AJ.65 Avon, 6,500lbf (28.9kN); 1B 2x reheated Napier E.131	2A 2x AJ.65 Avon, 6,500lbf (28.9kN); 2B 2x reheated Napier E.131	2x AJ.65 Avon, 6,500lbf (28.9kN)
Max speed	580kt (1,075km/h) at SL	570kt (1,055km/h) at SL	1A 537kt (994km/h) at SL, 497kt (920km/h) at 25,000ft (7,620m)	2A 535kt (991km/h) at 2,000ft (610m)	549kt (1,017km/h) at SL
Rate of climb	8,600ft/min (2,620m/min) at SL	8,500ft/min (2,590m/min) at SL	1A 7,740ft/min (2,315m/min) at SL; 1B 11,700ft/min (3,565m/min) at SL	2A 6,470ft/min (1,970m/min) at SL; 2B 9,850ft/min (3,000m/min) at SL	8,800ft/min (2,680m/min) at SL
Service ceiling	?	?	1A 51,400ft (15,665m); 1B 51,200ft (15,605m)	2A 49,000ft (14,935m); 2B 48,000ft (14,630m)	?
Armament	4x 30mm ADEN	4x 20mm Hispano	4x 20mm Hispano or 2x 30mm ADEN	4x 20mm Hispano or 2x 30mm ADEN	3x 30mm ADEN

1,000lb (454kg) or four 500lb (227kg) bombs or similar loads of mines, depth charges or flares.

Westland continued refining its original design with the PJD.142, PJD.143 and PJD.144. The main offering was PJD.144, similar to the PJD.129 but with reduced 38° wing sweep to increase the chord of the outer wing sections and larger tip fins were fitted. The fuel capacity was increased to 950gal (4,320L). Blown flaps using supersonic air – 'supercirculation' in mid-1950s parlance – were also considered. The PJD.142 had the engines mounted side by side and had a single vertical tail fin, while the similar PJD.143 gained a T-tail empennage. The RAE replaced the notional 4,860lbf engines with Avons, boosting the rate of climb to 8,800ft/min (2,680m/min).

The Design Study Conference was held on 15 December 1947, chaired by the Principal Director of Technical Development (Air) (PDTD(A)), Stuart Scott Hall. None of the submissions was considered to be an official tender; it was felt that six years of development would be required before the aircraft and AI equipment could be ready for service.

A low approach speed was more important than the AUW. On this basis the RAE had concerns about Westland's tailless offerings and the Director of Military Aircraft Research and Development (DMARD), JE Serby commented that Westland had been warned about the development hazards of opting for tailless designs at the previous Tender Design Conference. Westland was therefore quickly eliminated.

The DH.110 did not meet the approach speed limit, but the RAE felt that a 10% increase in wing area would be sufficient. The B.67 offered inferior performance to the DH.110 but with a comparable development risk. The conventional Fairey Scheme 1A had less risk and sacrificed some performance but still met the requirements. The conference was not impressed by Blackburn's offer to build a scaled prototype with a consequently lengthy development phase; therefore the B.67 was also eliminated.

The choice was now between the DH.110 and the Scheme 1A – a 40° or 25° sweep design. The DH.110 had a 40kt speed advantage at altitude, being capable of Mach 0.93 and easily matching land-based aircraft, whereas Fairey's Mach 0.86 would be obsolete within six years. The Fairey design had better catapult launch characteristics and could handle a 40in (102cm) diameter radar scanner without redesign. In terms of workload, DH's design team was busy but had spare capacity to take on the task and complete it as quickly as Fairey could. On the factory floor, DH was becoming overloaded but the potential of building the DH.110 for the RN and the RAF would bring economies of scale. The DH.110 was chosen and Serby fed back the 10% increased wing area suggestion to Chief Designer Ronald Eric Bishop. DH received a contract in October.

By August 1948 the 40in scanner requirement had been relaxed to 35in (89cm), easing installation problems. On the other hand, the Avon's weight had increased, pushing the AUW up by 900lb (408kg), which had knock-on effects for meeting the 90kt approach speed limit.

In January 1949 three naval prototypes were ordered, two NF and one strike (to Spec N.8/49), bringing the total DH.110 prototype order to 13. OR.246 was updated as Naval Staff Requirement NR/A.14 in March and a new Specification N.7/49 issued, only to be hastily revamped again as N.14/49 to match the performance requirements of the RAF's F.4/48 (as F.44/46 had become). Then in November, national economic problems forced the Treasury to cut the MoS's research and development programme and the naval DH.110 was axed.

"Lack of continuity can only lead to spasmodic efforts and a waste of money."

CHARLES HENRY CHICHESTER SMITH, DIRECTOR OF FAIREY AVIATION, 10 FEBRUARY 1950

Fairey's false start

Fairey was still very much in the picture. The CNR had hoped to leave the RAF to sponsor the DH.110 programme, while the Admiralty supported Fairey, which had continued to refine its designs to the updated N.14/49. The Admiralty worried that wartime emergency priority for the RAF might prevent DH.110 production for the RN, so a backup second prototype was considered. The Fairey design was the obvious choice, although the MoS considered asking Short Brothers to tender.

The Director of Research and Development (Navy), F Holroyd, had discussed increasing the wing sweep with Fairey in the summer of 1948, but they were not keen. By November the fighter's AUW had grown by 4,300lb (1,950kg), the dimensions increasing accordingly. Serby requested that the weight be trimmed by omitting some armament and equipment. The number of cannon was reduced to three. Chief Designer DL Hollis Williams' team considered reducing the wingspan and area but opted to keep the larger wing to increase the climb and ceiling performance. The cross-section of the fuselage was reduced. The AUW was 28,000lb (12,700kg) with an estimated maximum sea level speed of 519kt with a sea level rate of climb of 8,280ft/min (2,525m/min) and a service ceiling of 46,300ft (14,110m).

The Advisory Design Conference took place at the MoS on 5 April 1949, but not until 10 August did an MoS letter confirm that the project would go ahead with a likely order for three prototypes. This never happened. The Treasury's cutbacks that cancelled the naval DH.110 also paused N.14/49. DMARD was concerned about the development gap and suggested to Fairey that a single-engined fighter might stand a better chance of getting past the Treasury and would also offer superior performance.

Specification N.14/49 Fairey designs

	Fairey N.14/48 (ex-N.40/46 of 16.11.1948)	Fairey N.14/49 Scheme A	Fairey N.14/49 Scheme B
Span	55ft 0in (16.76m)	46ft 0in (14.02m)	48ft 6in (14.78m)
Length	50ft 0in (15.24m)	49ft 6in (15.09m)	46ft 6in (14.17m)
Wing area	583ft² (54.22m²)	470ft² (43.71m²)	?
All-up weight	29,300lb (13,290kg)	21,500lb (9,750kg)	21,300lb (9,660kg)
Powerplant	2A 2x AJ.65 Avon, 6,500lbf (28.9kN)	1x Avon RA.5, 8,300lbf (36.9kN)	1x Avon RA.5, 8,300lbf (36.9kN)
Max speed	537kt (996km/h) at SL, 509kt (943km/h) at 20,000ft (6,095m)	495kt (917km/h) at SL	503kt (939km/h) at SL
Rate of climb	8,280ft/min (2,525m/min) at SL	6,100ft/min (1,860m/min) at SL	?
Service ceiling	46,300ft (14,110m)	42,000ft (12,800m)	?
Armament	3x 30mm ADEN	3x 30mm ADEN	3x 30mm ADEN

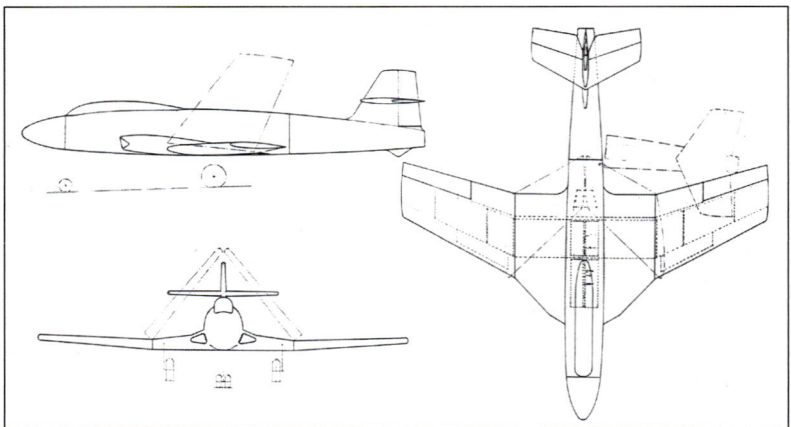

Fairey's Scheme A design to N.14/49 was in many respects a completely different aircraft from the earlier twin-engined N.40/46 designs.
Bill Harrison Collection via Tony Buttler

Williams sent a preliminary investigation to Serby on 23 December 1949. Scheme A was essentially the previous design, scaled down for a single unreheated 8,500lbf (37.8kN) Avon RA.5 with smaller wing root intakes and a tail jet pipe. Scheme B had a twin-boom layout and a shorter jet pipe. The latter was lighter and less draggy. Scheme A's estimated sea level rate of climb was 6,100ft/min (1,860m/min) with a ceiling of at least 42,000ft (12,800m). Consideration was given to fitting smaller 455ft² (42.2m²) wings without folding to save 900lb (408kg) and with a span of 43ft (13.1m) would fit on the lifts aboard the *Centaur*-class light fleet carriers. But the shorter span wing increased the fuel burn and adding extra fuel to compensate would negate the weight savings, especially if reheat was added.

Blackburn had drawn up its B.82 design in late April 1949 to meet N.14/49 but it never passed the preliminary design stage.

A meeting at Thames House on 3 April 1950 discussed N.14/49 in the light of recent changes to the requirements; the minimum speed being raised from 500 to 540kt at 30,000ft (9,145m) and the larger 35in (89cm) diameter AI.16 radar scanner was now preferred. A single-engined design could not meet the speed requirements and concessions on approach speed, combat ceiling and not using reheat in the climb provided little improvement. Fairey's conservative 25° wing sweep and 12% t/c ratio could not provide the required performance.

Fairey had been worried about the four months of silence from the MoS and infuriated by the constant stop-start of the NF project. On 5 April they were finally told to scrap the previous designs and start again with a higher angle of wing sweep and a fuselage big enough to fit the AI.16 – but also to wait until the Chiefs of Staff decided their priorities. Hollis Williams' team kept working on the twin-engined design until 19 May 1950.

The MoS was increasingly worried about the resources being funnelled into N.14/49 and N.9/49 (the Supermarine Types 508 and 525 – see Chapter 2.) They asked the Admiralty if both were really needed. The Admiralty replied in the affirmative. As the RAF's Hawker Hunter and Gloster Javelin were not carrier compatible the Admiralty argued that they had to develop their own aircraft. Maintaining sea communications in the Mediterranean by 1957 could mean potentially battling through waves of the latest transonic Soviet Air Force fighters and bombers like the Mikoyan-Gurevich MiG-17 *Fresco* and Ilyushin Il-28 *Beagle*. A December 1952 estimate of the likely Soviet aerial threat to Atlantic convoys in 1956 was 200 Tupolev Tu-14 *Bosun* jet-powered torpedo-bombers and 50 Tupolev Tu-4 *Bull* long-range piston-engined bombers (in fact only around 140 *Bosuns* were ever built for Soviet Naval Aviation). The MoS doubted whether the Fleet Air Arm (FAA) could sustain protracted air operations in those conditions, but agreed that if they had to, that only the best equipment would suffice. In addition, both N.9/49 and N.14/49 were seen as replacements for the turboprop-powered Westland Wyvern strike fighter, which was considered likely to be obsolete by 1957.

The impasse was broken on 19 July 1950, the Research and Development Programme Committee recommended withdrawing N.14/49 and Fairey ceased work on the design. The following month it was decided to write a new specification following the release of the government's paper *Defence Policy and Global Strategy*. After some debate it was decided to invite tenders from across the industry rather than relying on Fairey. Fairey was most displeased; seven years of design and development work since 1944 and expenses of £53,000 on its technical studies had come to naught. In a letter to the MoS the company warned, "If the matter is put to open tender, there is no reason to suppose that a repetition of the previous long periods of indecision will not recur before a start is finally made." As a consolation prize, MoS awarded Fairey the contract for the FD.2 delta-winged Mach 2 research aircraft.

Sea Venom

Waiting for the best could not go on indefinitely. The Sea Hornet was aging and needed replacement as soon as possible. Naval Staff Requirement NR/A.30 was raised in 1950 to cover a navalised de Havilland Venom NF.2 (as ordered for the RAF). It was also intended that the Royal Australian Navy (RAN) would operate the type.

Specification N.107 was issued on 18 September 1951. The specified take-off weight was 14,100lb (3,696kg) with a maximum speed of at least 502kt at sea level and 472kt at 30,000ft (9,145m), with a sea level rate of climb of 6,400ft/min (1,950m/min). Endurance was just over one hour including a patrol at economic speed, five minutes of combat and 20 minutes loitering before landing. The engine was a 4,850lbf (21.5kN) DH Ghost 103 centrifugal-flow turbojet. Armament was four 20mm Hispano Mk.V cannon with 150 rounds per gun, with provision for eight RPs under the wings for the night intruder role. An AI.10 radar was fitted along with a AN/APX-1 (ARI.5679) Identification Friend-or-Foe (IFF) transponder.

The prototype Venom NF.2 (flown by DH under B-Conditions identity G-5-3) was transferred to the FAA as WP227 for trials. Three Sea Venom NF.20 prototypes (WK376, WK379 and WK385) were ordered on 21 November 1950.

WK376 first flew at Hatfield on 19 April 1951 and following preliminary arrester hook trials at Farnborough, carried out a deck landing assessment aboard *Illustrious* during 9–12 July, totalling 53 landings. (Note that these trials took place before N.107 was formally issued.) Further catapult launch, arrester gear, deck handling and radio equipment trials took place during 1951–52 before the aircraft crashed near Farnborough on 25 July, when one of the rudders detached, killing the pilot Lt AE Facer.

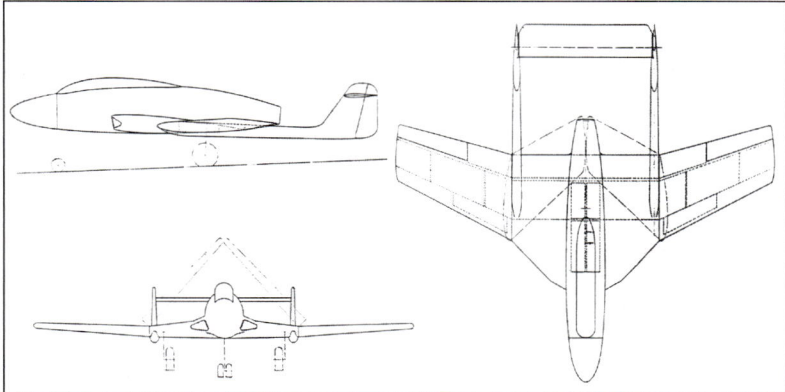

Fairey's Scheme B design had a twin boom layout. The booms look fairly thin for a fighter of this size. *Bill Harrison Collection via Tony Buttler*

DH Sea Venom FAW.21 WW204 of 809 NAS aboard the deck of a US Navy *Essex*-class carrier circa early 1959. At the top of the image is a Grumman S2F-2 Tracker of Sea Control Squadron 37 (VS-37) 'Sawbucks'. WW204 amassed 265.5 flying hours before it was stricken in May 1961. *Tony Buttler Collection*

The Sea Venom was very similar to the RAF's Venom NF.2 and NF.3 but with folding wings and naval features. Sea Venom XG612 was the seventh production FAW.22, conducting type trials at Hatfield in February 1956. In February 1958 it began *Blue Jay* handling test flights before conducting firing trials during 1959. It ended its career on engine trials until August 1960. *Tony Buttler Collection*

WK379 flew in June 1952 – also losing a rudder later that month but landing safely – and was used for catapult launch, arrester gear and carrier landing trials (including at night) and weapons clearance. WK385 was completed with power-operated folding wings, flying on 26 July 1952.

A single prototype of the NF.21 followed, XA539, flying from DH's Hurn factory on 21 May 1954 and carrying out carrier trials aboard *Bulwark* during 21–26 March 1955. It was damaged the following year in crash-barrier trials and struck off charge.

A production contract for 50 Sea Venom NF.20 aircraft was issued on 2 January 1951 (the NF.20 was redesignated FAW.20 – Fighter, All-Weather – in March 1953.) The first aircraft, WM500, flew on 27 March 1953. This was followed by orders for 167 NF.21 (redesignated FAW.21), which were broadly similar to the Venom NF.2A and NF.3 with a 4,950lbf (22.1kN) Ghost 104 engine, AI.21 radar (US-supplied AN/APS-57) and a strengthened long-stroke undercarriage. The last 39 were completed to FAW.22 standard with a 5,300lbf (23.6kN) Ghost 105 for improved high-altitude performance; some FAW.21 were later upgraded to this standard. XG737, the last new-build aircraft, was delivered in January 1958. The RAN received 39 Sea Venom FAW.53s and further export success came from France, where SNCASE (Sud-Est) licence-built 101 Sea Venoms as the Aquilon for the Aéronavale.

The Sea Venom entered service with 890 NAS at RNAS Yeovilton on 20 March 1954 (their assigned carrier was *Albion*). Sea Venoms saw action during the Suez Crisis (Operation Musketeer) in November 1956 with aircraft of 809, 891 and 893 NAS operating from *Albion* and *Eagle*, undertaking ground attack missions alongside Cyprus-based RAF Venoms.

In the summer of 1954, DH was awarded a contract to investigate the use of blown flaps to reduce the approach and landing speeds. A $^2/_7$th scale model was wind-tunnel tested, but nothing further came of the idea.

Thoughts turned to proving the AAM as a weapons system in 1956. The plan was to convert three FAW.21 aircraft (XG607, XG612 and XG662) for naval proof-testing of the *Blue Jay*/Firestreak missile before the Sea Vixen became operational. Two missiles would be carried under the wings, the estimated conversion cost being £100,000. DH had already made a Venom NF.2 conversion and the work carried out was similar: provision of two underwing pylons, the Ghost 105 engine and uprated hydraulic pumps; removal of the cannon to make space for the 'black boxes'; provision of air heating and air cooling for the missiles. Following

A Hawker Sea Hawk and a Sea Venom FAW.22 prepare for catapult launch aboard HMS *Bulwark* in 1958. One of the Sea Venom's roles was to provide navigational assistance to the Sea Hawks on long range strike sorties. *Tony Kilner via Tony Buttler*

catapult launch and landing trials at Bedford and carrier landing trials aboard *Albion* with 800 NAS in July, the three aircraft formed a test flight within 893 NAS. They embarked aboard *Victorious* in late 1958 for firing trials, scoring 80% success against target drones off Malta using trials batch missiles (fully-guided production missiles were unavailable at that time.) The firing and operational trials lasted into early 1960.

Seven FAW.21s were modified by the by the Naval Air Radio Installation Unit at RNAS Lee-on-Solent in 1958 as the ECM.21 for the electronic countermeasures role, with the ECM equipment replacing the cannon. The ECM fit included an AN/APR-9 search receiver with a AN/APA-69 direction finder and AN/ALT-6 and ALT-7 jamming equipment. These aircraft equipped 831 NAS at RAF Watton from 1963 to 1966. Some FAW.22s were also converted, becoming the ECM.22.

Swept wing interims

While the Sea Venom offered superior performance over the Sea Hornet, it was not a modern design and lacked a swept wing. The Director of Naval Air Warfare Division, Captain Charles Evans, was worried about the lack of a modern swept wing naval fighter. The straight wing Supermarine Attacker and Hawker Sea Hawk were only just entering production, while the swept wing Supermarine Type 510 had made brief carrier trials and the prototype Type 525 was still under construction. In March 1951 he proposed ordering interim swept wing day and night fighters without the usual prototype and evaluation stage to enable them to enter service in 1955 to equip the fleet carriers *Eagle* and *Ark Royal*.

At that time no suitable NF contender existed, but there were four day fighter contenders: a modified

Sea Venom FAW.22s of 891 NAS being prepped on *Bulwark*'s flight deck in early 1958. In the background is the Westland Whirlwind HAS.7 plane guard helicopter. The Sea Venom in the foreground is XG736, which made a heavy landing back aboard *Bulwark* on 2 May 1958, fracturing its nose leg oleo. Restored by the Ulster Aviation Society during the late 1980s, today it is believed to reside somewhere in the West Midlands. *Tony Kilner via Tony Buttler*

Sea Venom FAW.22 XG698 makes one of its final flights at Yeovilton in July 1970. On the 29th it left the Fleet Requirements Unit to be disposed of as a firefighting training aid at RNAS Culdrose. *Terry Panopalis Collection*

Sea Hawk, Hawker P.1087 (a navalised P.1081), a navalised Hawker P.1083 Hunter and the Supermarine Type 548, a navalised Swift. The latter was selected as the best choice, Staff Requirement NR/A.34 and Specification N.105D&P being written up for a batch of 20 aircraft and issued to Supermarine on 6 May 1952. The intended roles were day interception, strike support, combat air patrol and ground attack.

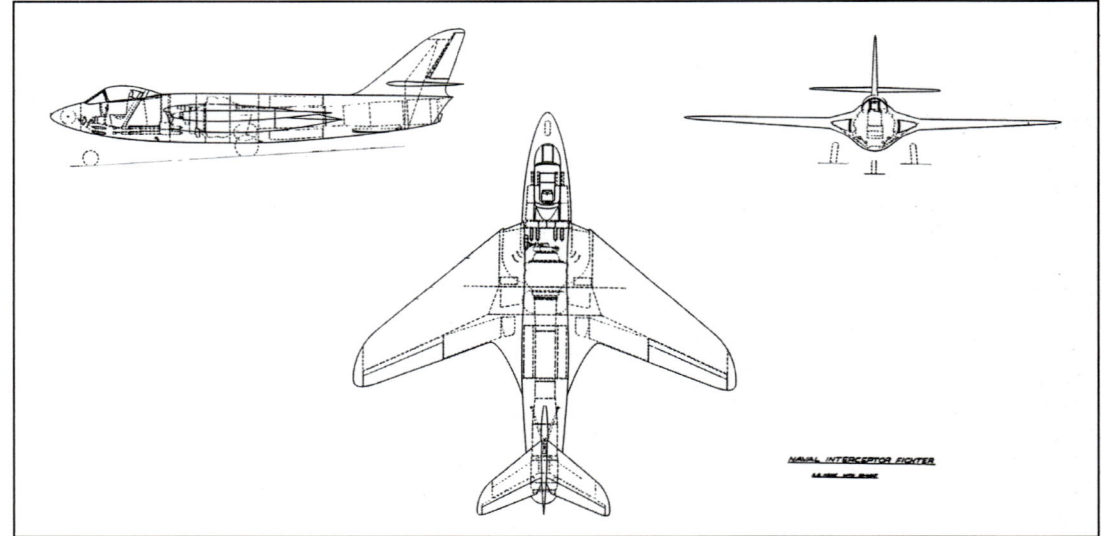

Hawker's P.1087 was essentially the P.1081 with naval features and a reheated Rolls-Royce Nene. *Tony Buttler Collection*

The Swift had to be modified with catapult attachments and arrester gear and an undercarriage capable of withstanding a rate of descent of 20ft/sec (6m/sec), but wing folding was not required given that the main role was for trials and familiarising pilots with swept wing aircraft. The maximum speed at 45,000ft (13,715m) was to be at least 515kt with a time from launch to 45,000ft of seven minutes with reheat. Launch would be from the 150ft (45.7m) and 138ft 6in (42.2m) long BS.4 catapults without using reheat and there would be provision for Rocket Assisted Take-Off Gear (RATOG).

Chief Designer Joe Smith had investigated navalising the Swift as early as November 1950 and foresaw no likely problems – but the priority of the RAF's needs meant that few compromises were made to include naval features into the Swift's basic design. The RAE had reservations about the conversion, although the Swift's development woes were yet to become apparent. The RAF fought the order, Assistant Chief of the Air Staff (Policy), Air Vice-Marshal Douglas Macfadyen claiming it was delaying their Swift F.3s, was too expensive and unjustified on strategic grounds given that the fleet was unlikely to be within range of land-based MiGs. (They also had concerns that Scimitar production would derail Swift deliveries until Supermarine and the MoS proved the firm could fulfil both orders.) The politicking and campaigning eventually backed the RAF's Swifts; design work on the 'Hooked Swift' ended in late 1952 and the requirements were withdrawn. In 1955 Hawker did complete a brochure of the P.1117, a radar-equipped Hunter armed with two Firestreak AAMs for the RN.

Interim Swept wing fighters

	Hawker P.1087	**Supermarine Type 548**	**Folland Gnat Mk.2**
Span	36ft 0in (10.97m)	32ft 4in (9.85m)	24ft 0in (7.31m)
Length	39ft 1in (11.91m)	41ft 5.5in (12.63m)	32ft 0in (9.75m)
Wing area	287ft² (26.66m²)	321ft² (29.82m²)	160ft² (14.86m²)
t/c ratio	?	10%	6% root, 4% tip
All-up weight	?	19,000lb (8,620kg)	9,130lb (4,140kg)
Powerplant	1x Nene with reheat	1x Avon RA.7R Mk.114, 7,500lbf (33.3kN) dry, 9,450lbf (42.0kN) reheat	1x Orpheus Or.6 with reheat, 8,000lbf (35.6kN) reheat
Max speed	605+kt (1,120km/h) at SL	610+kt (1,130km/h) at SL	Mach 1.5 at 35,000ft (10,670m)
Rate of climb	?	?	5min to 50,000ft (15,240m) with reheat
Service ceiling	?	?	45,000ft (13,715m)
Armament	4x 20mm Hispano	2x 30mm ADEN, 2x 1,000lb (454kg) bombs, 16x 60lb (27kg) RPs	2x 30mm ADEN, 2x AIM-9 Sidewinder

William Edward Willoughby 'Teddy' Petter was famous by the mid-1950s as the designer of the English Electric Canberra tactical bomber and P.1A supersonic research aircraft, which would become the P.1B Lightning interceptor. But Petter had become convinced that smaller and lighter fighters would be cheaper to produce in larger numbers. He left English Electric, joining Henry Folland at Folland Aircraft where he put his theory to the test with the Fo.139 Midge and the Fo.141 Gnat, which did not interest the RAF as a fighter but was later developed into the Fo.144 Gnat T.1 two-seat advanced trainer.

Petter continued to push his lightweight fighter concept and set his sights on obtaining supersonic performance with a new wing of 6% t/c ratio. The Fo.143 Gnat Mk.2 was a single-seat day fighter with AI.23 radar, armed with two Firestreak or AIM-9 Sidewinder AAMs and was also offered in two-seat night fighter, single-seat carrier-based, photo-reconnaissance and two-seat trainer variants. Originally planned with a 4,850lbf (21.5kN) Bristol Siddeley Or.4 Orpheus 701 with a Swedish-developed afterburner for a 30% boost in sea level static thrust, Bristol later offered the Or.6 Orpheus with 20% percent more thrust and an afterburner based on that of the Ol.22R Olympus for a maximum speed of Mach 1.5 at 35,000ft (10,670m). The new 40° swept wing had a similar planform to the original Gnat but with slightly less area. The empennage and undercarriage were unchanged.

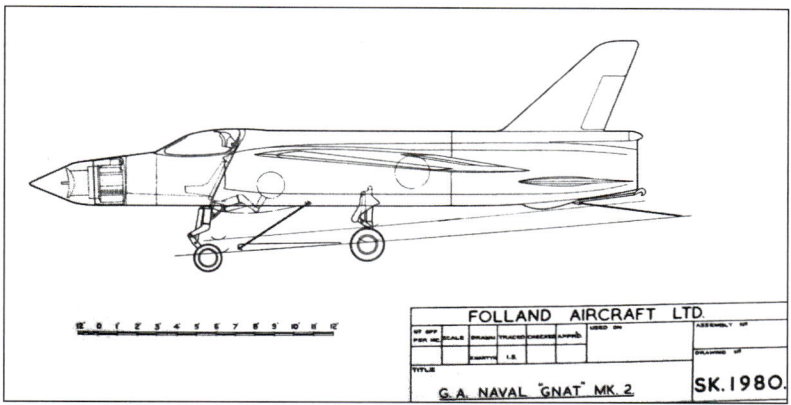

A technical drawing of the diminutive Folland Gnat Mk.2, which if it had been built would have been the smallest jet-powered manned aircraft ever operated from an aircraft carrier. *Author's Collection*

The AUW for the naval variant was 9,130lb (4,140kg) with a landing weight of 7,585lb (3,440kg). The radius of action for an interception at 45,000ft (13,715m) was 120nm (222km), or 215nm (398km) if reheat was not engaged. The FAA showed no interest in this dinky concept.

This photograph of the Folland Fo.139 Midge beside the Supermarine Type 525 VX138 indicates the size difference between Teddy Petter's Gnat and the latest naval fighters then being developed. *Terry Panopalis Collection*

Blackburn made this magnificent model of the B.89 in 1/24th scale to accompany its brochure. The detailed model shows the double hinge fold lines on the wings and the outlines of the ailerons, leading edge slats and trailing edge flaps. *Brough Heritage via Tony Buttler Collection*

N.114

Specification N.114 was written up to replace N.14/49 and issued on 22 February 1951. The normal AUW remained 28,000lb (12,700kg) and a crew of two was required, as were one or two reheated Avon RA.7 or Sapphire turbojets. The specified minimum speed at 30,000ft (9,145m) was 540kt with a minimum sea level rate of climb of 10,000ft/min (3,050m/min) and a minimum ceiling of 40,000ft (12,190m). Endurance was to cover the climb to 30,000ft, 90 minutes patrolling at economic speed (acceptable on one engine), five minutes combat at 20,000ft (6,1000m) and 20 minutes loitering at 2,000ft (607m) before landing.

The flying characteristics had to be suitable for nocturnal carrier operations with good combat manoeuvrability. The folded span had to be within 20ft (6m) to allow stowage in three rows aboard the carriers. The servicing and rearming turnaround period between sorties was not to exceed seven minutes.

The radar was further upgraded to the AI.18 set. GEC began developing the X-band AI.18 in 1951, at 880lb (400lb) it was a hefty piece of kit. The 29in (73cm) diameter paraboloidal scanner used conical scanning and was capable of tracking a target automatically in range and azimuth. By mid-1958 airborne tests demonstrated a 75% probability of detecting a bomber like the Il-28 *Beagle* or English Electric Canberra head-on at 25–28nm (46–51km), with lock-on at 20nm (37km).

Armament was to be a mix of: four 30mm ADEN with ammunition for eight seconds of firing, or two ADEN and an air-to-air RP battery, or two ADEN and four *Blue Sky* (Fairey Aviation Fireflash) beam-riding AAMs (later replaced by the active-homing Vickers *Red Dean*) – though carriage of AAMs did not have to be included in the actual tender (because there was little concrete data to provide to the designers.) The aircraft was to be fitted with the best all-weather flying equipment and instruments, including UHF air-to-air and air-to-ground homing and a lightweight rear warning radar set (no information regarding this existed either!) Deciding who to invite to tender was complicated by the MoS's new 'Size and Shape' policy which aimed at reducing the number of design centres in the industry to 10 companies to reduce dispersion of resources and excessive competition. Armstrong Whitworth, Blackburn and Westland were listed as production units only (Fairey and Handley Page were similarly

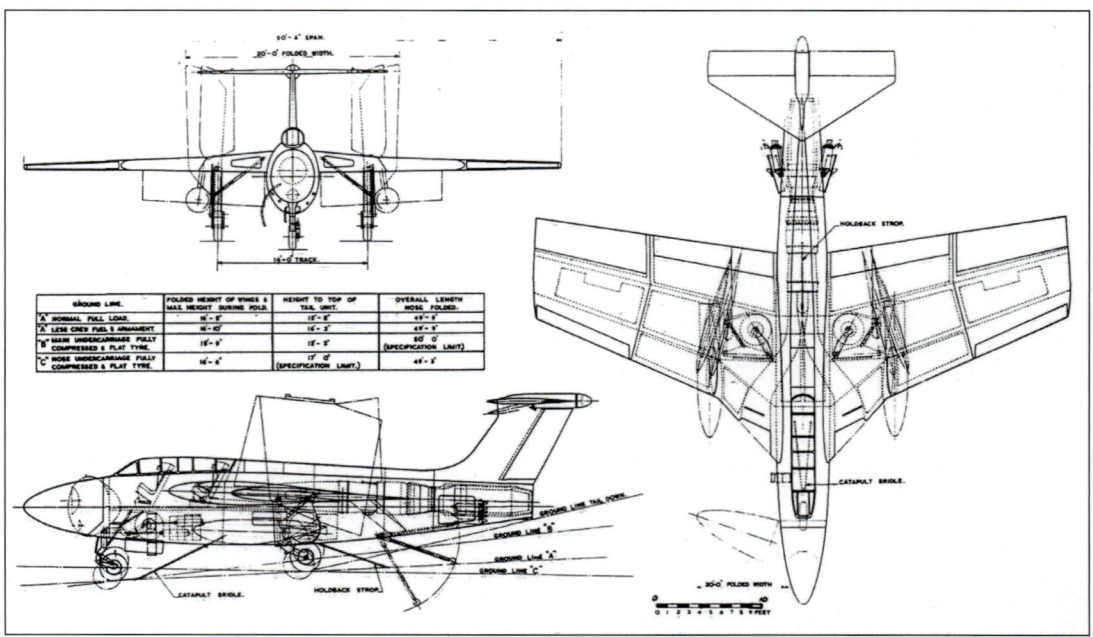

A technical general arrangement of the Blackburn B.89. *Brough Heritage via Tony Buttler Collection*

downgraded in 1954). The production-only companies were not meant to be involved in future tenders. At the very least they could not expect to recoup their design team costs from the MoS, but Industry was not officially informed about the policy. After some internal debate, Blackburn and Fairey were added to the original invitation list of DH, Fairey, Gloster and Vickers. Bristol, Percival, Saunders-Roe (Saro) and Short Brothers were also granted permission to tender (Bristol and Percival soon dropped out.)

Blackburn tendered the B.89 which was developed from the B.82. It had a mid-mounted, compound swept wing (20° inboard/40° outboard) with double wing folding and a t/c ratio of 10–6.5%. Blackburn had just completed the crescent-winged Handley Page HP.88 research aircraft, which had a scaled down version of the HP.80 Victor bomber's wing. This experience encouraged Chief Designer FJW Digby to utilise a compound wing to maintain a constant Mach number from the root to the tip. The wing had leading edge slats on the outboard sections and root intakes for the single reheated Sapphire Sa.4 turbojet (alternatives being the Avon RA.12R and Bristol Siddeley Olympus Ol.3.) The aircraft had a T-tail; the pilot and observer sat in tandem and the armament of three ADENs and 80 RPs in retractable packs was carried beneath the cockpit floor. The internal fuel capacity was 870gal (3,955L) with drop tanks expanding that to 1,170gal (5,320L). The AUW was calculated as 26,940lb (12,220kg). The estimated maximum speed at sea level was 606kt, 10,320ft/min (3,145m/min) rate of climb at sea level and a service ceiling of over 45,000ft (13,720m). Blackburn quoted a prototype first flight 42 months from an Instruction to Proceed (ITP). In October, Blackburn proposed the B.94 undercarriageless version for use with flexible decks – a concept that was still being seriously considered.

With the N.14/49 work under its belt, Fairey studied several layouts and submitted a single-

> *"Our own naval opinion is apparently that we could operate in the North Sea for not more than about three days on end. If our Navy are considering such operations they will require something even better than the N.113!"*

ASSISTANT CHIEF OF THE AIR STAFF (POLICY), AIR VICE-MARSHAL DOUGLAS MACFADYEN, 8 NOVEMBER 1951

engined design with a mid-mounted, swept wing with 40° sweep and 8% t/c ratio and had double wing folding. After examining all the available engines, the 12,500lbf (54.0kN) Olympus Ol.3 without reheat was selected. The two 30mm ADEN were fitted in the wings and 70 RPs in retractable packs were located ventrally in the fuselage; tandem racks would carry four *Blue Sky* AAMs under the fuselage or two *Red Deans* under the wings. The AI.16's secondary 10in (25cm) diameter scanner was fitted in a small bullet on the inner port wing. The internal fuel capacity was 700gal (3,182L) or 1,076gal (4,892L) with overload tanks. The AUW was 29,800lb (13,520kg). The estimated maximum speed at sea level was 601kt and 570kt at 20,000ft (6,100m) with a sea level rate of climb of 9,830ft/min (2,995m/min) and a ceiling of 44,000ft (13,410m). Performance figures were also given for the Avon RA.8 and Sapphire, both of which gave inferior climb outcomes. The required climb performance could not be met at the overload weight of 32,900lb (14,925kg). Fairey forecast that a prototype could fly in 156 weeks from receiving the ITP.

Saro's P.148 design was the most novel of the contenders, featuring a T-tail, a high-mounted 40° swept wing and a single Avon RA.10R mounted dorsally in its own nacelle above the rear fuselage. The

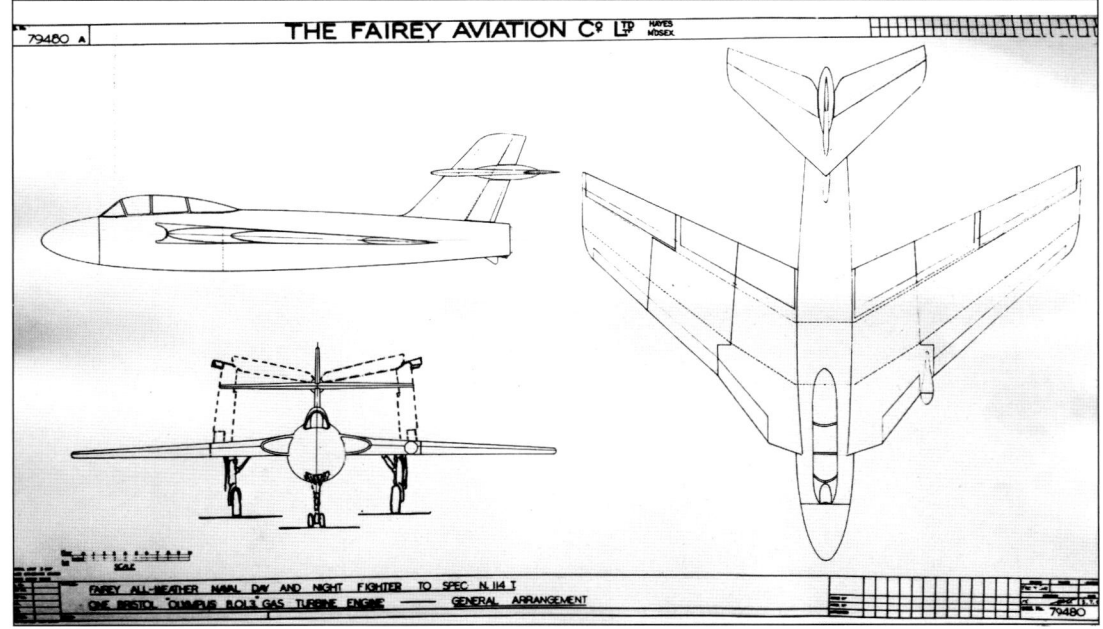

Fairey's N.114T design was conservative – a rather unexpected outcome to the MoS given the previous design work that the company had devoted to naval all-weather fighters since 1946. *Leonardo UK*

The Saro P.148 was the most novel of the N.114T tenders with a T-tail, 40° swept wing and a reheated Avon RA.10R mounted in its own nacelle above the rear fuselage. The crew sat side by side in an arrangement mirroring that of the DH.110 with the observer to starboard seated inside the fuselage. The small bullet on the starboard wing is the AI.16's 10in (25cm) diameter secondary ranging scanner. Four ADEN cannon were mounted below the cockpit and the large panel beneath the wing is an 18-round retractable RP pack. *Leonardo UK*

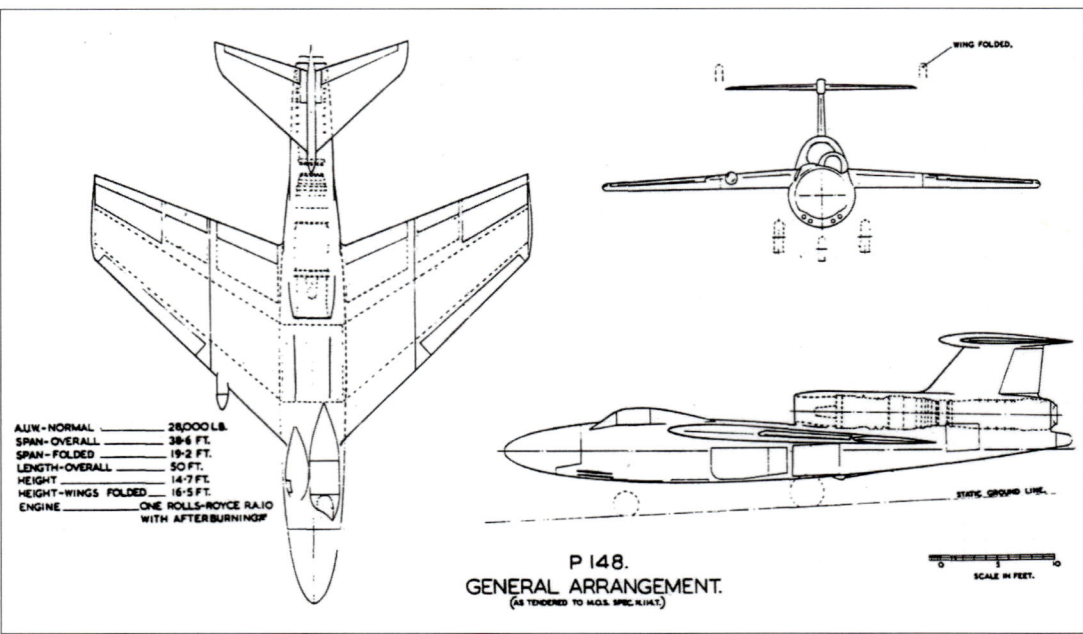

crew sat side by side in an arrangement mirroring that of the DH.110 with the pilot offset to port and the observer to starboard totally inside the fuselage with a 'coal scuttle' hatch. The main undercarriage retracted into the fuselage. The AI.16's 10in ranging scanner was fitted in a small bullet on the inner starboard wing. Four ADEN cannon were mounted below the cockpit, two batteries of 36 RPs were further aft in the fuselage sides below the wing. Four *Blue Sky* or two *Red Dean* AAMs could be carried under the wings. Total fuel capacity was 1,150gal (5,230L) in six tanks. RATOG could also be fitted. The estimated AUW was 28,000lb (12,700kg) with a sea level maximum speed of 600kt and 544kt at 30,000ft, a sea level rate of climb of 9,750ft/min (2,970m/min) and a 47,000ft (14,325m) service ceiling.

After submitting the brochure, Saro received the latest data on the Avon RA.12R from Rolls-Royce, so sent to the MoS with the more powerful engine. The sea level maximum speed increased to 606kt with 547kt at 30,000ft, the sea level rate of climb to 13,320ft/min (3,755m/min) and 49,500ft (15,090m) service ceiling. Saro calculated that the prototype would fly in 30 months from the ITP.

The Short PD.5 was a conventional design with a mid-mounted thin (6.5% t/c) low aspect ratio wing of 19.25° sweep and a mid-mounted tailplane. The vertical tail was all-moving and lacked a rudder; a pod at the tip housed the rear warning radar. Shorts also proposed an undercarriageless version for flexible decks. The single Sapphire Sa.4 was fed by wing root intakes; the total internal fuel capacity was 850gal (3,865L) and two rigid overload tanks could be fitted. Four ADEN cannon and a retractable battery of 52 RPs were mounted below the cockpit and four *Blue Sky* or two *Red Dean* AAMs could be

Saro later revised the P.148 with a more conventional layout and a delta wing. The engine was a single reheated Avon RA.14 and the armament was reduced to two cannon for a lighter 24,000lb (10,890kg) AUW. *Tony Buttler Collection*

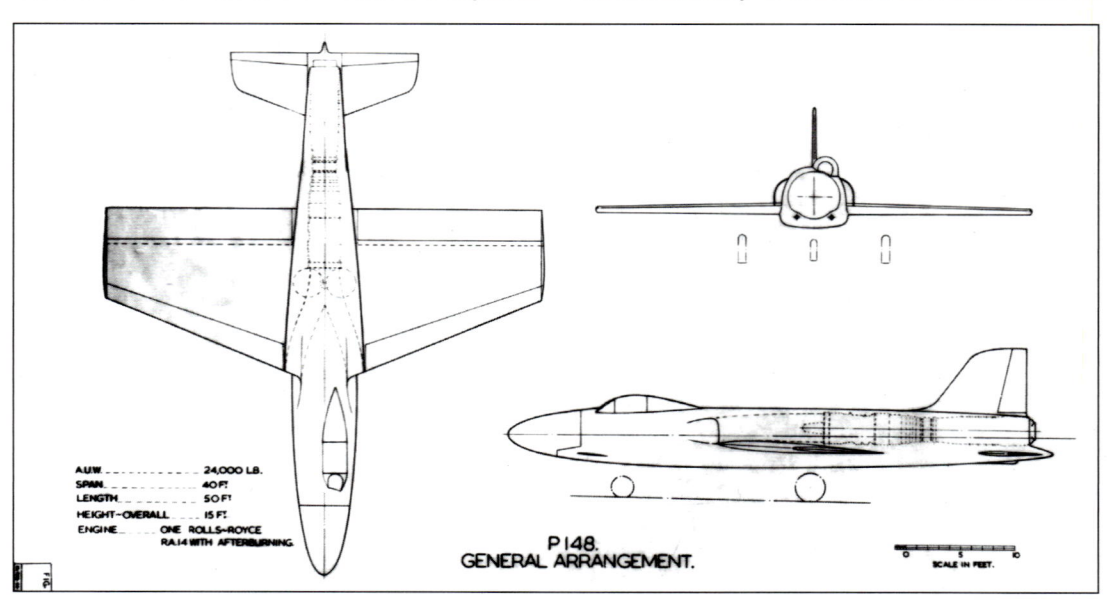

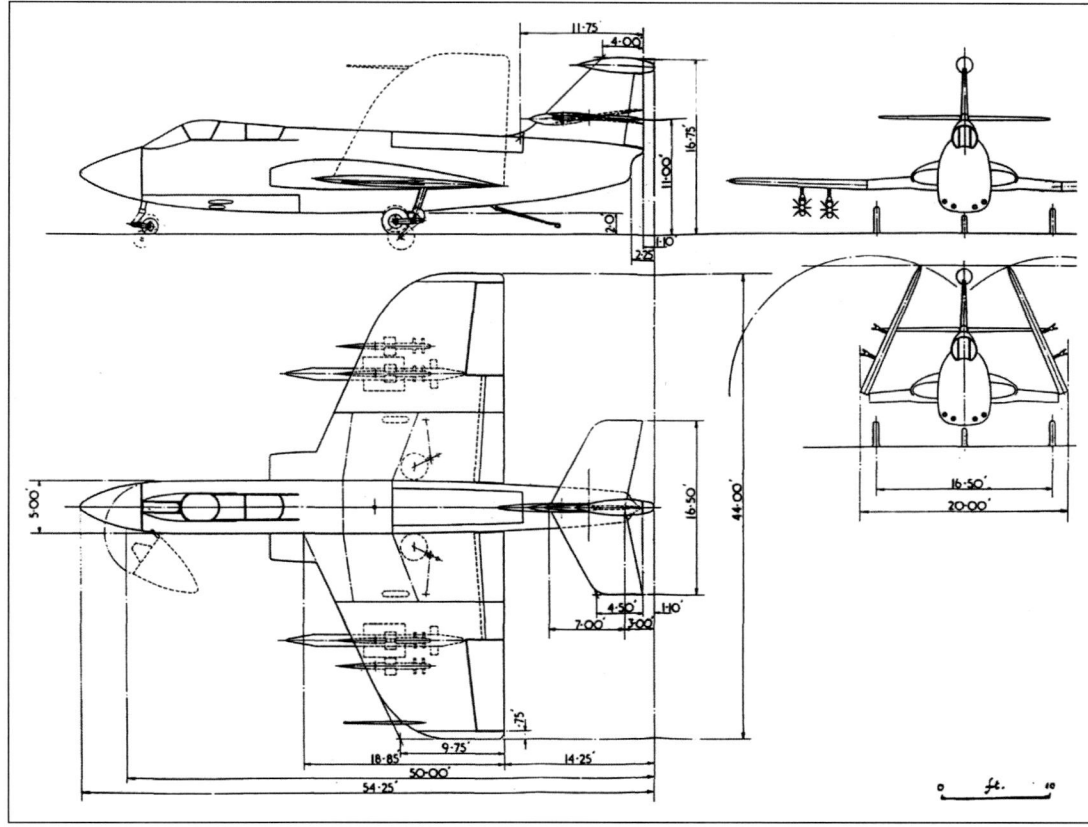

This general arrangement drawing of the Short PD.5 shows the low aspect ratio wing of 19.25° sweep. The vertical tail was all-moving and lacked a rudder, the tip pod housing the rear warning radar. The top view shows the possible alternative arrangement of four *Blue Sky* or two *Red Dean* AAMs. *Short Brothers via Author's Collection*

carried under the wings. The estimated AUW was 28,000lb (12,700kg) with a sea level maximum speed of 606kt, a sea level rate of climb of 9,910ft/min (3,020m/min) and 42,850ft (13,060m) service ceiling. Shorts predicted a prototype first flight 30 months from the ITP.

Westland's design was PJD.261. It had a cranked swept wing, effectively a delta with an average sweep of 40° with 8% t/c ratio, and a T-tail. Future developments envisioned boundary layer control using an air compressor rather than engine bleed air and blown flaps to reduce the approach speed by 20kt and a variable sweep wing was also considered. The AI.18 radar was housed in a folding nose to meet the carrier lift and hangar dimensional constraints. The powerplant was a single Avon RA.12R or Sapphire Sa.4 and the fuselage held 950gal (4,320L) of fuel, plus a 90gal (409L) ventral drop tank could be fitted. The armament was four 30mm ADEN, two RP packs and four underwing

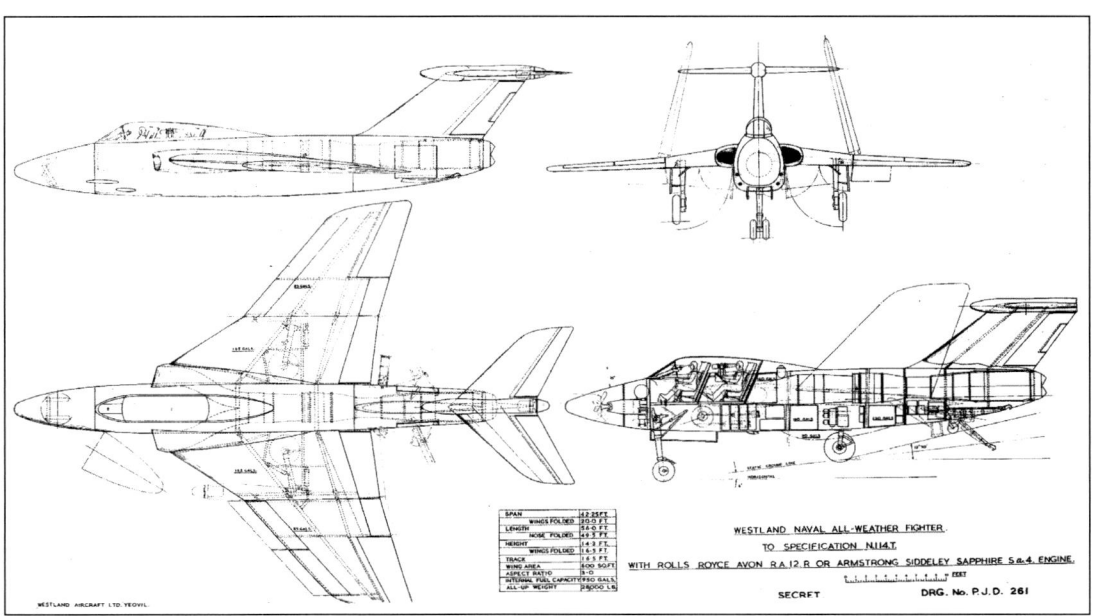

Technical drawing PJD.261 of Westland's N.114T tender. *Leonardo UK via Jeremy Graham*

Westland's tender was an attractive design with its compound swept wing and T-tail. *Leonardo UK via Jeremy Graham*

Blue Sky or two *Red Dean* AAMs. The estimated sea level maximum speed was 621kt with the Avon or 600kt with the Sapphire; the sea level rate of climb being 10,800ft/min (3,290m/min) and 10,500ft (3,200m) respectively. The service ceiling was 44,500ft (13,565m) and 43,400ft (13,230m) with the Avon and Sapphire. Westland predicted a prototype first flight 120 weeks following the ITP. A forward fuselage mock-up was built and Westland also proposed a conversion trainer variant.

The Tender Design Conference at Thames House took place on 9 October 1951. The RAE had looked at all the tenders, making comparison calculations as part of their assessment. They estimated that all the designs were 4,000–6,000lb (1,814–2,722kg) overweight; surprisingly in view of all its previous design work and experience, Fairey's design had the heaviest structural weight. A high approach speed of 117kt counted against the Saro P.148 and Short PD.5 – the latter being judged as having insufficient wing area. The Blackburn B.89 and Fairey's design were overweight but met the performance requirements. Blackburn's wing design was considered to be more careful and considered than Fairey's (Blackburn's wing was influenced by Dr Gustav Lachmann's compound sweep work at Handley Page.) The PD.5 could be improved by fitting more effective flaps. The P.148 had several negative points: high wing loading, the engine placement might have affected directional control on approach and the narrow 8ft (2.43m) wheel track would make deck landings tricky. Despite this, Saro impressed the assessors given that it was the company's first carrier-borne jet fighter design.

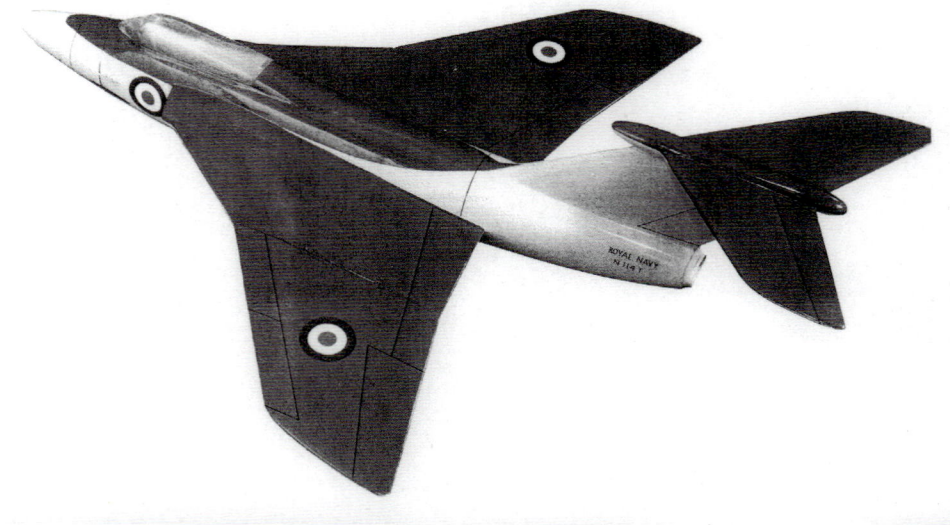

This rear quarter view of Westland's official model illustrates well the compound swept wing, which was almost a delta wing in layout. *Leonardo UK via Tony Buttler Collection*

Lower wing loading was an advantage for combat manoeuvrability, with the B.89 coming out on top.

When it came to engines the RAE felt the Olympus was the better choice at high altitude and RD Projects, J Cohen, argued its lower fuel consumption could reduce AUW by 2,600lb (1,180kg), but the conference did not state a preference. Production aspects would determine availability, with V-Bomber programme taking large numbers of Olympus, the Avon looked more likely to be available. In terms of armament, Fairey had only offered two cannon, Shorts three plus an insufficient number of RPs, while Westland's RPs were stowed externally, which increased drag.

Next the resources of the companies were scrutinised. Blackburn's Brough factory would be busy if the B.101 Beverley tactical transport was ordered and Chief Designer's George Edward Petty's design team would need to recruit additional staff. Short's Sydenham factory in Northern Ireland was already busy building English Electric Canberras and Fairey was focused on building the Gannet ASW aircraft. In technical terms the B.89 had narrowly won over Westland's design but no outcome was decided pending other considerations. A follow up meeting on 16 November to study concessions led to the Director of Naval Air Warfare (DNAW), Captain

The full-scale forward fuselage mock-up of Westland's design included a folding radome and accessible cannon bays to check the fit of the equipment to be installed. *Leonardo UK via Jeremy Graham*

Naval Requirement NR/A.14 & Specification N.114T designs

	Blackburn B.89	**Fairey N.114T**	**Saro P.148**	**Short PD.5**	**Westland PJD.261**
Span	50ft 6in (15.39m); 20ft 0in (6.10m) folded	46ft 0in (14.02m); 20ft 0in (6.10m) folded	38ft 7in (11.76m); 19ft 2in (5.85m) folded	44ft 0in (13.41m); 20ft 0in (6.10m) folded	42ft 3in (12.88m); 20ft 0in (6.10m) folded
Length	53ft 9in (16.38m); 49ft 9in (15.16) folded	50ft 0in (15.24m)	50ft 0in (15.24m)	54ft 3in (16.54m); 50ft (15.24m) folded	56ft 0in (17.06m); 49ft 5in (15.05m) folded
Wing area	700ft² (65.10m²)	645ft² (59.9m²)	500ft² (46.5m²)	641ft² (59.61m²)	600ft² (55.8m²)
t/c ratio	10% root, 6.5% tip	8%	8%	6.5%	8%
All-up weight	26,940lb (12,220kg)	29,800lb (13,515kg)	28,000lb (12,700kg)	28,000lb (12,700kg)	28,000lb (12,700kg)
Powerplant	1x Sapphire Sa.4, 9,760lbf (43.4kN) dry, 12,200lbf (54.2kN) reheat	1x Olympus Ol.3, 12,150lbf (54.0kN) dry	1x Avon RA.10, 9,150lbf (40.7kN) dry, 11,380lbf (50.6kN) reheat	1x Sapphire Sa.4, 9,760lbf (43.4kN) dry, 12,200lbf (54.2kN) reheat	1x Avon RA.12 or Sapphire Sa.4, 12,200lbf (54.2kN) reheat
Max speed	606kt (1,123km/h) at SL	601kt (1,113km/h) at SL; 570kt (1,055km/h) at 20,000ft (6,095m)	600kt (1,110km/h) at SL; 544kt (1,007km/h) at 30,000ft (9,145m)	606kt (1,123km/h) at SL	RA.12 621kt (1,150km/h) at SL; Sa.4 600kt (1,112km/h) at SL
Rate of climb	10,320ft/min (3,145m/min) at SL	9,830ft/min (2,995m/min) at SL; 4,930ft/min (1,500m/min) at 30,000ft (9,145m)	9,750ft/min (2,970m/min) at SL	9,910ft/min (3,020m/min) at SL	RA.12 10,800ft/min (3,290m/min) at SL; Sa.4 10,500ft/min (3,200m/min) at SL
Service ceiling	45,000+ft (13,715+m)	44,000ft (13,410m)	47,000ft (14,325m)	42,850ft (13,060m)	RA.12 44,500ft (13,565m); Sa.4 43,400ft (13,230m)
Armament	3x 30mm ADEN, 2x40 2in (50mm) RPs	2x 30mm ADEN, 70x 2in (50mm) RPs, 4 Blue Sky or 2 Red Dean	4x 30mm ADEN, 2x36 2in (50mm) RPs, 4 Blue Sky or 2 Red Dean	4x 30mm ADEN, 52x 2in (50mm) RPs, 4 Blue Sky or 2 Red Dean	4x 30mm ADEN, 2in (50mm) RPs, 4 Blue Sky or 2 Red Dean

RM Smeeton, refusing to concede anything but 30 minutes patrol time. The DH.116 'Developed Venom' (see below) was anonymously introduced in the meeting as an example of what might be achieved.

The PDTD(A), Stuart Scott Hall, on 5 November reported that the Admiralty had serious doubts about the N.114T aircraft and had no faith in Blackburn or Westland to produce it (awkwardly adding a postscript confessing that his predecessor NE Rowe had become Blackburn's Technical Director, which somewhat modified the MoS's view!) Blackburn and Westland's success in the face of the 'Size and Shape Policy' was awkward for the MoS to admit.

The DMARD, AE Woodward Nutt, confirmed the Admiralty's doubts over the size and weight and their idea to acquire an interim aircraft until something better came along, even though they had no idea what that 'something' was. He pointed out that the 'Developed Venom' could not be ready until 1957 (N.114T was estimated to begin production in autumn 1955). On 21 January 1952 all concerned were informed that their submissions had failed to meet N.114T and that the Admiralty was looking at less stringent requirements. In May a revised N.114T2 appeared, adding provision for jet deflection, but in reality, N.114T was dead.

Blackburn still had hopes for the B.89, fitting a much smaller 425ft² (39.5m²) wing and lightening the aircraft to 20,000lb (9,072kg) to create the B.95 in March 1952. Blackburn's board, however, declined to pursue the project as a private venture. But later that year the design evolved into the B.102 with two smaller Bristol Orpheus turbojets and a DH Spectre rocket motor for climbing and combat. A MoS visit in November revealed to Petty that the Admiralty was about to release a requirement for a strike aircraft – NA.39 (see Chapter 5) – and advising them to tender. In the New Year the design morphed into the Sapphire-powered B.103 – thus the Buccaneer was the unintended beneficiary of N.114T.

DH.116 developed Venom

Ronald Eric Bishop, DH's Chief Designer, had toured the USA's aviation industry in the summer of 1951 and returned home with innovative ideas about how to improve the Sea Venom. The resulting DH.116 'Developed Venom' was vastly different, only retaining the nose and cockpit (although the Admiralty insisted on ejection seats being added.) Bishop aimed for a modern aircraft that could operate from fleet and light fleet carriers. There was an element of modularity in that the forward fuselage could easily be redesigned with a new single-seat cockpit.

The twin boom layout was discarded in favour of a conventional rear fuselage with a tail jet pipe exhaust and a T-tail. The engine was to be an Avon RA.14 rated at 9,500lbf (42.2kN) in dry thrust and 14,000lbf (62.2kN) in reheat. A new swept wing of 5–7% t/c ratio was designed for a critical Mach number of 1.0. It had full-span, leading-edge slots and Fowler-type trailing edge flaps; all the controls were power-operated. Fuel capacity was 562gal (2,555L) in the fuselage plus provision for two 100gal (455L) drop tanks. Either AI.17 or the American AN/APS-21 radar could be fitted in the nose; under the cockpit were two 30mm ADEN cannon.

The estimated AUW was 21,405lb (9,709kg). The performance estimates were impressive: a

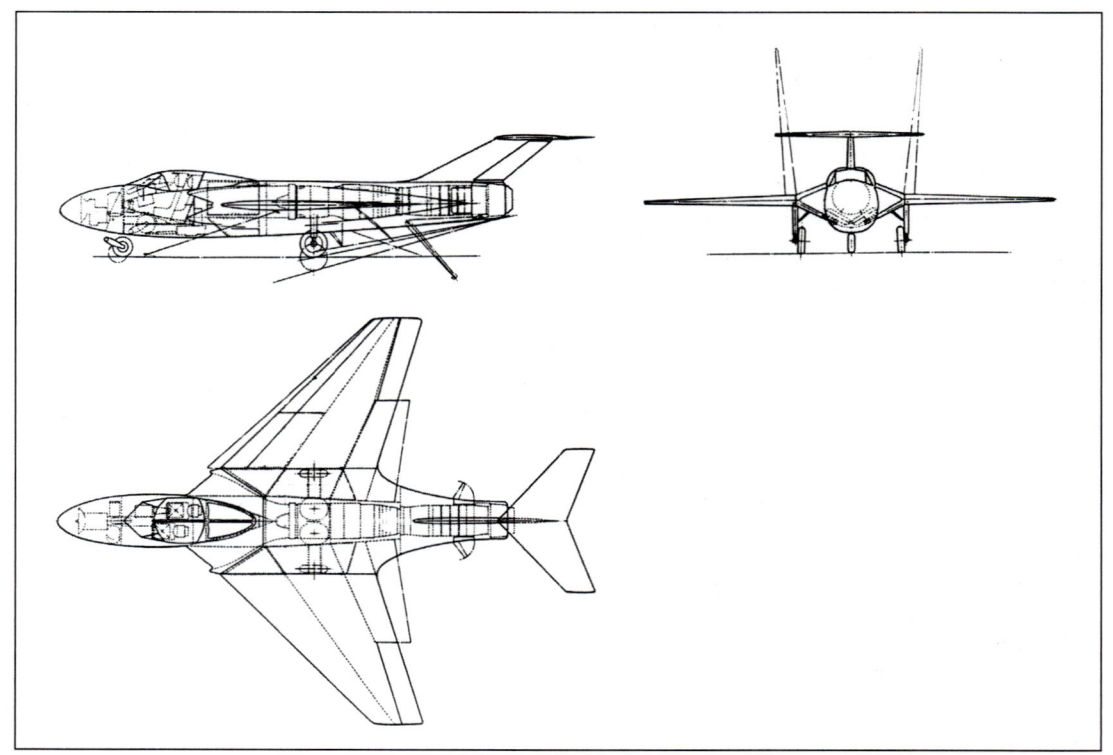

A general arrangement drawing of the DH.116 'Developed Venom', which essentially married the Sea Venom cockpit nacelle with a new centre and rear fuselage and wings. *de Havilland Hatfield via Tony Buttler Collection*

The DH.116 looked very different from the Venom on which it was loosely based. A lack of drawing staff prevented de Havilland pressing ahead with what might have been a very useful transonic fighter. de Havilland Hatfield via Tony Buttler Collection

maximum speed of Mach 0.92 in dry power at sea level or Mach 0.975 with reheat and Mach 1.01 at 30,000ft; a sea level rate of climb of 9,000ft/min (3,020m/min) on dry power or 29,600ft (9,020m) with reheat; a time to 45,000ft (13,720m) in 4.1min and an operational ceiling of 51,500ft (15,700m).

The Admiralty was sufficiently impressed to draw up Staff Requirement NR/A.38 around the DH.116 in March 1952 to replace NR/A.14; the MoS releasing Specification N.131T in May. Maximum speed was not to be less than 550kt at 40,000ft (12,192m) with a maximum rate of climb not less than 20,000ft/min (6,095m/min) and a ceiling of 48,000ft (14,630m). Endurance was to cover climbing to 40,000ft, one hour patrolling, five minutes of combat and 20 minutes loitering at 2,000ft (610m) before landing. Folded span was reduced to just 12ft (3.65m) and the AUW was to be 'kept as low as possible' and no limit was quoted to give the designers leeway.

Woodward Nutt suggested opening N.131T to tenders to appease the industry given the previous disappointments and it was sent to DH, Fairey, Saro, Short and Westland – interestingly the Admiralty stated it wanted the resulting aircraft to be 'produced by one of the leading fighter firms.' Perhaps luckily for the MoS and the Admiralty the other companies declined to tender.

The Admiralty considered ordering two prototypes, but then DH had to admit that its design team was overloaded and that it could not take the project further. Bishop, as a consolation prize,

Table heading please

	DH.112 Sea Venom FAW.22	**DH.116 'Super Venom'**
Span	42ft 11in (13.08m); 23ft 0in (7.01m) folded	34ft 0in (10.36m); 12ft 0in (3.66m) folded
Length	36ft 7in (11.15m)	44ft 0in (13.41m)
Wing area	279.8ft² (25.99m²)	370ft² (34.41m²)
t/c ratio	10%	7% root, 5% tip
All-up weight	15,400lb (6,985kg)	26,940lb (12,220kg)
Powerplant	1x Ghost 105, 5,300lbf (23.6kN)	1x Avon RA.14, 9,500lbf (42.2kN) dry, 14,000lbf (62.2kN) reheat
Max speed	500kt (925km/h) at SL; 482kt (893km/h) at 30,000ft (9,145m)	606kt (1,123km/h) dry at SL; 595kt (1,102km/h)/Mach 1.01 at 30,000ft (9,145m)
Rate of climb	5,750ft/min (1,750m/min) at SL	9,900ft/min (3,020m/min) dry at SL; 29,600ft/min (9,020m/min) reheat at SL
Service ceiling	39,500ft (12,040m)	51,500ft (15,700m)
Armament	4x 20mm Hispano, 8x 60lb (25kg) RPs, 2x 1,000lb (454kg) bombs	2x 30mm ADEN

The second DH.110 prototype was WG240, which was used for development work for the Sea Vixen but lacked naval features such as folding wings. *Terry Panopalis Collection*

dusted off the idea of a naval DH.110 – the Vixen had been rejected by the RAF in favour of the Javelin and its reputation was marred by the horrendous mid-air breakup of the prototype WG236 at the 1952 Society of British Aircraft Constructors Show at Farnborough.

A Vixen rises from the ashes

The MoS considered that nothing else off-the-shelf was likely to be suitable and going out to tender again would bring even more delay (and ire from the aircraft companies). The DH.110 was assessed at a meeting at St. Giles Court on 5 March 1953. There were several doubts; whether Eric Bishop's team at Christchurch could complete the work quickly, whether the AI.18 radar would fit, the low airframe strength factors for the ground attack role and the Admiralty wanted four – not two – *Blue Jays*. It was decided to revisit NR/A.38 in relation to the DH.110 as NR/A.38/3 and Specification N.139D&P was drafted to cover the development, while Bishop was asked to prepare a detailed brochure.

N.139D&P called for a performance of at least 600kt at sea level and 530kt at 40,000ft (12,190m) with a rate of climb of at least 14,000ft/min (4,270m/min) – N.139P of May 1955 for the production aircraft increased this to 18,000ft/min (5,485m/min) at sea level and 10,000ft/min (3,050m/min) at 20,000ft (6,100m) with time to 40,000ft in 5min 45sec.

On 6 November 1953 a third DH.110 prototype was agreed with DH, it would be constructed using existing F.4/38 components and the MoS assigned First Level Priority to its construction. The Avon RA.24 was originally selected but it was completed with Avon RA.28 engines. The Admiralty confirmed its intentions under the Radical Review by providing financial provision for 400 production aircraft in September: three aircraft for 1956/57, 27 in 1957/58, 95 in 1958/59, 130 in 1959/60 and 145 in 1960/61. The first production order was for 100, of which the Treasury only approved 75 – partly due to the Admiralty's interest in the two-seat Supermarine Type 556.

Bill Tamblin's design team at Christchurch redesigned 80% of the DH.110; a new all-moving tailplane was fitted and the fuselage was altered to fit the AI.18. It was the first British aircraft designed

DH.110 Sea Vixen FAW.1

Span	50ft 0in (15.24m); 22ft 3in (6.78m) folded
Length	55ft 7in (16.94m)
Wing area	648ft² (60.26m²)
t/c ratio	10%
All-up weight	42,000lb (19,050kg)
Powerplant	2x Avon Mk.208, 12,250lbf (50.0kN)
Max speed	560kt (1,037km/h) at 10,000ft (3,050m)
Rate of climb	16,900ft/min (5,150m/min) at SL
Service ceiling	48,000ft (14,630m)
Armament	2x14 2in (50mm) Microcell RPs, 4x Firestreak, bombs or RP pods

The Sea Vixen FAW.1 was the first all-missile armed aircraft in FAA service. First production aircraft XJ474 is carrying four Firestreak IR-homing AAMs. *Blue Envoy Collection*

to use AAMs as its primary weapon and during development the ADEN cannon were replaced by two 14-round retractable packs of Microcell 2in (5.1cm) RPs. Test firings of the ADENs revealed the mountings could not withstand the recoil, the only workable solution to which was to insert a baulk of timber! The RPs also caused initial problems with gas ingestion causing engine surging and flame outs. The Firestreak infrared seekers were cooled in flight by an ammonia refrigeration system and they were slaved to the AI.18 radar, locking-on before launch when the target came into range.

The DH.110 Mk.20X prototype, XF828, made its maiden flight at Christchurch on 20 June 1955. This aircraft was semi-navalised with an arrester hook and catapult attachments as well as reprofiled wing

A row of brand new Sea Vixen FAW.1 with the nearest aircraft being XJ484. Issued to 892 NAS, XJ484 suffered a number of minor accidents and by January 1961 was retired. *Blue Envoy Collection*

The Sea Vixen could carry a variety of weaponry. Shown here are four 1,000lb (454kg) HE bombs, four Firestreaks, two AGM-12 Bullpups, two pods of 2in (50mm) Microcell RPs (one with the frangible nose cap removed) and 32 60lb (27kg) RPs. The only weapon missing is the *Red Beard* tactical nuclear bomb. *Blue Envoy Collection*

The 1960 SBAC Show at Farnborough included factory fresh Sea Vixen FAW.1 XJ578 with Dayglo dummy Firestreaks, drop tanks and refuelling probe. *Terry Panopalis Collection*

The Sea Vixen had a 'buddy' refuelling capability using a Flight Refuelling Mk.20A pod to extend CAP endurance. In this image Sea Vixen FAW.1 XJ488 is refuelling FAW.1 XJ521 on 20 November 1959 during a de Havilland trial. *Blue Envoy Collection*

leading edges and structural strengthening, but without folding wings. The definitive production standard would add powered wing folding, a reinforced undercarriage with a steerable nose wheel and a revised empennage.

DH had wanted to name the aircraft Pirate in 1954 (the 1949 RAF/RN DH.110 was named Vixen) but the Admiralty demurred, eventually choosing the unoriginal name Sea Vixen in 1957; the designation FAW.1 denoted its all-weather capability. A total of 114 were built, the first aircraft, XJ474, flying on 20 March 1957. XJ474 and XJ475

Sea Vixen FAW.1 XJ585 of 893 NAS prepares to take-off from HMS *Centaur's* bow catapult. On 28 January 1963 the aircraft hit *Centaur's* roundown on a night approach, skidding along the deck, hitting four parked Sea Vixens and catching fire before crashing into the sea off the bows. Both Lt Cdr DF Fieldhouse and Lt SN Swift were killed.
Terry Panopalis Collection

Sea Vixen FAW.1 XJ486 with some of the ground attack ordnance used by the type: 1,000lb (454kg) bombs, 2in (50mm) Microcell RP pods, 3in (76mm) RPs and small practice bombs. This aircraft was also used in *Red Beard* and the Low Altitude Bombing System (LABS) clearance trials.
Blue Envoy Collection

XJ488 was used for most of its life on trials work, ranging from arrester gear tests, 'buddy' refuelling, AI.18R fire-control computer tests and towed-target winch evaluations. By 1967 the aircraft was assigned to the A&AEE's 'C' Squadron, painted black overall with white lightning flashes and 'RN Test Squadron' titles on the nose. Used as a Martel ASM trial support aircraft, it was retired in 1972 and today its cockpit survives at the Robertsbridge Aviation Society, East Sussex. *Blue Envoy Collection*

were used for trials alongside XF828. Service trials took place in November 1958 and the Sea Vixen entered service with 892 NAS in 1959.

In June 1963 20 FAW.1s were converted at Yeovilton with a wide-band radio homer, the Pilot Attack Sight and AGM-12 Bullpup air-ASMs. These aircraft were issued to 890, 893 and 899 NAS. The changes only added 50lb (22kg) weight but when loaded with four Bullpups the AUW could exceed 30,000lb (13,605kg). The Admiralty required the Sea Vixen to be cleared to carry the *Red Beard* tactical nuclear bomb as insurance against delays in the Blackburn Buccaneer's development, but it was never deployed in the nuclear strike role.

DH studied a 'thin-wing' supersonic development during December 1953 to the summer of 1954. These studies included three main options: a 810ft² (75.3m²) delta wing of 7% t/c ratio; thinner 6% t/c outer wing sections with .5ft (0.46m) tip chord to increase the area to 672ft² (62.5m²); reduced t/c ratio by extending the chord of the entire wing for an area of 794ft² (73.8m²). The engines would be upgraded to the Avon RA.24R with the afterburners in longer tail pipes. The second wing option coupled with the RA.24R was estimated to give a sea level rate of climb of 33,600ft/min (10,240m/min) and a level speed of Mach 1.0 at 36,000ft (10,970m) in clean condition.

In April 1954 another version had the 6% t/c wing modifications with an area of 450ft² or 500ft² (41.8m² or 46.5m²) and a single Rolls-Royce RB.106 or DH PS.25 Gyron turbojet to achieve Mach 1.49 or Mach 1.43 respectively at 36,000ft. A 7% t/c ratio wing of 750ft² (69.75m²) with a pair of RB.106 would reach Mach 1.55. These studies led to proposal for the RAF with a 10,000lbf (44.4kN) DH Spectre rocket added for high-altitude capability. Fitting reheated Rolls-Royce RB.168 Spey turbofans to the Sea Vixen FAW.1 was considered in 1960. The serious drawback for all these schemes was the possibility of acoustic vibration fatigue damaging the tail booms and tailplane from the use of reheat.

Supermarine Type 556

Span	37ft 2in (11.33m); 20ft 0in (6.09m) folded
Length	58ft 6in (17.83m, 51ft 0in (15.54m) folded
Wing area	478ft² (44.45m²)
t/c ratio	8%
All-up weight	41,852lb (18,984kg)
Powerplant	2x Avon RA.24
Max speed	665kt (1,232km/h) at SL; 600kt (1,110km/h) at 40,000ft (12,190m)
Rate of climb	43,000ft/min (13,105m) at SL with reheat
Service ceiling	52,150ft (15,895m)
Endurance	1hr 45 min at 40,000ft (12,190m)
Armament	4x 30mm ADEN, 2x Firestreak, 2in (50mm) RP pods

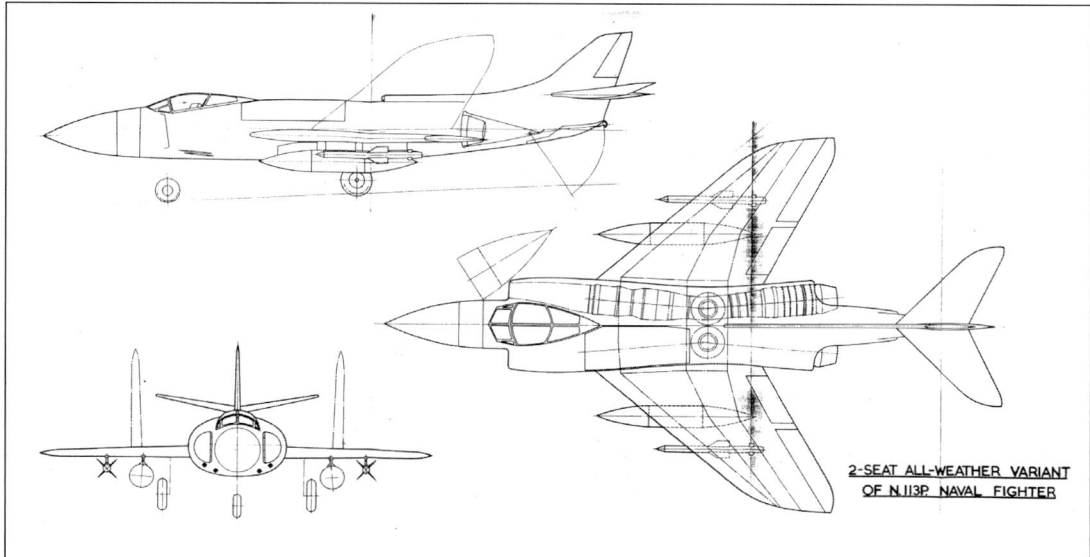

A general arrangement drawing of the two-seat Supermarine Type 556 all-weather interceptor developed from the Scimitar with a wider forward fuselage for side-by-side seating. *RAF Museum Hendon via Ralph Pegram*

Two-seat Scimitar

Although the Sea Vixen programme was progressing well, on 17 February 1954 the MoS had requested Supermarine to propose a two-seat, all-weather fighter version of the Type 544 Scimitar (itself still two years away from flight) to meet NR/A.38. Joe Smith's design team submitted a brochure the following month. The Type 556 had a wider and deeper nose to accommodate the AI.18 radar and side-by-side cockpit seating. This also enabled the engines and intakes to be splayed outwards to free up fuselage space for avionics and the internal fuel capacity was 1,210gal (5,502L), plus two 200gal (909L) drop tanks could be carried under the wings. Armament would be four *Blue Jay*, with or without ADEN cannon. The Avons were upgraded to the RA.24 and the supersonic flap blowing would be retained. The estimated maximum speed was 665kt at sea level and 600kt at 40,000ft (12,190m), the sea level rate of climb being 43,000ft/min (13,105m) using reheat and the service ceiling was 52,150ft (15,895m). The operating weight was 28,170lb (12,777kg) – 3,228lb (1,464kg) heavier than the DH.110 – but the performance was superior. The estimated development cost was £5 million.

Sufficiently impressed, the Admiralty and MoS ordered one prototype, XH451, in September. This had not been a forgone conclusion given the budget problems. The government was looking at cutting the Defence Vote and asking the FAA to make do with just one aircraft type – Scimitar or Sea Vixen – instead of a combined fleet of 900 aircraft. The Type 556 would be cheaper to develop and offered better performance, it looked like the Sea Vixen might be dropped again; although the Type 556's development was 18 months behind the Sea Vixen's and the Scimitar's blown flaps were unproven (timely arrival of trials data from the USN gave the Admiralty confidence that they would work.) A committee chaired by the Permanent Secretary of the Ministry of Defence, Sir Harold Parker, investigated the case and its report was marginally in favour of the Type 556. The plan was now to only order a small batch of Sea Vixens until the Type 556 was ready, if the money could be found then the Admiralty would proceed with all three programmes. The DNAW, Captain Duncan Lewin, feared that the entire Scimitar programme could be lost, leaving the RN without a strike aircraft. The Admiralty changed tack, pushing to maintain the Sea Vixen and Scimitar, and won the case.

The Treasury allocated £500,000 for a prototype, hoping that using as many stock Scimitar parts as possible would save money. A forward fuselage mock-up was built but work was suspended on 27 April 1955 following the Sea Vixen production order and was soon cancelled. The Type 556 was briefly reconsidered in early July to carry a pair of *Red Dean* AAMs, but the missile was cancelled the same month, signalling the end of the Type 556.

After 13 years of indecision, the FAA finally got the all-weather fighter that it wanted, but technology was already moving forwards and SAMs were increasingly seen as being the future of air defence and the Soviet naval threat was also evolving.

5 Buccaneer – Not just a weapon

By the early 1950s the Fleet Air Arm had several strike aircraft in prospect, among them the Supermarine Scimitar Mk.1. But the Admiralty wanted a dedicated strike aircraft with the capability to deliver a nuclear weapon. This desire was not simply a case of 'Keeping up with the Joneses' – the Royal Air Force and the US Navy. The Royal Navy had its own list of suitable targets, not least Soviet naval harbours and shore installations. Since the end of the Second World War, Joseph Stalin had restarted his naval expansion plans including four 35,900-ton Project 82 *Stalingrad*-class battlecruisers, four 26,230-ton Project 66 heavy cruisers, 25 13,230-ton Project 68bis *Sverdlov*-class light cruisers as well as 14,500-ton Project 85 anti-aircraft cruisers. These ships would pose a serious threat to resupply convoys from the USA in the advent of a Third World War. Aerial attack using torpedoes or 2,000lb (907kg) armour piercing bombs would be costly in the face of radar-guided anti-aircraft

Blackburn Buccaneer S.2 XT278 coming into land with everything down – flaps deflected with flap blowing active, undercarriage down, airbrakes open and venting fuel. At the time this photograph was taken in July 1966 the aircraft was with 809 Naval Air Squadron. *Terry Panopalis Collection*

artillery (AAA). Instead, they would have to be destroyed by air-to-surface missiles (ASMs) or nuclear bombs released from sea-skimming bombers flying under the ships' radar coverage. The resulting Naval Staff Requirement NR/A.39 gave rise to one of the most noted post-war British military aircraft – the Blackburn Buccaneer.

Tiresome appendages – Stand-off weapons

Following Stalin's death on 5 March 1953, much of the naval programme was cancelled, but 21 *Sverdlovs* were laid down, of which 14 were completed by 1955. These cruisers were capable of 32.5kt and had a gun armament of four triple 6in (152mm) calibre turrets, six twin 3.9in (100mm) secondary mounts and eight twin 37mm AAA mounts. They were protected by 3.9in (100mm) thick belt and 2in (50mm) deck armour, plus the turrets had armour up to 6.9in (175mm) thick. They were formidable vessels; the Admiralty planned a mix of cruisers (and even the battleship HMS *Vanguard*) and airpower to counter them before they could escape out into the North Atlantic to harry convoys.

The Admiralty realised (as the Germans had during the Second World War) that capital ships were best disabled by stand-off guided weapons. A surface-to-surface version of Sea Slug utilising a ballistic trajectory within the radar horizon of the Type 901 fire-control radar was proposed. Codenamed *Blue Slug* by the Ministry of Supply (MoS), it would be fitted with the 88lb (40kg) armour piercing warhead from the *Red Angel* rocket projectile (RP). Alternatively, Sea Slug armed with a lightweight 0.5-2kT Gwen nuclear warhead could have been used.

The 11¼in (28.5cm) diameter *Red Angel* RP weighed 1,055lb (478kg) and was carried by the Westland Wyvern S.4. It was designed to either penetrate the deck armour or hit the water short of the ship at a shallow angle to hole the target under the waterline – the most efficient way to sink a vessel is to make it flood. *Red Angel* only had a range of 15,000ft (4,570m), well within AAA range.

During the Second World War, Major-General Sir Millis Rowland Jefferis of the MoS's secret MD1 weapon research and development organisation had begun work on a television-guided (TV) bomb for the Air Ministry containing a High-Explosive Squash Head warhead to pierce warship armour. By 1947 the *Journey's End* bomb had acquired basic trajectory control using 'bonkers' (small explosive charges) but development was abandoned. The Air Staff remained interested in the concept and issued Operational Requirement OR.1059 for a TV-guided glide bomb. This led to *Blue Boar*, developed by Vickers with EMI being responsible for the TV-guidance and Smiths Aircraft Instruments developing the autopilot and control system. Originally intended as an anti-ship weapon, it evolved into a 5,000lb (2,267kg) bomb for the Vickers Valiant B.1 strategic bomber. Doubts over the effectiveness of the TV guidance system and the radio datalink's vulnerability to electronic countermeasures (ECM) saw *Blue Boar* being cancelled in August 1954.

On 21 March 1953, just a fortnight after Stalin's death, a meeting at the Ministry of Supply (MoS) discussed the Admiralty's requirement for an anti-ship homing bomb with a 1,000lb (454kg) warhead to destroy commerce raiders. The bomb would have active radar homing and be designed for underwater hits. This 'Naval Blue Boar' was intended to arm two-seat all-weather fighters like the de Havilland DH.110, but it was clear the resulting weapon would likely be too bulky and – at 3,300lb (1,497kg) – too heavy for that aircraft.

In response to the Air Staff's Operational Requirement OR.1123 issued in July 1953 and the Admiralty's requirements, Fairey Aviation asked Vickers to provide rough drawings and estimates for the guided bomb. On 1 September, Vickers Chief Designer for guided weapons, Henry Gardner, showed Fairey and the MoS a project using a shortened *Blue Boar* casing with the GEC X-band radar seeker from Vickers' *Red Dean* air-to-air missile (AAM). Fairey agreed with the proposal and found themselves becoming the lead contractor of the resulting *Green Cheese* glide bomb. A Valiant would carry four *Green Cheese* externally to allow the active seeker to home onto the target before launch. The MoS' Director (Guided Weapons Projects) Brigadier John Clemow was so impressed that he hoped it had "reached a stage where a missile was no longer regarded as a tiresome appendage and a nuisance to the aircraft designer."

The Admiralty issued Staff Requirement AW.319 for use with the Fairey Gannet anti-submarine aircraft and the future NA.39 aircraft. Sadly, Clemow's prediction did not come true and *Green Cheese* became a nuisance to the aircraft designer. Internal carriage required a change to flip-out wings and the bomb bay needed an extending launch rail to lower the bomb into the slipstream to allow the

A Westland Wyvern S.4 with a *Red Angel* anti-ship rocket. The weapon was 11¼in (28.5cm) in diameter, 10ft 9in (3.28m) long and weighed 1,055lb (478kg), of which 88lb (40kg) was the warhead. It was designed to pierce deck armour and for underwater attack, hitting just below the armoured belt. It was estimated that six *Red Angel* hits could cripple a *Sverdlov*-class cruiser. *Author's Collection*

radar seeker to lock-on to the target before release. The solution on some of the NA.39 designs was to use a rotating bomb bay door. Even worse, the 32in (18cm) diameter body prevented the Gannet's bomb bay doors being closed and at 3,800lb (1,724kg) it became too heavy for the Gannet – one might ask how Fairey managed to design a weapon that could not fit its own aircraft!

The Gannet was not a high-altitude bomber, so limiting the effectiveness of a glide bomb. Fairey also found it difficult to reduce the drag to maintain the 30° glide angle, so added a Smokey Joe boost/sustainer rocket from the English Electric Thunderbird surface-to-air missile (SAM), thereby turning *Green Cheese* into a missile.

Targeting data would be provided by the aircraft's ASV.19B, ASV.20 or later ASV.21 surface-search radar, cueing in the GEC active radar seeker to the target's location, then locking-on before release. A semi-active mode was proposed but rejected as the launch aircraft would have had to maintain radar contact with the target, exposing it to defensive fire. *Green Cheese* would have a 'jinker' to perform random weaving manoeuvres during descent to disrupt the target's SAM and AAA fire-control radars. Once the rocket burned out, the dive would increase to 40° and it would hit the water 150ft (45m) short of the target, the radome being sheared off and exposing an angled plate to force the speeding missile back upwards to explode under the keel. Getting the correct offset to hit 150ft short was technically problematic and this mode of attack was eventually replaced by a conventional deck-penetrating, armour-piercing warhead.

All this tinkering led to weight and cost increases and the Admiralty grew disenchanted with the weapon. By March 1955 work was slowing and cancellation followed in 1956. The improved *Cockburn Cheese* (named after the Principal Director of Scientific Research (Guided Weapons) Dr Robert Cockburn) and nuclear-armed *Green Flash* proposals went no further.

The Admiralty instead opted to use the *Red Beard* 25kT yield tactical nuclear bomb, or to give its official name the Bomb, Aircraft, HE 2,000lb, MC Mk.2 – its real weight was closer to 1,750lb (793kg) – or otherwise known by its cover name 'Target Marker Bomb', TMB. Delivery was via the Low Altitude Bombing System (LABS), which calculated the 'toss' manoeuvre to lob the bomb onto the target whilst keeping the aircraft out of anti-aircraft defence range. LABS trials began in June 1958 using Scimitar F.1 XD218 and the final trials began in September 1963, again using XD218, although the temperamental weapon was never fully cleared for use aboard aircraft carriers – no aircraft could land on a carrier whilst carrying a *Red Beard* (in an accident it may have exploded with a yield of 1kT!) *Red Beard* was an unboosted fission weapon with a composite core of plutonium and uranium-235 which was inserted shortly before take-off. It had two radar fuzes which were activated by a barometric 'gate' after release, this ensured that they only transmitted in the last few seconds during the freefall to the computed burst height for safety (also minimising exposure to ECM). There were back-up contact and graze fuzes to ensure detonation. The Mk.2 bombs used by the RN were improved to withstand the salty, cold and wet conditions when loaded onto aircraft sitting on carrier decks.

NA.39

By late 1951 the Admiralty was looking towards a future jet bomber weighing over 100,000lb (45,360kg) for its future aircraft carriers. The planned new ship, dubbed the '1952 Carrier', was a 52,000-ton ship with an overall length of 815ft (248.4m) and a flight deck width of 160ft (48.7m) and containing 50,000ft² (4,645m²) of hangar space. It was designed to operate a bomber 65ft (19.8m) long with a wingspan of 70ft (21.3m) (49ft (14.9m) folded) and a take-off weight of 70,000lb

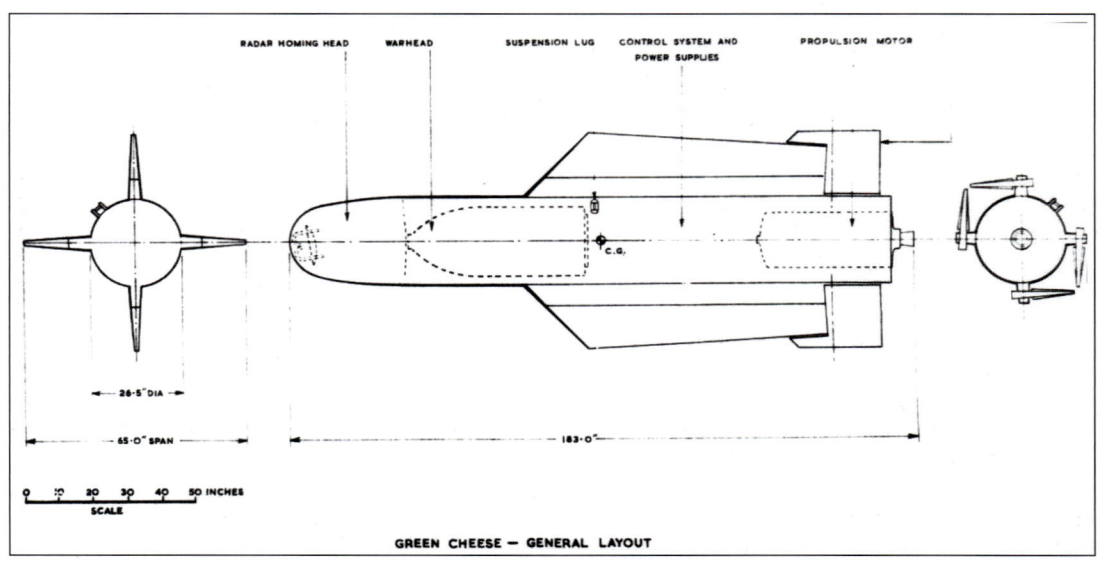

A general arrangement drawing of the *Green Cheese* guided weapon, showing the folding wings and internal layout including the location of the armour piercing warhead. In the nose was the EMI active radar scanner. *Via Joe Cherrie*

(31,750kg) – this was later reduced to 60,000lb (27,215kg) as the ship began to hit dock infrastructure limits. The bomber was to have a radius of action of at least 500nm (925km) against shore targets – more strategically ambitious members of the Naval Staff called for 1,000nm (1,852m). A flexible deck was considered, which led to the proposed trials using an English Electric Canberra tactical bomber (see Chapter 2). The cost of the carrier was too much for the defence budget to bear and the Controller, Admiral Sir Ralph Edwards, ordered all design work to cease on 8 July 1953. The FAA was going to have to obtain a strike aircraft that could operate from existing carriers.

Naval Air Requirement NA.39 was finalised in October 1953 for a two-seat strike aircraft capable of low-altitude attacks to enter service in 1960. In December 1952 the MoS had made studies of modified DH.110 Vixen and Supermarine N.113D designs to fulfil NA.39, estimating some 50% of the DH.110's airframe and 80% of the N.113's would require modification and impractically large drop tanks would be required to meet the range requirements. DH proposed a development programme using a modified Vixen prototype with a larger wing and all-moving tailplane, followed by a semi-navalised prototype (lacking folding wings) with Rolls-Royce RA.14 Avon engines and a fully navalised prototype with a cannon pack and the ability to carry *Blue Jay* AAMs and batteries of RPs. DH estimated entry into service in 1957. Early plans for a single jet-powered aircraft with a booster rocket motor were abandoned as impractical.

The decision was made to press on with a new aircraft and the MoS released Specification M.148T on 27 March 1954, which following discussions with the aviation industry was refined and re-released as Issue 2 on 18 June. The primary role was low-altitude visual attack followed by medium altitude attacks using radar-guided using *Green Cheese* against large targets. The capability to carry a 'packaged installation' to act as a refuelling tanker was also required.

The MoS indicated that a twin-engined design would be the most suitable solution, the MoS favouring a notional scaled-down Rolls-Royce RB.106 with 8–9,000lbf (35.5–40.0kN) thrust (designed as a replacement for the Avon, the RB.106 was cancelled in March 1957.) Maximum speed at sea level was to be not less than 500kt (ideally as fast as possible) and the service ceiling was 30,000ft (9,145m) – later raised to 32,000ft (9,750m) to provide adequate gliding range for *Green Cheese*. The maximum take-off weight limit was 40,000lb (18,145kg). A radius of action of 400nm (470km) was required for the 'Low Attack' sortie with a TMB and 800nm (1,480km) for the 'High Search and Attack' sortie. The aircraft was to be stressed for 60° dives from 20,000ft (6,100m).

The armament was to include one TMB (*Red Beard*) nuclear bomb or *Green Cheese* ASM, or more conventional loads of two 2,000lb (907kg) armour piercing bombs or four 1,000lb (454kg) bombs or four Mk.12 (later Type S) mines. Rocket payloads included 24 RPs or four *Red Angel* armour piercing RPs. Alternatively a gun pack with four 30mm ADEN (or 20mm Hispano Mk.V) with ammunition for 10 seconds' firing would be provided. Up to four underwing hardpoints would be fitted. The avionics included an EMI Electronics ASV.21 surface-search radar, a monopulse radar for targeting, *Yellow Lemon* Doppler navigation radar and AN/ARN-21 Tactical Air Navigation (TACAN).

Armstrong Whitworth Aircraft (AWA), Blackburn Aircraft, Fairey Aviation, Short Brothers and Westland Aircraft were invited to tender at the end of March. A development batch of 10–20 aircraft was envisioned. Percival Aircraft made a request to tender, this was granted on 13 April but in June the company had to drop out given the complexity of the requirements and Percival had little experience of combat aircraft (at the time it was building the Provost basic trainer.) Percival was instead contracted to draw up a 'ghost design' to investigate methods of using tapped engine compressor air to improve the aerodynamics, such as flap blowing, as a technical design exercise.

After the other companies submitted their tenders, another, partially completed, tender arrived from Hawker following a personal request from the Admiralty to Chief Designer Sydney Camm. Camm was not particularly interested in bombers, which probably explains the half-hearted nature of the submission which did not include full costings or delivery estimates. Saunders-Roe (Saro) did not officially tender but did design two naval strike aircraft around this time which were probably based on M.148T.

> "*I do want to emphasise to you the fundamental importance which I attach to equipping the Navy with the N.A.39 aircraft. This is not just a weapon. It is the major contribution of the Navy to deterring anyone who wishes to resort to the use of force.*"
>
> FIRST LORD OF THE ADMIRALTY, EARL OF SELKIRK, TO MINISTER OF DEFENCE DUNCAN SANDYS, 27 AUGUST 1958

The Designs

AWA's design team headed by HR 'Hal' Watson submitted the AW.168. The designers focused on keeping within the 40,000lb limit by saving weight wherever they could. The initial layout had the two 7,000lbf (31.1kN) thrust DH PS.43 Gyron Junior turbojets mounted adjacent to the fuselage, but not inside it due to the large bomb bay. Extensive wind tunnel testing was conducted to optimise the drag performance. Despite the high-speed drag figures being fairly reasonable, the engines were then moved outboard into underwing nacelles with the

WINGS OVER THE FLEET

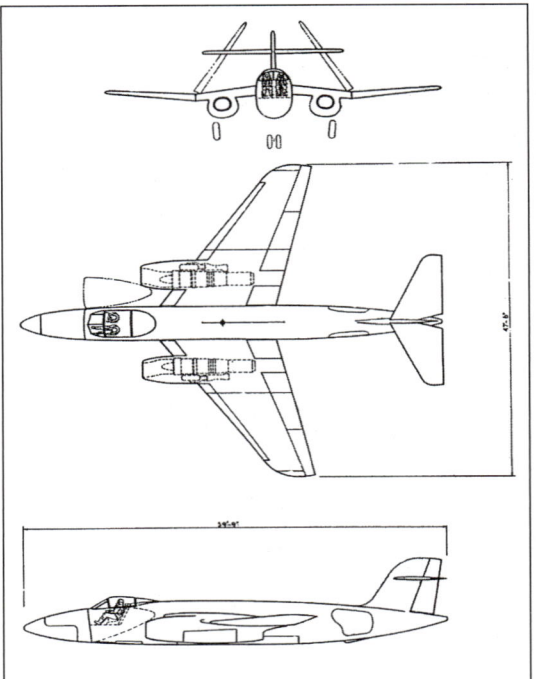

A general arrangement drawing of the AW.168. The large panel on the rear fuselage is the port air/dive brake. *Ray Williams Collection via Tony Buttler*

main undercarriage legs retracting into the inner wing sections. This gave poor handling in the event of asymmetric thrust following an engine shut-down, so the nacelles were moved further inboard and the forward-retracting undercarriage legs were moved to the outboard side of the engine nacelles.

The swept wings featured blown flaps using air tapped from the Gyron Junior compressor stages to reduce the approach and landing speeds and allow a higher landing weight. The two-spar wings also had full-span leading edge drooped slats and a single wing fold; folded span was 23ft (7.01m). The thickness-to-chord (t/c) ratio was 8.5%. Jet pipe deflection using cowls were fitted to divert the jet exhaust thrust 45° downwards to increase lift on take-off. Fuselage length was reduced by having side-by-side seating for the pilot and observer and the radar radome could be folded for carrier stowage. The bombs would be carried on the underwing hardpoints when the removable cannon pack was fitted into the bomb bay.

The estimated maximum speed was 585kt at sea level; a total of 1,690gal (7,683L) of internal fuel in the upper fuselage and inner wings gave a low-

Armstrong Whitworth made this handsome model of the AW.168 to supplement its brochure submission. In the days before CGI a model was a good way to give a visual impression of the final product that had visual impact. *Ray Williams Collection via Tony Buttler*

The AW.168's main undercarriage legs retracted into the engine nacelles beside the Gyron Juniors, note the offset intake. The nacelle also featured Jet pipe deflection using cowls to divert the jet exhaust thrust 45° downwards to increase lift. *Ray Williams Collection via Tony Buttler*

The AW.168 was an attractive looking aircraft, – not that beauty was part of the MoS's selection criteria. *Ray Williams Collection via Tony Buttler*

altitude radius of action of 510nm (945km). Additional range could be obtained by two 250gal (1,136.5L) underwing drop tanks or in-flight refuelling via a nose-mounted probe.

The proposal for the development batch included two initial 'flying shell' aircraft without cockpit pressurisation, bomb bay, jet deflection and wing and nose folding. The third aircraft would receive the jet deflection and the fourth and subsequent aircraft would be fully equipped and navalised. The estimated first delivery was 30 months from the Instruction to Proceed (ITP), with the 20th development aircraft being completed 14 months later. A full-scale mock-up complete with folding wings and nose was completed.

As related in Chapter 4, Blackburn's Chief Designer George Petty had learned about the impending NA.39 during an MoS visit to Brough in November 1952, during which he was encouraged to tender a version of the all-weather fighter concepts the company was working on. A single Rolls-Royce Avon-powered design was rejected as too small. The twin Armstrong Siddeley Sapphire-powered B.103 emerged on the drawing board in early January 1953. It had a large double-sweep wing with the engines either of the fuselage below the wing and a T-tail.

The design team led by Barry Laight and Roy Boot began to refine the design. Moving the engines outboard was rejected due to increased drag and asymmetric thrust issues. Instead, the engines were moved upwards into the wing roots, which reduced the frontal area, drag and allowed the main undercarriage to retract into bays below them. Two large, machined steel spars took the wing's structural load, combined with integrally stiffened machined skins on the wings and tailplanes.

The fuselage was redesigned to conform to the

The AW.168's wings had full-span leading edge drooped slats and the trailing edge had ailerons and three-piece flaps. The model was depicted with an external load of two 1,000lb (454kg) bombs. *Ray Williams Collection via Tony Buttler*

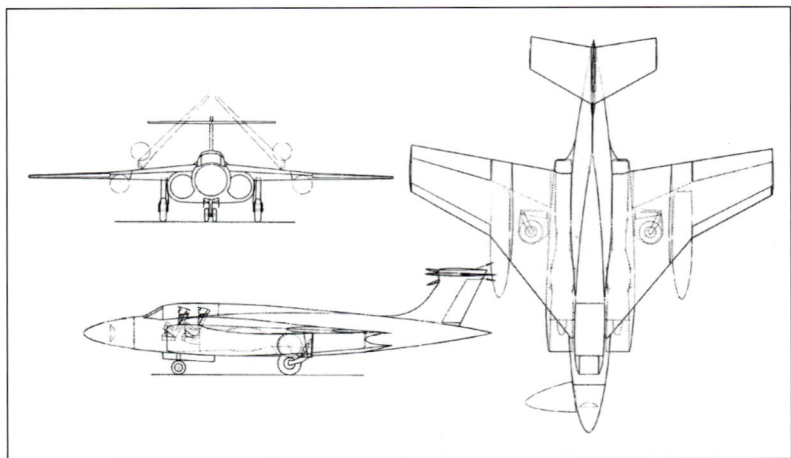

The original Blackburn B.103 design powered by two Armstrong Siddeley Sapphire turbojets. The wing is directly descended from the B.89 all-weather fighter to N.114T. The pilot and observer sat in staggered tandem to give the observer a forward field of vision. *Brough Heritage via Tony Buttler Collection*

The B.103 was soon refined into the shape that would become recognisable as the Buccaneer. At this stage, area rule had started to be applied and the tail clamshell airbrake was added.
Brough Heritage via Tony Buttler Collection

The manufacturer's model of the B.103. *Brough Heritage via Tony Buttler Collection*

principles of transonic area rule, which had recently been codified in the USA by engineer Richard Whitcomb at the National Advisory Committee for Aeronautics. Area rule makes the cross-sectional area of the fuselage as constant as possible to delay drag rise; this was very evident in the B.103 with a waisted fuselage at the wings, flattened fuselage sides below the cockpit and empennage and a distinctive rear fuselage hump.

Extensive supersonic air blowing – 'supercirculation' – was applied to the flaps, ailerons, tailplane and the outer wing sections from just behind the leading edge to give excellent low-speed handling characteristics with full lateral control down to the stall. The wings had a compound sweep of 40° at the root, 38° midspan and 30° outboard; the t/c ratio was 9% inboard and 6% outboard. The extremity of the fuselage was a two-piece clamshell dive/air brake.

The need to lower the *Green Cheese* before launch to acquire its target was problematic. The designers adopted a feature from the American Martin XB-51A bomber to remove the drag caused by opening the bomb bay doors, a rotating door onto which the missile was attached. Originally it would have rotated and lowered, but once *Green Cheese* was cancelled the door was simplified to rotate only.

The engine selected was the DH PS.43 Gyron Junior with the 11,400lbf (50.7kN) Bristol BE.33 and Armstrong Siddeley P.151N as alternatives. The estimated maximum speed at sea level was 640kt and Mach 0.98 up to 30,000ft (9,145m). The estimated gross weight was 39,308lb (17,830kg) with an overload weight of 46,000lb (20,865kg) with a rear bomb bay tank for a radius of action of 1,115nm (2,066km) or 1,300nm (2,410km) if the entire bay was used for fuel (as it would be for tanker operations).

Blackburn also proposed an all-weather fighter version using the BE.33 engine, increasing weight by 1,500lb (680kg) but increasing the speed to Mach 1.05 with a 45,000ft (13,715m) cruise ceiling and 22,500ft/min (6,858m/min) rate of climb.

The proposal for the development batch of either 10 or 20 aircraft included two or three 'flying shells'

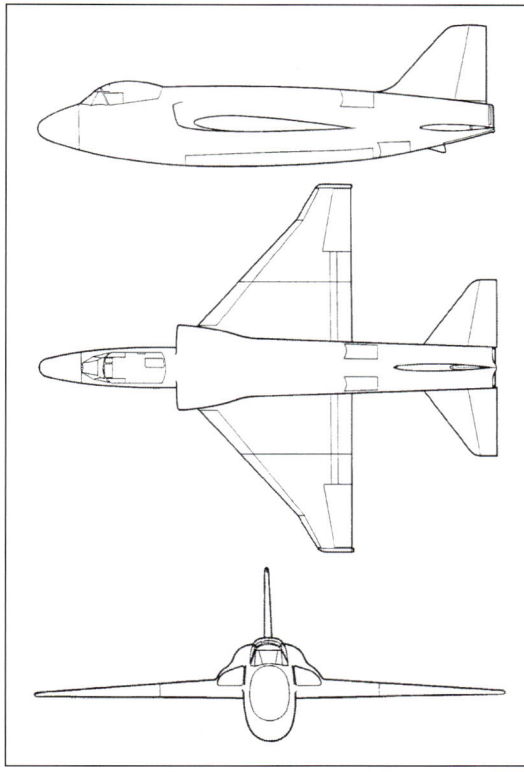

A general arrangement drawing of the delta-winged Fairey M.148T. *Leonardo UK via Tony Buttler Collection*

Fairey also made a scale model to accompany its tender, painted in Sky and Dark Sea Grey – the FAA's strike aircraft colours of the early 1950s. On this view of the surviving model can be seen the weapon bay doors and the upper and lower airbrakes. *Tony Buttler Collection*

Fairey's design was compact, a factor aided by the decision to fit a delta wing. The engines were mounted above the wing centre section with the weapon bay below the wing. *Tony Buttler Collection*

without cockpit pressurisation, bomb bay doors, radar and navigation equipment and wing and nose folding. The estimated first delivery was 33 months from the ITP, with the final development aircraft due for completion just under two years later.

Fairey studied numerous layouts before selecting a delta winged aircraft. The wing had a 9–5.3% t/c ratio to lower the structural weight. A low mounted tailplane was fitted aft and the two PS.43 Gyron Juniors were located in the upper rear fuselage with wing root intakes and tail pipe exhausts. The wings had a single fold point, leading edge slats and blown trailing edge flaps (no details on how this worked were presented to the MoS). The estimated approach speed with blowing was 112kt or 121kt without. The two crew sat side by side; the bomb bay in the lower fuselage had retracting doors with front and rear fairings to reduce drag when opened. Lowering gear and 'push off' equipment would be provided for *Green Cheese* and the TMB.

The estimated gross weight was 39,500lb (17,917kg). Maximum speed at sea level would be 571kt with a range of 1,442nm (2,670km) on full internal fuel or 1,850nm (4,430km) with two 300gal (1,364L) overload tanks, pushing the weight to 45,000lb (20,412kg). The estimated first delivery was three years from the ITP, with 69 months required before the 20th development aircraft was completed.

Fairey had wanted Rolls-Royce to develop a lightweight Avon instead of using the Gyron Junior. In lieu of this, they offered a single Avon with a larger 45ft (13.7m) span wing of 550ft² (51.2m²), the maximum sea level speed dropping to 560kt but the gross weight remaining unchanged.

Short Brothers & Harland aimed to produce a supersonic aircraft with high manoeuvrability to ensure a long service life (the author doubts that they would have foreseen the Buccaneer lasting to 1994!) The resulting PD.13 was the most technically advanced of the contenders. It was a tailless swept wing design based on earlier work for the S.B.1 jet bomber to Specification B.35/46 (a V-Force 'insurance') and S.B.4 research aircraft. The wing was an 'aero-isoclinic' unit as devised by Professor Geoffrey Hill back in the 1930s with all-moving wing tip controllers for lateral control (giving a theoretical 800°/sec rate of roll!) The wing had 40° leading edge sweep with t/c of 10% at the root and 6% at the tip and was made up of two spars, which took most of the bending and torsion stresses. Wing folded was provided. The inner wing had integral tanks forward of the spars, the main undercarriage retracted

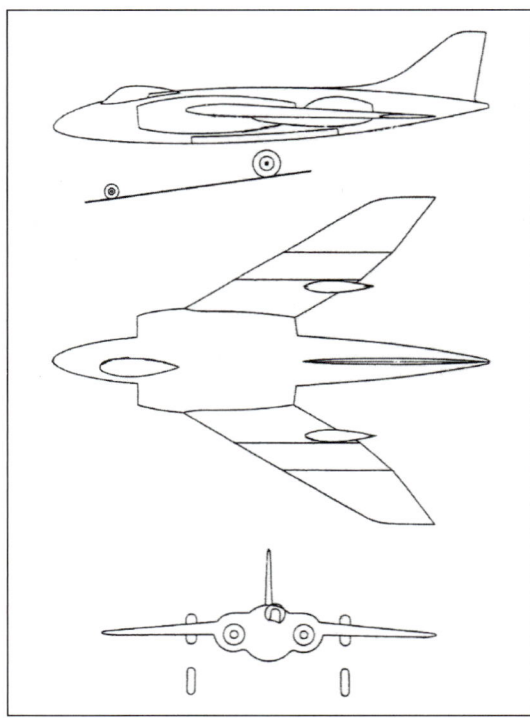

A general arrangement drawing of the Short PD.13. The pilot's cockpit was offset to port with the observer sitting in the fuselage to starboard. *Short Brothers via Author's Collection*

RIGHT The manufacturer's model of the PD.13 shows the layout of the aircraft with its raised offset pilot's canopy and the tailless swept wing layout with the all-moving wing tip controllers. *Short Brothers via Tony Buttler Collection*

CENTRE RIGHT This top-view of the model shows wing layout to effect. The trailing edge pods housed the main undercarriage. *Short Brothers via Tony Buttler Collection*

RIGHT The model reveals the deflected jet pipes at the 38.4° take-off setting. *Short Brothers via Tony Buttler Collection*

into underwing nacelles. At the wing roots were the 12,500lbf (55.6kN) Avon RA.19, providing ample thrust to use jet exhaust deflection to augment lift at low speeds, the exhaust pipes being deflected downwards 38.4° for take off and 52° for landing.

The fuselage was of conventional construction, the crew sat side by side; the pilot in a raised cockpit offset to port and the observer sat lower within the fuselage to reduce drag. The bomb bay featured a rotating door and a lowering floor. No in-flight refuelling probe was offered. Estimated gross weight carrying a TMB was 40,000lb (18,145kg), rising to 40,520lb (18,380kg) with *Green Cheese*. Maximum speed at sea level was 658kt and 616kt at 30,000ft (9,145m) and it attain Mach 1.0 in level flight using emergency power. The sea level rate of climb was 11,800ft/min (3,597m/min) at 39,600lb (17,960kg); the operational ceiling was 34,800ft (10,610m). The estimated first delivery was 30 months from the ITP, with almost five years elapsing before the 20th development aircraft was completed.

Westland had perhaps the best knowledge of jet deflection of any company within the industry, having converted Gloster Meteor F.3 RA490 in collaboration with the National Gas Turbine Establishment with exhaust deflecting cascades during 1953. The designers preferred jet deflection to flap blowing because there was no power loss from tapping the engine compressors and changes in the rate of descent could be made smoothly without change of trim or fore and aft accelerations. The jet pipes with two sequential rotating joints would deflect to 11° for normal flight, 28° for take off and 45° for landing. The 6,830lbf (30.4kN) PS.43 Gyron Junior was selected but Westland would have preferred a more powerful engine like the BE.33. Airframe heating was countered by steel and titanium panels under the wings.

A semi-delta wing was fitted with a broad chord inner wing section and the twin tail fins were located on two booms which separated the inner and outer wing sections as fences, which improved the stiffness of the wing at the fold hinge line. Large elevators of 3ft (0.91m) chord were fitted at the trailing edge of the inner wings for ample control at low speeds. The outer wings had ailerons and drooped leading edges to prevent tip stalling at high angles of incidence. The low wing loading gave good manoeuvrability. Brake flaps were fitted above and below the fuselage just behind the weapon bay, which had a lowering beam for the weapons. Fuel was carried in the upper fuselage and inner wings with a retractable refuelling probe on the portside of the cockpit. A two-position undercarriage gave a tail down attitude for take-off and a nose-down attitude for landing. The two crew sat in tandem in a staggered arrangement to provide the observer with a forward field of vision. The short fuselage meant that a folding nose was not required.

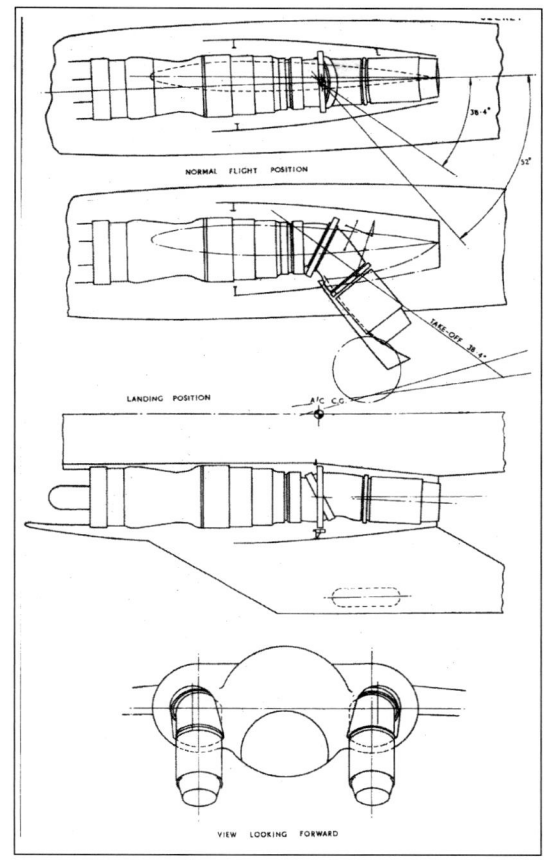

This technical drawing reveals the details of the jet pipe deflection system using sequential rotating joints. *Short Brothers via Tony Buttler Collection*

A conventional design with underwing podded engines and supersonic flap blowing was drawn up for comparative studies.

The estimated gross weight was 40,915lb (18,560kg). Maximum speed at sea level was 585kt and 490kt at 35,000ft (10,670m) with a sea level rate of climb of 8,300ft/min (2,530m/min) at 30,500lb (13,835kg). From a start date of January 1955, the estimated first flight of the aerodynamic

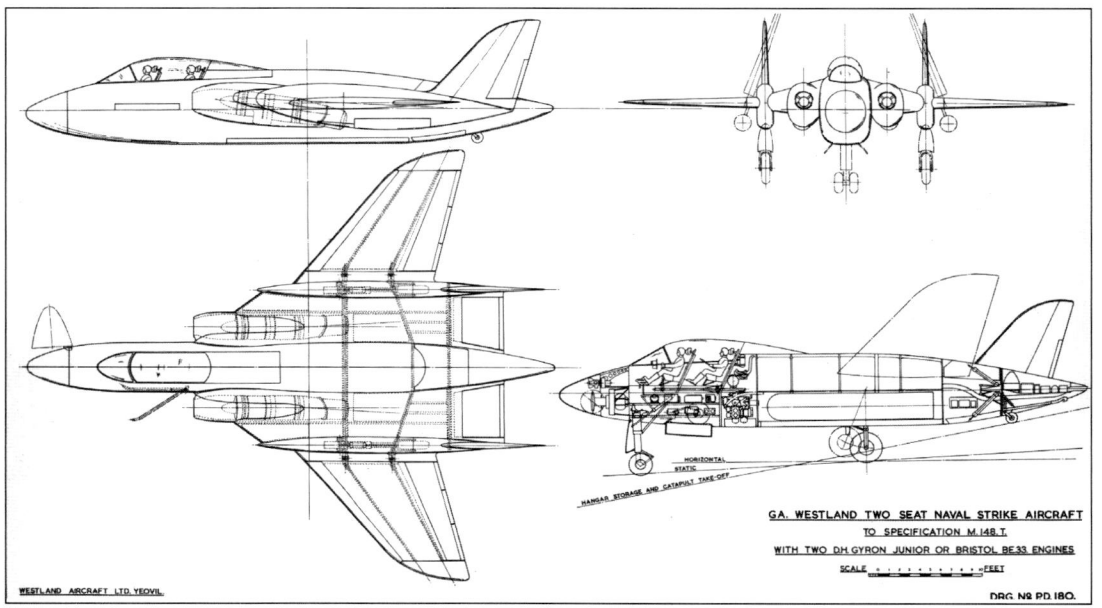

A general arrangement drawing of Westland's M.148T submission. The object in the weapon bay is *Green Cheese*. Note the retractable refuelling probe on the port side, beside the cockpit. *Leonardo UK via Jeremy Graham*

WINGS OVER THE FLEET

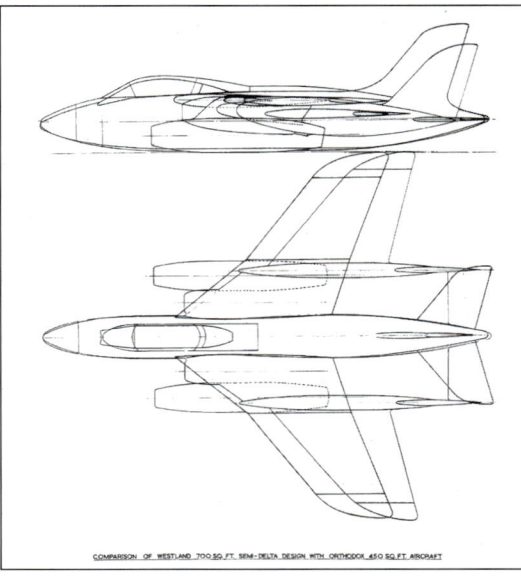

Westland compared its tailless delta design with a conventional swept-wing having underwing engine nacelles. The area of the delta wing was 700ft² (65.1m²) and that of the swept wing only 450ft² (41.8m²). *Leonardo UK via Tony Buttler Collection*

This ventral view reveals the deflecting jet pipe nozzle layout and the broad chord inner wing sections with large elevators for sufficient control authority when using deflected thrust. *Tony Buttler Collection*

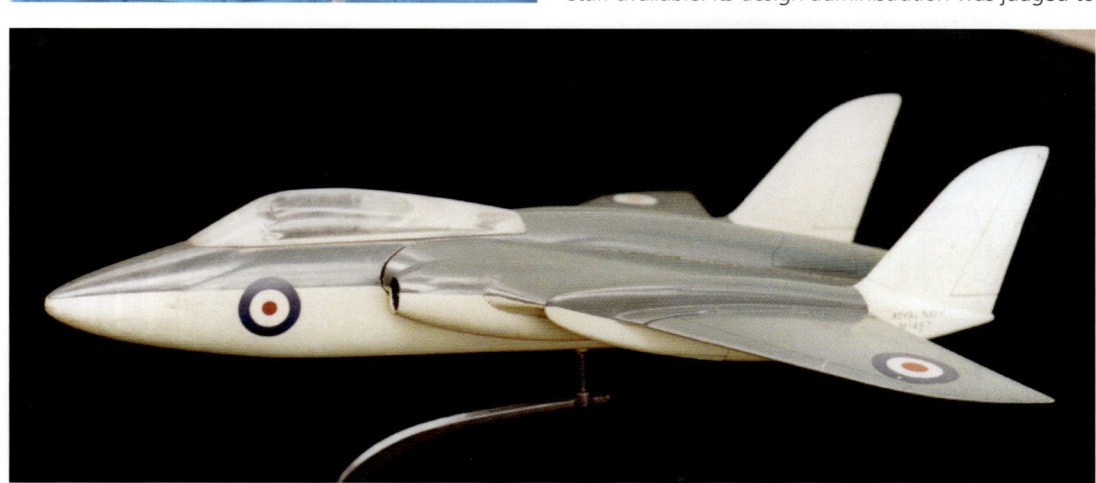

The manufacturer's model survives today. *Tony Buttler Collection*

of the delta wing – this small engine had a diameter of 20in (50.8cm). The wing had inner leading edge slats, the outer wing sections folding; the t/c ratio was 7%. The rest of the design was conventional, with side-by-side seating, a foldable nose for carrier stowage and the *Green Cheese* and the TMB would be semi-recessed into a shallow bomb bay. No weight or performance estimates have been found.

Saro's unsubmitted P.178 designs featured a swept wing of 8% t/c ratio with a gross weight of 40,000lb with a 4,000lb (1,814kg) bombload, which included a TMB. The fuselage was conventional and had side-by-side seating. The P.178/1 was powered by PS.37 Gyron Junior engines mounted dorsally in the upper fuselage with exhausts each side of the vertical tail. The slightly larger P.178/2 had the Gyrons Juniors in nacelles on the upper surface of the wings.

The MoS now had to assess the tenders and guidance was issued that Hawker and Westland should be reviewed last. JR Webber of the RD Projects Department began in early November by assessing the companies and their current workloads. AWA had recently begun submitting its own designs again, including the promising AW.166 supersonic research aircraft to Specification ER.134T in competition with the Bristol Type 188. The MoS judged the design team to be young and of good quality. Production-wise, the company was building Hawker Sea Hawks but had nothing else on the horizon and the design team required expansion by 40–60 staff. Blackburn's work on the B.101 Beverley tactical transport would cease by 1956, the company had extensive naval experience and had drawn with Westland for Specification N.114T, although there were some doubts about the quality of their manufacturing workmanship (pushing them into last place in this category.) Fairey was heavily involved in the Gannet, Ultra-Light helicopter, Rotodyne and the supersonic FD.2 Delta. Recruiting enough additional design staff was impossible and Fairey's suggestion of sub-contracting was rejected. This seemed to rule out Fairey. Shorts only had the S.B.6 Seamew light anti-submarine aircraft and S.C.1 VTOL research aircraft in development and had ample staff available. Its design administration was judged to

'flying shell' prototype was spring 1957 with the development batch completed by December 1959. The company admitted that additional design staff or a sub-contractor would be needed to meet the anticipated workload. A full-scale mock-up and a cockpit mock-up were built at Yeovil.

Hawker shared Fairey's desire to use a Rolls-Royce engine. Foregoing the Gyron Junior, the P.1108 had four RB.115 turbojets under the trailing edge root

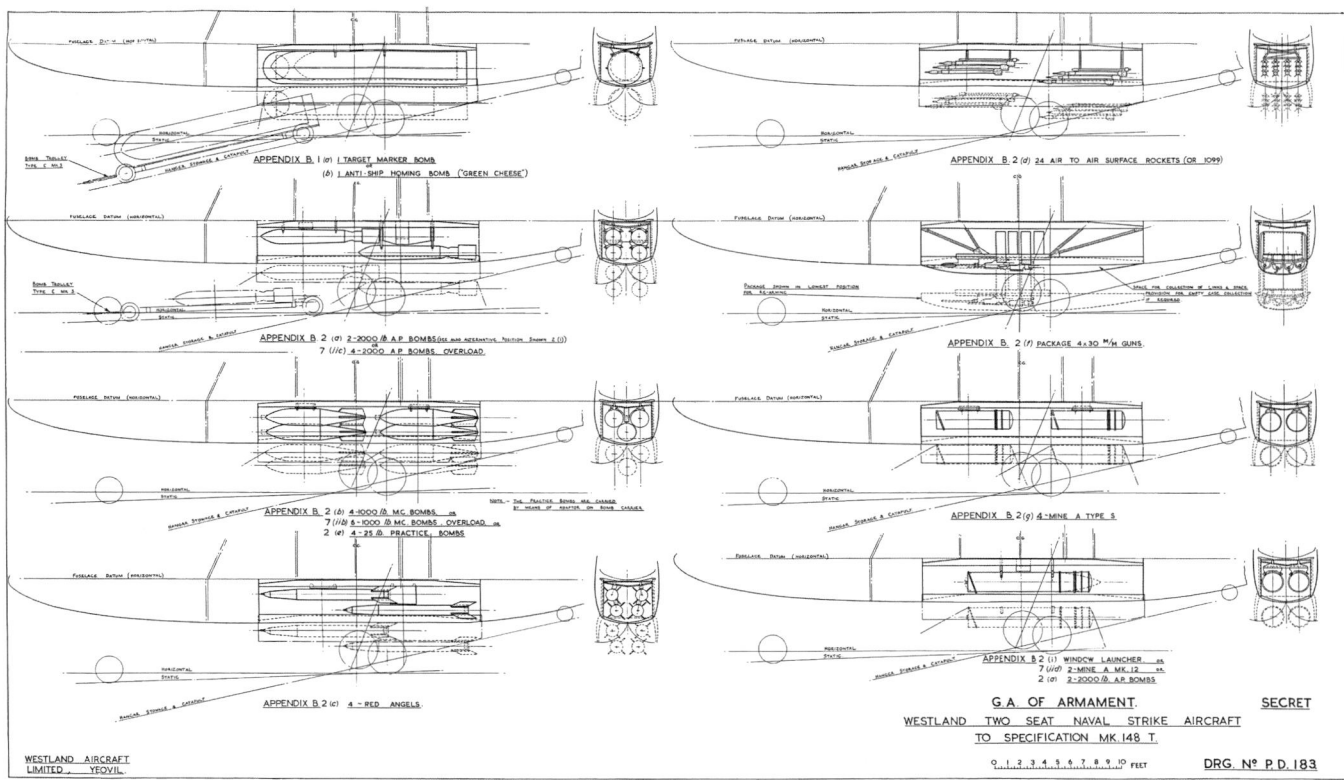

The loadout of the various weapons called for under M.148T were implemented by Westland. From top right clockwise: 60lb (27kg) RPs, quadruple 30mm ADEN cannon pack, four mines, two 2,000lb (907kg) mines or *Window* (chaff) dispensers, four *Red Angels*, six 1,000lb (454kg) bombs, four 2,000lb bombs or one *Green Cheese* or TMB. *Leonardo UK via Jeremy Graham*

Hawker and Sydney Camm had little interest in M.148T but were persuaded to sketch up a basic design. *BAE Systems via Tony Buttler Collection*

This official artwork of the P.1108 shows the layout of the four Rolls-Royce RB.115 turbojets and the ventral fairing which covered a semi-conformally carried *Green Cheese* missile. *BAE Systems via Tony Buttler Collection*

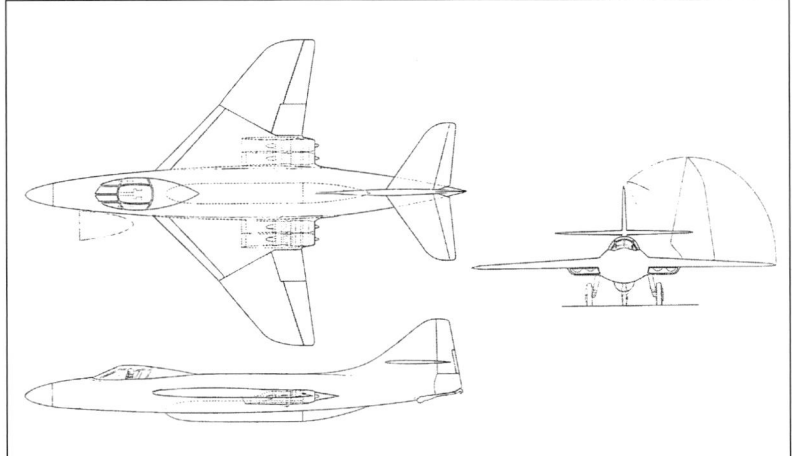

be the best in the industry. Hawker and Westland were only briefly assessed, the former was overworked with Hunters and other fighter work and Westland's admission of manpower shortages implied hiring another 100 staff or sub-contracting 60% of the detail design to another firm.

The Tender Design Conference took place at the MoS headquarters at St Giles Court on 3 December 1954 with GWH Gardner, the Director General Technical Development (Air) as Chairman. It began by immediately casting aside Hawker and Westland, the latter on account of insufficient resources and its proposal was assessed as having "little merit." The M.148T would prove to be Westland's last military fixed-wing design.

The remaining tenders had comparable; maximum dive speed limits, the PD.13 just failed the high-altitude cruise speed requirement and the Fairey

WINGS OVER THE FLEET

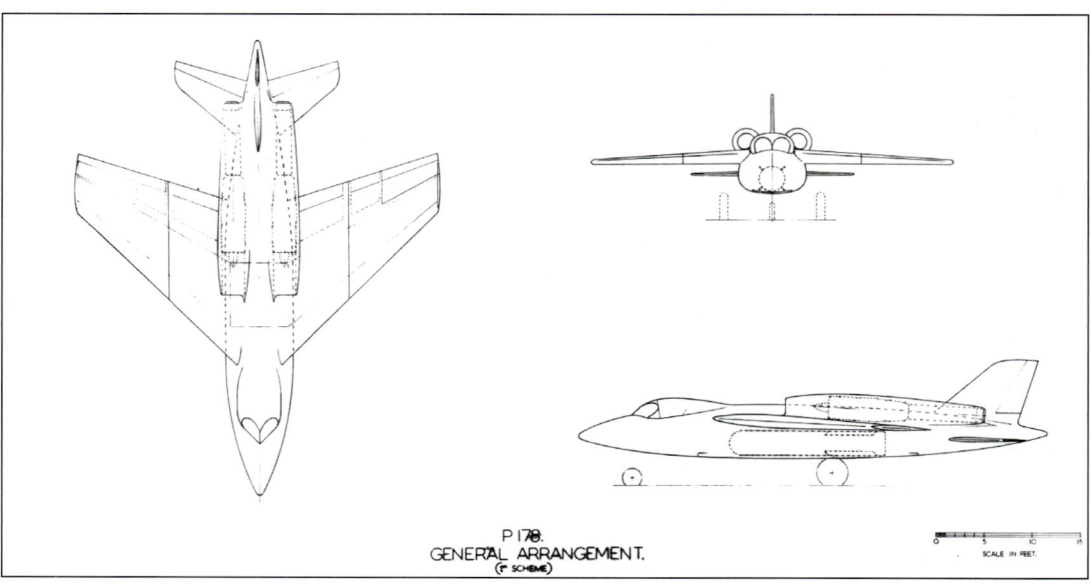

Saro did not officially tender the P.178 to M.148T and NA.39 but the design was obviously intended to meet those requirements. The P.178/1 was largely conventional apart from the dorsal engine location. *Tony Buttler Collection*

design missed it by a large margin. The B.103 and PD.13 had a large margin of maximum speed over the other contenders. The AW.168, B.103 and Fairey design had supersonic blowing, but did not rely on it to meet the performance requirements, whereas the PD.13 was reliant on jet deflection. Both the AW.168 and PD.13 were judged to be heavy.

The B.103 was favoured due to its extensive wind tunnel work and satisfactory blowing scheme, but it was also clear that more wind tunnel data would be required. The PD.13 with its 'aero-isoclinic' wing and jet deflection was advanced but had the most technical unknowns and was possibly over-engineered given that it was not a genuinely supersonic aircraft. Up to this point there had been no fully successful tailless aircraft and the MoS was worried about the implications for deck landing and any delays caused by the required additional flight testing.

Some concerns were raised by the lack of experience with rotating bomb bay doors with guided weapons specialist Commander RGB Roe wondering if *Green Cheese* would work properly if it was launched inverted in the rotated position. Fairey's bomb bay design was judged to be poor.

In terms of future growth, the B.103 seemed the best offering with a good equipment installation and ease of maintenance. The Royal Aircraft Establishment (RAE) preferred the more conventional AW.168, arguing that it was the only design likely to be ready to enter service in 1960. The Naval Staff's response was that it would prefer the B.103 in 1961 to the AW.168 in 1960. Fairey's design was dropped leaving the top three as B.103, AW.168 and PD.13.

A policy meeting was held immediately after the Tender Design Conference and some consideration was given to ordering the B.103 and AW.168 and halting whichever was judged to be inferior following completion of wind tunnel tests, but this still might have been a tough decision to make. AE Woodward Nutt, now serving as the Principal Director of Research

The Saro P.178/2 moved the Gyron Juniors to the wings, which were slightly enlarged in area and span. *Tony Buttler Collection*

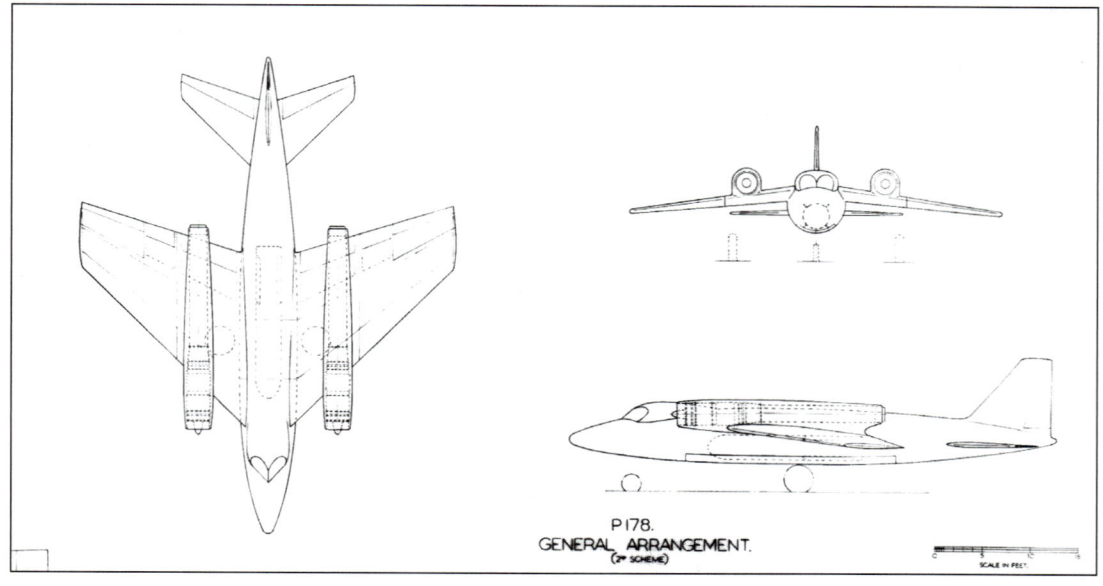

Naval Requirement NR/A.39 & Specification M.148T designs

	AW.168	Blackburn B.103	Fairey M.148	Short PD.13	Westland M.148	Hawker P.1108	Saro P.178	Blackburn Buccaneer S.1
Span	47ft 6in (14.48m); 23ft 0in (7.01m) folded	42ft 6in (12.95m)	42ft 0in (12.8m)	38ft 1in (11.61m)	43ft 0in (13.11m)	40ft 0in (12.19m)	P.178/1 37ft 6in (11.43m); P.178/2 39ft 0in (11.89m)	42ft 4in (12.90m); 19ft 11in (6.07m) folded
Length	59ft 9in (18.21m); 51ft 0in (15.54m) folded	61ft 6in (18.75m)	51ft 0in (15.54m)	51ft 0in (15.54m)	50ft 10in (15.49m)	58ft 0in (17.68m)	P.178/1 48ft 9in (14.86m); P.178/2 51ft 0in (15.54m)	63ft 5in (19.33m); 51ft 10in (15.80m) folded
Wing area	555ft² (51.6m²)	535ft² (49.7m²)	500ft² (46.5m²)	482ft² (44.8m²)	863ft² (80.3m²)	510ft² (47.4m²)	P.178/1 470ft² (43.7m²); P.178/2 520ft² (48.4m²)	514.7ft² (47.82m²)
t/c ratio	8.5%	9% root, 6% tip	9% root, 5.3% tip	10% root, 7% tip	?	7%	8%	9.25% root, 6% tip
All-up weight	40,000lb (18,145kg)	39,309lb (17,830kg)	39,500lb (17,915kg)	40,520lb (18,380kg)	40,915lb (18,560kg)	?	40,000lb (18,145kg)	45,000lb (20,410kg) full load
Powerplant	2x Gyron Junior PS.43, 7,000lbf (31.1kN)	2x Gyron Junior PS.43, 7,000lbf (31.1kN)	2x Gyron Junior PS.43, 7,000lbf (31.1kN)	2x Avon RA.19, 12,500lbf (55.6kN)	2x Gyron Junior PS.42, 6,830lbf (30.4kN)	4x RB.115	2x Gyron Junior PS.37	2x Gyron Junior DGJ.1, 7,100lbf (31.5kN)
Max speed	585kt (1,084km/h) at SL	640kt (1,186km/h) at SL; Mach 0.97-0.98 up to 30,000ft (9,145m)	571kt (1,059km/h) at SL; 502kt (930km/h) at 30,000ft (9,145m)	658kt (1,220km/h) at SL; 616kt (1,141km/h) at 30,000ft (9,145m)	585kt (1,085km/h) at SL, 490kt (907km/h) at 30,000ft (9,145m)	?	?	580kt (1,075km/h)/Mach 0.875 at SL
Rate of climb	?	?	5,010ft/min (1,527m/min) at SL	11,800ft/min (3,595m/min) at SL at 39,600lb (17,965kg)	8,300ft/min (2,530m/min) at SL at 30,500lb (13,835kg)	?	?	
Service ceiling	?	35,000ft (10,670m)	?	34,800ft (10,605m)	?	?	?	50,000ft (15,240m)
Range	510nm (945km) with max bombload	2,230nm (4,130km), overload; 2,600nm (4,815km) with max bomb bay tanks	1,442nm (2,671km); 1,851nm (3,428km) with 2x 300gal (1,364L) overload tanks	?	?	?	?	1,500nm (2,785km) normal range
Armament	1x Green Cheese or Red Beard, 4x Red Angel, 4,000lb (1,814kg) bombload, 24x RPs	1x Green Cheese or Red Beard, 4x Red Angel, 4,000lb (1,814kg) bombload, 24x RPs	1x Green Cheese or Red Beard, 4x Red Angel, 4,000lb (1,814kg) bombload, 24x RPs	1x Green Cheese or Red Beard, 4x Red Angel, 4,000lb (1,814kg) bombload, 24x RPs	1x Green Cheese or Red Beard, 4x Red Angel, 8,000lb (3,629kg) bombload (overload), 24x RPs	1x Green Cheese or Red Beard, 4x Red Angel, 4,000lb (1,814kg) bombload, 24x RPs	1x Red Beard, 4,000lb (1,814kg) bombload	1x Red Beard, 4,000lb (1,814kg) internal bombload, 4,000lb (1,814kg) external bombload, 4x AGM-12 Bullpup

WINGS OVER THE FLEET

Alternative NA.39 Part One. Armstrong Whitworth AW.168 Argonaut S.1s of 800 NAS attempt to send the crippled tanker SS *Torrey Canyon* to the bottom in an attempt to limit the fuel spill in March 1967. The AW.168 was the second place choice to fulfil NA.43, being pipped to the post by the Blackburn B.103's more sophisticated flap blowing and area-ruled aerodynamics. *Luciano Alviani*

Alternative NA.39 Part Two. A Short Brothers PD.13 Scythe S.1 tosses a *Red Beard* tactical nuclear weapon towards a Soviet surface task force supporting an amphibious assault in Northern Norway as another *Red Beard* explodes on the far side of the Soviet cruisers, including the helicopter carrier *Moskva*. The PD.13 finished third in the NA.43 evaluation, it offered the best speed performance but its tailless aero-isoclinic winged layout was judged technically risky. *Luciano Alviani*

and Development (Aircraft), felt that shorter development steps would be less ambitious and therefore reducing the risks of delay, in his view the AW.168 should be selected. The 'Size and Shape' policy also had to be considered; spending £400,000 assisting Blackburn seemed to send the wrong message but the Chairman reasoned the money would be spent elsewhere in the industry in any case and Blackburn's design was of sufficient quality to overrule the policy. The MoS and Admiralty opted for the B.103 on 9 December. Hal Watson at AWA was understandably disappointed with being runner-up for a third time.

Buccaneer

Barry Laight's team now worked on transitioning the B.103 – eventually named Buccaneer – from the drawing board to the factory floor. The Advisory Design Conference was held at St. Giles Court on 17 March 1955 to discuss the requirements of Specification M.148D, Issue 3, which was issued to Blackburn on 18 April. The planned entry into service was pushed back to 1961.

The airframe received its area ruling, which helped to reduce the stresses of low-altitude turbulence and provide a smoother ride for the crew. The stresses caused by the turbulent low level air required the wing structure – including single-piece wing skins – to be milled from solid billets of metal and several structural members were machined from steel forgings. This strong construction easily met the required fatigue life of 3,000 flying hours of low level flights and at least 1,000 carrier landings. There were some early corrosion problems with the dorsal magnesium fuselage skinning given the salty environment.

With an eye to what we would call stealth features today, M.148D called for careful design to minimise infrared radiation and the radar echoes produced by the aircraft. The RAE carried out radar echoing area measurements using scale models and an optical simulator in 1962, recommending using Plessey DX.3 Radar Absorbing Material (RAM) in the engine intakes to reduce radar returns at centimetric wavelengths. It was proposed to use air cooling for the jet pipes to reduce the infrared signature. More active defences were planned to include a radar warning receiver (RWR) and a bomb bay ECM pack and/or bomb bay chaff dispensers.

The DH Gyron Junior Mk.101 engines were rated at 7,100lbf (31.5kN) and capable of supplying air to the boundary layer control (BLC) blowing system at a rate of 14.2lb/sec (6.44kg/sec). In November 1955 it was decided to fit all aircraft with an in-flight refuelling probe.

Ferranti was subcontracted to develop the navigation/attack system. The radars were the EMI ASV.21, Radar Ranging Mk.4 and *Yellow Lemon* Doppler navigation radar. Defensive aids would include the ARI.18105 *Blue Saga* RWR. Development of a wide-band radar jammer proved technically challenging and was replaced by Admiralty Requirement AW.389 for an S-band jammer. The nav/attack system was designed to achieve a Circular Error of Probability (CEP) – the radius of a circle inside which the probability of an impact point is 50% – of 750ft (228m) with the TMB.

Spec M.148D&P was issued on 12 August 1960 to cover the production aircraft. The requirements barely changed, except that the maximum take off weight was not to exceed 41,450lb (18,801kg) and the maximum landing weight was not to exceed 31,000lb (14,061kg). Following the cancellation of *Green Cheese* the ability to carry AGM-12 Bullpup ASMs was added and the avionics were updated to the Ferranti ARI.5930 *Blue Parrot* radar and ARI.5880 *Blue Jacket* Doppler navigation with a computer and a Mk.3 roller map display. A Strike Sight was fitted for the pilot, with an associated Control and Release Computer and it received radar range data from *Blue Parrot* and groundspeed from *Blue Jacket*. There was no way to input the target's

Development batch Blackburn Buccaneer S.1 XK488 was used for engine testing and is seen with an example of the DH Gyron Junior Mk.101 turbojet. *Blue Envoy Collection*

velocity, an omission for targeting ships. *Blue Jacket* was only effective down to 200ft (61m) and lost signal in climbs above 13°, in dives steeper than 7° or in banking turns at an angle greater than 6°.

The X-band *Blue Parrot* radar was developed from the AI.23 radar for surface-search (maximum range 240nm [444km] at 35,000ft [10,670m]) and terrain-following. The radar was linked to the LABS analogue computer which had accelerometers to measure the aircraft's vertical, lateral and longitudinal *g* forces to plot the correct pull-up manoeuvre for the Elliott

Development batch Buccaneers XK489 and XK487 in formation. The construction of a development batch using production jigs rather than building a handful of dedicated prototypes and the weapons system concept whereby the designers were integrating various sub-systems rather than just concentrating on the airframe were new innovations for the industry. *Terry Panopalis Collection*

WINGS OVER THE FLEET

"Forgive us for teaching our grandmother how to suck eggs, but this is our chicken – to continue the metaphor – and we like it, believe in it and want it to be the success we are convinced it can be."

COMMANDER ALAN JOHN LEAHY, 700Z FLIGHT INTENSIVE FLYING TRIALS UNIT, REPORT NO.16, 19 DECEMBER 1962

Brothers autopilot to 'toss' the *Red Beard* up and forwards towards the target while the Buccaneer made a hasty retreat. *Blue Parrot* also had a Radar Dive Bombing mode for diving attacks with conventional bombs with automatic bomb release, achieving an accuracy of 60ft (18m).

For the 'buddy' tanker role, a Flight Refuelling Ltd. Mk.20A refuelling pod would be carried under the wings (a bomb bay unit had originally been planned). The weapons load was 8,000lb (3,630kg) in the bay or 12,000lb (5,545kg) under the wings. For the reconnaissance role a weapon bay pack would carry a fan of three vertical F.95 Mk.4 cameras or one forward-facing and two oblique F.95s or one F.97 night camera with 200 photoflash cartridges.

The batch of 20 development aircraft was ordered on 2 June 1955. Each aircraft introduced new features as the line progressed from the initial 'flying shell' aerodynamic prototypes, the eighth aircraft onwards being built on production jigs. The second aircraft, XK487, had thicker wing skins for aerodynamic and flutter tests; XK488 was used for engine development; the fourth, XK489, was fully navalised with powered wing folding, folding nose and arrester hook and a four-tank fuel system (XK486–88 had eight tanks); XK490 had the rotating bomb bay door and underwing hardpoints; XK491 had a retractable refuelling probe and a slightly longer fuselage. The seventh aircraft, XK523, was the first with full electronics and nav/attack avionics – beginning dummy TMB carriage trials by July 1960 – while XK524 and XK525 spent most of their time on catapult and arrester gear clearance trials. XK530 was used to clear the carriage and release of Bullpup ASMs.

XK486 made its maiden flight at RAE Bedford on 30 April 1958 with Blackburn's Chief Test Pilot Lieutenant Commander (Lt Cdr) Derek Whitehead and observer BJ Watson aboard. Blackburn's flight test team at Holme-on-Spalding-Moor also included Deputy Chief Test Pilot Gartrell Richard Ian 'Sailor' Parker, John Goodwin 'Bobby' Burns and FAA test pilot Lt Cdr Edward Rosebury Anson (who was destined to be *Ark Royal's* final Captain in 1976 and retired in 1984 with the rank of Vice Admiral). Carrier trials began on 19 January 1960 aboard *Victorious* with XK523 making 14 successful deck landings, the following day XK489 made a total of 17 landings. 700Z Naval Air Squadron (NAS) formed as the Intensive Flying Trials Unit (IFTU) at RNAS Lossiemouth under the command of Lt Cdr Alan John Leahy on 7 March 1961.

An early Buccaneer S.2 is shown in this publicity photograph of the stores that it can carry. Most of these items were also carried by the Buccaneer S.1. From top to bottom, left to right: Mk.20A refuelling pod, two slipper fuel tanks and one drop tank; four AGM-12 Bullpup, rear bomb bay fuel tank; four 1,000lb (454kg) bombs, forward bomb bay fuel tank; 16 3in (76mm) rocket projectiles, two 2.6in (68mm) Matra SNEB rocket pods with RPs, one heavily airbrushed Red Beard tactical nuclear bomb; remainder of the 68mm RPs, eight 25lb (11kg) practice bombs. *Blue Envoy Collection*

This formation of 700Z NAS Buccaneers shows the different colour schemes adopted. XK534 is in all-over high-gloss anti-flash white for the nuclear role while XK532 and XK533 have Dark Sea Grey upper surfaces to enable them to blend into the seascape while flying at low level, making it more difficult for fighters at higher altitudes to spot them. *Blue Envoy Collection*

Buccaneer S.1 XN965 takes off from HMS *Eagle's* waist catapult. First flown on 6 August 1963, it was operated by 809 and 736 NAS, being retired by January 1971. It was then used by the RAE for cockpit noise trials and MRCA Tornado avionics testing. It was scrapped by 1980. *Blue Envoy Collection*

The early carrier landing trials led to some rudder modifications to improve the response to the pilot's control column movements. The heavy aircraft had a high longitudinal inertia to overcome on landing. Flight tests revealed that if the ailerons were drooped beyond 10° at low speeds, trimming the resulting nose-down attitude was difficult, so an electrically actuated flap was fitted to the tailplane to restore trim authority. If the deflection was beyond 12°, BLC had to be in operation to avoid stalling the wing (the usual deck landing configuration was 45° flap, 25° aileron droop and 25° tailplane). A set of 21 vortex generators was also added to the outer wings to reduce buffeting and counteract any pitch-up trim, but at the cost of reducing range by 12%. Airflow problems around the base of the tailplane at high speeds which led to severe vibration were cured by a new area ruled bullet fairing.

The second phase of carrier trials was marred by the loss of XK529 on 31 August 1961; the BLC failed during the catapult launch and the aircraft pitched up and stalled, crashing into the sea 1,500ft (457m) ahead of *Hermes*. Sadly, Lt Cdr O Brown and observer TD Dunn were both drowned. Blackburn conducted wind tunnel tests and analogue computer simulations to investigate the causes and possible solutions. Catapult trials at RAE Bedford highlighted problems maintaining the correct 13–14° angle of incidence and pitching-up following catapult launches. Blackburn advised on new flap and aileron droop settings and encouraging pilots to use the 'free stick' method – letting the aircraft choose by itself the optimal aerodynamic attitude just after launch, a method used with many carrier-based aircraft fitted with mechanical flight controls. The tail skid also needed some redesign to avoid damaging the arrester wires. By July 1962 56 launches and landings had been made aboard *Hermes* using XK530 and XK536 at landing weights up to 43,500lb (19,730kg) without problems, despite the 130kt landing speed.

The IFTU had to work out the bugs with the *Blue Parrot* radar and *Blue Jacket* Doppler system in

WINGS OVER THE FLEET

Buccaneer S.1 XN928 in an all-over high gloss anti-flash white paint finish for the nuclear strike role. *Terry Panopalis Collection*

The Buccaneer was designed for low altitude penetration flights in all weathers in order to fly under defending early warning radar coverage. Soon after the Buccaneer's introduction most land and carrier-based attack aircraft adopted this flight profile in an effort to avoid defensive SAM systems and anti-aircraft artillery. *Blue Envoy Collection*

partnership with Ferranti engineers – not without some friction when the unit's ground engineers tinkered with the bombing system to improve accuracy. The first successful demonstration of the Buccaneer's potential was Exercise Fairwind VII in June 1962, 14 sorties being flown against a North Sea convoy with attacks against single ships, the *Blue Parrot* radar picking up its targets within 100–140nm (185–259km) in heavy cloud or 180nm (333km) in clear conditions while the Type 80 early warning radar station at RAF Buchan did not detect the Buccaneers over these ranges.

Buccaneers XK525 and XK528 carried out 'long toss' attack mode clearance trials at the RAE's ranges at West Freugh with the *Red Beard* tactical nuclear bomb during 17 February to 30 September 1964. The nav/attack system – using the refined preset release equation it contained – achieved a 50% CEP of 600ft (183m), accuracy relying on the groundspeed data provided by the *Blue Jacket* Doppler radar. The attacks were made at 550kt at heights between 300 and 500ft (91 and 152m), with the bomb release during the pull up manoeuvre around 3.3nm (7km) away from the target. This performance bettered M.148D's specified 750ft (228m) 50% CEP.

Construction, technical development and Service trials went reasonably smoothly (though with some delays), but several aircraft were lost in accidents; XK529 as detailed above and XK486 due to a failure of the artificial horizon while flying in cloud on 5 October 1960, 'Sailor' Parker and his observer D Nightingale ejected safely (as a result a standby artificial horizon was added to all Buccaneers.) Sadly 'Sailor' Parker and his observer Gordon Copeman were killed on 19 February 1963 when Buccaneer S.1 XN952 crashed at Holme-on-Spalding Moor airfield during a LABS demonstration. They had ejected but landed in the wreckage. XK524 was lost following a tailplane stall during a test flight on 13 May 1965, the pilot Paul Millett and observer JR Harris ejecting safely.

A production order for 40 production aircraft was placed in October 1959 – the official name and designation Buccaneer S.1 (S for nuclear strike) being approved on 26 August 1960. The initial production aircraft, XN922, made its first flight from Holme on 23 January 1962 with the last S.1, XN973, being completed in December 1963. (All except the prototype were towed, backwards, on their undercarriage from the Brough factory to Holme-on-Spalding Moor for test flying.)

The first squadron, 801NAS at Lossiemouth, formed in July 1962 and went on its first Far East tour aboard the newly refitted *Ark Royal* on 20 February 1963. At the end of the year, they undertook tropical trials from RAF Tengah at Singapore, the results of which required several modifications to reduce the temperatures in the bomb bay, avionics compartments and the undercarriage bays. 700Z NAS was renumbered as 809 NAS as the Operational Flying School in January

The crews of a quartet of Buccaneer S.1s, headed by XN956 of 800 NAS, scramble into their cockpits aboard HMS *Eagle* in 1964. *Terry Panopalis Collection*

1963 and embarked aboard *Victorious* and *Eagle* (in March 1965 it was again renumbered as 736 NAS.) 800 NAS reformed in March 1964, participating in the Beria Patrol oil blockade of Rhodesia aboard *Eagle* in 1965 with support from Scimitar tanker aircraft of 800B Flight. The last frontline squadron was 803 NAS at Lossiemouth, forming in July 1967 as the Buccaneer Headquarters Squadron with a mix of S.1 and S.2 aircraft, four of its Buccaneers joining *Hermes* in the Far East.

During the NA.39 tender phase several of the design teams, including Barry Laight's, had been concerned about the Gyron Junior's lack of thrust. The more powerful Bristol BE.33 was thought to be the better choice, but this did not complete development. In June 1956 the MoS had suggested a future 'Thin Wing' version to reduce drag and increase speed, but Blackburn's calculations revealed no worthwhile improvement. Once in service it was clear that the aircraft could not be catapulted at maximum take-off weight, the situation being worse when launching from *Centaur* or *Hermes* in tropical conditions the 2,750–4,500lb (1,245–2,040kg) weight reduction reducing the hi-lo strike radius from 290nm (537km) to just 135–100nm (250–185km). The only solution was to take-off with a reduced fuel load and top up the tanks from a Scimitar or Buccaneer 'buddy' tanker. It was also possible to stall the engine inlet guide vanes, a loss of thrust and a crash being the frequent outcome if there was insufficient altitude to effect recovery. Work began to find a new engine (see below) and consequently the Buccaneer S.1's service life was short, with replacement by the improved Buccaneer

After the Spey-powered S.2 entered service the S.1 was relegated to training duties. XN965 was on the strength of 736 NAS at Lossiemouth in August 1969. Following retirement in 1972, it went to the MOD for Panavia Tornado avionics testing until ending up on the Pendine Ranges by 1988. *Terry Panopalis Collection*

The Buccaneer S.1 was initially equipped with a retractable refuelling probe in the nose. Refuelling trials involved the sixth development batch aircraft XK491. A sortie on 3 July 1959 saw XK491 making approach and dry contacts (i.e. no fuel transferred) with Flight Refuelling Limited's converted English Electric Canberra B.2 WH734. *Blue Envoy Collection*

S.2 from 1965, although the last S.1s would not retire until December 1970. Being the first aircraft to embrace the hazardous world of fast low level flying meant that mishaps were common and a third of the 40 aircraft were lost in accidents.

Odds and sods

Despite the selection of the B.103 to meet NA.39 there were numerous other private ventures. Supermarine continued to offer a range of single and two-seat developments of the Scimitar during 1954–56 as an interim solution (see Chapter 3).

Sydney Camm at Hawker had been focusing his efforts on the P.1121 multi-role fighter which the company had pursued as a private venture since 1956. No official interest was shown by the RAF or the MoS who felt that Hawker had not grasped the concept of weapon system development which considered that the designers had to consider all the aspects of what made a military aircraft work including systems, engines, avionics and armament and integrate their development accordingly. Blackburn had mastered this for the Buccaneer programme with success.

In 1957 the US Naval attaché had visited Kingston to gather information on a potential carrier-based version for the USN. In April 1958 a two-seat, carrier-based version was drawn up, the two crew sitting side by side in a wider fuselage. The 37ft (11.2m) span wings were modified to fold from the roots for a folding span of 28ft (8.5m). The nose of the 60ft 6in (18.4m) long fuselage folded to 51ft (15.5m) for carrier stowage. The engine was a Bristol Siddeley Olympus 21R with fully-variable reheat. Internal fuel capacity was 1,200gal (5,455L) with provision for two 150gal (682L) drop tanks under the wings and a retractable refuelling probe was fitted on the port side of the fuselage below the cockpit. The armament comprised a semi-recessed TMB in the belly and RP pods or bombs under the wings. The radar was probably the AI.23 or *Blue Parrot*. No performance data is known, but the basic P.1121 was expected to reach Mach 1.3 at sea level and Mach 2.3 at altitude. Unable to continue financing the project without any orders in prospect, work on the half completed prototype stopped during 1958. Today the remains of the P.1121 reside at the Brooklands Museum in Surrey.

The RAF wanted its own low-altitude tactical nuclear bomber to replace the Canberra. Requirement GOR.339 began to be drawn up in 1956. Until it was formally released the industry pitched some interim ideas, many of which were based on the FAA's latest aircraft: a de-navalised B.103A, a strike version of the planned extended fuselage DH.110 Sea Vixen and the Type 565 Scimitar development. The RAF cast all these aside and GOR.339 was released, becoming ever more ambitious in its performance targets and avionic capabilities. In the summer of 1958 the Minister of Defence Duncan Sandys, with his usual keen eye for savings, asked whether NA.39 was justified given the apparent duplication with GOR.339. The Admiralty was unequivocal in its support for NA.39 as a means of deterrence and long-range strike in all weathers in 'Global' (i.e. nuclear) or 'Limited' wars around the world. Both sets of requirements went ahead with Sandys' (and the Treasury's) blessing. The eventual fate of the resulting British Aircraft Corporation (BAC) TSR.2 is well known and need not concern us here, except to note that several of the GOR.339 contenders had an eye towards naval use.

Blackburn refined the B.103A into the B.108 which kept its naval features but had a redesigned cockpit and D.GJ.4 Gyron Juniors with cooled turbine blades. Blackburn considered that a transonic aircraft was much cheaper and of less development risk, offering to modify the 11th Buccaneer development aircraft as the prototype – the contrasting fates of the Buccaneer and the TSR.2 would seem ample proof of that statement.

'Bill Tamblin's design team at DH Christchurch offered an advanced design with a variable-

BUCCANEER – NOT JUST A WEAPON

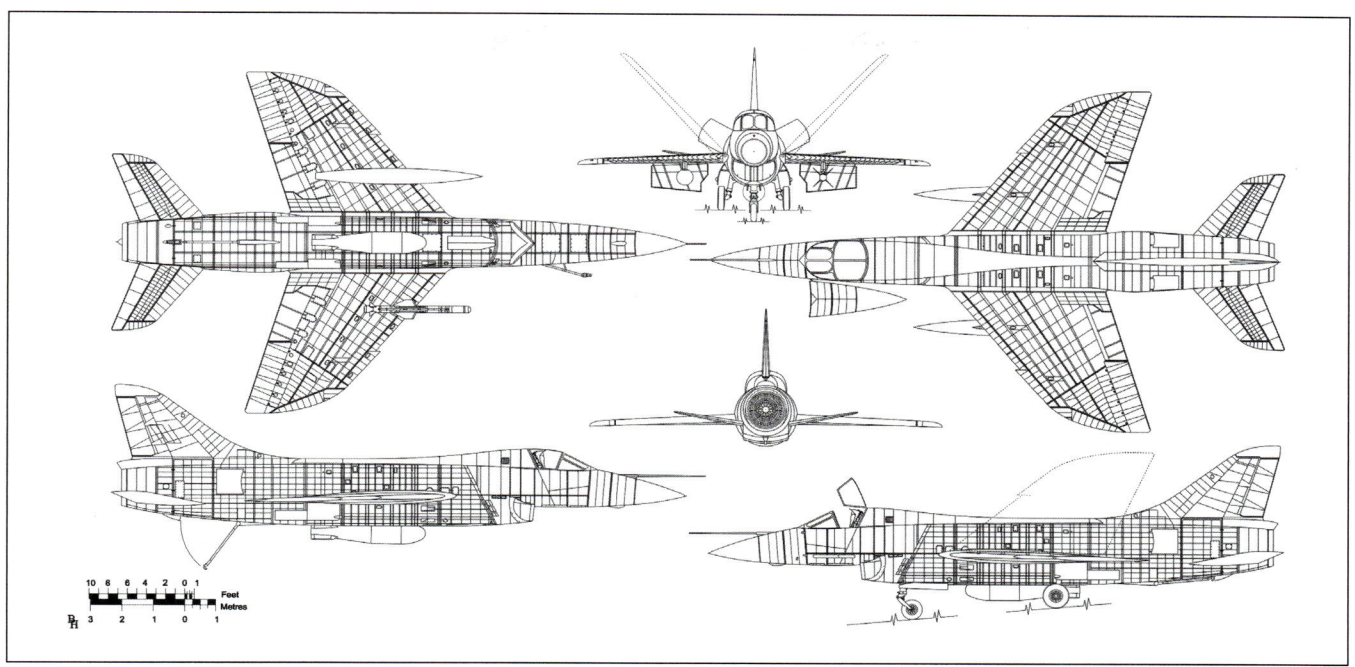

incidence wing like that of the American Vought F8U Crusader carrier-based fighter. Under the wings were two Rolls-Royce RB.142R Medway turbofans for a maximum speed of Mach 1.3 at sea level. Given the use of the variable-incidence wing well suited to carrier operations it is of little surprise that Tamblin made a brief study of the naval strike role, alongside use as a fighter.

Vickers Aviation completed a brochure in May 1958 on a naval strike fighter variant of its Type 571 submission, including swapping the single RB.142R with two smaller engines. None of these submissions had much impact on the Admiralty (and the last thing the RAF or MoS wanted was naval requirements further complicating GOR.339) but within a year they would be looking at similar aircraft (see Chapter 10).

This general arrangement drawing of the two-seat naval Hawker P.1121 variant is reconstructed from original Hawker technical drawings but includes some speculation to fill in the missing details. While this proposal may have offered a good supersonic replacement for the Sea Vixen or the Scimitar, it was not in the same league as the Buccaneer in regard to payload, range and low altitude attack capability. *Barrie Hygate & Paul Martell-Mead*

Interim Carrier-capable strikers

	Hawker P.1121 (naval)	Blackburn B.108	DH GOR.339
Span	37ft 0in (11.2m); 28ft 0in (8.5m) folded	42ft 6in (12.95m); 19ft 11in (6.07m) folded	34ft 0in (10.36m)
Length	60ft 6in (18.4m); 51ft 0in (15.54m) folded	65ft 6in (19.96m)	67ft 6in (20.57m)
Wing area	?	500ft² (46.5m²)	440ft² (40.9m²)
t/c ratio	5.1% root, 3.8% tip	7.5%	5%
All-up weight	?	49,000lb (22,225kg), 600nm (1,110km) range	48,750lb (21,115kg), 600nm (1,110km) range
Powerplant	1x Olympus 21R	2x Gyron Junior DGJ.4, 7,700lbf (34.2kN)	2x RB.142R, 14,000lbf (62.2kN) dry, 22,400lbf (99.6kN) reheat
Max speed	Mach 1.3 at SL; Mach 2.3 at altitude (estimated)	628kt (1,163km/h)/Mach 0.95 at SL; 650kt (1,204km/h)/Mach 1.05 diving	Mach 1.04 at SL, Mach 1.3 at SL with reheat; Mach 2.0 at altitude
Rate of climb	?	?	5,000ft (457m) to 50,000ft (15,240) in 1.4min
Service ceiling	?	?	60,000ft (18,290m)
Armament	1x Red Beard, bombs and RP pods	1x Red Beard, 4,000lb (1,814kg) internal bombload, 36x 3in (76mm) or 74x 2in (50mm) RPs internal, 4,000lb (1,814kg) external bombload	1x Red Beard, 2x 1,000lb (454kg) bombs internal, 24x 3in (76mm) or 84x 2in (50mm) RPs internal, 2x 1,000lb bombs external, 23x 3in or 74x 2in RPs external

Straining at the leash. With the nosewheel high in the area for the correct angle of incidence for a catapult launch this Buccaneer S.2 is held back by the catapult bridle as the two RB.168 Speys spool up to full power. In enlarged intakes and fixed refuelling probe are key distinguishing features of the S.2. *Blue Envoy Collection*

Buccaneer S.2

The Buccaneer S.1 was limited by the thrust available from its two Gyron Juniors and further development of the engine seemed unlikely to cure the situation. A 1956 proposal to fit the 10,000lbf (44.4kN) PS.50 Gyron Junior was abandoned as the wing spars needed modifications to fit the 3in (76cm) wider diameter jet pipes and increased the weight by 500lb (227kg). Blackburn began looking at alternatives (in May 1963 Blackburn was acquired Hawker Siddeley Aviation, becoming the Blackburn Division).

Bristol offered the 7,000lbf (31.2kN) BE.55A compound turbojet with a two-stage fan using the high pressure compressor from the Orpheus Or.3. Rolls-Royce had recently developed the RB.163 Spey turbofan for the Hawker Siddeley Trident airliner and Blackburn felt that a military version would be more suitable than the BE.55A. Rolls-Royce agreed, leading to the unreheated 11,200lbf (49.8kN) RB.168-1A Spey Mk.101 turbofan. The spars needed to be modified for the larger jet pipe diameter. Other changes included modifications to the BLC to cope with the hotter tapped air, a strengthened undercarriage, increased span tailplane, a new alternating current electrical system (enabling the troublesome air turbine alternator to be removed) and cockpit layout improvements included the new Mk.3 Pilot's Display Unit.

The Defence Resources and Policy Committee approved the proposal on 9 November 1960 and the Treasury also gave its assent for the £6 million price tag (£4.5 million for the RB.168, £1.5 million for production), although Prime Minister Harold Macmillan needed reassurance that this was not duplicating the TSR.2 programme before giving his assent on 13 December. During 1961 the Ministry of Aviation (MoA) were advocating the addition of reheat and an Airborne Interception radar to give the Buccaneer a secondary interception role, but the Admiralty (nor the Treasury) were keen and declared no intention to turn the Buccaneer into a fighter. But other provisions were added: carriage of the US Mk.28 70kT–1.1MT yield thermonuclear bomb (the USA had supplied a number of these weapons to the RAF under Project E); improvements to the wide-band homer; the new AW.389 L-Band and S-Band jammer; provision for RAM; nuclear flash protection for the crew; increased 10,000lb (4,535kg) weapons load including six Bullpups; a sideways-looking

The 1966 SBAC Farnborough Show featured brand-new Buccaneer S.2 XV157, which was still held by the Naval Aircraft Support Unit pending issue to a squadron. XV157 was surrounded by weaponry, including the AGM-12 Bullpup ASMs and their underwing pylons. *Terry Panopalis Collection*

BUCCANEER – NOT JUST A WEAPON

The Buccaneer was designed for low-altitude penetration flights in order to fly under defending early warning radar coverage. The first production Buccaneer S.2 XN974 is making landfall over the British. This aircraft spent its life on Hawker Siddeley and A&AEE test flying until 1970. On 4 October 1965 it was the first FAA aircraft to fly non-stop across the Atlantic (taking 4hr 16min) and on 9 December 1965 achieved an endurance of 8hr 40min. *Blue Envoy Collection*

radar for reconnaissance; carriage of AW.155 12in (305mm) diameter rocket-launched radar decoys (several of these items were later cancelled.)

Naval Requirement AW.396 was raised to cover the development and Specification M.232D&P was issued to Blackburn on 29 March 1963. The sea level maximum speed was to be at least 615kt with a rate of climb not less than 14,500ft/min (4,420m/min). The service ceiling was to be at least 40,000ft (12,190m). A radius of action of 600nm (1,110km) was required for the 'Low Attack' sortie and 1,000nm (1,852km) for the 'High Search and Attack' sortie – the Spey's lower fuel consumption increasing the range over the S.1. Take-off weight was to be no more than 44,700lb (20,270kg) with a maximum landing weight of 33,000lb (14,965kg).

The aircraft was to be capable of dive-bombing in a 60° dive from 20,000ft (6,095m). The 2in (50mm) Microcell RPs would be fired at 600kt in a 10° dive. Conventional bombs would be delivered by a dive toss, releasing at 10–20° in the climb at 400–600kt or in a depressed sight line attack diving at 10–20° at 400–600kt.

A Buccaneer S.2 production order was placed on 8 January 1962 (before the S.1 had entered service). Development aircraft XK526 and XK527 were converted with the new engines and larger intakes, XK526 making the first Spey-powered flight on 17 May 1963. XK527 also received a new non-retractable in-flight refuelling probe.

At the 29th Design Progress Meeting at St Giles Court on 25 October 1962, Roy Boot outlined some potential further developments: 430gal (1,955L) drop tanks or six underwing hardpoints; an increased 53,500lb (24,267kg), take-off weight; and an 8,000lbf (35.5kN) thrust Bristol Siddeley BS.605 twin-chamber rocket motor fuelled with High Test Peroxide (HTP) and kerosene. The Chairman, Captain JE Dyer-Smith, was impressed enough to ask Boot to work on an official brochure. Some of these features later appeared in the export Mk.50 for South Africa.

The Long Term Costings in 1965 envisioned a force of 184 Buccaneers: 40 S.1, 94 S.2 and 50 S.2* new-build aircraft, with 27 S.1s to be converted to S.2 standard during 1967–69 and some S.2 upgrades to S.2* standard during the early 1970s. The planned Frontline Aircraft Establishment (FAE) for 1970 was 15 aircraft aboard *Eagle* and 15 on *Ark Royal* in the Far East, 11 on *Victorious* in home waters, plus six ashore at Lossiemouth with 803 NAS and 12 for training.

The 1966 Defence Review affected this planning and only a total of 84 Buccaneer S.2 were built at Brough, with production immediately following the S.1. The first aircraft, XN974, made its maiden flight on 6 June 1964. The last delivery was in December 1968, the last batch being completed to Martel-armed configuration with some being delivered straight to the RAF (see below) and seven aircraft on order were cancelled as part of the Defence Review. Apart from the two S.2 prototypes, no other S.1 airframes were converted, the £550,000 cost of manufacturing new fuselage centre sections counted against the proposal.

The first aircraft were delivered in March 1965 with No.700B Flight being formed the following month as the IFTU. 801 NAS at Lossiemouth became

WINGS OVER THE FLEET

HMS *Hermes* was the smallest Royal Navy carrier to operate the Buccaneer. The Buccaneer S.2s here have a mix of colour schemes with the Dark Sea Grey either only on the upper surfaces or all-over. *Terry Panopalis Collection*

operational on 14 October 1965 and four days later XN980 marked Trafalgar Day by flying low over Nelson's Column in London. The squadron embarked aboard *Victorious* in June 1966. 809 NAS began receiving S.2s in January 1966, followed by 800 NAS in June and 803 NAS in January 1968. 800 NAS had a good showing during Exercise EDEN APPLE in 1968, being based ashore at RAF Luqa in Malta. The Buccaneer dropped bombs in anger in March 1967, trying to ignite the oil spill from the sinking tanker *Torrey Canyon* with aircraft from 800 and 736 NAS flying sorties from RNAS Brawdy in Wales. The last FAA S.2s were retired with 809 NAS in December 1978 when *Ark Royal* was decommissioned.

The long-range capability of the S.2 was demonstrated on 4 October 1965 when XN974 was flown by Cdr G Higgs and Lt Cdr A Taylor across the Atlantic from Goose Bay, Labrador to Lossiemouth non-stop without refuelling, covering 1,694nm (3,138km) in 4hr 16min. Further demonstrations included a low-level simulated nuclear attack against the airfield at Gibraltar flown from *Victorious* in the Irish Sea in May 1966, a 2,000nm (3,700km) round trip. In January 1972 the Buccaneers of 809

Buccaneer S.2 XV357 of 803 NAS at Lossiemouth in October 1969. *Terry Panopalis Collection*

Tales of Buccaneer crews' exploits at low level are legion. This is not the lowest flying Buccaneer but it can be appreciated that flying over the still waters of a lake required piloting skill and the terrain avoidance capabilities of the *Blue Parrot* radar. *Blue Envoy Collection*

NAS flew 1,300nm (2,400 km) from *Ark Royal* to mount a successful military presence over Belize City, the capital of British Honduras (Belize today), to deter a possible invasion by Guatemala over conflicting territorial claims. This was one of the most effective showcases of the geopolitical impact that the RN's carrier fleet could have.

New capabilities came on stream. Naval Staff Requirement NSR.6418 called for the ability to carry and launch the new Matra/Hawker Siddeley Dynamics Martel ASM by 1971. In August 1966 the Weapons Development Committee (WDC) gave approval to fit 50 S.2 aircraft for Martel, with 17 new-build and 33 conversions – reduced in 1967 to 16 and 32 respectively and then in 1968 to 7 and 27, with all the Martel aircraft ultimately due to transfer to the RAF (the provision of a stronger undercarriage for the RAF complicated the conversions and added costs). A total of 110 Martels were required, 78 for *Ark Royal* and 30 for *Eagle* – although in the event *Eagle* was never refitted with Martel facilities due to her impending retirement.

The main changes were the new underwing pylons and a TV screen and joystick controller for

A mixed formation including Buccaneer S.2A XT285 and Sea Vixen FAW2s XS589 (carrying a Mk.20 'buddy' refuelling pod under the starboard wing), XN694 and XN653. At this time XT285 was being operated by 736 NAS. In 1971 it became a flying testbed for the Panavia Tornado's avionics. *Blue Envoy Collection*

the observer in the rear cockpit. The typical fit was three TV-guided AJ.168 Martels plus a TV-guidance datalink pod or four passive radar-homing AS.37 Martel anti-radar ASMs, or a mix of both types. A training pod fitted with a TV seeker could also be carried to train the observers on how to acquire and track a target. The AJ.168 Martel would be fired 17nm (32km) from the target with the Buccaneer flying at 600kt. The new pylons also allowed the use of triple-ejector racks for 1,000lb (454kg) bombs, although these were not used in FAA service.

Other changes included provision for the new WE.177A variable 0.5–10kT yield tactical nuclear weapon (given the cover identity of HE 600lb MC bomb) to replace *Red Beard* (20 bombs were assigned to the Buccaneers), the Strike Sight Mk.4 weapon recording system and Martin Baker Mark 6MSB ejection seats with 'zero-zero' capability (zero airspeed/zero altitude). Fully upgraded aircraft were designated as S.2D, partially upgraded aircraft lacking Martel as S.2C. The upgrades took longer than planned, the first aircraft not being redelivered until October 1972.

Another planned upgrade was the provision of an EMI/Hawker Siddeley Dynamics Type 401 infrared linescanner (IRLS) under NSR.6425 to replace the nocturnal F.97 camera then in development for the tactical reconnaissance role (the IRLS had been developed for the TSR.2). The intention was to fit 47 aircraft for IRLS and to buy 16 IRLS sets and fit data receiver 'transcription' equipment to *Ark Royal* and

Development batch Buccaneer XK527 was converted as the second S.2 prototype in 1963 and took part in the Martel trials, being suitably adorned with 'Martel' titles on the nose. It had a long career as a test aircraft, being retired by the A&AEE in 1982. Today it is believed to be in private ownership somewhere in North Wales. *Blue Envoy Collection*

Another Martel testbed used by Hawker Siddeley Dynamics at Hatfield was Buccaneer S.2B XV350, seen here in in October 1969. XV350 had been transferred to RAF ownership the previous December and was the first S.2B conversion. *Terry Panopalis Collection*

The crew of Buccaneer S.2 XV867 are about to experience the effective deceleration of the *Ark Royal's* recently fitted DA.2 Direct Acting Arrester Gear as they catch the wire following a sortie in October 1970. *Terry Panopalis Collection*

Hermes. The post-Defence Review cutbacks whittled down this number until finally in February 1968 the Director of Naval Air Warfare (DNAW) felt that the shortened service life (at that time disbandment was scheduled for 1972) made the provision of IRLS unjustifiable (by the time of cancellation four of the final production batch had already received the bomb bay fittings, the RAF declined to continue with the project). At the same time the Navy Department cancelled NSR.6435 for a Tail Warner radar and withdrew from joint Naval Air Staff Requirements NASR.853 for active ECM, NASR.1354 for a new low-altitude day camera and NASR.1356 for in-flight film processing equipment for the F.95 camera.

There was some interest from potential export buyers, including the USN following the granting of Mutual Weapons Development Programme (MWDP) funding assistance for the NA.39's development, the West German Marineflieger in 1960 to replace its Hawker Sea Hawks and the Royal Canadian Air Force as a European-based tactical nuclear strike aircraft. The only customer to proceed with an order was the South African Air Force (SAAF) for 16 Buccaneer Mk.50. These differed in having manual wing folding and a retractable installation in the rear fuselage for an 8,000lbf (35.5kN) Bristol Siddeley BS.605 twin-chamber rocket motor with a 30-second HTP supply to boost take-off performance from hot-and-high airfields. Oversize slipper fuel tanks were also provided for ferry flights. The *Blue Parrot* was also modified with a different pulse rate and a map matching mode for navigation.

DH Sea Vixen FAW.1 XJ476 was used in the Martel development programme. Hawker Siddeley Dynamics was responsible for the TV-guided AJ.168 version. This AJ.168 test round is accompanied by the TV datalink pod which would receive the relayed TV camera image from the missile and transmit back the observer's course corrections via joystick in the cockpit. *Blue Envoy Collection*

137

The second prototype Buccaneer S.2 XK527 showing that the Buccaneer could carry four AS.37 anti-radar Martels, only three TV-guided AJ.168 could be carried due to the need to carry the TV datalink pod on one of the hardpoints. *Blue Envoy Collection*

Buccaneer S.2 XV357 of 809 NAS aboard HMS *Ark Royal*. This aircraft was transferred to the RAF as an S.2A in October 1973. *Terry Panopalis Collection*

No. 24 Squadron SAAF formed at Lossiemouth on 1 May 1965, training its crews before transiting home to Air Force Base Waterkloof in November. One aircraft was lost during its transit and was not replaced due to the arms embargo which was in place by then (likewise, a desire to buy a second batch of 14 aircraft failed.) The squadron disbanded on 28 March 1991.

Following the 1966 Defence Review and the January 1968 cancellation of the RAF's General Dynamics F-111K order, would see 62 Buccaneer S.2s being transferred to the RAF (who was a very reluctant recipient having argued consistently against adopting the Buccaneer since 1958 despite Blackburn's efforts to update and revise the aircraft.) In 1972 the FAA's non-Martel S.2 and S.2C aircraft transferred to the RAF became the S.2A, the Martel-armed S.2D becoming the S.2B. The RAF ordered another batch of 26 new-build S.2B aircraft and these were followed by further batches up to 1977 including three as trials aircraft for the RAE in 1973–74 and 20 attrition replacements. Following *Ark Royal's* reprieve until December 1978, 809 NAS retained 14 Buccaneer S.2s as well as 20 WE.177 nuclear weapons for them. On 27 November *Ark Royal's* Buccaneers and Phantoms began disembarking, making their final catapult launch and flying to RAF St Athan to be handed over to the RAF. The RAF's Buccaneers remained responsible for the maritime strike role in cooperation with RN warships under the new Joint Maritime Operating Procedures.

5 BUCCANEER – NOT JUST A WEAPON

The RAF maintained the 'buddy' tanker system with the Mk.20 refuelling pods and bomb bay tanks on four tankers; the S.2Bs gained additional bomb bay door tanks and with full auxiliary and drop tanks the Buccaneer could carry 2,815gal (12,709L) in the tanker role.

As the Panavia Tornado GR.1 entered service in the early 1980s, the Buccaneers continued fulfilling the maritime strike role, being upgraded under Air Staff Requirement ASR.1012 with the Ferranti FIN.1063 Digital Inertial Navigation System replacing *Blue Jacket* and Scanner Azimuth Angle added to the *Blue Parrot* to improve accuracy (other updates such as a Digital Multi-Function Scan Converter for *Blue Parrot* and a new display were not funded.) ASR.1226 was issued for the development of the British Aerospace Dynamics P3T Sea Eagle long-range sea-skimming ASM, a Martel development with an active radar seeker and a small turbojet sustainer engine. Following a starring role in the Gulf War (Operation Granby) in early 1991 as laser-guided bomb designators for Tornados, using a AN/AVQ-23E PAVE SPIKE pod mounted on the port, inboard wing pylon, the Buccaneer was finally retired in 1994.

Buccaneer Mk.3 and Mk.2*

As early as May 1960 Blackburn had submitted a brochure to the MoA for the B.112 Buccaneer Mk.3 with reheated RB.168 Spey engines. The Admiralty decided to focus on improved avionics rather than supersonic performance. In April 1961, the Admiralty released Naval Staff Target AW.162(T) to initiate feasibility studies for an improved blind-bombing system for conventional weapons with a new dual-band high-definition radar with moving-target indication and terrain avoidance and inertial navigation with an accuracy of 1.7nm (3.2km) drift per hour at altitudes below 250ft (76m). The observer would also receive a rolling-map display to aid navigation. The resulting Buccaneer Mk.3 was planned to enter service in 1965. £50,000 of funding was made available for the feasibility studies. The MoA received system proposals from Computing Devices Canada, Elliott Automation, English Electric, Ferranti, IBM, Litton and Sperry. Blackburn's integrated study featured the new Q-band radar proposed by Elliott. All the proposals were assessed by the RAE in 1963, which backed Blackburn's proposal (though not the selection of a Q-band radar.) The technological challenges of the avionics and the estimated cost of up to £30 million led to cancellation.

AW.162 was superseded by AW.418 in September 1963, leading to Naval Staff Requirement NSR.6148 to improve the nav/attack system, weapons release capabilities and crew survivability. The planned in-service date was the second quarter of 1969. The improved navigational accuracy was a consequence of the adoption of the Martel ASM which had to be launched within 10nm (18.5km) from the last visual fix with ¼° bearing accuracy. Development work on

The Buccaneer maintained a ground attack role; S.2 XV358 carries two pods for Matra 2.75in (68mm) SNEB rocket projectiles on the outboard hardpoints while part of the FAA detachment at RAF Honington in July 1977. XV358 was issued to 809 NAS the following month, transferring to the RAF in November 1978. *Terry Panopalis Collection*

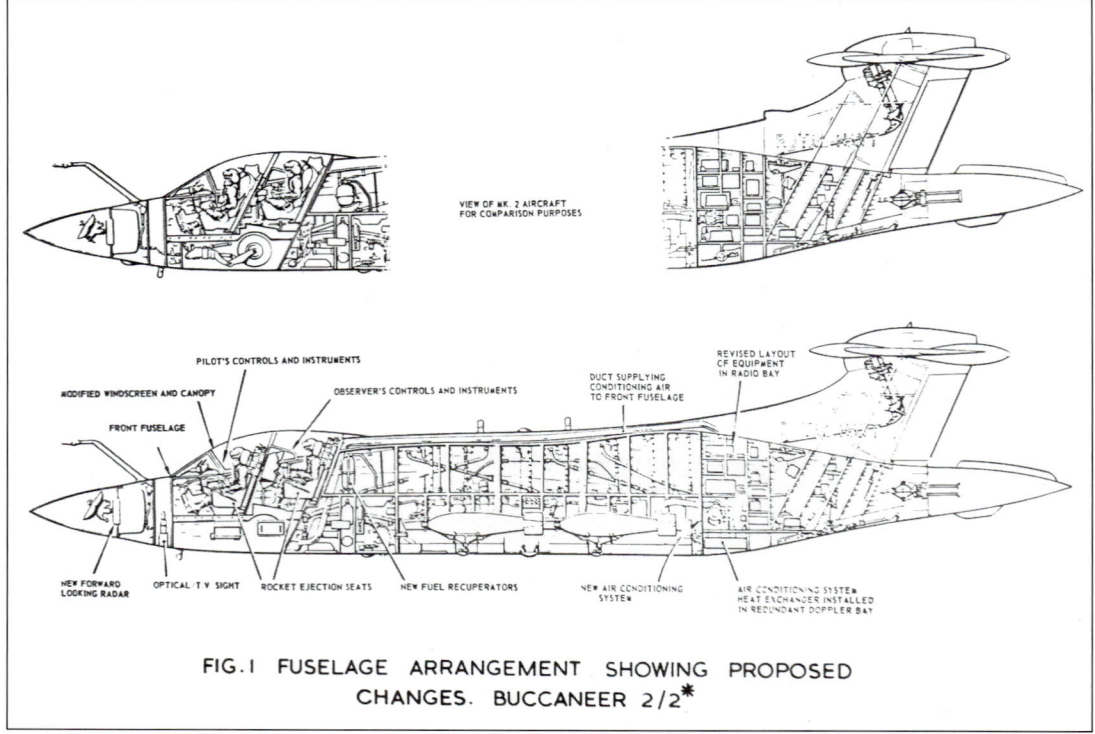

An internal arrangement comparison of the Buccaneer S.2 and S.2*. *Author's Collection*

the Buccaneer S.2 upgrade as the P.134 Buccaneer S.2*. began during August 1964 and £10 million was allocated to upgrade 50–60 aircraft.

NSR.6148 was endorsed on 30 July 1965 and Specification M.258D&P was issued to Hawker Siddeley on 16 November. The specified maximum design landing weight was 35,000lb (15,875kg). The Speys would be upgraded 19,000lbf (84.5kN). The radius of action for the low-altitude attack was 555nm (1,028km) or 925nm (1,713km) with a high-altitude search phase.

It was planned to modify the Ferranti FE540 inertial navigation system selected for the Hawker Siddeley P.1154 with an Inertial Reference System Computer and the P.1154's air data system. A rolling map display would be provided for the observer and the pilot's cockpit would receive the P.1154's Specto Head-Up Display (HUD). In addition, alignment equipment would be required for the aircraft carriers to accurately set the gyroscopes with the ship's position and speed (the carrier having its own Ship Inertial Navigation System) within 2.5 minutes before take-off. The FE540 was designed for operation at altitudes up to 50,000ft (15,240m) and speeds up to Mach 1.7. It could be programmed with five preset waypoints and would maintain its accuracy over 2,170nm (4,020km) and over a latitude range of 70° North to 70° South (this could be extended to 75°N to 75°S but at the cost of other operational limitations) The navigational requirements studied were:

- **Ship Target:** No fixes except on the target itself. Range from the parent carrier 520nm (965km); *Blue Parrot* radar fix 130nm (240km) from the target at 30,000ft (9,145m) before descent to low level; radar switched back on 26nm (48km) from the previously identified position of the target; AJ.168 Martel missiles fired 17nm (32km) from the target.

- **Airfield Target:** Parent carrier is 87nm (160km) offshore. A previous attack on enemy air defences would allow a high-altitude radar fix of the airfield 434nm (805km) inland; descend to low level 87nm from target; final Initial Point (IP) 26nm from the target.

- **Support of Army Ashore:** Parent carrier is 260nm (480km) offshore. Descent to low level before reaching the coast; final IP 43nm (80km) from the coast and 8.6nm (16km) from the target.

The radar would be upgraded to the ARI.23129 Ferranti forward-looking/terrain-following radar (FLR) – essentially an improved *Blue Parrot* – which was in development for the BAC TSR.2 (the second pre-production Buccaneer XK487 had been used as one of the TFR testbeds). The Buccaneer S.2's standard autopilot, magnetic compass, airstream direction detector and radio altimeter were retained. A steerable TV camera under the nose would feed a TV display in the rear cockpit for aiming the AJ.168 Martel. To improve the escape facilities, Martin Baker Mark 8 'zero-zero' ejection seats would be fitted.

Weapons compatibility with the nav/attack system included the future anti-armour and anti-personnel weapon being developed to Air Staff Target AST.1197 (this emerged as the Hunting BL.755 cluster bomb in the mid-1970s), napalm

The Buccaneer possibly never attained its full potential, having been denied major upgrades in FAA and RAF service. Buccaneer S.2 XV357 of 809 NAS is about to be hurled into the air from *Ark Royal's* waist catapult in 1970. Three years later it was transferred to the RAF as an S.2A. *Author's Collection*

tanks, 1,000lb (454kg) freefall and retarded bombs (the latter later being dropped from the requirements), 25lb (11.3kg) and 28lb (12.7kg) practice bombs, 2.67in (68mm) Matra SNEB and 2in (50mm) Microcell RPs, AJ.168/AS.37 Martel and AGM-12 Bullpup ASMs (the WE.177A nuclear bomb was not aimed by the nav/attack system.) A meeting at the MoA on 12 October 1964 discussed the equipment to be fitted. At this stage the Ministry of Defence (MOD) and the WDC had not committed to Hawker Siddeley's proposal. The Chairman, LHG Sterne, the Director Naval Aircraft and Helicopters, emphasised that a fixed development cost ceiling and reasonable timescale were essential to obtain approval. The Naval Staff accepted using the P.1154's inertial platform, despite issues with finding the best method of alignment aboard ship before take-off. Blackburn engineer Ken Essex-Crosby confirmed that the original proposal was unchanged (also representing Blackburn was Captain Duncan Lewin, an ex-FAA pilot who had commanded HMS *Glory* during the Korean War and *Eagle* before being appointed Director of Plans by First Sea Lord Admiral Lord Louis Mountbatten and who had been present at the original M.148T Tender Design Conference that had favoured the B.103 back in December 1954, he retired and joined Blackburn in 1957, becoming Managing Director in 1971).

An assessment of *Blue Parrot* paired with the AN/APN-149 TFR against the FLR, a General Dynamics TFR or the P.1154's Ferranti radar showed that a slightly modified FLR was the best choice, despite its search range only being 70–75% of *Blue Parrot's*. The DNAW, Captain Raymond Lygo, therefore wanted assurance that it could pick out a Soviet guided-missile destroyer at a minimum of 130nm (240km) (Lygo, like Duncan Lewin, would enter the aircraft industry following retirement with the rank of Admiral, becoming the Chief Executive of British Aerospace in 1986.) It was noted by the MoA that the decision not to modify *Blue Parrot* was due to cost but modifying the TSR.2's FLR looked just as expensive.

A separate programme was envisioned for improving the BLC system to reduce the catapult launching limits by 5–10kt. Roy Boot stated that 5kt could be achieved by a relatively simple modification of the wing trailing edge but that a 10kt improvement would also require leading edge modifications, which had to be compatible with carriage of Martel.

An RAE comparative assessment of the Buccaneer S.2 and S.2* in June 1965 showed the inertial navigation system was more accurate and the ability to input updated fixes was a huge improvement. The average weapons kill capability was improved by a factor of two for unguided weapons, the AJ.168 having a kill capability similar to four 1,000lb bombs. Martel also contributed to improved survivability, being launched outside the reach of defensive anti-aircraft weapons. The S.2*'s terrain avoidance capability in poor weather conditions was another positive factor.

The 1966 Defence Review meant the end for the S.2* upgrade (and Hawker Siddeley's attempts to interest the RAF in the supersonic P.150 Buccaneer S.2** which included additional TSR.2 systems), one Treasury official enthusiastically recording, "There is little to say except (sotto voce) 'I told you so.' The Treasury have consistently argued that the improved Buccaneer was not worth the money." Whether or not that was true, unforeseen by the Treasury, the Buccaneer still had nearly 30 years more service to go, much of it with the RAF.

6 Missile generation

Most Cold War historians and aficionados of post-war British aircraft will have April 1957 ingrained in their memory as the time of the now infamous Defence White Paper drawn up under the Minister of Defence Duncan Sandys and the influence of the Prime Minister Harold Macmillan. The White Paper is often labelled as killing off manned fighters in favour of missiles – a sweeping generalisation based upon the paragraph referring to Royal Air Force Fighter Command's future responsibilities. In fact, the White Paper cancelled several missile programmes, including the *Blue Envoy* surface-to-air missile (SAM) intended for the RAF and Royal Navy. The aim of the White Paper was to reduce spending on weapon systems research and development (R&D).

The RN faced an aerial threat from manned bombers releasing stand-off air-to-surface missiles (ASMs). By 1955 the RAF was drafting OR.329 for a two-seat all-weather interceptor capable of Mach 2 at 60,000ft. The Admiralty considered joining this effort but it soon became clear that the aircraft would be too large and heavy for carrier use. Instead, they decided to join the RAF's effort to develop a hybrid rocket and jet-powered interceptor – the Saunders Roe (Saro) P.177, another of Sandys' victims. Following Sandys' defence cuts the only remaining option was to improve the de Havilland

The *Red Top* AAM gave the Sea Vixen FAW.2 two advantages: a head-on intercept capability to engage targets quicker and a snap-up capability to engage high altitude targets. The factory-fresh Sea Vixen FAW.1 XN684 was partially converted to FAW.2 standard in early 1962 with the *Red Top* trial installation, proving the missile/aircraft combination in tests before being fully converted to FAW.2 standard in 1966–67. *Blue Envoy Collection*

Sea Vixen's AI.18 radar and AAM armament with 'snap-up' capability to tackle high-altitude supersonic targets. This stopgap would remain in service until the start of the 1970s.

The Threat

The main aerial threat facing the RN remained the manned bomber, but that threat was now flying faster and at higher altitudes and the air-to-surface missiles (ASMs) were replacing air-dropped bombs or torpedoes as the main danger to warships. The ideal solution was to destroy the bomber before it could launch its missile, implying high speed and climbing capability to ensure an interception using air-to-air missiles (AAMs). Failing that, warships would need shorter-range defences to shoot down any incoming missiles. The RN's first SAM, the Sea Slug (designed by the Project 502 team of Armstrong Whitworth Aircraft, Smiths and Sperry) entered service aboard the *County*-class destroyers in 1960.

In early 1954 the threat from first-generation subsonic bombers like the Ilyushin Il-28 (NATO codename *Beagle*) was being replaced in threat analyses looking ahead to 1962 by an assumed bomber capable of Mach 1.3 at 60,000ft (18,290m). This was remarkably prescient, the Soviet Air Force had just released the technical requirements for what became the Tupolev Tu-22; the prototype flying on 21 June 1958, the Tu-22A *Blinder-A* entering service in 1962 with the dual role bomber-reconnaissance Tu-22R *Blinder-C* following a year later and the ASM-armed Tu-22K *Blinder-B* entering production in 1964. The Tu-22K was capable of Mach 1.27 at 36,090ft (11,000m) and could cruise at Mach 1.06 when carrying a Kh-22 ASM. The *Blinder* was a relatively rare aircraft, however; Soviet Naval Aviation (Aviatsiya voyenno-morskogo flota, AVMF) only received 62 Tu-22R, and a mere 76 Tu-22Ks were built. The AVMF only equipped two regiments, one for the Baltic Fleet in 1962 and one for the Black Sea Fleet in 1965; they remained in service until the end of the Cold War.

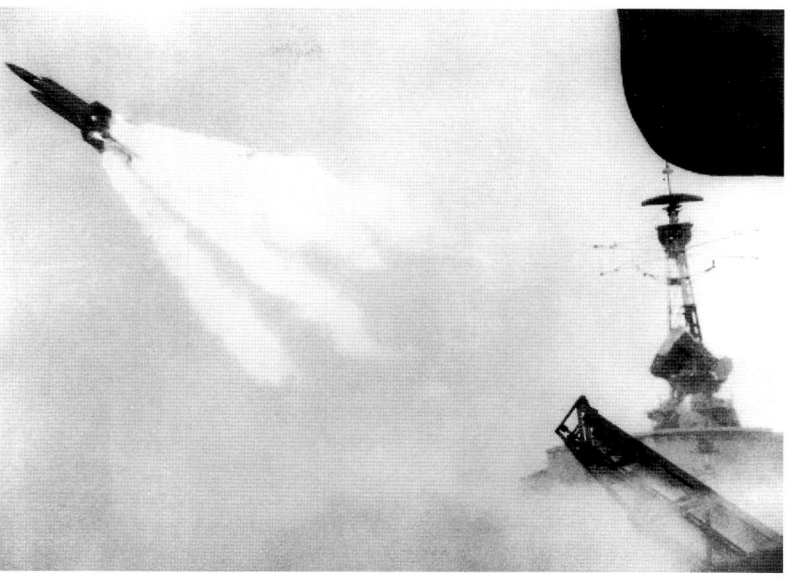

The Kh-22 ASM – known to NATO as the AS-4 *Kitchen* – had active radar homing and could engage a cruiser-sized target from 173nm (320km) away, reaching a speed of Mach 2.94–3.27. It was akin to a small aircraft; 38ft 2in (11.67m) long with a 9ft 8in (3m) wingspan and weighing 12,489lb (5,665kg). It was armed with either a 1,980lb (900kg) semi-armour piercing warhead able to burn its way up to 20ft (40m) inside a ship, or a nuclear warhead for area attacks.

The Kh-22 was the latest in a line of Soviet ASMs. They were all large, aircraft-like airframes with fixed swept wings with active radar homing and large semi-armour piercing warheads to attack large warships such as carriers or cruisers, or nuclear warheads to blast an entire carrier group. The MiG KS-1 Kometa (AS-1 *Kennel*) introduced in 1952 was essentially a shrunken MiG-15 powered by an RD-500K centrifugal-flow turbojet (a copied Rolls-Royce Derwent V); it could be released 48.5nm (90km) away from the target. It was first carried by the

The Armstrong Whitworth-led Project 502 team developed Sea Slug from 1946, it was the RN's first SAM. This is a Sea Slug test round, launched from the trials ship HMS *Girdle Ness* in 1956. The four booster rockets would be discarded and the missile's sustainer motor would take it to the target. *Crown Copyright*

The Tupolev Tu-22 *Blinder* was a distinctive looking aircraft and was the first supersonic bomber threat that the RN had to take seriously. This is the prototype, Samolet 105. *Author's Collection*

Tupolev Tu-4KS *Bull* (a copy of the Boeing B-29 Superfortress) and then by the medium-range jet-powered Tupolev Tu-16KS *Badger-B*, with several Tu-16KS and Kometas being exported to Indonesia and Egypt. The K-10S (AS-2 *Kipper*) of 1961 was carried by the Tu-16K and capable of Mach 1.6 and fitted with a nuclear warhead. The Kh-20 (AS-3 *Kangaroo*) armed the turboprop-powered Tu-95K *Bear-B* from 1959. It was capable of Mach 1.8, being launched 323–81nm (600–150km) from the target, making a 60° terminal diving attack. The Bereznyak KSR-2 (AS-5 *Kelt*) of 1962 was relatively smaller – still 28ft 4in (8.64m) long and weighing 8,988lb (4,077kg) – allowing a Tu-16KSR-2 to carry two under its wings. It had a maximum speed of Mach 1.02 and a 1,650lb (750kg) warhead. Egypt used them against Israel during the Yom Kippur War of 1973.

Missile defence

The planned air defence of the United Kingdom from 1949 concentrated on the 'Stage Plan'; a programme using three progressive stages of guided weapon and radar technology. Stage 2 was usurped by Stage 1¾, a 170nm (320km) range, Mach 3 capable SAM developed by Bristol Aircraft from the Stage 1 Bloodhound (codenamed *Red Duster*). It was intended for defence of the UK and for warships to provide long-range cover for a carrier group. The missile, codenamed *Blue Envoy*, was essentially a Bloodhound built out of stainless steel with a double-sweep delta wing (82° sweep on the inboard strakes, 75° inboard and 42° outboard) designed by the German-born (naturalised British) aerodynamicist Dietrich Küchemann and aerodynamicist and ramjet engineer Roy Hawkins of the Royal Aircraft Establishment (RAE). Two 18in (45.7cm) diameter Bristol BRJ.800 ramjets would sustain the missile at Mach 3 for 170nm. Guidance would be via continuous wave (CW) radar to overcome electronic countermeasures (ECM) and the warhead may have been the 5–10kT yield *Blue Fox* (later re-named *Indigo Hammer*) nuclear device.

The Admiralty had several doubts. The missile was too big to fit onto smaller warships and required assembly before launch which would reduce the rate of fire – the wingspan was 16ft 9in (5.15m). The minimum range of 8.6nm (16km) was nearly that of the carrier group's low-altitude search radar coverage. The RAF also had doubts, as bombers soon switched from high-altitude flights – trying to get over SAM defences – to low-altitude ground-hugging penetration flights. These issues contributed to Sandys' decision to cancel the project.

Post *Blue Envoy* and Saro P.177, the long-range SAM returned in 1958 as the New Naval Guided Weapons System – NIGS. The requirement called for a missile to counter a Mach 3 target at 70,000ft (21,340m) – on the face of it the requirements of *Blue Envoy* turned up another notch. The warhead included a nuclear option, the lightweight 0.5-2kT Gwen which had been intended for a nuclear-armed Sea Slug variant. At least 32 Gwen warheads were planned. NIGS was planned to arm missile destroyers DLG 07-10 (07 and 08 emerged as the last pair of *County*-class Batch II ships). The Ministry of Aviation (MoA) hoped for interest from the RAF, but this not forthcoming.

Several research studies under the WA.726 codename were conducted by the RAE and the Project 502 team of Armstrong Whitworth, Smiths and Sperry during 1959-60. They began by updating Sea Slug which emerged as a delta-winged 'dart' to which was attached a 14in (35.5cm) diameter, 10ft (3.05m) long solid-fuel booster rocket stage, the combined length being 27ft 7in (8.4m). Bristol learned of WA.726 and dusted off *Blue Envoy* with the sustainer ramjets upgraded to the 13in (33cm) diameter BS.1001 and adding a 10ft long solid-fuel booster, bringing the total length to 26ft 7in (8.1m). Bristol then offered the RP.25 powered by a single BS.1001 ramjet integrated into the missile body with two jettisonable booster rockets; the body had a Gothic delta wing with a curved leading edge. The RP.25 was the smallest of the missiles at 13ft 1in (3.98m) long and 5ft (1.52m) span. Range was only 43nm (80km) but it could reach Mach 4 and 110,000ft (33,530m). A third Bristol offering was a navalised Bloodhound Mk.2.

NIGS evolved into something approaching the US Navy's (USN) Typhon system designed to destroy high-altitude and sea-skimming targets, which would have used ramjet-powered RIM-50A Typhon LR and RIM-55A Typhon MR missiles guided by the complicated AN/SPG-59 passive electronically scanned array radar. Typhon was beyond the state-of-the-art and was cancelled in December 1963. NIGS was envisioned to have twin-arm launchers with a rate of fire of 20 seconds per missile. A series of 17 ship studies in 1958-59 spiralled to 7,400-ton destroyers and 7,700-ton nuclear-powered ships with magazine capacities of 16–80 missiles – the vertical stowage of the long missiles made these magazines very large (as a comparison with the 27ft long NIGS missiles, the hull depth of the *County*-class ships was around 38ft [11.5m]). Vertical launch was considered but would have required an even larger ship.

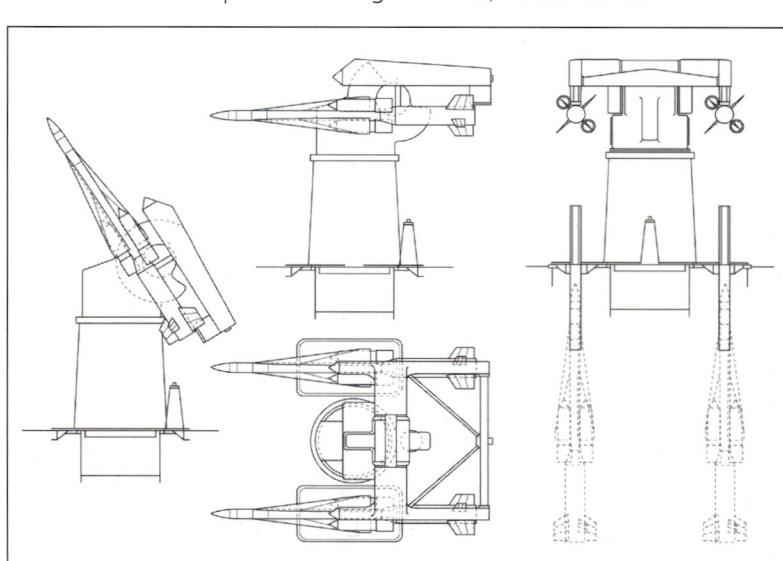

Drawn from plans held by The National Archives, this NIGS launcher and missile proposal is from Vickers-Armstrongs in 1960. It was around 32ft (9.75m) long (including the booster stage) and had two 14.5in (36.8cm) diameter ramjet sustainers. *Chris Gibson*

Two Sea Dart drill rounds on the GWS.30 launcher aboard the Type 42 destroyer HMS *Edinburgh*. The Bristol Siddeley BS.1003 Odin ramjet was integrated with the missile structure, hence the annular nose intake; the four spikes are the interferometer aerials which home onto the returns from the Type 909 fire-control radar (whose dome is atop the ship's bridge). *MOD/Open Government Licence*

The first Admiralty/MoA Working Party Meeting in February 1959 discussed the required S-band frequency scanning surveillance radar (FSR), which would have four 20 × 20ft (6 × 6m) fixed arrays with the capability to detect a 10.7ft² (1m²) sized target at 125nm (231.5km) range (it was described as comparable with the SPG-59.) The average transmitter power was to be 80kW, four CW illuminators of 5kW power would also be fitted; missile tracking was to be provided by the FSR – this radar was later scaled down (20 × 15ft [6 × 4.5m] arrays) as the New Surveillance Radar (NSR). The missile had mid-course command guidance with semi-active terminal homing with a 9in (22.8cm) diameter dish – the nuclear armed version would only use command guidance for safety. The performance against smaller targets was estimated to be superior to Typhon. The ship would need an electrical generation capacity of up to 1MW to power the radar suite.

No hardware materialised and the project ended around early 1961 in favour of the more urgent Small Ship Integrated Guided Weapon System (SIGS). Bristol had pre-empted this by considering NIGS too ambitious and proposing the 'Large PT.428', a development of the short-range PT.428 being developed for the British Army with an additional booster rocket and semi-active homing. The Admiralty was not impressed but SIGS appeared soon after. For the first time the missile was to be capable of being stowed and handled like a round of gun ammunition. Bristol – now part of the British Aircraft Corporation (BAC) – submitted the SIG-16, but its 13.9nm (25.7km) range was too short. Bristol replaced its sustainer rocket with the BS.1003 Odin ramjet (the Chow booster rocket was retained) and this was the winning contender (other tenders included PT.428 and Vickers-Armstrong offered a variant of the American RIM-24 Tartar). In 1962 the MoA assigned the code CF.299 to the project and design authority was handed to the Project 502 team at the insistence of the Admiralty. CF.299 entered production as the GWS.30 (Guided Weapon System) Sea Dart which armed the Type 82 and Type 42 air defence destroyers and was also fitted to the *Invincible*-class light aircraft carriers during the 1970s and 1980s.

The Admiralty was also interested in short-range SAMs which could engage low-altitude targets, including incoming ASMs. The first studies in 1946 led to the 1948 requirement GD 81/48 which resulted in Popsy A, a basic missile based on the CTV.1 rocket test vehicle with semi-active Q-band radar homing to intercept gliding bombs. This was superseded by the supersonic Popsy B to enable it to also deal with aircraft. It was proposed for frigates and merchant ships (with control from a 'command ship'), but the entire programme was cancelled in 1950. Requirement GD 165/55 married the Popsy Q-band homer with the US AAM-N-5 Meteor AAM, becoming Mopsy (also known as Popsy-Meteor) as an Anglo-American project. No progress was made and Meteor was cancelled in 1953.

Mopsy was succeeded in 1953 by *Orange Nell*, a missile capable of intercepting supersonic missiles and aircraft within a range bracket of 5–1nm (9.1–1.8km) with an ideal minimum impact point 1.4nm (2.7km) away from the ship. The 100lb (45.3kg) warhead would either be of blast-fragmentation or continuous rod type. The missile would need to attain at least Mach 1.2 and have a response time from acquisition to launch within 10 seconds. Acquisition data would come from an S-band volume scanning radar and an X-band or Q-band CW illuminator would guide *Orange Nell's* semi-active seeker. The proposed twin-rail launcher would replace a medium calibre gun

The Short Brothers Sea Cat was a replacement for the 40mm Bofors gun. This is the original GWS.20 system with visual aiming, the destroyer HMS *Decoy* trialling the system before it was installed (briefly) in HMS *Eagle*. The later GWS.21, 22 and 24 included radar-assistance. Even so, this subsonic missile was obsolete by the 1980s. *Crown Copyright*

turret with a magazine containing 40 missiles stored vertically in concentric rings. Parametric studies were made but no hardware materialised and little work was done before cancellation in 1957. This was partly because destroying an ASM and its warhead was difficult to achieve with the miss distances obtainable with 1950s era technology and it was therefore safer to destroy the bomber before it could release its missiles. An alternative was the USN's similar General Dynamics RIM-24 Tartar, which the Admiralty was keen to buy but the Treasury disliked the Dollar expenditure that would entail.

The RN instead made do with the Short Brothers & Harland Sea Cat from 1962 until the early 1990s. This was a basic subsonic and optically-guided SAM (later radar tracking assistance was added) developed from the Australian Malkara anti-tank missile. It had a range of 3.4nm (6.4km). It was an export success, being sold to several Western navies and a land-based version, Tigercat, was equally successful. Although a limited weapon, it did achieve eight kills during the Falklands Conflict in 1982 (ironically, the Argentine Army had Tigercat batteries on the islands). In 1962 Shorts proposed a supersonic Sea Cat II, essentially a new missile using the same launcher and targeting infrastructure. The missile was around 6.5ft (2m) long and had a two-stage booster/sustainer rocket motor. This private venture went no further.

Also released in 1962 was naval requirement GD.302 for the *Confessor* study into a new-generation point-defence SAM capable of destroying sea-skimming ASMs. This study led to the selection of the BAC PX.430 in 1967 which entered production in the late 1970s as Seawolf. Seawolf used differential tracking – the fire-control radar tracking the target and the missile and bringing both tracks together (up to two outgoing Seawolves could be tracked simultaneously.) With 1970s digital technology, rather than *Orange Nell's* 20ft (6m) miss distance, Seawolf could hit a 4.5in (11.4cm) diameter target, such as an artillery shell.

P.177 – The manned missile

The idea of using rocket motors to improve the climbing capability of interceptors was a popular concept at the end of the Second World War. In February 1945, one of the Ministry of Aircraft Production's technical experts, Handel Davies, had suggested adding auxiliary rockets to jet-powered interceptors to enable them to reach 45,000ft (13,715m) in three minutes. The Admiralty was not overly impressed with the idea (nor with the thought of stowing liquid oxygen aboard its carriers) but the RAF became seriously interested in the captured Messerschmitt Me 163 Komet rocket-powered interceptors and in 1946 Armstrong Siddeley and de Havilland (DH) began work on liquid-fuelled rockets. Development by 1951 allowed the issuing of Operational Requirement OR.301 and Specification F.124T for an interceptor capable of reaching

A GWS.25 Sea Wolf SAM is fired from the bow launcher of a Type 22 Batch 1 frigate during the early 1980s. *Crown Copyright*

60,000ft (18,290m) in 2min 30sec. In October 1952 two Avro 720 and three Saro P.154 (soon renamed SR.53) prototypes were ordered.

At this stage the Admiralty remained a bystander. By May 1954 the Ministry of Supply (MoS) and RAF were reshaping F.124T into a mixed jet and rocket-powered aircraft armed with two *Blue Jay* infrared (IR)-homing AAMs and equipped with airborne interception (AI) radar to intercept an assumed 1962 Soviet bomber capable of Mach 1.3 at 60,000ft.

The Avro 720 was redesigned and the company proposed a naval version, the Type 728, with the delta wing enlarged from 360 to 460ft² (33.4 to 42.7m²). It would be powered by an 8,000lbf (35.6kN) DH Gyron Junior turbojet and an 8,000lbf Armstrong Siddeley Screamer rocket fuelled by kerosene and liquid oxygen. The structure and undercarriage would be strengthened for arrested carrier landings. Avro also investigated fitting a canard foreplane to improve the maximum lift coefficient and reduce the angle of attack on landing and it would reduce supersonic trim drag with performance benefits. Economy measures and the SR.53's superior performance led to the Avro 720 being cancelled in April 1955.

The RAF then upped the stakes, OR.337 calling for Mach 1.6 at 65,000ft (19,810m) and reaching that altitude in four minutes with short bursts at Mach 2. Specification F.177D was issued on 17 May 1956 and the entry into service was to be by July 1959. This time the Admiralty joined the effort, raising Naval Staff Requirement NR/A.47 alongside OR.337. It was becoming clear that the RN required a high-altitude interception capability that the Sea Vixen could not provide and a complement to Sea Slug, which was limited mainly to subsonic targets below 50,000ft (15,240m).

While it wanted something approaching the RAF's OR.329/F.155T interceptor, the NA.47 type was to be a lead-in fighter as a shorter development step. The Admiralty considered the Saro P.177

"If we are to defend the Fleet in the early and middle sixties, the P.177 is essential."

FIRST LORD OF THE ADMIRALTY, QUINTIN HOGG, 2ND VISCOUNT HAILSHAM, 28 NOVEMBER 1956

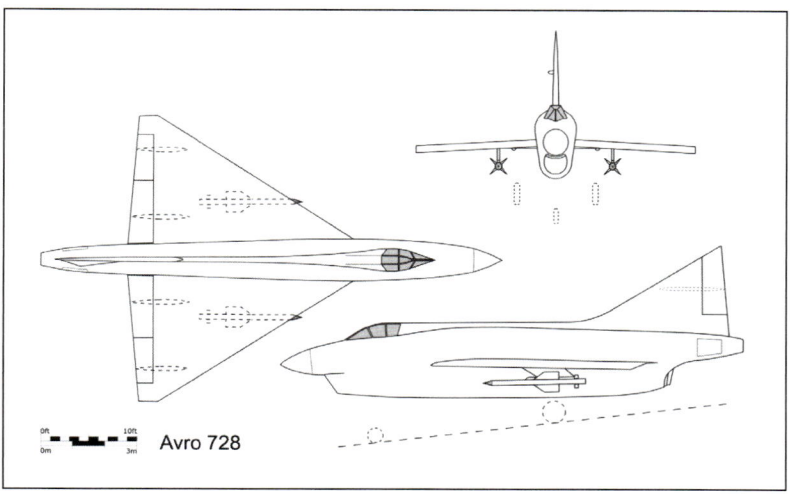

Avro 728

The Avro Type 728 was based on the RAF's Type 720 mixed rocket/jet-powered interceptor. The cancellation of the 720 in April 1957 also ended any chances of the 728 being selected by the Admiralty. *Author*

A 'what-if?' painting of an Avro Type 728 Sea Archer FAW.1 of 803 NAS taxying to HMS *Victorious*' waist steam catapult for take-off just beyond the Straits of Gibraltar. The converted helicopter cruiser HMS *Belfast* stands by with her Bristol Type 191 Belvedere HAS.1 ASW helicopters screening for Soviet submarines as a Westland Widgeon HC.7 mounts plane guard. *Luciano Alviani*

WINGS OVER THE FLEET

Naval requirement NR/A.43 contenders

	Avro 728	Bristol Type 188N	Hawker Study	Saro P.177N
Span	27ft 4in (8.33m)	33ft 0in (10.05m)	30ft 6in (9.3m)	30ft 3in (9.22m) over missiles
Length	48ft 0in (14.63m)	66ft 6in (20.26m); 52ft 0in (15.84m) folded	51ft 0in (15.54m)	50ft 6in (15.39m)
Wing area	460ft² (42.7m²)	383ft² (35.58m²)	430ft² (39.99m²)	327ft² (30.41m²)
t/c ratio	4.5%	4%	?	6%
All-up weight	23,885lb (10,835kg)	?	?	27,348lb (12,405kg)
Powerplant	1x Gyron Junior DJG.1, 8,000lbf (35.5kN) & 1x Screamer, 8,000lbf (35.5kN)	2x Gyron Junior PS.50/DGJ10R, 10,000lbf (44.4kN) dry, 14,000lbf (62.2kN) reheat	1x Gyron Junior & 1x rocket motor	1x Gyron Junior PS.50/DGJ10R, 10,000lbf (44.4kN) dry, 14,000lbf (62.2kN) reheat & Spectre D. Spe.5A, 8,000lbf (35.5kN)
Max speed	Mach 2.0	Mach 2.0	Mach 2.0	Mach 2.35 at 40,000ft (12,190m); Mach 2.75 at 70,000ft (21,340m)
Rate of climb	?	?	?	60,000ft/min (18,290m/min) at SL
Service ceiling	60,000ft (18,290m)	?	?	67,000ft (20,240m)
Armament	2x Blue Jay	2x Blue Jay	2x Blue Jay or 2in (50mm) Microcell RPs	2x Blue Jay Mk.3 or 2x48 2in (50mm) Microcell RP pods, 2x 1,000lb (454kg) bombs

alongside fighter developments of the Fairey Delta 2 supersonic delta wing research aircraft and the Bristol Type 188 Mach 2.5 stainless steel research aircraft. The 188N drawn up in March 1955 was powered by two DH Gyron Juniors with ECKO AI.20 *Green Willow* radar in the nose and two *Blue Jays* under the wings, the 35ft (10.67m) span wing did not need folding but the long fuselage had tail and nose/cockpit folding to fit onto the carrier lifts. Ralph Williams of Hawker's Kingston design office also made a brief design study of a Gyron and Spectre powered hybrid fighter to meet NA.47 armed with two Firestreaks. The Admiralty selected the P.177. An Assessment Group Meeting to discuss NA.47 at the MoS at St Giles Court on 19 August 1955 declared the maximum weight had to be kept below 30,000lb (13,610kg) and selected the *Blue Jay* Mk.3 as the best armament option.

Commonality between the RAF and Fleet Air Arm (FAA) P.177s was of prime importance. The

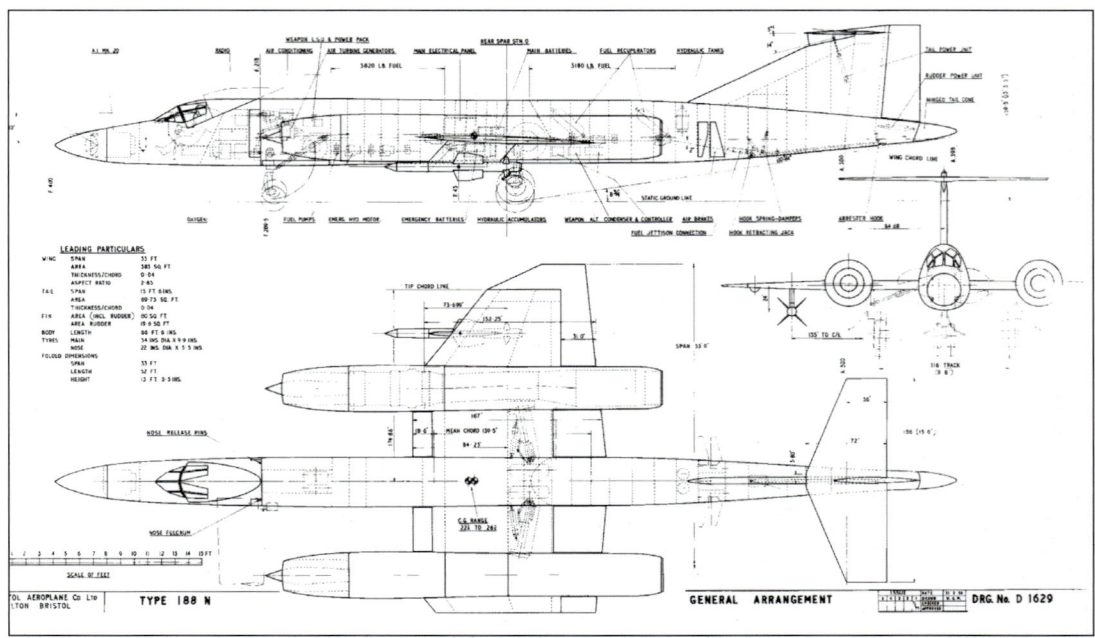

This general arrangement drawing shows minimal changes from the Type 188 apart from the nose folding, radar nose and arrester hook. *Tony Buttler Collection*

TOP RIGHT A period artistic impression of the naval Bristol Type 188N featuring the manufacturer's model. The Type 188 had an elegance of its own, but is one of the more unlikely contenders to be found on the deck of an aircraft carrier. It was, however, one of only two aircraft capable of Mach 2 in the UK at the time, which made it eligible to meet the need for an interceptor. *Tony Buttler Collection*

CENTRE RIGHT The manufacturer's model of the Type 188N features two Firestreak AAMs under the wings. The join line just visible behind the cockpit indicates where the entire cockpit and nose section would have folded for hangar stowage. *Tony Buttler Collection*

BOTTOM RIGHT One of the Saro P.177N's intercept profiles. *Leonardo UK via Joe Cherrie*

aircraft were to be fitted with the Ferranti AI.23 radar (the AI.20 was briefly considered as a stopgap), ARI.18059 Tactical Air Navigation (TACAN), a UHF and S-band or wide-band homers, ARI.5875 Identification Friend-or-Foe Mk.10 and AN/ARC-52 UHF radio (plus a standby set). The desired performance included a time of four minutes to Mach 1.4 at 60,000ft (18,288m) and a 75,000ft (22,860m) cruising altitude on reheat jet and rocket thrust. Two naval sortie profiles were outlined:

- A long warning interception of a Mach 0.9 bomber at 60,000ft (18,290m) detected 400nm (740km) away; initial climb to 36,000ft (10,970m); drop tanks jettisoned; 12 minutes cruising for towards the target; rocket ignition to climb at Mach 1.4 to 60,000ft; manoeuvring into a pursuit intercept course at Mach 1.6 (180° turning radius 4.2nm [7.7km]); target destroyed 165nm (305.5km) away from the centre of the fleet with 22 minutes flying time.

- A normal warning interception of a Mach 0.9 bomber at 60,000ft (18,290m) detected 200nm (370km) away; initial climb to 60,000ft; rocket ignition at 30,000ft (9,145m); level off and acceleration to Mach 1.4 within two minutes; manoeuvring into 180° pursuit intercept course at Mach 1.6; target destroyed 55nm (101.8km) from the centre of the fleet with 8min 38sec flying time.

There was no open tendering process, Saro being contracted to begin a design study on 18 May 1955. Chief Designer Maurice Brennan's team submitted interim brochures for the P.177N and P.177R in August and October respectively (note, some authors refer to the SR.177, archive Ministry documents only use P.177, which I shall maintain for consistency). The Director General of Technical Development (Air) at the MoS, GWH Gardner, felt

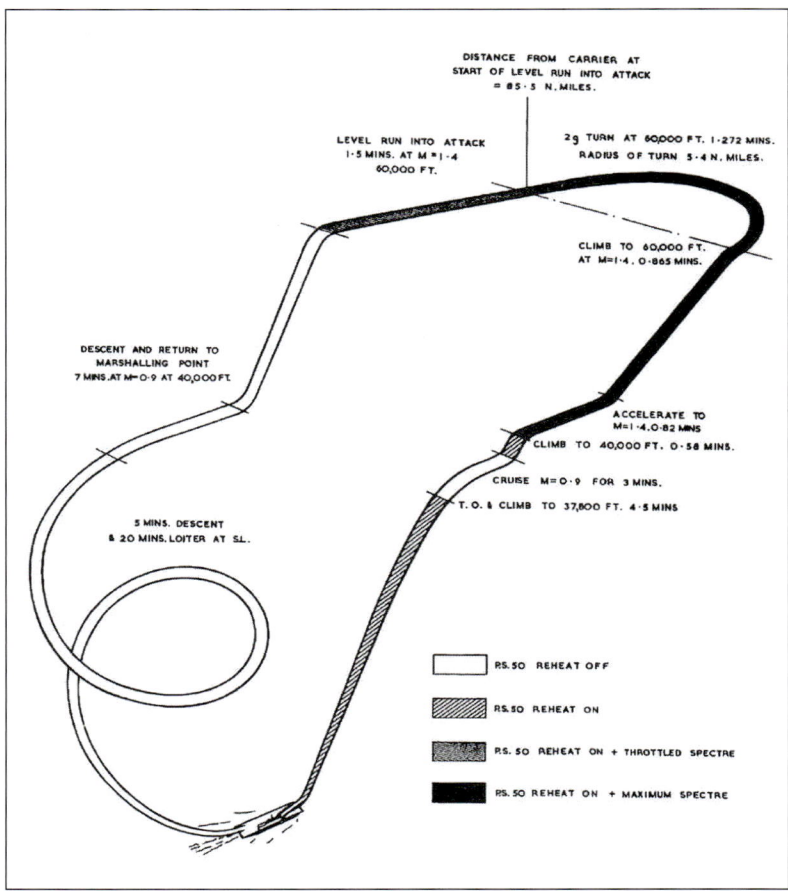

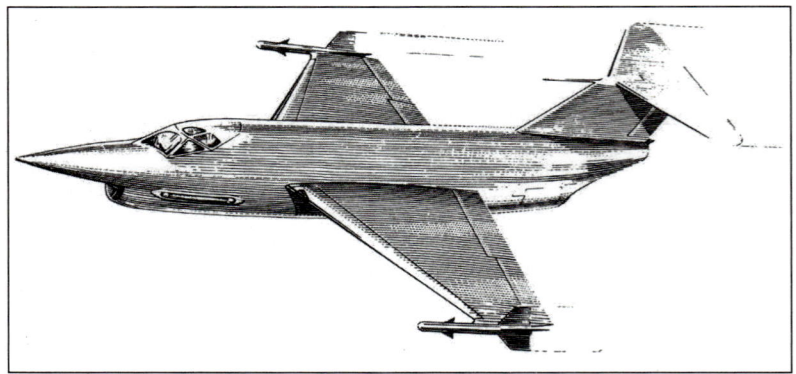

An early artist's impression of the Saro P.177. *Leonardo UK via Joe Cherrie*

Saro's resident artist created this impressive artwork of a P.177N loaded with *Red Tops* and two fuel drop tanks. The blown flaps are fully deflected, undercarriage and hook lowered, airbrakes open and the translating intake cowl open to ensure that the Gyron Junior can gulp enough air as the aircraft decelerates for landing. Less obvious is the thrust deflection from a diverter nozzle between the main undercarriage, its stream of hot exhaust air is just visible. *Leonardo UK via Tony Buttler Collection*

that using the new DH DGJ.10 Gyron Junior turbojet would give good performance, advice that Saro took. Originally the engine layout was that of the SR.53 – rocket in the lower fuselage with the jet above. The need to provide blown flaps required a reversal to make tapping the jet's airflow easier, in turn moving the jet intake to the ventral chin position. The alternative rocket motor choices to the DH Spectre were four Napier Scorpions or a pair of Armstrong Siddeley Gammas.

The P.177N differed from its land-based cousin in having an arrester hook, catapult hooks, a hold-back fitting, a larger diameter nosewheel and a landing flap on the tailplane of the T-tail (its deflection was coordinated with the trailing edge flaps.) Initially only the P.177N had a retractable in-flight refuelling probe, but this provision was later shared with the P.177R, as were the blown flaps.

One planned future development for the P.177N was deflected thrust – deflecting the jet exhaust 50° downwards to augment the blown flaps. This provision was deleted in January 1957, allowing the engine to be moved farther aft and the afterburner forward to shorten the jet pipe and reduce structural weight. The multi-spar wing formed an integral fuel tank, it had 39° leading edge sweep and full span leading edge flaps, blown trailing edge flaps and ailerons. The jet intake had a two shock inlet cone and a sliding cowl for a secondary intake slot for low speed operation.

The turbojet was a 10,000lbf (44.5kN) DH PS.50 DGJ.10 Gyron Junior and the rocket was an 8,000lbf (35.6kN) DH Spectre D.Spe.5A which used High Test Peroxide (HTP) as the oxidant. Within the Spectre a platinum gauze would decompose the HTP into 600°C (1,112F) steam, kerosene would be sprayed in and ignited for increased thrust. Enough HTP was carried for four minutes' endurance at full power. HTP also fuelled the Auxiliary Power Unit (a steam turbine spinning at 36,000rpm). A total of 10 fuel tanks were located in the wings and fuselage with between five and one tanks loaded with HTP depending on the interception profile. Two 150gal (682L) drop tanks could be carried under the wings.

Take-off performance at 28,300lb (12,835kg) weight with full rocket 'hot' thrust (i.e. decomposed HTP steam plus burning kerosene) plus the Gyron Junior's 5,500lbf (24.4kN) thrust and 15lb/sec (6.8kg/sec) blown airflow over the flaps at 45° deflection the aircraft would attain 123kt at the end of the BS.4 steam catapult with a windspeed over the deck as low as 10kt (or 16kt with 'cold' – steam only – rocket thrust or 10kt with no rocket at 21,500lb (9,750kg)). The aircraft was stressed for 5.5g acceleration which gave growth margin for more powerful steam catapults. With a landing weight of 17,000lb (7,710kg) the approach speed would be 131kt with an arrester wire contact speed of 110kt with 21kt wind over the deck (27kt wind and 16,900lb (7,665kg) weight in the tropics). Maximum landing weight was 19,000lb (8,620kg) with 28kt wind over the deck; the aircraft was stressed for 4g deceleration during arrested landings.

The two *Blue Jay* Mk.3 IR-homing AAMs or 48-round 2in (50mm) Microcell RP pods were fitted on the wing tips. The *Blue Jay* Mk.3 was developed specifically for launch at speeds of up to Mach 1.7 and altitudes up to 65,000ft (19,810m) – the minimum launch altitude was 15,000ft (4,570m). It had increased 36in (91.4cm) wingspan and a reduced thrust Magpie rocket motor to limit kinetic heating following launch (the further improved *Blue Jay* Mk.4/*Red Top* was also considered.) The AI.23 radar had a range of around 20nm (37km) with lock-on usually achieved within 15nm (27km) of the target, the Pilot Attack Sight signalling the required manoeuvres to the pilot. If the enemy bomber was employing ECM, the S-band and UHF homers could be used to guide the P.177 to within AI.23 range. ARI.18107 Tactical Air Navigation (TACAN) beacon homing was also provided.

Wasting no time, Saro was given the ITP on 29 September 1955. Development would follow the MoS's new procurement process of ordering a development batch from production jigs in five batches during January 1957 to February 1960: five aircraft for basic aerodynamic and engine development; three for weapons system development; five for testing the special features of the P.177N and P.177R (the 9th aircraft, originally due to test the thrust deflection, was reassigned as the West German P.177 prototype); six for the Aeroplane & Armament Experimental Establishment (A&AEE) for CA – Controller Aircraft – Clearance; and finally eight (four each of P.177N and P.177R) for service trials. Serials XL905–XL907 and XL920–XL925 were allocated for the first two batches. The first nine development aircraft would receive the 7,000lbf (31.3kN) PS.43 DGJ.1-4 development engine. Production orders of 150 aircraft each for the FAA and RAF was envisioned.

Saro was only a small company and lacked a proper flight test team and adequate development facilities at Eastleigh Aerodrome. Despite this the company promised to have the first aircraft flying in April 1958 with service entry in July 1960. By early 1957 the full-scale mock-up was well advanced with many production jigs completed. Despite subcontracting some draughtsman tasks to companies like Marshall of Cambridge and Miles Aircraft, the design phase schedule slipped by 11 weeks. The flight control system was originally subcontracted to Louis Newmark Limited, but they dropped out, being replaced by Smiths Instruments in partnership with Kelvin & Hughes.

During the summer of 1956, the West German Luftwaffe and Marineflieger began showing interest, a technical mission visiting Eastleigh in April. The USA had also shown interest and was funding the SR.53 (which first flew on 16 May 1957) via the Mutual Weapons Development Program (MWDP) and in February the Ministry of Aviation (MoA) requested $11.7 million from MWDP for the P.177. The justification in the application highlighted that the Supermarine Scimitar and DH Sea Vixen could not meet the specified threat, while the Sea Slug had limited range and no high-altitude capability and that only the P.177 could fill the gap until 1970. On 4 June the MWDP replied that the P.177 was within its production phase of development so was ineligible for MWDP funds. Time ran out before a revised application could be made.

The P.177 had faced an existential crisis since the Minister of Defence Duncan Sandys had unveiled the Defence White Paper in April 1957, which called for SAMs to take over the primary role of the UK's air defence and declared that "the RAF is unlikely to have a requirement for fighter aircraft of types more advanced than the supersonic P.1 and work on such projects will stop." The manned fighter was becoming obsolete – the threat was no longer a Mach 1.3 bomber at 60,000ft but ballistic missiles which no fighter – and few SAMs at that time – could

> "Whatever happens about the German order, I feel that we shall not be able to get this aircraft for the Navy. It will cost at least £10M over and above the cost of the 80 Plan and I suggest there is no point in holding on any longer."

WN HANNA, JOINT HEAD OF MILITARY BRANCH, ADMIRALTY, 7 NOVEMBER 1957

A manufacturer's model of the P.177N with a pair of *Red Tops* on the wing tips. The horizontal 'pipe' below the cockpit is the retractable refuelling probe. The model is marked XL905, the serial allocated to the first P.177 airframe. In reality XL905 would have been a 'flying shell' aerodynamic prototype. *Leonardo UK via Tony Buttler Collection*

Saro built a full scale P.177 mock-up at East Cowes. It was an impressive looking aircraft but the company's resources were hard pushed to deliver the necessary technical drawings, let alone embarking on full scale production. *Leonardo UK via Tony Buttler Collection*

Alternate horizons. A pair of Saro P.177N Skua F.1s of 899 NAS shepherd a Soviet Naval Aviation Myasishchev M-50 *Bounder-B* away from HMS *Furious* and her task force in the Iceland–Shetland gap in 1962. The P.177 was designed to intercept Mach 2.0-capable bombers such as the Myasishchev M-50, which like the P.177, was destined never to enter frontline service. *Luciano Alviani*

counter. Indeed, the head of the Defence Research Policy Committee, Sir Frederick Brundrett, considered whether it was unwise to offer P.177s to Germany as Bristol Bloodhound and *Blue Envoy* SAMs would be more effective. At sea, however, the RN faced the threat of stand-off anti-ship missiles launched from manned bombers, not ballistic missiles.

The newly appointed First Lord of the Admiralty, George Douglas-Hamilton, 10th Earl of Selkirk, manged to convince Sandys not to include the P.177N in the White Paper as the RN would lack any high-altitude interception capability – the *Blue Envoy* SAM had been cancelled as well. The only alternative would be to order additional – and costlier – Sea Vixens to fill the gap (the Admiralty argued buying P.177s instead of Sea Vixens had saved enough to balance out the costs of buying HTP stocks, building storage facilities and refitting the carriers.) There were also worries that cancellation might impact the development and delivery of Gyron Juniors for the Blackburn Buccaneers. The P.177R prototypes were immediately cancelled and the development batch cut to 18 P.177Ns.

The Minister of Supply, Aubrey Jones, succeeded in keeping the project alive in the hopes that the German order might materialise. In May the Royal Canadian Navy had issued a requirement for an interceptor for their *Majestic*-class carrier HMCS *Bonaventure*, with a weight of 24,000lb (10,885kg). Saro considered a submission, reducing the fuel capacity to meet the weight limit, but no RCN interest materialised. Saro asked the Admiralty if it would still place an order if the P.177 continued as a private venture with West German backing. Without the RAF's aircraft to help amortise the development costs, the unit price rose from £235,000 to £250,000. The Admiralty calculated an order for 140 aircraft would cost up to £12 million, which was unaffordable. They resigned themselves to cancellation with the priority being to protect the Buccaneer. Regardless of Germany's intentions, the Admiralty could not fund an order. Following rejection from the MWDP as the only other source of outside funding, the P.177N was cancelled on 8 November.

The SR.53 programme was to continue and plans envisioned five P.177 prototypes being completed for high-speed research programmes in an attempt to recoup something from the £3 million already spent. At that time, a first flight was scheduled for April 1958. West German interest waned in the face of the cancellations and having to contribute to the development costs and they walked away on 23 December. The entire project came to a stop, the SR.53 test flying programme continuing until July 1960. The blow led to Saro's exit from aircraft manufacture (combined with the MoA's enforced rationalisation of helicopter production by Westland Aircraft), the company instead focusing on space rockets and hovercraft. The cancellation gave impetus to plans to improve Sea Vixen, Sea Slug and the Airborne Early Warning Fairey Gannet AEW.3.

Sea Vixen FAW.2

In the post-P.177 world, the FAA would have to make the best use of the Sea Vixen. A new long-range naval SAM was unlikely to materialise before 1972. As early as November 1957 the Admiralty had decided which modifications would be required to improve performance: an extended fuselage for additional fuel tanks; new Rolls-Royce RB.141 Medway low-bypass turbofans; a lightweight AI.18 radar to correct the centre of gravity; flap blowing to maintain take-off and landing performance; redesigned wings; a new collision-course AAM with a snap-up capability against high-altitude targets. The move towards a collision-course weapon meant that the intercept would no longer require a tail-chase, thus saving time and enabling targets to be destroyed further away from the fleet. A development cost of £14 million (up to £20 million if the Admiralty had to fund the AAM too) and a production cost of £500,000 – double that of the P.177 – were meant to dissuade Sandys from pulling the plug on the Saro fighter. In that it failed, but it indicated the improvements required.

In 1958 the Admiralty settled on the extended fuselage, flap blowing and a collision-course weapon – the semi-active *Blue Jay* Mk.5/*Blue Dolphin*, along with adding a CW illuminator to the AI.18C (*Blue Dolphin* was later cancelled in favour of the IR-homing *Blue Jay* Mk.4/*Red Top* with an improved Indium Antimonide seeker for a collision-course capability). These developments would enable to Sea Vixen to engage supersonic targets between 15,000 and 60,000ft (4,570 and 18,290m) with a 15,000ft snap-up capability to intercept higher targets. The American Raytheon AAM-N-6 Sparrow III with semi-active radar homing was also looked at. In May 1958 £25,000 was authorised to begin development work.

Further impetus came in February 1960 as the Admiralty began drafting a Naval Air Staff Requirement for an interceptor/strike aircraft to enter service in 1965/70 – later brought forward to April 1964. The weapons system was to have a high kill probability of a Mach 1.3 bomber up to 55,000ft (17,765m) and subsonic bombers between sea level and 60,000ft (18,290m), plus a 'best possible' capability against Mach 2 targets up to 60,000ft.

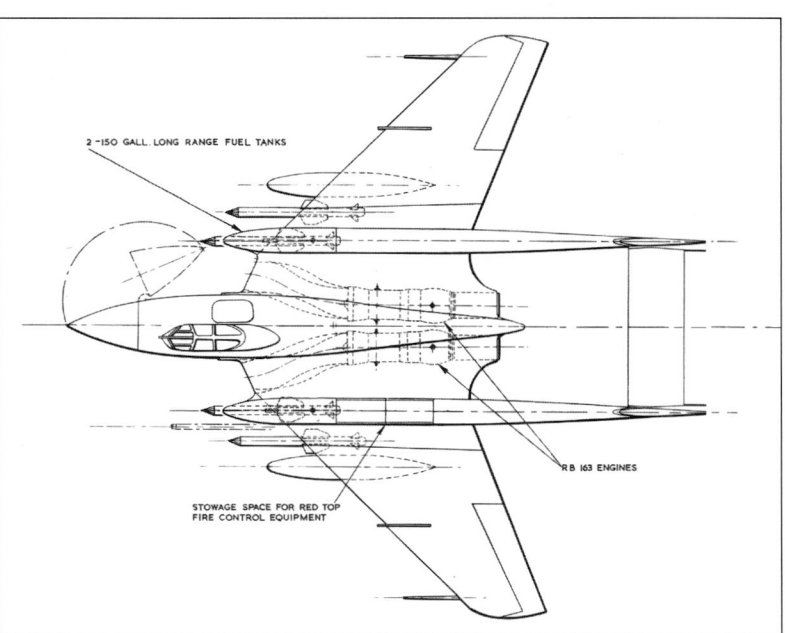

The Christchurch design office looked at ways of improving the Sea Vixen. This version has unreheated Rolls-Royce RB.163 Spey turbofans with minor rear fuselage nacelle changes. *de Havilland Hatfield*

Fitting reheated RB.168 Speys resulted in a longer and fatter rear fuselage in order to accommodate the afterburners. The thermoacoustic effects on the tail booms would have been a structural problem. *de Havilland Hatfield*

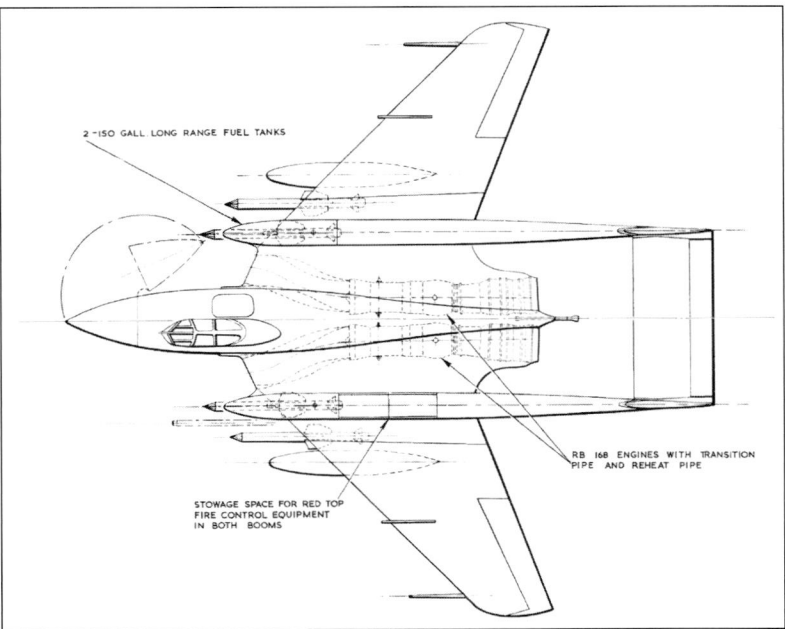

The de Havilland Division of Hawker Siddeley Aviation (DH had been acquired in 1960) began updating the Sea Vixen. The Avons were to be replaced by a pair of Rolls-Royce RB.168 Spey turbofans rated at 11,060lbf (49.1kN) dry and 19,250lbf (85.6kN) reheated to increase the maximum speed to Mach 0.985 in level flight and

Sea Vixen FAW.1 XJ488 was used by de Havilland at Hatfield to test the *Red Top* fire-control computer for the modified AI.18R radar. *Author's Collection*

Mach 1.5 diving. Eventually however, it was decided to retain the Avons. The forward section of the tail booms was extended ahead of the wing leading edge to provide an additional 250gal (1,136L) fuel tankage, increasing range by 52–87nm (96–160km) depending on the sortie profile.

Avionics and armament improvements included: the revised AI.18R radar (a Q-band version was also studied) with an intercept computer and revised fire-control computers for *Red Top* AAMs replacing the Firestreaks; the Pilot Attack Sight; a wide-band radio homer; and provision for four AGM-12 Bullpup air-to-surface missiles (ASMs). The basic weight increased by 682lb (309kg) and the maximum weight was now 46,341lb (21,020kg).

By the summer of 1963 Treasury approval had been given for 29 new-build airframes and 24 FAW.1 conversions. The new-build airframes were manufactured at Hawker Siddeley's Hawarden factory between late 1962 and 1966. The Director General Air (Navy) had requested 80 conversions in the Long Term Costing estimates for 1965, but only 71 were funded due to increasing costs. The unit cost of the new-build aircraft rose too, the Head of the Admiralty's Material Division 3 (Naval) noting that the costs, "have risen, like yeast, from £435,000 to £467,000." In addition, a new 'Partial Aircraft Rework' policy with a shorter 18-month maintenance cycle reduced the required fleet size by nine aircraft. A proposal to run on *Centaur* with Sea Vixen FAW.1s until 1970 would have further reduced the need by 22 aircraft. The final four conversions were cancelled in October 1966, leaving a fleet of 96 aircraft (37 conversions were carried out by the Civil Repair Organisation and 30 by the Naval Repair Organisation).

Service clearance trials of the weapons system took place at the A&AEE at Boscombe Down during May 1962 to June 1964. The weapons system requirements had been further refined to tackling (in order of priority): the subsonic Tupolev Tu-16 *Badger* at altitudes up to 45,000ft (13,750m); low-ltitude Mach 1 attackers between sea level and 500ft (152m); Mach 1.5 capable Tupolev Tu-22 *Blinder* bombers up to 55,000ft (17,765m); fighter versus fighter.

The trials included firings of *Red Top* and Firestreak AAMs (including a mixed load of a pair of each – the Firestreaks being carried on the starboard side), Bullpup ASMs, 2,000lb (907kg) and 1,000lb (454kg) bombs, napalm tanks, 2in (50mm) rocket pods and practice bombs.

The aircraft used were the partially converted FAW.1 XJ488 (for Hawker Siddeley Dynamics trials)

DH.110 Sea Vixen FAW.2

Span	50ft 0in (15.24m); 22ft 3in (6.78m) folded
Length	55ft 7in (16.94m)
Wing area	648ft² (60.26m²)
t/c ratio	10%
All-up weight	41,575lb (18,860kg)
Powerplant	2x Avon Mk.208, 12,250lbf (50.0kN)
Max speed	600kt (1,110km/h) at SL
Rate of climb	9,000ft/min (2,743m/min)
Service ceiling	48,000ft (14,630m)
Armament	4x Red Top, 2x AGM-12 Bullpup, 4x 1,000lb (454kg) bombs, 1x Red Beard, RP pods

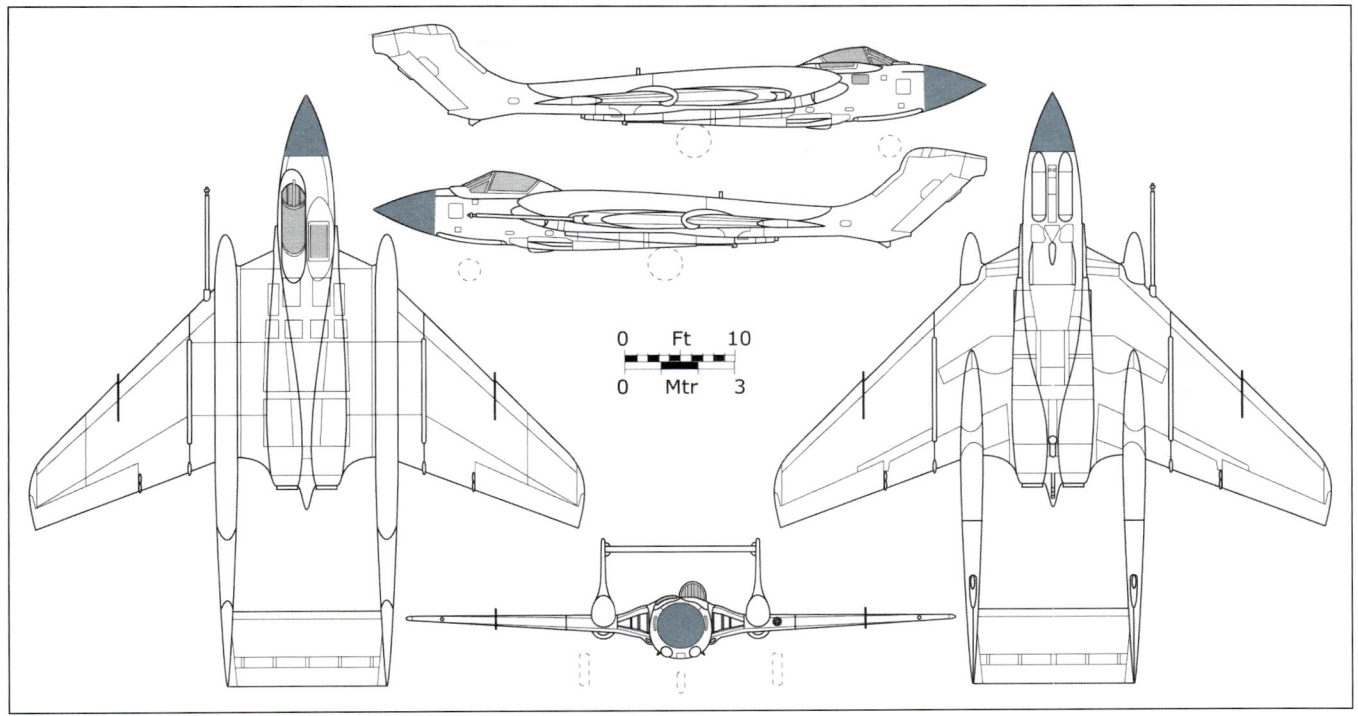

A general arrangement drawing of the Sea Vixen FAW.2. *Chris Gibson*

the interim FAW.2 prototype conversions XN684 and XN685 (first flights at Hatfield on 1 June and 17 August 1962) and the first two production aircraft XP919 and XP920 (XP919 first flew on 8 March 1963.) The decision not to fit new engines meant that the subsonic target altitude limit was restricted to 45,000ft – or 48,000ft (14,630m) with *Red Top's* snap-up attack capability. The fire-control system revealed the ability to plot an intercept course against Mach 1.7 targets up to 51,000ft (15,545m). The AI.18's inability to deal with clutter made snap-down or sea level intercepts reliant on the sea conditions.

The carrier deck trials included 43 catapult launches and arrested landings and 162 touch-and-goes, including night operations, aboard *Hermes* in February 1964. The landing all-up weight (AUW) limit was raised to 35,000lb (15,875kg)

Hermes' Captain, Captain WD O'Brien, complained to his superiors about the speculations concerning the FAW.2's increased AUW impacting

A *Red Top* drill round is fitted to Sea Vixen FAW.2 XJ610 of 892 NAS in this photograph taken in September 1967. *Terry Panopalis Collection*

The Sea Vixen FAW.2 could also be armed with the AGM-12 Bullpup ASM to give a secondary surface strike capability. *Blue Envoy Collection*

Additionally, the Sea Vixen had a potent ground attack capability. The pilot of Sea Vixen FAW.2 XN691 of 899 NAS has released a salvo of Matra 2.6in (68mm) SNEB rockets from four pods mounted on the wing hardpoints. The aircraft had passed into private ownership for preservation by 1988 but several aborted attempts at restoration sadly saw it being scrapped at North Weald in 2001. *Blue Envoy Collection*

A Sea Vixen powered by flower power. During 899 NAS's final Far East cruise aboard HMS *Eagle* in May 1971 to January 1972, the deck crews gave several of the Sea Vixens gaudy paint schemes, including XJ581 which gained flowers on the nose and tail booms and pink missile pylons. Other artistic endeavours included flowers and a sharkmouth on XS577; XJ608 gained a lipstick mouth and long eyelashes; while XN684 had 'For Sale' painted across the upper fuselage and Royal Australian Navy roundels under the wings. *Terry Panopalis Collection*

on the ability of his newly refitted ship to operate the aircraft. Flag Officer Aircraft Carriers (FOAC) also expressed concerns about the narrow recovery safety margins and the effect on aircrew morale, including resignations from the Service – concerns shared by the Admiralty. O'Brien highlighted that night landings were already nerve-wracking for his pilots. His ship could only maintain 24kt when catapulting in the tropics with a clean hull and for most of the time hull fouling and heavy air conditioning usage made attaining 24kt difficult.

FOAC pointed out that in high ambient temperature conditions with no wind that the FAW.2 could not operate from *Hermes* and *Centaur* and would have a marginal capability aboard *Eagle* and *Victorious* (*Ark Royal's* upgraded arrester gear could handle up to 37,000lb [16,780kg]). Following further trials, by 1966 the landing limits for *Hermes* in these climatic conditions had been lowered to allow a reduction of 2.5kt wind over the deck, or a reduction of 5kt with the newly introduced (Mod.1177) auto-throttle – which was initially unreliable but allowed a 125kt approach at 31,000lb (14,600kg) (128kt remained the nighttime landing limit.)

The first squadron to re-equip was 899 NAS at RNAS Yeovilton in February 1964, embarking on *Eagle* the following December as part of the Beira Patrol blockade of the self-proclaimed Republic of Rhodesia. Further proposals for new engines in 1965, the long-range coherent pulse AI.25 radar in 1966 and new long-range AAMs in 1968 never came to fruition. The Sea Vixen's intended retirement date of 1970 was looming and the 1940s-era design was becoming increasingly obsolescent.

A Sea Vixen FAW.2 comes in to land aboard HMS *Ark Royal* in the late 1960s. *Blue Envoy Collection*

7 Anti-submarine warfare

"It may be said that the Gannet is one of the most flexible weapons ever at the disposal of an operational commander."

FAIREY PRESS RELEASE, APRIL 1954

During both World Wars, the German U-boat had been one of the gravest threats to the United Kingdom's ability to remain an active belligerent by targeting the oceanic lifelines on which the nation relied for imports of food and supplies. The submarine threat had been overcome during both wars by a combination of new technology and strategies such as the introduction of defended convoys, Asdic (better known today by its American name Sonar), radio direction-finding, long-range patrol aircraft and smaller escort aircraft carriers. The Fleet Air Arm (FAA) had made a large contribution with its anti-submarine warfare (ASW) operations from escort carriers using Fairey Swordfish, Fairey Barracuda and Grumman Avenger aircraft (the latter supplied under Lend-Lease), providing ASW cover outside the range of shore-based RAF Coastal Command patrol landplanes and flying boats.

The state of maritime technology, even as late as 1945, meant that most submarines could not remain submerged for prolonged periods and could only travel slowly underwater. The adoption of the snorkel to allow diesel engines to run while submerged provided a means of increasing underwater speed and allowing the recharging of batteries. When combined with new high-endurance batteries and improved hull streamlining the resulting 'high-speed submarine' was a much more dangerous threat by 1950. One weakness, however, was that ASV (Air-to-Surface Vessel) radars could pick out the snorkels from among the ocean surface 'clutter' the radar echoes caused by the waves.. By 1960 the nuclear-powered submarine offered an almost invulnerable target capable of high speeds submerged and rapid changes of depth. As the Cold War deepened, the threat of the USSR's expanding submarine fleet grew.

The Fairey Gannet was the FAA's premier fixed-wing anti-submarine aircraft. This ventral view of AS.4 XG790 reveals the large weapon bay originally designed to house the massive *Pentane* homing torpedo, and aft of it, the retractable ASV.19B radar radome. Under the wings are eight racks for rocket projectiles, practice bombs or flares and marine markers. *Author's Collection*

ANTI-SUBMARINE WARFARE

Until the advent of thermonuclear weapons, the Royal Navy believed that it would be called upon to fight a third Battle of the Atlantic during a period of what was termed 'Broken-Back Warfare' following an initial exchange of atomic weapons which might lead to a stalemate. The Admiralty was worried that the new high-speed submarines would be able to evade ASW patrol aircraft, approaching a convoy undetected to make attacks beyond the screening escort ships using long-range torpedoes and making a second attack by using quick reloading gear before the escorts could reach them. Extending the surface escort screen beyond 4.3nm (8km) was impracticable, the only effective solution was an aerial platform.

By the early 1950s the helicopter had emerged as the leading contender to fulfil the role and the Admiralty sought to develop the concept of operating helicopters from ships. Until they could be developed, fixed-wing carrier-based aircraft would have to fulfil the ASW role.

Versatile Firefly: Fighter to Sub-Hunter

The Fairey Firefly had been originally designed in 1940 as a two-seat fighter to meet Specification N.5/40 to succeed the Fairey Fulmar. The Rolls-Royce Griffon V-12 powered Firefly had evolved into a multi-role aircraft during the war and the post-war Mk.5 was designed to be capable of easy conversion to the fighter, night-fighter and ASW roles, being designated FR.5, NF.5 and AS.5 respectively depending on the equipment fitted. A total of 338 Mk.5s were built. Armament comprised four 20mm Hispano Mk.V cannon in the wings plus underwing loads of eight 3in (76mm) rocket projectiles (RPs) or a pair of 1,000lb (454kg) bombs. In the ASW role these payloads also included depth charges, mines, air-sea rescue containers and eight to twelve sonobuoys.

The sonobuoy is an air-dropped expendable floating capsule that deploys a passive hydrophone into the water, sinking to a selected depth and transmitting the acoustic information back to the aircraft by radio. Modern sonobuoys are more complex and include active sonar versions, but development of hydrophone-equipped buoys began during the 1930s for survey work and the operational *High Tea* sonobuoy was first dropped from Short Sunderlands of No. 210 Squadron of Coastal Command in July 1942. Early hydrophones were not sophisticated and relied on the operator being able to distinguish the sound of a submerged submarine's motors and ballast pumps from the background noise of the ocean by ear alone. During the 1950s developments included directional hydrophones able to provide better target bearings and electronic assistance in interpreting the acoustic signals.

The Firefly AS.5 was equipped with American-supplied sonobuoys and AN/APS-4 ASH (Air-Surface, Model H) search radar. The Firefly AS.6 was fitted with British radar equipment and ARI.5286

Fairey Firefly FR.1 MB757 was delivered to Heston for conversion as the AS.7 mock-up with clipped wings, the Mk.4 tailplane and the underwing pods for AN/APS-4 ASH radar and fuel. It also undertook deck trials in 1949. In this photograph the aircraft is carrying a load of dummy mines and flares. *Tony Buttler Collection*

MB757 was modified with a mock-up of the enlarged rear cockpit bubble canopy and it carried out canopy jettison tests in a wind tunnel and in flight during 1950. It was retired in 1952. *Tony Buttler Collection*

This formation of 750 NAS Firefly T.7s is on a training sortie from RNAS Culdrose in 1953. In the rear cockpits can be seen the instructors keeping an eye on their student observers hunched over radar scopes. Nearest the camera is T.7 WJ192. *Terry Panopalis Collection*

sonobuoys (the ARI designation denotes an Air Radio Installation). No cannon were fitted but the Mk.5's wing hardpoints for rockets, bombs, depth charges, mines and sonobuoys were retained. A total of 133 were built (plus 56 Mk.5s were converted later); the first aircraft, serial WB505, flew on 23 March 1949. The type entered service with 814 Naval Air Squadron (NAS) in January 1951 and the last was retired in 1955.

It was clear by 1950 that the Fairey Gannet, being developed to meet Specification GR.17/45, would not enter service until the middle part of that decade and therefore an interim aircraft would be required, Naval Staff Requirement NR/A.28 being issued. The Firefly was again modified, the AS.7 reverting to a chin-mounted radiator and the full-span wings of the wartime Mk.I and Mk.II. It lacked any weapons capability, being intended as a search platform equipped with sonobouys and radar and carrying two observers in the rear cockpit, which gained a large, bulged canopy. A 1,965hp (1,465kW) Griffon 59 was fitted.

The first pre-production AS.7, WJ215, made its maiden flight on 22 May 1951 but trials soon revealed poor handling, especially at low speeds. Fitting a taller tail fin and rudder failed to cure the handling problems and it became clear that the AS.7 was not suitable for carrier operations. This led to a curtailment of the order from 337 aircraft and only 151 were completed at Hayes and Heaton Chapel with the first production aircraft, WJ146, flying on 16 October 1951. Production ended in December 1953.

Visitors to the SBAC Show at Farnborough in September 1951 were treated to Firefly AS.7 WJ216, complete with underwing stores (rocket projectiles not carried in FAA service) and rather ugly flame dampers for the Griffon's exhaust stubs for night landing trials. *Terry Panopalis Collection*

Due to the type's shortcomings – and the advent of the Gannet – many of the AS.7s were also issued directly to training units, including; the Naval Air Anti-Submarine School, 719 NAS, at Royal Navy Air Station Eglinton; and 750 and 796 NAS at RNAS St Merryn. A total of 43 aircraft were completed as T.7 trainers with an instructor and an observer student in the rear cockpit (these aircraft lacked an arrester hook). The other element of the Naval Air Anti-Submarine School, 737 NAS, used the armed Firefly T.2 trainer and Firefly AS.5 aircraft for weapons training.

The T.7 rapidly became surplus to requirements and six were converted at Heaton Chapel during 1953 into prototype T.8 pilotless radio-controlled drones, followed by 34 U.8 conversions to support various missile development programmes, many being expended by Firestreak-toting de Havilland Sea Vixens and Sea Slug surface-to-air missiles (40 older Mk.4 and Mk.5 Fireflies were also converted to similar U.9 standard).

Surplus Fireflies were not just expended as targets, however. This versatile airframe was adapted to conduct several training tasks. Fairey developed a tandem-seater advanced flying trainer conversion on a private-venture basis, the T.1 featuring a new rear cockpit raised by 12in (30.5cm) with a separate windscreen and canopy replacing the original observer's cockpit. The similar T.2 conversions retained two 20mm Hispano cannon and the underwing bomb racks for tactical weapons training. The main user was 737 NAS, the Naval Air Anti-Submarine School at RNAS Eglinton, where they were used for the instrument flying and anti-submarine weapons phases of the Operational Flying School Training Course. Around 50 surplus FR.I fighters were converted into unarmed T.3 observer trainers equipped with ASH radar. They were used by 796 NAS at St Merryn between July 1950 and June 1953 on the advanced phase of the observer training course (being a two-seat aircraft no instructor could be carried, unlike the three-seat T.7 which replaced it.)

The Avenger returns

The interim Firefly AS.7 lacked any offensive weapons capability and it was clear that additional ASW aircraft would be required. The solution came from the USA via the Mutual Defense Assistance Program (MDAP); a batch of 100 surplus General Motors TBM-3E Avengers. The FAA of course was no stranger to the Avenger, having operated over 900 as torpedo- and dive-bombers during the war.

The aircraft carrier maintenance ship HMS *Perseus* ferried the first six aircraft across the Atlantic in March 1953, these being delivered in US standard to 815 and 824 NAS. The remainder were modified by Scottish Aviation at Prestwick with British electrics; the AS.4 retained the ASH radar pod under the starboard wing while the AS.5 received British ASV.19A radar. The weapon bay was altered for British depth charges and bombs and underwing racks for eight 3in RPs were fitted. Most aircraft retained the dorsal turret but the machine gun was removed. One unforeseen problem was that towing the disembarked aircraft 30 miles (48km) from the port to Prestwick Airport caused damage to the wing root attachment points, which required repair work.

From January 1954 the AS.4 and AS.5 conversions began to be issued to 814, 815, 820 and 824 NAS. Service with these units was short, with 814 NAS being the last to convert to the Gannet in November 1955. The Avengers passed to second-line NAS for training and trials duties as well

Piston-powered ASW aircraft

	Fairey Firefly NF.5	Fairey Firefly AS.7	Grumman TBM-3E Avenger AS.4
Span	41ft 2in (12.55m) ; 13ft 6in (4.11m) folded	44ft 6in (13.56m) ; 13ft 6in (4.11m) folded	54ft 2in (16.51m); 19ft 0in (5.79m) folded
Length	37ft 11in (11.55m)	38ft 3in (11.65m)	40ft 0in (12.20m)
Wing area	330ft² (30.65m²)	342.5ft² (31.81m²)	490ft² (45.52m²)
Loaded weight	13,927lb (6,317kg)	13,970lb (6,335kg)	16,761lb (7,600kg)
Powerplant	1x Griffon 74, 2,245hp (1,674kW)	1x Griffon 59, 1,965hp (1,465kW)	1x Cyclone R-2600-20, 1,750hp (1,304kW)
Max speed	335kt (621km/h) at 14,000ft (4,265m)	260kt (482km/h) at 10,750ft (3,275m)	226kt (420km/h)
Rate of climb	2,050ft/min (625m/min) at SL	1,550ft/min (472m/min) at SL	?
Service ceiling	29,200ft (8,900m)	25,500ft (7,770m)	22,600ft (6,890m)
Max range	1,130nm (2,090km)	747nm (1,385km) at 144kt (267km/h)	982nm (1,820km)
Armament	4x 20mm Hispano, 2x 1,000lb (454kg) bombs, 8x 60lb (27kg) RPs	None	2,000lb (907kg) of bombs or depth charges, 8x RPs

The Grumman Avenger served as an interim solution until the Gannet was ready. This Avenger is ECM.6B XB446, on the strength of 831 NAS at Culdrose in 1960. The ventral radome is the radio jamming antenna. Today it resides at the Fleet Air Arm Museum at Yeovilton. *Terry Panopalis Collection*

as to Royal Navy Volunteer Reserve (RNVR) squadrons to replace their Fireflies. Following the disbandment of the RNVR squadrons in March 1957, the survivors were transferred to the Dutch and French navies (19 and 47 aircraft respectively).

There were also small numbers of specialist conversions. Four Avenger TS.5 aircraft received ARI.18144 *Orange Harvest* passive electronic support measures (ESM) equipment. *Orange Harvest* could detect radar emissions from RLK-101 Albatros (NATO codename *Snoop Tray*) and MRK-50 *Snoop Pair* surface-search radars used by Soviet submarines. These aircraft were operated by 745 NAS.

Five AS.6 aircraft were fitted with electronic countermeasures equipment (ECM) supplied under MDAP; an AN/APR-9 search receiver and AN/APT-1 and -4 radio jammers along with a British *Airborne Cigar* ABC voice jammer. The converted ECM.6 aircraft had a ventral radome for the jamming antenna. They were allotted to the Naval Air Radio Warfare Unit, 751 NAS, based at RAF Watton, the home of the Central Signals Establishment and the RAF's electronic reconnaissance and electronic warfare (EW) squadrons. The squadron's main role was EW training for the crews of RN warships and it participated in four carrier deployments: aboard *Illustrious* during 31 August to 2 October 1953, *Centaur* during 19 February to 15 March, *Bulwark* during 7-23 June 1955 and a week-long deployment aboard *Eagle* in November 1957.

Gannet – Atlantic hunter

Fairey had long been interested in aircraft layouts using two fuselage-mounted engines driving a common driveshaft with a contra-rotating propeller. Engineer Captain A Graham Forsyth (who would go on to work on the Rotodyne VTOL transport in the 1950s) proposed an engine comprised of two 12-cylinder horizontally-opposed engines sharing a common crankcase to drive a contra-rotating propeller – leading to the P.24 Prince engine. The idea was that one 'half' of the engine could be shut down during cruising flight to reduce fuel consumption and would be a more compact arrangement than a traditional twin-engine aircraft aboard aircraft carriers. The P.24 Prince was test flown but never entered production.

To meet Specification O.21/44 for a torpedo-bomber/reconnaissance aircraft, the formula was slightly altered to use two standard Rolls-Royce Merlin V-12 engines located below and behind the pilot's cockpit to drive a contra-rotating propeller. Two prototypes were ordered but were quickly superseded by a similar project, the Strike Fighter developed from August 1944. The Strike Fighter was refined in March 1945 under Specification N.16/45 but the prototypes were not ordered until June 1946 and by then a Rolls-Royce proposal to use their new AP.25 Coupled Tweed double-turboprop engine had been adopted. The Coupled Tweed would provide 3,020shp (2,252kW) plus 380lbf (1.7kN) of residual exhaust thrust. On 7 October 1946 Specification GR.17/45 was prioritised over the Strike Fighter and soon after Rolls-Royce cancelled further work on the Tweed to focus on its many other gas turbine engine projects and N.16/45 was shelved.

Specification GR.17/45 had been issued in 1945, alongside Operational Requirement OR.220, for a two-seat twin-engine carrier-based anti-submarine aircraft with a gross weight of 16,500lb (7,485kg) and a maximum speed of 265kt, capable of operating from the *Colossus* and *Majestic*-class light fleet carriers. It would be armed with homing torpedoes and would be equipped with ASV.15 search radar and eight American AN/CRT-1 sonobuoys, as well as their AN/ARR-3 sonobuoy radio receiver. Fairey's design team led by Chief

Tools for the Job: Homing torpedoes

The air-dropped, acoustic-homing torpedo was introduced by the US Navy during the Second World War and rapidly became the weapon of choice to destroy submarines. They were dropped into the general area of the target submarine as identified by sonobuoy or ASV contact and the weapon would perform its own search patten before homing onto the sound of the submarine's propellers or machinery.

The UK began its own development programme in the late 1940s with Zeta and Zoster, part of the Z-series of advanced homing torpedo concepts. Zoster the was air-dropped variant of the Zonal winged-torpedo to provide a stand-off range. Work on the Z-series ended in 1949 without any success, but Zeta gave rise to the Vickers-Whitehead Mk.21 torpedo, codenamed *Pentane*.

Development work began in 1949, becoming a joint Admiralty/Air Staff programme linked to Operational Requirements AW.59 and OR.1058 in October 1954. *Pentane* weighed 1,950lb (884.5kg) and a was large weapon of 21in (533mm) diameter (overall span 27in [685mm] including the air tail) and 14ft (4.26m) long (16ft 2.5in [4.95m] including the air tail and parachute assembly.) These statistics caused headaches for aircraft designers trying to provide a large enough weapon bay, which was essential as it had to be internally carried as the batteries and electronics needed to be kept warm in flight. Powered by silver-zinc batteries, it was capable of 30kt to ensure that no diesel-powered submarine could outrun it. Development dragged on, the Admiralty growing uneasy about the size and weight with few FAA aircraft or helicopters able to carry it. *Pentane* was finally cancelled in 1958, having cost £1.72 million and deprived lightweight homing torpedoes of much needed development funding.

The lightweight torpedo was the passive-homing Mk.30 Dealer-B. This was another joint Admiralty/Air Staff programme under AW.60 and OR.1094 for use with helicopters and ASW aircraft and was developed in parallel with the ship-launched Mk.20E Bidder anti-submarine homing torpedo. Of 18in (457mm) diameter and 8ft (2.4m) long, Dealer-B had a single propeller and eight control surfaces. Trials against submarines during 1953 revealed a high hit-rate and provisional service release was achieved in 1954. Dealer-B remained in service until 1970, being exported to several NATO nations, some of which used it until the early 1980s.

An improved Mk.30 Mod.1 with an estimated hit probability superior to any torpedo then existing was cancelled in 1955 in favour of licence-building the cheaper, but much inferior, US Mk.43 torpedo. A 1956 project for a 14in (355mm) diameter, active/passive torpedo for helicopters had begun prototype trials using a Dealer-B motor married to a new passive homer, but the programme was cancelled in 1957, along with a smaller 12in (305mm) diameter project.

Treasury approval was given to purchase 50 US Mk.43 Mod.1 torpedoes and Plessey was contracted to develop an 'Anglicised' version in 1956. The Mk.43 was 10in (254mm) in diameter, 7.6ft (2.3m) long and weighed 265lb (120kg). The acquisition range was 1,200ft (365m) with a 2.2nm (4.1km) effective range travelling at 21kt for six minutes. It had a 50% kill chance against a submarine travelling at 12kt.

The Mk.43 was followed by a licence-built US Mk.44 torpedo, 1,900 being produced as the UK Mk.44 Mod.1. This was of 12.75in (323mm) in diameter and weighed 430lb (195kg). The acquisition range was 1,500–2,100ft (457–640m) with a 3nm (5.5km) effective range travelling at 30kt and it was capable of engaging submarines as deep as 1,000ft (305m). It was a disappointing weapon, however, with poor acoustic performance in shallow water and an inefficient, helical acoustic search pattern.

Work began on an improved UK Mk.44 Mod.2 with shallow water improvements, an optional surface attack mode, dual homing frequencies (to allow a pair to be dropped together), improved endurance and a better search pattern. It would be capable of diving to 1,500ft (457m) and would have a new warhead using 90lb (41kg) of RDX explosive. Adding a 1,500–15,000ft (457–4,572m) forerun – the safety distance before the acoustic homer was activated – would allow use from surface ships and enable helicopters to attack without having to raise their dipping sonar and thus break sonar contact. This also fulfilled the minimum requirements of naval requirement NSR.6169 for a stand-off ASW weapon.

In 1965 the RN was given project oversight and the weapon was redesignated Mk.31. Development hit several technical problems and costs spiralled, GEC-Marconi taking over development before cancellation came in 1971. The US Mk.46 was procured instead to arm helicopters and the Ikara stand-off ASW missile. The Mk.46 weighed 490lb (222kg), had an acquisition range of 4,500ft (1.3km), with a 5.3nm (9.9km) effective range travelling at 45kt and was capable of engaging submarines travelling at 33kt as deep as 1,500ft (457m).

Designer Herbert Eugene Chaplin based their submission on the Strike Fighter and completed their first brochure on 14 December 1945, which contained two Type Q designs, Schemes A and C.

Although based on the Strike Fighter design the Type Q featured a large cockpit for the crew and an internal weapon bay for a single homing torpedo or six depth charges/bombs. Sixteen 3in RPs could be carried underwing. A second brochure on 12 March 1946 contained two revised designs, Schemes D and E. The wing area was increased from 445ft² (41.2m²) to 475ft² (44.2m²) to allow take-offs in low wind speeds at full overload weight – Scheme D 18,200lb (8,256kg), Scheme E 17,610lb (7,988kg). The landing approach speed while carrying a full ordnance load and two hours of fuel was reduced to 66kt.

Scheme D was powered by the AP.25 Coupled Tweed and Scheme E had the Armstrong Siddeley Double Mamba turboprop (the coupled version of the Mamba being developed at Fairey's request.) The two engines coupled to a contra-rotating propeller, each engine driving one of the propellers, provided twin-engine safety and the ability to cruise on one engine to save fuel. When the Tweed was abandoned the engine choice automatically fell to the Double Mamba, although that engine did not begin bench testing until 1948. One advantage of the Mamba was its ability to run on kerosene,

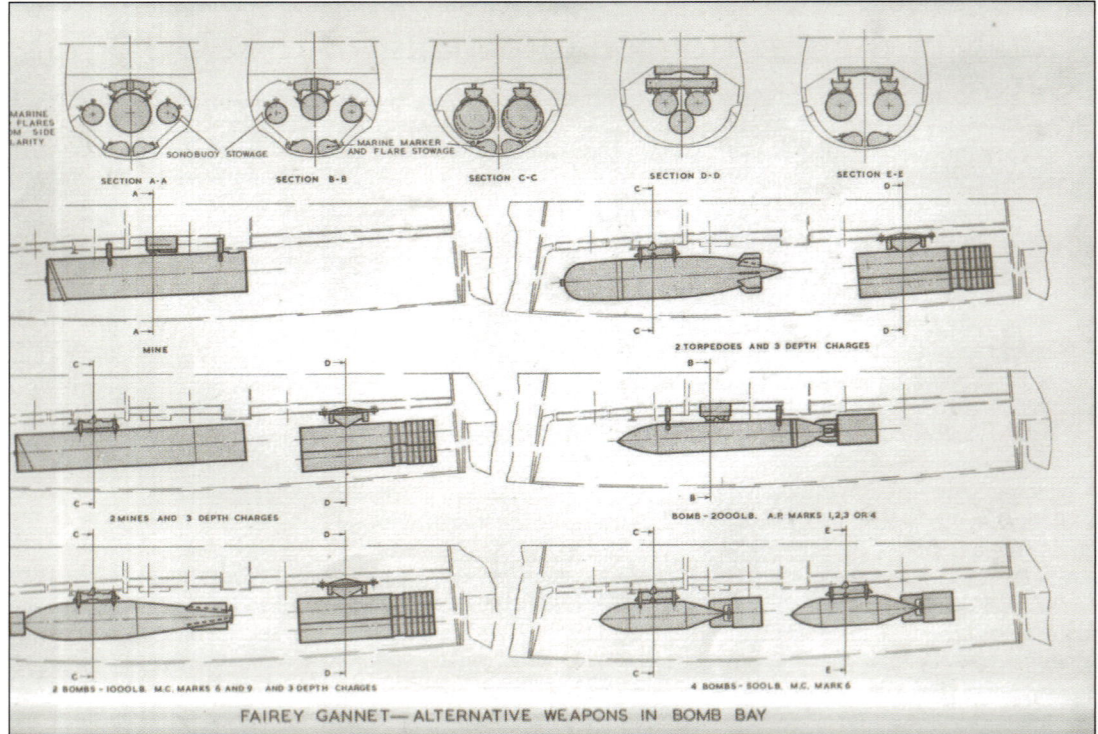

The Gannet's weapons bay could carry a wide variety of stores for the anti-submarine, anti-shipping and minelaying roles. *Leonardo UK*

AVGAS or naval grade diesel to avoid the need to provide separate fuel stowage aboard carriers.

The Ministry of Supply (MoS) placed an order for two prototypes on 12 August 1946. The Type Q was redesignated as the Fairey 17 in 1949 and the design was refined with separate tandem cockpits for the pilot and observer. Production would use a novel jigging technique developed by Fairey. The Envelope System built the stressed-skin structures inwards, the skin plating and internal structure being assembled to a drill template which was shaped to the external form of the section which allowed better control of the external contours.

The first prototype, VR546, was moved by road to Aldermaston for its first flight on 19 September 1949 with Chief Test Pilot Group Captain Richard Gordon Slade at the controls with the chief engineer DL Hollis Willis acting as observer. Handling problems soon became apparent during the flight with a lack of forward trim range and elevator power to hold the nose down at speeds over 147kt. Selecting the slow-flying position when the Fairey-Youngman flaps were

The first prototype Gannet, VR546, was fitted with a dummy third cockpit canopy for aerodynamic flight testing. All production aircraft would have three separate cockpits. *Crown Copyright*

The third prototype Gannet WE488 on display at Farnborough in September 1951. Note the larger canopy for the rear cockpit than on production aircraft. *Terry Panopalis Collection*

retracted also caused a sharp change in trim. The elevator hinge position and spring tab were altered but on 25 November VR546 crashed on take-off as Slade attempted to stop violent porpoising at unstick speed. Repairs took three months and flight trials resumed on 1 March 1950 but problems remained: the rudder was too light, the ailerons too heavy and on landing it proved impossible to maintain a nose-up attitude to keep the nosewheel off the runway once the engine power was cut.

Further improvements enabled the naval evaluation to begin at the Aeroplane & Armament Experimental Establishment (A&AEE) at Boscombe Down in June, where six FAA pilots completed 19 hours of Airfield Dummy Deck Landings (ADDLs). The first carrier landing occurred on 19 June aboard *Illustrious*, with 25 landings completed that day. The Type Q still showed a lack of elevator authority, this was finally cured by adding an inter-connection between the flaps and tailplane incidence gear to alter the trim when the flaps were lowered. The second prototype, VR557, flew on 6 July 1950.

In 1949 the new Naval Staff Requirement NR/A.9 had called for a second observer as a dedicated ASV radar operator. The need to incorporate a third cockpit in the rear fuselage (the requirements also stated the need for a simple means of conveying a written message of maximum folded size 2.75 × 1 × 1in (7× 2.5 × 2.5cm) between the centre and rear cockpits) as well as a longer weapon bay to stow *Pentane* led to the need for an additional production prototype. These changes also added weight, which made single-engine flying on one half of the Double Mamba increasingly difficult. The design changes were aerodynamically tested on VR546, a dummy third cockpit canopy being fitted and the dummy ASV radome was moved further aft. Two auxiliary fins were added on the tailplanes to increase the fin area to compensate for these changes.

The third prototype, WE488, incorporated these new features and flew on 10 May 1951. It carried out flight tests until it was seriously damaged in an accident on 9 October 1953. In January 1952 VR546 made five experimental flights (which the MoS was unaware of) with the tailplane moved to the top of the tail fin but a proposal to test this layout for production went no further. In May, the main undercarriage legs were fixed down and sloped backwards to simulate the 12in (30.5cm) rearward shift of the undercarriage on the production aircraft to correct a tendency to tip onto the tail due to the shift in the centre of gravity from adding the extra cockpit and moving the ASV. Carrier trials aboard *Eagle* went ahead despite the makeshift fixed undercarriage, totalling 66 take-offs and landings. The A&AEE concluded that, "the aircraft is exceptionally well suited to carrier operation." In all, the three prototypes accumulated over 250 carrier landings with further trials aboard *Illustrious* and *Eagle* being completed in October 1953.

Comparative trials against the Blackburn B.88/Y.B.1 during 1950 revealed some problems with accessibility for maintenance but 100 aircraft – now named the Gannet – were ordered on 14 March 1951 as a 'Super Priority' programme essential to the defence of the UK. Specification GR.117P was issued to Fairey on 24 October. It requested a maximum speed of at least 265kt at 5,000ft (1,525m) and the ability to fly on one engine at speeds 'well below 150kt'. Endurance was to be three hours at 5,000ft (down to sea level). The All-up Weight (AUW) was not to exceed 19,600lb (8,890kg). A Ferranti ASV.19B surface-search radar was mounted in the retractable 'dustbin' radome. The Admiralty then imposed a ban on further

Gannet AS.4 XA426 is carrying an interesting underwing load of 3in (76mm) RPs and sonobuoy dispensers at the SBAC Show at Farnborough in September 1956. Note the feathered rear coaxial propeller, signifying that one 'half' of the Armstrong Siddeley Double Mamba engine has been shut down. *Blue Envoy Collection*

requirement changes in order not to delay the development any further.

The Admiralty's desire to replace the Firefly was revealed in June 1950; with the Double Mamba still in development, it was proposed to fit the Rolls-Royce Griffon 57 instead to speed deliveries (and save money). In the event, the Grumman Avengers supplied under MDAP plugged the capability gap.

A Working Party was set up in November 1952 in response to requests from the Admiralty and RAF Coastal Command for more anti-submarine aircraft to cover the Atlantic and UK waters in order to determine the most economical solution – carrier-based Gannets or shore-based Avro Shackleton MR.2A aircraft. The RN's assessed wartime need was 76 Gannets and 40 ASW helicopters operating from nine light fleet carriers (three *Centaur*-class and six *Colossus*-class) and 10 Merchant Aircraft Carrier conversions (four light ASW aircraft or helicopters each); Coastal Command needed 163 Shackletons and 356 Lockheed Neptune MR.1s. The conclusion was that the provision of 235 Gannets should be unaltered.

Test pilot Peter Twiss flew the first production Gannet AS.1, WN339, on 9 June 1953. By October four aircraft had been completed. On 5 April 1954, 703X Flight of 703 NAS, the Service Trials Unit, took delivery of four Gannet AS.1 for intensive flight trials; the elevator control problems lingering on. The unit lost one Gannet when the Double Mamba failed on take-off and another was damaged in a belly landing following a hydraulic system failure.

The Gannet's weapon bay could accommodate a wide range of stores. Seen here is an array of mines, depth charges (the blunt end slows the descent in the water, allowing the aircraft to get clear of the blast when set to explode at shallow depths) and a US Mk.43 homing torpedo. *Blue Envoy Collection*

Fairey Gannet design evolution

	Type Q Scheme D	Type Q Scheme E	Gannet AS.1	Gannet Mk.4 (project)	Gannet Mk.5 (project)	Gannet AS.4
Crew	Two	Two	Three	Three	Three	Three
Span	55ft 0in (16.76m); 19ft 6in (5.94m) folded	55ft 0in (16.76m); 19ft 6in (5.94m) folded	54ft 4in (16.56m); 19ft 6in (5.94m) folded	54ft 4in (16.56m); 19ft 6in (5.94m) folded	54ft 4in (16.56m); 19ft 6in (5.94m) folded	54ft 4in (16.56m); 19ft 6in (5.94m) folded
Length	43ft 0in (13.11m)	43ft 0in (13.11m)	43ft 0in (13.11m)	43ft 0in (13.11m)	43ft 0in (13.11m)	43ft 0in (13.11m)
Wing area	475ft² (42.2m²)	475ft² (42.2m²)	482.8ft² (44.9m²)	482.8ft² (44.9m²)	482.8ft² (44.9m²)	482.8ft² (44.9m²)
All-up weight	16,750lb (7,600kg)	16,550lb (7,505kg)	19,600lb (8,890kg)	22,350lb (10,140kg)	21,680lb (9,835kg)	23,446lb (10,635kg)
Powerplant	1x AP.25 Tweed, 2,500shp (1,846kW)	2x coupled Mamba	1x ASDM.1 Double Mamba Mk.100, 2,950ehp (2,200kW)	1x P.156, 4,400shp (3,821kW)	1x ASDM.4 Double Mamba	1x ASDM.3 Double Mamba Mk.101, 3,035ehp (2,263kW)
Max speed	266kt (492km/h) at SL; 274kt (508km/h) at 15,000ft (4,570m)	274kt (508km/h) at SL; 265kt (491km/h) at 15,000ft (4,570m)	269kt (499km/h) at SL	?	?	259kt (481km/h)
Service ceiling	?	?	25,000ft (7,620m)	?	?	25,000ft (7,620m)
Armament	1x homing torpedo, 6x depth charges or bombs, 16x RPs	1x homing torpedo, 6x depth charges or bombs, 16x RPs	1x 2,000lb (907kg) mine, 2x 1,000lb (454kg) bombs or mines, 4x 500lb (227kg) bombs, 6x depth charges, 2x homing torpedoes, 16x RPs	1x Green Cheese, 2x 1,000lb (454kg) bombs or mines, 4x 500lb (227kg) bombs, 16x RPs	1x 2,000lb (907kg) mine, 2x 1,000lb (454kg) bombs or mines, 4x 500lb (227kg) bombs, 6x depth charges, 2x homing torpedoes, 16x RPs	1x 2,000lb (907kg) mine, 2x 1,000lb (454kg) bombs or mines, 4x 500lb (227kg) bombs, 6x depth charges, 2x homing torpedoes, 16x RPs

Tropical trials were conducted at Khartoum, Sudan in November using WN372.

On 17 January 1955 826 NAS formed at RNAS Lee-on-Solent followed by 824 NAS at RNAS Eglington on 21 February (it also absorbed 703X Flight) and 825 at RNAS Culdrose in July. In May, 826 NAS embarked aboard *Eagle* for the first operational deployment to the Mediterranean and Malta. By the end of 1955 33 AS.1s had been delivered to the Royal Australian Navy (RAN) with 816 and 817 NAS forming up at Culdrose before their delivery aboard HMAS *Sydney*. These aircraft were not retired until 1967.

The AS.1 production batch of 183 aircraft (264 had originally been ordered) also included 34 Gannet T.2s, a flying training version without armament. The second cockpit was converted for an instructor with a duplicated set of flying controls and a periscope and two passenger seats were fitted in the rear observers' cockpit. The RAN also received three T.2s.

The Gannet's armament capability was formidable. The weapon bay could carry in the Strike Role one *Pentane* or two Dealer-B homing torpedoes or six Mk.11 or Mk.16 depth charges – other bombloads included one 2,000lb (907kg) or two 1,000lb (454kg) or six 500lb (226kg) bombs – with external loads of 16 3in Mk.8 or 24 Mk.5 RPs, eight Illuminating Rockets or eight practice bombs (a Ferranti Gyro Rocket Gunsight was provided for the pilot). The Search Role included the carriage of eight anti-submarine training indicators, four T.1946 (DRSB1) directional sonobuoys or 18 × T.1945 (NDRSB) non-directional sonobuoys, six marine markers and four flares. In the Mining Role the bay would accommodate two A Mk.7 or four A Mk.8 or two A Mk.10 or A Mk.A Type S or one A Mk.12 mines plus four marine markers and four flame floats. The weapon bay could also be fitted with a 100gal (454lit) auxiliary fuel tank.

The maximum range in the Search Role, cruising on one engine was 653nm (1,210km); in the Strike Role with *Pentane* and a *Blue Silk* Doppler navigation radar external pod, this would decrease to 527–473nm (976–876km) cruising on both engines.

As good as the Gannet was, upgrades were soon investigated. In March 1952 plans had emerged for a Series II airframe, which by June 1953 had grown to cover the Mk.3 Airborne Early Warning (AEW), Mk.4 strike and Mk.5 ASW aircraft (the Gannet AEW.3 is discussed in Chapter 9). The Mk.5 would receive ARI.5885 *Blue Silk* Doppler navigation radar and Search Receiver SD.62 and modern alternating current electrics would be fitted. The two-seat Mk.4 would have ASV.20 search radar, *Blue Silk* and the 3,300lb (1,495kg) *Green Cheese* anti-ship missile (whose weight escalated to 3,800lb (1,725kg) – too

The Gannet ECM.6 was the second electronic warfare conversion of the type. The ASV.19B radar was replaced by the jamming antenna. Gannet XA460 was converted to ECM.6 standard in 1962. It was stripped of its ECM equipment in 1966 but returned to service in 1967 as a continuation trainer, due to a lack of serviceable Gannets. XA460 is seen here in February 1970 when it was assigned to the Gannet Support Unit at Lossiemouth. Retired in 1971 it today resides at the Ulster Aviation Society at Long Kesh, Lisburn. *Terry Panopalis Collection*

heavy for the Gannet – and being too large to enable the weapon bay doors to be closed around it). An alternative weapon was the *Yellow Sand* homing anti-ship bomb proposed by EMI and Smiths. The proposed engine was the ASDM.4 Double Mamba (a coupled ASM.6 Mamba, which was in development for the Short Seamew). The estimated AUW for the Mk.4 was 22,350lb (10,140kg) and 21,680lb (9,835kg) for the Mk.5. Fairey submitted its brochure to the MoS on 27 October.

The need for improved performance in tropical conditions and attain 20,000ft (6,095m) to release *Green Cheese* and greater fuel economy saw other engines being considered for the heavier Mk.4. The Napier Eland and Rolls-Royce RB.109 Tyne were ruled out as they were not coupled engines, leaving the Armstrong-Siddeley P.156, a 4,400shp (3,821kW) double engine with 20% lower fuel consumption than the Double Mamba. Although development would cost £3.5 million, money would be saved be using the same reduction gearing as the Double Mamba ASM.4

Surplus Gannets found use as Carrier On-Board aircraft ferrying modest amounts of important freight and personnel from shore to the carriers. This COD.4 framed by a Sea Vixen FAW.2 is aboard HMS *Eagle*. *Terry Panopalis Collection*

and the MoS pointed out that the 2,000shp (1,491kW) single-shaft P.160 derivative would be an ideal civil airliner and helicopter engine. Around this time the Admiralty accepted that exposing the slow Gannet to the formidable radar-guided anti-aircraft artillery aboard the *Sverdlov*-class cruisers was unacceptably hazardous and the requirement to carry *Green Cheese* was withdrawn. The resulting cancellation of *Green Cheese* and the Gannet Mk.4 strike version removed the rationale to fund a new engine and the P.156 was also cancelled in October 1955.

Fairey was awarded a contract in 1954 to investigate the use of blown flaps to reduce the approach speed by 12kt. The firm suggested a trials installation mounting a Turbomeca air compressor in the forward part of the weapon bay, but nothing further came of the idea.

The need to improve engine power to cope with the increases in weight during development led to the improved 3,035ehp (2,263kW) ASDM.3 Double Mamba 101. On its return from tropical trials at Khartoum, AS.1 WN372 was fitted with the new engine, flying on 12 March 1956. This became the prototype Gannet AS.4 (not to be confused with the proposed strike Mk.4 above).

The first production AS.4 followed in April and by August 824 NAS had begun re-equipping. The maximum normal take-off weight was 19,600lb (8,890kg) with an overload weigh of 21,600lb (9,797kg). Production was curtailed at 90 and its service life was short, with retirement coming by July 1960 when the ASW task was handed over to the Westland Whirlwind HAS.7 helicopter fleet. The early retirement also meant the cancellation of several pending improvements in 1958: certification of engine intake de-icing; provision of *Blue Silk* (in an underwing pod), ARI.18144 *Orange Harvest* ESM, the ARI.181008 Sonobuoy Mk.1C system; ARI.18120 *Violet Picture* UHF homing; and the upgrade of the radios from VHF to UHF.

Production also included eight T.5 trainers, similar to the earlier T.2 but with the ASDM.3 Double Mamba. The T.5s used for check flights and standards training by 849 NAS were the last Gannet trainers to retire in 1978. Five AS.4 were later stripped of mission equipment to serve in the Carrier Onboard Delivery (COD) logistical transport role with 849 NAS.

Seven aircraft were converted with ECM equipment to replace the Avenger ECM.6; one Gannet ECM.4 and six ECM.6 being operated by 831 NAS, the Naval Air Radio Warfare Unit, at Culdrose (originally an ECM variant of the AEW.3 had been desired but conversions were cheaper than new-build aircraft). These aircraft were fitted with US-supped AN/APR-5 and -9 search receiver and AN/ALT-6 and -7 jamming equipment by the Naval Air Radio Installation Unit at RNAS Lee-on-Solent.

The AS.4 was an export success, the West German Marineflieger ordering 15 aircraft, which were diverted from the RN's order and delivered in 1958. The Marineflieger also received one T.5 trainer and two surplus FAA T.2s upgraded to T.5 standard. The Indonesian Angkatan Laut Republik Indonesia (Naval Air Arm) acquired 20 refurbished Gannet AS.1 in 1959. The first batch of Indonesian pilots were trained by Fairey at White Waltham using WN365, which Fairey had converted to T.5 standard as a company communications aircraft (registered as G-APYO). It later re-joined the FAA with the new serial XT752. Attempts to interest the Royal Canadian Navy failed and a deal with Yugoslavia in 1957 could not be reached due to the Gannet's high price and the RN's reluctance to supply Mk.30 Dealer-B torpedoes.

Cross-decking with US Navy carriers was a vital part of NATO cooperation. Gannet ECM.4 XG798 of 831 NAS is visiting the USS *Forrestal* in June 1960 surrounded by (anti-clockwise) a Vought F8U Crusader, two Douglas AD4 Skyraiders, a Douglas A3D Skywarrior bomber and Grumman S2F Tracker ASW aircraft. *Terry Panopalis Collection*

WINGS OVER THE FLEET

GR.17/45 Also-rans

Blackburn and Short Brothers also submitted design proposals to meet Specification GR.17/45. Both proposals would fly but be denied production orders. Blackburn's initial proposal was a development of the B.48 Firecrest torpedo-bomber-fighter, the B.54 (soon redesignated Y.A.5 under the Society of British Aircraft Constructors system.) The B.54 had a similar inverted-gull laminar-flow wing and featured a ventral retractable ASV radome (initially a chin radome had been proposed), a weapon bay, tricycle undercarriage and would be powered by either an Armstrong Siddeley Python or Napier Double-Naiad turboprops driving a contra-rotating propeller. Blackburn's design philosophy was to offer higher engine power with a relatively high wing loading. Three Y.A.5 prototypes were ordered.

Like the Fairey Type Q, the design grew in weight. With the GR.17/45 gross weight limit raised to 17,500lb (7,940kg), the Y.A.5 was expected to weigh in at 17,100lb (7,755kg). Armstrong Siddeley was experiencing development problems with the Naiad and the coupled version was not expected before 1949. Blackburn therefore made the decision to fit the prototype with a 2,000hp (1,491kW) Rolls-Royce Griffon 56 to enable aerodynamic flight tests to begin. In the event, both the first and second prototypes were completed with Griffons, the redesignated Y.A.7, WB781, flying on 20 September 1949 (one day behind the Type Q's maiden flight) and Y.A.8 WB788 following on 3 May 1950.

Following catapult launch and arrested landing trials at Farnborough in January 1950 using WB871, the initial deck landing trials took place aboard *Illustrious* during 6–17 February. A total of 19 landings were made (on one landing the hook hit the carrier's round down and snapped.) The Royal Aircraft Establishment pilots assessed that the aircraft was unusually directionally stable during arrested landings with no tendency to swing, even if the wire was caught off-centre.

Specification GR.17/45 designs

	Blackburn B.54/ Y.A.5	Blackburn B.54/ Y.A.7 & 8	Blackburn B.88/ Y.B.1	Type Q Scheme D	Type Q Scheme E	Gannet AS.1	Short Brothers S.B.3
Crew	Two	Three	Three	Two	Two	Three	Three
Span	43ft 5in (13.23m); 19ft 6in (5.94m) folded	43ft 5in (13.23m); 19ft 6in (5.94m) folded	44ft 2in (13.46m); 19ft 6in (5.94m) folded	55ft 0in (16.76m); 19ft 6in (5.94m) folded	55ft 0in (16.76m); 19ft 6in (5.94m) folded	54ft 4in (16.56m); 19ft 6in (5.94m) folded	59ft 9in (18.21m); 19ft 10in (6.04m) folded
Length	42ft 6in (12.95m)	42ft 5in (12.92m)	42ft 8in (13.01m)	43ft 0in (13.11m)	43ft 0in (13.11m)	43ft 0in (13.11m)	44ft 8in (13.62m)
Wing area	?	?	?	475ft² (42.2m²)	475ft² (42.2m²)	482.8ft² (44.9m²)	560.4ft² (52.1m²)
All-up weight	17,100lb (7,757kg)	?	13,091lb (5,938kg) unarmed	16,750lb (7,600kg)	16,550lb (7,505kg)	19,600lb (8,890kg)	23,600lb (10,705kg)
Powerplant	1x Python or Double Naiad	1x Griffon 56, 2,000 hp (1,491 kW)	1x ASDM.1 Double Mamba Mk.100, 2,950ehp (2,200kW)	1x AP.25 Tweed, 2,500shp (1,846kW)	2x coupled Mamba	1x ASDM.1 Double Mamba Mk.100, 2,950ehp (2,200kW)	2x Mamba, 1,475shp (1,100kW)
Max speed	?	?	278kt (515km/h) at 10,000ft (3,050m)	266kt (492km/h) at SL; 274kt (508km/h) at 15,000ft (4,570m)	274kt (508km/h) at SL; 265kt (491km/h) at 15,000ft (4,570m)	269kt (499km/h) at SL	278kt (515km/h) at 10,800ft (3,290m)
Service ceiling	?	?	?	?	?	25,000ft (7,620m)	?
Range	?	?	?	?	?	816nm (1,515km)	621nm (1,150km)
Armament	1x homing torpedo, 6x depth charges or bombs, 16x RPs	1x homing torpedo, 6x depth charges or bombs, 16x RPs	1x homing torpedo, 6x depth charges or bombs, 16x RPs	1x homing torpedo, 6x depth charges or bombs, 16x RPs	1x homing torpedo, 6x depth charges or bombs, 16x RPs	1x or 2x homing torpedoes, 6x depth charges or bombs, 16x RPs	1x or 2x homing torpedoes, 6x depth charges or bombs, 16x RPs

ANTI-SUBMARINE WARFARE

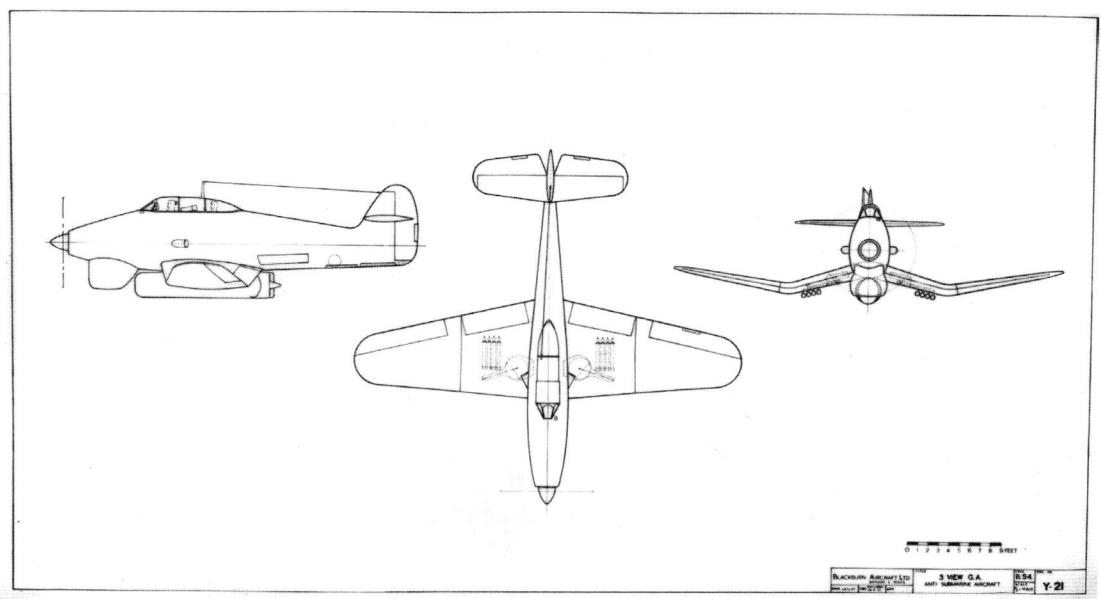

The original B.54 design of November 1945 was much closer to its Firecrest origins. The design lacked an internal weapon bay, a faired ventral pannier being used instead. The ASV radar was mounted under the nose which meant the Firecrest's tailwheel undercarriage was used unchanged. Wing span was 37ft 6in (11.46m) unfolded and the overall length was 35ft 4in (10.76m). *Tony Buttler Collection*

The Naiad's delays forced Blackburn to follow Fairey in selecting the Double Mamba. The third prototype, now designated B.88 and Y.B.1, was fitted with the 2,950shp (2,200kW) ASDM.1 Double Mamba and WB797 made its maiden flight on 19 July 1950. With the two piston-powered prototypes having carried out the major portion of the test flying, WB797 was ready to begin preliminary carrier trials only three months later.

Despite this timely development schedule, Fairey had the benefit of three Mamba-powered prototypes and the Admiralty – which probably favoured the Type Q all along given their strong involvement with its antecedents as far back as 1944 – lost interest in the ungainly-looking B.88. Despite the change in the requirements for a third crew member all the prototypes were completed as two-seaters. In addition, take-off performance with the flaps down was poor and this counted against the aircraft during the service evaluations. Despite some positives, such as better accessibility for maintenance and a 50% greater load of sonobuoys, no production order was received.

The decision to add a second observer and relax GR.17/45's gross weight limits to led to the decision to examine a third aircraft as an interim type. The S.A.1 Short Sturgeon torpedo-bomber reconnaissance aircraft had been developed to Specification S.11/43 but had not flown until 1946 and was left without a role, apart from a modest production order as a high-speed target tug. Short Brothers proposed an ASW variant. At a MoS meeting on 8 March 1949 it was agreed to convert two Sturgeons off the production line as prototypes and Specification M.6/49 and OR.275 were written around the design.

The resulting S.B.3 had a redesigned forward fuselage with a new bulbous nose section containing a

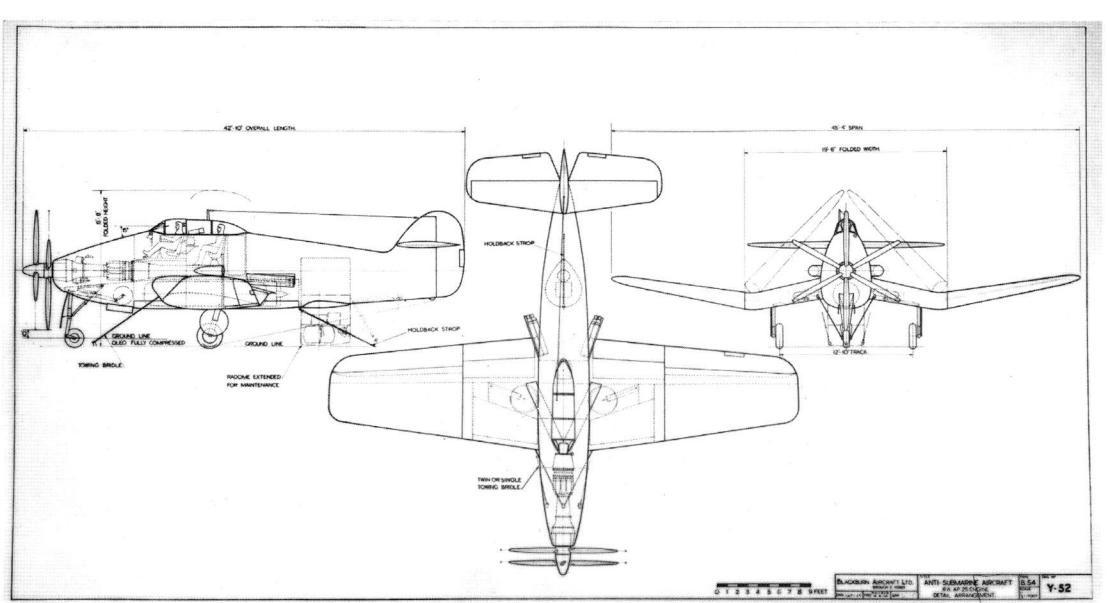

By March 1948 the addition of a ventral weapon bay beneath the wing centre section created the definitive B.54 design. The engine is the Rolls-Royce AP.25 Tweed. The wing span was now 45ft 4in (12.81m) unfolded and the overall length was 42ft 10in (13.05m). *Tony Buttler Collection*

171

The prototype Blackburn B.54/YA.7 WB781 powered by a Rolls-Royce Griffon 56 V-12 engine driving a six-blade contra-rotating propeller. Note that the lateral exhaust ports for the original turboprop powerplant remain in the fuselage above the wing. One claim to fame for WB781 was its use in angled deck approach trials with HMS *Triumph* in February 1952. *Author's Collection*

The Blackburn B.88/Y.B.1 WB797 received the intended 2,950shp (2,200kW) ASDM.1 Double Mamba turboprop. Handling trials continued until April 1951, followed by Mamba development flying until July. Used for ground instruction at RNAY Fleetlands, it was finally scrapped in 1963. *Author's Collection*

Y.B.1 WB797 was on display at the SBAC Show at Farnborough in September 1950. *Terry Panopalis Collection*

cabin for the two observers with a chin ASV radome. The 2,080hp (1,550kW) Rolls-Royce Merlin 140 engines were replaced by two 1,475shp (1,100kW) ASM.3 Mamba turboprops in longer nacelles.

Despite the need for an interim type evaporating due to the appearance of the Firefly AS.7 and Avengers, it was decided to continue with the S.B.3 as an ASW testbed. A combination of Short's move from Rochester to Belfast and a large number of design defects meant that the prototype, WF632, did not fly until 8 December 1950. It was decided to build a new airframe for the second prototype, WF636, rather than convert another unfinished Sturgeon airframe, but it was never completed due to the Mamba's unavailability before the programme was cancelled on 11 April 1951. The cancellation was due to result of the early flight trials which had revealed poor longitudinal and directional stability at low speeds and it proved extremely difficult to trim when flying on one engine. Both airframes were scrapped in 1951.

Photographs of the SB.3 flying are rare, but a spectator at Farnborough in September 1950 managed to capture WF632 during its display. The deep nose with its radar and windows of the two observers is evident. *Terry Panopalis Collection*

This rearward view of Short SB.3 WF632 is arguably the safest for the reader's eyes given how ungainly it looked. Designed as a twin-engine torpedo bomber it had a compact folded arrangement for carrier stowage. *Tony Buttler Collection*

Short Seamew

The Admiralty became concerned that however effective the Gannet was, it could not be operated from the light fleet carriers which would function as escort carriers. What was needed was a smaller more basic aircraft which could also be operated by the RNVR squadrons to replace their Fireflies and Avengers. Naval Staff Requirement NR/A.32 was raised in 1950 to find a solution.

The three-seat aircraft had to have folded dimensions to fit the lifts of *Colossus* and *Majestic*-class ships. The economic cruising speed was to be at least 120kt with a maximum level speed of at least 200kt. It was to be able to take off, climb to 5,000ft (1,525m) and patrol for four hours at economical cruising speed and land aboard an aircraft carrier at low speeds in all weathers, which meant providing low wing loading. The free take-off distance was to be within 440ft (134m) with 12kt wind blowing down the deck.

Attacks against submarines would only rarely be made above 1,500ft (457m) and with relatively sedate 30° diving attacks. An ASV.19B radar would be fitted in a fixed radome and armament consisted of six 3in (76mm) RPs (including Glow Worm illuminating RPs), T.1945 NDRSB sonobuoys, anti-submarine flares, marine markers or one Dealer-B homing torpedo, four sonobuoys or four Mk.11 or Mk.16 depth charges. The Admiralty foresaw wartime production would total 1,200 aircraft at a rate of 20 per month.

Blackburn, Short Brothers and Westland entered tenders. In July 1950 Blackburn proposed the B.83, an unusual looking design with the pilot and an observer sitting back to back under a large sideways-opening bubble canopy with the radar operator in a separate cockpit below and ahead of the main cockpit with a separate windscreen and sideways-opening canopy. The engine was to be a Merlin 35 and behind the ASV radome was a weapon bay for a homing torpedo and four underwing racks for light stores were also provided. Blackburn drew up the Mamba-powered B.91 in March 1951 but decided not to submit a formal tender; they had misgivings that the specified low wing loading would cause problems in turbulent wind conditions and that the required flaps to provide sufficient lift would affect the lateral control.

The Short PD.4 designed by a team led by Chief Designer David Keith-Lucas was powered by a Merlin engine and had a tricycle undercarriage. Westland submitted two designs sharing the same wing and T-tail but with different fuselages and retractable or fixed undercarriage options. Either a Mamba or a Rolls-Royce R.Da.3 Dart turboprop could be fitted. The mid-position wing had a double-folded layout with the wing tips folding to match the height of the T-tail. Below the wing was a weapon bay for a homing torpedo.

In October 1951 Fairey offered a two-seat Gannet variant, the Project 45 with a single ASM.5 Mamba and the retractable radar radome moved ahead of the shortened weapon bay.

Shorts was awarded the development contract, Specification M.123D being issued on 10 April 1952 and three prototypes ordered six days later. The design – now redesignated as the S.B.6 – was changed, the second observer being removed to save weight, the undercarriage altered to a tailwheel layout (the tailwheel extended when the flaps were lowered to give a horizontal attitude on the deck) and powered wing folding was added as well as an emergency air system for lowering the flaps. The 1,475ehp (1,100kW) ASM.3 Mamba was selected as the engine (production aircraft received the 1,770ehp [1,320kW] ASM.6.) The weapon bay was 14ft (4.26m) long and could be extended to 17ft (5.18m) to allow *Pentane* to be carried by removing the radome. There was also a

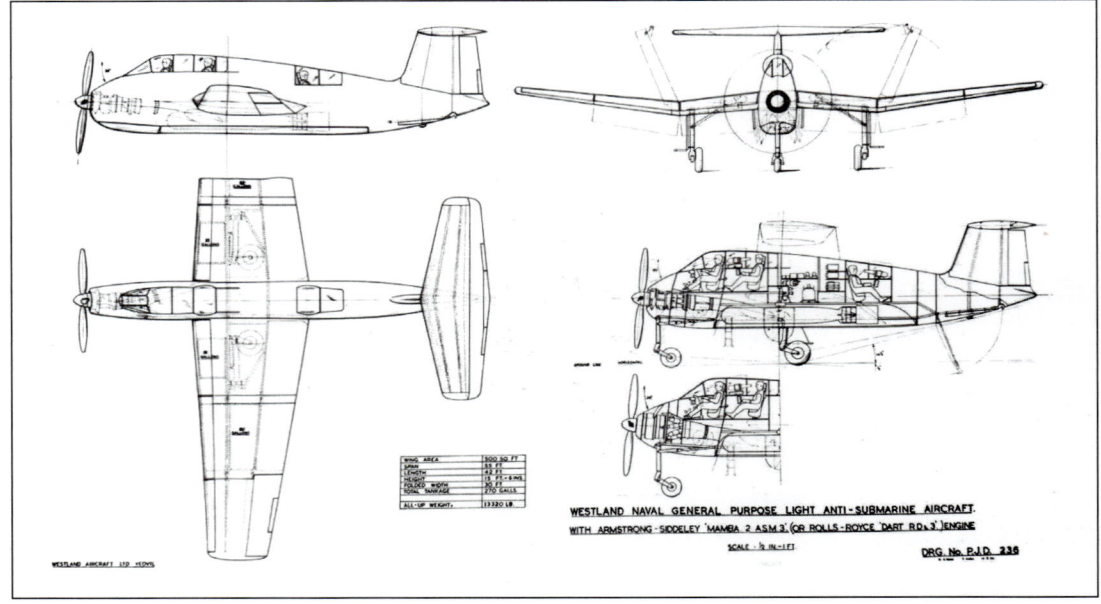

Westland design, as shown on technical drawing P.J.D.236, was a neatly packaged three-seat aircraft with the crew sat above the turboprop engine and the torpedo bay. This is the version with a retractable tricycle undercarriage. *Leonardo UK via Jeremy Graham*

ANTI-SUBMARINE WARFARE

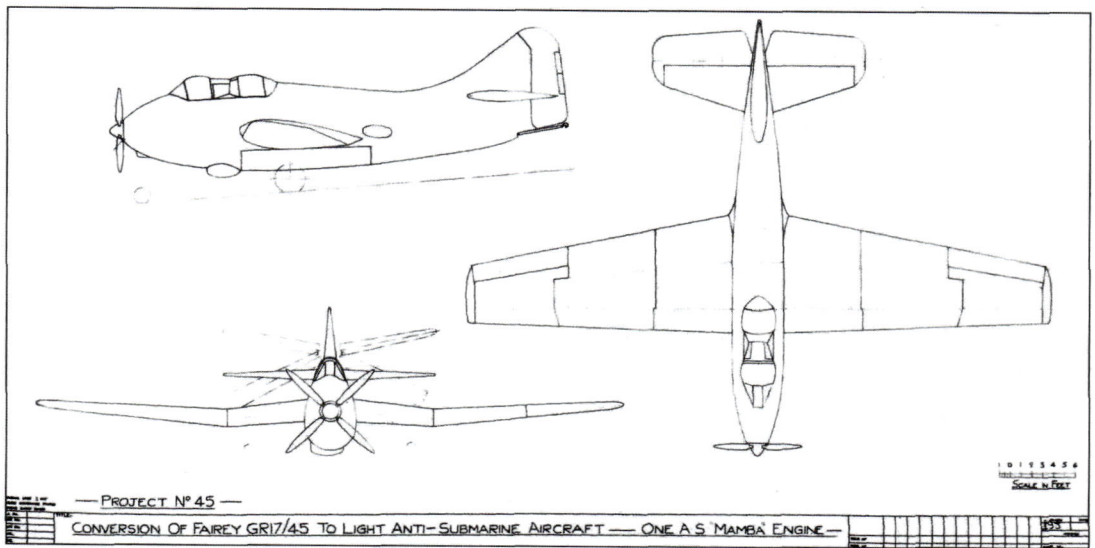

Fairey's Project 45 was a revised two-seat Gannet with the Double Mamba replaced by a single ASM.5 Mamba and a shorter fuselage and weapon bay. Note that the retractable ASV.19B radar radome was located ahead of the weapon bay – the opposite of the Gannet's layout. *Leonardo UK*

proposal to replace the ASV.19B with a removable sonobuoy receiver pack.

The first of three Seamew prototypes, XA209, made its maiden flight on 23 August 1953, with test pilot Squadron Leader Walter J 'Wally' Runciman experiencing control problems and making a crash landing. Three weeks later Runciman displayed the repaired XA209 at the 1953 Society of British Aircraft Constructors Show at Farnborough. The second prototype, XA213, was used for successful carrier trials aboard *Bulwark* in July and December 1955. The third prototype, XA216, was never completed, instead being used as a structural fatigue test article.

During flight tests Wally Runciman soon found that the Seamew had excellent performance in crosswinds, a low stalling speed of 50kt and could maintain level flight on half power, but it also had some very poor handling characteristics, especially at the stall. The airflow from the radome caused issues when the weapon bay doors were open. The prototypes were modified with fixed leading-edge slats; slots were added to the trailing edge flap; and slats were added to the tailplane roots (later replaced by a 'vented fillet' V-shape slot.) The rudder horn balance and trim tabs were altered several times and the ailerons were modified before the handling was acceptable, although its problems

Specification M.123 designs

	Blackburn B.83 and B.91	Short Brothers S.B.6 Seamew AS.1	Westland M.123
Crew	Three	Two	Two
Span	45ft 0in (13.7m); 27ft 10in (8.48m) folded	55ft 0in (16.76m); 26ft 1in (7.95m) folded	55ft 0in (16.76m)
Length	41ft 7in (12.70m)	41ft 0in (12.50m)	42ft 0in (12.80m)
Wing area	?	585ft² (54.4m²)	500ft² (46.5m²)
All-up weight	?	14,400lb (6,530kg)	13,320lb (6,040kg) with retractable undercarriage; 13,240lb (6,005kg) with fixed undercarriage
Powerplant	B.83 1x Merlin 35; B.91 1x Mamba	1x ASM.6 Mamba, 1,590shp (1,186kW)	1x ASM.3 Mamba, 1,400shp (1,044kW); or 1x Dart RDa.3, 1,320shp (984kW)
Max speed	?	204kt (378kt) at 10,500ft (3,200m)	?
Range	?	651nm (1,207km)	?
Armament	1x homing torpedo, 4x depth charges, 6x RPs	1,844lb (836kg) weapon load, 1x homing torpedo, 4x depth charges, 6x RPs	1x homing torpedo, 4x depth charges or bombs, 6x RPs

ABOVE The second prototype Short Seamew XA213 in formation with one of the production aircraft. *Tony Buttler Collection*

RIGHT A detailed view of the Seamew's underwing racks, each carrying three 60lb (27kg) RPs. These would have been used to engage surfaced submarines or small vessels. These RPs are fitted with dummy warhead sections. *Crown Copyright*

The second prototype Short Seamew XA213 made the type's first carrier trials aboard HMS *Bulwark* in July 1955. *Author's Collection*

were never fully overcome. Blackburn's initial pessimism about the low wing loading requirement may have been fully justified.

Seamew XA209 was used for ADDLs at Boscombe Down in August 1954. The conclusion was that the low-speed handling was not "up to the standard required for a deck landing clearance in regard to the lateral and directional control." The A&AEE also criticised poor taxying control with the wings folded and the flaps could foul the weapon bay doors if they were opened with the flaps down. Engine surging issues cancelled a planned assessment aboard *Albion*.

Specification M.123P was issued on 19 May 1954 for the 60 Seamew AS.1 production aircraft which had been ordered a year earlier. Specification M.123P2 followed on 9 November 1954 for RAF Coastal Command's Seamew MR.2 for the inshore maritime patrol role countering fast attack craft and submarines lurking around the coast. These aircraft would omit the arrester hook but retained manual wing folding and had low-pressure tyres. The RAF agreed to take half of the production batch as MR.2s.

By 1956 the Admiralty had reduced their order to 24, most of the *Colossus*-class ships had by then decommissioned (or were shortly due to) and helicopters were already seen as the better option. In addition, the cost of the Gannet fleet left no money to fund any additional Seamews. The RAF had also lost interest in the inshore patrol requirement and cancelled their half of the order. Of the four MR.2 aircraft already completed (XE173–XE176), three were converted to AS.1 standard.

One these aircraft, XE175, was used by Shorts as a demonstrator and Wally Runciman made a

Prototype Seamew XA209 at the SBAC Show at Farnborough in 1954 with the arrester hook down and the weapon bay doors open. *Terry Panopalis Collection*

European sales tour, stopping at Italy in March 1956, Yugoslavia in April and ending in West Germany in May. Sadly, not long after its return, performing at the Sydenham Air Display on 9 June 1956, XE175 entered a slow roll at 100ft (30m) and while attempting a half loop the nose fell and struck the runway, killing Runciman.

The final straw came with the 1957 Defence White Paper which not only axed the Seamew but also its intended recipient, the RNVR squadrons. By that time XE219 had completed service flight trials with 700 NAS in November 1956 with around 200 take-offs and landings on HMS *Warrior*. Four Seamews had been delivered but not issued, these and three others were scrapped at RNAS Lossiemouth with eleven more undelivered aircraft being scrapped at Sydenham. Shorts saved one, XE180, for its Apprentice Training School as a ground instructional airframe, until it too was scrapped in 1967. In an effort to recoup something, the Admiralty considered offering the completed aircraft for sale to Brazil and Argentina, but nothing came of this idea.

This frontal view of a production Seamew AS.1 with its wings folded shows the fixed slats on the wings, the slats and the tailplane root 'vented fillet' – all attempts to remedy the low-speed handling. Note that the aileron takes up most of the trailing edge of the outer wing. *Tony Buttler Collection*

177

The Seamew was displayed at Farnborough in 1955 along with its array of payloads including sonobouys and RPs. *Terry Panopalis Collection*

The high cockpit perched above the Mamba turboprop gave the pilot an excellent view on landing. *Terry Panopalis Collection*

8 Anti-submarine helicopters

By 1945 the Admiralty was no stranger to rotary-wing aviation. The Cierva Autogiro Company's Chief Test Pilot, Wing Commander Reginald Brie, had carried out a landing and take-off from the carrier HMS *Furious* in 1935 with one of the company's autogyros. The Admiralty in 1938 issued Specification S.22/38 for a shipborne three-seat reconnaissance rotary-winged aircraft; contracts being awarded to designer Raoul Hafner for his AR.V Gyroplane and G & J Weir Limited for their W.7 helicopter. The events of 1940, however, halted all work. Around the same time there was strong interest in acquiring Pitcairn autogyros from the United States of America for convoy maritime patrol use. In 1942 Brie, by now part of the British Air Commission in Washington DC, witnessed a demonstration of Igor Sikorsky's VS-300 helicopter and persuaded Sikorsky to let him fly the YR-4 prototype.

Brie became enthused by the anti-submarine warfare (ASW) potential that the helicopter offered and persuaded the Commission to order two. The Admiralty planned to fit merchant ships with landing platforms and made available the *Empire Jersey* and the SS *Daghestan* for deck landing trials in the USA. Lieutenant Alan Bristow RNVR flew the initial trials in a YR-4B fitted with pontoon floats. Two YR-4Bs,

Where it all began. Sikorsky R-4 Hoverfly FT835 touching down onto the makeshift landing pad aboard the freighter SS *Daghestan* during Convoy HX 274 on 16 January 1944. At the controls is US Coast Guard pilot Lt Stewart Ross Graham. The R-4 lacked the lifting capability to carry depth charges and was only useful for visual observation. *US Navy via Terry Panopalis Collection*

179

The RN's post-war ASW concepts in operation. The Type 12 frigate HMS *Rothesay* would hunt for submarines using its Type 170 and Type 174 sonars, bearing information from which would be used to vector its Manned Torpedo-Carrying Helicopter (MATCH) in order to release a pair of homing torpedoes onto an enemy submarine. *Rothesay's* Westland Wasp HAS.1 can be seen in the background returning to the ship. The ship was armed with a triple-barrel Limbo Mk.10 mortar to engage close-range submarine targets as a last-ditch defence. The Westland Sea King HAS.1 in the foreground had its own Type 195 dipping sonar to localise contacts or as part of an outer defensive screen. The Sea King – as shown here – could carry four Mk.46 homing torpedoes, sufficient to attack at least two targets. *Blue Envoy Collection*

serialled FT833 and FT834, were embarked during convoy HX 274 returning to Britain in January 1944, but the poor weather provided few opportunities for operational flying. In 1946 Lt Bristow successfully flew from a platform fitted to the *River*-class sloop HMS *Helmsdale*, which was serving as an anti-submarine trials ship. The main problem was that the R-4 was underpowered which limited it to a visual search role. The Sikorsky S-51, licence-built by Westland Aircraft as the Dragonfly, offered no improvement and was used for search and rescue (SAR) and training duties.

The potential was there but the helicopter needed more technical development. Such was the rate of progress that by 1969 the RN had retired its Fairey Gannets from the ASW role and had homing torpedo-armed ASW helicopters, such as the Westland Wasp HAS.1 based aboard its anti-submarine frigates, supported by the larger Westland Wessex HAS.3 and Sea King HAS.1 capable of search operations with dipping sonars. This chapter outlines that progression from the initial experiments to the realisation of the helicopter fleet.

Early steps

In December 1949 the Admiralty, the Air Staff and the Ministry of Supply (MoS) began studying future anti-submarine helicopters. The MoS's Research Director Projects prepared several preliminary design studies. The optimum design had a 60ft (2.7m) diameter rotor, 9,000lb (4,080kg) all-up weight (AUW) and an 850hp (633kW) piston engine. No suitable British engine then existed in this power bracket, the closest being the 520–560hp (377–417kW) Alvis Leonides nine-cylinder radial engine. The Leonides was underpowered, however, and in 1950 Westland rejected its use in the Sikorsky S-55 because it offered insufficient payload (the lack of suitable engines forced Westland to consider fitting the 1930s-era Bristol Perseus nine-cylinder radial).

The Bristol Type 173 tandem-rotor helicopter powered by two Leonides had been designed by Raoul Hafner to meet Specification E.4/47 for an experimental ten-seat helicopter. Bristol submitted a brochure for a Naval Type 173 in December 1950 with a crew of three, four hours' endurance with a payload including 600lb (272kg) of sonar equipment

This evocative artwork illustrates Raoul Hafner's Naval Type 173 proposal for the ASW role operating from Fleet carriers. Note the Supermarine Seafire on the carrier deck – a rather anachronistic feature, even for 1950! *Leonardo UK via Bruce Sellers*

and 850lb (385kg) of weapons (Mk.30 Dealer-B homing torpedoes, flares and Marine Markers). The estimated AUW was 10,600lb (4,810kg). Folding rotor-blades and a folding tailplane would enable the Type 173 to be accommodated in a 40 × 44ft (12.1 × 13.4m) hangar space if parked diagonally. Hafner envisaged operations with 'hunter-killer' pairs and proposed an 'Admiral's Barge' transport variant with extra fuel tanks for long sorties, for example to the Mediterranean. The RAF's Air Staff was not entirely satisfied, wanting a co-pilot and dual controls, ASV.19 search radar, increased fuel tankage and additional stowage for flares, Marine Markers and dinghies.

Westland proposed an ASW version of its advanced W.81 30-seat private-venture in 1951, which combined the S-55's rotor with two Armstrong Siddeley Mamba turboshafts with a double epicyclic final drive to power the rotor. It would have a crew of four and be equipped with a dipping sonar and two Dealer-B torpedoes.

The Admiralty favoured what it termed a 'single package' helicopter capable of conducting both search and strike operations with the ability to carry sonar equipment and anti-submarine armament together. Naval Staff Requirement NA.43 was drafted during mid-1952 for the 'single package' helicopter carrying a *Pentane* homing torpedo and dipping sonar, with a crew of four, four hours endurance and an AUW of 14,000lb (6,350kg). In December 1952, the AUW was increased to 17,000lb (7,710kg) because it proved impossible to

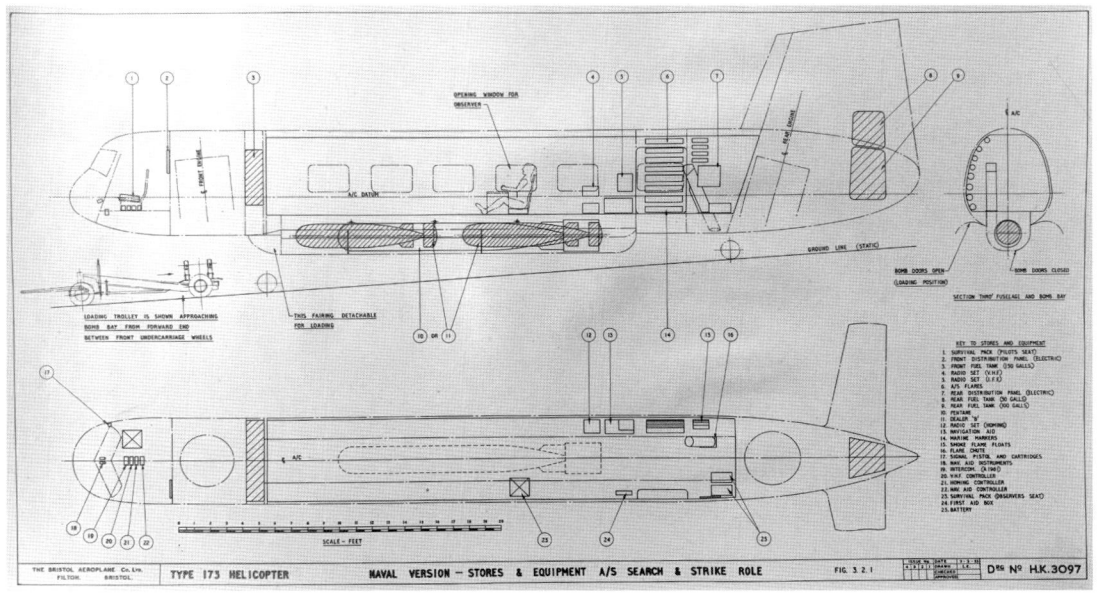

A technical drawing showing the internal layout of the Naval Type 173 proposal. It is similar in several respects to the later Type 191 to requirement NA.43 *Leonardo UK via Bruce Sellers*

WINGS OVER THE FLEET

The Admiralty's hopes of acquiring the purpose-built Bell HSL-1 as an interim 'Single Package' helicopter were dashed when the USN cancelled the programme. The aircraft illustrated here is production HSL-1 BuNo 129162. *Terry Panopalis Collection*

meet the endurance requirements with the original weight limit. This new AUW, however, exceeded the maximum deck lift strength limit of the *Colossus*-class light fleet carriers, thus ruling them out as convoy escorts. Coastal Command issued similar requirements as Operational Requirement OR.326.

Britain had no suitable helicopter or sonar equipment; the only choice was to buy American. The US Navy's (USN) Experimental Squadron VX-3 had been evaluating the Piasecki HRP-1 Rescuer with AN/AQS-1 dipping sonar since 1947. At least one AQS-1 set was supplied to the UK in 1950 to enable evaluation of the technology and to allow designers like Raoul Hafner – now heading Bristol Aircraft's helicopter design team at Weston super Mare – to appreciate the bulk of the equipment. By 1951 development of the first production standard dipping sonar, the Raytheon AN/AQS-4, was underway. The AQS-4 consisted of a winch with 90ft (27m) of cable, at the end of which was a rotating transducer head with a separate receiver. The power pack, chemical paper recorder and the control panel were mounted in the main cabin. The complete equipment weighed 300lb (136kg). RN observers participated in the trials with Experimental Squadron VX-1 at Key West, Florida using the Sikorsky S-55 HO4S-1.

The Admiralty submitted a Mutual Defense Assistance Program (MDAP) bid for 15 Sikorsky HO4S-1 helicopters and 13 AQS-4 sonars (this was later increased to 40 helicopters but 25 were cancelled once Westland licence-production began). They also bid for 45 Bell HSL-1 tandem-rotor ASW helicopters, but this was reduced to 18 (serials XB453–XB470 were reserved in October 1952). The prototype HSL-1 first flew on 3 March 1953 but following a difficult development programme the USN pulled the plug. In Britain, Rank-Pullin was responsible for licence-building the AQS-4 sonar as the Type 194 (they later produced the improved Type 194B for the Westland Wessex HAS.1) pending the start of Plessey's production of the Type 195 sonar, which had been developed by the Admiralty Underwater Weapons Establishment – AUWE.

An Anti-Submarine Warfare Development Unit was formed jointly with Coastal Command at RAF St Mawgan for trials and evaluation work. The RAF ordered four Bristol Type 171 Sycamore HR.Mk.12 helicopters for the unit. It was found the ARI.5487 sonobuoy receiver equipment would not fit inside the Sycamore's cabin, so the initial trials used a hydrophone lowered into the water on a 100ft (30m) long cable. A shore-based radio receiver picked up the transmissions, but the signals were unrecognisable.

A second trial in July 1952 used a T.1945 (NDRSB) non-directional sonobuoy on a 140ft (42.6m) cable. The diesel-powered submarine HMS *Ambush* was the target, using its snorkel – 'snorting' – just below the surface at 5kt. The result was a failure, the rotor noise and airframe vibration travelling down the cable and the sound waves reflecting off the surface of the sea masked the submarine's sounds, even at close range. Thus, the dipping hydrophone was abandoned.

The first eight of the AQS-4 equipped Sikorsky HO4S-3 helicopters (designated HAS.22 in British service) arrived in September 1953, allowing the formation of an evaluation unit, 706 Naval Air

Whirlwind HAS.3 XJ402 was modified for a minesweeping trial in July 1961. The towing gear was fitted beneath the tailboom, replacing the stabilising keel plate. The trial was carried out by 771 NAS based at RNAS Portland. *Terry Panopalis Collection*

A photo of an anti-submarine sweep perhaps? No, Lt Cdr GGR Miller of 705 NAS is starting to tow the 450-ton minesweeper HMS *Gavinton* with his Whirlwind in an experiment off the Isle of Wight. The slack of the tow rope has not yet been taken up, so remains submerged in this image. *Gavinton* was towed at the speed of 5kt, the idea being that without its engines running, the minesweeper could safely sweep acoustic mines. *Charles E. Brown via Terry Panopalis Collection*

Squadron (becoming 845 NAS in March 1954), which included exchange officers from the USN and the Royal Canadian Navy (RCN). Despite problems due to lack of spares, trials by the Joint Anti-Submarine School at Londonderry were followed by carrier-based trials to determine the best methods of command and control from the parent ship. AQS-4 trials revealed that autopilots were required to relieve the pilots of the physical demands of hovering for prolonged periods at 15–20ft (4.5–6m) during sonar search operations.

During April 1954 to August 1955, 845 NAS was based at RNAS Hal Far on Malta, for an extensive series of trials. Despite a shortage of spares 2,800 hours were flown, including 90 hours of night flying and exercises aboard HMS *Eagle* conducted covered a broad spectrum of possible operational roles – the Director Naval Air Warfare Division (DNAW), Captain Frank HE Hopkins, was sceptical about non-ASW duties – as well as exploring the technical aspects of the sonar equipment. It was discovered that experienced ex-Fairey Firefly observers required 80 hours of operational helicopter flying to achieve the standards required to operate the dipping sonar effectively and that Doppler radar navigation would be vital for measuring drift in windy conditions. The lessons were gathered into a publication issued by the Commander-in-Chief Mediterranean in March 1956, titled *Instructions for Operating A/S Helicopters* (informally known as 'Dipper'). This document was accepted as the RN's interim standard doctrine pending further tactical trials and its contents were disseminated to the RCN and the USN.

The trials also confirmed the best method of helicopter direction using radar plotting from ships. Informative Direction was the usual method, with the helicopter's crew being fully responsible for the search pattern and the parent ship only stepping in if they wandered too far away. Positive Direction differed in that the ship provided the vector to the target and the instructions when to hover and lower the sonar. Unsurprisingly, the crews of 845 NAS preferred the more autonomous Informative Direction, but this method was recognised as being problematic – and potentially dangerous – when trying to screen aircraft carriers with multiple aircraft movements going on in the area. During Exercise TFX 19/5, the destroyer HMS *Whirlwind* successfully used Positive Direction and this method became standard for all shipboard operations.

This Westland Whirlwind HAS.7 illustrates well the Sky and Extra Dark Sea Grey colour scheme initially worn by the Whirlwind HAS.7 during the 1950s. Later the grey was replaced by Golden Yellow to improve detectability if the helicopter ditched. *Terry Panopalis Collection*

The Piasecki HPR-2 was the USN's version of the H-21 Workhorse. Had Fairey and Piasecki chosen a different turboshaft engine it might have been procured instead of the Type 191. *Terry Panopalis Collection*

The Fleet Air Arm (FAA) had to rely on the S-55 as an interim ASW helicopter until the NA.43 'Single Package' helicopter was ready. Westland had already secured a production licence for the S-55 in 1950 on its own initiative. The Alvis Leonides Major-powered Whirlwind HAR.6 would form the basis of the Whirlwind HAS.7. Westland secured a contract and prototype XG589 first flew on 17 October 1956 at Yeovil. A total of 120 were built. 700H NAS began intensive trials in June 1957 with 820 NAS becoming operational in January 1958.

The HAS.7 was operated as a 'hunter-killer' pair; a 'hunter' equipped with Type 194 dipping sonar and the 'killer' armed with a Mk.30 *Dealer-B* (later a US Mk.44) homing torpedo or depth charges carried in a shallow trough beneath the raised cabin floor. The 780hp (580kW) Leonides Major 755/1 14-cylinder radial engine and the transmission clutch suffered from poor reliability and several failures led to fatal accidents. The HAS.7 was relegated to transport and amphibious assault duties during 1959 as the HAR.9, forcing the Fairey Gannet to briefly resume carrier-based ASW duties.

The Single Package

Following the issue of invitations to tender for Requirement NA.43 in March 1953 Bristol submitted the Type 191 design. Hafner hoped that developing the Type 191 from the Type 173 would reduce development risk and time. Bristol estimated that if a contract was placed during November 1953, that the prototype would first fly in May 1957 with the first production deliveries in 1960.

The Type 191 was based on the Type 173 Mk.3 airframe but with several structural modifications; the removal of two 1ft (30cm) fuselage bays and a blunter rear-end profile to ensure that the helicopter could fit on a 45 × 34ft (13.7 × 10.3m) deck lift with 18in (45cm) all-round clearance. Another structural change was the inclusion of a ventral weapon bay for a single 21in *Pentane* or two Dealer-B torpedoes. The two four-blade metal rotors were powered by two 850hp (633kW) Leonides Major 751/1 engines. The specially designed undercarriage had castoring wheels for easier deck handling and could withstand an emergency descent of 10ft/sec (3m/sec). The AQS-4 console, winch and 96ft (29m) cable reel was mounted in the forward cabin. The estimated 100kt maximum speed and 87kt cruising speed fell short of the requirements (150kt and 100kt respectively). Endurance would be sufficient to carry one *Pentane* for 69.5nm (128km), two Dealer-B for 147nm (274km) or two US Mk.43 torpedoes for 226nm (418km). The crew comprised a pilot, co-pilot, sonar operator and observer. The pilots would be assisted by an autopilot during the hovering phase of sonar dipping.

The Admiralty and the MoS endorsed NA.43 at a Naval Aircraft Design Committee meeting on 30 September 1953, the Treasury subsequently sanctioning the purchase of 65 aircraft. Another three helicopters for development and airworthiness certification work were added later, bringing the total to 68. Specification HR.146D&P was issued on 18 December to cover development. Four essentially identical helicopters were ordered for RAF Coastal Command to meet OR.326 and Specification HR.149. The RCN ordered their own Type 193 variant and there was also interest from Australia and France. The Type 192 Belvedere tactical transport for the RAF to meet OR.325 also shared several features with the Type 191 (most notably the stalky undercarriage).

Fairey Aviation offered another option in August 1953. It had already reached agreement with Piasecki to licence-build the H-21 Workhorse tandem-rotor transport helicopter. Fairey now offered an ASW conversion (a similar Piasecki proposal had been rejected by the USN in favour of the HSL-1.) A conversion seemed feasible given Piasecki's experience in fitting sonar and autopilots in the HUP Retriever, but the airframe would require some redesign to shorten it to fit on carrier lifts. Fairey would be responsible for the modifications for dipping sonar and external stores and the installation of an Armstrong Siddeley ASM.6 Mamba. The Admiralty hoped that airframes could be obtained via MDAP quite cheaply. The MoS rejected the fixed-wheel turbine Mamba as a suitable powerplant due to rotor instability concerns and a poor margin of power for safety and therefore the proposal was rejected.

The Type 173 Mk.1 prototype (registered as G-ALBN but assigned serial XF785 for the trials) carried out carrier compatibility trials aboard HMS *Eagle* during 10–13 November 1953. The trials literally went too smoothly as *Eagle* was a very steady ship which prevented a full assessment of deck motion effects on landings. Starting and

'Single Package' Helicopters & Naval Requirement NR/A.43 designs

	Bell Model 61 HSL-1	Bristol Type 191/1	Bristol Type 191/2	Piasecki/Fairey H-21	Westland Wessex HAS.1
Rotor diameter	2x 51ft 6in (15.70m)	2x 48ft 11in (14.91m)	2x 48ft 11in (14.91m)	2x 44ft 0in (13.41m)	1x 56ft 0in (17.07m)
Length	39ft 11in (12.17m) fuselage	50ft 3in (15.31m) fuselage	50ft 3in (15.31m) fuselage	52ft 6in (16.03m) fuselage	65ft 10in (20.07m); 38ft 2in (11.63m) folded
Rotor area	3,840ft² (356.7m²)	3,270ft² (303.8m²)	3,270ft² (303.8m²)	3,041ft² (282.5m²)	2,463ft² (228.8m²)
All-up weight	16,958lb (7,692kg) search; 16,853lb (7,644kg) attack	17,660lb (8,010kg)	17,800lb (8,070kg)	14,600lb (6,620kg)	12,600lb (5,715kg)
Powerplant	1x P&W R-2800-50, 2,100hp (1,565kW)	2x Leonides Major 751/1, 850hp (633kW)	2x Gazelle 100 N. Ga.2, 1,650shp (1,230kW)	1x Mamba, 1,600shp (1,193kW)	1x Gazelle 13 Mk.161, 1,450shp (1,081kW)
Max speed	107kt (200km/h)	100+kt (185km/h)	120kt (222km/h)	110+kt (203km/h)	117kt (217km/h)
Service ceiling	14,400ft (4,390m)	?	12,000ft (3,655m)	8,100ft (2,470m)	14,100ft (4,300m)
Search endurance	3hr 30min	2hr 30min	3hr	2hr	Up to 3hr
Armament	2x US Mk.43 homing torpedoes	1x *Pentane* homing torpedo, or 2x Mk.30 Dealer-B or US Mk.43 homing torpedoes	2x Mk.30 Dealer-B or US Mk.43 homing torpedoes	2x Mk.30 Dealer-B or US Mk.43 homing torpedoes	2x Mk.30 Dealer-B or US Mk.43 homing torpedoes

stopping the rotor blades in varying wind conditions defined the wind speed limits to prevent blade motion – which risked the blades striking the fuselage. It was found that a 30kt headwind caused problems and during stationary tests the rear blades were lifted clear of the droop stops when *Eagle* turned out of a 20kt headwind.

During deck handling trials the helicopter could be rotated 360° using its castoring front wheels by lifting the rear wheels off the deck using the rotors under engine power. The rear wheels were non-castoring but the trials report advocated fitting castoring front and rear wheels to ease manual handling when manoeuvring into tight spaces, especially inside the hangar. Folding the rotor blades was time consuming and the folded arrangement was bulky, being wider than the undercarriage track and risking damage to the blades when in the hangar.

The increase in weight became the main development problem during 1954, which combined with insufficient engine power seriously affected the estimated endurance, despite Bristol's initial assurances that all requirements would be met within the AUW limit. At its worst, the empty weight increased from 13,369lb (6,064kg) to 14,773lb (6,700kg). Later it was discovered that the 200lb (90kg) weight of the sonar operator had been overlooked in the loading calculations, which cancelled out all the weight savings made during the detail design review. Achieving the specified 400nm (740km) range required an AUW of 17,660lb (8,010kg).

The Admiralty was not prepared to offer additional concessions and further efforts to reduce weight included deleting the rotor de-icing, *Pentane* (still required for the turboshaft-powered Series 2) and redesigning the undercarriage and rotor hubs. Bristol eventually achieved a reduction of 400–450lb (180–205kg).

The MoS suggested that a turbine-powered Type 191 could meet NA.43 with a concessionary increase to 18,000lb (8,164kg) AUW. The Ministry's

Bristol Type 173 Mk.1 G-ALBN/XF785 being pushed towards the aft lift aboard HMS *Eagle* during the carrier compatibility trials in November 1953. *Crown Copyright*

WINGS OVER THE FLEET

Bristol Type 191 Series 2 estimated performance vs requirements

Search and Strike Role

Weapons	Basic weight	Requirement	17,000lb AUW	17,500lb AUW	18,000lb AUW
1x *Pentane*	14,420lb (6,540kg)	300nm (555km)	186nm (344km)	229nm (424km)	271nm (502km)
2x Mk.30 Dealer-B	12,820lb (5,815kg)	400nm (740km)	243nm (450km)	286nm (529km)	328nm (607km)
2x US Mk.43	12,970lb (5,885kg)	400nm (740km)	326nm (603km)	369nm (683km)	411nm (761km)

Close Support Role (Screening)

Weapons	Basic weight	Requirement	17,000lb AUW	17,500lb AUW	18,000lb AUW
1x Mk.30 Dealer-B	13,135lb (5,600kg)	2hr 30min	2hr 30min	2hr 54min	3hr 18min
2x US Mk.43	12,990lb (5,890kg)	2hr 30min	2hr 36min	3hr 0min	3hr 24min
None	12,450lb (5,650kg)	3hr 30min	3hr 6min	3hr 30min	3hr 36min

The Type 191 production line at Bristol's Old Mixon works in 1955. *Leonardo UK via Bruce Sellers*

choice was the Napier E.156 Gazelle free-turbine, which could be fitted without substantial airframe modifications. The Treasury approved funding for 94 turbine-powered Type 191 and Type 192 Series 2 helicopters in April 1954 and funding for the Gazelle in July. The Series 2 would be lighter with a basic operational weight of 11,265lb (5,110kg) versus the 11,937lb (5,415kg) of the piston-powered Series 1 – but the 17,800lb (8,070kg) AUW still exceeded the requirement. Suggested solutions to overcome the carrier lift strength limit were to carry out weapon loading or fuelling on the flight deck. The range when carrying two Dealer-B was increased to 200nm (372km).

The third Leonides Major-powered Type 173 Mk.3 XE288 was the naval prototype with a shortened fuselage and modified undercarriage. It was intended for naval handling and deck landing trials and the development of folding blades, but completion was delayed and it remained a static test aircraft. Three Series 1 and two Series 2 development aircraft were planned (a dedicated Type 193 Series 2 airframe was rejected by the Treasury). It was planned to fly the Series 1 helicopters during

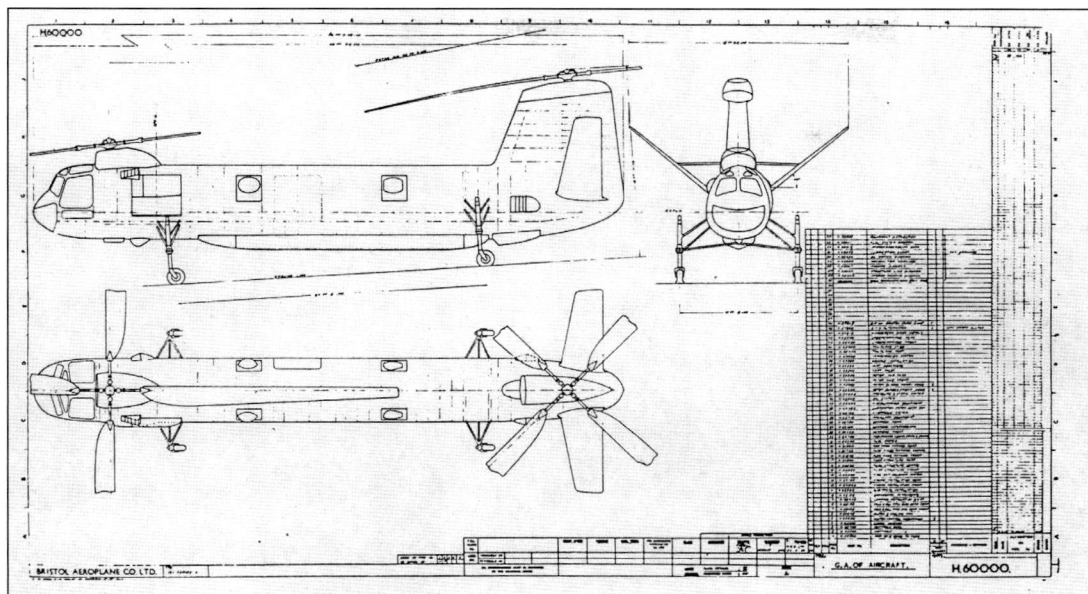

A general arrangement drawing of the Type 191 Series 1 powered by two Alvis Leonides Major radial engines. The bulged ventral weapon bay is evident. *Leonardo UK via Bruce Sellers*

November 1957–January 1958, followed by the Series 2 in April–May 1958. Only the Series 1 airframes were completed, being converted as Gazelle and rotor transmission ground running test rigs for the Type 192 Belvedere programme.

Dissatisfied that the Type 191 Series 2 could not meet NA.43, the Admiralty cancelled all 68 production aircraft in May 1955 (serials XG354–

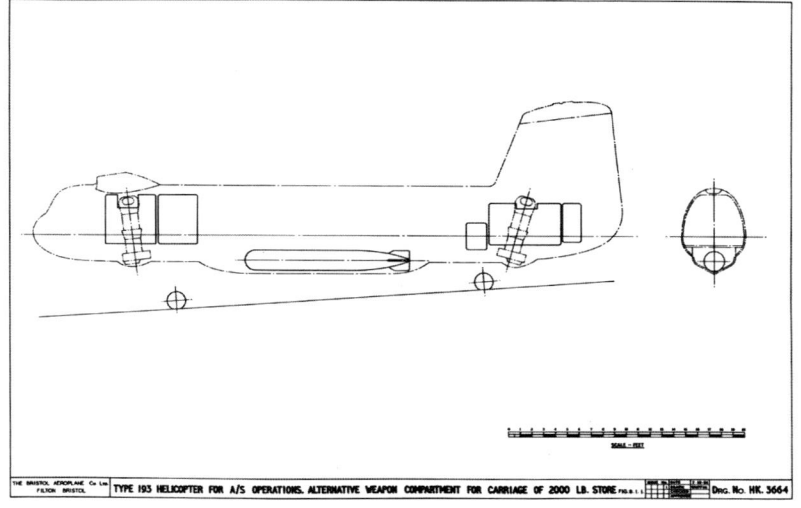

RIGHT This internal general arrangement layout of the Type 193 variant for the Royal Canadian Navy shows the position of the two Leonides Major engines and also the bulk of the *Pentane* homing torpedo in the weapon bay. *Leonardo UK via Bruce Sellers*

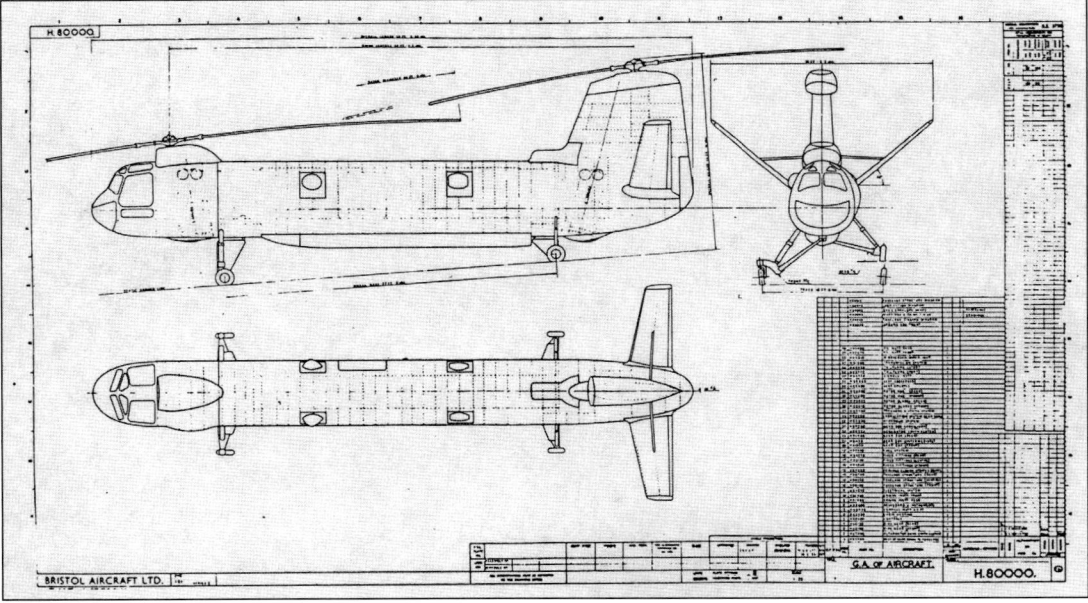

A general arrangement drawing of the final Bristol Type 191 Series 2 powered by two Napier Gazelle turboshafts and a revised undercarriage and horizontal stabilisers. *Leonardo UK via Bruce Sellers*

WINGS OVER THE FLEET

ABOVE Only the Series 1 airframes were completed, being converted as Gazelle ground running test rigs for the Type 192 Belvedere programme. Ground test rig No.1 is seen here on the test stand at Old Mixon in 1957. This view shows well the reprofiled rear fuselage to assist fitting the fuselage onto aircraft carrier lifts. *Leonardo UK via Bruce Sellers*

TOP RIGHT A never-were that nearly was. A Bristol Belvedere HAS.1 releases a *Pentane* homing torpedo during an anti-submarine exercise in the Clyde in October 1962. *Luciano Alviani*

XG398 and XG419–XG441 had been allocated in April 1954). Bristol in its defence argued the Admiralty's insistence on the ability to take-off with zero wind over the flight deck and full performance in tropical conditions were unrealistic requirements.

Wessex

During the climax of the Type 191 saga, the Flag Officer Aircraft Carriers, Rear Admiral AR Pedder, had argued that helicopters aboard fleet carriers would interfere with fixed-wing deck operations. The Admiralty now substantially modified NA.43 to enable a smaller single-rotor helicopter to be used.

The revised NA.43 Issue 4 deleted the now-cancelled *Pentane*; added 15 minutes of sonar search in the Search and Strike Role; made minesweeping a firm requirement; and turbine engines mandatory. Time-on-station was reduced to two hours with a maximum endurance of three hours. Range was reduced from 400nm to 150nm (740 to 277km) with two Dealer-B or 200nm (370km) with two Mk.43 Mod. 1 torpedoes. In the Close Support Role the weapons load would be one Dealer-B or two Mk.43 Mod.1 and two Marine Markers, increasing to two Dealer-B or Mk.43 Mod.1 torpedoes and two Marine Markers in the Search and Strike Role. The dipping sonar was the improved Rank-Pullin Type 194B but American avionics would be fitted until the planned British equivalents were ready – AN/APN-22 (later AN/APN-117) substituting for the ARI.23062 Mk.7A radio altimeter and AN/APN-97 Doppler drift measuring radar for *Blue Orchid*.

Westland tendered a Sikorsky S-58 variant in February 1956 and Specification HAS.170D&P was issued on 26 June to cover development. After considering the Rolls-Royce Dart, Westland selected the 1,450shp (1,081kW) Gazelle N.Ga.13 Mk.161. The prototype, an imported Sikorsky-built airframe, was reassembled at Yeovil and flown on 24 June 1956 by Westland's Chief Test Pilot, WH 'Slim' Sear,

being passed to the Aeroplane and Armament Experimental Establishment – and serialled XL722 – for evaluation the following month. It was re-engined with a Napier N.Ga.11 Gazelle in 1957, flying again on 17 May for trials. The smaller and lighter Gazelle altered the centre of gravity, enabling some of the avionics to be moved from the aft fuselage to the nose. This aircraft was followed by 12 Westland-built pre-production aircraft and 99 HAS.1 production aircraft – the name Wessex was officially bestowed on 30 January 1959. The first pre-production helicopter XL727 made its maiden flight on 20 June 1958. Intensive flying trials began in April 1960 with 700H NAS and 815 NAS became operational in July 1961. The HAS.31 for the Royal Australian Navy (RAN) was similar except for the 1,575shp (1,174kW) Gazelle 13/2 Mk.162 engine; from 1968 these were upgraded to HAS.3 standard as the HAS.31B.

The HAS.1 was an interim type, the full ASW weapons system being introduced with the Wessex HAS.3, which was developed to meet Specification HAS.227D&P issued on 19 July 1963. The engine was upgraded to the 1,600shp (1,193kW) Gazelle 18 Mk.161 and the avionics included an upgraded ARI.5595 Ekco AW.391 lightweight search radar, Plessey Type 195 dipping sonar, Marconi Doppler navigation and a Newmark/Westland duplex automatic flight control system (AFCS). The latter could carry out an entire sortie automatically, including hovering and transits between sonar dips.

The Wessex HAS.3 was the first FAA helicopter to carry a nuclear depth bomb. The WE.177A (anonymised as the Bomb, Aircraft HE 600lb MC)

Westland Wessex HAS.1 XM871 of 706 NAS. Note the base of the Type 194B dipping sonar transducer protruding from the helicopter's belly. XM871 was later converted to HAS.3 standard and was lost in the Red Sea on 21 August 1975 when operating from the *County*-class destroyer HMS *Glamorgan*. *Phil Butler Collection*

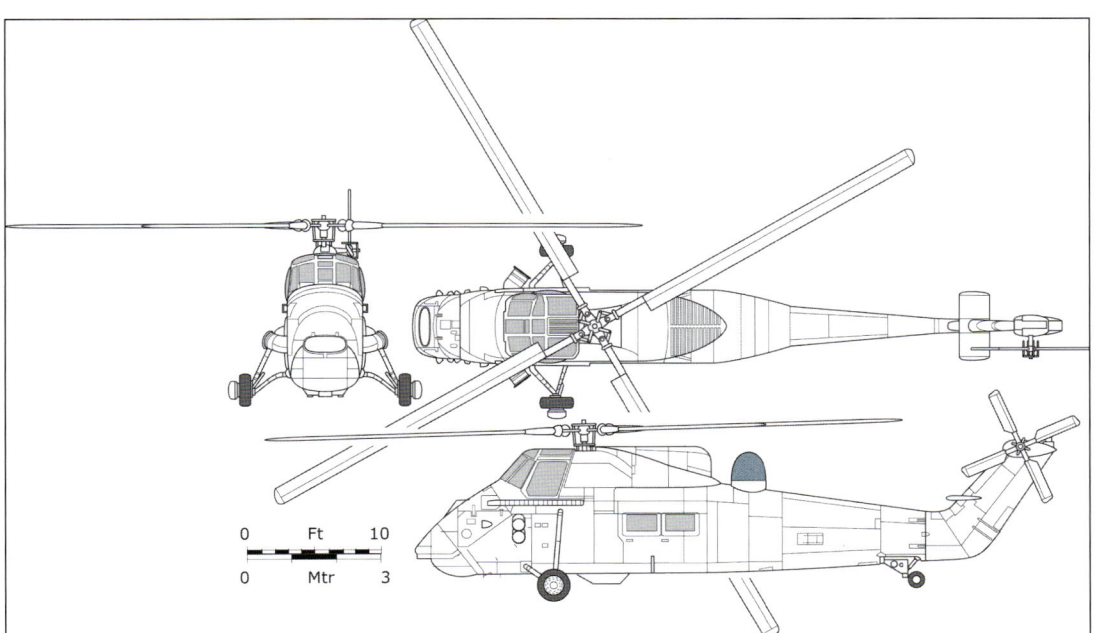

ABOVE A general arrangement drawing of the Wessex HAS.3. *Chris Gibson*

Wessex HAS.1 XS880 of 826 NAS based aboard HMS *Hermes* with its Type 194B dipping sonar transducer dangling in mid-air in September 1966. The Wessex was initially painted in RAF Blue Grey with Golden Yellow upper surfaces. XS880 ditched following engine failure during plane guard duties alongside *Ark Royal* on 22 May 1975. *Terry Panopalis Collection*

LEFT The Wessex could carry a 15kT WE.177A depth bomb to deal with deeply submerged targets. HAS.3 XS882 is fitted with an inert training round. *MOD via Terry Panopalis Collection*

BELOW The second prototype Wessex HAS.3 XT256 was a ground instructional airframe by the time of this July 1978 photograph at RNAS Lee-on-Solent, but the open cabin door reveals the large Type 195 transducer and its associated cable drum and winch filling the cabin. *Terry Panopalis Collection*

Wessex HAS.3 XS121 was first flown on 28 May 1963, being assigned to the A&AEE at Boscombe Down for electromagnetic compatibility trials before being issued to 820 NAS in October 1964. It survived a ditching on 25 March 1965 to be repaired and sent to the Far East for assessment trials in September 1967. Returning to the UK in early 1968, XS121 finally succumbed to another ditching on 16 February 1972 following engine failure off Portland Bill. *Author's Collection*

The Wessex could extend its range by refuelling from a ship without having to land by means of a cable and hose system. This Wessex HAS.3 of 737 NAS is practicing the technique in the English Channel from the flight deck of the helicopter training ship RFA *Engadine* in 1978. *Terry Panopalis Collection*

replaced RAF Coastal Command's Project N US-supplied dual-key 11kT Mk.101 Lulu and 15kT Mk.57 nuclear depth bombs. It had a hydrostatic fuze and a variable yield warhead of 0.5kT for use in shallow waters down to 130ft (40m) or 1.0kT for deeper waters. The casing was designed to flood and sink at 20ft/sec (6m/sec). The bomb was 16.5in (41.9cm) in diameter, 112.25in (285cm) long and weighed 600lb (272kg). The delivery profile was to turn into the wind following release and accelerate to maximum permissible speed to escape the blast area.

Development of the HAS.3 was protracted by various problems with the engines and autopilot, development costs doubling to £18 million and the 43 HAS.1 conversions averaged £270,000 each.

Three prototypes were built; XT255 making its first flight on 3 November 1964 at Yeovil with XT256 and XT257 following on 27 January and 10 May 1965. Trials with 700H NAS at RNAS Culdrose began in January 1967 and 814 NAS became operational in October. The Wessex's main shortcoming was poor endurance in the screening role and its operational life was quite brief, being replaced by the Westland Sea King HAS.1 from 1970 – except for a few carried aboard the *County*-class guided-missile destroyers into the 1980s. From late 1967 some HAS.1 were assigned to the carriers as plane guards for SAR duties with the ASW equipment removed.

Wessex HAS.3 XM836 with the *County*-class guided-missile destroyer HMS *Devonshire* in the background; this class of ships operated the Wessex HAS.3 until the early-1980s. XM836 had been completed as a HAS.1 in May 1960, being converted as the prototype HAS.3 conversion and flying as such on 15 June 1966. XM836 was issued to *Devonshire's* sistership *Fife* in October 1971. An emergency landing on 22 September 1980 ended this helicopter's varied career. *HMS Osprey via Terry Panopalis Collection*

Ultra-Light G-APJJ was the fifth built and is seen here at the SBAC Show at Farnborough in September 1958 with Fairey test pilot John Morton at the controls, shortly after its use aboard the frigate HMS *Undaunted* in Exercise SHOPWINDOW. *Phil Butler Collection*

The compact design of the Ultra-Light and its Blackburn/Turbomeca Palouste compressor are nicely illustrated in this second view of G-APJJ at Farnborough in September 1958. *Phil Butler Collection*

Ultra-Light

By the mid-1950s a new generation of anti-submarine frigates was entering service. The Type 15 and Type 16 conversions of Second World War-era destroyers were supplemented by the Type 12 *Whitby*, Type 14 *Blackwood* and Type 81 *Tribal* classes. The main shipborne anti-submarine weapon was the triple-barrelled Mortar Mk.10 Limbo, with a range of 3,000ft (914m). The Mk.20E Bidder homing torpedo was in development with an effective range of 3.95-8nm (7.3-14.6km) but the Admiralty required a weapon to fully exploit the new Type 177 long-range sonar's detection range. A basic lightweight helicopter was seen as the ideal way to deliver a homing torpedo over longer distances.

In 1955 the Director of Under Surface Warfare, Captain Edward Bayldon, had his attention was drawn to the Fairey Ultra-Light, which had been designed to meet the Air Staff's OR.319 for an ultralight reconnaissance helicopter for the Army. Swapping the weight allowance for a passenger for a lightweight torpedo seemed feasible. The DNAW, Captain Frank Hopkins, confirmed that the concept was feasible; the RCN had conducted a similar exercise aboard HMCS *Labrador* using a Hiller helicopter.

The first Ultra-Light prototype (XJ924) ordered under Specification HR.144T had made its maiden flight on 14 August 1955 but within a year the Army and the MoS had withdrawn official support and Fairey continued development on a private venture basis. The RN's interest helped to revive the fortunes of the programme.

The Ultra-Light's structure was basic but robust. A licence-built Blackburn/Turbomeca Palouste 505 air compressor supplied air through the rotor hub and blades to two tip-mounted Fairey pressure jets, where the air was mixed with fuel and burnt, giving an equivalent thrust of 150hp (111kW). The rotor's speed limits were a minimum of 380rpm to 490rpm maximum, the normal operating speed being 460rpm. There was sufficient payload to carry single Mk.43 homing torpedo and fuel for an 8.6 nm (16km) radius of action with 15 minutes spent loitering.

Sea trials aboard the Type 15 frigate HMS *Grenville* took place during 4-12 February 1957 using Fairey's fourth prototype Ultra-Light, G-AOUK. *Grenville* was fitted with a wooden platform 9ft (2.7m) above the quarterdeck and four 50gal (227lit) fuel drums on the quarterdeck enabled refuelling via hand pumps. The trial began by G-AOUK flying off the back of a 3-ton lorry on the quayside on to the ship. A total flying time of 29hr 50min was recorded with 72 deck landings, of which 64 were at sea. The pilots found no issues operating from the heavily rolling and pitching platform in wind speeds up to 62kt – the naval liaison pilot from 705 NAS stating that no other helicopter could have operated in such conditions. The precise power control, excellent stability of the rigid rotor at low airspeeds and the ski undercarriage, which eliminated movement between the aircraft and the deck, were notable features.

Preliminary operational assessments during 20–22 February experimented with the Frigate Controlled Approach procedure; the ship's Helicopter Controller guiding the helicopter to a submerged target via the helicopter's radar transponder, the submarine being tracked by sonar. The trial was hampered by technical issues with the *Aster* radar transponder, but even so, *Grenville*'s Type 293 target-indication radar could track the Ultra-Light at an altitude of 20ft (6m) out to 10.6nm (19.7km) and the ship's Type 974 navigation radar achieved 1.8nm (3.5km) when the helicopter was flying at 200ft (60m).

During the autumn G-AOUJ made more than 70 take-offs and landings from *Grenville*. Other related

MATCH alternatives: Hydrofoils

Saunders-Roe also designed marine craft and the company was awarded a study contract in January 1957 to investigate a remotely-controlled, hydrofoil, anti-submarine weapons carrier. The result was the P.200, two of which could be carried in davits on the quarterdeck of a frigate. Its hull featured a planing bow with a tunnel aft which carried a *Pentane* homing torpedo. Aft of the bow step was the sonar – either a helicopter dipping sonar (which would require the craft to slow down considerably) or a retractable strut-mounted sonar (which could be used at speeds up to 30kt.)

The P.200 was powered by a 1,200shp (894kW) Napier Gazelle N.Ga.3 turboprop driving a four-blade, pusher propeller (a 'boosted' version was proposed with a Gazelle and two small Rolls-Royce RB.93 Soar turbojets). The weight was 11,000lb (4,990kg), with a length of 30ft (9.1m) and 16ft (4.8m) beam. The maximum speed was 70kt in calm conditions or 60kt in rougher seas; radius of action was up to 25nm (46km).

The intended sequence of deployment for the 20–50 minute long sortie was:

- Frigate sonar contact with a submarine target at a range of 5–10nm (9–18km) in North Atlantic conditions or 25nm (46km) in shallow waters;
- One P.200 deployed via davits (frigate moving at low speed);
- Hydrofoil accelerates to maximum speed towards the target bearing;
- Slowing or stopping enroute to deploy dipping sonar to acquire a fix on the target;
- Homing onto the target's bearing at high speed (slowing/stopping to deploy sonar again if required);
- *Pentane* (or another homing torpedo type) released over the target's position;
- Hydrofoil cruises back to frigate at 40–70kt for recovery via davits.

Ultimately the concept was abandoned. Despite previous experience with the larger R-103 *Bras D'Or* hydrofoil built for the Royal Canadian Navy, model water tank tests in simulated rough sea conditions obtained poor results and cavitation over the foils (which would have affected sonar performance) remained a problem.

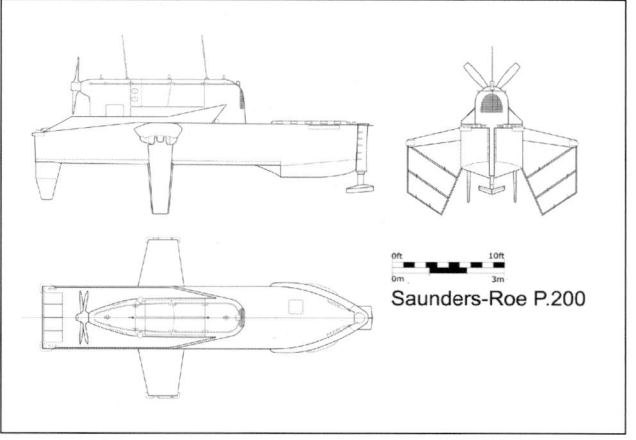

A general arrangement drawing of the Saro P.200 hydrofoil torpedo carrier. *Author*

The P.200 was an innovative concept, being the forerunner of the Unmanned Surface Vessel (USV) that is becoming popular with navies today. The helicopter was far more versatile and less limited in regard to rough seas. *Author's Collection*

trials involved sistership *Undaunted* vectoring a Whirlwind HAS.7 to the ship's sonar contact using the Type 974 radar, followed by a similar trial by the radar training ship *Fleetwood* using the improved Type 978 navigation radar.

During 30 June to 4 July 1958 Ultra-Light G-APJJ was operated from *Undaunted*, the ship receiving a lightweight steel platform, which was slightly smaller than *Grenville's* at 21ft × 26ft (6.4 × 7.9m). The platform's light construction caused problems with the skid undercarriage due to the undulating deck. A radar plotting test achieved 3.8nm (7.2km) with the helicopter flying at 300-500ft (91-152m).

Following the successful trials which proved the feasibility of the concept, the MoS issued Specification HAS.191D on 8 August 1958. With an AUW of 1,650lb (748kg) with a crew of two the helicopter was to be capable of a maximum continuous cruising speed of not less than 70kt at heights up to 3,000ft (914m) with a radius of action of 8.6nm (16km). The sea level vertical rate of climb was to be at least 200ft/min (61m/min). It had to be capable of landing with the ship sailing at up to 20kt in wind speeds of up to 40kt. Meeting these requirements led to 4ft (1.2m) additional rotor diameter to reduce disc loading, more efficient circular tangential type tip-jets as fitted to the Rotodyne, a 3ft 6in (1m) taller undercarriage to provide adequate clearance for a torpedo and extension of the allowable shift of the centre of gravity. Three development aircraft were ordered.

The Director of Naval Construction (DNC) began studying how the Ultra-Light could be accommodated aboard frigates. The helicopter would require a platform and a simple hangar or inflatable screen to enable maintenance under

WINGS OVER THE FLEET

A Fairey Ultra-Light races a Saro P.200 hydrofoil torpedo carrier in June 1959 at the Needles off the Isle of Wight. The Ultra-Light inspired the MATCH concept using ship-directed helicopters armed with lightweight homing torpedoes; the P.200 remote-controlled hydrofoil was a similar concept but carrying the much larger *Pentane* homing torpedo. *Luciano Alviani*

cover, plus stowage for 500gal (2,273L) of AVCAT (sufficient for 15 hours flying), 16 Mk. 43 torpedoes and equipment for battery charging and weapon loading. Six extra personnel, including the pilot, would be required. Initial thoughts for the Type 12 *Whitby*-class envisaged a hangar in the hull (replacing one of the two Limbo mortars usually fitted) with a lift to bring the helicopter onto the upper deck. This scheme was replaced by a topside hangar. Ideally all ships equipped with the Type 177 would have received helicopters, but the estimated £6.12 million cost saw this plan reduced to 18 Type 12 and seven Type 81 ships. The additional costs per ship were £205,000: £25,000 for the helicopter, £80,000 for the torpedoes, £80,000 for the Type 177 sonar and £20,000 for ship fitting work.

The Isle of Wight Rival

Two months after Specification HAS.191D was issued the more capable Saunders-Roe P.531 helicopter appeared. The P.531 had been designed to a Joint Services Requirement for a general purpose helicopter with full tropical performance and soon attracted the Admiralty's attention given its ability to carry two torpedoes rather than one, as well as greater

The Saro P.531 prototype in its original wheeled configuration in 1958. It was later serialled XN333 for naval evaluation in October 1959. It was lost during a trial of MAD equipment off Portland Bill on 19 July 1961 when the tail rotor driveshaft failed, Lt CRC McClure was killed and Lt BR Allen injured. *Phil Butler Collection*

Lightweight helicopters

	Fairey Ultra-Light	**Saro P.531-0**	**Westland Wasp HAS.1**
Rotor diameter	28ft 3½in (8.61m)	32ft 6in (9.91m)	32ft 3in (9.83 m)
Length	15ft 0in (4.57m) fuselage	29ft 0in (8.84m) rotors folded	40ft 4in (12.29m) overall; 30ft 4in (9.24 m) fuselage; 25ft 9in (7.84m) folded
Rotor disc area	?	3,270ft² (303.8m²)	816.9ft² (75.80m²)
All-up weight	1,800lb (817kg)	3,800lb (1,724kg)	5,500lb (2,495kg)
Powerplant	1x BnPe.2 Palouste 50 gas generator; 2x Fairey pressure jets, 150hp (111kW) equivalent thrust	1x Turmo 601, 320shp (238kW) derated	1x Nimbus 103 or 104, 1,050shp (783kW), derated to 710shp (529kW)
Max speed	85kt (158km/h) cruising	105kt (194km/h)	104kt (193km/h)
Service ceiling	4,800ft (1,463m) hovering ceiling in ground effect	2,300ft (700m)	12,200ft (3,720ft)
Range	160nm (290km)	210nm (390km)	263nm (487km)
Armament	1x US Mk.43 homing torpedo	1x Light Series Bomb Carrier for 4x flares & Marine Markers	2x UK Mk.44 or US Mk.46 homing torpedoes; 4x AS.12

endurance and potential for future development. The interest was economic too; Saro quoted a price of £147,250 for three prototypes, compared to £180,000 for three Ultra-Lights. By the end of 1958 the Admiralty was firmly behind the P.531 and the Ultra-Light order was cancelled and Specification HAS.194D issued on 15 April 1959 to cover the P.531 development batch.

The specification called for an AUW of 3,000lb (1,360kg) with 1,000lb (453kg) disposable load (fuel, crew, radio and two Mk.43 or Mk.44 torpedoes). Maximum speed without external stores was to be at least 87kt at 2,000ft (609m) with a continuous cruising speed of at least 80kt. Range when cruising at 70kt was to be 200nm (370km). The vertical rate of climb, free of ground cushion effect at sea level at maximum power, was to be at least 180ft/min (54.8m/sec) with the ability to hover in the ground cushion in still conditions at 3,400lb (1,540kg) maximum take-off weight. The service ceiling was to be not less than 12,000ft (3,660m). The crew consisted of a pilot and co-pilot/observer/passenger in the front of the cabin with provision for a three-passenger bench seat in the rear.

Saro offered three versions. The P.531-0 was the naval evaluation prototype with a 320shp (238kW) Turbomeca/Blackburn Turmo 601 turboshaft (capable of running on AVCAT, AVTUR or diesel) married to a modified Saro Skeeter 12 transmission system and a four-blade main rotor. Saro estimated that the first helicopter could be delivered in six months following an order. The P.531-1 had a 425shp (316kW) Turmo 603 with a 650shp (484kW) rated transmission for future growth. A prototype was estimated to fly in April 1959 with the first production aircraft following within five months. The P.531-2 was the ultimate development with a 1,000shp (745kW) turboshaft to deliver 650shp (484kW) in tropical conditions to meet all future FAA and Army requirements.

Following manufacturer's trials from 24 June 1958, the three P.531-0 helicopters (XN332, XN333 and XN334) were delivered during October and November 1959 (at this stage they were informally named Sea Sprite).

The DNC was asked to investigate if any changes were required to accommodate the P.531 aboard the Type 12 and 81 frigates. No problems were foreseen in enlarging the Type 12's facilities; the Type 81 received an innovative hangar with an integrated roof lift, the five ton weight increase being subtracted from the 34-ton Board Margin built into the design (the changes cost

Saro P.531-0 XN334 making an approach to land aboard HMS *Undaunted*'s early flight deck during Frigate Controlled Approach Trials in late 1959. Note the empty Light Series Carriers mounted under the fuselage which would be used with practice weapons and flares. *Phil Butler Collection*

WINGS OVER THE FLEET

Saro P.531-0 XN334 making a landing aboard HMS *Ashanti*. Note the suction pads on the ski undercarriage to prevent the helicopter sliding on the deck. XN334 was lost on 4 March 1962 in a take-off accident aboard *Ashanti*, the helicopter losing height and the skid clipping the flight deck which made the aircraft topple inverted into the water. Both crewmen were rescued. *Phil Butler Collection*

£5,000 per ship). Using the ship's bunkers to refuel the helicopter reduced the ship's cruising endurance by 130nm (240km). The Admiralty was concerned about the available Mk.43 torpedo stocks given that the P.531 could carry two per sortie and were worried about the Dollar expenditure involved in direct purchase or licence royalties to buy additional weapons.

The evaluation batch was delivered to 700 NAS. Over five weeks during November and December 1959, one of the helicopters was embarked aboard *Undaunted*, completing 15 flying days with 290 day and 31 night deck landings in various sea-states – the weather varying from calm to 35kt winds and 15-20ft (4.5-6m) high waves. Following the problems encountered during the Ultra-Light trials, *Undaunted's* landing platform was given a wooden deck, but now the P.531 slid on its skids as the ship pitched and rolled in heavy seas. This was later cured by fitting suction cup pads.

The Frigate Controlled Approach directed attacks were practised during the tactical trials against the submarine HMS *Tireless* at ranges between 1.8–7.7nm (3.4–14.4km) away from *Undaunted*. Of the 117 valid attacks carried out, 98 simulated torpedoes fell within 1,200ft (365m) of the point of aim, achieving a Circular Error Probability (CEP, the area within which at least 50% of the weapons released would hit) radius of 600ft (182m). The Aster radar transponder was still causing problems so two rearward-facing radar reflectors were fitted to the undercarriage legs which enabled the helicopter to be tracked up to 7.7nm (14.4km) away. The trials proved that the Frigate Controlled Approach was a practical method to engage enemy submarines.

Night flying operations were conducted without any difficulties – red light floodlights and other lighting for the landing platform was improvised, including duty-free tobacco tins containing a 4-Watt bulb with a slit cut into them taped to the deck!

In 1961, 771 NAS reformed out of 700 NAS as a dedicated helicopter trials and training unit. The unit flew 18 months of trials with the three P.531s and this experience led to the improved Westland Wasp HAS.1 and the Manned Torpedo-Carrying Helicopter (MATCH) weapons system.

MATCHing the Wasp

With the Ministry of Aviation (MoA) led rationalisation of the helicopter industry, Westland absorbed the helicopter divisions of Bristol, Fairey and Saunders-Roe. The P.531 was developed further under Specification HAS.216D&P, which was issued on 29 April 1961.

The performance requirements were more exacting. Take-off weight was to be 5,500lb (2,494kg) with a freight capability of 300lb (136kg). The maximum cruising speed was to be at least 95kt at sea level at 5,000lb (2,270kg) maximum AUW – later increased to 5,200lb (2,360kg). The vertical rate of climb was to be at least 180ft/min (54.8m/min) with a service ceiling of 12,000ft (3,660m). The radius of action for an anti-submarine sortie was to be at least 20nm (37km), plus 30 minutes loiter on station, 15 minutes loiter on return to the ship and five minutes hovering. The helicopter's folded length was not to exceed 26ft (7.9m), the folded width 7ft (2.1m) and the folded height 10ft (3.3m).

The Wasp's main anti-submarine armament was a pair of UK Mk.44 homing torpedoes, as carried by XV627, assigned to the *Leander*-class frigate HMS *Hermoine* in 1979. Captain F5 refers to *Hermoine* being the Flagship of the 5th Flotilla. All Wasp Flights assigned to ships belonged to 829 NAS. Well-travelled Wasps tended to pick up collections of stickers in the lower cockpit windows, as XV627 has here. *MOD via Terry Panopalis Collection*

The P.531 became the Westland Wasp HAS.1 (initially known as the Sea Scout) and received several improvements, including a folding tail to reduce the fuselage length to 25ft 9in (7.84m) and a 1,050shp (782kW) (de-rated to 710shp (529kW)) Bristol Siddeley Nimbus 103/104 turboshaft. The revised tail pylon carried a two-blade rotor on the port side with a stabiliser to starboard. Experience from the deck handling trials and a special-built experimental rolling platform at the Royal Aircraft Establishment's Bedford site led to the development of a four-wheel fully castoring undercarriage along with a harpoon-type deck securing system. A radio altimeter and an autopilot providing height, roll, yaw and pitch control were also fitted.

The Wasp could carry two Mk44 or one Mk46 torpedo and carriage of the WE.177A nuclear depth bomb was trialled, the cabin doors being removed to compensate for the potential blast pressure.

The Wasp was also armed to counter Fast Patrol Boats (FPBs) to meet Naval Staff Requirement NSR.6623 for an interim air-to-surface missile (ASM)

Another anti-submarine option was the WE.177A depth bomb, the 0.5kT weapon being able to crush a submarine's pressure hull within a large radius. The cabin doors were removed to lessen the effects of blast overpressure on the airframe. NATO planners debated at length whether such weapons could be used in the early stages of a conflict with the Soviet Union without risking a general nuclear exchange. This Wasp HAS.1 is XT788, of 829 NAS assigned to HMS *Minerva* hovering alongside HMS *Eagle* in 1969. *Terry Panopalis Collection*

WINGS OVER THE FLEET

For the anti-Fast Patrol Boat role the Wasp could be armed with four Nord AS.12 ASMs with an APX Bezu gyro-stabilised sight fitted in the cockpit roof for the co-pilot. XT790 is seen in 1976 when it was assigned to 703 NAS. A landing accident on 15 July 1982 saw its retirement but XT790 had a second life, being sold to the Malaysian Navy in August 1982, becoming M499-09. *MOD via Terry Panopalis Collection*

capability with two Nord AS.12 ASMs mounted on pylons either side of the cabin. The co-pilot aimed the wire-guided missiles via an APX Bezu gyro-stabilised sight in the cockpit roof. The AS.12 had been selected in preference to the Short Hellcat development of the Sea Cat surface-to-air missile (SAM). The AS.12's range of 22,500ft (6.8km) and 30 seconds powered flight time exposed the helicopter to the FPBs' defensive armament. It was also limited to daylight operation, requiring flare illumination of the target from another helicopter at night (trials using Sea Kings to control night attacks had limited success), but its simplicity and low cost outweighed its limitations. All the Wasp-equipped frigates could swap four Sea Cats for eight AS.12 missiles in their magazines.

An order for two Sea Scout HAS.1 pre-production aircraft with 685shp (510kW) Nimbus Mk.101 turboshafts was placed in September 1961. The first, XS463, was flown on 28 October 1962 by Westland test pilot Ron Gellatly, XS476 following on 21 January 1963. The Sea Scout name was soon dropped in favour of Wasp and the first of 96 production aircraft flew during January 1963 (30 more were cancelled). In late February XS463 was used for preliminary deck trials aboard the Type 81-class frigate *Nubian*. In May 1964 Specification HAS.126 was amended for a higher AUW of 5,500lb (2,494kg) to allow the safe carriage of heavier weapons. This had some knock-on effects; tropical trials were conducted by XS527 from RAF Khormakasar in Aden and aboard the Type 81 frigate *Mohawk* laying offshore during August and September. With the higher AUW the vertical performance in tropical conditions failed to meet the specifications.

The complete MATCH weapons system aboard a frigate comprised: one Wasp HAS.1; a Type 177M or Type 184M hull-mounted long-range sonar (the latter having pulse-Doppler capability); Type 199 towed variable depth medium-range sonar; Type 978 X-band navigation radar for helicopter tracking; Outfit RRA transponder receiver; a sonar marker system feeding the JYA electronic plotting table and the Helicopter Controller's dedicated JUA Display; Outfit QQA true motion helicopter and submarine course tracker for the JUA Display; the Optical Plot Attachment for the JUA which provided an 'attack graticule' with which the Helicopter Controller 'aimed' the attack.

MATCH provided a frigate with a 50% chance of successfully dropping a torpedo within 1,500ft (457m) of a submarine at ranges of up to 8.8nm (16.4km) in all-weathers – the Circular Error of Probability (CEP). It was found that the main limit to a successful kill was the capability of the Mk44 torpedo, which is why the more destructive WE.177A nuclear depth bomb was considered for

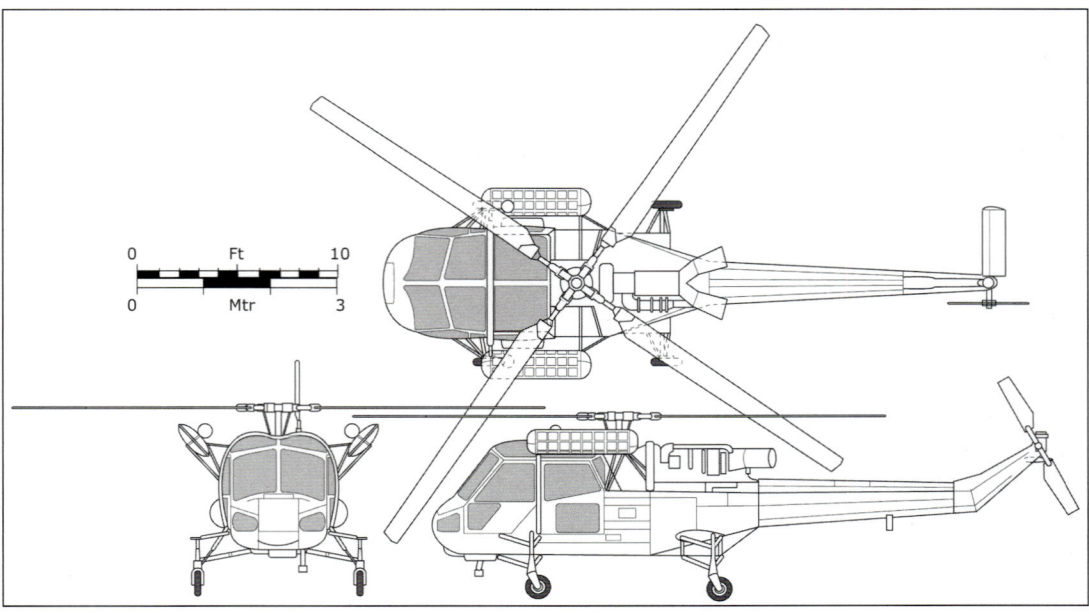

A general arrangement drawing of the Wasp HAS.1. *Chris Gibson*

Wasp XT780 of 703 NAS in June 1974 carrying two AS.12 but without the gyro-stabilised sight. Presumably, this was just a handling training flight. XT780 had first flown on 22 June 1966 and was withdrawn from service in January 1980. *Terry Panopalis Collection*

use against deeper targets. It must be remembered, however, that MATCH's accuracy depended on the performance of the ship's sonar.

An evaluation at the Atlantic Underwater Test and Evaluation Centre at Andros Island in the Bahamas was conducted during September and October 1968 to fully analyse the performance of the MATCH system. The *Leander*-class frigate *Sirius* was used alongside the diesel submarine HMS *Tiptoe*. The 50% CEP was calculated as 1,206ft (367m); but Wessex HAS.3 attacks were more accurate, because the Wessex had a two-man observer team with better crew co-ordination and its own Type 195 dipping sonar to verify the target's location. The performance of the Wessex HAS.3's sonar proved to be superior in some situations than the ship's Type 184M – being stationary in the hover made plotting underwater contacts easier than aboard a moving ship.

An Operational Evaluation was conducted the following month by the *Leander*-class frigates *Juno* and *Sirius*, with Type 177M and Type 184M sonars respectively, against the new nuclear hunter-killer submarine *Valiant*. Due to problems associated with

Wasp XT782 flying a display during the 1960 SBAC Show at Farnborough with two dummy Mk.43 torpedoes and with the emergency floatation gear inflated. Later named 'Scrumpy the Cider Glider', XT782 was transferred to the Royal New Zealand Navy in 1989. *Terry Panopalis Collection*

MATCH lternatives: Missiles

By the late 1950s several navies were investigating stand-off missiles capable of delivering a homing torpedo. The USN's Rocket Assisted Torpedo (RAT) programme entered service in 1960 as the RUR-5 ASROC; France developed Malafon (Marine Latécoère Fonds); the Soviet Union began development of the RPK-1 Vikhr (codenamed FRAS-1 by NATO) in 1960.

The Admiralty's Joint Underwater System Assessment Group investigated three private ventures during 1959–1960, leading to Naval Staff Targets 110(T) and 111(T) in 1960.

Armstrong Whitworth and GEC proposed Project 525, a 9ft (2.7m) long rocket booster with a 6ft (1.8m) span wing and powered by an unspecified 300lbf (1.46kN) thrust turbojet mounted above the missile body; underneath was slung a 550lb (249kg) homing torpedo. Effective range was 1–14.8nm (2.2–27.4km), it would use command guidance and was intended to be launched from fixed box launchers (a trainable launcher with an 18 missile magazine was designed later).

Napier's Air-Flight A/S Weapon Vehicle (also called Seahorse) was offered in two variants with the Mk.44 homing torpedo either being mid-mounted or underslung. The rocket booster was 9ft 1in (2.7m) long with a 6ft 1in (1.8m) span wing and had a 450lbf (2kN) sustainer rocket motor, which was unusually located ahead of the torpedo with side vents. Maximum range was 9.8nm (18km), it could be guided via command guidance or pre-programmed if tracking radar emissions were undesirable. Either two single-rail or one twin-rail fixed high-elevation launcher would be used with 20 reloads

Vickers designed ASBUG, a 12ft (3.6m) long rocket carrier for a US Mk.44 torpedo, which would be released after the missile impacted the water. Command guidance would be used, launching of the 1,250lb (567kg) weapon was via a trainable launcher. These three weapons only offered 50% success against non-manoeuvring submarine targets and were not taken further.

In 1959 the Australian Government Aircraft Factory (GAF) began work on the Ikara (Aboriginal for throwing stick), a 1,400lb (635kg) development of the Malkara anti-tank missile, 16ft (4.8m) long with the warhead in the nose replaced by a Mk.44 homing torpedo. Ikara soon evolved into a new missile powered by a Bristol Aerojet Murawa two-stage solid-fuel rocket booster/sustainer to achieve a range of 9.8nm (18.2km) with the torpedo semi-recessed underneath. The Admiralty selected Ikara, a joint Admiralty/MoA working party recommending carriage of the heavier – but superior – US Mk.46 torpedo and the WE.177A nuclear depth-bomb. Requirement USW368 (later becoming NSR.7668) was issued to deal with a submarine with capable of 40kt (later reduced to 35kt) with a 2,000ft (609m) depth limit and 30ft/sec (9.1m/sec) change of depth. Ikara complemented MATCH, overcoming the latter's restrictions due to wind, sea state, visibility and providing a much quicker 30 seconds reaction time and superior re-attack capability with 24 missiles. The main drawback was that the frigates' sonars often lacked the acquisition range to take advantage of Ikara's reach. GAF continued development; the M4- (minus) being developed for the *Leander*-class frigates in 1966; the M6 'Super Ikara' with a modified Murawa for increased range and the NASR.7511 (Sting Ray) homing torpedo was cancelled in 1976; the M7 proposal of the early 1980s would have added a turbojet sustainer to further increase range.

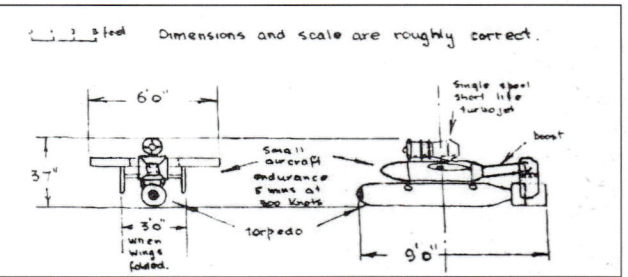

Armstrong Whitworth's Project 525 was an ungainly looking torpedo-carrying glider with a small turbojet strapped on top. *Via Chris Gibson*

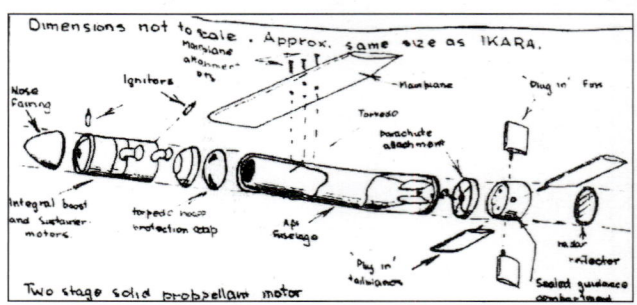

Napier's Seahorse sandwiched the homing torpedo between the sustainer and booster rocket motors. *Via Chris Gibson*

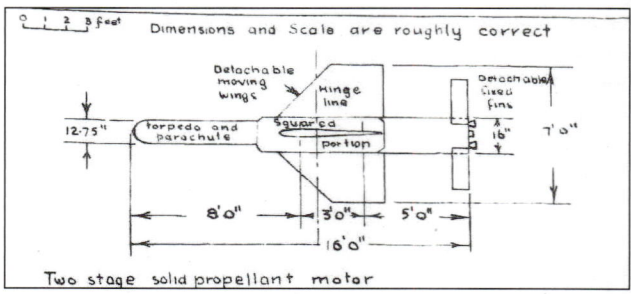

The Government Aircraft Factory's initial Ikara design, showing much of its Malkara heritage. *Via Chris Gibson*

This Ikara test round on display at the National Cold War Exhibition at the RAF Museum Midlands shows the final design. The Bristol Murawa two-stage solid-fuel booster/sustainer is at the rear and a dummy Mk.46 torpedo payload is carried beneath. The wings and tail fin were attached in the ship's magazine before launch. *Author*

Wasp XT788 which was still assigned to the *Leander*-class frigate HMS *Minerva* when this picture was taken. Following a landing accident at Roosevelt Roads in Puerto Rico in June 1973, it was assigned to the Type 21 frigate HMS *Antelope*. XT788 was withdrawn from service in September 1979. *Phil Butler Collection*

safety in the sea conditions, *Valiant* only exceeded 12kt during five out of 24 MATCH attacks, so preventing conclusive results but the success rate was 77%. In reality, an unrestricted nuclear submarine able to dive and manoeuvre at high speed would be difficult to detect or hit with homing torpedoes.

The FAA operated the Wasp from June 1963 until November 1985, being supplanted by the Westland Lynx HAS.2 from 1977. Although the Wasp was being replaced by the Westland Lynx HAS.2 by the time of the Malvinas/Falklands Conflict in 1982, the Wasp played an important part in hostilities. On 25 April, a Wessex HAS.3 from the destroyer *Antrim* spotted the Argentinian submarine ARA *Santa Fe* on the surface. The Wessex and a Lynx HAS.2 from the Type 22 *Broadsword* frigate *Brilliant* attacked the *Santa Fe* with depth charges, a Mk 46 torpedo and strafed it with a machine gun. A Wasp from *Plymouth* and two more Wasps launched from the Antarctic/ice patrol ship HMS *Endurance* fired AS.12 ASMs, damaging *Santa Fe* seriously enough to prevent her from submerging. The crew abandoned the submarine at South Georgia and surrendered to British forces. The Wasp was retired in 1988 when the last of the Type 12 frigates adapted with hangars was decommissioned.

Exports were made to Brazil (three new-build and seven ex-FAA airframes), Indonesia (10 ex-Dutch), Malaysia (12 ex-FAA), Netherlands (13), New Zealand (four new-build and 13 ex-FAA) and South Africa (16 out of 18 ordered).

NASR.358: The Tandems return

By 1962 the Admiralty was looking for a replacement for the Wessex and issued Requirement AW.165. The Air Staff had need of a similar helicopter to replace its Belvedere HC.1 transports and therefore both requirements were merged as Naval Air Staff Requirement NASR.358, which was issued on 17 December 1962. The requirement called for a general purpose helicopter to enter service by 1970. The primary role was ASW with secondary roles covering logistic and tactical transport, Commando assault operations, crane lift, minelaying and minesweeping – the last two roles being added by the Deputy Director of the Naval Air Division, Captain Eric 'Winkle' Brown. A fleet of 114 helicopters was desired; the aircraft carriers and escort cruisers each carrying five, three or four in each *Tiger*-class cruiser conversion and six to eight aboard a 'Helicopter Garage Ship', a support ship concept which was abandoned but later revived as the smaller RFA *Engadine* commissioned in December 1967. Each commando carrier would accommodate eight NASR.358 helicopters – four for heavy lift and four for ASW – alongside 14 Wessex HU.5.

NASR.358 called for dimensions – with the blades folded – of 51 × 17 × 17ft (15.5 × 5.1 × 5.1m). The AUW was not to exceed 30,000lb (13,610kg) (increased to 32,500lb [14,740kg] in 1964). Maximum speed was to be at least 150kt and cruising speed, 130kt. Endurance for ASW operations was to be three hours (increased to four hours in 1964.) Sufficient reserves of power were required to maintain performance under tropical conditions and

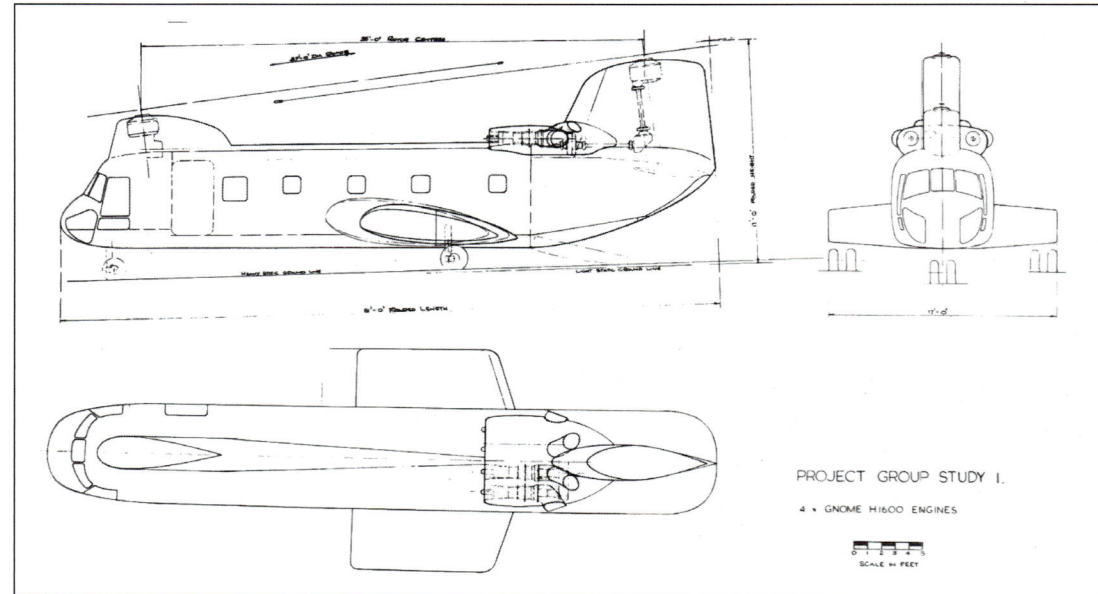

The WG.1 of Project Group Study No.1 bore a strong resemblance to the Boeing Vertol CH-46 Sea Knight. *Leonardo UK*

to allow cruising flight with one engine switched off to save fuel (also providing one engine-out safety in an emergency.) Specified flight weather minima were a 100ft (30m) cloud base, 900ft (274m) visibility and −26°C to +45°C (−14.8°F to +113°F) temperatures. The aircraft was to be amphibious and buoyant, remaining upright in Sea State 3 with rotors running and Sea State 2 with rotors stopped. Dipping sonar performance considerations imposed limits on external noise, the rotor sound received by the sonar transducer while hovering at 50ft (15m) was not to exceed the ambient noise of Sea State 3 conditions.

The ASW requirement was aimed at dealing with a nuclear-powered submarine capable of 40kt (later reduced to 35kt), diving to 2,000ft (609m) and making rapid changes in direction and depth for evasion. The ASW system was to comprise Type 195 dipping sonar (ultimately a new 360° scanning sonar weighing an estimated 5,000lb (2,267kg) was planned), a Magnetic Anomaly Detector (MAD) or an alternative passive localisation/classification device, an all-weather AFCS, *Blue Orchid* Doppler radar navigation, surface search radar, radar transponder, an automatic display system and a ADAWS compatible datalink (ADAWS was a ship-based digital combat control system.) The crew comprised two pilots, an observer and a sonar operator, with accommodation for a spare crew member.

The armament was to comprise four UK Mk.44 or two US Mk.46 torpedoes or two Mk.44 torpedoes plus a WE.177A nuclear depth bomb or one Mk.46 and one WE.177A. Provision was also made for a future stand-off weapon being developed under Naval Staff Target NST.6169 (a 1965 requirement for a stand-off weapon with a maximum range of 30,000ft [9.1km] and a minimum range of 3,000ft [914m] with at least 75% kill probability; the idea was dropped in favour of the Mk.31 homing torpedo then under development.) Other stores included four Marker Marine N5 Mk.1, eight practice depth charges, two emergency ground illuminating flares or four smoke and flame floats.

The ASW screening sortie included a 30nm (55 km) transit and three hours on station (50% of the time spent hovering) before returning to the ship at maximum economic cruising speed and landing with 10% remaining fuel. The datum investigation sortie was similar except that the transit was for 80nm (148km) at not less than 140kt with 2.5hr on station (50% time spent hovering.) The Commando role required a 65nm (120km) radius of action carrying 20 troops (15 in tropical conditions) or a Land Rover and towed 4.7in (120mm) calibre L6 WOMBAT recoilless gun, together weighing 4,000lb (1,814kg).

The NASR.358 helicopter would be operated in pairs as no current weapon enabled a single helicopter to make an effective attack whilst maintaining the sonar contact, unless the target approached within torpedo acquisition range, typically 2,100ft (640m). The need to raise the sonar and transit to, or vector another helicopter to, the last known or predicted sonar position was time consuming and reduced the kill probability against a fast, evading submarine. This was the rationale for pursuing the NST.6169 stand-off weapon for the NAST.358 helicopter.

There were several contenders for NASR.358. The Boeing Vertol V.107M was a version of the CH-46A Sea Knight tactical transport with a palletised ASW system, using the 3 × 5ft (0.9 × 1.5m) ventral hatch for sonar dipping. NASR.358 was similar in several respects to United States Air Force requirement SOR.190 which had been met by the Sikorsky S-61R CH-3B Pelican, essentially an SH-3 Sea King with a rear tail ramp. Sikorsky also had the much larger S-65A CH-53A Sea Stallion, but this did not meet the required AUW and folded dimensions requirements and lacked powered rotor blade folding. The Sud Aviation SA 321 Super Frelon was likewise too large and had insufficient crane lift

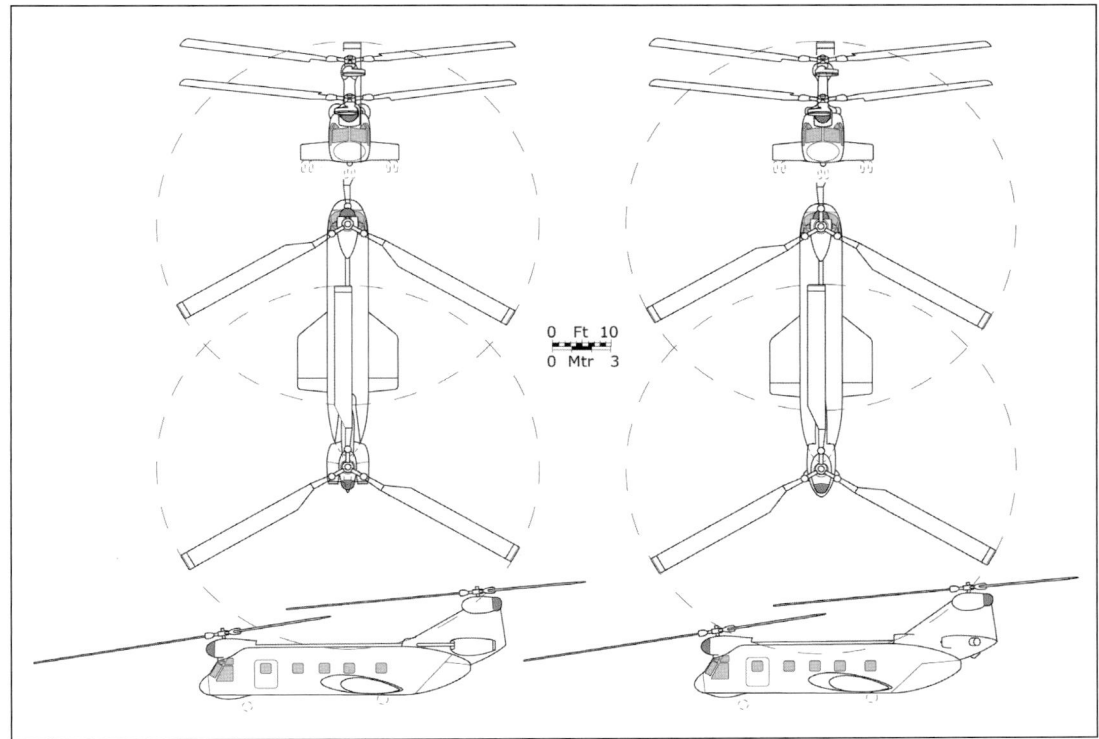

The WG.2 designs B and C differed in their engine choices; three H.1600 Gnomes or two GE T64-6 turboshafts respectively. To keep the overall dimensions as compact as possible an unusual split radar arrangement fore and aft was used to provide 360° coverage unobstructed by the rotor pylons. Both had clamshell rear doors for the transport role. *Chris Gibson*

capacity and ferry range. NASR.358's endurance and engine-out requirements could only be realistically met by a four-engine helicopter, so Boeing Vertol also offered a version of the CH-47A Chinook tandem-rotor helicopter with four Bristol Siddeley Gnome H.1400 turboshafts.

Westland's former Bristol design team at Weston-super-Mare went for a fresh design building on experience from the Belvedere with input from the Fairey Division's Aerodynamics Department. The WG.1 development programme began in October 1962 and during the following May six initial designs (labelled A to E) were examined in *Group Study No.1*. All six shared a common layout with two 57ft (17.3m) diameter three-blade rotors and four 1,600shp (1,193kW) Gnome H.1400 engines. Each had 4,500lb (2,040kg) fuel capacity in the undercarriage sponsons with provision for additional internal bag tanks for up to 5,500lb (2,495kg) capacity.

Design A was the baseline RAF tactical transport of 30,000lb (13,610kg) AUW (when assessed as a naval helicopter it was relabelled 'F'). Design B for naval operations had a 35,750lb (16,215kg) AUW and a 4,830bhp (3,600kW) rated transmission system for the rotors. Design C had a further uprated transmission of 5,000bhp (3,730kW) transmission to handle the power of four H.1800 Gnomes; the AUW was 37,000lb (16,780kg). Design E had the required AUW of 30,000lb and had a 3,900bhp (2,910kW) transmission.

Design B could carry the Type 195 Sonar plus weapons for the specified three hours on station or the notional 5,000lb sonar for 1hr 48min. 'C' could carry 2,700lb (1,225kg) of sonar equipment plus weapons, or the 5,000lb sonar without weapons, for 2hr 8min. Both 'B' and 'D' could carry a 2,000lb (907kg) sonar plus weapons for three hours, while using H.1800 Gnomes allowed 'C' to carry a 2,800lb (1,270kg) sonar. 'E' and 'F' were limited to two hours on station with Type 195 sonar.

The subsequent *Group Study No.2* focused on three naval designs designated WG.2. Design A attempted to minimise weight and fuselage size by designing the fuselage around the sonar and three operators with the weapons and flares stowed in the undercarriage sponsons. A dorsal structural boom and a swept fin pylon carried the tandem rotors (the front rotor overhanging the cockpit) and contained the fuel tanks. Three Gnome H.1600 were fitted in the base of the pylon. Design B had a conventional forward fuselage with an internal weapon bay with a rotating door, the undercarriage sponsons providing fuel stowage. Design C was similar but with two 2,650shp (1,976kW) General Electric T64-6 turboshafts (Bristol Siddeley held a T64 production licence) which reduced the transmission weight and fuel consumption. Rolls-Royce proposed a new 2,400shp (1,789kW) turbine to suit a three-engine layout but Westland declined this offer. All three variants had Type 195 sonar and 6,800lb (3,085kg) of weapons at 30,000lb AUW and all three achieved three hours on station or could carry the 5,000lb sonar for one hour. The layout of Design A prevented its use for transport but 'B' and 'C' could carry 32 troops or two Land Rovers in the Commando role. Overall, Design C came the closest to meeting NASR.358.

In 1965 Westland offered the WG.9, an alternative with 26,000lb (11,795kg) AUW and a single, five-blade rotor of 69ft (21m) diameter, powered by three

Westland design studies to meet NASR.358

Westland WG.1 (Group Study No.1)

	Design A	Design B	Design C	Design D	Design E	Design F
Role	Tactical transport	ASW	ASW	Design B for transport role	ASW	Design A for ASW role
Rotor diameter	2x 57ft 0in (17.37m)	2x 57ft 0in (17.37m)	2x 57ft 0in (17.37m)	2x 57ft 0in (17.37m)	2x 57ft 0in (17.37m)	2x 57ft 0in (17.37m)
Blade chord	33in (83cm)	36in (91cm)	37in (93cm)	36in (91cm)	30in (76cm)	33in (83cm)
Engines	4x Gnome H.1400, 1,600shp (1,193kW)	4x Gnome H.1400, 1,600shp (1,193kW)	4x Gnome H.1400, 1,600shp (1,193kW)	4x Gnome H.1400, 1,600shp (1,193kW)	4x Gnome H.1400, 1,600shp (1,193kW)	4x Gnome H.1400, 1,600shp (1,193kW)
Transmission rating	4,500bhp (3,355kW)	4,830bhp (3,600kW)	5,000bhp (3,730kW)	4,830bhp (3,600kW)	3,900bhp (2,910kW)	4,500bhp (3,355kW)
All-up weight	30,000lb (13,605kg)	35,750lb (16,215kg)	37,000lb (16,780kg)	33,000lb (14,970kg)	30,000lb (13,605kg)	30,000lb (13,605kg)
Fuel & payload	10,986lb (4,980kg)	14,012lb (6,355kg)	15,069lb (6,835kg)	12,718lb (5,768kg)	10,105lb (4,580kg)	9,780lb (4,435kg)
Crane role payload	9,300lb (4,220kg) over 30nm (55km)	N/A	N/A	10,500lb (4,760kg) over 30nm (55km)	N/A	N/A
Search endurance	N/A	3hr 0min with Type 195 sonar	2hr 8min	N/A	2hr 0min with Type 195 sonar	2hr 0min with Type 195 sonar
Dash speed	150kt (277km/h)	137kt (277km/h)	144kt (266km/h)	143kt (264km/h)	138kt (255km/h)	150kt (277km/h)

WG.1 Group Study No.2 variant

	Design A	Design B	Design C
Role	ASW & transport	ASW & transport	ASW & transport
Rotor diameter	67ft 0in (20.42m)	67ft 0in (20.42m)	66ft 0in (20.11m)
Engines	3x Gnome H.1600, 1,600shp (1,193kW)	3x Gnome H.1600, 1,600shp (1,193kW)	2x GE T64-6, 2,650shp (1,976kW)
All-up weight	30,000lb (13,605kg)	30,000lb (13,605kg)	30,000lb (13,605kg)
Fuel & payload	10,679lb (4,843kg)	10,940lb (4,960kg)	10,881lb (4,935kg)
Crane role payload	?	?	?
Dash speed	132kt (244km/h)	132kt (244km/h)	150kt (277km/h)

Final Proposals

	WG.9	WG.11A
Role	ASW & transport	ASW & transport
Rotor diameter	1x 69ft 0in (21.03m)	2x 57ft 0in (17.37m)
Engines	3x Gnome H.1600, 1,600shp (1,193kW)	4x Gnome H.1600, 1,600shp (1,193kW)
All-up weight	26,000lb (11,795kg)	32,000lb (14,515kg)
Fuel & payload	?	?
Crane role payload	10,150lb (4,065kg) over 20nm (37km)	20,000lb (9,070kg) over 30nm (55km)
Dash speed	?	?

Gnomes. The fuselage featured a ramp tail door and could accommodate 40 troops. The ASW equipment would be that of the Wessex HAS.3; the ASW mission endurance was three hours. The WG.9 marginally missed the crane lift requirement, being able to lift 10,150lb (4,065kg) over 20nm (37km), instead of the specified 12,000lb (5,445kg).

Westland's final offer for NAST.358 was the WG.11A, a military version of the stretched fuselage WG.11 tandem rotor design (itself based on the WG.1). It had a maximum gross weight of 32,000lb (14,515kg), or 35,200lb (15,965kg) in the crane role. When ferrying with maximum fuel the 40,000lb (18,145kg) weight would be offset by with stub wings providing increased lift. It could carry 34 troops (a civil version with the stub wings could carry 60 passengers) and could lift 20,000lb (9,070kg) in the crane role. With a notional 2,500lb (1,135kg) advanced sonar it could remain on station for over three hours.

The MoA doubted Westland's ability to develop and produce a tandem-rotor helicopter on budget or schedule and favoured a quicker and cheaper off-the-shelf purchase. The Gnome-powered Chinook would be available in 1968, some two to four years sooner than the WG.11.

The naval configured CH-47A Gnome Chinook incorporated several changes: powered rotor blade folding and spreading, power kneeling for the aft landing gear, shipboard tie down points, crash resistant main fuel cells with pressure refuelling, revised electrics including two 40kVA AC generators, a 6,000shp (4,474kW)-rated transmission and four Gnome H.1600 turboshafts with intake anti-icing and hydraulic starting. Provision was made for a ferry fuel system with pressure refuelling whilst hovering and in-flight oil replenishment. British equipment included a Louis Newmark-developed AFCS with a limited authority four-channel autopilot. In the Commando role would have provision for 12 paratroopers or simultaneous roping of two sticks of 12 troops. Other improvements included jettisonable overload fuel tanks, armour protection and stowage for three Type MS 9 dinghies.

The anti-submarine weapons were carried externally along with four Light Series Bomb Carriers for Marine Markers and flares and it was proposed to use a new practice depth charge dispenser developed for maritime patrol aircraft. Provision was made for defensive armament using podded guns on removable stub pylons as trialled on the experimental ACH-47A gunship variant. Vertol also offered a version with two 2,650shp (1,976kW) Lycoming T55-L-7 turboshafts with a 32,500lb (14,740kg) AUW. The research and development cost would be £20–30 million with a £1 million unit cost. Despite the doubts surrounding NASR.358 the Chinook development plan was approved in July 1964.

NASR.358's naval requirements proved tough to meet and doubts soon began to surface. In May 1963 Bristol Siddeley Engines made performance studies of four Gnome-engined helicopters and

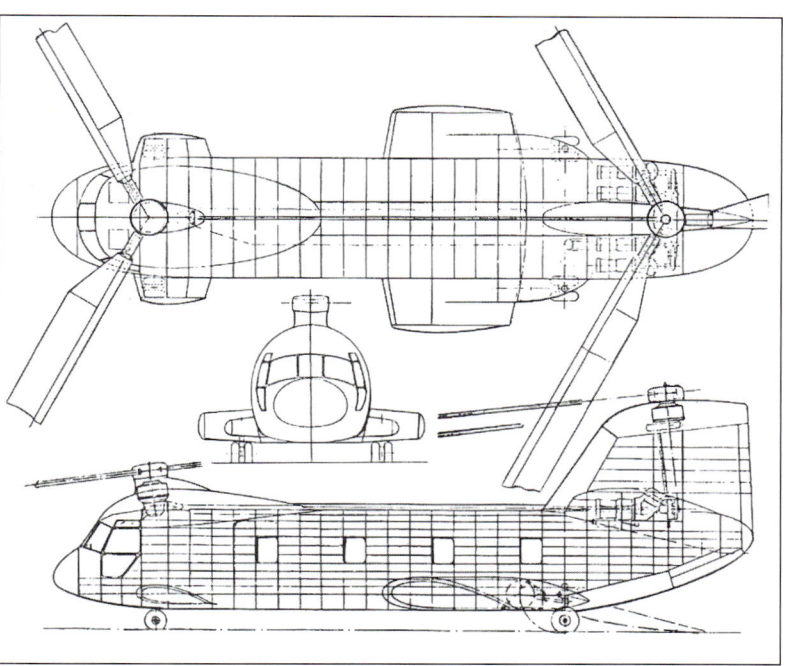

The WG.11 was developed from the WG.1 studies and had a longer fuselage. *Leonardo UK*

In this 'what-if?' painting HMS *Queen Elizabeth* prepares to receive a trio of Westland WG.11 Commando HC.3s while a WG.11 Cougar HAS.1 lifts clear of the flight deck for an anti-submarine sweep. The proceedings are being watched by the First Sea Lord in his Cougar HCC.2 'Admiral's Barge' VIP transport. *Luciano Alviani*

concluded that the naval requirements could not be met without hindering the RAF variant with excess structural weight. The MoA considered that the need for four engines was expensive in both initial and operating costs, weighed against this the improved engine-out reliability reduced the total buy by 12 airframes (based on analysis showing five helicopters had been lost over the sea each year since 1957.) The MoA concluded that no helicopter could carry the Admiralty's future 5,000lb sonar. The Admiralty backtracked to 2,500lb (1,130kg) – sufficient for one Type 195 or a 2,300lb (1,040kg) Double Type 195 with two transducers mounted back to back for 360° coverage. The Chinook and WG.11 were too large for shipborne and tactical roles, as the Type 191 had indicated a decade earlier. In addition, NATO requirements were now calling for four hours endurance for future ASW helicopters.

In December 1964 the new Navy Department within the newly unified Ministry of Defence (MOD) reviewed the developments in doctrine and sonar and weapon development since the inception of NASR.358. This identified additional needs for a new tactical plot and passive radar detection equipment but there were several setbacks; the helicopter-to-ship Data Transmission System to meet NSR.7276 was in abeyance and the 360° sonar lacked sufficient justification to warrant urgent development and was postponed beyond 1970. By July 1963 the Admiralty had been considering a smaller helicopter and in May 1965 the Navy Department withdrew from NASR.358, the Chinook becoming an RAF programme while the Navy sought a smaller single-role helicopter.

NASR.365

Air Staff Requirement ASR.365 was drawn up in 1963 for a medium transport helicopter to replace the RAF's Whirlwind HC.10 and Wessex HC.2 and to complement the NASR.358 heavy lift helicopter. Worried about the size and performance of the NASR.358 helicopter, the Navy Department issued AW.168 for a smaller helicopter and both requirements were merged as NASR.365 in 1965.

The helicopter had to be capable of tactical troop lift (including operations from commando carriers), logistic support, air ambulance, SAR, light crane lift, paratrooping, armed support and minelaying. The helicopter was to be in RAF service by 1970 and ready for commando carrier operations by 1975.

Maximum speed was to be at least 150kt with a cruising speed of at least 135kt. Internal payloads were to comprise 4,000lb (1,815kg) (16 troops) over a 75nm (138km) radius of action or 3,000lb (1,360kg) (12 troops) over 100nm (185km). External payload capacity was to be 4,000lb (1,815kg) (for example a ¼ ton Mk.8 Land Rover) carried over a 50nm (92km) radius or 4,800lb (2,177kg) for 20nm (37km) in the Crane Lift role. Ferry range was to be 700nm (1,300km) with additional internal fuel tanks.

For naval operations a folding tail and fixings for floatation gear were required. This equipment had to keep the helicopter buoyant and upright in Sea State 2 with the rotor stopped or Sea State 3 with rotors turning. The helicopter was to be equipped with a comprehensive AFCS/navigation system, with autopilot approach capability being developed under Naval Air Staff Target NAST.517, building on work undertaken for NASR.358.

The MoA contracted Westland to complete a feasibility study. Westland produced two versions of their WG.7 design and studied a range of variants of the Sud Aviation SA 330 – then under development to become the Puma. The WG.9 drawn up for NASR.358 was too large for the requirements, so was not reconsidered.

The WG.7 was based on the earlier WG.4 24-troop tactical transport and had a take-off weight of 11,500lb (5,220kg), being powered by two Gnome turboshafts. Adding the RN's ASW and SAR requirements led to the 17-seat WG.7E with a 14,000lb (6,350kg) take-off weight, a folding tail, hull floatation and the NAST.517 avionics. It offered little advance over the Wessex and was abandoned. The WG.7G with a take-off weight of 15,500lb (7,030kg) offered superior performance to the SA 330 and greater endurance than the Wessex HAS.2, only falling marginally short in some aspects of NASR.365. The estimated payload over a 75nm (138km) radius was 3,990lb (1,810kg), ferry range was 760nm (1,410km) and endurance on station was almost two hours. The MoA estimated that the development cost would be £26.25 million, production costs being £426,000 for

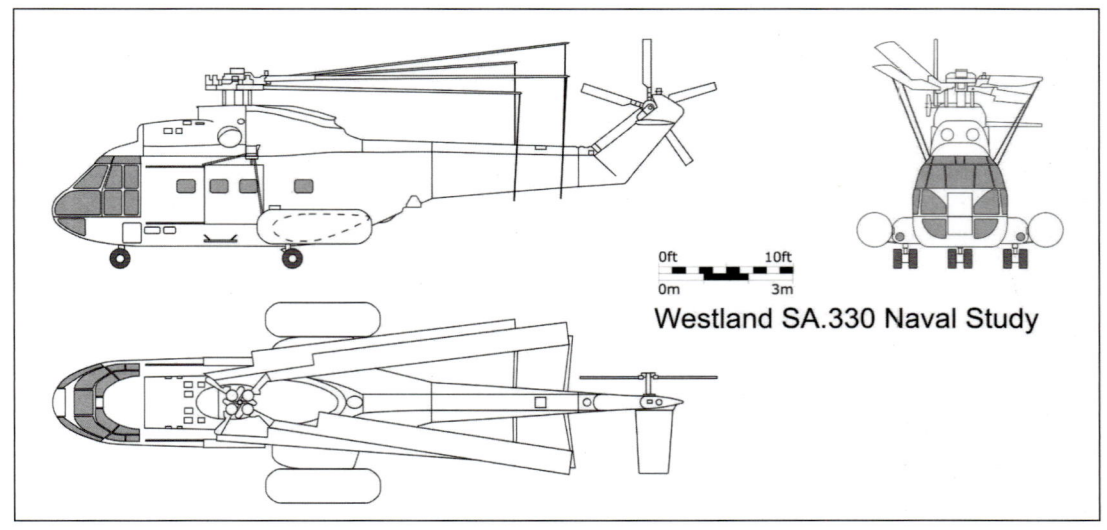

Sud Aviation proposed a navalised SA 330 Puma with folding rotor blades, folding tail boom and additional floatation gear. Westland used this as a basis for a further six studies. *Author*

Westland SA.330 Naval Study

Westland design studies for NASR.365

	SA.330 Study Variant 6A	SA.330 Study Variant 6B	SA.330 Study Variant 7A	SA.330 Study Variant 7B	SA.330 Study Variant 8A	SA.330 Study Variant 8B	WG.7E	WG.7G
Role	RAF tactical transport	RAF tactical transport	Commando	Commando	ASW	ASW	ASW & Commando	ASW & Commando
Engines	2x Turmo III C4, 1,328shp (990kW)	2x Gnome H.1400, 1,600shp (1,193kW)	2x Turmo III C4, 1,328shp (990kW)	2x Gnome H.1400, 1,600shp (1,193kW)	2x Turmo III C4, 1,328shp (990kW)	2x Gnome H.1400, 1,600shp (1,193kW)	2x Gnome H.1400, 1,600shp (1,193kW)	2x Gnome H.1400, 1,600shp (1,193kW)
Undercarriage	Tricycle	Tricycle	Tricycle	Quadricycle	Quadricycle	Quadricycle	Tricycle	Tricycle
Flight Control System	French	British NAST.517	French	British NAST.517	British NAST.517	British NAST.517	British NAST.517	British NAST.517
Auxiliary Power Unit	No	No	No	Yes	No	Yes	?	Yes
Take-off weight	14,110lb (6,400kg)	?	?	?	?	?	14,000lb (6,350kg)	15,500lb (7,030kg)
Tactical payload (75nm/139km radius)	3,490lb (1,580kg)	3,680lb (1,670kg)	3,300lb (1,495kg)	3,080lb (1,400kg)	N/A	N/A	?	3,990lb (1,810kg)
Crane payload (20nm/37km radius)	4,190lb (1,900kg)	4,370lb (1,980kg)	4,010lb (1,818kg)	3,770lb (1,710kg)	N/A	N/A	?	?
Endurance on station	N/A	N/A	N/A	N/A	1.30hr	1.35hr	?	Around 2hr
Estimated development cost	£6.65M	£18.275M	£6.8M	£18.95M	£13.1M	£20.0M	?	£26.25M
Estimated production cost	£347,000	£432,000	£352,000	£452,000	£507,000	£514,000	?	£426,000 RAF; £441,000 Commando

the RAF version and £441,000 for the Commando helicopter with service clearance estimated for early 1973. The WG.7G was disproportionally expensive and technically riskier than the SA 330 so was eliminated as a serious contender, barring any political considerations favouring an all-British design.

The six SA 330 variants covered the full range of development options for the tactical, Commando and ASW roles. The basic French version exceeded the payload/range requirements but fell short of British design standards and lacked allowance for weight growth. The MoA considered retaining the French flight control system to avoid the need to develop the expensive NAST.517 avionics. Detachable undercarriage sponsons were needed to meet the air-portability requirements. Preliminary carrier deck motion data seemed to indicate that a new quadricycle undercarriage might be required for adequate stability. The new undercarriage imposed a 240lb (108kg) weight penalty and added £400,000 to the production cost. Adding a folding tail, floatation gear and an auxiliary power unit further reduced the payload, so Westland proposed replacing the Turbomeca Turmo III C4 turboshafts with the lighter Gnome H.1400, which also had slightly lower fuel consumption. The estimated development costs varied depending on the engine and avionics choices but the likely cost was up to £400,000 plus £10,000 per aircraft in licence royalties. Fully developing the H.1400 Gnome was estimated to cost up to £8.5 million but the commonality with the existing Gnome-powered helicopter fleet was attractive.

The Navy Department had doubts over NASR.365, especially when it was found that the Type 195 sonar equipment was too tall to fit inside the cabin of the WG.7 or SA 330. Increasing the cabin height seemed impossible given NASR.365's air-portability and deck stability requirements and repackaging the Type 195 could take up to five years to complete. The DNAW argued that the SA 330 was not suitable for operations from ships. The Sikorsky SH-3D Sea King was by now the Navy Department's desired solution for the ASW role and they withdrew from NASR.365 in mid-1965 to avoid delaying the RAF's SA 330E tactical transport, acquired under the Anglo-French Helicopter Agreement signed in January 1967 and which entered service as the Puma HC.1 in 1971.

Although sporting a Westland logo at the SBAC Show at Farnborough in September 1968, XV370 was actually the first of four Sikorsky-supplied SH-3D Sea Kings which were reassembled by Westland. *Terry Panopalis Collection*

Sea King

During March 1965 Westland had approached the Navy Department to promote the Sikorsky S-61D SH-3D Sea King, having held a production licence since 1959. The Sea King offered twin-engine reliability, carriage of more weapons for re-attack capability and over three hours' endurance. This encouraged the RN to reject the NASR.358 Chinook and NASR.365 and Westland was awarded a study contract. Following the submission of the brochure to the MoA and the MOD in June, the initial development programme was approved in December. Naval Staff Requirement NSR.6429 was formally approved in June 1966 to cover development and the MoA issued Specification HAS.261D&P to Westland on 9 June. In September the Treasury endorsed the development and procurement of 56 helicopters. The MoA also encouraged Anglo-German collaboration, offering West Germany a heavy/crane and ASW helicopter package deal during 1966.

The Sea King would replace the Wessex HAS.3 with secondary roles in tactical transport, all-weather SAR and vertical replenishment. It would be operated aboard aircraft carriers, commando carriers, the planned Escort Cruisers and the *Tiger*-class cruiser conversions. At the time HMS *Eagle* and *Ark Royal* each carried eight Wessex, which fitted into hangar spaces which the Blackburn Buccaneer and Hawker Siddeley Sea Vixen could not use. It was accepted that with future aircraft and new DAG arrester gear taking up more hangar space, that carrying Sea Kings would displace some fixed-wing aircraft. The commando carriers *Albion* and *Bulwark* had sufficient space for Sea Kings until their planned replacements arrived during 1974/75 (these ships never got beyond the planning stage following the withdrawal East of Suez post-1966.) The *Tiger* conversions were originally designed for four Wessex but four Sea Kings were accommodated by extending the hangar during the conversion. The *County*-class destroyers each retained a Wessex, their unique sideways-facing hangar door prevented a Sea King being stowed, but they could operate from the flight deck with some limitations.

The Escort Cruiser had origins in a 1959 study for a helicopter carrier with 22 helicopters. By 1960 it had become an anti-submarine and anti-aircraft cruiser with a conventional aft flight deck layout of around 5,400 tons displacement armed with eight Wessex and GWS.1 Sea Slug SAMs. The advent of the larger NASR.358 helicopter and Sea King, plus modern weapons systems such as the GWS.30 Sea Dart SAM and the Ikara anti-submarine missile led to a larger 10,500-ton design with a higher internal hangar and an offset carrier-like flight deck, but the air group shrank to five Wessex or Sea Kings. Its £16.8 million cost contributed to the eventual decision to defer them in favour of the *Tiger*-class conversions.

Maintaining two helicopters on task required only five or six Sea Kings compared to eight Wessex. Over 24 hours this would require 16 Sea King sorties and seven flight crews compared to 48 Wessex sorties and 12 crews. The saving of 40 aircrew personnel in peacetime (72 in wartime) would give welcome relief to the ships' cramped accommodation.

NSR.6429 and HAS.261D&P called for maximum folded dimensions of 50 × 16.5 × 17ft (15.2 × 5 ×

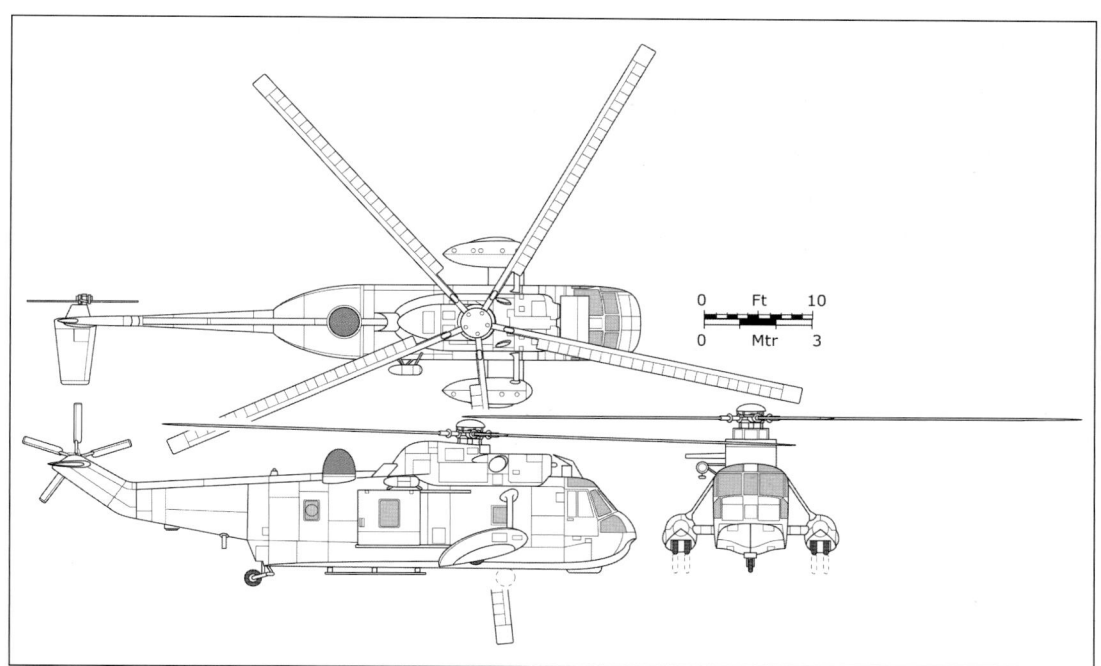

A general arrangement drawing of the Sea King HAS.1. *Chris Gibson*

5.1m). The required performance was to be attained carrying a crew of four, full ASW system and four Mk.44 torpedoes at sea level. Maximum speed was to be at least 120kt, the cruising speed at least 100kt with vertical climb performance of at least 180ft/min (54m/min). The three hours endurance (four hours was desirable) would consist of numerous short sorties plus 15 minutes' reserve. In the transport role with 11 troops the radius of action was to be 43nm (80km), or 17nm (32km) when carrying a 4,000lb (1,815kg) external load. Removing the sonar enabled 16 troops to be carried over 130nm (240km) or a 6,000lb (2,720kg) external load for 43nm. The stated flight weather minima were a 100ft (30m) cloud base, 900ft (274m) day and night visibility, −26°C to +45°C (−14.8°F to +113°F) temperature range and wind speeds up to 60kt.

The Sea King HAS.1's ASW system was based on that of the preceding Wessex HAS.3 with the main ASW sensor being the Type 195M dipping sonar. The rotor downwash is visible on the water; the rotor noise radiated downwards affected the performance of early-generation dipping sonar transducers. *Blue Envoy Collection*

The Sea King's main role was to screen the RN's carrier forces. Sea King HAS.1 XV699 flies past HMS *Ark Royal* in 1971. XV699 had an accident prone life. A spurious engine fire warning led to a single-engined sea landing in February 1972. A night-time engine failure resulted in a ditching in the Caribbean on 19 March 1975; on recovery by *Ark Royal*, the smoke floats and Marine Markers spontaneously ignited as it was lifted out of the water! A tail rotor drive failure over North Wales on 5 June 1989 resulted in a heavy landing on Pont Henri's village football pitch and a broken undercarriage. At Prestwick, an airport tug reversed XV699 into an RAF HS.125 Dominie in November 1996. Another forced landing, this time in the Grampians during mountain rescue practice, occurred on 20 April 1998, a Chinook airlifting the unlucky airframe to Prestwick. It saw out the remainder of its service without further mishap! *MOD via Terry Panopalis Collection*

To aid sonar performance the noise radiated downwards within the 6–10kHz frequency range was to be reduced to a minimum. The sound received by the sonar transducer at a depth of 50ft (15m) while hovering at an altitude of 40ft (12m) was not to exceed the ambient noise level of Sea State 3 conditions. Cabin noise levels were to be no higher than 85dB.

The ASW System was based on that of the Wessex HAS.3 and comprised the Type 195M sonar, ARI.5955 Ekco AW.391 radar, ARI.5954 transponder, AW.96 Doppler navigation and the Louis Newmark Mk.31 AFCS. Future provision was also to be made for data links, MAD and sonobuoys. Armament was four Mk.44, or two Mk.46 or NASR.7511, homing torpedoes, or a pair of Mk.44 (or one Mk.46) with a WE.177A depth bomb. Two conventional Mk.11 Mod.2 depth bombs could be carried alongside two torpedoes. Light Series Bomb Carriers could accommodate four Marine Markers, 12 practice depth charges or four smoke floats.

The SH-3D's General Electric T68-10 turboshafts were replaced by two Bristol Siddeley Gnome H.1400. The 70% commonality with the Wessex's H.1200 Gnome offered economies in spares support, maintenance and training.

Alternatives briefly examined included the Agusta 101G, Sud Aviation SA 321 Super Frelon, Boeing Vertol CH-47B Chinook and the Sikorsky CH-53A Sea Stallion but none met all the requirements, which were written around the Sea King. Export prospects looked bright given that the Wessex HAS.3 ASW system was already generally acknowledged to be superior to the equipment fitted in the USN's Sea Kings. Italy, West Germany, the Netherlands and Australia were all identified as potential customers.

Four Sikorsky-supplied SH-3D (XV370–XV373) were reassembled by Westland. XV370 had flown from Avonmouth Docks to Yeovil on 11 October 1966 and was used for performance and handling trials; XV372 was fitted with Gnomes for testing, flying on 8 September 1967; XV371 did not fly until 16 February 1968 with the Louis Newmark Mk.31 AFCS and XV373 did not begin its mission systems trials until June 1968. The first Westland-built HAS.1, XV642, flew on 7 May 1969, being displayed at the Paris Air Show the following month and making the first deck landing aboard *Engadine* on 2 July. Following 1,500 hours of manufacturer's trials the Sea King Intensive Flying Trials Unit, 700S NAS, used six Sea Kings for 2,700 hours of trials from August 1969. The first operational unit, 824 NAS, formed in February 1970. The 56 HAS.1 aircraft were followed by 15 new-build and 37 converted HAS.2 aircraft from 1976 with 1,535shp (1,144kW) Gnome H.1400-1 turboshafts and a revised tail transmission with a six-blade tail rotor.

The Sea King HAS.1 had to rely on its dipping sonar and in poor weather conditions its effectiveness – and that of ship sonars too – dropped dramatically. For example, during Exercise Hɪɢʜ Wᴏᴏᴅ ɪɴ 1971, the nuclear hunter-killer HMS *Churchill*, pretending to be a Soviet anti-ship missile-armed *Charlie*-class nuclear submarine was not detected, let alone attacked. The Sea Kings failed to achieve any sonar detections and even when the frigates were vectored to a target their Limbo mortars, Wasp HAS.1 MATCH and simulated Ikara missile attacks were all judged to be misses. This was a particular low point, but it shows how bad results could be in the 1970s. The introduction of sonobuoys for ASW helicopters later in the decade gave an immense improvement in detection capability.

The success of carrier screening operations was equally mixed. A carrier only carried up to seven

The Sea King could carry up to four Mk.44 homing torpedoes, as illustrated here by HAS.1 XV703 of 824 NAS in May 1972. The Type 195M dipping sonar transducer has been lowered. All Sea King HAS.1s were painted in overall RAF Blue Grey. XV703 was upgraded three times: to HAS.2 standard in 1977, HAS.5 in 1985 and finally as a HAS.6 in 1988. *Terry Panopalis Collection*

Following the Falklands Conflict, Detachment 'A' of 826 NAS was deployed to provide ASW and SAR services. The Sea King pictured here in March 1984 is HAS.5 ZA137. This helicopter had taken part in hostilities, having been aboard *Hermes* and transferred to RFA *Fort Austin* on transport duties. The rescue hoist can be seen fitted above the cabin door. ZA137 withdrew to the UK later in March 1984, returning to the Falklands in November. A gearbox seizure saw ZA137 being shipped back to the UK in June 1985. *Terry Panopalis Collection*

helicopters, only sufficient to maintain two on operations simultaneously, which did not provide an effective screen. The Type 195M dipping sonar did not provide enough detection range for the screening role and its average time between technical failures was only 30 hours. The Sea King's improved endurance over the Wessex helped, as did the conversion of the cruisers *Tiger* and *Blake* to accommodate four Sea Kings each. With one of these cruisers plus one or two escorting *County*-class destroyers with their Wessex HAS.3, a carrier group might have 10–14 large ASW helicopters, adequate for a screen but with no slack for other contingencies. There were just not enough helicopters and ships to operate them from.

Modernised Sea Kings

The continually evolving Soviet submarine threat saw the Sea King updated under NSR.6666 to introduce a sonobuoy monitoring capability – a much superior way to gather acoustic detection and targeting information. Westland began development work on the HAS.5 in 1978. Structural changes included moving the cabin rear bulkhead 6ft (1.8m) aft, a strengthened cabin floor, stiffer hull structure and a revised underfloor fuel tank layout. A new nav/attack system was fitted using Decca TANS G coupled to a Decca Type 71 Doppler and a MEL Sea Searcher radar. A new GEC LAPADS acoustic processing and display system was fitted for use with passive SSQ-801 Barra sonobuoys and it could also monitor sonobuoys laid by the RAF's Nimrod MR.2 maritime reconnaissance aircraft. The Australian Weapons Systems Research Laboratory began development on the Barra (Aboriginal for 'listening') in 1964 and it entered production in 1971. Racal MIR-2 Orange Crop electronic support measures (ESM) was fitted for passive radar/radio detection along with ARI.23363 Yellow Veil electronic countermeasures (ECM). The Type 195M dipping sonar was retained. Some HAS.5s later received AN/AQS-81 towed MAD kits acquired from Sikorsky.

The first of 30 new-build HAS.5 helicopters, ZA126, was flown on 26 August 1980 and 820 NAS became operational with the new mark in June 1981. 55 older HAS.2 airframes were also converted to the new standard. During the Gulf War (Operation GRANBY) in early 1991, specific operational upgrades were fitted for the combat environment, including; GPS,

Sea King HAS.6 XV677 of 814 NAS aboard HMS *Invincible* in September 1993. The HAS.6 was a late 1980s upgrade with a GEC Avionics AQS-902G-DS digital sonar processing system, Type 2069 dipping sonar and an internal CA/ASQ-504(V) AIMS (Advanced Integrated MAD System). *Terry Panopalis Collection*

AN/ALQ-157 Matador infra-red (IR) countermeasures jammers, M-130 30-round chaff/flare launchers, a radar warning receiver, Menagerie ECM, HAVE QUICK secure radio communications, a GEC Sandpiper forward-looking IR sensor, hand-held thermal imagers and Demon video-based mine-hunting equipment.

The HAS.5 lasted in service longer than originally planned, given the delayed development of the EHI Merlin HM.1 to replace it. Further upgrading of 73 airframes and six new-build aircraft resulted in the HAS.6 with the GEC Avionics AQS-902G-DS digital sonar processing system with a Type 2069 dipping sonar (a heavily upgraded Type 195 with solid-state electronics) capable of being lowered to 700ft (210m) and an internal CA/ASQ-504(V) AIMS (Advanced Integrated MAD System). Other improvements included improved GEC-Plessey IFF, Orange Reaper ESM and encrypted *Lamberton* secure radio communications. New composite main rotor blades and an emergency gearbox lubrication system were also fitted along with 1,660shp (1,238kW) Gnome H.1400-1 engines. The initial conversion, XZ581, first flew on 15 December 1987.

Some of the HAS.5 were converted for SAR duties as the HAR.5 with an external winch and medical equipment; the ASW systems were removed but the Sea Searcher radar was retained. These aircraft served with 771 NAS at RNAS Culdrose and HMS *Gannet* SAR Flight at Prestwick Airport in Scotland. They were replaced by civilian operated SAR helicopters operated by Bristow Helicopters (founded in June 1955 by Alan Bristow, who had flown the initial YR-4B trials back in 1944.) Other variants in British service included the AEW.2A, AEW.5 and ASaC.7 AEW conversions (see Chapter 9) and the RAF's HAR.3 for SAR operations. As foreseen, numerous exports were made, including: West Germany (23 Mk.41 for SAR), India (42 Mk.42), Norway (11 Mk.43 for SAR), Pakistan (six Mk.45), Egypt (six Mk.47), Belgium (five Mk.48 for SAR) and Australia (10 Mk.50).

9 Airborne Early Warning

The defence of the fleet from aerial attack relied on excellent situational awareness of potential threats and effective command and control. As we have seen in Chapter 4, the introduction of radar from 1939 was as revolutionary for the Royal Navy for air defence as it was for the Royal Air Force on land. The main drawback to aerial search radars aboard warships is their limited range due to the curvature of the earth. In principle, the higher a radar is mounted the further it can 'see over the horizon'. Putting a radar on an aircraft seems the logical solution. The RAF experimentally fitted a Vickers Wellington Ic in 1942 with a modified ASV Mk.II radar with a rotating Yagi antenna atop the fuselage with 360° coverage, with a radar operator and interception controller aboard the aircraft. The US Navy fitted General Motors TBM-3 Avengers with AN/APS-20A search radars to create the *Cadillac I* airborne early warning (AEW) aircraft in February 1945, which proved very useful in providing early warning of Japanese Kamikaze attacks. This soon caught the Admiralty's attention, but a lack of resources and suitable aircraft – especially in the post-1978 period when the fleet carrier force was no more – led to a rather improvised approach to providing AEW coverage, including American-supplied Douglas Skyraiders, the Fairey Gannet AEW.3 and various Westland Sea King helicopter conversions since 1982. Today, the Merlin HM.2 based Crowsnest system has proved troublesome and its operational capability has been delayed – by the time you read these words it may have been achieved, some four years behind schedule.

Early steps to AEW

Knowledge of the USN's TBM-3W *Cadillac I* AEW system encouraged the Admiralty to seek a similar capability. A committee of experts from the Admiralty Signals Department and the Directorate of Naval Aircraft Committee was chaired by Rear Admiral WG Benn in late 1944. Although originally developed by Radiation Laboratories as an S-band surface search set capable of detecting snorkels, the USN's *Cadillac I* experiments proved that the AN/APS-20A could detect small ships and aircraft formations within 87nm (160km). Due to the technological limits of the time, search radars worked better over the sea, because of the reduced effect of ground clutter creating false returns. Even so, the Signals Department was not satisfied with the APS-20's resistance to clutter, nor its range. They wanted a range of 148–174nm (273–322km) with the capability of providing bearing information on a four-aircraft formation with accuracy within 5,280ft (1.6km) of the bearing. They also wanted height finding with an accuracy within 1,000ft (305m) at a range of 60nm (113km). This would require a large, stabilised antenna and a Doppler system to remove

A Fairey Gannet AEW.3 of 849 NAS has the steam catapult bridle attached prior to taking off from HMS *Ark Royal*. The Gannet AEW.3 is perhaps the quintessential airborne early warning aircraft that springs to mind when thinking about RN carrier aviation. Within the next decade a new fixed-wing AEW platform may enter service, but it will be unmanned. *Blue Envoy Collection*

the clutter. Data transmission back to the ship would probably have used the *Cadillac's* AN/ART-28 *Bellhop* data transmission system – a television camera aboard the aircraft which filmed the radar scope and transmitted the picture by radio to the parent ship.

The Director of Air Warfare and Training, Captain Philip Yorke, nominated the Fairey Spearfish torpedo-bomber as the only suitable British naval aircraft in prospect to lift the required payload. Fairey got wind of this, but rather than waiting for the speculative British radar, they opted to fit the APS-20A radar in a ventral radome replacing the torpedo bay. Whether the USN could supply enough sets under Lend-Lease was an unknown factor. The prototype Spearfish did not fly until July 1945 and the end of the war shortly afterwards ended the project. The Telecommunication Research Establishment (TRE) focused its research and trials on providing the RAF with an AEW capability (which remained stillborn).

While the Admiralty was keen to acquire AEW aircraft – equipping the Type 61 *Salisbury*-class Air Direction frigates with the AN/SRR-4A AEW video datalink in readiness – there was neither money nor aircraft available. Following the outbreak of the Korean War in June 1950 defence spending rose rapidly as rearmament began in earnest. This was aided by US funding under the Mutual Defense Assistance Program (MDAP). Among the RN's equipment requests were 50 Douglas AD-4W Skyraiders equipped with the latest APS-20E radar. These aircraft were delivered from November 1951, being designated Skyraider AEW.1.

The Skyraiders initially equipped 778 Naval Air Squadron (NAS) at RNAS Culdrose for operational training and trials aboard HMS *Eagle* before 849 NAS formed at Culdrose in 1952 with five flights of four aircraft, each being assigned to a carrier. Following a report from the Captain of *Eagle*, pilot and aircrew numbers (two operators per aircraft) were increased to allow continuous 24-hour operations. Training was stepped up with four

"They represent, in my opinion, the most important contribution to Naval Aviation – and indeed to naval tactics in general – for many, many years. There are few forms of naval operations on which they cannot exert a profound effect."

REAR ADMIRAL SIR ALEXANDER BINGLEY, CAPTAIN OF HMS EAGLE, 2 APRIL 1953.

The Douglas AD-4W Skyraider was supplied from the USA with MDAP funding. An AN/APS-20E radome was mounted below the fuselage, giving 360° radar coverage around and below the aircraft. WT944 (ex-BuNo 127942) was received in November 1951, being used for catapult and arrester gear trials before going to 778 NAS. It was modernised in 1959 and retired in February 1960. It was sold to Scottish Aviation and cannibalised for spare parts for Sweden. *Blue Envoy Collection*

courses of four crews per year, with flexibility to add a fifth crew. A lack of spares, especially for the engines, saw a temporary reduction to 20 operational aircraft in the summer of 1954.

Early experience with AEW aircraft was mixed. Operations with the four Skyraiders and six crews of

This view reveals how wide the APS-20E radome was. Providing aerodynamic housings for ever larger radar antennae was one of the major problems in designing new AEW aircraft. This Skyraider AEW.1 is WT985 (ex-BuNo 124104). *Blue Envoy Collection*

Skyraider AEW.1s WT961 (on the right) and WT947 (left), behind a group of Sea Hawk FGA.6s of 806 NAS aboard HMS *Albion* in 1960. *Terry Panopalis Collection*

Skyraider AEW.1 WT121 (ex-BuNo124121) was delivered in September 1953. It had already flown 802 hours in US Navy service and served 849 NAS well until September 1960. It appeared at Culdrose Navy Days on public display and in 1972 went to the Fleet Air Arm Museum (by sea and Sea King airlift). It is extant in store at the FAA Museum's Cobham Hall store. *Blue Envoy Collection*

'A' Flight aboard *Eagle* from January 1953 revealed the value of AEW. The Skyraiders were used for detecting low-altitude aerial targets, detection of surfaced submarines and snorkels as well as surface reconnaissance (doing the work of six Fairey Fireflies in one hour) and direction of air strikes against surface ships (a strike over 234nm [434km] was directed during Exercise Cross Bar. The APS-20E achieved better detection ranges against propeller-driven aircraft than jets due to the greater radar return from the former, a piston fighter being detected up to 34nm (64km) away and a heavy bomber up to 70nm (128km). The need for a simple but secure method of reporting ranges and bearings of targets over the radio was also highlighted.

Despite this initial enthusiasm, their overall contribution to USN 6th Fleet Exercises in the Mediterranean was judged to be "negligible.". Out of 230 raids upon the task force 17% were undetected and the Skyraiders only detected six attacks. The assessment of the APS-20 radar after Exercise Phoenix I in 1956 was that it was "disappointingly inaccurate and inconsistent." The results of Exercise Phoenix II in 1958 were equally poor, *Ark Royal's* Skyraiders were misused which led to them flying at lower than ideal altitudes and incoming low-altitude attacks were lost in the sea clutter. Exercises Dawn Breeze IV and Phoenix III in 1959 fared no better. They reported 200 enemy contacts but fighter direction was pointless as the carriers had radar contact themselves due to the short detection range of the APS-20. Despite these shortcomings, they were used in action during the Suez Crisis, flying from *Eagle* and *Albion* during Operation Musketeer in November 1956. The Skyraiders were replaced by the Fairey Gannet AEW.3 from December 1960 – becoming the last piston-engined, fixed-wing aircraft operated by the Fleet Air Arm (FAA).

Gannet AEW.3

The Skyraider was only seen as an interim solution and Naval Staff Requirement NA.64 was raised in 1954. The roles of the aircraft were to provide early warning of approaching enemy aircraft at sea, assist in fighter direction, submarine snorkel detection, surface reconnaissance and the direction of strikes. The aircraft would be based on one of the carrier-

The deck crew help position Skyraider AEW.1 WV180 (ex-BuNo 124116) for take-off. The Skyraider was originally built as a single-seat attack aircraft but was also built with a wider fuselage for support roles, the two radar operators sitting side by side in the rear fuselage. *Blue Envoy Collection*

borne anti-submarine warfare (ASW) aircraft then under development to meet Specification GR.17/45, the Fairey Project 17 (which became the Gannet AS.1) or the Blackburn B.88/Y.B.1. These aircraft were powered by turboprops, an important factor as the RN was phasing out the stowage of petrol aboard its carriers in favour of less volatile AVTAG and AVCAT jet engine fuels. Both had 'coupled' engines, two separate turboprops driving coupled gearing for co-axial propellers, each engine driving one half of the propeller, thus providing twin-engine safety and the ability to cruise on one engine to save fuel. Two operators were required due to the 5.5hr patrol duration.

Blackburn proposed an AEW version of the B.54/Y.B.7, the earlier Rolls-Royce Griffon piston-powered version of the B.88, with the APS-20E radar installed in a ventral fuselage radome in line with the wing leading edge. The two-seat tandem cockpit was retained unchanged. Fairey's proposals began as a similar easy conversion, but the resulting Gannet AEW.3 was essentially a new aircraft. The rear fuselage was modified to accommodate the two radar operators. The original proposal had them seated in tandem, back to back. The RN's doctors rejected this, citing the 2–3ft (60–90cm) gap between them which precluded non-verbal communication via the intercom and two operators were required for the 5.5hr patrol duration. The RN insisted on side-by-side seating, requiring a wider cross-section (which also eased the headaches of trying to fit all the equipment in.) This led to the Mamba's exhaust pipes being shortened to exhaust beneath the leading edge of the wing; the engine itself being upgraded to the 3,875ehp (2,889kW) Armstrong Siddeley Double Mamba 102. The former second cockpit structure was retained to minimise the changes required to the jigs and allowed easier access to the radar's electronics for maintenance. The tail fin was modified and the dihedral of the wing was slightly increased. The undercarriage was lengthened to provide enough deck clearance for the ventral radome.

The Advisory Design Conference was held at the MoS offices at St Giles Court on 26 July 1955. Here the draft specification was scrutinised in light of the final design. Chief Designer Herbert Eugene Chaplin queried the planned approach speed of 95kt, doubting that a strong enough arrester hook could be supplied, and the 380kt maximum diving speed limit, given that the strength of the radar's radome was an unknown quantity.

AEW aircraft

	Douglas Skyraider AEW.1	Gannet AEW.3
Crew	Three	Three
Span	50ft ¼in (15.25m); 23ft 10in (7.26m) folded	54ft 4in (16.56m); 19ft 6in (5.94m) folded
Length	39ft 3¾in (11.96m)	44ft 0in (13.41m)
Wing area	400ft² (37.16m²)	482.8ft² (44.9m²)
Loaded weight	17,311lb (7,852kg)	25,000lb (11,340kg)
Powerplant	1x Cyclone R-3350-26WA, 3,300shp (2,460kW)	1x ASDM.8 Double Mamba Mk.102, 3,875ehp (2,890kW)
Cruising speed	217kt (402km/h)	120kt (225km/h)
Service ceiling	36,000ft (10,970m)	25,000ft (7,620m)
Max range	754nm (1,400km)	695nm (1,290km)
Radar	AN/APS-20E	AN/APS-20F

The prototype Gannet AEW.3 was XJ440, seen here on an early test flight with an unpainted fuselage. The wider fuselage of the AEW.2 enabled the two radar operators to sit side by side in the rear fuselage (the compartment can be identified by the escape hatch just aft of the wing). This required new engine exhaust pipes which vented under the wing leading edge. The tail was also modified for better stability. *Blue Envoy Collection*

The Fairey Gannet AEW.3 was slightly more aerodynamic than the Douglas Skyraider and the radar was upgraded to the APS-20F, but the radome was little changed. *Blue Envoy Collection*

The Gannet AS.1 entered production and by default it would become the basis of the AEW aircraft. Specification AEW.154D was issued to Fairey on 11 August 1955. Unlike the original Gannet, the development was to follow the Weapon System concept which made Fairey responsible for the integration of the avionics and sub systems.

In addition to the APS-20E radar, other avionics included a GPI Mk.5 ground position indicator and ARI.5885 *Blue Silk* GPI Mk.4A Doppler radar, ARI.5875 IFF Mk.10 Identification Friend-or-Foe, AN/APX-7 IFF Interrogator, ART-28 *Bellhop* video datalink, ARI.18048 *Green Salad* wide-band homing and AN/ARN.21 Tactical Navigation (TACAN). Underwing carriers were fitted for four Marine Markers or reconnaissance flares or Type G Air Sea Rescue cannisters as well as two 150gal (682L) fuel drop tanks. In 1963 the aircraft was also cleared to carry Mk.44 homing torpedoes.

By the autumn of 1955 it had been decided to order 31 Gannets initially but the total requirement was for 80 aircraft. By May 1956 the requirement looking ahead into the early 1960s had grown to 100 aircraft. The defence cutbacks a year later cut this number and only 44 aircraft were built.

There was a question of whether to licence-produce the required 69 APS-20E sets for the initial order (plus spares) or buy them direct from the USA. Home production was estimated to cost £1.91 million, including a payment of $564,000, whereas buying from the USA would be cheaper at £1.48 million but at the outlay of $4.14 million from the UK's Dollar reserves. An initial order of 40 sets was to be placed with Elliott Brothers, but on 5 December 1955 the Treasury agreed to buying them from the USA for $2.75 million. This order was later amended to the improved APS-20F and included the ART-28 *Bellhop* datalink and AN/APX-7 IFF. Elliott integrated the *Blue Silk* Doppler navigation system with the APS-20F.

Such were the differences between the Gannet AS.2 and AEW.3 that the Director of the RN Tactical School, Captain RG Swallow, considered the AEW.3 to be a new aircraft and proposed the new name Albatross in December 1954 (naval reconnaissance aircraft were named after sea birds). This proposal was not taken up.

A Gannet T.5 trainer converted with the new longer undercarriage completed its carrier trials aboard *Ark Royal* in July 1957 and the new AC electrics were trialled in a converted AS.1. The prototype Gannet AEW Mk.3, XJ440, made its first flight at Northolt on 20 August 1958. Flight trials revealed good handling with similar stability to the Gannet AS.4 and stalling and low speed flight was accomplished without problems. Controller Air clearance was obtained on 27 November 1959 with tropical clearance following in January 1961. Initial deck landing trials with XJ440 aboard *Centaur* took place from 18 November 1958 with full clearances obtained the following May.

The first production example, XL449, flew on 2 December 1958 with the first fully equipped aircraft completed at Hayes in January 1959; production ended in June 1963. 700G Flight at Culdrose was formed as the Intensive Flying Trials Unit on 17 August 1959 under the command of Lieutenant Commander W Hawley. The unit flew 600 sorties and 1,900 hours, achieving availability of 71%. The detection ranges of the APS-20F while flying at 3,000–5,000ft (915–1,525m) were assessed as "most encouraging;" antenna tilt was found to be critical in obtaining the best range against low flying targets. Weather and sea state affected range too, as did interference from other APS-20F and ship radars (it was recommended pairs of Gannets should fly at least 52nm [96.5km] apart).

On 1 February 1960 700G Flight became 849 NAS 'A' Flight. The squadron had 18 aircraft, assigning its five flights to individual carriers. A flight of four aircraft with five crews could maintain one airborne and one standby aircraft for 96 hours, with good serviceability it was possible to have two airborne for up to 18 hours a day. The squadron averaged well over 400 flying hours per month during the peak of Gannet AEW operations. The Gannets were able to provide interception control for Combat Air Patrol (CAP) fighters independent of the carrier and could guide strike aircraft onto surface targets.

As part of the research into a successor system under Naval Air Staff Requirement NASR.6166, in 1967 the Ministry of Defence (MOD) Directorate of Operational Analysis carried out an assessment of APS-20 performance going back to 1951. The report was critical of several failings in several exercises during this period (those relating to the Skyraider are recounted above.) During Exercise CROSSBOW in 1962 a total of 73 interceptions were made, 11 being unsuccessful but the AEW controlled CAP made 10 successful low-altitude interceptions. The Gannet fared well in Exercise POKER HAND later that year, flying three AEW barriers around the task force. Performance against low level targets during Exercise PHOENIX two years later was disappointing due to congested airspace and poor equipment serviceability. Two AEW barriers were successfully established but out of 26 low-altitude raids approaching the barriers only four were reported. Later that year Exercise FOTEX

The fourth production Gannet AEW.3 XL452 coming in to land during the 1959 SBAC Show at Farnborough with one propeller feathered. The Double Mamba consisted of two turboprops driving coaxial propellers. One engine could be shut down and its propeller feathered to reduce fuel consumption and extend range. *Terry Panopalis Collection*

Penultimate production Gannet AEW.3 XR432 is taxying under the power of one 'half' of its Double Mamba. When this photograph was taken in 1966 it was assigned to 849 'A' Flight and HMS *Victorious*. It was retired from service in November 1976. *Blue Envoy Collection*

WINGS OVER THE FLEET

In March 1978 Gannet AEW.3s XL450 (coded 042R) and XL471 (043R) prepare for take-off aboard HMS *Ark Royal* to begin a patrol sortie. *Blue Envoy Collection*

achieved better detection performance but the ranges were low and many targets were engaged by Sea Slug and guns. The *County*-class missile destroyer *Hampshire* often achieved first warning and identification using its Outfit UA8/9 passive electronic support measures (ESM) equipment. In 1965 Exercise IRON GATE a total reliance was placed on AEW, but the Gannets' operators only plotted four out of 13 low level raids in Phase A and 11 out of 15 in Phase B when only one Gannet was airborne. Destruction or probable destruction of 28% of Phase A and 39% of Phase B raiders was achieved by the Sea Vixens, but again rough seas had affected radar performance and the Gannets had not made a significant contribution to the effectiveness of the CAP.

Despite these criticisms, the AEW.3 was kept updated. In 1964 *Bellhop* was modified under Naval Staff Requirement NSR.1894 to enable it to transmit a stabilised radar picture to the ship receiver. The APS-20F was upgraded in 1968, the IFF also being upgraded to the ARI.23134 set and passive ECM fitted. Gannet AEW.3 XR433 was used for the trial installation and clearance tests. By 1970 Elliott Automation and Marconi were working on providing the APS-20 with airborne moving target indication (AMTI). Airframe refurbishment was undertaken by Westland at Weston-Super-Mare until early 1976 and Rolls-Royce maintained its Mamba workshop until 1978.

By this time only *Ark Royal* was the sole fleet carrier and AEW.3s XL482, XL494, XP229 and XR433 were assigned to the ship in the summer of 1970. They served with 849 NAS at RNAS Lossiemouth until the end of December 1978 when *Ark Royal* was paid off.

NA.107

Naval Requirement NA.107 was issued in 1957 for a Gannet AEW.3 replacement as a picket aircraft to extend the range of aerial radar surveillance around the fleet. A force of 40 aircraft was desired. The USN remained far ahead in AEW development with the Hazeltine Corporation AN/APS-82 radar equipped twin-engine Grumman WF-2 Tracer in service (redesignated E-1B in 1962) and the new General Electric AN/APS-96 and Grumman W2F-1 Hawkeye (redesignated E-2A) in development. The Admiralty was prepared to acquire either US or British radars. What was desired was something like the Hawkeye, a twin-turboprop powered aircraft which could operate from the fleet carriers.

Building upon previous work on a potential AEW variant of its Type 748 feederliner for the Swedish Air Force, Avro proposed the Type 768 in March 1959. The basic 748 airframe was heavily modified with a shortened and strengthened 55ft (16.7m)

Gannet AEW.3 XL471 in 1964 when it was assigned to HMS *Victorious* with 849A Flight in the Far East; it spent 1963–67 based at Singapore. *Blue Envoy Collection*

long fuselage, shorter 81ft (24.6m) double-folding outer wings, a new twin fin empennage, stronger undercarriage, catapult spools and an arrester hook. Like the 748, it was powered by two Rolls-Royce Dart turboprops. The radar was mounted in a 'mushroom' radome atop the fuselage, supported on a short pylon and struts to the rear fuselage and engine nacelles; the overall height was 17ft 6in (5.33m) to fit inside existing carrier hangars. The estimated all-up weight (AUW) was 38,000lb (17,235kg) with enough fuel for a five hour patrol 200nm (370km) from the carrier. The approach speed at 30,000lb (13,610kg) was 90kt.

Despite the double folding which tucked the wing tips inboard of the engine nacelles, the folded span of 40ft (12.19m) exceed the specified maximum folded width by 10ft (3m). Avro had to go back to the drawing board. The wings were extended to 85ft (25.9m) and retained the double folding, but the outboard hinge line was angled so that the starboard outer wing folded forwards and the port outer wing backwards to lie on top of the new APS-96 radar rotodome, which was faired into the upper fuselage. The Darts were also moved inboard by 2ft 4in (72cm) and the propeller diameter was reduced from 12ft (3.66m) to 10ft (3m). This not only achieved the 30ft (9.14m) folded width but improved the propellers' deck clearance to 3ft (90cm).

Blackburn Aircraft proposed a smaller aircraft with a crew of just three, a pilot and two radar

> *"It seems doubtful if the carrier-borne APS-20 AEW aircraft can be expected to produce worthwhile results against low-flying aircraft in the North Atlantic sea states."*
>
> VICE ADMIRAL ALEXANDER BINGLEY, FLAG OFFICER AIRCRAFT CARRIERS, EXERCISE PHOENIX II REPORT, 1958.

operators sitting side by side, all seated on ejection seats. The low-mounted wing carried two 4,600shp (3,440kW) Rolls-Royce Tyne 12 turboprops. A twin fin empennage was fitted aft. The AN/APS-96 radar rotodome was placed on a short pylon over the rear fuselage for aerodynamic reasons, the trailing edge being between the tail fins. This design would have offered good speed, but lacking any airborne controllers it would have relied on *Bellhop* or Link-11 datalinks to transfer the radar data to the carrier.

The Admiralty looked at buying the Grumman Hawkeye in the summer of 1960. The cost of buying 40 aircraft was £100 million, plus Grumman wanted a £37 million contribution to the research and development costs. On top of that, the Hawkeye was too large to fit onto the lifts of any existing RN carrier. This scuppered any chance of a purchase. Grumman later offered a package deal of a small number of E-2A Hawkeyes for delivery in 1965 with the newer AN/APS-120 radar equipped E-2C following in 1970 when the first of the new CVA-01 class carriers would

Gannet AEW.3 XL479 of 849 NAS 'D' Flight aboard HMS *Eagle* in 1965. XL479 was retired in 1976 having accumulated 2,990 flying hours. *Terry Panopalis Collection*

WINGS OVER THE FLEET

AEW aircraft designs to NA.107

	Avro Type 768	Blackburn NA.107	Grumman E-2A Hawkeye	Blackburn P.119	Blackburn P.39 AEW	Blackburn P.139/1 to /5	Vickers Type 582 AEW	Vickers Type 583 AEW	HS.125 AEW
Crew	?	Three	Five	Two	Two	Two	Two	Two	?
Span	Originally 81ft 0in (24.68m); 40ft 0in (12.19m) folded; revised 85ft (25.90m) 30ft 0in (9.14m) folded	?	80ft 7in (24.6m); 29ft 4in (8.94m) folded	42ft 4in (12.90m); 19ft 11in (6.07m) folded	32ft 0in (9.75m); 20ft 10in (6.35m) folded	42ft 4in (12.90m); 19ft 11in (6.07m) folded	40ft 0in (12.19m); 45ft 0in (13.72m) with AAMs; 29ft 0in (8.84m) folded	49ft 0in (14.94m) extended, 27ft 0in (8.23m) swept	Originally 47ft 0in (14.33m); 32ft 0in (9.75m) or 26ft 0in (7.92m) folded; revised 50ft 0in (15.24m) or 54ft 0in (16.45m); 26ft 0in (7.92m) folded
Length	55ft 0in (16.76m)	?	57ft 7in (17.58m)	63ft 5in (19.33m); 51ft 10in (15.80m) folded	61ft 9in (18.82m); 51ft 6in (15.70m) folded	63ft 5in (19.33m) (68ft 5in (20.87m) P.139/4); 51ft 10in (15.80m) folded	65ft 4in (19.91m); 52ft 0in (15.84m) folded	53ft 0in (16.5m); 50ft 0in (15.24m) folded	49ft 10in (15.18m) excluding refuelling probe
Wing area	Originally 720ft² (66.89m²)	?	700ft² (65.03m²)	514.7ft² (47.82m²)	526ft² (48.90m²)	514.7ft² (47.82m²)	405ft² (37.70m²)	?	Originally 353ft² (32.79m²); revised 369.6 ft² (34.33m²) or 405ft² (37.62m²)
All-up weight	38,000lb (17,235kg)	?	52,000lb (23,590kg)	45,000lb (20,410kg) estimated	?	Up to 56,000lb (25,400kg) estimated	45,000lb (20,410kg) estimated	43,300lb (19,640kg)	?
Powerplant	2x Dart	2x Tyne 12, 4,600shp (3,440kW)	2x T56-A-8/8A, 4,050shp (3,020kW)	2x Gyron Junior DGJ.1, 7,100lbf (31.5kN)	2x RB.153-61, 6,850lbf (30.5kN); & 2x RB.162 lift engines	2x RB.168-1A Spey Mk.101, 11,100lbf (49.3kN)	8x RB.163 (scaled), 1,800lbf (8.0kN) dry	2x RB.153-61R	2x RB.172 or M45
Speed	?	?	325kt (602km/h)	580kt (1,075km/h)/ Mach 0.875 at SL	Mach 0.95 at SL; Mach 2.5 up to 60,000ft (18,290m)	580kt (1,074km/h)/ Mach 0.95	Mach 2.0 to 2.5 at altitude	Mach 1.1 at SL, Mach 2.5 at 55,000ft (16,765m)	?
Service ceiling	?	?	40,000ft (9,190m)	50,000ft (15,240m)	?	50,000ft (15,240m)	60,000-65,000ft (18,290-19,810m)	?	40,000+ft (9,190m)
Endurance	5hr 0min	?	4hr 0min	?	?	?	?	?	?
Radar	AN/APS-96	AN/APS-96	AN/APS-96	SLAR	Ferranti SLAR	SLAR	4x SLAR antennas	Ferranti or Hughes/EMI SLAR	Dorsal radome

222

be completing. But again, the cost and the required Dollar expenditure prevented an order.

The development of the new CVA-01 carrier, designed to operate larger and heavier aircraft, resulted in a change of emphasis in the requirements. A jet-powered aircraft became more desirable and the folded width limit was reduced to 27ft (8.2m). The intent seems to have been to acquire an AEW aircraft closer in size to the latest naval strike aircraft. With purchase of aircraft or radars from the USA ruled out due to the costs involved, it was clear that British industry would have to come up with indigenous solutions.

Blackburn saw the opportunity to investigate commonality with the B.103 Buccaneer S.1 then in development. The P.119 design study by the Project Office fitted a sideways-looking airborne radar (SLAR) into the bomb bay. The aircraft would have used a racetrack orbit over the fleet to obtain 360° coverage. A second proposal used a rotating antenna inside an inflatable radome.

Chief Designer Barry Laight offered another option, retaining the Ferranti *Blue Parrot* radar in the nose and fitting another in the tail, the split airbrakes being moved to elsewhere on the airframe. This provided 360° coverage but the Royal Radar Establishment (RRE) highlighted that the *Blue Parrot* lacked sufficient range – to meet NA.107 it would need an 8ft (2.4m) diameter antenna. The resulting 'Dumb-bell Buccaneer' was so hideous that Laight promptly threw his sketch into the bin! Looks aside, the de Havilland Gyron Junior-powered Buccaneer S.1 lacked the thrust and high-altitude endurance required for an AEW aircraft.

Brough would later offer another fast AEW aircraft, a variant of the P.39 carrier-based strike aircraft. This was a Dassault Mirage IIIV V/STOL fighter with its eight RB.162 lift engines replaced by fuel and with two RB.162 mounted in tandem behind the cockpit to counteract the pitch-down moment created by the delta wing on landing. The main engines were to be a pair of 6,850lbf (30.5kN) Rolls-Royce/MAN RB.153-61. A large dorsal fairing extending from the root of the vertical fin contained a Ferranti radar using a 15 × 2ft 4in (4.6 × 0.7m) antenna with roll stabilisation, mechanical vertical scanning and electronic 60° scanning in azimuth (30° forward and 30° aft), which could be electronically 'flipped' to look to either starboard or port. The estimated radar range was 150nm (280km).

Vickers-Armstrong proposed a version of the Type 582 twin-fuselage strike aircraft that had been tendered to Operational Requirement OR.346 in March 1960. This futuristic design had two fuselages joined by a high tailplane and the wing centre section contained eight Rolls-Royce RB.163 turbojets. The pilot and observer sat in a tandem cockpit in the port fuselage, the starboard fuselage being devoted to electronics and fuel. Vickers fitted an S-band Doppler SLAR on the lower outboard sides of both fuselages for lateral coverage and another antenna was mounted onto a new spanwise

One of the Blackburn P.139 proposals of September 1963 with ventral SLAR antennas mounted on the Buccaneer S.2. *Brough Heritage*

The highly unconventional Vickers Type 582 twin-fuselage strike aircraft was offered as an AEW platform with S-band Doppler SLAR antennas on the lower outboard fuselage sides with a mini wing-type structure joining the forward fuselages with fore and aft-facing antennas. The wing tip missile hardpoints were replaced by tip tanks for additional fuel. This manufacturer's model of the basic strike version shows the tip tanks. *Tony Buttler*

structure between the fuselages mounted ahead and below the main wing for forward and aft coverage. The wing tip missile hardpoints were replaced by tip tanks for additional fuel.

In May 1960 Vickers offered an AEW version of the Type 583 two-seat strike/Sea Vixen replacement aircraft which had variable-geometry wings. A 23ft (7m) long ventral pylon housed back-to-back antennas which were 18in (46cm) tall. The radar would be either a Ferranti or Hughes/EMI pulse-Doppler set with a Vickers Guided Weapons Division-designed antenna with mechanical scanning in elevation and electronic azimuth scanning of the 150 slotted elements. This aerial had been developed for a reconnaissance radar for the RAF's R.156 supersonic reconnaissance aircraft requirement in the late 1950s. The SLAR lacked 360° coverage, Vickers explaining that the aircraft would have to fly 90° turns in a square orbit or a 120nm (241km) long arc with a

A model of the HS.125 AEW proposal alongside the standard HS.125 business jet, showing the extent of the changes to the fuselage, empennage and wings as well as large Rolls-Royce RB.162 or SNECMA M45 turbojets. *de Havilland Hatfield via Joe Cherrie*

180° turn at each end.

Blackburn (now part of Hawker Siddeley Aviation) revisited the P.119 in May 1963, now using the Rolls-Royce RB.168 Spey-powered Buccaneer S.2 as the basis. The first P.139 study, P.139/1, carried two 22ft (6.7m) long pods inboard of the wing fold hinge, replacing the usual slipper fuel tanks. Each pod was 2ft (0.6m) deep and the electronics were housed in the former bomb bay. To restore endurance, the P.139/2 retained the slipper tanks and moved the 25ft (7.6m) long antennas to the lower fuselage, the pods folding outboard to allow sufficient ground clearance for take-off and landing.

The P.139/4 had the antenna moved to the nose, which was redesigned to be 5ft (1.5m) longer and 3ft (0.9m) deeper, with slab faces on the sides and below. The P.139/5 of June 1963 had a ventral pod 27ft (8.2m) long, 2ft (0.6m) wide and 3ft (0.9m) deep which retracted into a centreline recess in the belly.

The Admiralty by now wanted an AEW that had fighter controllers aboard to avoid the reliance on datalinks and 360° coverage without recourse to orbiting flight patterns was a must. The Blackburn Division designers at Brough cast around for another aircraft in the Hawker Siddeley stable, selecting the HS.125 business jet which had been designed by de Havilland. The HS.125 had just been ordered by the RAF as the Dominie T.1 navigation trainer and a navalised version had been offered to replace the Gannet COD.4 in the Carrier On-Board Delivery support role.

Brough considered the best radar layout, opting for a mushroom antenna with a 2ft 6in (0.8m) high pylon that doubled as a 150gal (682L) fuel tank. The elliptical antenna was modelled on a similar proposal Avro had drawn up for the HS.748AEW the previous year. It had a length of 12ft 9in (3.9m) and width of 4ft (1.2m). Due to the aerodynamic effects this would create, a new double fin empennage was fitted aft. The fuselage and undercarriage were strengthened and the usual catapult spools and arrester hook added. The DH.125's Bristol Siddeley Vipers would be replaced by a pair of Rolls-Royce RB.172 or SNECMA M45 turbofans, which would also feature higher-rated generators. An in-flight refuelling probe was fitted to the nose to extend endurance beyond the three hours possible on internal fuel. The wings were provided with powered folding (folded span was 32ft [9.75m]) and the span was later increased by 3ft (0.9m) to improve endurance at altitude. Brough also suggested fitting a new 34ft (10.3m) span wing using the planform of the Handley Page HP.130 laminar-flow research aircraft for increased fuel capacity. Brough was not particularly happy with the outcome and concluded that a clean sheet design was the only way forward. The Admiralty was happy to agree.

FMICW and the Flying Pig

The Defence Operational Analysis Establishment began Project 125 in 1961 to investigate the UK's future AEW needs. The report concluded that a joint RN-RAF aircraft would be the most cost-effective solution. This led to the RN's Naval Requirement AW.166 of February 1962 becoming Naval Air Staff Requirement NASR.6166 in December for a new AEW aircraft to enter service in 1969 and the associated NASR.6167 for a COD transport and aerial refuelling tanker for the FAA and an assault transport for the RAF. To add a further layer of collaboration, the aircraft was to be developed in cooperation with France to equip the Marine Nationale's carriers under the Memorandum of Understanding (MoU) *Collaboration in the Aeronautical Field*, which was signed by Secretary of State for Defence Denis Healey, Minister of Aviation Roy Jenkins and the Minister of the Armed Forces Pierre Messmer on 17 May 1965. Interest in NASR.6166 was also received from Sweden, Japan and India but both the UK and France were reluctant to divulge radar technology secrets with some or all of these nations.

Research by the RRE and Elliott Brothers had led to a new radar technique that could eliminate ground clutter and provide AMTI – Frequency Modulated Interrupted Continuous Wave (FMICW) radar. FMCW radars transmit a continuous wave signal with a frequency that varies over time. The frequency of the return signal is compared with the originally transmitted signal, the frequency triplets created provide the range and range rate. Instead of using separate transmitter and receiver antennas, FMICW used one antenna by interrupting the signal. Another advantage was less reliance on signal processing computers. Originally intended for air interception radars for fighters, the FMICW was equally applicable to AEW and was suitable for the fore and aft scanner system (FASS) layout favoured by Brough. The FMICW did not operate well with propeller-driven aircraft as the propellers attenuated the signal, as well as creating spurious returns. The radar's performance was also linked to airspeed; ideally the AEW aircraft would have to fly at 1.2 times the stalling speed – targets approaching from astern had to be flying twice as fast as the AEW

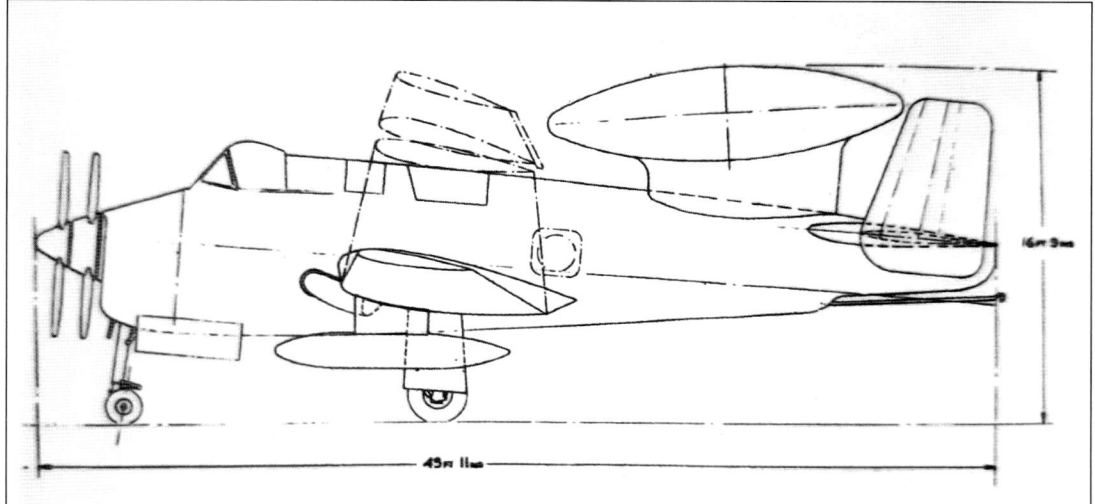

Fairey assisted with BAC's feasibility studies, including a proposal to fit the FMICW radar in a dorsal radome on the Gannet with a new twin tail arrangement. *Leonardo UK*

aircraft in order to be detected among the ground clutter. The 10kW S-band radar had an estimated detection range of 200nm (370km). The RRE favoured using a separate L-band secondary radar for sea surveillance.

For the aircraft designers the main constraint was the maximum wingspan of 60ft (18.3m), which would have knock-on effects in attaining a high enough altitude to ensure that the endurance requirements were met. The NASR.6167 COD/tactical transport version was to carry 5,000lb (2,270kg) of cargo (such as a crated jet engine) or up to 28 passengers in rear-facing seats. Design study contracts were issued to the British Aircraft Corporation (BAC) and Hawker Siddeley's Blackburn Division in 1965.

BAC assigned the design task to the former Vickers Aviation team at Weybridge. The feasibility study revealed that the likely AUW would be 40,000lb (18,145kg), requiring 80ft (24.4m) span wings. Conforming to the 60ft span limit would restrict the AUW to 30,000lb (16,610kg), which would lack enough internal fuel to meet the endurance requirement. Having extendable, folding, outer wing sections were offered as a solution, albeit at the cost of more complexity.

Westland's Fairey Division at Hayes collaborated with BAC on the feasibility study, offering two developments of the Gannet. The first was based on the AEW.3 with an updated radar and systems. The second proposal but with a new rear fuselage with a twin tail empennage to accommodate the 16ft diameter dorsal rotodome for the FMICW radar. The wingspan would be increased to 60ft to improve endurance. Given the Anglo-French collaboration, BAC also examined a conversion of the Dassault MD.410 Spirale light transport with a dorsal antenna (perhaps similar to Dassault's own plans, see below) and a conversion of the forthcoming Dassault Mystère small business jet, which like Brough's HS.125 conversion, entailed radical changes with a new empennage, dorsal antenna, increased span wings and uprated engines with additional electrical generation capacity. The result was a decision to pursue a clean-sheet design.

The RRE studies led to six antenna options for the radar system:

- **A:** 8ft (2.43m) diameter circular antenna, for nose and tail installation (FASS)

- **B:** 10ft (3.04m) diameter circular antenna, FASS

- **C:** 16ft (4.87m) wide antenna, 20ft (6.09m) diameter circular rotodome

- **D:** 20ft (6.09m) wide antenna, 25ft (7.62m) diameter circular rotodome

- **E:** 16ft (4.87m) wide antenna, 20ft (6.09m) diameter elliptical rotodome

- **F:** 12ft × 16ft (3.65 × 4.87m) elliptical antenna, FASS

The elliptical antennas were rejected on aerodynamic grounds and Option F would have led to excessive fuselage width.

BAC divided its designs into two categories of systems:

- **System I:** full specification, AEW and control, on-board data processing, interception control, separate L-band sea surveillance radar, four crew, aircraft AUW 40,000lb

- **System II:** reduced specification, AEW, basic interception control, no sea surveillance radar, two crew, aircraft AUW 30,000lb.

Each system came in three subvariants: I(i) the full-spec aircraft with 6,850lbf (30.5kN) RB.153 aft-fan turbojet/low-bypass turbofans; I(ii) with lighter equipment; I(iii) powered by 3,400shp (2,600kW) General Electric T64-P4 turboprops (for which Bristol

AEW aircraft designs to NASR.6166

	BAC Design A1	BAC Design A2	BAC Design B1	BAC Design C1	BAC Design C2
Span	73ft 0in (22.25m) fully spread; 60ft 0in (18.28m) take-off; 22ft 0in (6.70m) folded	54ft 0in (16.45m); 20ft 0in (6.09m) folded	71ft 0in (21.64m) fully spread; 60ft 0in (18.28m) take-off; 25ft 0in (7.62m) folded	70ft 0in (21.33m) fully spread; 58ft 6in (17.83m) take-off; 22ft 0in (6.70m) folded	60ft 0in (18.28m); 22ft 0in (6.70m) folded
Length	52ft 0in (15.84m)	52ft 0in (15.84m)	36ft 0in (10.97m); 40ft 0in (12.19m) wings folded	44ft 6in (13.59m); 49ft 0in (14.93m) wings folded	43ft 6in (13.25m)
All-up weight	40,000lb (18,145kg)	40,000lb (18,145kg)	40,000lb (18,145kg)	30,000lb (13,605kg); 40,000lb (18,145kg) with RB.153	40,000lb (18,145kg)
Powerplant	2x Dart R.Da.15; or 2x RB.153 aft-fan, 6,850lbf (30.5kN)	2x RB.153 aft-fan, 6,850lbf (30.5kN)	2x Dart R.Da.15	2x Dart R.Da.15; or 2x PLF1B-2, 5,220lbf (23.2kN); or 2x RB.153 aft-fan, 6,850lbf (30.5kN)	2x RB.153 aft-fan, 6,850lbf (30.5kN)
Radar	FMICW, 8ft (2.4m) FASS	FMICW, 8ft (2.4m) FASS	FMICW, 10ft (3.3m) FASS	FMICW, 20ft (6.1m) rotodome	FMICW, 20ft (6.1m) rotodome

	Hawker Siddeley P.139B-2	Hawker Siddeley P.139C-1	Hawker Siddeley P.139C-3	Hawker Siddeley Brough P.139C-4	Hawker Siddeley Brough P.139C-5
Span	60ft 0in (18.28m); 27ft 0in (8.22m) folded	60ft 0in (18.28m); 27ft 0in (8.22m) folded	60ft 0in (18.28m); 27ft 0in (8.22m) folded	64ft 0in (19.50m); 27ft 0in (8.22m) folded	62ft 0in (18.99m); 27ft 0in (8.22m) folded
Length	53ft 0in (16.15m)	63ft 0in (19.20m); 50ft (15.24m) folded	54ft 6in (16.61m)	55ft 0in (16.76m)	54ft 0in (16.45m)
All-up weight	45,000lb (20,410kg)	40,000lb (18,145kg)	40,000lb (18,145kg)	40,000lb (18,145kg)	40,000lb (18,145kg)
Powerplant	2x RB.172, 6,500lbf (28.9kN)	2x RB.172, 6,500lbf (28.9kN)	2x RB.172, 6,500lbf (28.9kN); 4x RB.162 optional lift engines	2x Dart; or 2x T64-P4D, 3,400shp (2,535kW); or 2x coupled Gnome	2x Dart; or 2x T64-P4D, 3,400shp (2,535kW);
Radar	FMICW, 8ft (2.4m) FASS	FMICW, 9ft 6in (2.9m) FASS	FMICW, 8ft (2.4m) FASS	FMICW, 8ft (2.4m) FASS	FMICW, 16ft (4.8m) ventral

Siddeley had a production licence); II(i) a modified Gannet; II(ii) with simplified navigation radar and 5,220lbf (23.2kN) Avco Lycoming PLF1B-2 turbofans; II(iii) with pulse-compression radar and Dart turboprops. BAC favoured II(ii) in terms of development cost and risk.

The need for a flying radar testbed saw BAC examining the Percival P.66 Pembroke, which would be modified into the BAC 169 with a 16ft (4.9m) diameter dorsal rotodome and the Alvis Leonides engines replaced by 4,320lbf (19.2kN) thrust PLF1A-2 turbofans or the Rolls-Royce RB.162 or RB.153.

Weybridge formulated a series of designs. Designs A1 and B1 had the FASS installation and featured high-mounted straight wings and a tail boom with endplate fins, the only difference being fuselage width and depth to accommodate the 8ft and 10ft diameter antennas respectively. The aft antennas were of elliptical shape with 1ft (30cm) less height to accommodate the arrester hook beneath the radome. They were powered by two Dart R.Da.15 turboprops, the nacelles being over the wings to keep the propellers well clear of the forward radar's arcs. The outer wing sections folded axially 90° and then 90° backwards to lie flat along the fuselage – the so-called 'Grumman fold' method. A refuelling probe was fitted on the nose cone.

Design F1 was very similar but was equipped with the elliptical FASS antennas. The excessive drag of the elliptical radomes and similar-shaped lower fuselage cross-section saw this design being rejected. A2 was a flying wing development of A1 with a mid-mounted

BAC Design C3	BAC Design C5 (Dart)	BAC Design C5 (T64)	BAC Design D1	BAC Design F1	Improved Gannet
60ft 0in (18.28m); 22ft 0in (6.70m) folded	70ft 0in (21.33m) fully spread; 58ft 6in (17.83m) take-off; 22ft 0in (6.70m) folded	70ft 0in (21.33m) fully spread; 58ft 6in (17.83m) take-off; 22ft 0in (6.70m) folded	70ft 0in (21.33m) fully spread; 58ft 6in (17.83m) take-off; 22ft 0in (6.70m) folded	72ft 0in (21.94m) fully spread; 60ft 0in (18.28m) take-off; 23ft 0in (7.01m) folded	60ft 0in (18.28m); 19ft 6in (5.94m) folded
44ft 6in (13.59m)	48ft 0in (14.63m)	46ft 0in (14.02m)	46ft 6in (14.17m); 49ft 0in (14.93m) wings folded	52ft 0in (15.84m)	49ft 11in (15.21m)
40,000lb (18,145kg)	40,000lb (18,145kg)	40,000lb (18,145kg)	40,000lb (18,145kg)	40,000lb (18,145kg)	?
2x T64-P4D, 3,400shp (2,535kW)	2x Dart R.Da.15	1x coupled T64-P4D, 6,800shp (5.070kW)	2x Dart R.Da.15	2x Dart R.Da.15	1x ASDM.8 Double Mamba Mk.102, 3,875ehp (2,890kW)
FMICW, 20ft (6.1m) rotodome	FMICW, 16ft (4.8m) ventral	FMICW, 16ft (4.8m) ventral	FMICW, 25ft (7.6m) rotodome	FMICW, 12ft (3.65m) FASS	FMICW, 16ft (4.8m) rotodome
Hawker Siddeley Brough P.139C-6	**Hawker Siddeley Brough P.139C-7**	**Hawker Siddeley Brough P.139F-7**	**Hawker Siddeley Brough P.139F-8**	**Hawker Siddeley Brough P.139G**	**Breguet Br.123A & Br.123B**
63ft 0in (19.20m); 30ft 0in (9.14m) folded	60ft 0in (18.28m); 27ft 0in (8.22m) folded	63ft 0in (19.20m); 27ft 0in (8.22m) folded	71ft 0in (21.64m); 27ft 0in (8.22m) folded	70ft 0in (21.233m)	60ft 0.5in (18.30m); 25ft 3in (7.70m) folded
54ft 6in (16.61m)	54ft 6in (16.61m)	55ft 0in (16.76m)	54ft 0in (16.45m)	55ft 0in (16.76m)	Br.123A 52ft 0in (15.85m); Br.123B 52ft 6in (16.0m)
40,000lb (18,145kg)	40,000lb (18,145kg)	40,000lb (18,145kg)	40,000lb (18,145kg)	40,000lb (18,145kg)	39,685lb (18,000kg)
2x Dart; or 2x T64-P4D, 3,400shp (2,535kW);	2x RB.172, 6,500lbf (28.9kN); or 2x M45	2x RB.172, 6,500lbf (28.9kN)	2x RB.172, 6,500lbf (28.9kN)	2x RB.172, 6,500lbf (28.9kN)	2x T64 4,000shp (2,985kW); or 2x M46 turbofans
FMICW, 14ft (4.2m) or 16ft (4.8m) or 20ft (6m) rotodome	FMICW, 14ft (4.2m) or 16ft (4.8m) rotodome	FMICW, 9ft 6in (2.9m) FASS	FMICW, 8ft (2.4m) FASS	FMICW, 9ft 6in (2.9m) FASS	Br.123A FMICW, 8ft (2.4m) FASS; Br.123B 24ft 11in (7.6m) rotodome

swept wing with wing tip fins and was powered by two RB.153 in underwing nacelles.

Design C1 had the 20ft diameter rotodome and the aircraft resembled the Hawkeye with a sleek fuselage, high-mounted wing with nacelles for two Dart R.Da.15 and twin tail fins. The rotodome was 4ft (1.2m) deep to improve the height finding capability, at the cost of exceeding the 17ft (5.2m) clearance limit for carrier hangars. The rotodome could be raised and lowered on its large pylon and was mounted quite far back on the fuselage to minimise the blanking caused by the propellers. The 'Grumman fold' was used with 20ft (6m) of the outer wing also folding to meet the 60ft unfolded span limit. A refuelling probe was fitted above the cockpit. The D1 was very similar except for a 2ft (0.6m) fuselage stretch for the 25ft diameter rotodome. Two further versions of the C1 and D1 were sketched with PLF1B-2 and RB.153 jets, the latter requiring new nacelles and the main undercarriage was relocated to fuselage sponsons; dihedral was added to the tailplane to keep it out of the jet efflux (the Lycoming engine had a forward fan and the turbine section had bifurcated exhausts allowing the same nacelle structure to be used.) The C1 with PLF1B-2 was BAC's favoured choice.

The C2 was a tailless design, taking the wings of the A2 with the 20ft diameter rotodome mounted right aft on a pylon that doubled as the fin and rudder (the endplate fins lacking control surfaces). It also retained the A2's twin RB.153s. The C3 looked very similar but was a completely new design thanks to its use of two

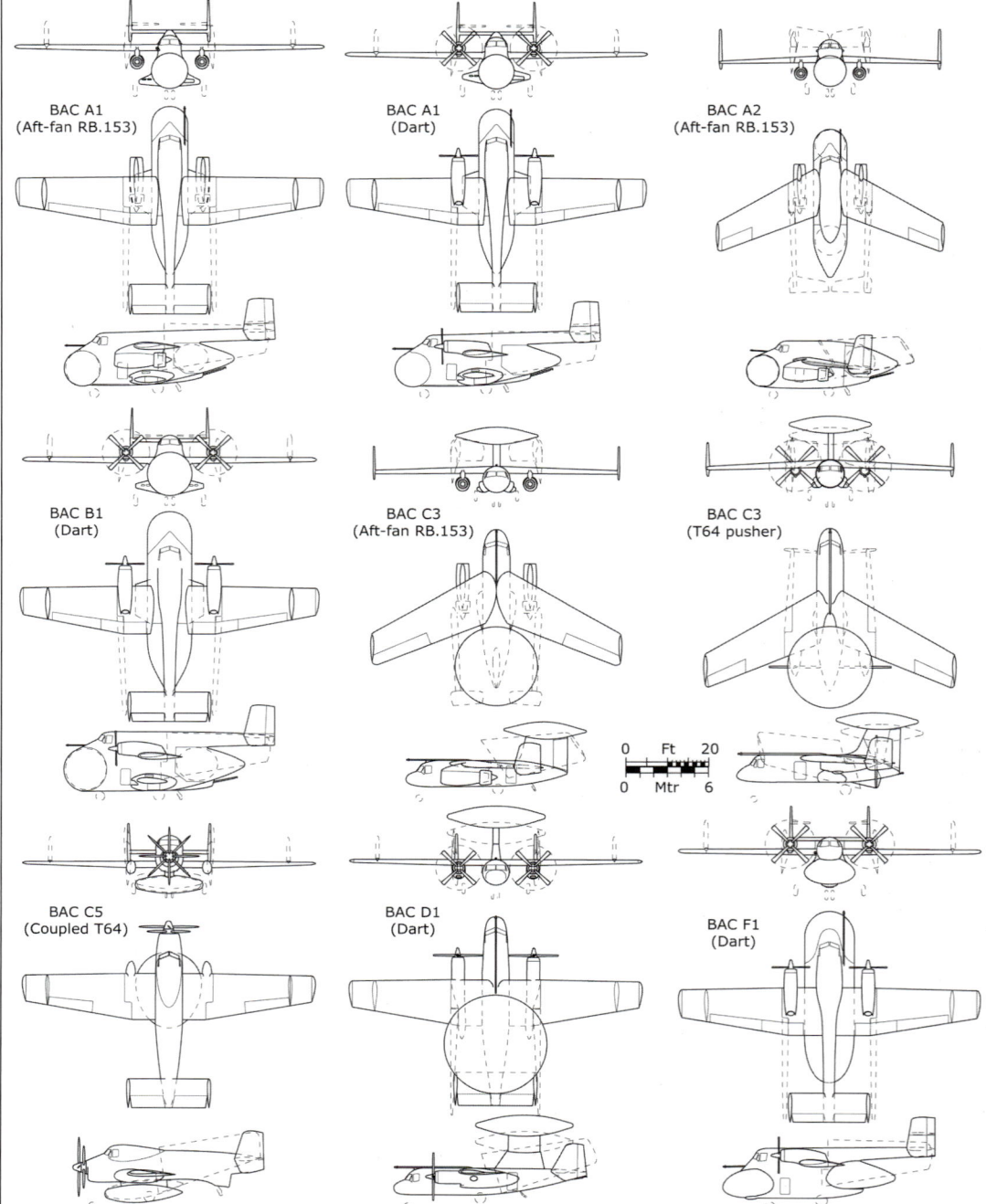

A compilation of some of BAC's numerous design studies to meet NASR.6166. BAC favoured the dorsal rotodome layout but ultimately the Admiralty preferred Hawker Siddeley Brough's FASS antenna layout. *Chris Gibson*

T64-P4 turboprops in a pusher configuration. The radar had to be raised on a taller, but narrower chord, tail fin to keep it out of the propeller arc. This would have precluded hangar stowage, so the fin and a section of the rear fuselage could swing through 180° to the rear and downwards to reduce the height by 3ft (0.9m).

Another way to keep the radar away from the propellers if turboprops were fitted was to mount it ventrally. The C5 used the 20ft diameter rotodome, which could be raised and lowered for adequate deck clearance. The fuselage was similar to the C1 but the radar was now ventrally mounted and the R.Da.15 Darts were mounted in nacelles above the wing. The main undercarriage legs were 5ft (1.4m) long, beefing it up for carrier landings cost an additional 810lb (327kg) in weight over the C1's undercarriage. The 508lb (230kg) weight penalty of the ventral rotodome was a further drawback. The second C5 design was in essence a redesigned Gannet AEW.3 with coupled T64-P4 turboprops driving a co-axial propeller and twin tail fins. In both cases, the 'Grumman fold' was used with 20ft (6m) of the outer wing also folding to meet the 60ft limit. The main undercarriage was housed in small wing nacelles.

BAC submitted another design based on its previous work with SLAR aerials. The airframe was

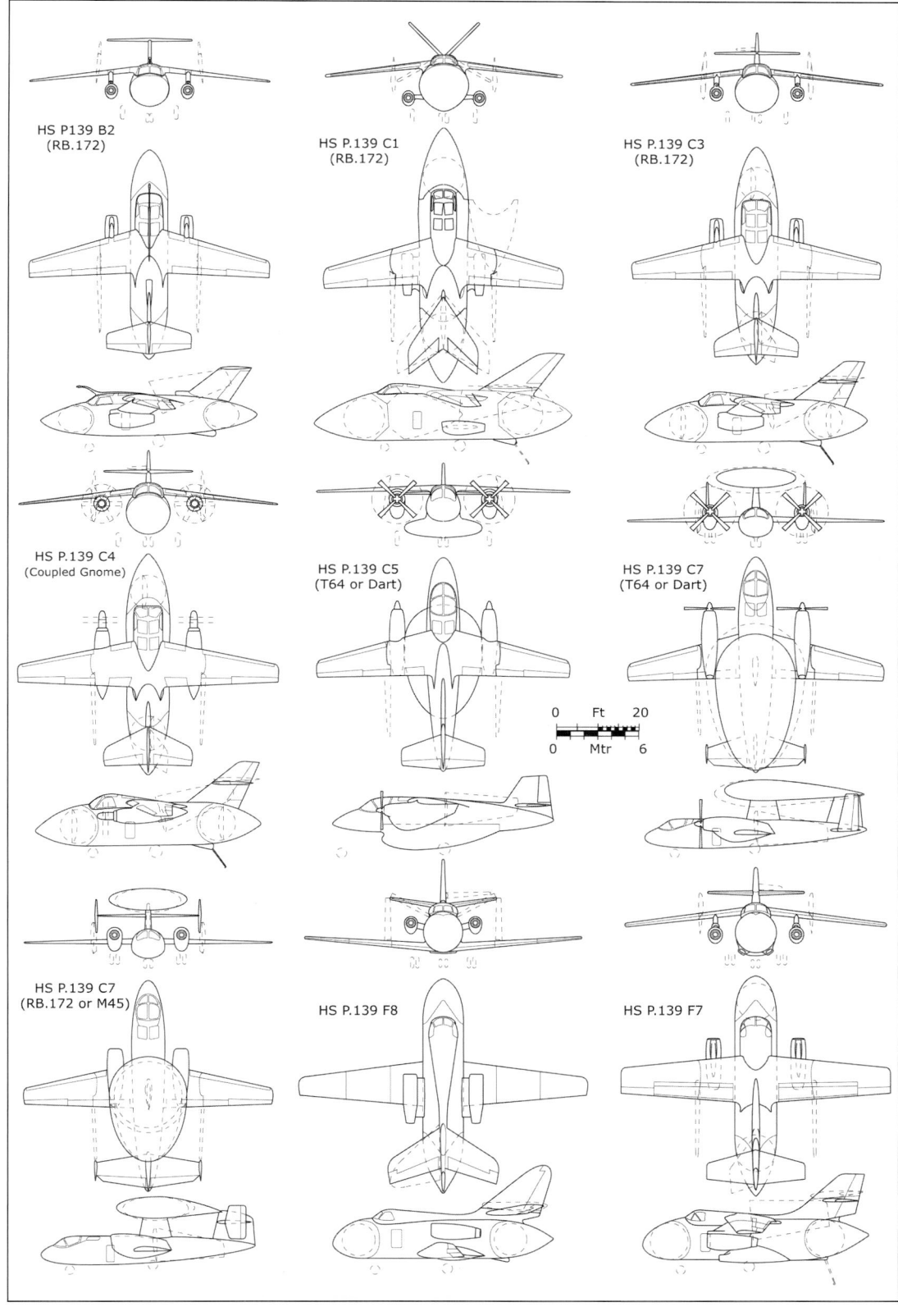

Hawker Siddeley Brough Division's P.139 studies would not win any aeronautical beauty contests but the FASS radome layout required the aircraft to be little more than winged radar carriers. *Chris Gibson*

that of the NASR.6167 COD variant but fitted with four radar antennas, a pair of 11 × 3ft (3.6 × 0.9m) antennas on the rear fuselage sides and pairs of 18ft × 1ft (5.5 × 0.6m) antennas in the wing leading and trailing edges with radar-transparent surface material to cover those portions of the wing. Each antenna would cover a 60° sector with 30° scanned fore and aft. This drag-reducing radar layout was married to a novel new propulsion concept – the tip fan. This General Electric engine would use a 4ft

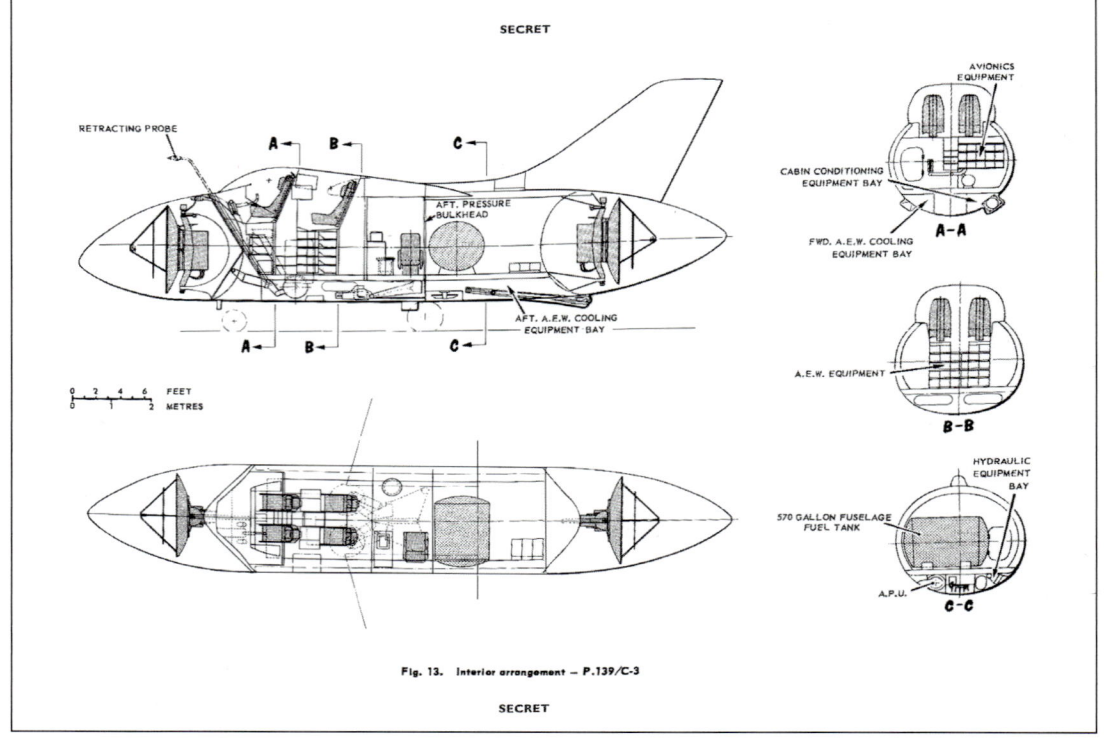

The internal layout of the P.139 C3 showing the arrangement of the radar equipment, crew stations and the retractable refuelling probe. The P.139B was very similar except for having a T-tail empennage.
Brough Heritage via Chris Gibson

(1.2m) diameter gas generator in a fairing ahead of the wing root which drove a larger fan section in an 8ft (2.4m) long duct under the wing root, which had a bi-conical centrebody, the air being compressed and then expanded – just like a convergent/divergent exhaust duct.

Blackburn's P.139 project studies covered at least a decade's work on various AEW aircraft for the RN and the RAF from 1963. Only the NASR.6166 designs need concern us here. The starting point of the new airframe studies was the P.139 'Ab Initio' – which some wag at Brough later called 'The Flying Pig' due to its portly dimensions. Brough and the RRE selected the 8ft (2.4m) diameter antenna, giving a fuselage width of 10ft (3.7m) (or 12ft (3.7m) if the 10ft antenna was used). The FASS layout would give 360° coverage and a compact airframe was designed around the radars – described as a 'cigar with a lump', the lump being the cockpit canopy. The engine choices were both turbofans, the 6,500lbf (28.9kN) Rolls-Royce RB.172 (which was developed into the RR-Turbomeca RT.172 Adour) and the 6,500lbf Bristol Siddeley BS.116, a scaled Olympus 320 which was developed into the BSEL/SNECMA M45. A crew of four would be carried, all provided with ejection seats.

The 'Ab Initio' was refined into the P.139B with a single T-tail and underwing nacelles for the turbofans. The airframe changes were minimal for the COD role: a light metal fairing for the nose radome, the radar space being used for baggage and the rear radome becoming a cargo door (swinging open to the left). The portly fuselage could easily accommodate the specified 5,000lb (2,270kg) of cargo or 28 passengers.

The P.139C-1 had high-mounted wings and a V-tail, which could be folded downwards. The two RB.172 turbojets were mounted on short pylons low on the aft fuselage. This allowed the wing fold hinges to be located further inboard, meeting the 27ft (8.2m) folded width requirement. The radar antennas were of 9ft 6in (2.9m) diameter.

A proposal to provide short-field performance similar to that of the Hawker Siddeley HS.681 tactical transport then in development for the RAF saw the addition of two pods under the outer wings, each holding a pair of 6,000lbf (26.7kN) RB.162 lift engines (or a single 10,163lbf (45.2kN) RB.193). These were mounted horizontally with rotating thrust-diverting cascades (as used by the Hawker Siddeley P.1127). The undercarriage was changed to a paired tandem mainwheel layout for rough field operations. This version was presumably tailored to the RAF's assault transport element of NASR.6167, although it was drawn up in AEW form.

The P.139C-4 introduced turboprop power, either two Darts or T64-P4s driving 9ft (2.7m) diameter six-blade contra-rotating propellers or four Bristol Siddeley Gnomes in a coupled arrangement which may have allowed one engine per side to be shut down during cruising to reduce fuel consumption. The limited 30,000ft (9,145m) altitude, increased cabin noise and incomparability with the FMICW radar were serious problems, however.

The P.139C-5 mirrored BAC's efforts with a ventral radome with a similar 16 × 4ft (4.9 × 1.2m) antenna. The new fuselage was much sleeker and of elliptical cross-section. The radome was broad but the rear section was faired into the lower fuselage to improve the aerodynamics. Two Dart or

T64 turboprops were mounted in wing nacelles. The long main undercarriage legs would have proved as troublesome as BAC's proposal to meet the carrier landing requirements.

The dorsal rotodome version of the C-5 was the C-6, a twin tail being fitted with a central fin retained to support the aft end of the radome structure. The turboprop nacelles were also different, the engines being mounted over the wings. The radome could accommodate a 14 × 4ft 6in (4.3 × 1.4m), 16 × 4ft (4.9 × 1.2m) or 20 × 5ft (6 × 1.5m) antenna. The C-7 swapped the turboprops for RB.172 or M45 turbofans mounted over the wings. The absence of propellers meant that the 60ft (18.3m) span wing folded to the specified 27ft (8.2m). The tail was further modified, returning to a broader-chord tail fin with large endplate fins mounted on the tailplane away from the jet efflux. The C-7 could carry either the 14 × 4ft 6in (4.3 × 1.4m) or 16 × 4ft (4.9 × 1.2m) antenna.

A low-mounted wing layout was studied with the P.139F-5 which had a gull wing, with nacelles for the RB.172 or M45 at the elbow of the inboard gull section. A T-tail was fitted, which included small endplates. The F-5's wing and basic layout was used as the basis of an airliner study, retaining the 10ft fuselage diameter and capable of seating 40 passengers. Brough saw this as a way to amortise some of the development costs.

The P.139F-8 had high-mounted wings and the engines were mounted in mid-fuselage-mounted nacelles, similar in concept to the C-1. The P.139G had a T-tail and the engines were installed under the wing roots with extended intakes and exhausts. Two fuel tanks could be carried on underwing pylons.

Given that NASR.6166 was an Anglo-French collaboration, Breguet Aviation undertook two series of studies, and consulted the electronics companies CSF (Compagnie générale de la télégraphie sans fil) and CFTH (Compagnie Française Thomson-Houston), as well as Elliott and Marconi in the UK.

The three Br.123A studies covered the FASS layout and strongly resembled Brough's P.139B, but with twin tail booms. The high-mounted 60ft 0.5in (18.3m) span wings had folding outer wings that laid on top of the inner wing section, the folded span being 25ft 3in (7.7m). The three versions differed only in the engines offered, the two turboprop-powered designs having two Dart or T64-P4 engines and the jet-powered version having a pair of SNECMA M46 turbofans.

The three Br.123B studies were much sleeker with a dorsal rotodome and a low-mounted wing with a V-tail. The rotodome was of 24ft 11in (7.6m) diameter and could be raised and lowered on its pylon. A retractable ventral SLAR surface surveillance radar was also fitted in the lower rear fuselage. The engine choices were identical to the Br.123A, the jet-powered version moving the M46 turbofans to the rear fuselage beneath the V-tail fins.

Other AEW studies around 1963–64 included a Breguet Br.1050 Alizé carrier-borne ASW aircraft

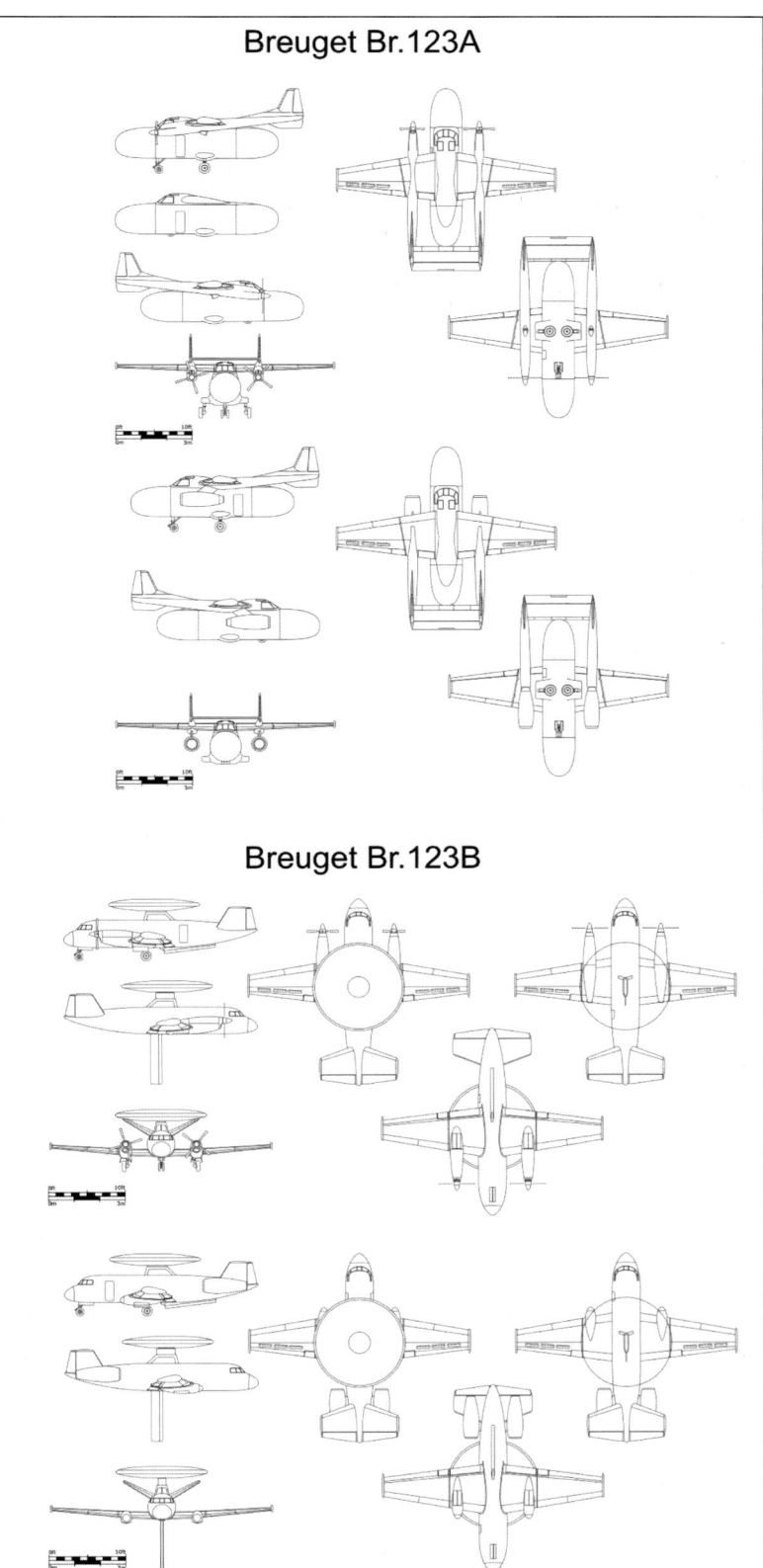

A compilation of Breguet's Br.123 designs to NASR.6166. The Br.123A had the FASS layout and both turboprop and turbofan propulsion was considered. The Br.123B had a dorsal rotodome, again with turbofan or turboprop options. The Br.123B had a V-tail while the Br.123A had two tail booms. *Jens Baganz*

WINGS OVER THE FLEET

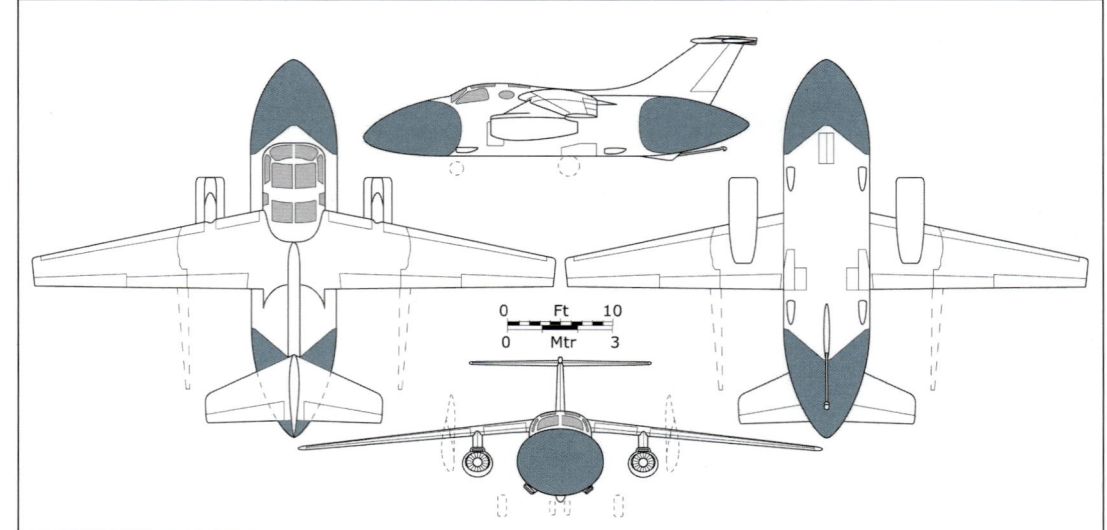

The Hawker Siddeley P.139B was selected as winner of NASR.6166 but was cancelled along with the CVA-01 in early 1966. *Chris Gibson*

modified with a dorsal radome and Dassault investigated an AEW version of the MD 410 Spirale III with a dorsal radome and large endplate fins on the tailplane, its high-mounted wings and Turbomeca Turmo IIID turboprops being retained unchanged.

The MOD now had to decide on a winner. The need for a stabilised antenna had been stressed many times but BAC's C1 design lacked this feature and therefore its dorsal rotodome suffered from airframe obscuration. The P.139B met the requirements and was selected in 1965. The RAF was not keen on the P.139, which had been tailored for shipborne use with a compact airframe. The RAF's assault transport idea also seems to have faded away. The French Marine Nationale would not obtain its AEW capability until it received three E-2C Hawkeyes in 2000 (to be replaced by three E-2D Hawkeye aircraft in 2027).

Just as it looked like the FAA would get the AEW capability it had always wanted a hammer blow came. The 1966 Defence Review cancelled the CVA-01 carrier and signalled that the existing carriers would be phased out by 1975. The provision of AEW cover for RN operations supporting NATO forces in the North Atlantic and UK waters would then fall to the RAF. P.139B was now surplus to requirements and cancelled. Another attempt to purchase the Hawkeye also failed.

The RAF drew up Air Staff Requirement ASR.387 in April 1966. Its extended development led to ASR.394 and Specification 274D&P in December 1970 for an interim type to replace the Gannet AEW.3. The result was the Avro Shackleton AEW.2, 12 MR.2 maritime patrol aircraft being refitted with APS-20F radars taken off the retired Gannets, modified with AMTI by Elliott Automation. They entered service with No. 8 Squadron at RAF Kinloss in September 1972 (the AMTI capability was added in 1973). Unforeseen at that time, the RAF would remain using the Shackleton until 1991.

AEW goes rotary

The use of helicopters for AEW has a surprisingly long history. In early 1947 the TRE had proposed fitting a helicopter with a radar antenna, trailing a cable back to the parent ship, which was equipped with the transmitter and receiver electronics. This plan was obviously infeasible and quickly thrown out by the Admiralty. The TRE came back with another plan, miniaturising the 'black boxes' so the total weight of the equipment, plus two operators, would weigh less than 5,500lb (2,495kg), which a tandem rotor helicopter like the Bristol 173 could lift. Such a role was not included as part of Naval Requirement NA.43; the Admiralty had put its faith in fixed-wing aircraft to meet its AEW needs.

In 1967 the picture was very different. The carriers would be gone by 1975, the Gannet and its APS-20 radars were due for replacement and the RAF's ASR.387 was looking at relatively short-ranged Hawker Siddeley Andover AEW derivatives that would be heavily reliant on tanker support to operate over the fleet. The Naval Staff was keen to hold onto some form of AEW capability and the only realistic option was to use a helicopter from its planned Command Helicopter Cruiser (the CCH which became the *Invincible*-class). As noted above, the FMICW radar was incompatible with rotating propellers and rotor blades, so a pulsed radar would be required.

ASR.387 was modified to include a 'Separate Sea/Land Solution' to provide an AEW helicopter. Initial proposals considered the Boeing Vertol CH-47B Chinook – which had recently been considered for the ASW role – but it was too large and expensive. The obvious solution was to modify the Westland Sea King HAS.1 then in development.

Westland was contracted to carry out a design study in 1967, looking at four options using a pulse-radar from Elliott. The first had an elliptical 8 × 2 × 2ft 9in (2.4 × 0.6 × 0.84m) antenna that could retract into a well cut in the lower fuselage. A radio datalink pod would be fixed to the lower port side of the rear fuselage. The rotating elliptical antenna caused aerodynamic problems with drag cycling and buffeting at the antenna's tips. The solution was to enclose the scanner in a circular inflatable nylon radome. The third study moved the radar and its nylon radome to the nose. The fourth had a fixed nose antenna providing only 240° coverage.

The mission profile involved a climb to 10,000ft (3,050m), patrolling for three hours before returning to the ship. This was less onerous than the usual ASW mission so only one pilot would be required. The retractable radar was the best solution to reduce drag and fuel consumption while transiting to the patrol area. To provide sufficient coverage three helicopters would be required, two in operation and one in maintenance.

The main problem was providing the three AEW helicopters aboard the CCH. At this stage the CCH was a cruiser with an aft landing deck with two landing spots and a hangar for six Sea Kings. The Director of Naval Construction pointed out that adding three helicopters, plus the necessary command and control space, would mean lengthening the ships by 60ft (18.3m), increasing the deep load displacement by 1,000 tons and increasing the cost by £8.4 million. The Navy Department could not afford this (the CCH itself being in a delicate political position given some of its variants resembled an aircraft carrier).

The AEW helicopter was quietly dropped from ASR.387, but that requirement was replaced by ASR.400 in 1970 and the question was re-opened. Westland suggested a 'clip on' system for a pulsed AMTI radar to avoid structural changes and minimised weight increase. Ferranti took Westland's initial rotating scanner idea and made it foldable rather than retractable. Elliott used a folding 9 × 3ft (2.7 × 0.9m) framework antenna under the belly; Westland favoured this option, despite potential icing issues. The MOD insisted that the RAF could provide all the AEW cover that the RN required and the AEW Sea King proposal was filed away. The results of Exercise High Wood in 1971, when the Shackleton's were judged to have "made little contribution", having only detected a third of the 27 incoming low-altitude attacks, provided evidence that the RN's lack of faith was not entirely misplaced.

Indeed, in 1974 the Vice Chief of the Naval Staff, Vice Admiral Sir Raymond Lygo, reopened the case but the First Sea Lord, Admiral Sir Edward Ashmore closed it, not wanting to start a battle with the RAF when he wanted to secure Sea Harrier and the Sea King Replacement. Another study was carried out in 1978 as the Gannets faced imminent retirement. The Director of Naval Air Warfare, Captain Linley Middleton, pointed out the operational shortcomings of the Sea King's 75kt search speed and that the 120–140nm (220–260km) radar search range from 10,000ft (3,050m) was less than the distance from which Soviet bombers would release their anti-ship missiles. The cost and potential Whitehall battles did not seem worth the capability that would result and so the idea was abandoned.

Corporate lessons

In April 1982 the RN found itself at war, facing a well-trained adversary equipped with modern fighters and anti-ship missiles off the Falkland/Malvinas Islands, 7,000nm away from home and at least 6,000nm beyond the RAF's AEW coverage by the elderly Shackletons. The British Aerospace (BAe) Sea Harrier FRS.1 fighters aboard *Invincible* and *Hermes* (ironically Middleton was now *Hermes'* Captain) had to rely on the escorts' Type 965M and Type 1022 air search radars for early warning, supplemented by Sea Harriers on CAP and other means such as the ships' ESM kit and communications interception of the Argentine pilots' radio chatter by nuclear-powered submarines loitering off the Argentine coast. Much debate on whether an AEW capability could have reduced the losses of ships to aerial attack has taken place in the years since.

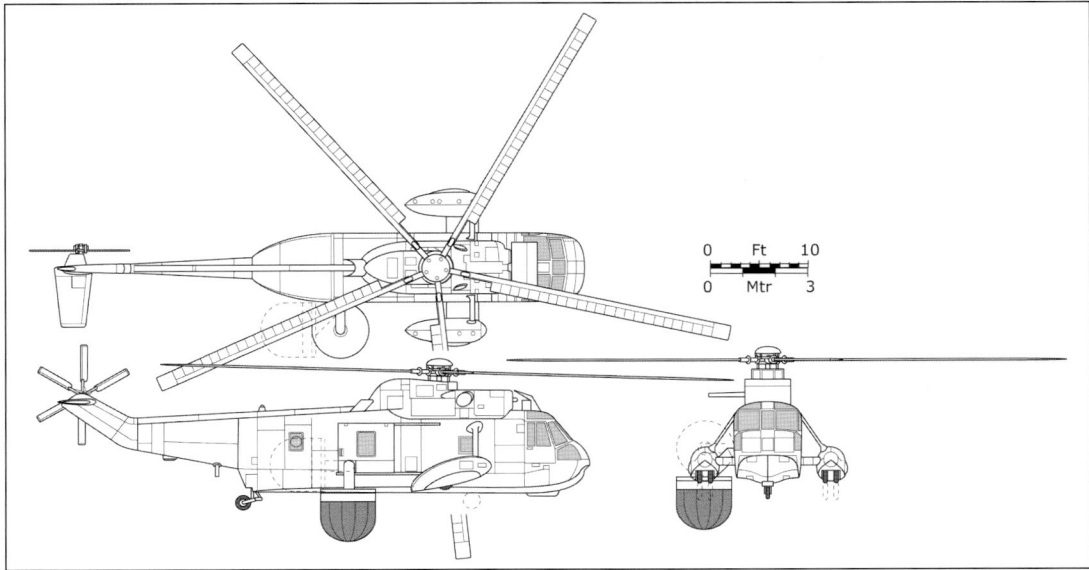

A general arrangement drawing of the initial Westland Sea King AEW.2 conversion with the inflatable Searchwater radome in the operational position, extended below the fuselage. *Chris Gibson*

WINGS OVER THE FLEET

Sea King AEW.2 XV704 of 824 NAS in 1984. The Searchwater radar mounting equipment and avionics racks can be seen through the open cabin door. The radome is deflated. *Blue Envoy Collection*

The Naval Staff recognised the need quickly and dusted off the 1970s plans. One of the many crash programmes enacted by the Armed Services during April to June was the Sea King HAS.2 (AEW). Westland began development in May and the first two aircraft attained operational status in August with D Flight 824 NAS, sailing south aboard HMS *Illustrious* as part of the relief force. The basic conversion removed the ASW equipment, replacing it with radar displays for two operators. The antenna of the ARI.5980/3 Thorn-EMI Searchwater radar (an X-band frequency-agile surface-search set from the Nimrod MR.2) was stabilised and mounted inside an inflatable radome on the starboard side, just aft of the main cabin door. The mounting was retractable to allow deck clearance for landing and when lowered it provided 360° coverage.

The conversion worked well, despite some issues with ground clutter, and could track up to 250 targets. The main limitation was that the Sea King could not operate above 10,000ft (3,050m) and had limited patrol endurance. The initial aircraft were followed by eight production standard conversions as the AEW.2A. These were operated by 849 NAS, which reformed at Culdrose on 8 November 1984.

Project Cerberus saw the AEW.2A fleet upgraded by Westland and GEC-Marconi with the Searchwater 2000 radar and the Cerberus system from 1997 as the AEW.7. This included upgraded secure

In 1994 Sea King AEW.2A XV664 received D-Day stripes as part of the 50th anniversary celebrations. The Searchwater radar is being lowered into position. Later converted to ASaC.7 standard it served in Afghanistan during 2009. *Terry Panopalis Collection*

234

A Sea King ASaC.7 of 849 NAS participating in Exercise Neptune Warrior in 2007. MOD/Open Government Licence

communications, improved navigation equipment, Joint Tactical Information Distribution System (JTIDS) (Link-16) datalink, video data recording and Active Noise Reduction. Three additional Sea Kings were also converted to increase the size of the fleet, although 13 aircraft was still three fewer than required. The Cerberus system was capable of simultaneously tracking 400 targets and JTIDS allowed the radar data to be shared with other aircraft and ships. The AEW.7 was redesignated as the ASaC.7 just before it entered service with 849 NAS, the change of designation to Airborne Surveillance and Control reflecting that the aircraft was capable of real-time battlefield control and reconnaissance gathering.

During the March 2003 invasion of Iraq, Operation Telic, 849 NAS deployed Sea King ASaC.7 aircraft aboard *Ark Royal*. On 22 March 2003, two of the aircraft collided over the Persian Gulf, killing seven of the crews. The Board of Inquiry called for night vision goggle (NVG) compatibility to be fitted – previous plans to improve the anti-collision lighting and provide NVG capability had been cancelled in 1994 to cut costs. Delays in finding a successor saw seven ASaC.7 being retained in service until 26 September 2018, being the final Sea Kings in British military service (and making the Sea King the longest serving FAA aircraft in its history.) 849 NAS briefly operated a single Merlin HM.2 in 2020 but the Crowsnest programme delays saw the squadron disband on 21 April 2020, ending a long (intermittent) service in the AEW role since 1953.

Fast AEW: Reprise

The immediate post-Falklands era threw up some odd concepts. BAe's Kingston Division, the former Hawker Aircraft at Kingston upon Thames, was designing the supersonic P.1216 V/STOL fighter to succeed the Sea Harrier (see Chapter 13). To overcome the Sea King's limitations, the Kingston Projects Office sketched up the P.1216-6 AEW with a podded SLAR. Being a single-seat aircraft, presumably all the radar data would have been beamed back to the carrier by datalink. The main structural change was the provision of new slightly tapered outer wing sections, giving an aspect ratio of 7.3 for a high-altitude endurance of four hours at subsonic speeds. Due to the 68ft (20.7m) wingspan, the wing was provided with double folding,

WINGS OVER THE FLEET

AgustaWestland's initial Merlin-based options for FOAEW included fitting stub wings to increase lift to offset the rotor to reduce fuel burn and increase endurance. The AEW system was the Thales Cerberus from the Sea King ASaC.7 with a retractable inflatable radome under the rear fuselage.
Leonardo UK

although it is unclear how such a large aircraft could have operated from the *Invincible*-class light carriers. A defensive armament of two 27mm Mauser BK-27 cannon and two AIM-9L Sidewinder IR-homing air-to-air missiles was retained.

In 1990 BAe's Military Aircraft Division at Warton proposed the Sidetrack concept, an unusual staggered tandem biplane wing single-seat fighter-type aircraft with large endplates joining the wings and carrying phased-array SLAR antennas. This led to the more realistic idea of fitting the Sea Harrier FA.2 with a version of the Siemens Plessey MESAR (Multi-functional Electronically Scanned Adaptive Radar), which had been developed for the RN's future air defence destroyers to replace the Type 42 *Sheffield*-class – Project Horizon and then the Type 45 *Daring*-class (as the Type 1045 SAMPSON radar). The MESAR antennas would be mounted in wing tip pods, each one covering a 120° sector, the 60° blind spots fore and aft being filled by flying a racetrack orbit at 35–40,000ft (10,670–12,190m). The rear fuselage would be swapped for the longer tail cone of the two-seat Harrier T.8N trainer to balance the shift in the centre of gravity. Wind tunnel tests were carried out – including scale models of the Boeing X-32 and Lockheed Martin X-35 Joint Strike Fighter contenders – but nothing further came of the concept.

Crowsnest

The emergence of the CVF programme in the late 1990s (which led to the *Queen Elizabeth*-class) reopened the need for a modern AEW system. Complicating matters was that the CVF was still fluctuating between carriers with steam catapults and arrester gear for conventional aircraft or ski-jump equipped ships for STOVL (short take-off vertical landing) aircraft. The former would enable AEW aircraft like the E-2C Hawkeye to be procured (as France did in 2000 to equip its new carrier *Charles de Gaulle*), the latter would require helicopters or the Bell Boeing V-22 Osprey tiltrotor.

In 2001 Staff Requirement ST(S)6849 led to the Future Organic Airborne Early Warning System (FOAEW). The total number of airframes required was not officially released but was between six and 12 aircraft. BAE Systems and Thales Defence were awarded concept phase study contracts worth around £500,000 in total. AgustaWestland teamed with Thales to offer a conversion of the Merlin HM.1 using the Cerberus systems from the Sea King ASaC.7 with the Searchwater 2000 radar mounted on the tail ramp. Stub wings would be fitted to offload the rotor when cruising to improve endurance. Another Merlin option was the Marina Militare Italiana's EH-101A with the HEW-784 ventrally mounted radar replaced by Searchwater 2000.

Bell Boeing offered the CV-22 Osprey in partnership with BAE Systems, fitting the Cerberus system with a retractable Searchwater 2000 radome on the tail ramp. Another option was to use a triangular dorsal radome with fixed electronically scanned arrays, but potential aerodynamic issues saw this being replaced by a single SLAR antenna which could be mounted dorsally or ventrally (if retractable/foldable). There was even a FASS proposal with nose and tail radars.

Northrop Grumman and BAE Systems offered the E-2C Advanced Hawkeye. The Hawkeye had undergone ski jump take-offs in the 1980s so was suitable for a STOVL carrier if arrester gear was fitted. Thales went for a 'bargain basement' deal, looking at upgrading ex-USN Grumman S-2E and S-2G Tracker ASW aircraft – which had been languishing in storage in Arizona for decades – with turboprop engines, glass cockpits and Searchwater 2000. Similarly, the MOD asked their US counterparts for prices for retired Lockheed Martin S-3 Viking ASW aircraft. More exotic options considered included light aircraft, gyrodynes, unmanned aerial vehicles (UAVs) (which from 2004 included the JUEP, the Joint UAV Experimentation Programme), airships and tethered aerostats.

The Merlin with Cerberus was selected as the lowest risk option but in 2005 FOAEW was recast as Maritime Airborne Surveillance and Control (MASC) with an entry into service date of 2012. A £3.4 million 15-month study contract was awarded to Lockheed Martin UK in partnership with Thales UK and AgustaWestland. At this time Thales was still looking at other platforms for Cerberus, including the Eurocopter NH90 or V-22 Osprey, the latter with support from the USN, including a demonstration flight of a US Marine Corps MV-22B from HMS *Illustrious* in July 2007. EADS Defence & Security Systems UK received a similar study contract worth £250,000 in July 2006.

Budget issues delayed MASC and the in-service date slipped to 2015, then 2018 and finally 2022 and project study work slowed. Thales still preferred to re-use the Cerberus system but Lockheed Martin looked

In the new and out with the old. Given the limited resources available to the RN, retrofitting the Sea King ASaC.7's Cerberus equipment into the Merlin was the most cost-effective solution, even if it is not the most optimal. *MOD/ Open Government Licence*

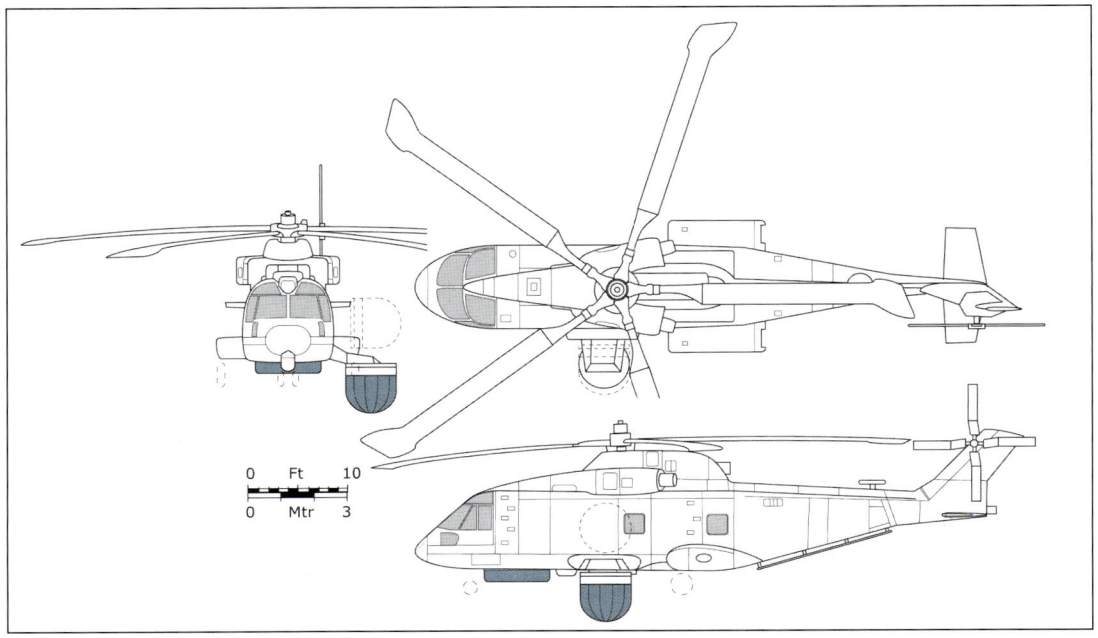

A general arrangement drawing of the Merlin HM.2 Crowsnest with the Searchwater radome in the deployed position. *Chris Gibson*

Crowsnest was not deployed until May 2021 with Carrier Strike Group 21 for HMS *Queen Elizabeth's* maiden deployment to the Pacific. Technical issues encountered during the deployment delayed the initial operating capability clearance until July 2023 and full operational capability was expected in 2025. *MoD/Open Government Licence*

Could an unmanned platform like the General Atomics Mojave – seen here under evaluation aboard HMS *Prince of Wales* – replace Crowsnest as the fleet's eye in the sky? Reliance on datalinks and radar processing on board the carriers is a technical risk, but there is no denying that UAVs offer an endurance unmatched by manned aircraft. *MoD/Open Government Licence*

at a derivative of the Northrop Grumman AN/APG-81 active electronically scanned array radar used on the F-35 Lightning II. In 2014 flight trials were carried out using Searchwater 2000 and an Elta radar, leading to the selection of Thales on 22 May 2015. The podded Searchwater system was named Crowsnest – a fitting name given the naval AEW role. Initial operating capability was significantly delayed and Crowsnest was not deployed until May 2021 with Carrier Strike Group 21 on its maiden deployment to the Pacific. Technical issues delayed the initial operating capability clearance until July 2023 and full operating capability was not expected until 2025. In September 2023, 820 NAS embarked two Crowsnest systems for its five Merlins aboard *Queen Elizabeth* for Operation FIREDRAKE in northern European waters. Current MOD plans foresee equipping just five Merlins with Crowsnest, with three aircraft being assigned to the high readiness aircraft carrier.

Unmanned AEW

Problems with Crowsnest have led the MOD to look for a replacement; in April 2025 the MOD issued a Request for Information notice seeking industry feedback on the potential solutions offered to replace Crowsnest. The requirements cover 24-hour surveillance of air and sea targets, including anti-ship missiles. The MOD had indicated that a contract may be awarded in 2027 for entry into service during 2030-2035. So what are the potential solutions on which the MOD wants feedback?

Project Vixen was revealed on 24 March 2021 to evaluate the use of fixed-wing maritime uncrewed air systems (MUAS) from the *Queen Elizabeth*-class for the surveillance, air-to-air refuelling, electronic warfare and strike roles. Project Vixen became linked with the RAF's existing Lightweight Affordable Novel Combat Aircraft (LANCA) programme, until the latter's cancellation on 24 June 2022. Project Vixen seems to be continuing; recent RN presentations have used the Boeing MQ-28 Ghost Bat UCAV with an arrester hook as a placeholder image. The plan is for Vixen to carry two 1,100lb (500kg) modular payloads. Vixen may well be an existing UCAV or a new design.

A potential platform is the General Atomics Mojave (developed from the MQ-1C Gray Eagle), which has been tested aboard HMS *Prince of Wales* on 15 November 2023. The Mojave has an endurance of over 25 hours and has been designed to carry electronic reconnaissance sensors as well as weapons.

Another contender is Projects Proteus, a rotary-wing MUAS being funded under the Spearhead programme for ASW capable of carrying two 1,102lb (500kg) modular payloads. It could be used to carry a radar to complement Crowsnest but would lack the altitude and endurance of a jet-powered UAV to become a permanent replacement. Leonardo has been awarded a 4-year £60mil contract to build a demonstrator that was scheduled to fly in 2025.

10 CVA generation

In 1960 the Admiralty was looking forward to obtaining a new class of modern fleet carriers equipped with advanced supersonic interceptors and strike aircraft using the latest aeronautical technologies such as variable-geometry (VG) wings, thrust vectoring for vertical take-off and landing (VTOL), guided weapon armaments and modern radars. Yet in early 1966 that dream was shattered, not only was the new carrier cancelled but the entire carrier fleet was destined for retirement by 1975 and Fleet Air Arm (FAA) personnel were looking ahead to a very uncertain future given that its fixed-wing aircraft were to be transferred to the RAF.

The cancellation of CVA-01 is one of the most contentious issues of British post-war defence

"We neither don't want to pay the penalty inherent in a V.T.O.L. capability we don't need nor do we want to be saddled with an expensive, single-seat (and single-engine) aircraft."

CAPTAIN DESMOND VINCENT-JONES, DIRECTOR OF NAVAL AIR DIVISION, MARCH 1962

With its RB.168-25R Mk.201 Speys at full power, McDonnell Douglas F-4K Phantom FG.1 XV567 is about to be thrust airborne by the combined power of the Speys and HMS *Eagle's* steam catapult during trials in 1969. *Eagle* lacked the extensive jet blast protection plates that *Ark Royal* received in her refit to operate Phantoms.
Gerald H. Balzer via Tony Buttler

WINGS OVER THE FLEET

This official painting of the final CVA-01 design illustrates its innovative features for aircraft operations: the 3° parallel deck; the two 250ft (76.2m)-long BS.6 steam catapults with retractable blast protection plates; deck edge lift aft of the island; two Deck Landing Projector Sights (to port amidships and immediately aft of the island); the four-wire Direct-Acting Arresting Gear (DAAG) using water retardation; and the open quarterdeck space beside the Sea Dart SAM launcher allowing jet engines to be tested on the hangar deck. *Crown Copyright*

planning. The Admiralty failed to justify the need for a carrier fleet at a time of national economic troubles and competing defence priorities within and beyond the RN. The Royal Air Force was pushing its 'Island Bases' strategy to maintain British geopolitical power 'East of Suez' in the Far East. Yet in 1971 the Far East Fleet itself was disbanded and the UK began a post-colonial retraction to the NATO sphere of operations in Europe and the North Atlantic.

The FAA did succeed in obtaining the outstanding McDonnell Douglas F-4 Phantom II from the United States of America in defiance of the Ministry of Defence (MOD) and the Ministry of Aviation (MoA), which was keen to meld together the disparate needs of the FAA and RAF into a common airframe, the Hawker Siddeley P.1154. This supersonic vertical/short take-off and landing (V/STOL) fighter would itself fall victim to defence cutbacks. The advanced strike aircraft to Operational Requirement OR.346 never materialised, which given that it was a mini-TSR.2 in terms of capability with additional technological risks was probably a good thing. The

The official painting of the starboard side shows the 'Alaskan Highway' along the outer edge of the island, with its multiple refuelling and rearming points to allow rapid turnaround of aircraft. The large dome atop the island is the Type 988 'Broomstick' 3-D radar, an Anglo-Dutch joint venture. The two smaller domes are the Type 909 fire-control radars for the GWS.30 Sea Dart system. The air group depicted is a mix of Phantom FG.1 and Buccaneer S.2. *Crown Copyright*

Airborne Early Warning (AEW) aircraft programme covered in Chapter 9 did not survive the CVA-01's cancellation. Although most of these projects never got off the ground, the research and development work undertaken was arguably the peak of the British aircraft industry's capabilities.

CVA-01

Design work on a new carrier to replace HMS *Victorious* began in November 1958. By 1963 plans foresaw *Centaur*, which was now obsolete as a light fleet carrier, becoming a third commando carrier with the new CVA-01 (the RN had adopted the US Navy's CVA designation to denote an Attack Aircraft Carrier) replacing both *Victorious* and *Ark Royal* in 1972 with CVA-02 and CVA-03 scheduled to replace *Hermes* and *Eagle* during the mid-1970s.

The key factors to any carrier design were cost – what the UK economy could afford – and size – the infrastructure constraints of dry docks etc., the same as those which had hindered the 1952 designs and the *Malta*-class as far back as 1944.

The design studies ranged from 42,000 to 68,000 tons at deep displacement, with 50,000 tons considered as the optimum size for capability and affordability. Design Study 53 was taken forwards as the baseline design with a displacement of 53,000 tons and an overall length of 870ft (265.2m). Two lifts were to be fitted, one being a deck-edge lift, and two steam catapults, one on the angled landing deck and one on the bows. Defensive armament included two GWS.30 Sea Dart surface-to-air missile (SAM) launchers on the quarterdeck and an Ikara anti-submarine missile launcher on the starboard side aft of the island.

The parallel deck was selected, the design growing to an overall length of 925ft (281.9m) and a flight deck beam of 189ft (57.6m). One Sea Dart SAM launcher and the Ikara were removed. The Sketch Design was approved by the Admiralty on 17 July 1963 and the public announcement of the go-ahead followed on 30 July. As the ship progressed to the Final Design of December 1965 a series of changes took place. The overall dimensions of the ship remained the same, but the deep load displacement grew to 54,500 tons.

Provision of de Havilland Sea Vixen FAW.2 fighters had been replaced by the larger and heavier F-4K Phantom FG.1; in fact, the ship could operate aircraft weighing up to 70,000lb (31,750kg) (twice that of the refitted *Eagle*). Two 250ft (76.2m)-long BS.6 steam catapults could accelerate a 60,000lb (27,200kg) aircraft up to 150kt or a 15,000lb (6,800kg) aircraft to 110kt without exceeding an acceleration of 5*g*. Both the Phantom FG.1 and Buccaneer S.2 could be launched without reheat. A novel Direct-Acting Arresting Gear (DAAG), which used pistons travelling through water pipes below the flight deck for the retardation effect, could arrest a 40,000lb (18,145kg) aircraft at 125kt or a 15,000lb aircraft at 100kt without exceeding a

"It is very questionable whether we should 'rock the boat' while the Carrier replacement programme is in the balance."

VICE ADMIRAL SIR FRANK HOPKINS, DEPUTY CHIEF OF NAVAL STAFF, 7 MAY 1963

deceleration of 5*g*. Both features gave ample future growth potential. A Deck Landing Projector Sight was fitted for landing assistance and night operations would be aided by a new system of 'Bedford Lighting Pattern' red floodlighting.

The aircraft capacity was sufficient for 12 Phantoms, 24 Buccaneers, four Airborne Early Warning aircraft, five Wessex HAS.3 anti-submarine warfare (ASW) helicopters and another pair of Wessex for search and rescue 'plane guard' duty. Enough ammunition, AVCAT and spares were carried for three days of intensive operations without resupply (four replenishment at sea stations were provided for easy resupply of stores and fuel.)

Other advanced features included: the use of nuclear submarine grade high-strength QT35 steel in the flight and hangar decks; high-pressure oil-fired steam boilers; a new 16.2mW electrical power supply system with turbo-generators and substations throughout the ship (a first for a warship of any navy, in contrast the refitted *Eagle* had a generation capacity of 8.25mW); electro-hydraulic scissors-type lifts; Agouti noise suppression for the propellers and an underwater protection system of bulkheads and voids to withstand a 1,800lb (816kg) torpedo warhead.

In terms of weapons and systems the CVA-01 would have a GWS.30 Sea Dart system with 38 missiles; digital Action Data Automation (ADA) data handling system with three Ferranti F1600-series computers, which could react to threats in 11 seconds and handle 12 simultaneous air interceptions; and the Anglo-Dutch Type 988 'Broomstick' 3-D search radar with automatic height-finding and 208nm (386km) range.

An additional Commando role requirement was added to carry 1,125 troops plus vehicles and equipment as well as 14 Westland Whirlwind or Wessex tactical transport helicopters for the cost of only four of her normal fixed-wing aircraft. Provision to carry aircraft like the USN's Grumman F-111B carrier-borne interceptor version of the General Dynamics F-111A fighter-bomber (the TFX programme). This required the lifts to be widened to 35ft (10.7m) at the cost of 15 tons of additional weight, the loss of accommodation for 20 sailors and costing an additional £45,000 (this was done for future cross-decking with USN squadrons, although the overweight F-111B was later cancelled and replaced by what became the Grumman F-14A Tomcat).

There was no doubt that CVA-01 was a modern, in some respects too novel, aircraft carrier and did everything that the RN wanted it to, within the constraints of physical size and cost. CVA-01 would be expensive, costing £70 million (excluding research and development costs.) It was planned to lay down

An artist's impression of the impressive looking Vickers ER.206/2 from the brochure. The square hatch just aft of the windscreen is the observer's cockpit entry/ejection seat hatch. The stacked pairs of Rolls-Royce RB.153 turbojets were fed by a common dorsal intake. *Tony Buttler Collection*

the keel in September 1967 with the hull launched two years later with acceptance following builder's trials by December 1971 and full operational status attained by June 1973. The name *Queen Elizabeth* was reserved, pending Royal assent. Final Board approval was received on 27 January 1966 and the formal invites to tender were ready to be sent out to the shipbuilders when the Cabinet sat on 14 February to approve the Defence Review.

Strike fighter

The Admiralty had to decide how many aircraft and what new types it would need for the 1960s. In 1957 the Cabinet Defence Committee had decided under the '88 Plan' that the RN should have three operational carriers, one based at Singapore with a balanced air group of strike, fighter and ASW aircraft, while the remaining pair would be predominantly equipped for ASW duty in the eastern Atlantic and European waters. In December 1959 approval was given for an embarked force of 38 fighters to give two carriers a full fighter complement, with the third having a self-defence capability (no numerical target was agreed for strike aircraft.) The report *Study of Military Strategy for Circumstances Short of Global War* had recommended having two carriers East of Suez, but the Cabinet rejected this. A similar 1960 study for an East of Suez Tactical Air Unit called for 32 fighters and 64 strike aircraft plus eight AEW aircraft, which would require two or three carriers. In May 1961 the Admiralty proposed providing all three carriers with a balanced air group to improve the ability to send a second carrier eastwards if circumstances required. This would reduce the number of frontline carrier-based ASW helicopters from 44 to 24 and AEW aircraft from 14 to 12 while providing a total of 86 fighter and strike aircraft. The Chiefs of Staff agreed but Harold Watkinson, the Minister of Defence, disagreed given the cost implications and instead proposed altering the limit to 38 fighters and 41 strike aircraft to give 79 aircraft, saving £18 million up to 1970. The Defence Committee approved the change, but in reality the RN's plans showed that attaining this combined force of Sea Vixens and Buccaneers would not be achieved before late 1965.

The Naval Aircraft Research Committee reported in January 1959 on its thoughts for fighter requirements for 1965–70. It postulated a long endurance subsonic fighter with a VG wing to give it a supersonic dash capability. It would be armed with air-to-air missiles (AAMs) capable of four-hour patrols to deal with enemy reconnaissance aircraft and bombers at least 87nm (160km) away from the fleet and would also be suitable for adaptation to the strike role. The all-up weight (AUW) limit was to be 48,000lb (21,770kg) with a landing speed of 130kt or less.

A draft Naval Staff Target was circulated on 17 March 1959 for a strike fighter to enter service in 1970. Funding this project alone would be impossible and talks with the Air Staff the following month led to the joint RN and RAF Operational Requirement OR.346. It would predominantly be a strike aircraft with an interceptor role, being able to switch between roles within 12–24 hours. The strike role would require a forward-looking terrain avoidance radar (FLR) plus a sideways-looking airborne radar (SLAR) for navigation and reconnaissance, while the interceptor would need an Aerial Interception (AI) radar. The naval version would have an AUW of 50,000lb (22,680kg), carrying 6,000lb (2,270kg) of bombs or missiles (or a single tactical nuclear bomb) over a radius of action of 1,000nm (1,852km), with the last 200nm (370km) to the target being a low-altitude penetration. In the interceptor role it would have four hours endurance and carry four AAMs to deal with a Mach 2.0 target at 80,000ft (24,385m). The maximum speed was to be Mach 2.5 while the approach and landing speed was to be no greater than 80kt. The internal weapon bay was to be 4ft (1.22m) high.

Admiralty Requirement GDA.103 and Air Staff Target AST.11983 were also issued around this time for a new long-range radar-homing AAM. Engineer John Forbat at Vickers designed a semi-active homing AAM, weighing 750lb (340kg) with a length of 12ft (3.66m). It had a flattened body with two low aspect ratio wings with twist-and-steer controls (the fins folded for internal stowage.) It was powered by a solid boost/sustainer rocket motor for a range of 30.4nm (55.5km).

de Havilland Propellers (soon to become Hawker Siddeley Dynamics) began its 'Family' studies, a series of missiles around 15ft (4.5m) long, with fuselage diameters of 12–15in (30–37.6cm), 4ft (1.22m) span wings (either *Red Top*-type fins or deltas) for internal stowage and weights varying between 500–1,500lb (227–680kg). They all had four solid rocket boosters and a DH Spartan sustainer rocket for a speed of Mach 4.

Other AAMs looked at included CW *Red Top* (also known as *Blue Dolphin* and 'Radar Red Top' – in abeyance since 1959 on economy grounds) using continuous wave homing, the semi-active Raytheon AAM-N-6 Sparrow III, Matra R.530, HM.45 (a Swiss licence-built Hughes GAR-11 Falcon) and an air-launched version of the BAC CF.299 (Sea Dart.) The requirements of OR.346 were similar to the RAF's

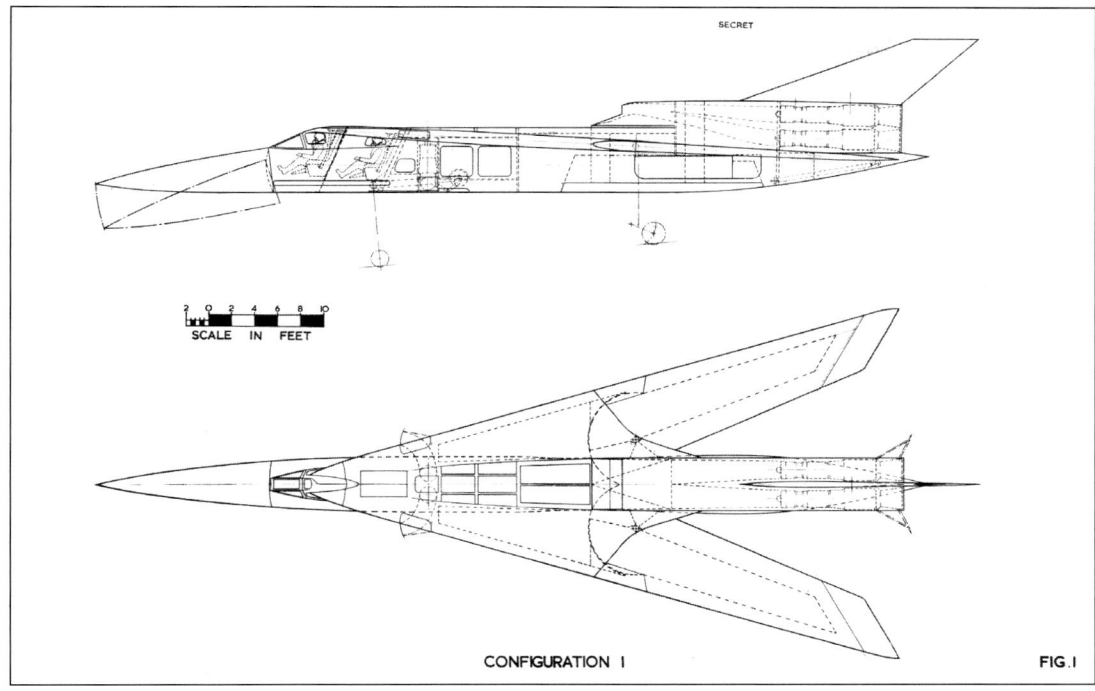

This technical drawing of the Vickers ER.206/2 shows the layout of the stacked pairs of Rolls-Royce RB.153 turbojets in the rear fuselage. Two lift engines are behind the cockpit with flip-out intakes in the wing root leading edges. The large wing root blocks any view upwards and rearwards for the pilot and observer. *Tony Buttler Collection*

GOR.339 Canberra replacement (later to become TSR.2) but with the interceptor and low-speed requirements adding another layer of technical risk and pushing the bounds of aeronautical development at that time. Specification ER.206 was issued in May 1959 to cover research and development, with Vickers Aircraft receiving the first study contract.

Vickers' initial thoughts in June 1959 were essentially a scaled down Type 571 (Vickers' TSR.2 proposal) with a delta wing as the Type 577. Scheme A had a high-mounted wing and a low-mounted tailplane. It was powered by two 7,250lbf (32.2kN) BE.61 ducted fan engines (an early form of turbofan) and the internal fuel load was 1,980gal (9,000L), plus two underwing 400gal (1,820L) drop tanks. The take-off weight was 48,000lb (21,775kg). Three further versions were drawn up in January 1960 with differing wing sizes.

Vickers eventually submitted four proposals under the designation Type 581. The ER.206/1 based on the Type 571 and Vickers estimated that it could be ready to enter service in 1966. Scheme A had a high-mounted wing of 41ft (12.5m) span with wing tip fuel tanks, while Scheme B had longer 43ft 8in (13.3m) span wings, again with tip tanks. Scheme C

An impression of the ER.206/2 coming into land on a carrier deck. The wing is at 25%° sweep with the three-piece blown flaps fully deflected, the wing tip elevons also being drooped. The airbrakes at the rear are open and the arrester hook is lowered. The two lift engines behind the cockpit are operating to counteract the nose-down pitching moment created by the flaps. The radar nose cone has been lowered to improve the pilot's forward view. *Tony Buttler Collection*

WINGS OVER THE FLEET

Vickers proposals to Operational Requirement OR.246 & Specification ER.206

	Type 577 Scheme A	Type 577 Scheme B	Type 577 Scheme C	Type 577 Scheme D	Type 581 ER.206/1 Scheme A	Type 581 ER.206/1 Scheme B
Span	41ft 0in (12.50m); 29ft 0in (8.84m) folded	43ft 6in (13.26m) with tip tanks; 29ft 0in (8.84m) folded	?; 29ft 0in (8.84m) folded	44ft 0in (13.41m) with tip tanks; 29ft 0in (8.84m) folded	41ft 0in (12.50m) with tip tanks	43ft 8in (13.31m) with tip tanks
Length	?	66ft 7in (20.29m)	66ft 7in (20.29m)	66ft 7in (20.29m)	66ft 7in (20.29m)	66ft 7in (20.29m)
Wing area	312ft² (29.0m²)	419ft² (39.0m²)	?	399ft² (37.10m²)	284ft² (36.4m²)	400ft² (37.20m²)
t/c ratio	?	?	?	?	5%	5%
All-up weight	48,000lb (21,775kg) strike and interceptor	48,000lb (21,775kg) strike and interceptor	?	47,860lb (21,710kg) interceptor	48,800lb (22,135kg) strike; 48,000lb (21,775kg) interceptor	48,800lb (22,135kg) strike; 48,000lb (21,775kg) interceptor
Powerplant	2x BE.61, 7,250lbf (32.2kN)	2x BE.61, 7,250lbf (32.2kN)	2x BE.61, 7,250lbf (32.2kN)	2x BE.61, 7,250lbf (32.2kN)	2x RB.142-4, 8,000lbf (35.6kN) dry, 13,000lbf (57.8kN) reheat	2x RB.142-4, 8,000lbf (35.6kN) dry, 13,000lbf (57.8kN) reheat
Max speed	?	?	?	?	Mach 2.0+ at altitude	Mach 2.0+ at altitude
Service ceiling	?	?	?	?	?	?
Radius of action	?	?	?	?	?	?
Armament	Strike: 1x Red Beard, bombs, RPs, AGM-12 Bullpup; interceptor: 2x AAMs	Strike: 1x Red Beard, bombs, RPs, AGM-12 Bullpup; interceptor: 2x AAMs	Strike: 1x Red Beard, bombs, RPs, AGM-12 Bullpup; interceptor: 2x AAMs	Strike: 1x Red Beard, bombs, RPs, AGM-12 Bullpup; interceptor: 2x AAMs	Strike: 1x Red Beard, 6x 1,000lb (454kg) bombs, 2x Bullpup internal, bombs & RPs external; interceptor: 2x 750lb (340kg) AAMs internal	Strike: 1x Red Beard, 6x 1,000lb (454kg) bombs, 2x Bullpup internal, bombs & RPs external; interceptor: 2x 750lb (340kg) AAMs internal

used a delta wing for additional area (being very similar to the Type 577). All three designs had all-moving tail surfaces (the delta using the tailplanes for differential roll control) and identical fuselages which contained an avionics bay behind the tandem cockpit, weapon bay for bombs or two AAMs and two engines. The selected engine was the Rolls-Royce RB.142/4 rated at 8,000lbf (35.6kN) dry and 13,000lbf (57.8kN) reheated. An alternative was two Bristol Siddeley BE.61 low-bypass turbojets or four Rolls-Royce/MAN RB.153 turbojets. The compressors were tapped for blowing over the leading edge and trailing edge flaps to reduce the approach and landing speeds. The avionics included an FLR and SLAR for the strike role, or a 36in (91cm) diameter AI radar. The estimated AUW was 48,000lb (22,135kg).

Barnes Wallis had been working on VG wings at Weybridge since the late 1940s, culminating in the graceful Swallow concept as well as collaboration with NASA during 1959 with Mutual Weapons Development Program funding. The spherical pivot mechanism was an important novel feature. The ER.206/2 used a derivative of Wallis' Swallow wing attached to a fuselage with a 'drooping' nose to

	Type 581 ER.206/1 Scheme C	Type 581 ER.206/2	Type 581 ER.206/3	Type 581 ER.206/4 (for RAF)	Type 582 (twin fuselage)	Type 582 (single fuselage)
	28ft 3in (8.61m)	57ft 6in (17.53m) extended; 31ft 0in (9.45m) swept	58ft 0in (17.68m) extended; 31ft 0in (9.45m) swept	59ft 10in (18.24m) extended; 32ft 6in (9.94m) swept	40ft 0in (12.19m); 45ft 0in (13.72m) with AAMs; 29ft 0in (8.84m) folded	40ft 0in (12.19m); 45ft 0in (13.72m) with AAMs
	66ft 7in (20.29m)	76ft 4in (23.27m)	76ft 1in (21.79m)	66ft 1in (20.14m)	65ft 4in (19.91m); 52ft 0in (15.84m) folded	65ft 8in (20.02m); 52ft 0in (15.84m) folded
	410ft² (38.10m²)	554ft² (51.50m²) extended; 552ft² (51.40m²) swept	528ft² (49.10m²) extended; 526ft² (49.0m²) swept	430ft² (40.0m²) extended; 600ft² (55.80m²) swept	405ft² (37.70m²)	408ft² (37.90m²)
	3.6%	11.5% extended, 4.19% swept	4.1% swept	11.5% extended, 4.1% swept	12.6% centre section	12.6% centre section
	48,800lb (22,135kg) strike; 48,000lb (21,775kg) interceptor	50,000lb (22,680kg) strike; 48,000lb (21,775kg) interceptor	45,114lb (20,464kg) strike with 4x bombs; 44,574lb (20,219kg) interceptor	47,850lb (21,705kg)	46,230lb (20,970kg) strike	46,087lb (20,905kg)
	2x RB.142-4, 8,000lbf (35.6kN) dry, 13,000lbf (57.8kN) reheat	4x RB.153; & 2x lift engines	2x RB.163 (0.7 scale), 7,740lbf (34.4kN) dry, 13,480lbf (59.9kN) reheat	2x RB.165, 8,850lbf (39.3kN) dry, 15,400lbf (68.4kN) reheat	8x RB.163 (scaled), 1,800lbf (8.0kN) dry	8x RB.163 (scaled), 1,800lbf (8.0kN) dry
	Mach 2.0+ at altitude	Mach 3.0 between 43,000-70,000ft (13,105-21,335m)	Mach 2.5 between 60,000-75,000ft (18,290-22,860m)	Mach 2.5 at altitude	Mach 2.0 at altitude, strike; Mach 2.5 at altitude, interceptor	Mach 2.0 at altitude
	?	70,000ft (21,335m)	?	?	60,000-65,000ft (18,290-19,810m)	60,000-65,000ft (18,290-19,810m)
	?	?	1,000nm (1,850km) with 4,000lb (1,814kg) bombload	?	1,200nm (2,225km) with 1x nuclear bomb	?
	Strike: 1x Red Beard, 6x 1,000lb (454kg) bombs, 2x Bullpup internal, bombs & RPs external; interceptor: 2x 750lb (340kg) AAMs internal	Strike: 1x Red Beard, 6x 1,000lb (454kg) bombs, 3x Bullpup, RP packs internal; interceptor: 3x 600lb (272kg) AAMs internal	Strike: 1x 2,000lb (907kg) nuclear bomb, 6x 1,000lb (454kg) bombs, 3x Bullpup internal; interceptor: 4x AAMs internal	Strike: 1x 2,000lb (907kg) nuclear bomb, 6x 1,000lb (454kg) bombs, 3x Bullpup internal; interceptor: 4x AAMs internal	Strike: 1x 2,000lb (907kg) nuclear bomb, 6x 1,000lb (454kg) bombs, 4x Bullpup; interceptor: 4x AAMs	Strike: 1x 2,000lb (907kg) nuclear bomb, 6x 1,000lb (454kg) bombs, 4x Bullpup; interceptor: 4x AAMs

improve visibility on landing from the tandem cockpit. The 4ft (1.22m) high weapon bay could accommodate six 1,000lb (454kg) bombs, three AGM-12 Bullpup air-to-surface missiles (ASMs) or four of John Forbat's GDA.103 AAMs.

The aircraft was powered by four RB.153 engines mounted in two stacked pairs in a large nacelle above the rear fuselage (an alternative design had them side by side in the rear fuselage fed by lateral underwing variable-ramp intakes). A single tail fin was fitted and the wing had wing tip elevons. The wing could be swept from 25° to 75° (the fixed forewing also had 75° leading edge sweep). Blown flaps were provided, the nose-down moment they created would be offset by two small Rolls-Royce lift engines mounted side by side behind the cockpit and fed via retractable wing root leading edge intakes (their control was automatic based on the elevons' position.) The estimated performance was impressive, attaining Mach 3.0 above 43,000ft (13,105m), the AUW being 50,000lb in the strike role and 48,000lb as an interceptor.

An extended submission deadline of March 1960 led to two further refined designs. The ER.206/3

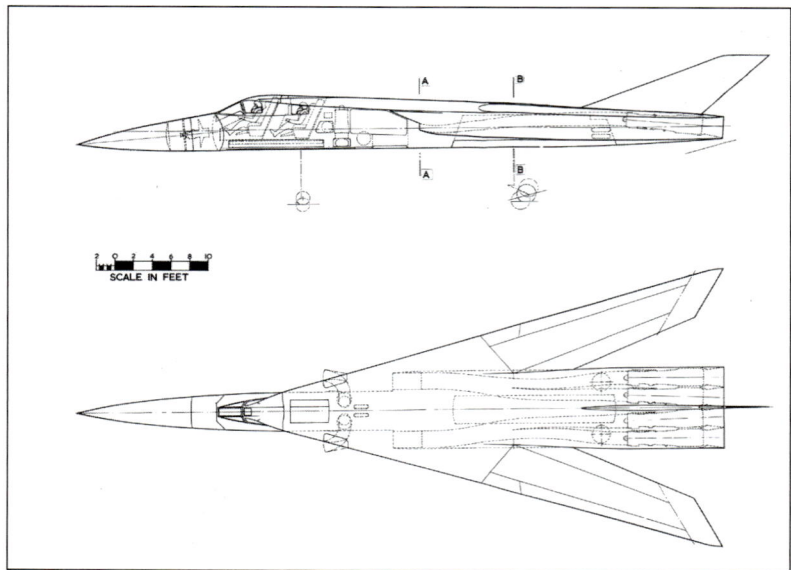

The alternative configuration for Vickers' ER.206/2 had the four Rolls-Royce RB.153 turbojets side-by-side in the rear fuselage, fed by underwing variable-ramp intakes. *Tony Buttler Collection*

A Vickers impression of the ER.206/2 with the underwing intakes. *Tony Buttler Collection*

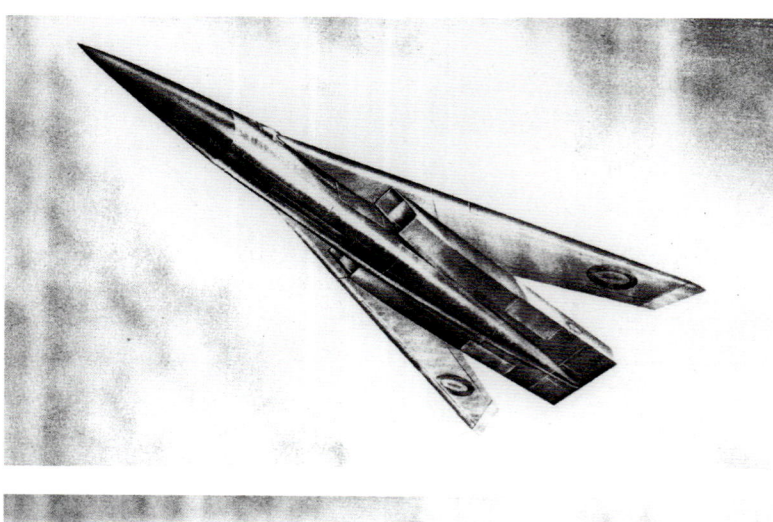

incorporated the findings from NASA's Langley Field wind tunnel tests. The tailplane was deleted to save weight and increase the lift/drag ratio to save fuel. It was also decided to make the previously fixed forewing folding or retractable to remove a tendency to pitch up at low speeds as wing sweep was increased, by removing the forewing as a producer of lift. The weapon bay could carry six 1,000lb bombs or three Bullpups or four AAMs. Two scaled thrust RB.163s rated at 7,740lb (34.4kN) dry or 13,480lbf (59.9kN) reheated would provide sufficient power for Mach 2.5 above 60,000ft (18,90m).

ER.206/4 was a de-navalised version for the RAF able to operate from semi-prepared airstrips with low-pressure tyres and it could carry the full 6,000lb weapons load with additional fuel due to the weight saved by removing the naval features. The engines were two RB.165 rated at 8,850lb (39.3kN) dry or 15,400lbf (68.4kN) reheated.

Vickers offered another futuristic design in March 1960 to replace the earlier ER.206/1 – the twin-fuselage Type 582. The fuselages were joined by a high tailplane and the wing centre section formed an 'integrated power section' containing eight scaled-thrust 1,800lbf (8.0kN) Rolls-Royce RB.163, the exhaust forming a jet flap to provide short take-off and landing (STOL) performance via a downwards deflecting trailing edge flap. This allowed a take-off speed of 100kt and an approach speed of 106kt. Leading and trailing edge flap blowing was provided for the outer wings (which folded downwards for carrier stowage); the all-moving tailplane also had a blown flap for use at low speed. The pilot and observer sat in a tandem cockpit ahead of the weapon bay in the port fuselage, the starboard fuselage being devoted to radar, avionics and fuel (two 200gal (909L) wing tip tanks were also fitted.) At 40,000lb (18,145kg) the aircraft could attain 60,000ft (18,290m) at Mach 2.5 or 65,000ft (19,810m) at 31,000lb (14,060kg). An AEW variant was also drawn up (see Chapter 9.)

A single-fuselage version with the engines divided into two inner wing sections with large nacelles outboard for fuel and the undercarriage was studied (largely for the RAF), but its increased drag was a drawback.

The MoA assessed the Vickers proposals in June. The VG wing was deemed to have substantial

The Vickers Type 581 ER.206/3 had a refined VG wing design with retractable wing roots that folded flat against the intake ducting to reduce the inherent pitch-up instability that the VG wing created at low speeds. In this view can just be seen the open lift jet intake above the main intakes and the exhausts immediately aft of the nosewheel. The lift jets were also a remedy, in this case against the pitch-down moment created by the wing flaps in the absence of a tailplane. The wing has its leading edge slats and trailing edge flaps deployed and the airbrakes aft are open. *Tony Buttler Collection*

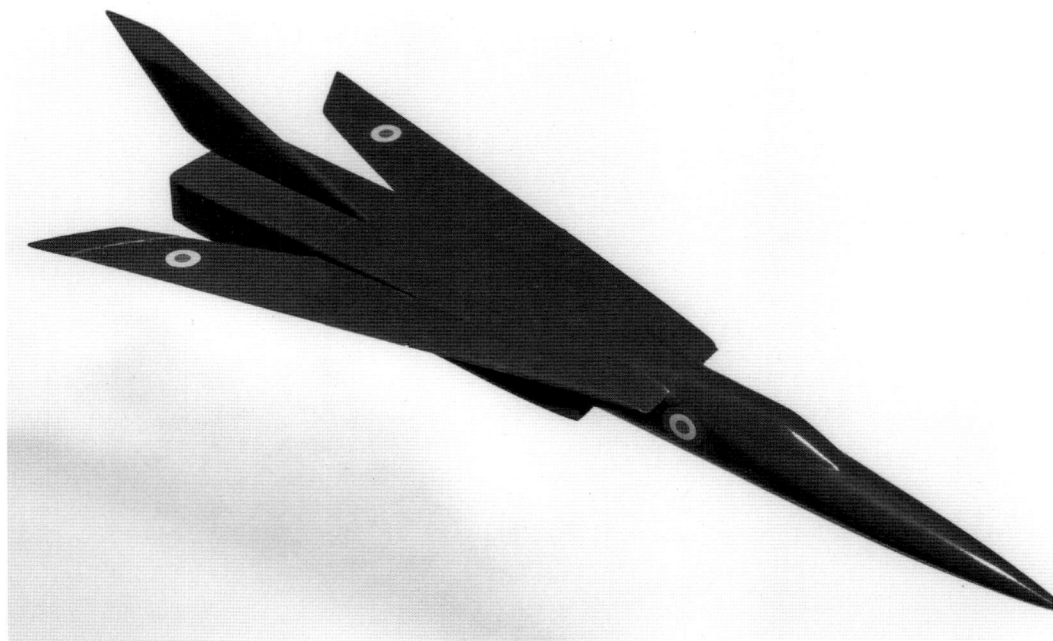

A model of the Type 581 with the wings at minimum and maximum sweep. Note that this version of ER.206/3 has fixed wing root sections. *Tony Buttler Collection*

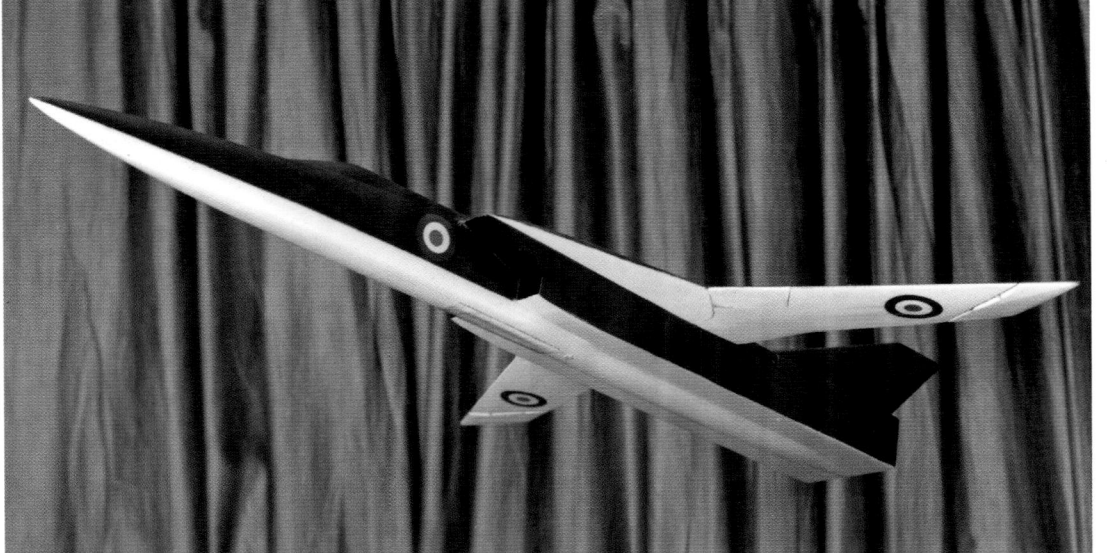

A ventral view of the showing the ramp intakes and boxy engine nacelle fairings. *Tony Buttler Collection*

RIGHT This original Vickers Type 582 model has been beautifully restored. The twin-fuselage design with its integrated power wing with the eight Rolls-Royce engines in the centre wing structure was certainly novel. *Sir George Cox via Tony Buttler*

TOP RIGHT The starboard fuselage contained the large AI radar. The substantial AAMs on the wing tip were notional representations of the Vickers semi-active AAM being developed to meet Requirement GDA.103 alongside OR.346. *Sir George Cox via Tony Buttler*

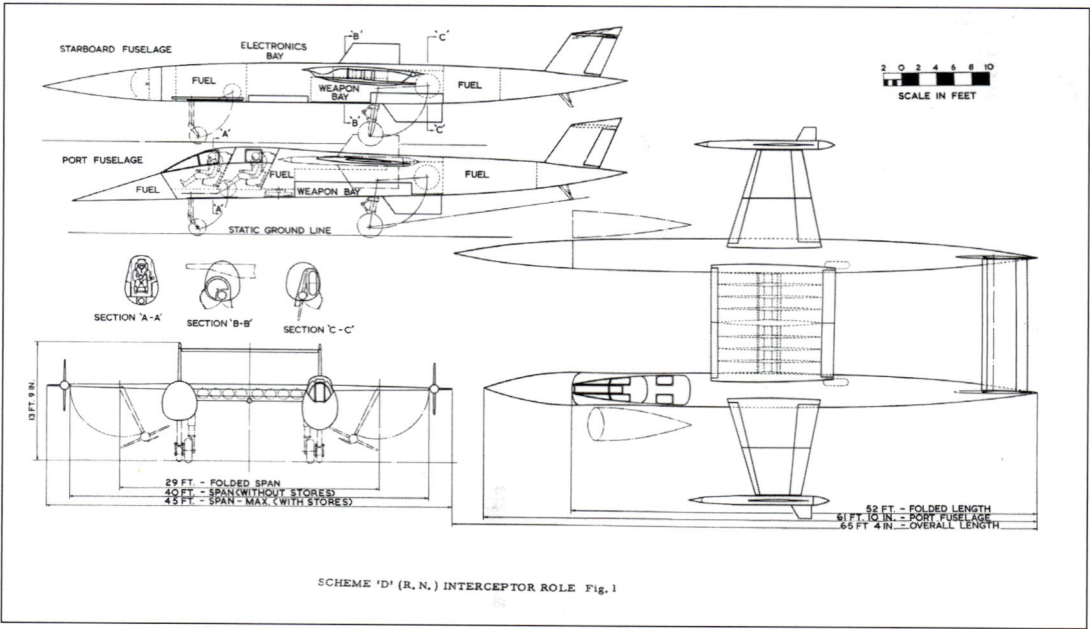

CENTRE This general arrangement drawing of the Type 582 reveals the internal layout. The folding nose cone of the port fuselage holds a fuel tank, the radar being to starboard. Note the unusual downwards folding outer wings. *Tony Buttler Collection*

The alternative single fuselage Type 582 configuration with the large fuel/undercarriage nacelles. *Tony Buttler Collection*

advantages over a fixed wing, although the Type 582 did offer a larger diameter radar with a lighter structure to be a viable contender. But development of the VG wing was seen as the most important feature. Further MoA funded research by Vickers began in August and in October the Air Staff began talks with the MoA on future exploitation of the technology. The MoA and the Aeronautical Research Council pressed for a research aircraft to be built. On 1 April 1962 a design study contract was issued for the Type 589, with the desire to build two aircraft. By April 1964 the estimated £10–20 million cost and ongoing technical issues regarding the structure and aerodynamics saw the Type 589 cancelled.

The former English Electric team at Warton also seems to have made some studies of a joint RAF/RN strike fighter of 40,000lb AUW in January 1961. P.37 Preliminary Scheme 3 had a mid-mounted 500ft² (46.5m²) delta wing; no tail surfaces were provided. The main undercarriage had tandem wheels. The engines were four Orpheus; two 5,610lbf (24.9kN) thrust engines mounted each side of the weapon bay (each with two rotating nozzles) and two 7,770lbf (34.5kN) engines in wing tip pods – not the most suitable layout for a naval aircraft. Preliminary Scheme 5 had a 31ft 3½in (31.29m) span double delta wing and two scaled Olympus 591/2 engines, again with two rotating nozzles for each engine. The intakes were extended to just aft of the radome (as were the wing roots.)

Hawker Siddeley strike fighters

The Admiralty briefed the Hawker Siddeley Group about OR.346 on 13 December 1960. A subsequent internal meeting chaired by Stuart Davies in February 1961 confirmed that the Group's combined OR.346 effort should come from de Havilland's team at Hatfield under William 'Bill' Tamblin, although the Blackburn team at Brough and the Hawker designers at Kingston would also offer alternatives.

The DH.127 (later renumbered DH.128) was a tailless delta wing design. It was designed to operate from the *Eagle*-class carriers using deflected thrust and lift engines for a STOL capability. The delta wing gave excellent strength and was fitted with elevons and flaps and lacked any high-lift devices. The outer wing sections folded upwards. Two rotating cascades on the sides of the aft fuselage for the RB.156-1R turbofans (in horizontal flight these were sealed by an aerodynamic fairing) and the two RB.162 lift engines (in the nose ahead of the cockpit) enabled an approach speed of 85kt. Using reheat a rolling take-off at 40,000lb (18,145kg) weight would be possible with 31kt wind over the deck.

A total internal fuel capacity of 2,390gal (10,870L) in wing, fuselage and tail fin tanks provided a radius of action of 1,390nm (2,575km) with a nuclear weapon or 900nm (1,670km) with an 8,000lb (3,630kg) bombload. The 'cab rank' close air support sortie had a 200nm (370km) radius with 2.7hr loiter time. The Combat Air Patrol (CAP) endurance at maximum weight was four hours. The internal fuel could be augmented by two 250gal (1,137L) drop tanks or a 300gal (1,365L) or 1,050gal (4,775L) auxiliary tank in the weapon bay.

The DH.127 as an interceptor could engage a Mach 3.0 target flying at 80,000ft (24,385m) some 100nm (185km) away from the carrier. A shallow conformal bay carried the weapons, plus two underwing hardpoints. The ASM options included DH's RG.10 TV-guided project, a 1,000lb (454kg), 12ft (3.66m)-long missile with a range of 9nm (16.7km). Four AAMs could be carried ventrally, as could a reconnaissance pack.

Blackburn was the naval specialist within Hawker Siddeley and it was no surprise that they were keen to offer something to OR.346. The minimal change

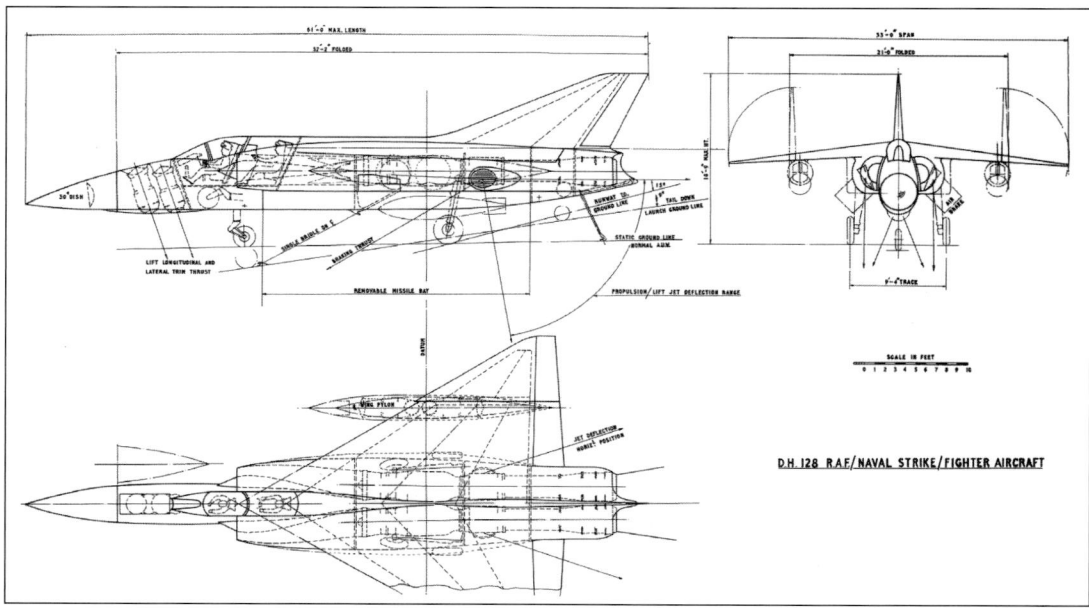

The de Havilland DH.128 was essentially identical to the DH.127 tailless delta-winged aircraft. The main engines were a pair of Rolls-Royce RB.156-1Rs with thrust diverters assisted by two lifting RB.162s in the nose. Note the semi-recessed *Red Beard* tactical nuclear bomb. *Author's Collection*

WINGS OVER THE FLEET

An original display model of the DH.127 survives in the Sir George Cox collection. This attractive tailless delta could easily be mistaken for a Dassault product at first glance. *Sir George Cox via Tony Buttler*

The DH.127's delta wing was simple in design and construction, it had no high lift devices, just trailing edge elevons and flaps. The entire inner wing section was devoted to integral fuel tanks. *Sir George Cox via Tony Buttler*

Hawker Siddeley Group proposals to OR.346 and Specification ER.206

	de Havilland DH.127/DH.128	Blackburn B.123 (July 1961)	Blackburn B.123 (Sept 1961)	HSG Brough P.135	Hawker P.1152
Span	33ft 0in (10.06m)	37ft 0in (11.28m); 20ft 0in (6.09m) folded	40ft 0in (12.19m); 20ft 0in (6.09m) folded	60ft 0in (18.29m) extended; 30ft 0in (9.14m) swept	40ft 0in (12.19m) RN; 45ft 0in (13.72m) RAF
Length	60ft 0in (18.29m); 51ft 2in (15.59m) folded	81ft 0in (24.69m)	Naval: 68ft 9in (20.95m); 60ft 0in (18.28m) folded	59ft 0in (17.98m)	68ft 6in (20.88m)
Wing area	560ft² (52.1m²)	550ft² (51.2m²)	600ft² (55.8m²)	?	?
t/c ratio	5%	5%	5%	?	?
All-up weight	49,100lb (22,270kg); 56,000lb (25,400kg) overload	56,500lb (25,630kg) max deck weight with 1x 2,000lb (907kg) nuclear bomb	61,380lb (27,840kg)	60,000lb (27,215kg) max take-off weight	50,000lb (22,680kg)
Powerplant	2x RB.156-1R, 11,065lbf (49.2kN) dry, 18,650lbf (82.9kN) reheat; & 2x RB.162 lift engines, 4,400lbf (19.6kN)	2x reheated RB.168 Spey; & 2x RB.162 lift engines, 5,000lbf (22.2kN)	2x RB.168-1R Spey, 15,000lbf (66.7kN) dry, 25,500lbf (113.3kN) reheat; & 2x RB.162 lift engines, 5,000lbf (22.2kN)	2x reheated RB.168 Spey; & 8x lift engines	2x RB.177 lift/cruise engine; & 4x RB.162 lift engines
Max speed	Mach 2.5 at altitude	Mach 2.0+ at altitude, clean	Mach 1.4 at SL, clean; Mach 2.5+ at 36,000ft (10,975m)	Mach 2.0+ at altitude	Mach 2.0 at altitude
Service ceiling	?	?	54,000ft (16,460m) with reheat	?	?
Radius of action	1,390nm (2,575km) with nuclear bomb; 900nm (1,670km) with 8,000lb (3,630kg) bombload	1,000nm (1,855km) with 4,000lb (1,814kg) bombload	1,000nm (1,855km) with 4,000lb (1,814kg) bombload	?	?
Armament	Strike: 1x 2,000lb (907kg) nuclear bomb, 8x 1,000lb (454kg) bombs, 4x AGM-12 Bullpup or RG.10; interceptor: 4x Red Top AAMs	Strike: 1x 2,000lb (907kg) nuclear bomb, 6x 1,000lb (454kg) bombs, AGM-12 Bullpup; interceptor: AAMs	Strike: 1x 2,000lb (907kg) nuclear bomb, 6x 1,000lb (454kg) bombs, 5x Bullpup or 3x RG.10; interceptor: 3x AAMs	Strike: 1x 2,000lb (907kg) nuclear bomb, bombs or ASMs; interceptor: AAMs	Strike: 1x 2,000lb (907kg) nuclear bomb, 6x 1,000lb (454kg) bombs; interceptor: AAMs

Blackburn offered a modified Buccaneer S.2 in 1958 as a Combat Air Patrol Fighter armed with four Firestreak AAMs. Two of the missiles were mounted on lower fuselage pylons to reduce drag. Ferranti AI.23 AIRPASS radar would be fitted. *Brough Heritage*

B.112 development of the Buccaneer S.2 with four *Red Tops* (a pair underwing and a pair carried on the lower forward fuselage to reduce transonic drag) and the high-altitude B.117 with an extended 49ft 6in (15.1m) wingspan and four underwing *Red Tops* were initial ideas in 1960.

The B.123 of July 1961 had a delta wing with longitudinal stability aided by diverting some of the thrust from the two reheated Rolls-Royce RB.168 Speys downwards and two lift jets mounted beneath the cockpit also aided the low approach speed. A T-tail was fitted, the designers favouring a tailplane to improve the longitudinal response and pitch damping in low-altitude terrain-following flight. Like the Buccaneer, solid billets would be used for the wing skins for a long fatigue life. The outboard sections of the wing folded, the inboard sections featuring large internal fuel tanks. A 36in (91cm) diameter radar antenna was mounted in the nose. A ventral pannier could carry a single nuclear weapon, while a longer pannier would hold eleven 1,000lb (454kg) bombs with four more mounted in tandem on two underwing hardpoints. The estimated maximum deck weight was 56,500lb (25,630kg). An alternative low-mounted tailplane version and a smaller 40,000lb (18,145kg) aircraft with a single Rolls-Royce RB.141 Medway turbofan were also studied.

In September a refined design was offered, which settled on the low-mounted tailplane layout. The RB.168-1R Speys were given two stages of reheat: immediately after the turbine section with thrust diverters/rotating cascades to enable 18,000lbf (80.0kN) thrust to be deflected downwards; in the tail pipes with variable area exhaust nozzles, providing 25,000lbf (133.3kN). The two lift engines were the 5,000lbf (22.2kN) RB.162. The armament was carried externally with semi-conformal ventral hardpoints with optional fairings plus two underwing hardpoints for the 6,000lb bombload, up to five Bullpups or three large AAMs or RG.10 ASMs. The estimated maximum deck weight was 61,380lb (27,842kg). Maximum speed was Mach 1.4 at sea level or Mach 2.5 at 36,000ft (10,975m). With a subsonic Mach 0.9 cruising speed and 22,100lb (10,025kg) of fuel a 4,000lb (1,815kg) bombload could be carried over 1,000nm (1,855km). The CAP endurance was 2.5hr. An alternative tapered swept wing was also studied, as was a version for the RAF with a longer fuselage and four RB.162 lift engines.

Brough also designed the P.135, which it considered to be a more practical solution, using a pivoting and translating VG wing, with angles between 63 and 25°. The aircraft was powered by two RB.186R Speys with reheat and had a maximum take-off weight of 60,000lb (21,215kg).

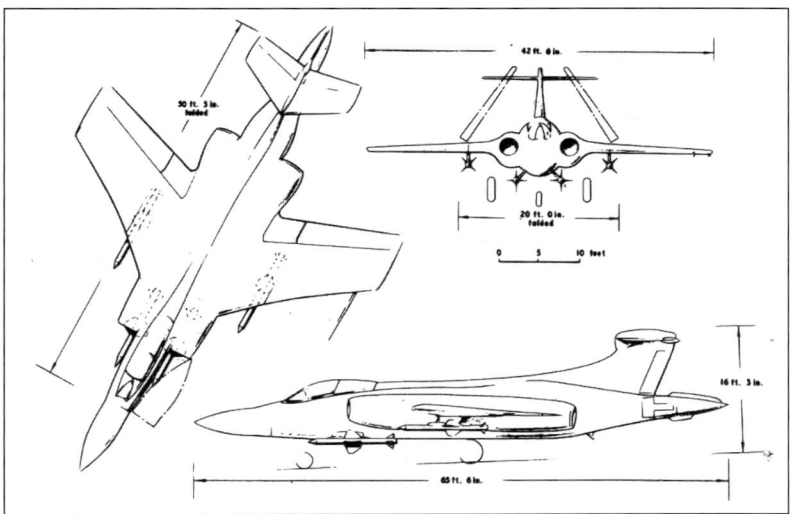

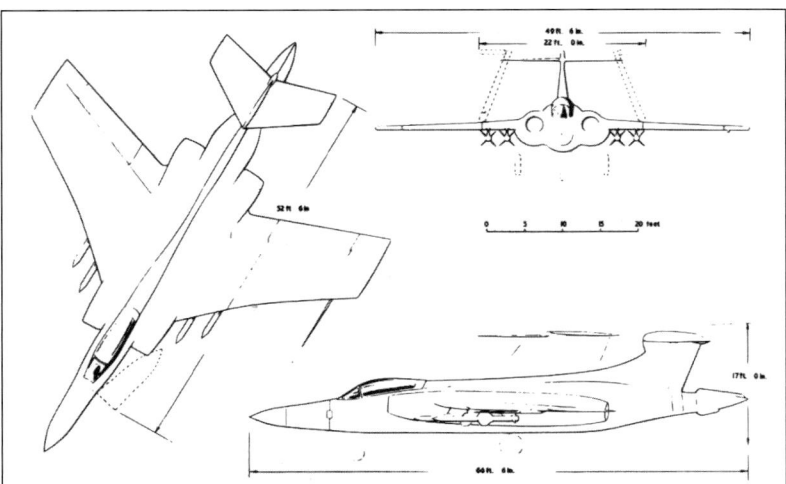

The P.117 was a high altitude Buccaneer interceptor with an extended wingspan of 49ft 6in (15.08m). Four *Red Top* or *Blue Vesta* AAMs were fitted under the inner wings. *Brough Heritage*

A general arrangement drawing of Blackburn's B.123. The overall design is reminiscent of the TSR.2 but with a delta T-tail. The two lift jets to counteract the pitching motion of the delta wing are below the cockpit. *Brough Heritage*

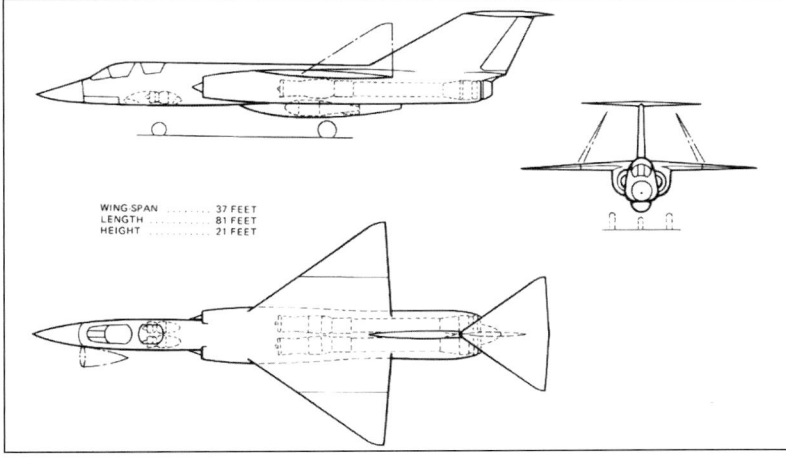

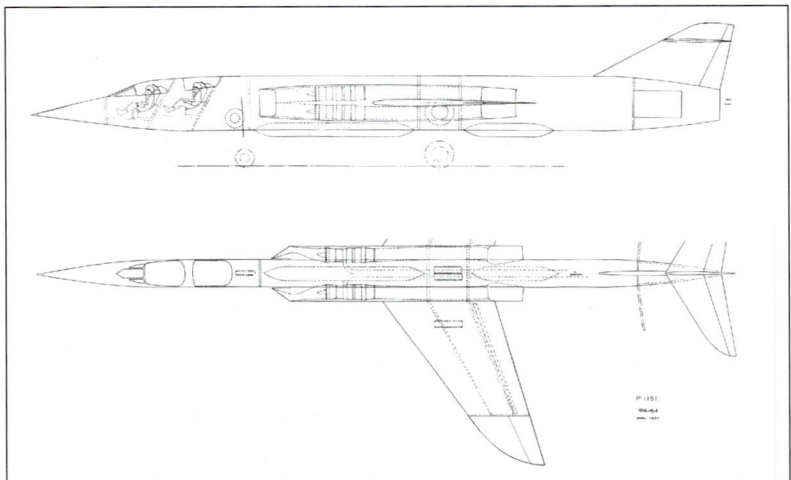

ABOVE The Hawker P.1151 was not one of Kingston's most elegant designs. Unusual features include the stacked pairs of RB.153 turbojets ahead of the wing and the semi-conformal blisters for the weapons. *Chris Farara via Tony Buttler*

RIGHT Brough further developed its P.123 concepts into the P.135 with a VG wing, with sweep angles between 63 and 25°. The aircraft was powered by two RB.186R Speys with reheat, each engine having a thrust diverting cascade under the wing root. Two banks for four RB.162 lift engines were also fitted. *Brough Heritage*

BELOW The Hawker P.1152 had four RB.162 lift engines (located in the wing roots, fore and aft of the wing), which had thrust vectoring nozzles. The main engine was a reheated RB.177 with two vectoring nozzles behind the compressor at the location of the centre of gravity, and a 'clang box' aft to divert the exhaust downwards. The swept wing had variable incidence. The six 1,000lb (454kg) bombs were carried in tandem pairs, semi-recessed along the centreline. *Chris Farara via Tony Buttler*

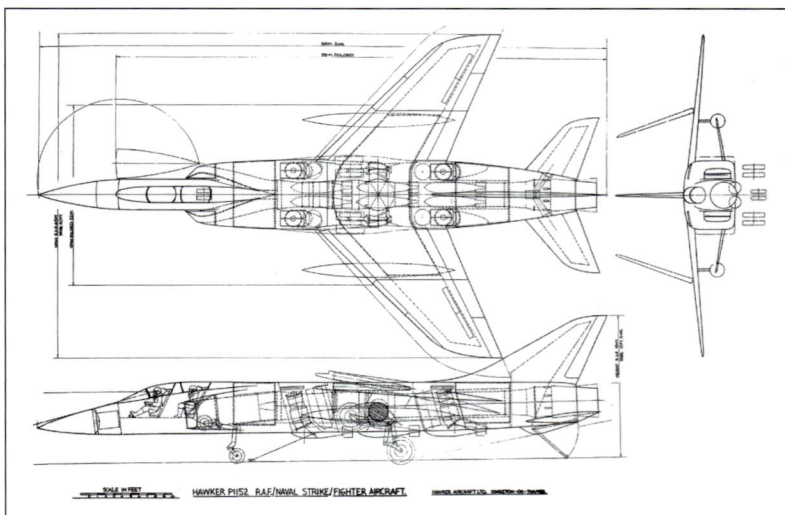

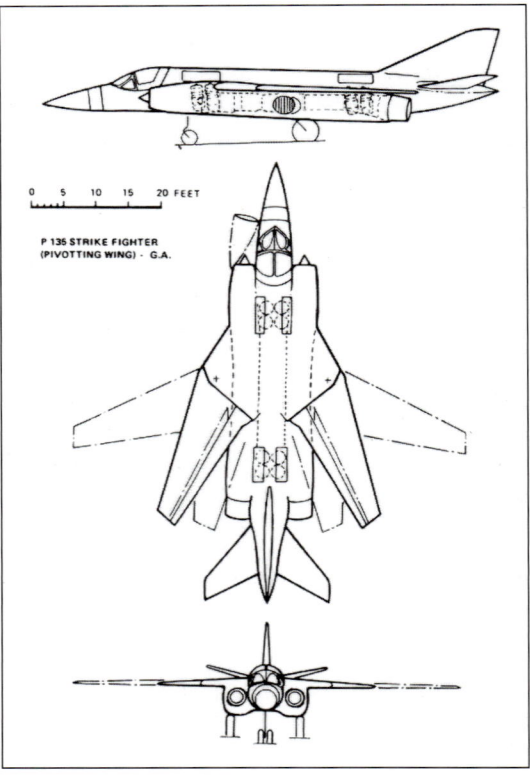

Kingston's Projects Office in December 1960 sketched up the P.1147 STOL strike/interceptor powered by a pair of reheated RB.173 and four RB.162 lift engines. This was followed in January 1961 by the P.1148 which added a VG wing. John Fozzard had three other designs in mind during April to June 1961. All were swept-wing designs with single tail fins. The P.1151 utilised the jet flap technique, using tapped air from the four reheated RB.153s which were in stacked pairs on either side of the fuselage. The crew sat in tandem and a T-tail was fitted along with a bicycle undercarriage with stabilising wheels retracting into the wings. Two ventral semi-conformal blisters were provided for the weapons.

The P.1152 was a V/STOL type using four RB.162 lift engines at the wing roots (two forward, two aft), which had thrust vectoring nozzles. The main engine was an RB.177 with reheat, it had two vectoring nozzles behind the compressor at the aircraft's centre of gravity and a 'clang box' aft to divert the exhaust downwards, a variable area nozzle being fitted. The swept wing had a variable incidence mechanism and had three-piece leading edge flaps, plain trailing edge flaps and two-piece ailerons with outboard spoilers. The all-moving tailplane was mounted low on the rear fuselage. The six 1,000lb (454kg) bombs were carried in tandem pairs, semi-recessed on the centreline.

The P.1153 was an unusual looking aircraft, having a Bristol Siddeley Olympus Ol.22R mounted ventrally with a ramp intake and a large cascade deflector exhaust under the wing. A bicycle undercarriage with stabilising wheels retracting into the wings was fitted. A total of 10 1,000lb bombs were carried in tandem pairs inside the fuselage from behind the cockpit all the way aft to the tail, quite how they were released is unclear.

Replacing Sea Vixen

While studies were underway for the supersonic strike/interceptor to meet OR.346, the Admiralty issued requirement AW.406 for a Sea Vixen replacement to enter service by 1970. The aim was to destroy a Mach 2.5 target flying at 65,000ft (19,810m) as well as low-altitude subsonic and supersonic targets. The armament would initially be four de Havilland Propellers *Red Top* infrared (IR)-homing AAMs until a new radar-homing AAM (being developed under Requirement GDA.103 and Joint Staff Target AST.1193) was ready. A secondary strike role required 8,000lb (3,630kg) of weapons carried on six external hardpoints, including the new WE.177A tactical nuclear bomb and anti-submarine depth bomb. The pulse-Doppler radar was to have a radar scanner diameter of 30in (76cm) and a range of 60nm (111km) against a medium bomber-sized target. The aircraft also had to be capable of reconnaissance. Maximum speed at sea level was to be Mach 0.92 with a supersonic dash capability and Mach 2.0 at altitude. A crew of two would be carried, and the desired maximum AUW was 40,000lb (18,145kg). The RAF became interested, seeing the requirements as being ideal for a Hawker Hunter replacement and in April 1962 requirements were combined under OR.356/AW.406 and proposals were sought from industry.

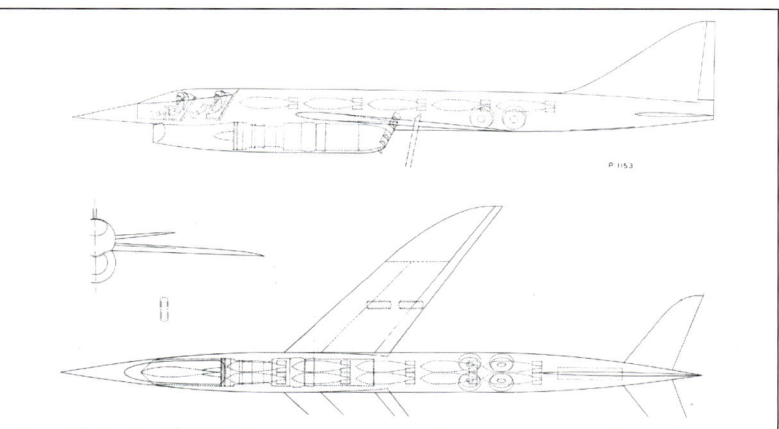

The P.1153 was a quirky design with its single ventral Bristol Siddeley Olympus Ol.22R with a large cascade deflector exhaust, a bicycle undercarriage arrangement and the long thin fuselage. Quite how the ten 1,000lb bombs were released is a mystery to the author – there is a single ventral hatch ahead of the tailplane which looks barely big enough for one bomb and which would require a complicated conveyor system. The centre of gravity and trim changes would leave a lot to be desired. *Chris Farara via Tony Buttler*

Operational Requirement OR.356 designs

	BAC VG Lightning Phase III	BAC Type 583	BAC Type 583V	BAC (English Electric) P.39	Hawker Siddeley P.1154B
Span	48ft 2in (14.68m) extended, 36ft 7in (11.16m) swept	49ft 0in (14.94m) extended, 27ft 0in (8.23m) swept	43ft 0in (13.11m) extended, 25ft 0in (7.62m) swept	32ft 0in (9.75m); 20ft 10in (6.35m) folded	30ft 0in (9.14m); 22ft 0in (6.70m) folded
Length	50ft 0in (15.24m)	53ft 0in (16.5m); 50ft 0in (15.24m) folded	52ft 0in (15.85m)	61ft 9in (18.82m); 51ft 6in (15.70m) folded	58ft 6in (17.83m); 52ft 0in (15.84m) folded
Wing area	?	?	250ft² (23.25m²) at 25° sweep	526ft² (48.90m²)	287ft² (26.66m²)
All-up weight	44,950lb (20,390kg)	43,300lb (19,640kg)	45,100lb (20,455kg)	38,896lb (17,643kg)	41,150lb (18,665kg)
Powerplant	2x RB.168-1R Spey, 10,360lbf (46.0kN) dry, 18,000lbf (80.0kN) reheat	2x RB.153-61R	2x RB.168-32D Spey	2x RB.153-61C; & 2x RB.162 lift engines	1x BS.100/8, 35,170lbf (156.4kN) PCB
Fuel capacity	2,000gal (9,094L)	?	?	15,000lb (6,804kg)	1,250gal (5,682L), plus 2x 200gal (909L) drop tanks
Max speed	Mach 1.43 at SL, Mach 2.2 at 44,000ft (13,410m)	Mach 1.1 at SL, Mach 2.5 at 55,000ft (16,765m)	Mach 1.1 at SL, Mach 2.5 at altitude	Mach 0.95 at SL; Mach 2.5 up to 60,000ft (18,290m)	Mach 1.75 at altitude
Armament	4x Red Top	4x Red Top	2x Red Top	4x Red Top, 4x 2,000lb (907kg) bombs, 6x 1,000lb (454kg) bombs, 4x AJ.68 Martel	4x Red Top, bombs, RPs

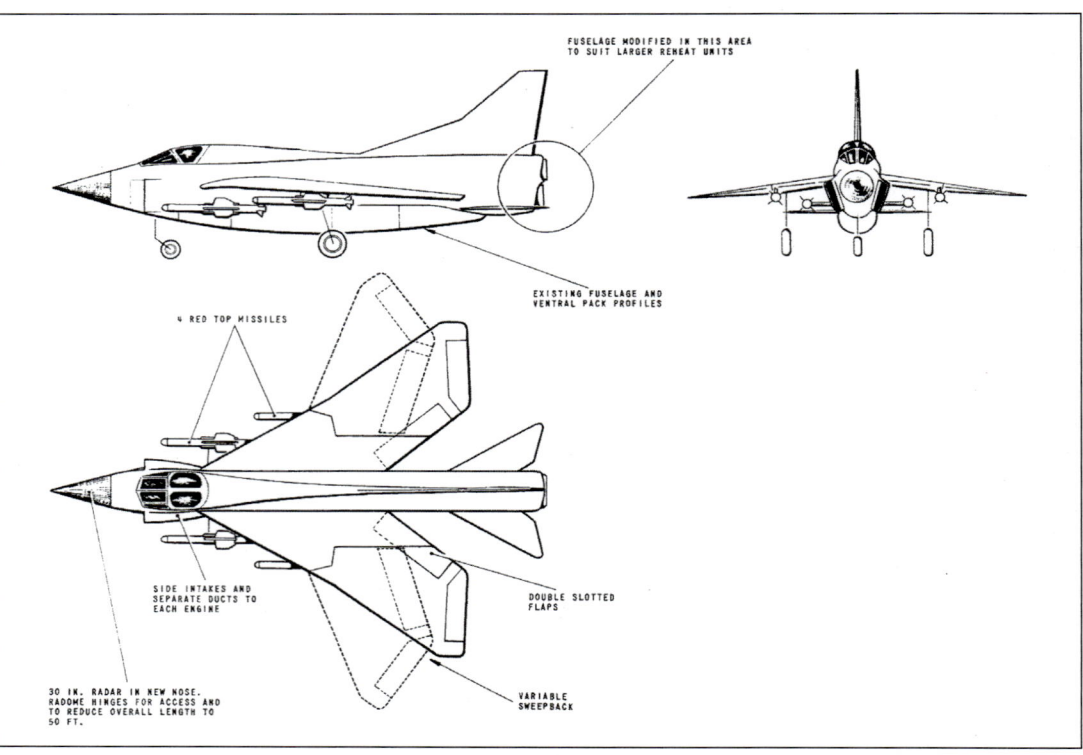

The Phase III VG Lightning was an ambitious development, it looked like a P.1A Lightning but was heavily modified with the T.5 two-seat trainer fuselage, a new VG wing retaining the fixed-wing planform, new nose radome and two Rolls-Royce RB.153-61C engines in a redesigned rear fuselage fed by new lateral variable-ramp intakes. *North West Heritage Group via Tony Buttler*

The BAC Type 583 was the closest the RN came to having its own F-14 Tomcat. It was the Admiralty's favoured choice before it settled on the F-4K Phantom. *Tony Buttler Collection*

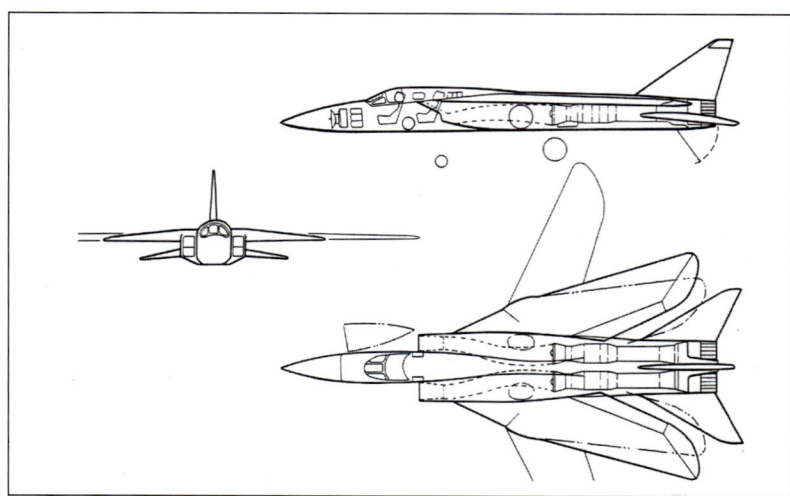

Vickers was understandably keen to offer the VG wing for OR.356 and AW.406. Weybridge had looked at several conversions of existing aircraft such as the Supermarine Swift and Scimitar and the English Electric Lightning under the Type 588 designation since 1961. By now Vickers was part of the British Aircraft Corporation (BAC) following a merger with English Electric and during 1964 the VG wing programme was transferred from Weybridge to Warton. A year before this transfer, Warton offered the Naval Lightning. This was based on the two-seat T.5 conversion trainer, which had side-by-side seating, with an enlarged dorsal spine and tail fin (which folded for carrier stowage) and an extended ventral pack containing 810gal (3,680L) of fuel – the total internal fuel load was 1,000gal (4,550L). The outer wing sections were replaced by variable sweep wings, with a range of 25–60°, which when fully swept, maintained the original wing planform to avoid any aerodynamic changes. Double-slotted flaps were fitted, the variable sweep giving a low approach speed. The Ferranti AI.23B AIRPASS radar was retained, the armament being two *Red Top*, Firestreak, Matra R.530 or AIM-9 Sidewinder AAMs on the lower fuselage pack and another pair under the fixed inner wings. Alternative ground attack options included two 30-round packs of 2in (50mm) Microcell rocket projectiles, 1,000lb (454kg) bombs, napalm tanks or AGM-12 Bullpup or Nord AS.30 ASMs. Warton estimated that with a start date of January 1964 that a VG-winged prototype could be flying by spring 1966.

In July 1963 the proposal was enhanced by the Phase III development. This involved fitting a new solid nose for the 30in-diameter radar AW.406 called for which meant that new lateral intakes had to be provided; these were equipped with double shock variable-ramps, one intake feeding each engine. The ventral pack became integral with the fuselage structure and the rear fuselage was modified to accommodate the larger diameter afterburners for a pair of RB.168-1R Spey engines (or alternatively the 7,820lbf (34.7kN) RB.153-61C). The fuel capacity was increased to 2,000gal (9,095L).

Weybridge offered the Type 583 based on the OR.346 VG wing studies. This was an attractive design with a single tail fin and tandem seating. It was designed to operate from the existing *Eagle*-class carriers with the wings set at 25° for take-off, landing and low speed flight and 74° for supersonic flight, with 'over-sweep' available to reduce the width for hangar stowage. The outer wing sections had blown trailing edge flaps, leading edge slats and ailerons. The wing's torsion box was sealed as a fuel tank. The engines were two RB.153-61R, providing a maximum speed of Mach 1.1 at sea level and Mach 2.5 at 55,000ft (16,765m); the strike radius was 1,000nm (1,850km) with a CAP endurance of 4.3hr. The estimated normal take-off weight was 43,300lb (19,640kg). Four *Red Top* AAMs would be carried. With the experience of the planned Type 589 research aircraft and the TSR.2, BAC estimated that development would be cost effective at £35 million and less technically risky (especially since the RB.153 was an Anglo-German project.) Tthe MoA estimated the development cost to be £85 million including the engine and radar development costs. An AEW variant was also drawn up (see Chapter 9).

Weybridge submitted another brochure on 23 August 1963 for the Type 583V. This was a V/STOL version, swapping the RB.153s for two RB.168-32D Speys with each engine feeding two swivelling nozzles like the Harrier. The fuselage was new, with a tapered rear end and the intakes moved forward and equipped with double shock variable-ramps. The VG wings were unchanged. The estimated gross weight was 45,100lb (20,455kg). The estimated entry into service was 1971. Further developments were a single-seater for the RAF with revised intakes with half-cone centre bodies and single-engine versions with the Bristol Siddeley Pegasus or RB.141 Medway.

Hawker Siddeley's Blackburn division offered the P.39 in February 1963. This was the Dassault Mirage IIIV V/STOL fighter with its eight 5,250lbf (23.4kN) RB.162 lift engines in the centre fuselage replaced by fuel tanks and two RB.162 mounted in tandem behind the cockpit to counteract the pitch-down moment created by the delta wing on landing. The main propulsive engines were to be a pair of 6,850lbf (30.5kN) RB.153-61C. The outer wing sections and the nose folded for carrier stowage (the nose also drooped to improve visibility on landing). Four *Red Tops* or 4,000lb (1,815kg) of bombs or ASMs would be carried on external hardpoints. The radius of action with a full bomb load was 800nm (1,480km). An AEW variant was also drawn up (see Chapter 9).

Hawker Siddeley's Advanced Project Department group at Kingston drew up a series of RAF/RN 'Bi-Service' designs using VG wings and thrust vectoring. These had novel layouts and notional AAM armaments. The APD.1017 designs were large twin-engined aircraft, 65ft (18.8m) long and 60ft (18.2m) span (at minimum sweep) wings with either a T-tail or a folding V-tail ; the 1017C had conformal fairings on each nacelle for either four RB.162 lift engines or 300gal (1,363L) of fuel. The undercarriage was unusual in having a single centreline four or two-wheeled bogie with twin forward undercarriage legs retracting into the sides of the intakes. The interceptor armament was four GDA.103 AAMs of

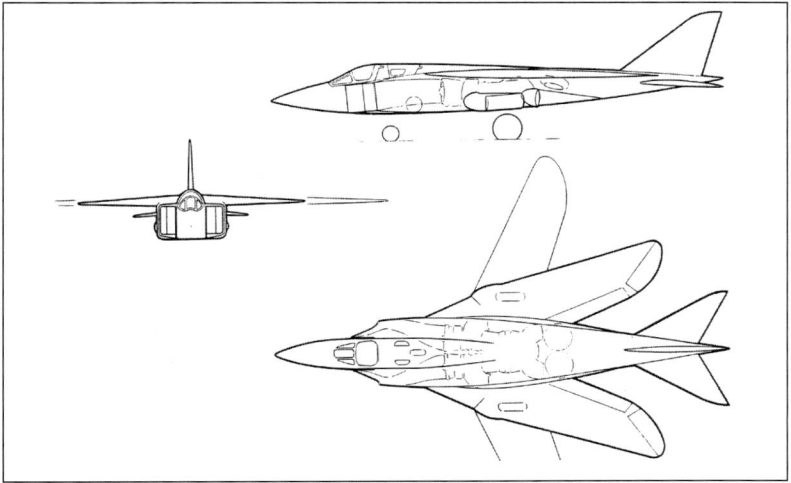

The Type 583V used two RB.168 Speys with thrust vectoring nozzles to provide a V/STOL capability. The complicated and heavy arrangement had little advantage over the single BS.100 of the Hawker Siddeley P.1154. *Tony Buttler Collection*

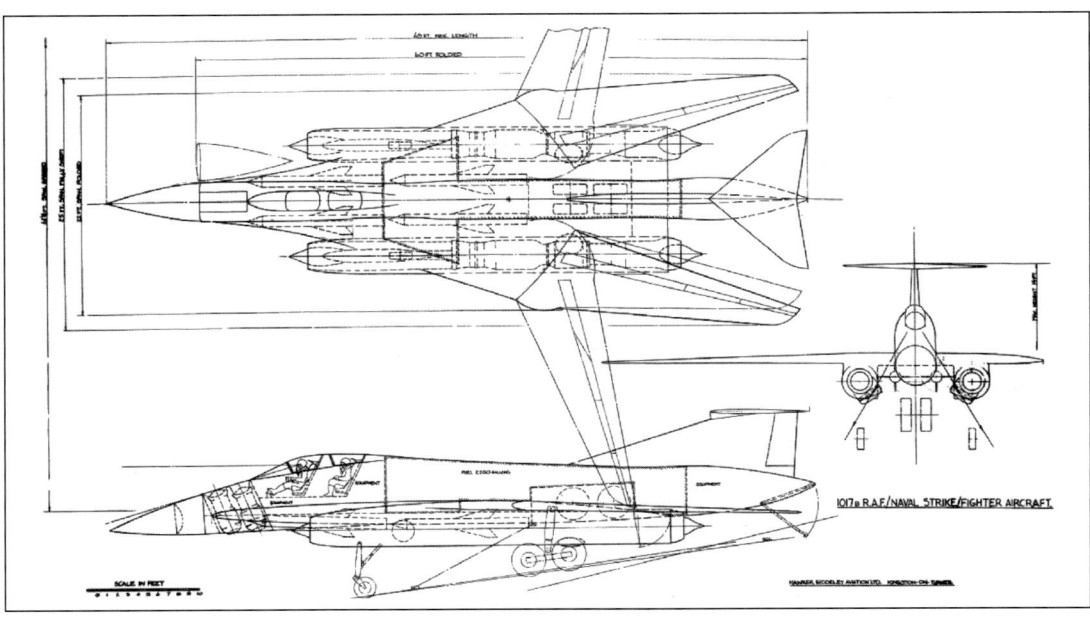

The two-seat APD.1017B had the main engines in nacelles under the wings, leaving the fuselage free for semi-conformal AAMs. Two lift engines were fitted in the nose ahead of the cockpit to assist during take-offs. The deep fuselage held 2,200gal (10,000L) of fuel. The moving outer wings had full-span spoilers. *BAE Systems via Author's Collection*

The APD.1017C lacked the nose lift engines and had two internal weapon bays, each capable of accommodating two AAMs (the missiles shown are probably de Havilland's 'Family' series of designs) or five 1,000lb (454kg) bombs. Note that one wing of the AAMs was left in the slipstream. Fuel tankage was 1,500gal (6,820L) in the fuselage and 720gal (3,273L) in the wings.
BAE Systems via Author's Collection

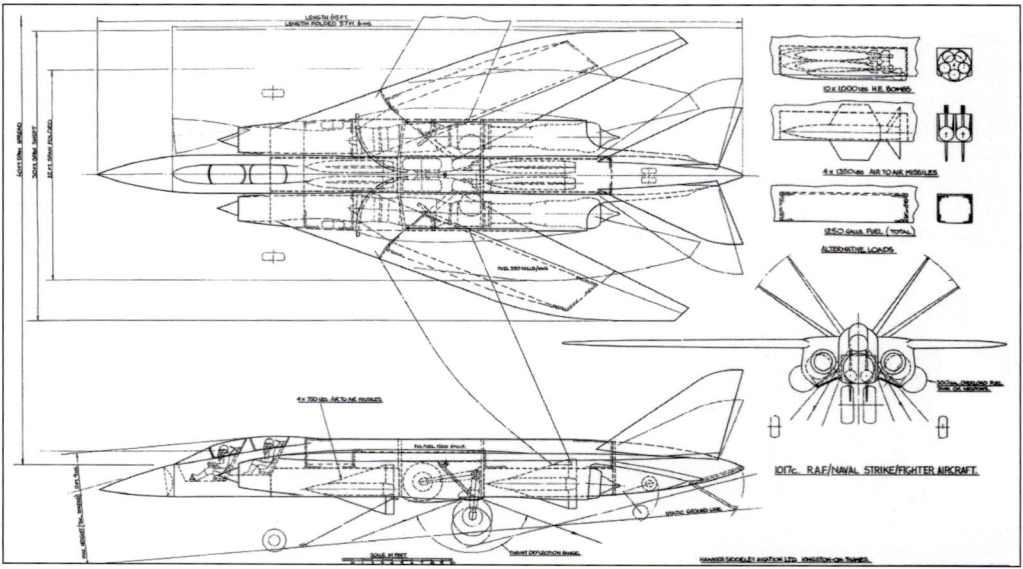

The APD.1022 was another unusual design of a rather hunchback appearance with low-mounted intakes and an unusual dorsal mounting of the AAMs to reduce drag. The angle of the V-tail could be increased to reduce height for hangar stowage.
BAE Systems via Author's Collection

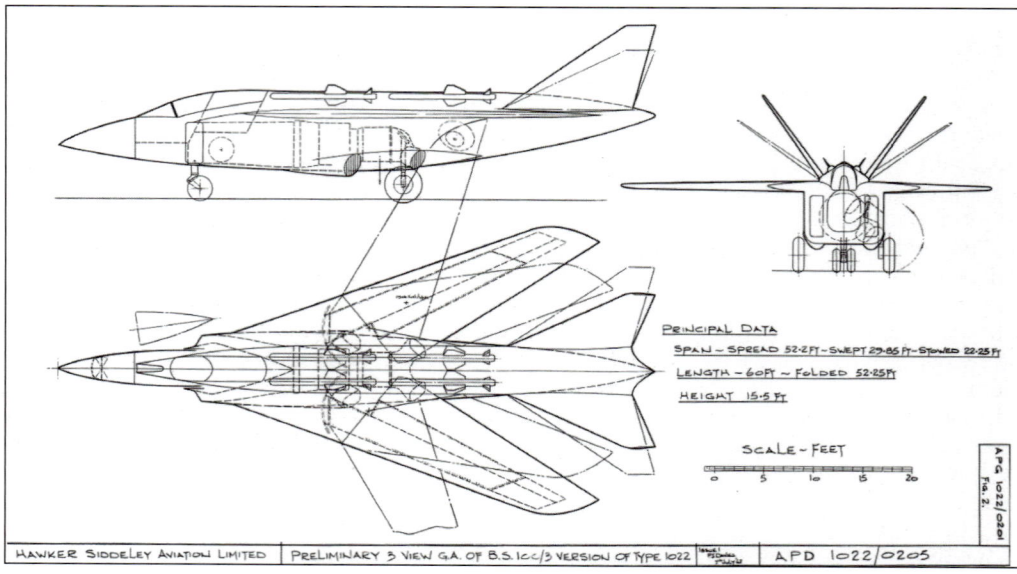

The Bristol Siddeley Olympus-powered APD.1022 featured a conventional tail jet pipe but also had a 'clang box' diverter in the centre of the fuselage to provide vertical thrust.
BAE Systems via Author's Collection

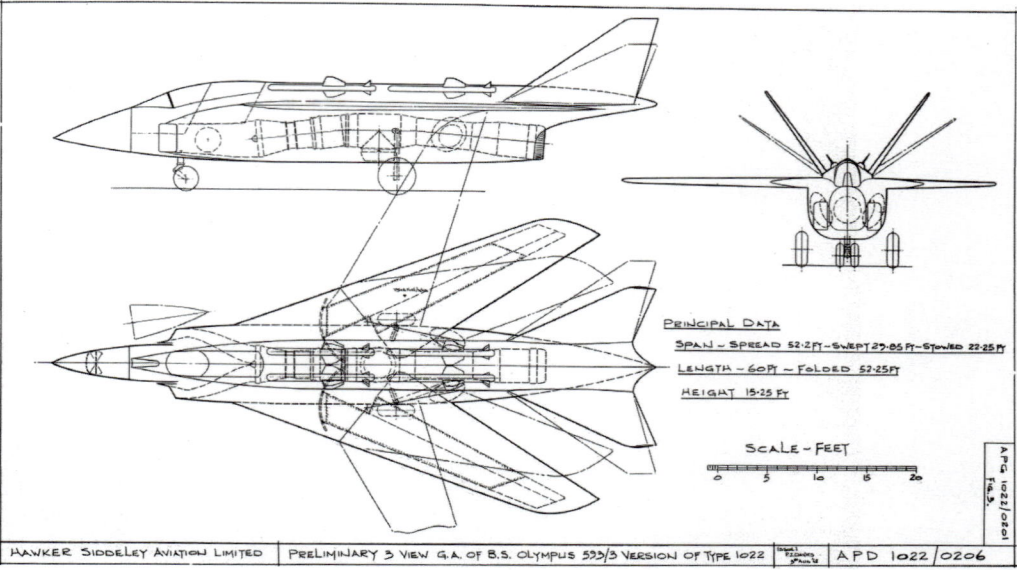

the DH Family series (weighing either 750 or 1,350lb (340 or 612kg); strike armament was four 1,000lb (454kg) bombs; the 1017B having two five-bomb rotating launchers.

The APD.1022 featured four dorsally-mounted *Red Tops* or *Blue Vestas*, high-mounted VG wings and folding V-tail. Length 60ft (18.2m) with a maximum span of 52ft 2in (15.9m); the engine choices were either a single BS.100/3 with four-poster thrust vectoring or a single Olympus 593/3 with a 'clang box' to divert the thrust vertically at the centre of the gravity.

Commonality and Verticality

By 1963 it looked likely that the BAC Type 583 would meet the requirements of AW.406 but other developments were taking place that forced the Admiralty into a new direction. As early as August 1961 the RAF had become interested in a supersonic V/STOL fighter-bomber. NATO Basic Military Requirement 3 (NMBR.3) for such an aircraft had been circulated around the aviation industries of Western Europe in June. The Cabinet Defence Committee meeting on 6 December ruled that future aircraft should be jointly developed to meet the needs of the RAF and FAA. Consequently, the Admiralty was asked to consider taking a common version of whatever aircraft won NMBR.3 alongside the RAF. The Admiralty rejected this proposal as NMBR.3 lacked endurance and weapons payload and was only a single-seater. They argued that modifying the NMBR.3 aircraft into a two-seat interceptor would be just as costly as AW.406 and was therefore pointless. The existence of the TSR.2 pushed the joint RN/RAF OR.346 strike aircraft back into the late 1970s, meaning that the Buccaneer S.2 would have to remain in service until 1980.

"It can hardly be doubted that Mr. Thorneycroft would be very hard to persuade. On the other hand, if he was adamant we could still accept the P.1154B: it is arguable that we should lose nothing by trying."

MEMORANDUM BY DEPUTY CHIEF OF NAVAL STAFF, MAY 1963

NMBR.3 was a hugely political project and selection of a winning design was contentious. There were two leading contenders, Dassault's Mirage IIIV – with eight lift engines and two propulsive engines – and the Hawker Siddeley P.1154 developed from the P.1127 research aircraft with a 33,150lbf (147.4kN) thrust Bristol Siddeley BS.100/9 engine with four-poster thrust vectoring and plenum chamber burning (PCB) – a method of reheat for the forward 'cold' nozzles. The Mirage IIIV did not meet the RAF's or the FAA's needs, while France had always intended to pursue the IIIV regardless of the outcome. Approval was given to proceed with the P.1154's development in April 1962 – which was later declared the technical winner of NMBR.3, which by then was a moot point. The government now put pressure on the Admiralty to acquire a version of the P.1154, but the saga of replacing the Sea Vixen was only just beginning.

The RAF had been strongly interested in the P.1154 to meet OR.356 and as political pressure to accept the aircraft if it won NMBR.3 grew, it became clear the RN would also be acquiring the aircraft regardless of the performance of the other AW.406 proposals. The First Sea Lord, Admiral Sir Caspar John, acquiesced to the wishes of the Minister of Defence, Harold Watkinson, but under protest. The Director of the Naval Air Division (DNAD), Captain Desmond Vincent-Jones, was equally unhappy, he did not want the complications of V/STOL or an

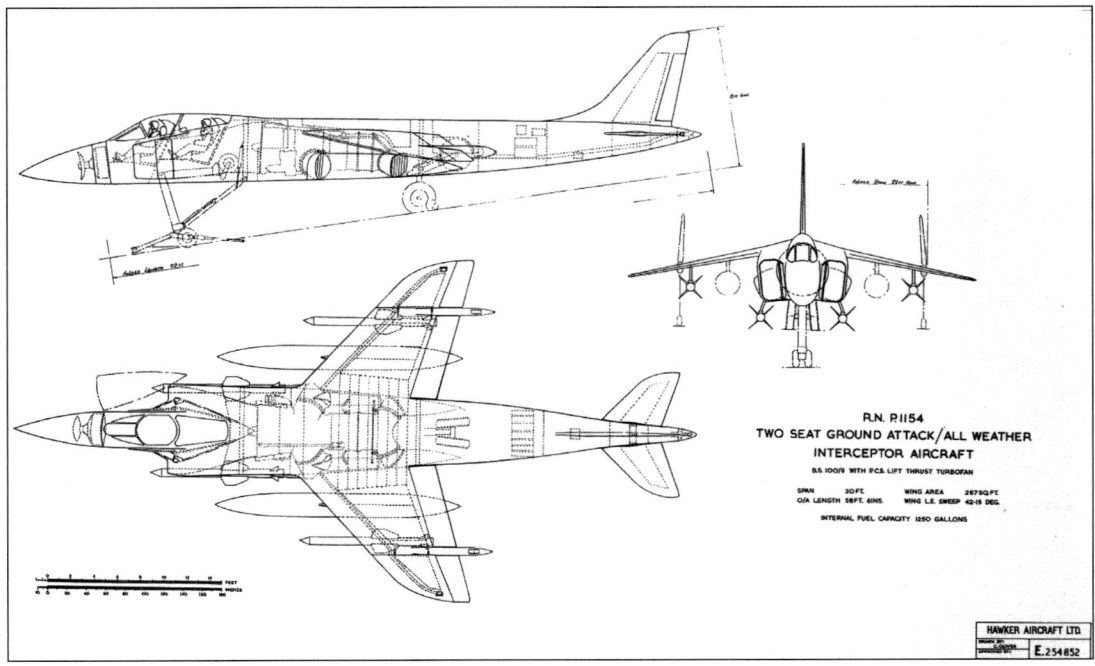

This is the original P.1154B with its two-seat cockpit, increased span folding outer wings, variable-ramp intakes and folding nose cone. The longer nosewheel leg complicated the use of a catapult bridle as the angle of the cable exceeded the 30° maximum limit usually allowed. The *Red Top* AAMs were carried underwing and on lower forward fuselage pylons. *BAE Systems via Chris Farara*

WINGS OVER THE FLEET

Hawker Siddeley P.1154 designs

	P.1154B Original	P.1154B Revised	P.1154B Big Wing	P.1154-34	P.1154 Bi-Service
Crew	Two	Two	Two	Two	One
Span	30ft 0in (9.14m); 22ft 0in (6.70m) folded	30ft 0in (9.14m); 22ft 0in (6.70m) folded	36ft 0in (10.97m); 22ft 0in (6.70m) folded	36ft 0in (10.97m); 22ft 0in (6.70m) folded	28ft 4in (8.63m); 22ft 0in (6.70m) folded
Length	58ft 6in (17.83m); 52ft 0in (15.84m) folded	58ft 6in (17.83m); 52ft 0in (15.84m) folded	58ft 6in (17.83m); 52ft 0in (15.84m) folded	58ft 6in (17.83m); 52ft 0in (15.84m) folded	57ft 7in (17.55m); 52ft 0in (15.84m) folded
Wing area	287ft² (26.66m²)	287ft² (26.66m²)	350ft² (32.55m²)	350ft² (32.55m²)	269ft² (24.99m²)
All-up weight	41,150lb (18,665kg)	?	48,000lb (21,775kg)	49,000lb (22,225kg)	?
Powerplant	1x BS.100/8, 35,170lbf (156.4kN) PCB	1x BS.100/9, 33,150lbf (147.4kN) PCB	1x BS.100 39,700lbf (176.4kN) PCB	2x RB.163-32D Spey, 19,200lbf (85.3kN) reheat	1x BS.100/9, 33,150lbf (147.4kN) PCB
Fuel capacity	1,250gal (5,682L); plus 2x drop tanks	1,600gal (7,273L); plus 2x drop tanks	1,900gal (1,638L); plus 2x drop tanks	1,900gal (1,638L); plus 2x drop tanks	1,200gal (5,455L); plus 2x drop tanks
Max speed	Mach 1.75 at altitude	Mach 1.75 at altitude	Mach 1.75 at altitude	Mach 1.8 at altitude	Mach 1.75 at altitude
Armament	4x Red Top, bombs, RPs	4x Red Top, bombs, RPs	4x Red Top, bombs, RPs	4x Red Top, bombs, RPs	2x Red Top, bombs, RPs

inferior single-seat fighter. Vincent-Jones' Deputy, Captain Eric 'Winkle' Brown visited Kingston on 2 April 1962 to see what the aircraft designers could offer. Chief Engineer Ralph Hooper was equally uneasy, his P.1154 design had been designed to meet the RAF's needs and he foresaw the entire project collapsing.

The first joint OR.356/AW.406 submission was made on 8 August 1962. Hawker Siddeley would develop two variants, the single-seat P.1154A fighter-bomber for the RAF and the two-seat P.1154B interceptor for the FAA. The P.1154A was scheduled to enter service in 1968 with the P.1154B following by 1970. The RN was looking at acquiring around 165 aircraft (plus 25 conversion trainers). The cost of developing the P.1154 was estimated in May 1963 at £200–230 million, £90–100 million being for the P.1154B. The USA, via the Mutual Weapons Development Program (MWDP) agreed to fund half of the BS.100 engine development costs. Kingston estimated that the first of four P.1154B prototypes would be ready to fly in October 1966 with the last flying by July 1967.

Specification F.242D was issued to cover development of both types. The CAP endurance was to be 2.5hr with a maximum speed at altitude of Mach 2.0. Ferry range was to be 2,170nm (4,025km). The wings of the P.1154B were larger and incorporated folding. The fuselage was stressed to 6.5g and take-offs would be via the carrier's steam catapult. The intakes were modified with two-stage variable-ramps for the higher speed requirements. The arrester hook would be for use if a vertical landing was not possible, but only at speeds up to 65kt and was rated for 1.5g deceleration. The P.1154B would receive the uprated 35,170lbf (156.4kN) BS.100/8 Phase II engine, allowing an AUW of 41,150lb (18,665kt).

The avionics included a Head-Up Display (HUD), GEC digital inertial navigation/attack system, an air data computer, semi-automatic datalink and tactical air navigation (TACAN). The 200W X-band pulse-Doppler radar would conform to the requirements of AW.406 with a 60nm range and a 30in-diameter scanner. A reconnaissance pod with cameras could also be carried. Four underwing and three ventral hardpoints would be provided for four *Red Top* AAMs, Bullpup or OR.1168 TV-guided ASMs (the later would become Martel), a single WE.177A (bomb or depth bomb), napalm tanks, 2in (50mm) rocket pods and drop tanks totalling 4,000lb (1,815kg).

The RN criticised the bicycle undercarriage arrangement as being unsuitable for catapulting, deck strength limits and stability. The Kingston Projects Office team under Ralph Hooper – and under the watchful eye of Sir Sydney Camm – agreed to fit a wing-mounted tricycle undercarriage to the P.1154B, which retracted into trailing edge nacelles. The undercarriage was stressed for a 12ft/min (3.65m/min) rate of descent. The nosewheel tow method of catapult launch was also untried in RN service and trials using a Sea Vixen would be required. The longer nosewheel leg for the correct take-off attitude complicated the use of a catapult bridle as the angle of the cable exceeded the 30° maximum limit.

An assessment by the Royal Aircraft Establishment (RAE) highlighted other shortcomings: an inadequate margin of thrust over the landing weight for vertical landing; lack of adequate control at approach speeds of 0–90kt; doubts over night all-weather recovery; and the excessive weight caused rotational problems after a catapult launch at the normal strike AUW. Additionally, Deputy DNAD Captain Eric Brown highlighted that the P.1154 only marginally met the endurance requirements at 2.5hr and that the

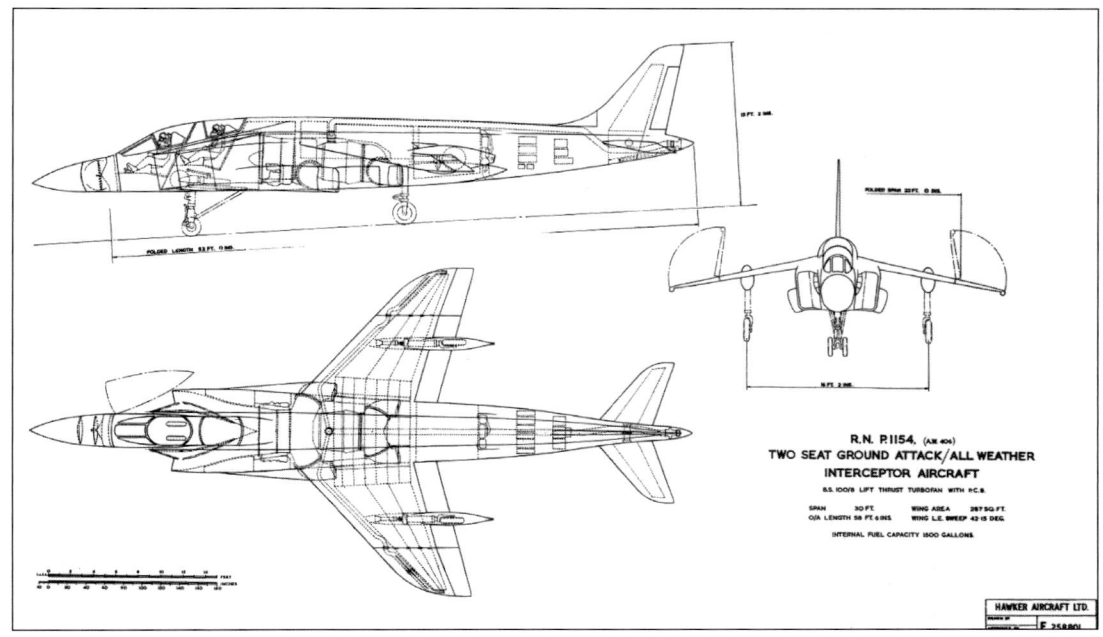

The revised P.1154B had a shorter nosewheel leg, repositioned undercarriage nacelles for a narrower track and a refined rear fuselage cross-section to reduce drag. The vectoring nozzles were also modified to improve their efficiency.
BAE Systems via Chris Farara

acceleration was poor. John Fozzard of Kingston's Projects Office (promoted as Chief Designer P.1154 in October 1963) quoted 5.25min to accelerate from Mach 0.85 to Mach 1.8M at the tropopause. In order to reach a more accurate acceleration requirement Brown asked the RAE to clarify the optimal CAP radius required to deal with high and low-altitude targets, the previous estimates varying between 60–150nm (111–277km).

When the two lower fuselage AAM positions proved to be problematic due to centre of gravity concerns, the wing was altered with two additional outboard hardpoints. Camm disliked this solution as wing twist would cause misalignment of the outer missiles and higher drag and he wanted to revert to the four hardpoint wing. This would mean no drop tanks could be fitted if four AAMs were carried – although a ventral tank was possible if the undercarriage legs were lengthened by 6in (152mm).

The major problem was weight growth. Between March and July 1963 the weight increased by 3,000lb (1,360kg) due to 'natural' growth, naval features and changes in requirements (each contributing around a third of the growth). At a weight of 42,000lb (19,050kg) it had no VTOL capability (the RN insisted on a vertical landing capability with 2,000lb [907kg] of weapons and 1,000lb [454kg] of fuel aboard) and Camm wanted to limit the weight to 40,000lb (14,145kg). 80lb (36kg) could be saved by shortening the nose undercarriage leg, but the 3° shallower incidence on catapult take-off would require steeper rotation.

The RN also wanted a twin-engine aircraft for increased safety, claiming that such aircraft saved the FAA a squadron's worth of aircraft from potential loss each year. In December 1962 Rolls-Royce proposed fitting two RB.168 Spey engines mounted side by side, each engine feeding two nozzles (with PCB) and cross-over pipes to maintain symmetrical thrust in the event of an engine failure (BAC's Type 583V was very similar in concept.) The performance was inferior to the BS.100-powered design and it was dropped, although the P.1154-34 of January 1964 returned to this concept. John Fozzard's team remained unhappy with this layout and work on it was halted when the Admiralty withdrew from the P.1154 project the following month.

There were also doubts about the aircraft's effectiveness in the air defence role. The February 1963 report *Air Defence of a Carrier Task Group in Limited War in the 1970s* assessed various methods of air defence for a single carrier group against a range of Soviet aircraft threats ranging from Tupolev Tu-16 *Badgers* to Tu-22 *Blinders* equipped with various real and notional future ASMs. The systems assessed were the new CF.299 SAM (Sea Dart), a notional improved CF.299 Mk.2, GWS.2 Sea Slug Mk.2, notional LRGW (Long Range Guided Weapon, a revival of NIGS – New Naval Guided Weapons System) and the P.1154 armed with the GDA.103 AAM.

Against a very low-altitude attack, two frigates and a carrier armed with Sea Dart SAMs could destroy 20–30 aircraft before the carrier was sunk by three ASM hits; nuclear warheads increased this to 100% of the bombers being destroyed before releasing their ASMs. The CF.299 Mk.2 assisted by AEW aircraft improved the kill ratio to 30–60. Adding either GWS.2 Sea Slug Mk.2 or a two-aircraft P.1154 CAP contributed little to improving the kill ratio (unless nuclear warheads were used.) Against a high-altitude attack a combination of two P.1154s on CAP and three Sea Dart systems would destroy 11–23 enemy Mach 1 bombers before the carrier was hit by an ASM – dropping to 5–6 Mach 2 bombers with the CAP unable to intercept a surprise raid before the ASMs were released 87nm (160km) away. In contrast a mix of LRGW and Sea Dart could destroy 13–30 Mach 1.0 bombers or 7–17 Mach 2.0

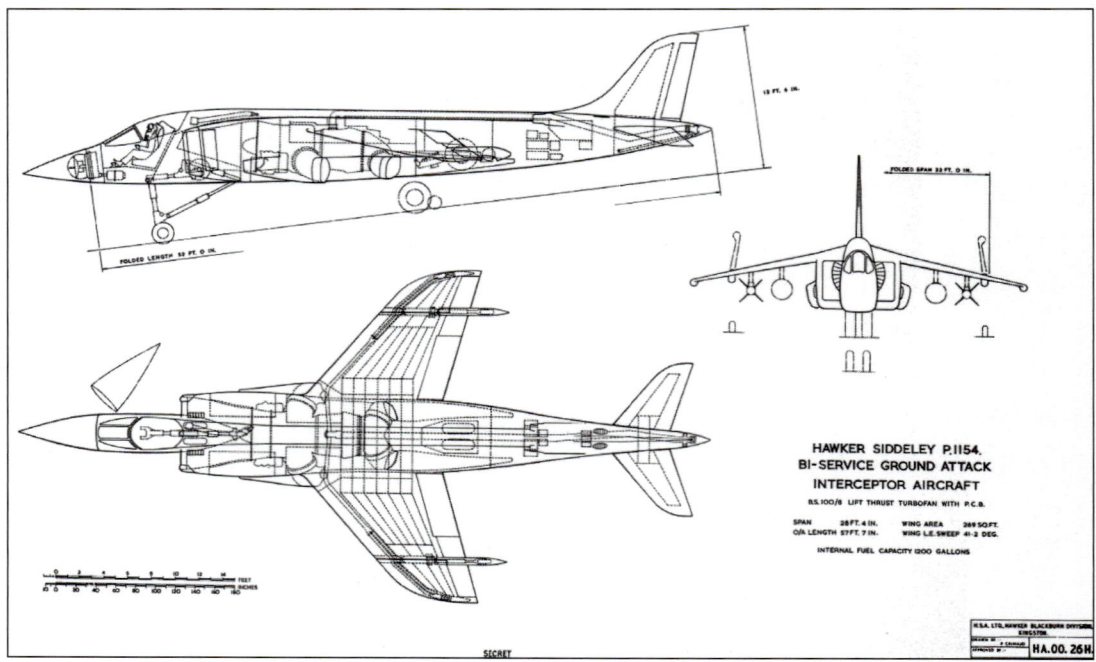

The final stage. The common airframe P.1154/2 was based on the RAF's single-seat P.1154A with the P.1154B's X-band pulse-Doppler radar, undercarriage, folding outer wings and the BS.100/8 Stage II engine. It suited neither potential operators' requirements, leading to the decision to let the RN pursue the McDonnell Douglas F-4K Phantom.
BAE System via Chris Farara

bombers. The conclusion was, "It is most doubtful whether the P.1154 should be considered acceptable as outer defence against a stand-off attack."

The RN was adamant that it wanted a VG wing aircraft of 50,000lb (22,680kg) AUW, believing that the RAF was wrong in sticking with V/STOL, which had several operational, logistical and command drawbacks. Vice Admiral Sir Frank Hopkins, the former Director of Air Warfare and now the Deputy Chief of the Naval Staff advocated making one last attempt to change Thorneycroft's mind. Captain Eric Brown and other Admiralty officers still found the BAC Type 583 very attractive, being a potential replacement for the Sea Vixen, Buccaneer and the Gannet AEW.3. The Vice Chief of the Naval staff, Vice Admiral Sir John Frewen, argued that the Vickers Type 584, a V/STOL version which was offered to NMBR.3, would be a better than the P.1154 and no more expensive to develop. The Admiralty estimated that developing the Type 583 alongside the RAF's P.1154A would save £15 million in development costs, partially offsetting the £25 million greater production cost for both aircraft combined.

Another short-term fix would be to fit the tentative AI.25 radar to the Sea Vixen FAW.2. There were possible non-aircraft solutions to air defence as well; additional Sea Dart frigates or developing the LRGW system. There were still worries that if the new carriers were not approved by the government that the Sea Vixen replacement would also be cancelled.

July was busy with negotiations and assessments to obtain a common airframe (by this time only 20% of the two versions were common) as demanded by the Defence Research Policy Committee. Two choices were offered, the P.1154/1 which was a single-seat P.1154B with just two *Red Tops*, a modified undercarriage and some of the navigational and radio homing equipment removed. The P.1154/2 was the RAF's P.1154A with a modified version of the P.1154B's X-band pulse-Doppler radar, stronger undercarriage, folding wings and nose and the BS.100/8 Stage II engine. The P.1154/1 had no VTOL capability, so was of no use to the RAF and was ruled out immediately. The P.1154/2 had a smaller diameter radar with only 40nm (74km) range and the CAP endurance was only 1.5hr. It offered significant advance over the Sea Vixen though and became the de facto common airframe. The First Lord of the Admiralty, Lord Carrington, accepted this solution on 9 July and on the 30th the Minister of Defence, Peter Thorneycroft, told the House of Commons that the RN and RAF had reached agreement on a common aircraft.

Commonality proved difficult to achieve in practice. The Admiralty on 22 August declared the P.1154 to be a 'second-rate interceptor' and the RAF was equally disenchanted with the reduced performance in the strike role. The RN continued to argue that having a dedicated radar operator in the low level interception role was superior, safer and more resistant to ECM as the back-seater could concentrate on trying to counteract its effects. By October the MoA was becoming concerned about the project and Hawker Siddeley told the Ministers of Defence and Aviation that the compromise design was unacceptable. The Chief Scientist's Committee now agreed that attempting to combine the disparate requirements would not work.

Kingston did not stop all V/STOL studies, the Special Projects team led by Ralph Williams drew up the SP.113 in November 1965, a land/naval strike aircraft in single and two-seat forms with folding wings and six underwing hardpoints for bombs, Bullpups and fuel tanks. The rear fuselage was notably thinner than that of the P.1154 to reduce drag. Wingspan was 37ft (11.27m), length 51ft (15.54m) and the wing area was 325ft² (30.19m²).

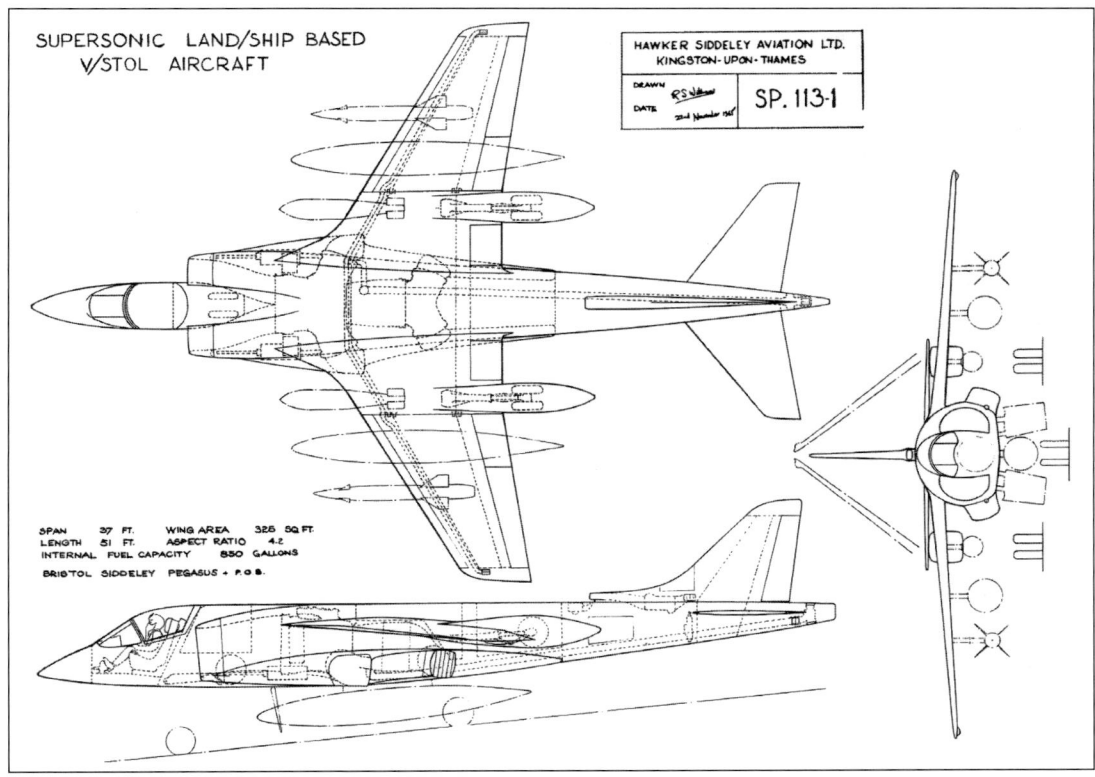

Despite the failure of the P.1154 Kingston did not stop developing the basic concept. The SP.113-1 of November 1965 was a much refined design with improved folding wings and seven hardpoints for a variety of ground attack weapons. The engine was a Pegasus with PCB. *BAE Systems via Author's Collection*

Phantomisation

The MoA's Research and Development Board had discussed a suggestion to buy the McDonnell F4H Phantom II for the RN instead of the P.1154B in June 1962. McDonnell had proposed a version powered by the RB.168-1R Spey turbofan. The cost of £8–13 million to develop the Spey and Phantom airframe was a big saving on the P.1154B's £30 million price tag. The Phantom's larger size and weight posed questions about deck strength, take-off and landing performance and fitting onto existing carrier lifts, but there was enough interest to pursue technical studies.

An exploratory visit to the USA in February 1963 (which was leaked to the press, causing political embarrassment) was followed by meeting in April in London with McDonnell representatives to discuss the feasibility of operating the Phantom from the RN's carriers. McDonnell proposed several versions (Models 98EQ, ER, ES and ET) with a longer nosewheel leg, RB.168-1R Speys and maximum landing weights of 34–38,000lb (15,420-12,235kg). The company's figures suggested that it could be operated from all current carriers as a fighter and from *Eagle* and *Ark Royal* as a strike aircraft. The Admiralty's more accurate BS.5 catapult performance figures suggested otherwise. Using the Spey would improve the climb to ceiling by 25%, increase the combat ceiling by 7,000ft (2,135m) and the radius of action by 40%.

A paper by the Admiralty and Air Staff for the Chiefs of Staff Committee in June identified only two possible off-the-shelf replacements for the Sea Vixen: the F-4B Phantom (in 1962 the F4H was redesignated F-4) and the nascent TFX programme. Both were ruled out as they could not operate from the RN's existing carriers. Opinions on the Phantom would soon change.

The MoA studied numerous alternatives during January 1964, the three main ones being: continuing the P.1154 for the RAF and letting the RN procure Phantoms and developing an RAF/RN VG wing aircraft in the late 1970s; P.1154 for both services and the late 70s VG wing aircraft; P.1154 for the RAF and running on Sea Vixen until 1975, thereby bringing forward the VG wing aircraft.

As part of this analysis, Deputy DNAD Captain Eric Brown, the Head of the RAE's Naval Aircraft Department R Duddy and Mr Moore of the Chief Scientific Adviser's team visited Washington during 1–4 January. This was followed by a second visit to Washington and McDonnell's St. Louis factory beginning on the 23rd by Captain Brown, a member of the Admiralty's Materials Branch, the MoA's Assistant Secretary and its Director of Contracts and the Assistant Director of the Scientific Research (Air) Department.

McDonnell now offered the Model 98FB based on the USN's new Model 98EV F-4J with the Westinghouse AN/AWG.10 weapons control system (but without the AN/AAA-4 infrared detector) and RB.168-25R Speys, which would necessitate structural changes to accommodate 20% larger intakes and a 6in (152mm) wider rear fuselage to accommodate the afterburners. Other structural changes included auxiliary intake doors on the rear fuselage to increase airflow at low airspeeds and a folding nose cone. The nosewheel leg extended to 40in (100cm)

The YF-4K prototype XT595 outside McDonnell's St. Louis factory in June 1966. *Gerald H. Balzer via Tony Buttler*

A close-up of the McDonnell Douglas F-4K Phantom's extended nose undercarriage and catapult strop. This feature was vital in enabling the F-4K to take-off safely from the smaller decks of British carriers. *Blue Envoy Collection*

to provide a 9° take-off attitude suited for the comparatively short BS.5 catapults. It retained the F-4J's STOL features, including drooping ailerons, enlarged leading edge flaps, slotted tailplane and flap and leading edge blowing.

McDonnell estimated that the first production aircraft could be delivered in early 1967. The UK's share of the development cost was estimated at £26–30 million. The AWG-10 system gave a superior intercept capability over the P.1154 and would be available three to four years sooner. The estimated total programme cost of £130 million was £100 million less than the P.1154 and the Phantom was almost production ready. The AIM-7 Sparrow missiles would cost £52 million, half the price of *Red Top* and were a superior all-weather AAM. The only negative point was the lack of inertial navigation for the secondary strike role.

The carriers also needed modifications to operate Phantoms. Only the new water spray DAAG arrester gear was suitable for the heavier Phantom, especially in tropical conditions. A trial fit (DAX.2) with one arrester wire was fitted to *Eagle* in 1967 and 600 landings were successfully made. Only *Ark Royal* received the full four-wire DA.2 with 228ft (70m) long water-filled tubes during her 1967–70 refit due to the defence cuts of 1966. Other requirements included the provision of extra workshop space, additional liquid oxygen production capacity and magazine changes to accommodate the Sparrow AAMs.

Hermes, as the smallest carrier, posed problems as landings in tropical conditions would be impossible – the ship could only make 25kt, and 30kt would be required in zero-wind conditions for a Phantom approaching at 140kt. USN F-4 Phantoms had conducted successful touch-and-go landings on both *Hermes* and *Victorious* during tests, which offered some optimism that a solution could be found. Given the differences in BS.5 catapult lengths (and thus differences in how much fuel could be carried), it was estimated that in tropical conditions CAP endurance would be 2.3hr from *Eagle* and 1.8hr from *Hermes*. Extending *Hermes*' BS.5 catapult to 175ft (53.3m) was proposed. It was optimistically planned that the ship could carry 11–12 Phantoms and up to eight Buccaneers. The modifications to *Hermes* and *Victorious* were estimated to cost up to £2 million per ship. Neither ship in fact would operate the Phantom; *Victorious* due to her early decommissioning in 1967 (during her 1966 Far East deployment she had successfully operated USS *Ranger*'s Phantoms) and *Hermes* was just too small for safe operations. (McDonnell proposed the Model 98HL in December 1965 with RB.168-27R engines, increased span wings with reduced leading edge sweep and larger tailplanes in an effort to improve take-off performance and lower the approach speed.)

On 26 February 1963, Peter Thorneycroft announced in the Commons that the development contract for the P.1154 would go ahead for the RAF and that the RN was free to pursue negotiations for the Phantom, soon to be designated the F-4K. Shortly after this announcement BAC sent the MoA another Type 583 brochure extolling the virtues of VG wings over the Phantom, quoting an in-service date of 1970 if an Instruction to Proceed (ITP) was received in May 1965. BAC's last-ditch attempt failed.

A Memorandum of Understanding with McDonnell in March was followed by a visit by the Minister of Aviation, Julian Amery, and Captain Brown in April, the Letter of Intent being signed on the 25th by Thorneycroft and Secretary of Defense Robert MacNamara. An RN technical team was set up in the USA to help oversee the project. The desire for industrial offsets to reduce the Dollar expenditure and secure British jobs resulted in around 40% of the F-4K's structure and equipment being produced in the UK and shipped to St. Louis for assembly by McDonnell.

The third production Phantom FG.1 of 700P NAS flying over HMS *Hermes*. The worries about whether *Hermes* could operate the Phantom led to the decision to go with McDonnell Douglas' proposed changes for the F-4K. Although deck trials were carried out *Hermes* was realistically too small to operate Phantoms safely. *Blue Envoy Collection*

Sub-assemblies were manufactured by BAC (rear fuselage) and Short Brothers & Harland (outer wing sections). Earlier proposals for final assembly in the UK by Short Brothers were rejected as too costly and logistically complicated, as was a MoA proposal for Canadair to assemble the Phantoms in return for Speys for any future Canadian Phantom order.

The AWG-10 fire-control system was licence-built by Ferranti as the AWG-11 and was modified with the AN/APG-60 radar and compatibility with AGM-12 Bullpup and WE.177A (it was envisioned that the TV-guided AJ.168 Martel ASM would be added later). A study was made during March 1965 into fitting *Red Top* IR-homing AAMs instead of AIM-9C Sidewinders to provide a superior all-aspect interception capability (assuming that the *Red Top* IR seekers were slaved to the AWG-11 system.) The drawbacks were additional cost, the need for hardpoint pylon modifications and increased drag. These outweighed the advantages and the Sidewinders were retained.

The expensive P.1154, TSR.2 and Hawker Siddeley HS.681 V/STOL tactical transport were causing a severe drain on the defence budget at a time of national economic problems and the incoming Labour government took a hard look at the programmes. The RAF's P.1154 had consumed £21 million and was cancelled on 2 February 1965 by the Secretary of State for Defence Denis Healey in favour of the cheaper, subsonic, P.1127 (Harrier GR.1) and the Phantom.

Initially it was planned to procure up to 400 Phantoms, 140 for the FAA to form five squadrons and 260 for the RAF. But the UK-specific changes led to higher than forecast development and production costs (up to three times the price of a standard F-4J) and the defence budget did not allow spreading the order across a longer production run. The 1966 Defence Review reduced the RN's needs and the order was reduced to 48 F-4K FG.1 for the FAA (seven aircraft were cancelled) and 116 F-4M FGR.2 for the RAF (in addition there were two prototype YF-4K and two YF-4M plus two pre-production FG.1 aircraft). The reduced FAA requirements saw 20 of the FG.1s being diverted directly to the RAF to equip No. 43 Squadron, although some were loaned back to equip the Phantom Training Unit, 767 Naval Air Squadron (NAS).

The first YF-4K prototype, XT595, made its maiden flight on 27 June 1966 at McDonnell's St. Louis facility. The second, XT596, followed on 30 August 1966. The

The first YF-4K Phantom XT595 makes its maiden flight at St. Louis on 27 June 1966. *Terry Panopalis Collection*

YF-4K Phantom XT597 during the trials aboard the USS *Coral Sea* in July 1968. *Terry Panopalis Collection*

two pre-production F-4K aircraft, XT597 and XT598, were used for fit check trials of the various systems. XT597 was used for catapult, arrester gear and deck landing trials, while XT598 was primarily used for AWG-10 and Sparrow AAM trials. All four aircraft were delivered to the UK by 1970 for continued trials with the Aeroplane and Armament Experimental Establishment (A&AEE), Rolls-Royce and BAC.

The first production aircraft, XT857, flew on 18 September 1967. The first three FG.1s were delivered to RNAS Yeovilton on 25 April 1968, being assigned to the Intensive Flying Trials Unit 700P NAS the following day. The Phantom Training Unit, 767 NAS, was formed on 14 January 1969, training both RN and RAF crews; 700P disbanded two months later.

Initial trials of the Phantom FG.1 on the USN carrier USS *Coral Sea* in July 1968 were followed by tests of a stick positioning device/limiter to stop the control stick being pulled right back during a catapult launch and testing of a pre-production audio angle-of-attack system. These took place in September aboard the USS *John F. Kennedy* using FG.1 XT597 with some success (the trial was stopped after four launches by an engine failure). These were followed by the A&AEE's deck trials aboard *Eagle* during 10–20 March 1969 to investigate approach speeds and an assessment of the handling and controllability during the approach, overshoots and 'bolters' (failing to catch an arrester wire). The trials with XT857, XT865 and XV567 went well but the pilots, Cdr Hefford and Lt Cdr Burn, noted poor longitudinal characteristics and the Spey's poor throttle and power response. The approach speed was more accurately determined to be around 138kt at 36,000lb (16,330kg). The trials had used *Eagle's* 199ft (60.6m) waist catapult, the absence of water-cooled blast deflectors meant that a 'lash-up' fitting of a thick steel plate chained to the deck behind the catapult was used, cooled by fire hoses after each launch before the next aircraft was readied for take-off.

The RB.168-25R Spey Mk.201 (rated at 12,800lbf (56.9kN) dry and 21,350lbf (94.9kN) reheated) gave the F-4K FG.1 a 30% shorter take-off distance, 20% faster climb to altitude, better acceleration at low speed and higher top speed compared with the standard F-4J, combined with longer range at lower altitudes due to its lower fuel consumption. This was demonstrated when 892 NAS deployed aboard the USS *Saratoga* in 1969 in the Mediterranean, the F-4K being quicker off the deck than the *Saratoga's* F-4Js. At higher altitudes, however, the Spey was less efficient and increased drag of the re-designed fuselage made the aircraft slower. The Spey also suffered from unacceptable throttle lag and reheat ignition problems (it used a catalyst system with a 2in (5cm) diameter platinum-rhodium gauze to ignite the fuel). This was fixed in the improved Mk.203 (rated at 12,250lbf dry (54.4kN) and 20,515lbf (95.2kN) reheated) which had a modified reheat control system for quicker ignition – especially useful during a 'bolter' landing to enable the pilot to make a go-around. An early modification was a

The A&AEE conducted a deck trials programme aboard HMS *Eagle* in June 1969. Here the bridle has fallen away and the reheat exhaust is scorching its way over the end of the angled flight deck. *Terry Panopalis Collection*

Deck trials were carried out aboard several US Navy carriers during 1968–69, including the USS *America* on 14 January 1969. *Gerald H. Balzer via Tony Buttler*

variable bleed air system which took the boundary layer control air from the 7th stage compressor, rather than the 12th stage, when full Military Power was engaged.

The initial plan for five frontline squadrons plus a training unit and reserve pool was reduced to just a single frontline squadron following the 1966 Defence Review. 892 NAS formed at Yeovilton on 31 March 1969 under the command of Lt Cdr Brian Davies. In May 892 NAS entered three Phantoms

It is a tight fit as Phantom FG.1 XV567 descends on *Ark Royal's* forward lift. On the deck beside the lift can be seen the retractable blast deflector plates of the bow BS.5 steam catapult. *Author's Collection*

carrier fleet until 1975 and proceeding with *Ark Royal's* refit. Much to the Treasury's chagrin the plans were upgraded to include the capability to operate Phantoms. The refit lasted from March 1967 to February 1970 and cost £32 million.

The modifications included a full 8.5° angled flight deck (which increased deck parking space, the fixed-wing aircraft capacity having fallen to 30), one 199ft (60.6m) and one 151ft (46m) BS.5 steam catapult with water-cooled exhaust blast deflectors, bridle catchers (a cost saving measure to avoid losing the bridles on each launch), DA.2 DAAG arrester gear and the Mk.9 safety barrier net which could safely stop a 36,000lb (16,330kg) Phantom at up to 130kt. The ship's electronics were partially updated, two Type 965P air-search radars were fitted but the original Type 982 target indication and Type 983 height finding radars were retained. An American AN/SPN-35 carrier approach radar was fitted to provide increased operational capability and safety for nighttime operations. Provision was made to mount three Sea Cat SAM launchers and Corvus decoy launchers were fitted. The old ship's wiring was somewhat decrepit; the equivalent of 1,200 miles (1,930km) was replaced, but much of the original electrics were retained. Given the planned five-year life remaining, only an overhaul of the steam turbines and boilers was carried out.

into the Daily Mail Transatlantic Air Race, with Davies in XT858 setting the fastest eastbound transatlantic crossing time of 4hr 46min 57sec from Floyd Bennett Field, New York, to Wisley, averaging Mach 1.44. This record stood for five years. The initial carrier deployment was aboard the USS *Saratoga* in the Mediterranean in 1969. During the initial catapult launches the heat from the Spey's reheat caused the deck plates to distort, leading to subsequent catapult launches being undertaken at reduced weight without reheat. 892 NAS finally embarked aboard *Ark Royal* on 14 June 1970.

Ark Royal had been scheduled to enter a £13.5 refit during 1967–68 to operate the Buccaneer S.2 and Westland Sea King HAS.1. The Treasury had ruled this uneconomical given her planned retirement in 1972. But Denis Healey's public announcement regarding the 1966 Defence Review had committed to retaining the

Eagle had been scheduled to receive her Phantom refit during 1968–70. *Eagle's* existing BS.5 catapults were powerful enough to launch the Phantom at its maximum take-off weight, but the steel plate jet blast deflectors required replacement with water-cooled deflector plates. The refit was estimated to cost £5 million in 1968, but by January 1972 that estimate had risen to £25–30 million and instead the ship was paid off. *Ark Royal's* three-year

Between the Phantoms serialled XV573 and XV585 only one was delivered to the FAA, the remainder were all completed for the RAF. XV579 was that aircraft, but seemingly McDonnell Douglas completed the aircraft with RAF camouflage. It served with 767 NAS for FAA and RAF conversion training duties until 1972 when it was transferred to the RAF. *Terry Panopalis Collection*

extension to 1978 made serviceability a serious problem, given her worse material state compared with *Eagle*. The laid up *Eagle* was gradually stripped of spares to keep *Ark Royal* operational, finally being sold for scrapping in October 1978.

892 NAS soon moved to RAF Leuchars in Scotland; during periods of shore duty the crews and aircraft participated in Quick Reaction Alert – QRA – duties alongside No. 43 Squadron RAF. In July 1972 767 NAS was disbanded and Phantom operational conversion training became the responsibility of the Phantom Training Flight at RAF Leuchars. From early 1974 the Marconi ARI.18223 radar warning receiver was fitted in a housing at the tip of the vertical fin. As 892 NAS believed that they would be the FAA's final carrier-based fixed-wing squadron, the adopted the Greek letter Omega (Ω) as a tail marking to symbolise this. The last Phantom catapult launch was on 27 November 1978 by XT870 during the squadron's final disembarkation flight from *Ark Royal* to RAF St Athan. There the aircraft were handed over to the RAF, being issued to No. 111 Squadron. During the Phantom's FAA service, 10 aircraft had been lost in accidents.

HMS *Ark Royal* made a special visit during the USA's Bicentennial Year in April 1976. Famously several of 892 NAS's Phantoms were zapped with US Star and 'Colonial Navy' markings. A pristine XV591 is seen here at Naval Air Station Oceana. *Terry Panopalis Collection*

For the Queen's Silver Jubilee in July 1977 Phantom XV568 of 892 NAS sported special '77' nose art on the radome. It retained the Omega symbol on the tail fin, selected by the squadron as the (believed to be) last fixed-wing fighter squadron. *Terry Panopalis Collection*

What might have been. Had the national economy not been in such dire straits, then this painting may have become a reality in the 1970s. A Hawker Siddeley Osprey FAW.2 of 800 NAS (armed with *Red Top* IR-homing and *Blue Vesta* radar-guided AAMs) and a Hawker Siddeley Buccaneer S.3 overflying HMS *Queen Elizabeth* and Type 82 destroyer HMS *Bristol*. On the carrier's deck sits a Westland WG.1 Cougar tandem rotor ASW helicopter. *Luciano Alviani*

The End?

The 1966 Defence Review was one of the most important events in the RN's post-war history. All its plans for future power projection and aerial defence of the fleet seemed to be in tatters and it faced the abrogation of fixed-wing aviation altogether.

Shortly after the October 1964 election of the Labour government led by Prime Minister Harold Wilson, the Cabinet Secretary Burke Trend unveiled his desire to begin a defence review with the aim of reducing the UK's defence expenditure to £2,000 million by 1970. This would require a saving of £400 million. Wilson was convinced of the need and Denis Healey as Secretary of State for Defence was responsible for getting the review done. The RAF had sacrificed the P.1154, TSR.2 and the HS.681 in favour of cheaper American aircraft (F-4M Phantom, F-111K and Lockheed C-130 Hercules), saving £200 million. The Army had little left to cut and could only offer to trim its reserve forces by a third, so Healey looked to the RN to make most of the remaining £200 million saving. That figure was similar to the estimated cost of building CVA-01.

The Naval Staff would have to fight their corner. The Chief of the Defence Staff, Admiral of the Fleet Lord Louis Mountbatten was nearing the end of his tenure and his political machinations on many issues – including the formation of the unified MOD which Healey now led – had made him unpopular in some parts of Whitehall, so his support for the carriers was not automatically a good thing. In addition, Mountbatten and the First Sea Lord, Admiral Sir David Luce, had conceded the inclusion of the RAF's F-111K as an essential part of the defence programme. This made the new carriers look like additional, rather than essential items.

During the negotiations the Naval Staff laid down two unnegotiable 'red lines'; that the maritime air defence and strike roles could not be separated from the role of power projection on land; secondly, that the number of fleet escorts (destroyers and frigates) could not drop below 80.

The first red line opened a serious vulnerability in the argument to retaining carriers by tying them closely to power projection, for which the land-based F-111K was already earmarked. While the 'East of Suez' amphibious landing requirement had been a key defence requirement earlier in the decade, with decolonisation in full swing and less political appetite to act without allies, Healey was less wedded to this policy. Focusing on power projection also made the vital role of air defence of the fleet seem of lesser importance. An increasingly heated and bitter series of arguments with the RAF over land-based fleet protection and power projection made the Naval Staff even more blinkered (as did the implicit threat to younger FAA staff officers that their careers were on the line.)

The new Chief of the Defence Staff, General Richard Hull and Healey's private secretary (a former Admiralty civil servant) offered a compromise 'maritime role' carrier capable of operating just Phantoms for air defence, with a secondary strike role. The resulting 30,000–35,000-ton carrier would be cheaper but the RN rejected this compromise, being determined to retain the Buccaneers. A decade of design studies had already ruled out small carriers and given the fears surrounding operating the Phantom from *Hermes*, the maritime carrier may have proved unworkable or would have spiralled in size had it gone ahead.

The second red line (only relaxed in the last few weeks of negotiations) sounded like a refusal to contribute anything to the review at a time when poor personnel recruitment and retention were growing problems, manning new carriers would be increasingly difficult in these circumstances.

Seeking to end the deadlock, in October 1965 Healey convened a Defence Council meeting to launch defence studies based on the Treasury's hypothetical cancellation of CVA-01 to bring the budget below £2,000 million. Luce refused to consider even a hypothetical cancellation. In December, Healey (with the Treasury's backing) offered one maritime carrier, but the carrier force would be retired in 1980. The Admiralty Board pushed for CVA-01, petulantly advising that if they could not have it, that the RN should give up all the carriers as soon as possible.

Healey decided to call their bluff, giving the Cabinet's Overseas Policy and Defence Committee two options to consider; decommissioning all carriers by the end of 1969 or building one large carrier and running on *Eagle* and *Hermes* until the 1980s (pointedly the maritime carrier was not offered.) The Treasury favoured decommissioning to save £88 million and free up 6,460 personnel. Burke Trend was sceptical that relying on the RAF for maritime control was feasible and offered the compromise of maintaining the carriers until 1975. Healey cancelled the Buccaneer 2** in favour of the F-111K, thus ending the FAA's long-term strike capability.

> *"We cannot be certain yet that the carriers will survive the Defence Review; and if they do not, the carrier fleet could well come to an end before 1970 through sheer inability to sustain FAA recruitment."*
>
> HEAD OF DS4, 6 AUGUST 1965

There was no Iron Curtain dividing East and West at sea. The desire to observe what the other side was doing – or stopping the other side seeing – led to close encounters, even as close as collisions between ships and submarines. Here a Kamov Ka-25 *Hormone* anti-submarine helicopter observes a Hawker Siddeley Buccaneer S.2 and a McDonnell Douglas Phantom FG.1 parked on the bows of HMS *Ark Royal*. Blue Envoy Collection

WINGS OVER THE FLEET

Victor K.1A XH590 refuelling Buccaneer S.2 XN982 and Sea Vixen FAW.2 XJ854. In the post-Defence Review years the RN would have to rely more heavily on RAF maritime patrol, airborne early warning and tanker support. The only problem was that the Air Staff assigned a lower priority to these roles and there were never enough tankers available until the late-1980s. Blue Envoy Collection

The Naval Staff were given a final opportunity to present a case to the Cabinet Committee. Their resulting plan was a mess: halving the number of Phantoms and operating Sea Vixens into the early 1970s; reducing the number of Buccaneers below those proposed in Trend's compromise plan; cancelling the TV-guided AJ.168 Martel for the anti-ship role; buying 25 navalised SEPECAT Jaguar M attack fighters from 1973; and a navalised version of the Anglo-French Variable Geometry (AFVG) strike aircraft. This proposal gave less capability for more money! The Jaguar M was under development for the French Marine Nationale but lacked a radar (the Marine Nationale cancelled it in 1973); the AFVG was similar to the earlier OR.346 and was the culmination of BAC's VG wing research but the collaboration fell apart a year later.

The Cabinet meeting of 15 February opted to cancel CVA-01 and retire the remaining carriers in 1975. Admiral Luce and the Navy Minister, Christopher Mayhew resigned in protest, but in reality the Naval Staff had talked themselves out of obtaining a compromise small carrier and talked themselves into giving up their existing ones. The alleged remark by Professor Louis Rydill, the CVA-01 Project Leader, that "cancellation was the happiest day of my life," sums up what the Ship Department felt about the chances of CVA-01 being a success. The devaluation of Pound Sterling in 1967 and the accelerated withdrawal from 'East of Suez' by 1971 made the carrier fleet's rationale even less secure.

The election of Edward Heath's Conservative government in June 1970 brought about the extension of *Ark Royal's* service until 1978 (avoiding her being refitted as a commando carrier alongside *Hermes*) but with fiscal and manning implications for the RN's long-term plans. Pleas from the USA and NATO during 1977–78 to reprieve *Ark Royal* fell on deaf ears. The increasingly unserviceable *Ark Royal* and the already-earmarked transfer of Phantoms and Buccaneers to the RAF made this option impossible without further cutbacks in other vital operational areas, such as ASW. It was not the end for the RN's fixed-wing carrier fleet; Hawker's P.1127 and a cruiser would fortuitously come together to provide the fleet's air defence.

11 Fly vertical

The outcome of the 1966 Defence Review was the reorientation of the United Kingdom's defence policy away from 'East of Suez' to focus on supporting NATO and Atlantic operations. The Naval Staff began planning other ways to provide naval air support for the fleet. This led to the era of the Hawker Siddeley Sea Harrier FRS.1 vertical/short take-off and landing (V/STOL) fighter and the 'through-deck cruiser.' The events of April and May 1982 in the South Atlantic following the Argentine invasion of the Falkland Islands/Malvinas cemented the Sea Harrier's place in history and reaffirmed the need for naval forces to have their own air cover. During the late 1970s and early 1980s the newly nationalised British Aerospace (BAe) began studying supersonic V/STOL fighters, taking up where the Hawker Siddeley P.1154 had left off in 1963. None of these concepts progressed off the drawing board, but as the Cold War ended in 1990 the RN had maintained the capability to defend the fleet and project strike power against land targets in the post-fleet carrier era. During the post-Cold War years, the Sea Harrier FA.2 brought world-leading interception capabilities, but its tenure was brief, the confused geopolitical situation of the early 21st century with its interventions and anti-terrorism campaigns required sea-to-shore strike power and the Sea Harrier was eclipsed by the Royal Air Force's Harrier GR.7 and GR.9A within the Joint Force Harrier. Both Fleet Air Arm and RAF pilots flew together on land and sea. Another round of defence cuts in 2010 saw the Joint Force Harrier being disbanded and the Harrier fleet withdrawn from service. The RN was left without sea-based fixed-wing air support for the first time since 1915.

Following the demise of the Fleet Carriers and the Phantoms and Buccaneers, the carrier fleet was renewed with the *Invincible*-class anti-submarine carriers and the Hawker Siddeley/BAe Sea Harrier FRS.1. HMS *Illustrious'* flight deck is busy in October 1986 with Sea Harriers of 800 NAS and Westland Sea Kings. *Terry Panopalis Collection*

WINGS OVER THE FLEET

VTOL

The RN was no stranger to VTOL aircraft. As early as 1953 they had been seen as a potential alternative to the flexible deck concept using undercarriageless aircraft. The same year, the Director of Air Warfare (DAW), Captain Arthur Bolt, sketched up a light fleet carrier with a flight deck 695ft (211.8m) long and 144ft (43.8m) wide, equipped with a single lift amidships and a 180ft (54.8m) long steam catapult on the 6.5° angled deck. The carrier could operate 16 Supermarine Scimitar F.1 fighters and later be converted to operate VTOL fighters with a 72ft (22m) radius landing area replacing the arrester gear.

This idea was not developed but the concept of VTOL had taken hold in the Admiralty and in the US Navy (USN) – which went as far as building prototypes of the Lockheed XFV-1 and Convair XFY-1 tailsitter VTOL fighter prototypes in 1954 (Supermarine had sketched up a remarkably similar Type 1040 back in February 1944 with a 24-cylinder Rolls-Royce Eagle piston engine.) The main obstacle was the lack of technical progress in obtaining reliable VTOL flight – taking off vertically, transitioning to horizontal flight and then transitioning to make a vertical landing, all under manual control. There was a multitude of ways of achieving this:

- Traditional helicopters or compound helicopters with additional propulsive propellers;

- Tilting rotor blades that function as rotors when vertical and as propellers in horizontal flight;

- Swivelling engine pods on the wing tips, either for turboprops or turbojets;

- Tilting wings, the incidence of the entire wing being altered from the horizontal to vertical (and vice versa), including the engines attached to it;

- Tailsitters with undercarriages on the tail surfaces and a tilting seat for the pilot (who must look over his shoulder to land!);

- Lift fans using large rotors within the wings to create vertical lift and usually covered by louvres in horizontal flight;

- Flat risers, aircraft with a battery of lift jets in the fuselage which are shut down in horizontal flight, which then become deadweight and take up fuselage space which could otherwise be occupied by fuel tanks or weapon bays;

- Zero-Length Launch (ZELL), blasting an aircraft airborne from a short rail using a massive rocket booster and landing conventionally.

British aircraft designers studied several of these concepts with naval applications in mind. In mid-1946 Fairey's Chief Designer, Herbert Eugene Chaplin, had drafted the Type K tailless swept wing tailsitter. It was powered by a pair of Rolls-Royce AJ.65 axial-flow turbojets for a maximum speed of 564kt. Originally pitched to the RAF, a naval version was also offered with the fighters attached to rails along the sides of the aircraft carrier for take-off. The pilot was sat in an independently swivelling cockpit to make landing easier. The Ministry of Supply (MoS) supplied research funding for rocket-propelled scale model testing (named Beta), resulting Type R – otherwise known as the FD.1 or Fairey Delta 1 – which flew as a delta-winged research aircraft with a normal tricycle undercarriage in March 1951. There is no evidence that Chaplin's

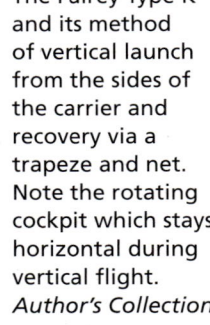

The Fairey Type K and its method of vertical launch from the sides of the carrier and recovery via a trapeze and net. Note the rotating cockpit which stays horizontal during vertical flight.
Author's Collection

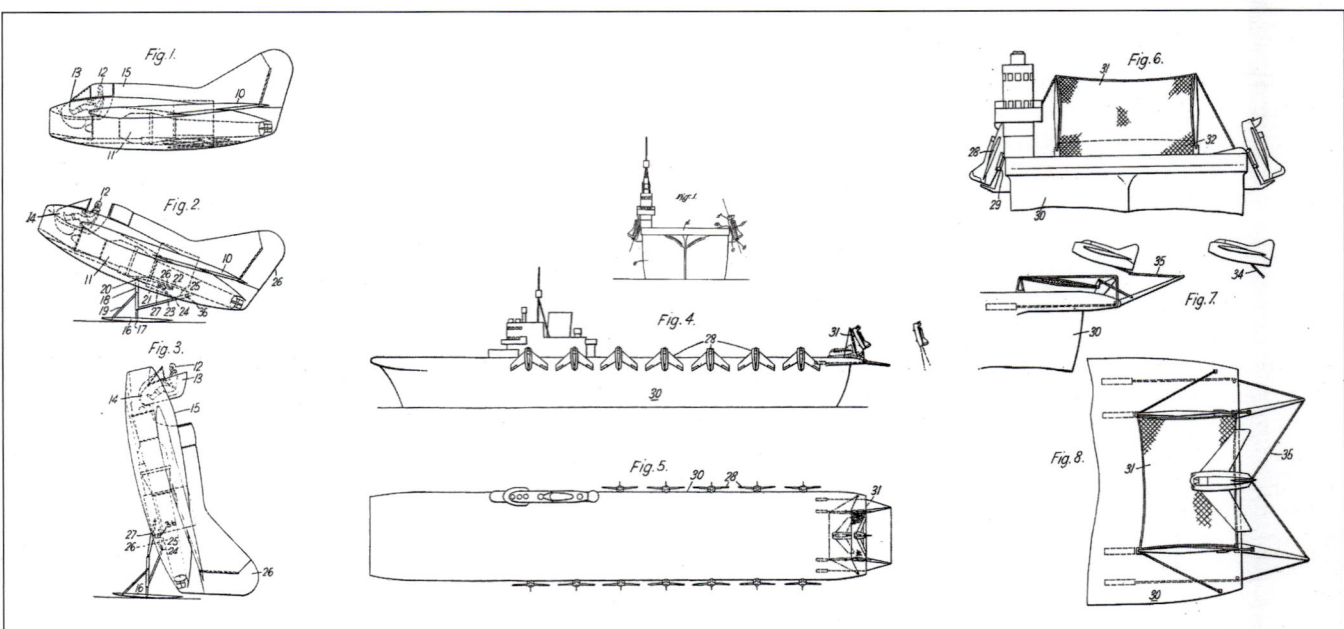

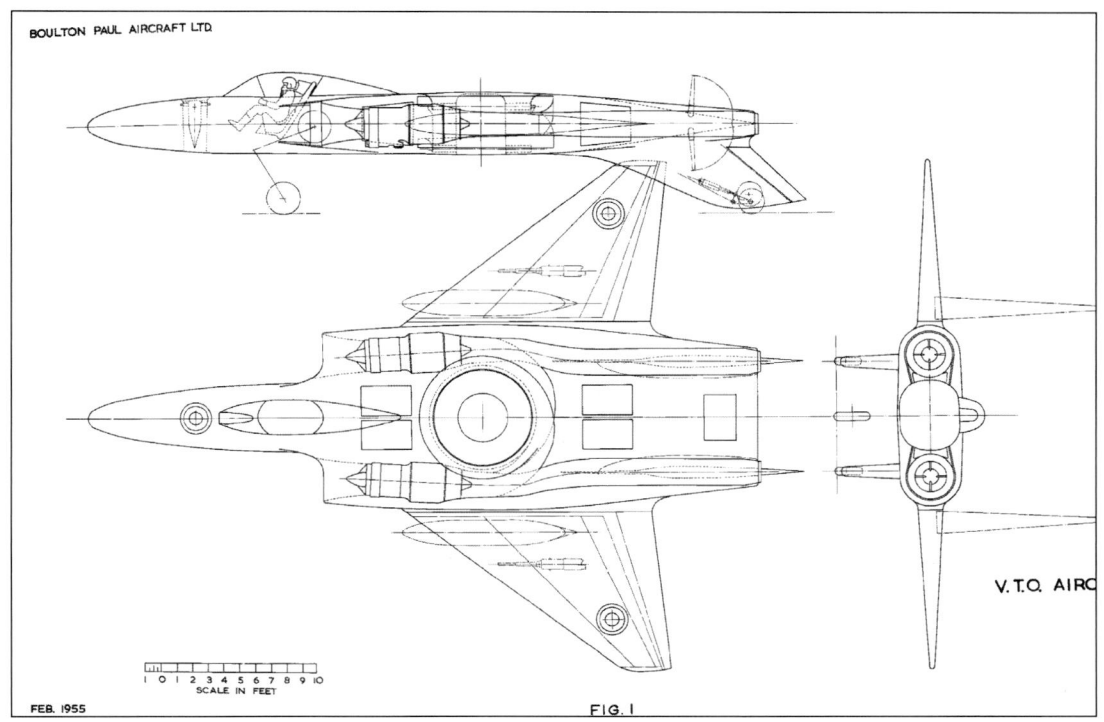

Boulton Paul's P.130 Scheme 8 design study was designed in February 1955 as a naval fighter with two Bristol Orpheus turbojets powering the main fan and three smaller control fans for attitude control in the nose and wing tips. *Boulton Paul Archive via Les Whitehouse*

naval VTOL concept was seriously entertained by the Admiralty.

Boulton Paul received research contracts from the MoS to study lift fans powered by jet exhaust bleed air, which had been proposed by RA Shaw, the Assistant Director of the Royal Aircraft Establishment's (RAE) Research Department in October 1954. The bleed air was used to drive a turbine to rotate the blades of the 42-blade ducted fan to provide vertical lift, equivalent to 550lbf (2.44kN) thrust at 6,000rpm. Being 6in (152mm) deep and weighing 52lb (23.5kg) each, they fitted inside the wing structure and in horizontal flight were blanked off via louvres. Prototype fans were built in collaboration with the National Gas Turbine Establishment (NGTE) and static tested at the RAE's facilities at Bedford, including a test rig with four fans which could be re-arranged in several ways to check for interference effects using multiple fans.

Boulton Paul's initial P.130 design studies were five-engine, single-seat, fighter-type aircraft with delta wings and a single large 75in (190.5cm) diameter fan in the centre fuselage. Scheme 8 of February 1955 was sketched as tentative naval fighter with folding delta outer wings with 53° leading edge sweep and the two ventral tails carried the main undercarriage legs. Two Bristol Orpheus turbojets in the wing roots powered the main fan and three smaller control fans for attitude control in the nose and near the wing tips. The wingspan was 34ft 2in (10.4m) and length 46ft 5in (14.1m).

The P.133B was a 'naval search and strike' aircraft designed in November 1956 around the requirements of NA.39, which had led to the Buccaneer. It was a large delta flying wing of 76° leading edge sweep with a large vertical tail, with the two 10,000lbf (44.4kN) de Havilland Gyron Junior turbojets in nacelles buried in the wings. The 28ft (8.53m) span did not require folding for carrier operations. The Gyron Juniors drove two turbines, located inboard of the engines, which powered four 32in (81.2cm) diameter fans in the wings via driveshafts; these were inboard of the engines and at the wing tips, just ahead of the ailerons. The trailing edge had a large elevon. Differential thrust and controllable inlet vanes on the control fans provided attitude control in the pitch and yaw planes.

The two crew sat in tandem and the weapon bay could accommodate one *Red Beard* tactical nuclear bomb or up to four 1,000lb (454kg) bombs. Five or eight external triple rocket projectile packs could be fitted for ground attack missions. The 40,120lb (18,200kg) P.133B was designed for catapult

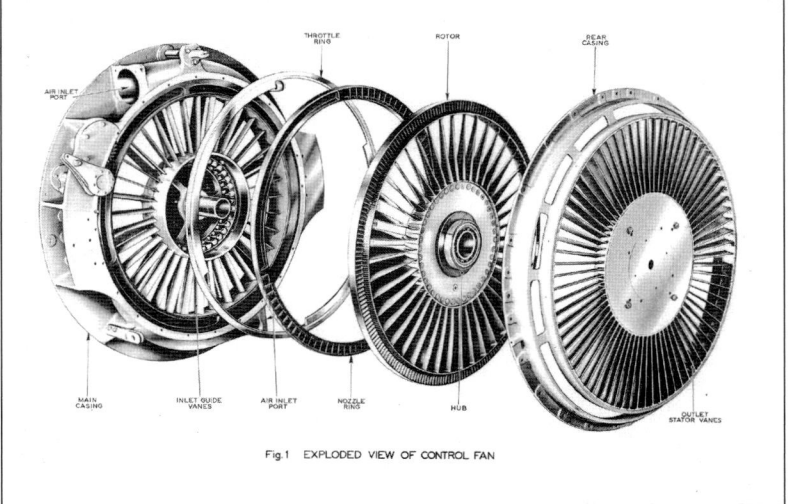

An exploded view of Boulton Paul's control fan driven by engine bleed air to spin the rotor. The bleed air impinged the vanes on the outer rim of the rotor disc. *Boulton Paul Archive via Les Whitehouse*

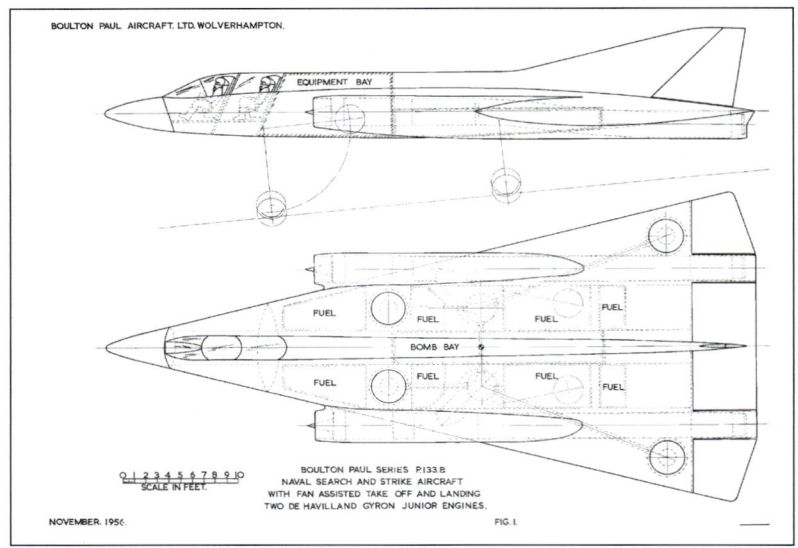

Boulton Paul's P.133B was designed around the requirements of NA.39. The two de Havilland Gyron Junior turbojets drove two turbines, located inboard of the engines, which in turn powered four 32in (81.2cm) diameter fans via driveshafts. *Boulton Paul Archive via Les Whitehouse*

launching in zero wind conditions or could take off at 100kt with the fans – the fans and turbines produced 34,000lbf (151.2kN) of lift. The minimum landing speed was 50kt. The all-up weight (AUW) was later re-estimated by NGTE to be 46,225lb (20,980kg).

The MoS requested a comparison design to the P.133B using lift engines. Again, the design was based around NA.39 and used two Gyron Juniors. Instead of the lift fans the centre fuselage section held 10 Rolls-Royce RB.108 lift engines (five each side of the weapon bay), giving 40,000lbf (177.8kN) vertical thrust. The wing thickness/chord ratio was increased; the leading edge sweep was 75°. The 31ft (9.44m) span wing did not need folding, although the nose cone of the 56ft (17m) long fuselage did fold for carrier stowage. The estimated AUW was 46,465lb (21,075kg) – only 210lb (95kg) more than the P.133B. The estimated maximum speed at sea level was 822kt with a take-off speed of 100kt, the radius of action being 348nm (643km).

Boulton Paul went on to design many other aircraft using this fan technology, including airliners, freighters and 'Jumping Jeep' reconnaissance vehicles for the Army, but none of them was built.

Short Brothers & Harland, which flew the S.C.1 V/STOL research aircraft in 1956, made several naval V/STOL studies later that year. The PD.23 two-seat strike aircraft had a small 28ft (8.53m) span delta wing with a gross weight of 62,000lb (28,125kg). It

VTOL designs

	Fairey Type K	Boulton Paul P.130 (Scheme 8)	Boulton Paul P.133B	Boulton Paul P.137	Short PD.23	Hawker P.1158
Crew	One	One	Two	Two	Two	One
Span	?	34ft 2in (10.41m); 15ft 0in (4.57m) folded	28ft 0in (8.53m)	31ft 0in (9.44m)	28ft 0in (8.53m)	?
Length	?	46ft 5in (14.14m)	58ft 0in (17.67m)	56ft 0in (17.06m); 51ft 0in (15.54m) folded	72ft 6in (22.10m)	?
Wing area	?	?	?	?	300ft² (27.9m²)	?
All-up weight	13,500lb (6,125kg)	?	40,120lb (18,200kg)	46,465lb (21,075kg)	62,000lb (28,125kg)	?
Powerplant	2x AJ.65 Avon	2x Orpheus, driving 1x 75in (190.5cm) diameter fan & 3x small control fans	2x Gyron Junior 10,000lbf (44.4kN), driving 4x 32in (81.2cm) diameter fans	2x Gyron Junior 10,000lbf (44.4kN); 10x RB.108 lift engines, 4,000lbf (17.7kN)	2x Avon RA.29; 20x RB.108 lift engines, 4,000lbf (17.7kN)	3x RB.153R; 6x RB.153 lift engines
Max speed	565kt (1,046km/h) at SL	?	?	822kt (1,522km/h) at SL	Mach 1.0	Mach 3.0
Armament	1x recoilless gun or 2x 30mm ADEN	2x 30mm ADEN, 2x bombs or RP pods	1x Red Beard, 2x 2,000lb (907kg) bombs, 4x 1,000lb (454kg) bombs, 5x3 or 8x3 RP packs	1x Red Beard, 4x 1,000lb (454kg) bombs	1x Red Beard	1x Red Beard, bombs, RP pods and other stores

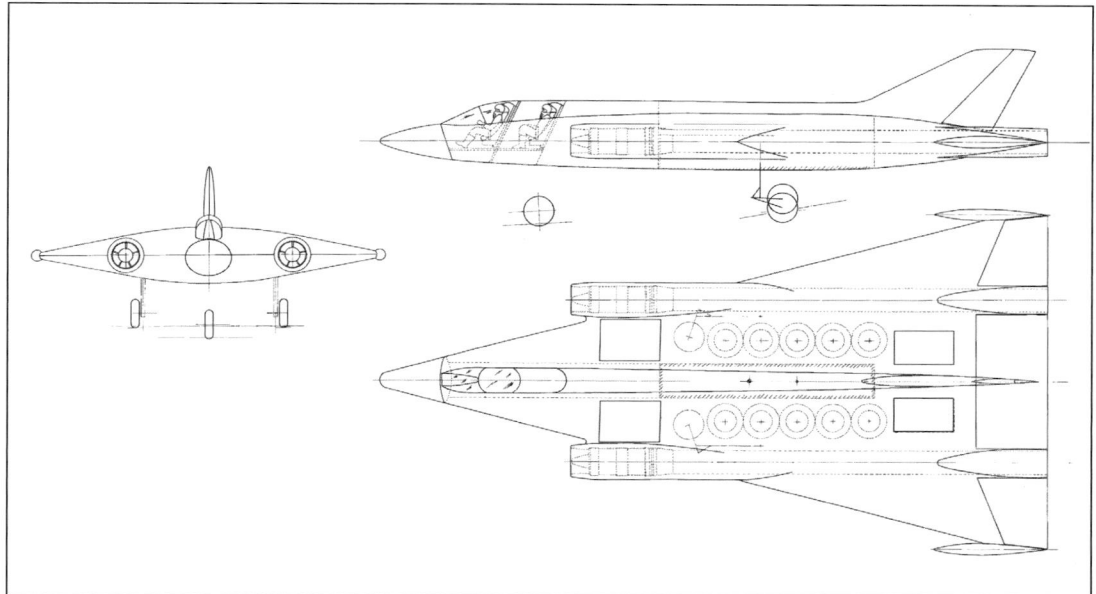

The P.137 comparison design to the P.133B had two Gyron Juniors for normal propulsion and ten Rolls-Royce RB.108 lift engines giving 40,000lbf (177.8kN) of vertical thrust. These studies were research projects to investigate what VTOL might achieve in the sphere of naval aviation. *Boulton Paul Archive via Les Whitehouse*

was powered by two Rolls-Royce Avon RA.29 turbojets mounted on the sides of the lower fuselage beneath the wings and had no fewer than 20 RB.108 lift engines in two banks ahead and aft of the wing. The estimated maximum speed was Mach 1.0 and range was 390nm (725km) with 2,783gal (12,652L) of internal fuel. The weapon bay carried one nuclear weapon.

The Hawker Siddeley P.1138 interceptor design of September 1959 was drawn up by Roy Braybrook of the Hawker Project Office at Kingston upon Thames. It had a tailless canard layout, the canards controlling the pitch. Forward-swept intakes above the wing root trailing edge fed three RB.153R engines, another six unreheated RB.153 were lift engines. The estimated maximum speed was Mach 3. Kingston was having fun doodling all kinds of futuristic V/STOL designs at this time. One of them would prove to be a winner.

Harrier

The breakthrough was vectored thrust. The French aircraft designer Michel Wibault had a brainwave in 1954; instead of using separate lift engines why not simply fit a jet engine with swivelling nozzles to divert the thrust? For vertical thrust the nozzles swivelled downwards, being rotated to face aft for horizontal flight. The nozzles would use 'cold' air tapped from the engine's compressor stage. He designed an aircraft around this design, but there was no official interest in France.

Undeterred, Wibault approached the Mutual Weapons Development Program (MWDP), which offered to pay 75% of the development costs and put Wibault in touch with Bristol Engines in 1956. Technical Director Stanley Hooker assigned the talented engineer Gordon Lewis to assist Wibault to refine the design. Wibault had originally intended to use the Bristol BE.25 Orion engine core but this was too heavy. Swapping it for the Or.3 Orpheus and fitting the first two stages of an Ol.21 Olympus low pressure compressor on a coaxial shaft created the BE.52. It had two nozzles and the exhaust vented aft as a normal jet engine. It was still too heavy, but further refinement with an Or.6 Orpheus core and the compressor was moved aft to reduce the length led to the BE.53 – which became the Pegasus. At this stage Hawker entered the picture. Sir Sydney Camm was becoming interested in V/STOL concepts and was looking around for an engine, getting wind of the BE.53. Chief Engineer Ralph Hooper began penning the P.1127 aircraft around the engine. It was Hooper who backed Lewis' earlier suggestion of having four nozzles (pairs fore and aft of the aircraft's centre of gravity). The compressor fan would feed the forward pair, the jet exhaust venting through the aft nozzles.

Bristol and Hawker worked as a team, developing the BE.53 Pegasus and the P.1127 together. Despite the defence cuts of 1957, the availability of MWDP funds, wind tunnel test assistance from NASA and support from NATO's Supreme Headquarters Allied Powers Europe ensured that the P.1127 went ahead as a research aircraft. Hawker had been pursuing the construction of a prototype as a private venture since May 1959 but the Ministry of Aviation (MoA) finally issued Specification ER.204D on 29 February 1960 and ordered two prototypes, followed by four more in November.

The first prototype, serial XP831, made its first untethered hover on 19 November 1960 at Hawker's Dunsfold factory. XP831 then made its first conventional flight on 13 March 1961, by Hawker's Chief Test Pilot Bill Bedford. Translations from hovering to forward flight began in September, on the 18th a complete transition sequence from vertical take-off to wing-borne flight and then a vertical landing was accomplished. The display at the 1962 Society of British Aircraft Constructors

WINGS OVER THE FLEET

HMS *Bulwark* took part in an RAE carrier trials programme in mid-June 1966 and this was followed in 1969 by the landing of Harrier GR.1 XV758 aboard the ship. *Blue Envoy Collection*

Hawker Siddeley Dunsfold's Chief Test Pilot Hugh Merewether landing Harrier GR.1 XV742 aboard helicopter cruiser HMS *Blake*. Despite high crosswinds the landings and take-offs went smoothly. *Blake*'s landing deck was 117ft (35.6m) long, 56ft (17m) wide at the forward end, tapering to 30ft (9m) at the stern. *Blue Envoy Collection*

(SBAC) Show at Farnborough introduced the public to the 'jump jet' that would become familiar to airshow audiences for the next 48 years.

Despite the early Pegasus engines lacking thrust and some accidents during test flying, the P.1127 proved to be a success and was the first V/STOL prototype to show that a practical military aircraft could result from the concept. Designed for ground support missions operating from fields and forest clearings, there was no reason why the P.1127 could not fly from the small decks of helicopter-equipped warships or aircraft carriers.

The first carrier-based trial was not related to any direct naval requirement. The Treasury approved £20,000 to carry out trials using XP831 on HMS *Ark Royal* to establish what features would be required on the naval Hawker Siddeley P.1154B supersonic V/STOL interceptor then under development (see Chapter 10.) Bill Bedford flew out to *Ark Royal* in the English Channel on 8 February. Bedford and fellow Hawker test pilot Hugh Merewether made six take-offs with deflected thrust at different nozzle settings and vertical landings. An observer from the USN was also present.

The FAA did not participate in the Tripartite Squadron evaluation of the six P.1127 Kestrel FGA.1 during 1964–65 – although the USN did. When the USN took its Kestrels home (as the XV-6A) in 1966, they were flown from the carrier USS *Independence* and the amphibious transport dock ship USS *Raleigh*, leading to the subsequent purchase of the Harrier by the US Marine Corps (USMC).

The successful Kestrel evaluation led to the RAF receiving the Harrier GR.1 in April 1969. As part of the Harrier development programme, P.1127 XP984 was fitted with the larger Harrier wing in 1966 for aerodynamic flight trials. Part of the RAE trials programme involved flight trials from HMS *Bulwark* in the English Channel in mid-June 1966, Harrier GR.1 XV758 also landing aboard *Bulwark* in 1969. This proved that fixed-wing V/STOL aircraft and helicopters could operate from the same deck. Another lesson was that the magnesium in the Harrier's airframe should be replaced with less reactive metals to better cope with corrosive salty environments.

While Hugh Merewether (now Dunsfold's Chief Test Pilot) was conducting tropical performance trials in Sicily with XP984, another naval test was performed, this time for the Italian Navy. They had built two *Andrea Doria*-class helicopter cruisers, armed with RIM-2 Terrier surface-to-air missiles (SAMs), small calibre guns and a hangar and landing deck aft for four anti-submarine helicopters; the larger *Vittorio Veneto* capable of operating nine helicopter was under construction and plans for a fourth ship (to be named *Trieste* or *Italia*) included 12 helicopters with provision for V/STOL fighters. Merewether performed a landing and take-off from *Andrea Doria*'s 98 × 52ft (30 × 16m) helicopter deck on 24 October 1967, while the ship was moored at La Spezia. This interest eventually led to *Trieste* transforming into light aircraft carrier *Giuseppe*

HMS *Ark Royal* was also used for Harrier GR.1 compatibility trials. A rolling take-off is made from the angled deck; in practice nearly all V/STOL aircraft employ rolling take-offs to save fuel. The Sea Harrier concept was born from these successful trials. *Author's Collection*

Garibaldi, which commissioned in 1985. McDonnell Douglas-built AV-8A Harriers were not received until a 1937 law which prevented the Italian Navy buying fixed-wing aircraft was repealed in 1989.

Repeating this feat for the RAE's Naval Air Department on 2 August 1969, Merewether landed Harrier GR.1 XV742 aboard the newly converted helicopter cruiser HMS *Blake*. *Blake*'s landing deck was 117ft (35.6m) long, 56ft (17m) wide at the forward end, tapering to 30ft (9m) at the stern. One of the ship's four Westland Wessex HAS.3 anti-submarine helicopters kept station as a rescue plane guard as Merewether conducted 33 landings and take-offs during eight sorties. During these flights the ship rolled 6° to either side with a 30kt wind over the deck, the Aeroplane and Armament Experimental Establishment (A&AEE) accepting this as the practical roll limit for Harrier landings. This event also celebrated the 52nd anniversary of Squadron Commander Edwin Dunning's 'world's-first' landing onto a moving ship, by manoeuvring his Sopwith Pup to alight on HMS *Furious'* forward deck in 1917. The confirmation that Harriers could operate from a cruiser was good marketing material for Hawker Siddeley. While the Naval Staff was still not convinced of the Harrier's utility as a naval aircraft, the RAF began working up a wartime carrier deployment capability and No. 1(F) Squadron flew service release trials during 1970 aboard *Eagle*.

The *Daily Mail* Transatlantic Air Race in May 1969 led to two Harrier GR.1s being available in the USA at the time that the USMC were assessing the Harrier following the trial operations from USS *Raleigh* (Squadron Leader Tom Lecky won the race in Harrier GR.1 XV741 with the fastest London-New York flying time of 6hr 11min). Hawker Siddeley test pilot John Farley decided to make a demonstration tour. On arrival at Naval Station Norfolk, Virginia, Farley proposed flying out and landing aboard the *Raleigh's* sistership *La Salle* which happened to be in harbour. Farley landed aboard, the groundcrew fitted drop tanks and rocket pods which had been delivered by helicopter, then he flew back to the

The compact Harrier GR.1 easily fits on the deck lift aboard *Ark Royal*. *Blue Envoy Collection*

WINGS OVER THE FLEET

Demonstrating No. 1(F) Squadron's ability to operate from carriers is Harrier GR.1 XV749 aboard *Ark Royal* in May 1971. *Terry Panopalis Collection*

shore to impress upon the USN and USMC staff officers watching that the Harrier could be operated independently of ground or ship facilities. This helped to clinch the USMC's order for the AV-8A Harrier in 1970.

Hawker Siddeley went one further when John Farley landed Harrier GR1 XV757 aboard the Argentine carrier ARA *Veinticinco de Mayo* on 4 September 1969, during the ship's delivery voyage from the Netherlands (originally the *Colossus*-class HMS *Venerable*, the ship had served the Dutch navy as HNLMS *Karel Doorman* during 1948-68). The marketing ploy impressed the Argentine Navy, but no order for the Harrier was forthcoming, nor from later South American marketing tours, including a jaunt aboard Brazil's *Colossus*-class ship *Minas Gerais* (ex-HMS *Vengeance*) in 1973.

In 1972 Hawker Siddeley's own two-seat Mk.52 trainer demonstrator, registered G-VTOL, made a Far East sales tour. On its way back to the UK, the aircraft visited the Indian Navy's base at Cochin. From there John Farley flew aboard the Indian carrier INS *Vikrant* (a M*ajestic*-class ship), generating 17 sorties in two days, plus two ferry flights from Cochin. The first day was devoted to obtaining handling and performance data relevant to the ship and the local conditions (the monsoon season had just begun) and the second day was devoted to flying Indian Navy pilots. Further demonstrations were flown at Goa and Delhi, including a low level mission and pilot familiarisation.

In 1973 John Farley fired a Matra/Hawker Siddeley Dynamics AS.37 Martel anti-radar missile from a Harrier GR.1 over Lyme Bay, Dorset. This trial highlighted that the Harrier had a potential anti-ship capability if air-to-surface missiles (ASMs) were fitted.

CCH to *Invincible*

The *Invincible*-class had its origins as far back as the Escort Carrier concept of 1959 carrying 22 anti-submarine warfare ASW helicopters. This was partly brought about by the criticisms of Rear Admiral AR Pedder, the Flag Officer Aircraft Carriers, that helicopters aboard fleet carriers would interfere with fixed-wing deck operations. Between 1960 and 1966 the Escort Cruiser married the ASW role with between eight and five helicopters with the traditional cruiser Task Force Flagship role with command spaces, a medium calibre gun for naval gunfire support and a GWS.1 Sea Slug – later GWS.30 Sea Dart – SAM launcher for area defence. It was similar in concept to the Italian *Andrea Doria* and *Vittorio Veneto* before becoming a 10,500-ton ship with an offset axial flight deck. The £16.8 million price tag contributed to the decision to defer new construction in favour of converting *Tiger* and *Blake*.

Following the 1966 Defence Review the need for a Command Cruiser (CCH) remained to replace the retiring carriers and the cancelled Type 82 guided-missile destroyers. The Future Fleet Working Party went back to a 10,000-ton design with an aft landing deck for six to eight helicopters. The design by 1968 was 12,000 tons with Sea Dart, a 4.5in (114mm) gun and six Westland Sea Kings. The Treasury did not demure, seeing it as equivalent to an Army divisional headquarters and Secretary of State for Defence Denis Healey also supported its inclusion in future planning.

The following year the number of Sea Kings increased to 12 to ensure a fully effective ASW screen around a Task Force. The Treasury accepted the enlarged helicopter complement and the fact that the CCH had regained its axial flight deck – the 'through-deck'. Much has been written about the use of the 'through-deck cruiser' moniker as a backdoor means to get the acquisition of carriers past the politicians. This is a red herring, as Denis Healey fully supported the larger design. There was no political doubt that the RN would receive a cruiser which was to all intents and purposes a mini-carrier in design. There was also no doubt that the ships would be capable of fixed-wing operations. The Admiralty Board had added the ability to operate RAF Harriers instead of Sea Kings in emergencies on a one-to-one replacement basis, this capability only costing another £1 million. Healey agreed that if the idea was practical that the order should go ahead. This was the real subterfuge – the Naval Branch historian Edward Hampshire has written that he has not yet discovered a 12-helicopter CCH design in the archives. It seems by sleight of hand the RN acquired a ship that in reality would only carry nine Sea Kings with space left over for a trio of Harriers.

Naval Staff Requirement NSR.7097 for the CCH was approved in February 1970. Its roles were to: command a naval task force and control the operation of land-based aircraft; operate large ASW helicopters for area defence; deploy area defence SAMs; and provide a quick-reaction contribution to strike, probe and limited air defence capability with V/STOL aircraft. The magazines would hold 54 homing torpedoes (a portion could be swapped for up to 24 Mk.11 depth charges) and 12 WE.177A nuclear depth bombs for the Sea Kings and 40 SNEB rocket pods and 18 1,000lb (454kg) bombs for the Harriers (provision for missiles was only "required for the Harrier Successor.") The orders for the ships were delayed by the 1970 General Election and change of government, the first ship finally being ordered in April 1973 as the CAH – a Cruiser, Helicopter. By this time, it was planned to operate five Harriers alongside nine Sea Kings and the ship had grown to 19,500 tons with a flight deck 550ft (168m) long, which later featured a ski-jump ramp at the bows. The ski-jump had been proposed by Lt Cdr Douglas Taylor in his university thesis as a means to allow a Harrier to make a rolling take-off to increase its payload. Hawker Siddeley backed the idea and with Ministry of Defence (MOD) funding a ramp was built at RAE Bedford and successfully tested in August1977 using pre-production Harrier GR.1 XV281, followed by another ramp at Yeovilton

in early 1981 which was variable between 7–15° to find the optimum setting for use aboard the carriers.

The first two ships, *Invincible* and *Illustrious* were commissioned on 11 July 1980 and 20 June 1982 and both had a 7° ski-jump. *Illustrious* set sail for the Falklands immediately on commissioning, arriving to relieve *Invincible* on 28 August. The third vessel, *Ark Royal* commissioned on 1 November 1985 and had additional Flag facilities and a 12° ski-jump which allowed the Sea Harrier to lift an extra 2,500lb (1,135kg) or reduce its take-off run by up to 60% with the usual 5,000lb (2,270kg) payload (12° ski-jumps were later retrofitted to *Invincible* and *Illustrious*). Courtesy of Falklands Conflict experience, *Ark Royal* also had improved close-in weapon systems for anti-missile self-defence.

The 1981 Defence White Paper, *The UK Defence Programme: The Way Forward*, was the product of Margaret Thatcher's Conservative government, the Secretary of State for Defence John Nott being keen

This is HMS *Illustrious* after the GWS.30 Sea Dart SAM system had been removed in the early 2000s to create additional deck space. The helicopters on the flight deck are two Westland Lynx AH.7 of 847 NAS supporting the Royal Marines and a Lynx HMA.8. MOD/Open Government Licence

The Sea Harrier's adversary. The Tu-95RT *Bear*-D would provide mid-course targeting information for the anti-ship missiles fired from Soviet cruise-missile submarines and warships well beyond the defensive screen of NATO carrier groups. By the 1980s the *Bear*-D was being superseded by Soviet EROSAT and ROSAT surveillance satellites. *US Navy*

to rebalance the Services' procurement plans within the available defence budget. The Navy Department's response was to look at cancellations of uncompleted ships, including *Ark Royal*. The political embarrassment of scrapping a ship just launched with much pomp by the Queen Mother was avoided by swapping it for *Invincible*, which was offered to the Royal Australian Navy in July 1981 for £175 million as a helicopter carrier. Events in the South Atlantic nine months later saw this deal being torn up. Two of the three *Invincibles* would be operational at any one time in rotation, the third being in refit.

Resurrecting Fixed-wing aviation

The RAF had not objected to the *Invincible*-class having Harrier capability, in their eyes it gave them a strategic reach and No. 1(F) Squadron had been carrier-capable since 1970 for wartime deployments. The Treasury was wary of the FAA being resurrected as a fixed-wing force, which it saw as duplicating the RAF. But having faced little opposition to the new ships and with the CVA-01 cancellation-era politicians out of the picture with Edward Heath's Conservative government winning the 1970 General Election, the RN had scope to manoeuvre.

The Naval Staff wanted its own Harriers to provide a quick-reaction capability to complement the RAF's long-range patrols by McDonnell Douglas Phantom FGR.2 fighters supported by Handley Page Victor tankers and Avro Shackleton AEW.2 early warning aircraft. All too often there were gaps in RAF coverage as aircraft transited to and from the patrol area or if the weather prevented aerial tanking. A naval Harrier could fill these gaps, with five aircraft aboard a CAH, one aircraft would be on Combat Air Patrol (CAP) 97% of the time with another ready to launch 91% of the time, providing a pair of Harriers over the fleet within 10 minutes.

Their role was to target Soviet Naval Aviation (Aviatsiya voyenno-morskogo flota, AVMF) Tupolev Tu-95RT *Bear-D* reconnaissance aircraft, which were used to provide midcourse targeting information for Soviet cruise-missile submarines and cruisers to update their anti-ship missiles. The *Bear-D* was equipped with Uspech-1A *Big Bulge-A* surface-search radar (maximum range 260nm [481.5km]) as well as Kvadrat-2 and SRS-4A Rhomb electronic intelligence, SRS-5 Vishnya communications intercept and SPS-2 electronic countermeasures equipment. The *Bear-D* would usually have to get within 60–80nm (110–150km) of the fleet for 10–15 minutes to get accurate enough passive ELINT targeting information, the aim was for the Harrier to intercept and destroy the *Bear-D* before it could transmit its data. Attacking supersonic Tu-22K *Blinder* and Tu-22M *Backfire* bombers before they could release their missiles would a less effective – but still very valid – role. The secondary role was visual, radar and electronic reconnaissance, with a tertiary role of attacking enemy ships or ground attack. One initial concept that was not taken forward was using the Sea Harrier to lay sonobuoy barriers to support the Sea Kings and the RAF's Nimrod maritime patrol aircraft.

Heath's government had been mildly supportive of the idea when it came into power and Naval Staff Requirement NSR.6473 was drawn and a project definition study took place during August 1972 to April 1973. The MOD Operational Requirements

Committee approved the project, as did the Chiefs of Staff in November 1973.

The Sea Harrier survived the 1974 Defence Review and the incoming Labour government of that year. There was strong opposition from the other Services but First Sea Lord Sir Edward Ashmore offered to spend less in other areas to fund the aircraft. With the RAF having cut its aerial tanker fleet – reducing its ability to maintain Phantom FGR.2 patrols in the Greenland-Iceland-UK (GIUK) Gap – the RAF's objections had little impact.

Another positive factor was that India and Iran were looking at purchasing the type. The Shah of Iran was interested in acquiring an *Invincible*-class ship and Sea Harriers, the £200 million price tag easily offsetting the £102 million cost of providing the RN with Sea Harriers. The Secretary of State for Defence Roy Mason was a keen backer, whereas the Chancellor of the Exchequer, Denis Healey, could see his work of 1966 being undone and was against the RN acquiring fixed-wing aircraft. The perceived critical need and the export prospects led the Defence and Overseas Policy Committee approve the purchase of 24 aircraft, a public announcement being made on 15 May 1975.

The Naval Staff's *Concept of Operations* planning document of 1975 covered the period 1985–99 and was the first such study into the RN's strategy and future requirements since 1968. It focused on supporting NATO's key operational needs – operations in the eastern Atlantic and the GIUK Gap. The following *Size and Shape* paper to determine future equipment needs took the threat from the new Tu-22M *Backfire* was taken especially seriously, the AVMF eventually operating around 200 *Backfires* of all variants.

The paper estimated that two regimental *Backfire* attacks each launching 20–60 ASMs (the supersonic Kh-22 AS-4 *Kitchen* with an effective range of 173nm [320km] armed with a 1,980lb [900kg] semi-armour piercing warhead or a nuclear warhead) would need to be countered by 37 modernised Sea Dart SAM systems, 45 Sea Harriers and 40 land-based interceptors to ensure that half the ships of both NATO task forces deployed in the eastern Atlantic area survived. The intelligence analysis suggested that the Soviets could launch one regimental strength attack per day (the Northern Fleet's 5th Maritime Air Division had two Regiments, each with 20 *Backfires*).

This meant a large financial outlay for a RN surface fleet that might survive for only four days of combat. The 21 additional Sea Harriers and the provision of a naval airborne early warning (AEW) capability would cost £112 million annually to run, the three *Invincibles* costing another £47 million per year – something like 21% of the RN's annual budget (based on 1973 budget costs).

The Naval Staff succeeded in getting the production order raised to 34. This was only sufficient to equip two squadrons of five aircraft each, potentially leaving the third carrier without any fighters. Therefore, another 13 aircraft were requested in mid-1979. The Minister of State for Defence Procurement disagreed, arguing that the FAA should train extra pilots instead. Given the looming 1981 Defence White Paper, no success was forthcoming as the politicians began eyeing up the third carrier for the axe.

Nestled beneath a Tupolev Tu-22M *Backfire* is a Raduga Kh-22 ASM (NATO codename AS-4 *Kitchen*). The Kh-22 had entered service in the mid-1960s on the Tu-22K *Blinder-B*. It was almost as long as a Sea Harrier – 38ft 2in (11.67m) versus 47ft 7in (14.51m) – and could reach speeds up to Mach 3.27. Armed with either a nuclear or 1,980lb (900kg) semi-armour-piercing warhead, the Kh-22 was a deadly threat to NATO ships operating in the Norwegian Sea and Eastern Atlantic. *US DoD*

The 'Shar'

The design team at Kingston had first proposed a 'Maritime Harrier' in 1969 and were soon able to develop the Harrier's basic design for the FAA. Specification 287D&P to cover the development and production of the Sea Harrier FRS.1 (FRS denoting Fighter, Reconnaissance and (nuclear) Strike – originally the name Osprey had been proposed) to meet NSR.6473 Issue 3 was issued to Hawker Siddeley on 30 July 1976.

The Sea Harrier was broadly constructed to the same standards as the Harrier GR.3, but with several differences. The nose was modified for a Ferranti ARI.5982 Blue Fox radar, with a folding nose cone to fit onto the carrier lifts. The fuselage was strengthened to Harrier T.4 trainer standards with other modifications including a cranked leading edge on the tailplanes and removal of all magnesium from the airframe to prevent corrosion in the salty environment. The cockpit floor was raised by 11in (28cm) to provide improved all-round vision for the pilot for aerial combat and additional space for the avionics beneath the floor. The ejection seat was the upgraded Martin-Baker Mk.10A. The inboard wing pylons were strengthened and a detachable, in-flight refuelling probe was provided.

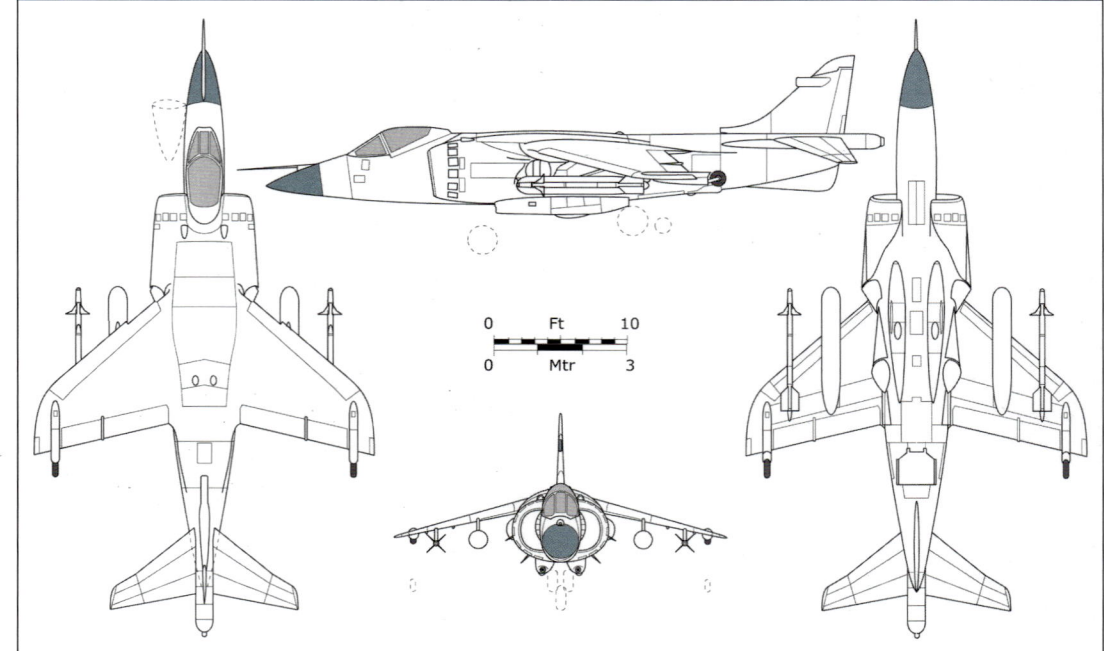

A general arrangement drawing of the Sea Harrier FRS.1 with the original interception armament of two AIM-9L Sidewinders on the outer hardpoints.
Chris Gibson

The 21,500lbf (95.6kN) Rolls-Royce Pegasus Mk.104 turbofan was also 'marinised' with a new aluminium casing replacing the original magnesium/zirconium case to prevent corrosion. The engine was also fitted with an increased capacity gearbox. An emergency pop-out dorsal ram air turbine was fitted to provide emergency electric power in the event of an engine flameout (this was later removed – it being deemed safer to eject if the engine quit.) The Blue Fox monopulse radar was developed from the ARI.5979 Seaspray surface-search radar fitted to the Westland Lynx HAS.2. It operated in the I-band and had frequency agility to improve resistance to jamming. It could detect small air and sea targets against the background clutter of poor weather or rough sea states. The radar was optimised for single pilot control with the flight parameters, such as speed, heading and attitude, superimposed on the head-down radar display so that the pilot could see all the information in one place. A Smiths Head-Up Display/Weapon Aiming Computer (HUDWAC) was fitted for fire-control. Doppler navigation was added, which was used in conjunction with the Ferranti NAVHARS twin-gyro inertial platform, which could be aligned on a moving carrier deck before take-off. An autopilot and a radar transponder was fitted, as was a Vinten F.95 oblique camera in the lower starboard fuselage for reconnaissance. A Marconi ARI.18223 radar warning receiver (RWR) was fitted with the aerials on the leading edge of the tail fin and in the tail cone. Built-in test equipment for the avionics also improved serviceability at sea.

Weapons comprised two 30mm ADEN cannon mounted externally in fuselage pods, each carrying 100 rounds of ammunition. The original AAM loadout was a pair of AIM-9L Sidewinder infrared (IR)-homing AAMs on the outboard pylons, shortly after the Falklands Conflict twin-rail adapters became available to double the AAM loadout. The inboard pylons were rated at 2,000lb (907kg) and usually carried 100gal (455L) or 190gal (864L) drop tanks but could also carry 300gal (1,364L) ferry

Sea Harrier FRS.1

Span	25ft 3in (7.70m); 29ft 8in (9.04m) ferry tips
Length	47ft 7in (14.51m); 41ft 9in (12.73m) folded
Wing area	201ft² (18.68m²)
t/c ratio	10% root, 5% tip
Max take-off weight	26,200lb (11,884kg)
Powerplant	1x Pegasus Mk.104, 21,500lbf (95.6kN)
Max speed	640kt (1,185kt) at SL; Mach 1.25 at height, diving
Service ceiling	52,150ft (15,895m)
Radius of action	400nm (740km) high altitude intercept; 250nm (463km) strike
Armament	2x 30mm ADEN, 2x or 4x AIM-9L Sidewinder, 2x Sea Eagle, 1x WE.177A, 1,000lb (454kg) bombs or 2.75in (68mm) Matra RP pods

tanks (that had to be dropped before the flaps could be lowered), or 1,000lb (454kg) freefall or retarded bombs, 36-round Matra pods for 2.75in (68mm) SNEB rocket projectiles or a single WE.177A tactical nuclear bomb. A single ventral hardpoint could also carry a 1,000lb bomb. The Phase 1 upgrade in the 1980s added the capability to carry two BAe P3T Sea Eagle ASMs for the anti-ship role to meet Naval Air Staff Requirement NASR.1226 (the introduction of Sea Eagle was delayed when the trial installation aircraft XZ450 was shot down over the Falklands).

Three Hawker Hunter T.8s (XL580, XL602 and XL603) were converted under Specification 288D&P for the Blue Fox radar development programme as the Hunter T.8M. The design changes included grafting the Harrier FRS.1's complete radome and nose section onto the Hunter along with updated avionics including two HUD units and a radar scope in the right-hand seat position. The outer underwing pylons could either carry two 22-round rocket pods or two AIM-9L Sidewinder acquisition training rounds to simulate live firing. Structural modifications were also made to allow the use of two 230gal (1,045lit) underwing drop tanks. On completion of the Blue Fox programme, XL580 and XL603 were converted for the training role and were delivered to 899 Naval Air Squadron (NAS) in August 1981.

Three Sea Harriers were assigned to development work, but the maiden flight was actually made by the first production aircraft XZ450 on 20 August 1978 at Dunsfold with John Farley at the controls (by this time Hawker Siddeley had become part of the nationalised British Aerospace – BAe). Only a week later Farley displayed XZ450 at SBAC Show at Farnborough, using a specially constructed temporary ski-jump ramp to full effect. XZ450 made the first landing aboard *Hermes* on 13 November 1978.

Landing approach techniques were devised and refined by the RAE, using two-seat T.2 XW175 fitted with a programmable Smiths Flexihud HUD and Microwave Digital Guidance Equipment (MADGE) landing assistance, as well as a radio altimeter and experimental three-axis autostabilisers. Land-based trials were followed by sea trials aboard *Hermes* in November 1978. An approach speed of 120kt was selected, slowing to a hover stop within 2,735ft (833m) at 200ft (61m) altitude parallel to the carrier off the port beam. The pilot would then fly sideways over the deck to make the vertical landing. The traditional Deck Landing Projector Sight was modified into the Harrier Approach Path Indicator (HAPI), two of them being fitted 300ft (91m) apart on the port deck edge with a third – the Close Approach Indicator (CAI) – atop the Flying Control position (FLYCO.) These were later replaced by the Deck Approach Projector Sight (DAPS) calibrated for a 40ft (12m) hover. The Landing Safety Officer also had a stabilised IR sight for night landings.

The first of the development batch, XZ438, made its initial flight, with test pilot Mike Snelling at the controls, on 30 December 1978. The aircraft made

Three Hawker Hunter T.8Ms were used as testbeds for the Ferranti Blue Fox radar with a HUD and radar display in the cockpit. They were later issued to 899 NAS as radar trainers. T.8M XL580 is overflying Yeovilton during a training sortie in May 1984. It was not retired until 1993. *Terry Panopalis Collection*

The second production Sea Harrier FRS.1 XZ451 of 700 NAS sits on the apron at RNAS Yeovilton in August 1979. During the Falklands Conflict it shot down a Canberra, a Pucara and a C-130E Hercules as well as damaging a Beechcraft T-34 Mentor. XZ451 crashed into the sea off Sardinia on 1 December 1989 due to a control restriction in flight. *Terry Panopalis Collection*

Sitting on the apron in August 1982 at Yeovilton is FRS.1 ZA176 of 809 NAS. For the Falklands campaign the Shars were quickly toned down with all-over Medium Sea Grey and low-vis roundels. Squadron markings were also removed. ZA176 was ferried south by SS *Atlantic Conveyor* and operated from *Hermes* during the war. Squadron Leader Ian Watson landed ZA176 aboard the Spanish container ship *Alfraigo* in June 1983 following radio failure. *Terry Panopalis Collection*

ski-jump trials aboard *Hermes* during 13–23 July 1981. Mike Snelling also made the maiden flights of XZ439 and XZ440 on 30 March and 6 June 1979. Both aircraft were used by the A&AEE for carrier trials aboard *Hermes* in the Irish Sea between 24 October to 8 November 1979; then aboard *Invincible,* Snelling making the first ski-jump take-off at sea on 30 October 1980 with test pilot (and former FAA pilot) Humphrey Taylor-Scott in XZ440 performing the second take-off. Ski-jump take-off clearance whilst carrying Sea Eagle was achieved by XZ440 in June 1982 aboard the brand-new *Illustrious*.

The Intensive Flying Trials Unit, 700A NAS, was formed at RNAS Yeovilton under the command of Lt Cdr Nigel 'Sharkey' Ward, receiving Sea Harrier XZ451 on 18 June 1979 and making its first carrier deployment aboard *Hermes* during October-November. Early pilot conversion was assisted by BAe's two-seat Mk.52 demonstrator G-VTOL, along with its regular BAe pilot Chris Roberts. 700A NAS was reformed as 899 NAS on 31 March 1980, becoming the headquarters and training unit. Alongside the two Blue Fox-equipped Hunter T.8M, by 1983 the squadron also operated a Harrier T.4A and three T.4N two-seat trainers, the T.4N having avionics more representative of the FRS.1.

Two frontline squadrons were formed at Yeovilton, 800 NAS in March 1980 and 801 NAS in January 1981. Each had five aircraft, which post-Falklands was increased to eight to ensure that a two-aircraft CAP could be maintained for 24 hours. The first operational deployment was by 800 NAS aboard *Hermes* in June 1981 and 801 NAS was assigned to *Invincible*. The 1981 defence cuts saw the abandonment of plans to form 802 NAS for *Illustrious*. The squadrons were assigned to SACLANT (Supreme Allied Commander Atlantic) with 800 and 801 NAS having 48-hour availability and 899 NAS could deploy as a combat squadron within 5–15 days. Quickly the pilots and deck crews adopted the shortened name 'Shar' for the Sea Harrier.

Combat exercises against the RAF's Phantom FGR.2 and US Air Force McDonnell Douglas F-15A and Northrop F-5Es revealed how agile the Sea Harrier was in combat and the benefits of its shrouded jet exhausts against IR-homing AAMs. Much has been written about the Sea Harrier's success during Operation Corporate to retake the Falklands in 1982. There is not space here to recap all the Sea Harrier's exploits and several books have already been devoted to the subject. Suffice to say that the three squadrons – plus 809 NAS specially formed out of a cadre from 899 NAS – managed to amass 28 serviceable Sea Harriers aboard *Hermes* and *Invincible* (14 Harrier GR.3s from No.1(F) Squadron were also ferried south and joined the carriers in the South Atlantic). During the conflict they flew 1,100 CAPs and 90 ground support sorties, totalling 2,675hr 25min flying time and 2,088 deck landings. Only 1% of planned sorties were cancelled due to unserviceability with an

> *"Without Sea Harrier there could have been no Task Force."*
> FIRST SEA LORD, ADMIRAL SIR HENRY LEACH

Harrier T.4N XW268 sporting special 899 NAS 50th anniversary markings in 1993. On 27 June 1994 a landing accident at RNAS Yeovilton ended XW268's flying career. The aircraft is now on display at the City of Norwich Aviation Museum. *Terry Panopalis Collection*

The pilot of Sea Harrier XZ455 of 800 NAS begins the take-off roll aboard HMS *Illustrious* in October 1986. XZ455 shot down two IAI Daggers during the Falklands hostilities. It was lost following a landing accident in the Adriatic following a mission over Bosnia on 31 February 1996. *Terry Panopalis Collection*

average aircraft availability of 80% despite the cramped conditions aboard the carriers and the poor weather. This was partly a reflection of the fact that the aircraft were still reasonably factory-fresh and that the Harrier and the Pegasus were proven pieces of kit.

Like many other British military aircraft, the Sea Harrier was subjected to urgent clearance trials for new stores and roles during the Falklands Conflict. The development batch aircraft XZ439 conducted AIM-9L Sidewinder firing trials at West Freugh during 8–14 April. Chaff/flare dispensers were hurriedly fitted to the aircraft. Efforts to clear the usage of 330gal (1,500L) ferry tanks ended with XZ438 crashing during a ski-jump take-off at Yeovilton due to fuel load imbalance on 17 May (Lt Cdr David Poole ejected safely.) Development of the 'Blue Eric' electronic countermeasures (ECM) pod – a miniaturised development of the Marconi Skyshadow small enough to replace one of the ADEN cannon pods – was completed but never fielded. Taylor-Scott volunteered for active service, but his greater value as a test pilot saw him being tasked with helping to re-form and train 809 NAS as well as AIM-9L trials work.

Two Sea Harriers were shot down by anti-aircraft fire over the islands; XZ450 was lost over Goose Green, Lt Nick Taylor being killed (this aircraft had been used for Sea Eagle trials, it has been suggested that Argentine military intelligence may have assumed all Shars were so fitted following investigations of the wrecked cockpit); XZ456 was shot down by a Roland SAM, RAF pilot Flight Lieutenant Ian Mortimer ejecting safely. Another four were lost in accidents; XZ452 and XZ453 possibly colliding in cloud or crashing into the sea with Lt Cdr John Eyton-Jones and Lt Al Curtis killed; an unexplained explosion (perhaps due to a faulty fuze on one of the 1,000lb bombs) following take-off destroyed ZA192 and killed Lt Cdr Gordon Walter James Batt; ZA174 rolled off *Invincible's* deck in heavy seas during preparations for take-off (the pilot ejected safely). None was lost in air-to-air combat however, excelling with the AIM-9L Sidewinder, shooting down 23 Argentine aircraft (nine IAI Daggers, eight McDonnell Douglas A-4 Skyhawks, two Dassault Mirage III, one English Electric Canberra and one Lockheed C-130 Hercules). They also damaged the Argentine patrol craft *Río Iguazú*, the spy trawler *Narwal* (used for ELINT) and the supply ships ARA *Bahía Buen Suceso* and *Río Carcarañá*.

The Sea Harrier fleet was augmented post-Falklands with two further orders, bringing the FRS.1 fleet to 57, the last being delivered in August 1988. These incorporated Phase 1 updates which were retrofitted to the older aircraft: AN/ALE-40 chaff/flare dispensers aft of the airbrakes, MADGE, twin electrical generators, twin-rail adapters for Sidewinder, Sea Eagle capability and an autotrim feature for the autopilot. Problems with engine surging limits saw ZE690, 691 and 692 being loaned to the A&AEE for tests during 1986–87. Aerial refuelling clearance trials were flown with the RAF's

'Shars' also operated from the decks of other navies' carriers. FRS.1 ZE692 is aboard the French carrier *Clemenceau* in October 1993. The detachable refuelling probe normally used for ferry flights is fitted above the port intake. ZE692 became the 24th FA.2 conversion in 1994. *Terry Panopalis Collection*

new Lockheed Tristar tanker conversions in 1985. Problems with safe jettisoning of the 190gal drop tanks led to them being redesigned. During 1988 the improved AIM-9M Sidewinder was integrated, the missile having greater resistance to decoy flares. Updated HUDWAC software was cleared in 1992 to avoid false lock-ons and to improve the head-on intercept capability (the AIM-9M lacked the CHIRP feature – the audio indication of lock-on – which was retrospectively removed from the AIM-9L for compatibility reasons).

One odd project was Skyhook. This was the brainchild of BAe Dunsfold test pilot Heinz Frick to enable Sea Harriers to be operated from destroyers and frigates and allow the undercarriage to be removed to save weight for an increased fuel or weapons payload (akin to the flexible deck concept.) A large computer controlled crane would be used to lift the aircraft airborne and capture the returning aircraft in the hover to bring it safely back aboard ship. The crane could even be used for mid-air refuelling at a rate of 1,000lb/min (454kg/min) whilst the Sea Harrier hovered. It was envisioned that a large destroyer with up to six Sea Harriers would have two Skyhook cranes, one on each beam. Engineer Dennis Mottram was assigned to work out the technical details. A coupling unit was tested using a large mobile crane and successful flight trials were carried out but a lack of official interest saw the project being abandoned.

As mentioned earlier, exports played a key role in the government sanctioning the Sea Harrier's development. While the Iranian order was a pipedream (the Shah was shortly to fall from power), India placed its order for six Mk.51 fighters and two Mk.60 two-seat trainers in November 1979. Later orders increased the fleet to 25 Mk.51 and five Mk.60 aircraft. The main difference between the Mk.51 and the FRS.1 was that the former was armed with Matra Magic IR-homing AAMs instead of Sidewinders. Sea Eagle ASMs were also carried.

The first aircraft flew on 6 August 1982 at Dunsfold and the Indian Navy formed No. 300 Squadron at Goa on 22 December 1983 when the first three aircraft arrived, allowing the final examples of the venerable Hawker Sea Hawk to retire. They operated aboard the carrier INS *Vikrant* before the acquisition of *Hermes* in 1987 which became INS *Viraat*. A shortage of Mk.60 trainers during the early 1990s saw a significant amount of the pilot training syllabus being conducted in the UK. The accident attrition rate was remarkably high; seven pilots were killed in 17 crashes and half the fleet was written off. With ex-FAA FA.2s being too expensive to acquire, Hindustan Aeronautics Limited upgraded 15 Mk.51 aircraft with assistance from

A Sea Harrier frigate concept by Vosper Thornycroft and BAe, equipped with two skyhooks. *Vosper Thornycroft/ BAE Systems via Joe Cherrie*

Israel, including Elta EL/M-2032 multimode radar, Elta cockpit displays and Rafael Derby active-radar beyond-visual-range (BVR) AAMs. Sea Harriers operated from *Viraat* for the last time on 6 March 2016 and they were retired on 11 May after 33 years of service, being replaced the Mikoyan MiG-29K *Fulcrum-D* multirole fighter.

Sea Harrier FA.2

The outcome of the Falklands Conflict not only opened the funding taps for the Phase 1 upgrade but also for a more thorough Phase 2 to incorporate all the lessons learned from Operation Corporate. The two most important items were an improved pulse-Doppler radar that could operate in high clutter environments overland with a look-down shoot-down capability and BVR AAMs to extend the interception range. Naval Staff Requirement NSR.6451 (Issue 4) was formulated to cover the airframe upgrades while the new radar and missiles came under NSR.6118 and NSR.6124 respectively. BAe received a feasibility study contract for the Sea Harrier FRS.2 in 1983, followed by political approval to go ahead in 1984 and a project definition phase during 1985.

The Blue Fox radar was replaced by the GEC-Ferranti Blue Vixen pulse-Doppler track-while-scan radar, which gave an all-weather, look down shoot down capability against multiple targets. This I-band radar was claimed to be the first in the world to be designed with compatibility with the Hughes AIM-120A AMRAAM – the selected BVR AAM. It had automatic track-while-scan with electronic countermeasures and air combat modes; selection of the ideal pulse repetition frequency was also automatic, dependent on the background clutter and target density. It could detect up to 128 targets, track 10 of those and could transmit targeting information to four AMRAAMs simultaneously. The average detection ranges against fighters at medium and low altitudes was 54nm (100km) and 30nm (55km) respectively. The active-radar homing AMRAAM was a 'fire-and-forget' weapon with a range of 57–65nm (105–120km). The larger Blue Fox antenna required a reprofiled nose radome (requiring the nose pitot probe to be replaced by pitot probes on the fuselage sides). Flight testing on a modified BAC One-Eleven airliner began in 1986 and from 1988 in the modified BAe 125-600B ZF130 which featured a facsimile FRS.2 cockpit which was built around the starboard cockpit seat.

BAe originally planned to fit pairs of AMRAAMs under the outer wings with AIM-9L Sidewinders on new wing tip launch rails. This proved to be unworkable due to the adverse effects on longitudinal stability. The two outer hardpoints had a Fraser Nash Common Launcher Rail for one AMRAAM or Sidewinder and another pair of AMRAAM could be carried under the fuselage, replacing the 30mm ADEN cannon pods (the cannon could still be carried for ground attack missions.) The Navy Department estimated a need for 330 AMRAAMs. Ground attack ordnance included 1,000lb (454kg) bombs (freefall and retarded), 540lb (245kg) bombs, 2.75in (68mm) CRV-7 rockets and Lepus flares. The FA.2 was also cleared to carry Paveway II laser-guided bombs,

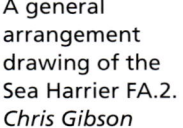

A general arrangement drawing of the Sea Harrier FA.2. *Chris Gibson*

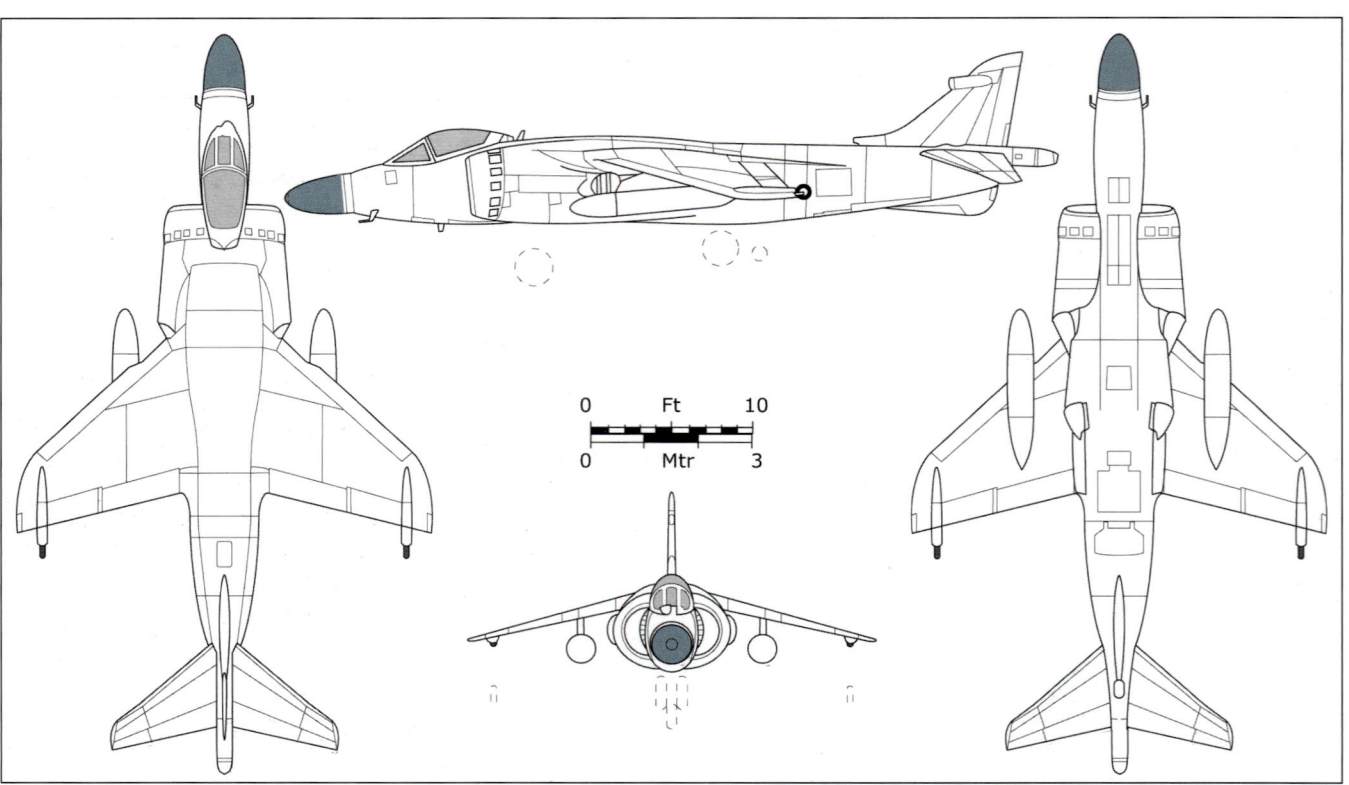

HS.125 ZF130 was converted to test the Blue Vixen radar and the FA.2 cockpit avionics, including complete Sea Harrier cockpit around the starboard seat. *Terry Panopalis Collection*

although it could not self-designate onto a target. Sea Eagle was still the anti-ship weapon, itself receiving updates to the radar homing seeker for improved resistance against jamming and decoying. The new GEC-Marconi Sky Guardian 200 RWR was fitted, along with an AN/ALE-40 chaff/flare dispenser. The internal starboard-facing oblique F.95 camera was retained for reconnaissance.

An entirely new rear fuselage section with a 13¾in (35cm) plug was fitted to improve longitudinal stability and provide additional avionics space (for weight distribution reasons the Blue Vixen's signal and radar processors were located here), along with liquid cooling equipment for the avionics racks. This new rear fuselage section had structural changes to mitigate the effects of thermo-acoustic fatigue caused by the rear jet exhaust nozzles. The cockpit was upgraded with two multi-function Head-Down Displays and Hands-On-Throttle-and-Stick (HOTAS) controls to reduce the pilot's workload; these were controlled by the Bus Control Interface Unit, which also contained the AMRAAM targeting modes (HUDWACS remained responsible for the Sidewinder and air-to-ground targeting modes). A MIL-STD-1553B databus was fitted and the Joint Tactical Information Distribution System (JTIDS) Link 16 datalink was added under Staff Requirement SR(S)7110. The cockpit avionics were trialled on the Advanced Cockpit Rig at Weybridge and aboard BAe 125 ZF130. Much of the Sea Harrier's electrics were rewired to improve reliability.

Aerodynamic improvements for the wings including moving the 'dogtooth' leading edge further inboard, the addition of a third wing fence and reducing the number of vortex generators to 11. Extended 'ferry tips' could still be fitted to increase range when required (and stability when carrying four AMRAAMs) – the span increasing to 29ft 8in (9.04m). The engine was upgraded to the 21,750lbf (96.7kN) Pegasus 11-21 Mk.106, a navalised version of the Mk.105 fitted to the RAF's Harrier GR.5 and GR.7.

Two FRS.1s were rebuilt as prototypes: XZ439 and ZA195. ZA195 was the first to complete, being flown on 19 September 1988 at Dunsfold with test pilot Heinz Frick at the controls, followed by XZ439 on 8 March 1989. In addition, XZ497 was converted as the Trials Installation aircraft in 1991 (the first two aircraft did not receive Blue Vixen radars until 1990). Carrier qualification trials with XZ439 and ZA195 aboard *Ark Royal* took place during 6–15 November 1990. Following the removal of WE.177A capability and an increased focus on ground attack, the FRS.2

The tools of the trade. This Sea Harrier FA.2 is carrying a pair of AIM-120A AMRAAMs under the fuselage, two Sea Eagle anti-ship missiles on the inboard pylons and a pair of AIM-9L Sidewinders outboard. *Terry Panopalis Collection*

WINGS OVER THE FLEET

This head-on view shows some of the changes made to the FA.2. The wings now have six leading edge fences to improve the aerodynamics and the extended ferry tips are also fitted. The enlarged radome contains the Blue Vixen pulse-Doppler multi-mode radar. The bulge below the windscreen houses the motor for the windscreen wiper – an essential feature in the salt laden marine environment. *MOD/Open Government Licence*

was redesignated FA.2 in 1994 (although officially designated F/A.2 in line with NATO nomenclature, it was usually styled FA.2). On 7 December 1988, the MOD ordered 29 FRS.1 rebuilds (costing £170 million), 18 new-build aircraft (at £12 million each) in March 1990 and another five conversions were ordered in 1994. (Another four – plus two T.8Ns – were sought in 1995 to bolster the RN's air defence capabilities, but were ruled out on cost grounds.) The upgrading of each aircraft took around 12 months to complete. The first FA.2 conversion ZE695 was delivered on 2 April 1993 and the first new-build aircraft ZH796 was first flown in late 1995. XZ439 and ZA195 were brought up to full operational standard in 1997.

The Operational Evaluation Unit (OEU) was formed at Yeovilton out of 899 NAS in June 1993, receiving FA.2 XZ497 on the 23rd. The Blue Vixen/AMRAAM combination was extensively tested, including 10 live firings by XZ439 at Eglin, Florida against subsonic Beechcraft MQM-107 Streaker and supersonic Convair QF-106A Delta Dart target drones from 29 March 1993. An early setback was the loss of XZ495 (one of only two FA.2s fitted with radars at that time) on 5 January 1994, which ditched into the Bristol Channel, the pilot Lt P Wilson ejecting safely. The OEU embarked four aircraft aboard *Invincible* in August 1994 for a limited combat cruise. Both 800 and 801 NAS received the FA.2, the former squadron making its first full scale deployment aboard *Illustrious* in January 1995.

Training was assisted by four T.8N two-seat trainers fitted with the FA.2 cockpit avionics (minus Blue Vixen and AMRAAM), which had been developed to meet Staff Requirement SR(S)6453. A static Sea Harrier Operational Radar Trainer simulator for the FRS.1 and FA.2 was completed at Yeovilton in 1989. Yeovilton's Full Mission FRS.1 Simulator was also modified to FA.2 standard.

The provision of the FA.2 did not solve all the shortcomings. A 1993 study into the Sea Harrier FRS.1's operational constraints reported ten issues, some of which required wider improvements within the FAA. They included: a shortage of trained aircrew with lack of frontline experience and a lack of surge capability (increasing the capacity of the training system was the only realistic solution); incomplete compatibility with allied naval air forces; the cost of ownership had increased from the specified 11.45

first line maintenance manhours to 37; lack of nighttime and stand-off daytime reconnaissance capability; lack of tactical night formation flying lighting. In addition, the Commanding Officer of RNAS Yeovilton called for a BVR imaging device (either magnified visual or IR) to allow the pilots to visually confirm their targets before firing their long-range AMRAAMs. This would allow the restrictive rules of engagement to be relaxed to allow the most effective use of BVR missiles, especially since fitting the Blue Vixen with an IFF interrogator was found to be too difficult. Given the costs involved it was decided to rely on nav system upgrades with embedded GPS and laser-ring gyros and JTIDS to overcome some of these issues.

The carriers embarked eight aircraft, enabling two to be on CAP 24 hours a day, with a third at 15 minutes' readiness. CAP endurance was 1hr 40min on station. The FRS.1 and FA.2 were deployed during the conflict between Serbia and Bosnia Herzegovina following the breakup of Yugoslavia. RN carriers were deployed to the Adriatic to participate in Operation DENY FLIGHT to enforce the United Nations' No-Fly Zone imposed over Bosnia. 800 NAS aboard *Invincible* was tasked with 1,007 missions from early 1993 to October 1994 and carried out all of them despite only having six aircraft; serviceability and the weather did not dent this impressive performance.

The FRS.1 was one of the few NATO aircraft assets used as a 'swing-role' fighter, being able to

An aerial refuelling capability remained essential for the relatively short-ranged Sea Harrier FA.2 to extend CAP endurance and strike sortie radius. The 800 NAS pilot of FA.2 ZH804 is about to make contact with the refuelling drogue being trailed by an RAF Lockheed Tristar tanker. *MOD/Open Government Licence*

A four-ship formation of Sea Harrier FA.2s of 801 NAS on a training sortie out of RNAS Yeovilton, comprising (from front to rear): ZH797, ZH811, ZH813 [the last production aircraft] and ZH808). The fin-less AIM-120 AMRAAMs on the outer hardpoints are for training purposes, allowing the full missile lock-on sequence to be practiced but without an actual missile launch. *MOD/Open Government Licence*

carry out offensive counter-air, close air support and battlefield air interdiction. Having only one radio was a drawback, the pilot having to switch between transmissions from the wingman and forward air controllers on the ground. Lessons learned led to upgrades for Sky Guardian, modified Fraser Nash Common Launcher Rails with BOL chaff dispensers in the rear, buying RT-1489/ALE GEN-X disposable radar decoys for the AN/ALE-40 dispenser and trialling the Marconi Apollo radar jamming pod.

One Sea Harrier was shot down on 1 February 1994, a shoulder-launched 9K32 Strela-2 (SA-7 *Grail*) IR-homing SAM hitting FRS.1 XZ498, Lt Nick Richardson ejecting and being rescued by an SAS team and a USAF Combat Search and Rescue helicopter. FA.2 XZ455 was lost on 13 February 1996 following the failure of the starboard nozzles while on landing approach to *Illustrious*, Lt G Phillips ejecting safely (XZ455 had been converted to FA.2 standard less than three years previously.) The last FRS.1 was retired at the end of 1995. The FA.2 took part in NATO Operation A‌LLIED F‌ORCE in March 1999 in response to Serbian repression of the Albanian population of Kosovo, again flying from *Invincible*.

Joint Force Harrier

During the 1990s, 'jointery' – joint Service cooperation – became one of the mainstays of the UK's defence policy for operational and cost reasons. The RAF maintained its carrier deployment capability with its new Harrier GR.7s, providing a precision strike and air interdiction capability that the Sea Harriers lacked. The GR.7 had to be cleared for carrier operations and the RAF pilots inducted into the RN's world. (This was not just a case of learning carrier deck operating procedures; preparations went down to the seemingly mundane level of whether the RAF's standard issue socks made from artificial fibres were fire-resistant enough to be worn aboard ship.) The carriers also required minor modifications to stow the RAF's weapons in the magazines (even the ADEN cannon ammunition was different, the FA.2 using the original 30mm calibre ammunition, the GR.7 having the newer 25mm version). Even the GR.7's 250gal (1,136L) drop tanks were different from the Sea Harriers' 190gal (864L) tanks. The wider span (non-folding) GR.7 wings just fitted onto the *Invincible*-class deck lifts. Provision of the correct spares and tools were necessary as the FA.2 and GR.7 used

BAe Sea Harrier FA.2

Span	25ft 3in (7.70m); 29ft 8in (9.04m) ferry tips
Length	46ft 6in (14.17m); 42ft 10.25in (13m) folded
Wing area	201.1ft² (18.68m²)
t/c ratio	10% root, 5% tip
Max take-off weight	26,200lb (11,884kg)
Powerplant	1x Pegasus Mk.106, 21,500lbf (95.6kN)
Max speed	618kt (1,145km/h)/Mach 0.94 at SL; 578kt (1,070km/h)/Mach 0.97 at altitude; Mach 1.25 diving
Rate of climb	50,000ft/min (15,240m/min) at SL
Service ceiling	51,000ft (15,545m)
Radius of action	400nm (740km) high altitude intercept; 300nm (555km) strike
Armament	2x 30mm ADEN, 4x AIM-120A AMRAAM or AIM-9L/M Sidewinder, 2x Sea Eagle, 1,000lb (454kg) bombs or 2.75in (68mm) CRV-7 RPs

BAE Systems Harrier GR.9A

Span	30ft 4in (9.25m)
Length	46ft 4in (14.12m)
Wing area	243ft² (22.6m²)
t/c ratio	Supercritical, 11.5% root, 7.5% tip
Max take-off weight	31,000lb (14,060kg); 18,950lb (8,595kg) short take-off
Powerplant	1x Pegasus 11-61 Mk.107, 23,400lbf (104.0kN)
Max speed	575kt (1,065km/h)
Rate of climb	14,715ft/min (4,485m/min)
Service ceiling	50,000ft (15,240m)
Radius of action	600nm (1,110km) with 2x 1,000lb (454kg) bombs, 3x BL.755 & 2x drop tanks
Armament	2x 25mm ADEN, 4x AIM-9L/M Sidewinder, 8,000lb (3,630kg) bombs, missiles, 2.75in (68mm) CRV-7 RPs and other stores

different parts and the mechanics worked to different regulations.

During 28 June to 7 July 1995 Trial Hornpipe was conducted aboard *Illustrious* using GR.7s ZG472, ZG475 and ZG501. It was discovered that the GR.7's Ferranti FIN1075 and FIN1075G (with a GPS receiver feed) inertial navigation systems suffered from reduced accuracy at sea due to issues with aligning the gyros aboard the ship before take-off. (As a result the improved FIN1075GEM with embedded GPS was fitted from late 1997.) Take-off performance with the larger Harrier II wing was particularly good but the lack of engine thrust would prevent vertical landings with any weapons still aboard the aircraft; in addition, in tropical conditions any unused underwing pylons would need to be removed to save weight. Range was also poor, the RAF suggesting that a 'buddy' refuelling capability should be investigated.

Further operations in 1996 aboard *Illustrious* and take-off trials using Yeovilton's ski-jump revealed concerns over pitch-up when the GR.7's 100% leading edge extensions (LERX) were fitted (the smaller 65% area LERX gave acceptable handling). In 1998 BAe Dunsfold conducted further trials with GR.7 ZD318 to allow the 100% LERX to be fitted along with the use of auto flap on take-off. Landing tests were made with just the intermediate pylons fitted, reducing weight and enabling the use of drop tanks with a pair of Sidewinders.

A major training deployment saw four GR.7s and servicing personnel from No. 1(F) Squadron joining *Illustrious* for Exercise Hot Funnel 97 from 28 February to 31 March 1997, embarking from Muscat in Oman and disembarking at Butterworth in Malaysia. The first full scale operational deployment the following year involved six GR.7s of No. 1(F) Squadron joining ten FA.2s of 800 and 801

"The CVS in the Gulf is giving visibility and understanding of the powerful capabilities of the FA2/GR7 mix and warming both politicians and the public to further developments of a joint Harrier force before the arrival of their replacements."

CHIEF OF NAVAL STAFF, ADMIRAL SIR JOCK SLATER, 4 FEBRUARY 1998

NAS aboard *Illustrious* (along with four 849 NAS Westland Sea King ASaC.7) for Exercise Strong Resolve 98. (*Invincible* also took part as a commando carrier with ten Sea King HC.4s and a detachment of Royal Marines Lynx AH.7s.) Around this time the GR.7 began using the GEC-Marconi Thermal Imaging Airborne Laser Designator (TIALD) 400 Series pod, TIALD stowage and maintenance equipment being installed aboard *Ark Royal* during her refit in 1998. (Plans to fit TIALD to the FA.2 never came to fruition.) By 1999 No. 1(F) Squadron had attained a 10 days' notice to embarkation capability. This was first demonstrated during Operation Bolton in January 1999 as a show of strength to force Saddam Hussein to comply with United Nations Special Commission inspections of suspected Weapons of Mass Destruction sites. Four GR.7s joined six FA.2s aboard *Invincible*. One modification made to eight aircraft was the addition of a second radio to improve communications.

The Labour government began an extensive Strategic Defence Review during 1997–98. The SDR advocated the creation of a 'Joint Force 2000' comprising the Harrier GR.7s and Sea Harrier FA.2s to complement each other and to provide a force able to "deploy from land and sea, capable of precision attack of sea, land and air targets, able to undertake timely reconnaissance, and air escort of

To celebrate 25 years of Sea Harrier operations, in July 2004 FA.2 ZH809 of 899 NAS revised this gloss finish reminiscent of the original FRS.1 colour scheme. ZH809 was one the 18 new-build FA.2 airframes. *Terry Panopalis Collection*

Returning Home. A Sea Harrier FA.2 of 801 NAS about to touch down aboard HMS *Invincible* during Exercise MAGIC CARPET 05 in the Middle East. Note that in the high temperatures only empty drop tanks remain hung under the wings to lighten the weight sufficiently for a vertical landing. *MOD/Open Government Licence*

joint and allied assets." This proposal built on the operational capability already demonstrated by Operation BOLTON. The Joint Force Harrier (JFH) was formed on 1 April 2000, controlling all RAF and FAA Harrier squadrons. It was initially part of the RAF's No.3 (Maritime) Group, but under the command of Flag Officer Maritime Aviation (FOMA). In 2004 the JFH was transferred to No. 1 Group and RN command ended.

A proposal by Rolls-Royce/BAe in 1997 to fit the more powerful Pegasus 11-61 to the FA.2 (alongside the Harrier GR.9) by 2003 for improved take-off and combat performance (costing £260 million) was not taken forward (and neither were plans to integrate anti-armour and precision guided munitions.) In the Gulf the FA.2 could land vertically with two AIM-120 AMRAAMs, without the need to jettison the expensive (£447,439) missiles, in the summer this reduced to one or none. A proposal to fit the Harrier II's zero-scarf cold nozzles (which provided an extra 200lbf (0.88kN) thrust) was put forward in 1996, but would have required flight testing, costing up to £500,000. Other more drastic measures such as lengthening the intakes with a 12in (30cm) fuselage plug or new wings were rejected as unfeasibly expensive.

The Sea Harrier FA.2 had been planned to serve until 2012, when it would be replaced by the Joint Combat Aircraft (JCA). It had been planned to move the Sea Harrier squadrons from Yeovilton to RAF Cottesmore and Wittering during 2003, but in February 2002 the MOD instead decided to retire the Sea Harrier during 2004–06. The MOD felt that the GR.7's ground attack capability was the JFH's most required role and they would be upgraded to GR.9 standard with modern precision attack ASMs like the MBDA Brimstone anti-armour weapon. In contrast the FA.2 was seen to be 'increasingly obsolescent', a somewhat odd statement given that it was still one of the best equipped fighters in Europe at that time and that the oldest new-build airframes were only seven years old. The MOD also welcomed the cost savings that the 'simplified logistics' from only having one Harrier variant would bring about. The GR.7s continued to be based on the carriers; retiring the FA.2 shrank the JFH from 77 to 51 aircraft.

The FA.2 squadrons remained at Yeovilton until they disbanded. 800 NAS was disbanded on 31 March 2004, reforming at Cottesmore on 31 March 2006 with ex-No. 3 Squadron GR.7's. The Sea Harrier training squadron, 899 NAS, was disbanded on 23 March 2005 and merged into No. 20(R) Squadron at Wittering. It was left to 801 NAS to bring the Shar's 28 years of service to an end on 31 March 2006 – the final flight having occurred four days earlier. It reformed on 1 October 2006 on the Harrier GR.9 and from March 2007 800 and 801 NAS operated as the Naval Strike Wing. One positive is that the Actual Establishment (AE) of the two naval squadrons was increased from seven to nine aircraft. The JFH had a 50/50 RAF/FAA personnel split, with the RAF's No.1(F) and IV Squadrons having a slightly higher proportion of RAF personnel, while shortages of FAA pilots hampered full manning of 800 and 801 NAS, leaving the Naval Strike Wing with an effective AE of nine Harriers.

Harrier GR.9 ZG506 of 800 NAS in the hover at RAF Cottesmore in November 2010, shortly before the demise of the Harrier and the Joint Harrier Force. *Terry Panopalis Collection*

Harrier GR.9 of No.1(F) Squadron taking off from HMS *Ark Royal* in 2010. *MOD/Open Government Licence*

Harrier T.12A ZH657 wearing the markings of 800 NAS under a moody sky in July 2010, five months before the Harrier's retirement. *Terry Panopalis Collection*

The GR.9 upgrade programme was contracted in January 2003 to BAE Systems, the total cost being £500 million. The upgrade included 'smart weapon' capability with Brimstone, 500lb (227kg) Raytheon Paveway IV laser-guided bombs and AGM-65D Imaging Infra-Red (IIR)-guided Maverick ASMs. Several other weapon options were not taken forward to save money, including the MBDA ASRAAM AAM (the AIM-9L/BOL Sidewinder being retained instead.) The capabilities were added in stages: Cap A with an in-service date of February 2005; Cap B added Brimstone the TIALD 500 targeting pod and MIL-STD-1760 stores management system in December 2005; Cap C1 provided Phase III dynamic weapon aiming for Enhanced Paveway III from September 2006; Cap C2/D integrated the AGM-65G2 Maverick IIR/TV-guided ASM and Paveway IV and Raytheon Mk.12 Successor Identification Friend-or-Foe (IFF) system. No. 20(R) Squadron had 10 of its T.10 two-seat trainers upgraded with the GR.9 avionics, becoming the Harrier T.12.

A total of 30 aircraft were of GR.9A standard with an upgraded engine. Back in December 1999 forty 23,400lbf (104kN) Pegasus 11-61 Mk.107 engines had been ordered for £150 million. The increased power enabled a higher maximum take-off weight of 34,000lb (15,420kg), improving performance for hot-and-high environments and carrier operations, enabling pilots to complete vertical landings with weapons still fitted (avoiding the need to ditch the expensive ordnance.) Installing the Pegasus Mk.107 required a new rear fuselage to be fitted; 20 GR.7s were raised to GR.7A standard, later being upgraded as GR.9As, while another 10 GR.7s were rebuilt to GR.9A configuration. These aircraft were mainly issued to 800 and 801 NAS.

The JHF and the Harrier GR.9 had short lives. The new Conservative-Liberal Democrat coalition government of 2010 conducted a Strategic Defence and Security Review (SDSR) which disbanded the JFH and retired the GR.7 and GR.9s in December 2010. The remaining 72 aircraft were sold to the USMC as spares the following year. For the first time since 1912, the RN had no fixed-wing combat aircraft capability.

12 New generation helicopters

By 1970 the helicopter had come of age. The Westland Whirlwind, Wessex, Sea King and Wasp had given the Royal Navy experience in the use of helicopters for anti-submarine warfare (ASW) as well as heliborne Commando amphibious assault and other roles such as search and rescue (SAR) and transport. In technical terms they had progressed from underpowered, vibrating novelties to gas turbine-powered aircraft capable of lifting useful payloads over reasonable distances. In seeking replacements for the Wasp and Sea King, the RN would turn to the latest aerodynamic and mechanical developments to develop two state-of-the-art helicopters for the 1970s and beyond, the Westland WG.13 Lynx and the European Helicopter Industries EH101 Merlin. Both would have long development periods but they emerged as world-leading designs with sales success and indeed are still in service today around the world. The RN also adapted the helicopter to new roles, the Lynx being designed to destroy Fast Patrol Boats (FPBs) in addition to submarines, with Merlin being tailored to task of laying and assessing lines of sonobuoys listening out for Soviet nuclear submarines passing between Greenland, Iceland and the UK – the 'GIUK Gap.'

Lynx

The Westland WG.13 completed the trio of designs pursued under the Anglo-French Helicopter Agreement of January 1967. While Sud Aviation had a majority stake in the development of the SA 330 Puma and SA 340 Gazelle, Westland led the development of the WG.13. The WG.13 had evolved from the WG.3A tactical helicopter project of 1963 to replace the Westland Scout (the Army Air Corp's

One of the RN's most important projects of the 1970s and 1980s was the Sea King Replacement (SKR), which finally entered service as the EH101 Merlin HM.1 in 2000 and will serve with the FAA until at least 2040. This is Merlin HM.2 ZH827 of 820 NAS escorting HMS *Queen Elizabeth* as she exits Rosyth dockyard for the first time to begin her sea trials. *MOD/Open Government Licence*

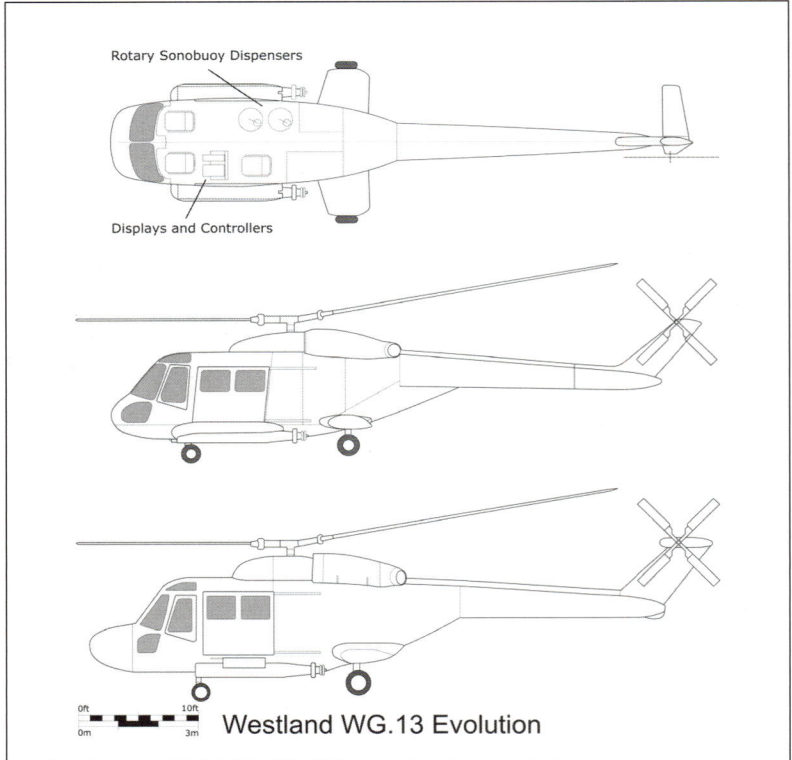

Westland WG.13 Evolution

Westland's WG.13 rapidly evolved to the familiar shape of the Lynx. Shown here is the Naval WG.13 as it evolved during 1966–68, the earlier design having two rotary sonobuoy launchers in the cabin and large streamlined pylons for the two homing torpedoes. By 1968 the Ferranti Seaspray radar had led to a revised nose with a distinct radome. *Author*

version of the Wasp). It had a single Type 192 Belvedere main rotor married to a Whirlwind gearbox, powered by two 750shp (559kW) Pratt & Whitney PT6A turboshafts. By 1966 the WG.3 had been further refined and encompassed several variants, including the WG.13V naval version which interested the Navy Department as a Wasp replacement and as a successor to the Aéronavale's Sud Est SE 319B Alouette III Astazou in the ASW role.

Naval General Air Staff Requirement NGASR.3335 was issued in 1968 to cover the development of the WG.13 to replace the Army's Scouts, the RN's Wasps, the Aéronavale's Alouettes and the RAF's Whirlwind HC.10s (which were operated as advanced flying trainers). During April 1968 Italy showed some interest in a tri-national programme but the talks were abandoned as it was felt that Italian interest was for industrial reasons rather than fulfilling any genuine military requirement. A design team at the Fairey Division at Hayes, led by Chief Designer Tadeusz 'Ted' Ciastula, was formed for the detailed design and engineering. The Engineering Director Vic Rogers and Chief Aerodynamicist David Balmford were critical in developing the semi-rigid hub and transmission.

Specification 273D&P was issued to Westland in May 1970 to cover the development of the naval variant for the RN and the Marine Nationale. It was to be capable of localising, classifying and attacking underwater contacts; surface reconnaissance using radar; the anti-FPB role; SAR; vertical replenishment; and troop carrying operations. The original in-service date was 1975 to allow the formation of an Intensive Trials Unit before the first Type 42 *Sheffield*-class guided missile destroyers commissioned in 1976 (this date subsequently slipped by a year.) The estimated number required was between 79 and 118 aircraft.

The economic cruising speed was to be at least 140kt with a maximum speed of at least 160kt. Endurance at sea level while carrying two crew, full all-weather equipment and 1,760lb (798kg) of ASW equipment was to be 1hr 30min (including 30min of hovering) or 2hr 30min carrying 1,000lb (453kg) of equipment. The chosen engines were two new 900shp (671kW) Bristol Siddeley BS.360 Gem turboshafts. Novel features included a semi-rigid rotor head, stainless-steel/glass-reinforced plastic rotor blades and the use of circular arc (CIRCARC) conformal gears in the main gearbox. The semi-rigid hub allowed high speeds (the Lynx claimed closed circuit speed records in 1972 and 1986) and agility, including the ability to fly loops. A folding tail reduced length by 8ft 6in (2.6m) and a wheeled undercarriage and a Fairey harpoon system provided safe deck landings in rough seas.

Avionics included an Elliot automatic flight control system (AFCS) and the Decca TANS self-contained navigation system. The RN version would have a Ferranti ARI.5979 Seaspray radar for surveillance and missile guidance. The ASW systems to be fitted at that stage were quite vague and the only suitable contact classification equipment was a Magnetic Anomaly Detector (MAD). The Aéronavale intended to fit sonobuoys for the target relocation role, but the RN argued that the performance of current sonobuoys was inferior to dipping sonar. An acoustic location device was to be developed under Naval Staff Requirement NSR.6434 but this never materialised. Provision was made to retrofit a datalink and electronic countermeasures (ECM).

In the anti-FPB role, the armament would be four British Aircraft Corporation (BAC) CL.834 Sea Skua air-to-surface missiles (ASMs) (the Sea Skua's development is discussed below.) Armament in the ASW role would be two UK Mk.44 or Mk.31 homing torpedoes or a single NAST.7511 homing torpedo (this became Sting Ray), two Mk.11 depth charges or one WE.177A nuclear depth bomb.

Early potential export users were the Royal Australian Navy (RAN), which had a similar staff requirement, and the United States Navy (USN) which was formulating its Light Airborne Multi-Purpose System II (LAMPS II) requirement. Although it lost to the Kaman SH-2F Seasprite, the Lynx (powered by the Pratt & Whitney PT6A) had been the favoured 'off-the-shelf' LAMPS contender. In response to the following LAMPS III requirement, Westland re-tendered the Lynx in August 1976, this time powered by the Gem 4 to handle the 10,500lb (4,760kg) weight and IBM Federal Systems would supply the ASW fit. The licence-production agreement with Sikorsky seems to have lapsed and Westland would have teamed up with another US company had it won the contract. The Lynx was too small to fulfil the LAMPS III requirements and lost out to the Sikorsky SH-60B Seahawk. Argentina would be the first export customer in 1972 as part of that nation's Type 42 destroyer deal.

Development was delayed by several technical problems and the unit price increased from £230,000 to £500,000 during 1968-69, the partners and Services agreeing to economies in the required equipment and fittings (France cancelled its planned three-seat Armed Escort gunship version.) The Ministry of Aviation even suggested cancelling the WG.13 in favour of acquiring the Bell 212 (better known in its US Army UH-1N Iroquois guise as the 'Huey'). The Model 212 could not meet the naval requirements, however, and would have required fundamental redesign for a new undercarriage, folding tail and folding rotor blades. Critically, all current and future frigate classes would have required major redesign for larger hangars and landing decks.

The BS.360 Gem also proved troublesome during its development and the French pressured Westland to fit the early production aircraft with PT6A engines (these had been fitted to the initial prototypes in the absence of flight-ready Gems.) The PT6A's greater fuel consumption would limit the ASW sortie to 2hr 10min. By 1972 the Gem was making satisfactory progress and its development became assured. The estimated total airframe development cost had risen to £40.52 million (the UK's share was £26.53 million) and £36.75 million for the Gem (UK share £33.62 million).

A development batch (DB) of 13 aircraft was ordered, including five naval WG.13s. Westland test pilots and observers Ron Gellatly, Roy Moaxam and David Gibbings made the first flight in the first DB aircraft, XW835, at Yeovil on 21 March 1971. The first naval DB aircraft XX469 made its first flight from Yeovil on 25 May 1952 with JGP Morton and David Gibbings in the cockpit. Rolling platform trials at the Royal Aircraft Establishment site at Bedford were undertaken in June before the helicopter flew to Marignane in France the following month for hot temperate trials and demonstration flights, making a successful deck landing aboard the French destroyer *Tourville*. A loss of tail rotor control and a heavy landing at Yeovil on 21 November 1972 saw the aircraft written off.

The second naval DB WG.13 XX510 made its maiden flight on 5 March 1973. It conducted dummy Sea Skua ASM drop tests and deck landing trials aboard RFA *Engadine* as well as various armament trials. Westland test pilots, supported by the Aeroplane and Armament Experimental Establishment (A&AEE) and the Centre d'Essasis en Vol (Flight Test Centre – CEV), made successful deck landing trials aboard *Tourville* during March 1974.

The third naval Lynx was XX910, first flown on 23 April 1974 and used for radar and system trials. The fourth, XX911, became the French Mk.2 prototype. XZ166 was the final naval DB aircraft, first flying on 5 March 1975 and used for Sea Skua armament trials. By 1976 the thirteen DB aircraft had amassed 2,800 flight hours (XX510 was subsequently written off in a heavy landing during engine-off trials on 20 March 1978.) The Lynx performed well and a speed of 190kt was achieved, but problems were encountered with yaw instability, collective and cyclic control coupling and vibration at speeds above 120kt.

During December 1973 30 Lynx HAS.2 were ordered, another 30 being ordered in August 1976. The first production aircraft XZ227 flew on 10 February 1976. The joint RN/Royal Netherlands Navy Intensive Flight Trials Unit at RNAS Yeovilton, 700L Naval Air Squadron (NAS), became operational with five aircraft during September and deck handling trials were carried out aboard the Type 42 destroyer HMS *Birmingham* in February 1977. 700L NAS became 702 NAS on 3 January 1978 as the Lynx training squadron, making the first shipborne deployment aboard the *Leander*-class frigate HMS

The Type 21-class frigate HMS *Amazon* is seen here with Lynx HAS.2 XZ234 aboard in 1979. At this time the helicopter was assigned to 702 NAS at RNAS Yeovilton. Converted to HAS.3 standard in 1987, it was withdrawn from use in November 2011 and became a donor airframe for the AW159 Wildcat programme. MOD via Terry Panopalis Collection

The DB2 Lynx HAS.2 XX510 during the deck landing trials aboard the new French destroyer *Tourville* in March 1974. XX510 was used for development testing until issued to the Empire Test Pilots' School at Boscombe Down in November 1981 and from 1984 becoming a ground instruction airframe. Leonardo UK via Terry Panopalis Collection

Resplendent in Oxford Blue is the third production Lynx HAS.3, serial ZD251 of 702 NAS at RNAS Portland in July 1983. At this time the Lynx fleet was beginning to be repainted in overall semi-gloss Dark Sea Grey. *Terry Panopalis Collection*

Phoebe from 8 February. The Lynx Headquarters unit for all the ship-based Flights was 815 NAS, based at RNAS Portland from 1981.

Initially the ASW role was to function as a ship-guided torpedo carrier with no provision for the search and relocation roles – in effect reprising the Wasp HAS.1's basic MATCH role. Aboard the new Type 22 *Broadsword*-class anti-submarine frigates, the Lynx was guided by the ships' new Type 2016 active/passive sonar which had an average detection range of 7.4nm (13.7km). From 1983 the Lynx was armed with a pair of GEC-Marconi Sting Ray Mod.0 homing torpedoes, which had been in development since 1976 (see later in this Chapter.)

The HAS.2 saw combat during the Falklands/Malvinas Conflict in 1982, some Lynxes receiving a towed MAD. On 3 May a Lynx conducted the first combat-firing of a Sea Skua missile, damaging the Argentinian patrol boat ARA *Alférez Sobral*. Other duties included carrying ECM pods and releasing bundles of chaff in sharp climbing flights from wavetop height to spoof and divert incoming AM.39 Exocet ASMs fired by the Argentine Navy's Dassault Super Étendard fighters. Although none

First flown on 1 June 1983, Lynx HAS.3 ZD259 was upgraded to HAS.3S standard in May 1992 and is seen here the following month as '342' assigned to the Type 22 frigate HMS *Brilliant*. The paint scheme is semi-gloss Medium Sea Grey, which was adopted from 1988. In 2001 ZD259 upgraded to HMA.8 standard, receiving the DAS upgrade in 2005. *Terry Panopalis Collection*

was shot down in combat, three aircraft were lost aboard vessels that were sunk by attacks from Argentine aircraft, the frigates HMS *Coventry* and *Ardent* and the container ship SS *Atlantic Conveyor*.

An updated version was delivered as the HAS.3 from March 1982, totalling 20 aircraft (three more were later added to replace the Falklands losses.) The first, ZD249, flew on 4 January 1982 and was used for handling and performance tests by the A&AEE. The HAS.3 had 1,120shp (835kW) Gem 41-1 engines to allow a greater 10,500lb (4,762kg) all-up weight (AUW). Other changes included a new four-bag emergency floatation system, a towed MAD for the contact relocation role, Racal MIR-2 Orange Crop electronic support measures (ESM) and *Lamberton* encrypted secure radios. Some of these features were refitted to the HAS.2 fleet. The third production batch of seven aircraft in 1987–88 received dual GEC-Marconi AD3400 UHF secure speech radios and were designated HAS.3S (two of them were actually completed for the Portuguese Navy to Mk.95 standard).

During the Gulf War in 1991(Operation Granby) around 18 Lynx were fitted with Loral Challenger IR jammers (later removed in-theatre to save weight), M-130 30-round chaff/flare launchers, Challenger ECM, a GEC Sandpiper forward-looking IR (FLIR) sensor and a FN-Herstal 0.50in machine gun in the cabin doorway, being redesignated HAS.3GM. During the mid-1990s several HAS.3 were converted for use aboard the Antarctic survey/ice patrol ship HMS *Endurance* with surveying equipment added and all weaponry removed as the HAS.3ICE.

Lynx developments

Naval Staff Targets NST.6678 and NST.6679 were issued during 1977 for an 'Uprated Mk.4 Lynx' to enter service in 1984. NST.6679 covered the ASW localisation and attack system, a sonobuoy processor based on that being developed for the Sea King Replacement (SKR) capable of monitoring SSQ-801 Barra passive and SSQ-963A CAMBS III active sonobuoys. It was discovered that this system could not be fitted within the desired timescale and the only alternative was to fit a dipping sonar. The off-the-shelf choices were the Bendix AQS-18, Bendix AQS-13F with additional sonobuoy monitoring capability or the Alcatel HS-12, which had been developed from the French DUAV-4 for the Dutch Navy's Lynx Mk.27s. Analysis showed that the AQS-18 was the most effective due to its reasonable range and good dip rate (12 per hour). The project was subsequently abandoned in favour of the SKR, however.

The Lynx's dynamic system was used to develop the WG.30 light transport helicopter, which entered production as the civilian W30-100. In 1982 the Swedish Navy issued a requirement to replace its Kawasaki/Boeing Vertol KV-107-II fleet and Westland proposed a W30-160 naval variant. It could be equipped with Alcatel HS.12 or Bendix ASQ-18 dipping sonar and a 360° scanning Ferranti

This Lynx HAS.3GM was operated by the frigate HMS *London* (seen in the background) during Operation Granby in February 1991. The urgent operational modifications included Loral Challenger IR jammers (later removed to save weight), M-130 chaff/flare dispensers and FN-Herstal 0.50in machine guns mounted in the cabin doorways. This helicopter is carrying an ECM jamming pod and the box atop the nose contains the forward hemisphere receivers for the Orange Crop ESM. *MOD via Terry Panopalis Collection*

Seaspray or MEL Sea Searcher radar under the nose. A removable beam under the cabin floor would carry the same weaponry as the standard Lynx, including Sea Skua ASMs. A stronger undercarriage and a deck harpoon system would also be fitted. No sale materialised, but Westland later offered a similar navalised W30-300 (an improved W30 with five-blade BERP III rotor and General Electric CT7 or Rolls-Royce Turbomeca RTM.322 engines) to West Germany and Canada without success.

The Lynx 3 was a 1982 private-venture created out of research work completed for the Franco-German PAH-2 attack gunship helicopter programme. The design team was led by Chief Designer Richard Case with Derek McMullan. The Lynx 3 featured 1,260shp (939kW) Gem 60-3 engines, a longer forward fuselage, W30 tail boom, a relocated tailplane and BERP III (British Experimental

WINGS OVER THE FLEET

Westland Lynx progression

	Lynx HAS.2 & HAS.3	Naval Lynx 3 (Project)	W30-300 & W30-400 Super Lynx (Project)	Lynx HMA.8	AW159 Wildcat HMA.2
Rotor diameter	42ft 0in (12.80m)	42ft 0in (12.80m)	42ft 0in (12.80m)	42ft 0in (12.80m)	42ft 0in (12.80m)
Length	49ft 9in (15.16m) overall; 35ft 7¼in (10.85 m) folded	37ft 3in (11.35m) fuselage	52ft 2in (15.90m) overall	50ft 0in (15.24m) overall; 35ft 7¼in (10.85 m) folded	50ft 0in (15.24m) overall; 44ft 3in (13.49 m) folded
Rotor disc area	1,385.4ft² (128.71m²)	1,385.4ft² (128.71m²)	1,385.4ft² (128.71m²)	1,385.4ft² (128.71m²)	1,385.4ft² (128.71m²)
All-up weight	10,500lb (4,760kg)	12,000lb (5,440kg)	W30-300, 15,700-16,000lb (7,120-7,260kg); W30-400, 18,000lb (8,165kg)	10,747lb (4,874kg)	13,228lb (6,000kg) max
Powerplant	HAS.2, 2x RS.360-07 Gem 2, 900shp (671kW); HAS.3, 2x Gem 41-1, 1,200shp (894kW)	2x Gem 60-3, 1,260shp (939kW)	W30-300, 2x CT7-2B, 1,712shp (1,276kW); W30-400, 2x RTM322-0, 2,100shp (1,566kW)	2x Gem 42-1, 1,000shp (746kW) max, 920shp (686kW) continuous	2x LHTEC CTS800-4N, 1,361shp (1,015kW)
Max speed	125kt (231km/h) max continuous cruising	165kt (306km/h)	149kt (276km/h)	175kt (324km/h)	168kt (311km/h); 143kt (264km/h) max cruising
Service ceiling	8,450ft (2,575m) hovering ceiling	?	?	10,600ft (3,230ft)	12,000ft (3,655m)
Range	320nm (592km)	538nm (997km)	365nm (676km)	280nm (518km)	280nm (518km)
Armament	2x Mk.44, or Mk.46 or Sting Ray homing torpedoes, 2x depth charges, 1x WE.177A, 4x Sea Skua	2x Mk.46 or Sting Ray homing torpedoes, 2x depth charges, 4x Sea Skua	2x Mk.46 or Sting Ray homing torpedoes, 2x depth charges	2x Sting Ray homing torpedoes, 2x depth charges, 4x Sea Skua, 1x 0.50in (12.7mm) MG	2x Sting Ray homing torpedoes, 2x depth charges, 4x Sea Venom, 20x Martlet, 1x 0.50in (12.7mm) MG

The Lynx 3 Naval mock-up was displayed at the 1984 SBAC Show at Farnborough. The W30 tail boom and lowered tailplane gave the Lynx 3 a different look. The BERP technology rotor blades were an improvement on the Lynx's original semi-rigid blades. *Terry Panopalis Collection*

The Lynx 3 Naval mock-up as completed in 1983. The nose is fitted with a generic Passive Identification Device and a 360° coverage radar radome. Dummy Sea Skuas are fitted. *Author's Collection*

Rotor Programme) rotor blades. The maximum take-off weight was increased to 13,000lb (5,895kg.)

The Naval Lynx 3 featured the new Ferranti Seaspray 3 radar with digital signal processing for track-while-scan capability in a new 360° coverage radome. Other equipment included a nose-mounted infrared (IR) passive identification device, Orange Crop ESM, sonobuoys and towed MAD or dipping sonar. Gross weight was 12,000lb (5,440kg) and overall length was 37ft 3in (11.3m).

The Naval Lynx 3 and the ASW version of the W30-300 'Super Lynx' were unsuccessfully offered to the RAN in February 1983 for its Destroyer Utility Helicopter requirement to equip its new *Adelaide*-class frigates, losing out to the Sikorsky S-70B-2 Seahawk. A full-scale mock-up of the Naval Lynx 3 was exhibited at the Society of British Aircraft Constructors Show at Farnborough in September 1985 and a standard land-based Lynx 3 demonstrator had flown in June 1984, but no interest was received and the programme was abandoned in 1987. These abortive developments would not be entirely wasted, however.

In April 1985 Racal was awarded a contract to develop the RAMS 4000 CTS central tactical system to reduce crew workload. This led to the introduction of the Lynx HMA.8 which featured several upgrades

The Super Lynx followed the Lynx 3. This early artist's impression features the 360° Seaspray radome and the nose-mounted Passive Identification Device. The mixed weapons load is one Sting Ray torpedo and a pair of Sea Skua ASMs. *Leonardo UK via Blue Envoy Collection*

The GEC Sea Owl FLIR in its steerable nose turret and the 360° radar radome below were key distinguishing features of the Lynx HMA.8. The Sea Owl gave the Lynx an all-weather passive identification capability of surface targets. The ship is one of the Type 23 *Duke*-class frigates. *Author's Collection*

including 920shp (686kW) Gem 42 Series 200 engines, an improved composite tail rotor, BERP III composite main rotor blades and a greater 11,300lb (5,125kg) AUW. Equipment changes included a nose-mounted GEC Sea Owl Forward-Looking Infrared (FLIR) and a 360° radome for the Seaspray radar (which retained its 180° scanning arc for budgetary reasons). The armament remained the same: four Sea Skua or two Sting Ray Mod.1 homing torpedoes or two Mk.11 Mod.3 depth charges (the WE.177A had been withdrawn in 1992).

Three HAS.3 were converted as development aircraft but the original plan to rebuild the HAS.3 fleet to HMA.8 standard was curtailed at 39 aircraft. The development machines had their operational evaluation undertaken by a reformed 700L NAS at RNAS Portland between 6 July 1990 and 17 July 1992. The first production HMA.8 became operational with 815 NAS in mid-1995, making a deployment aboard the Type 23 *Duke*-class frigate HMS *Montrose* later that year.

Some HMA.8s received digital processing for the Seaspray 3000 radar as the HMA.8(DSP) and later received the Defensive Aids Subsystem, being redesignated HMA.8(DAS). The fleet was standardised as the HMA.8(CMP) under the Combined Mods Programme, later re-designated as the HMA.8(SRU) when the SATURN (Second-generation Anti-jam Tactical UHF Radio for NATO) radio upgrade was fitted. The last HMA.8s were retired from FAA service on 23 March 2017, being replaced by the Leonardo AW159 Wildcat (see later in this chapter.)

The HMA.8 was broadly similar to the export Super Lynx, which had a reverse-direction composite tail rotor and stronger structure with later examples being powered by 1,334shp (994kW) LHTEC CTS800 turboshafts. Most export Lynxes have been naval versions: French Aéronavale (26 Mk.2(FN) and 14 Mk.4(FN)); Brazil (nine Mk.21); a Mk.22 order for Egypt was never completed; Argentina (two Mk.23 plus eight undelivered Mk.43); Netherlands (six Mk.25, 10 Mk.27 and eight Mk.41); South Africa (four Super Lynx Mk.64); Denmark (eight Mk.80 and four Mk.90 – two were rebuilds); Norway (six Mk.86 plus one rebuild); Germany (12 Mk.88 and seven Mk.88A plus 17 conversions); Nigeria (three Mk.89); Portugal (five Super Lynx Mk.95); South Korea (12 Super Lynx Mk.99); Malaysia (six Super Lynx Mk.100); Thailand (four Super Lynx Mk.110) and Algeria (four Super Lynx Mk.130.)

The Ship Killer: Sea Skua

By the late 1960s the RN had become concerned about the threat from Soviet FPBs armed with anti-ship missiles such as the P-15 Termit (NATO designation SS-N-2 *Styx*), especially after Egyptian-operated Project 183R (NATO codename *Komar*)-class FPBs sank the Israeli destroyer *Eilat* (the former HMS *Zealous*) during the Six-Day War in 1967. The *Komars* were basically wooden motor torpedo boat hulls with missiles, but the Soviet Navy was building much larger types, such as the Project 1234 Ovod *Nanuchka*-class which featured a defensive 4K33 (SA-N-4 *Gecko*) surface-to-air missile (SAM) system.

The 1966 Defence White Paper stated the intent to equip the RN with short-range anti-ship missiles for use against these vessels and the most cost effective solution was to equip the ASW helicopters aboard frigates with ASMs. The WG.13 Lynx was the cornerstone of this concept, the existing Wasp HAS.1 receiving the short-range Nord AS.12 ASM with visual command line-of-sight guidance as an interim solution.

Naval Staff Requirement NSR.6449 was raised to develop the search and targeting radar (the Ferranti Seaspray) and NSR.6624 was issued in 1967 for the all-weather ASM. In November 1968 a collaboration agreement was signed with France but they preferred a heavier missile with a large fragmenting shaped-charge warhead and retaining visual command line-of-sight guidance. Eventually both sides went their own ways, France developing the Aérospatiale AS.15TT.

The Ministry of Technology (Mintech) feasibility study completed in July 1969 recommended a semi-active/sea skimming missile with at least 5nm (9.1km) range. Mintech considered several off-the-shelf alternatives: the Norwegian IR-homing Kongsberg Penguin, Contraves Italiana Sea Killer Mk.1 and a modified Raytheon AIM-7E Sparrow with semi-active continuous-wave homing; but none of them met the requirements. Short Brothers unsuccessfully offered the Hellcat development of the Sea Cat SAM.

Hawker Siddeley Dynamics (HSD) and BAC were awarded project study contracts in April 1970 and GEC was contracted to design the homing head. Both designs were broadly similar, with a 66lb (30kg) semi-armour-piercing warhead, 291lb (132kg) weight and a range of 8nm (15km.) The BAC design was of canard configuration with a two-section body for ease of handling. A Wagtail booster rocket motor was proposed (production missiles used a Redstart motor) along with a Matapan sustainer rocket motor. BAC used several existing sub-systems to reduce costs, including gyros and hot gas actuators from the Rapier SAM, gas generators from the Sea Wolf SAM, the Nord AS.30 ASM's UHF command link and the TRT-AV7 radio altimeter developed for the MM.38 Exocet. HSD's SAMM-10 design was related to the Taildog/SRAAM missile family with conventional cruciform in-line controls and a modified Wagtail boost-sustainer motor. HSD proposed fitting its own radio-altimeter and a new GEC microwave frequency radio command link and favoured using a proximity fuze to ensure the required 90% hit probability.

BAC's design emerged as the winner in 1971 and became the CL.834 Sea Skua. Production was

Lynx HMA.8 XZ719 of HMS *Manchester* flies past the Flagship of the USN's 6th Fleet, USS *Mount Whitney*, in the Mediterranean in 2005. First flown as a HAS.2 on 1 April 1980, it was upgraded to HAS.3 standard in 1988 and first flew following the HMA.8 conversion on 21 June 2000. The semi-gloss Medium Sea Grey paint has been worn by Lynxes since 1988. It was scrapped for parts in 2014 and the airframe is now used for firefighting practice at RNAS Yeovilton. *US Navy via Terry Panopalis Collection*

This 1964 diagram shows the BAC Sea Skua's flight profile, an accurate sea-skimming attack in all weathers guided by the Ferranti Seaspray radar to counter the threat posed by the Soviet Union's large fleet of missile-armed fast attack craft. *Blue Envoy Collection*

WINGS OVER THE FLEET

authorised in October 1975 and the first trial launches took place at Aberporth in November 1979. It entered service in 1981 and was subsequently exported to Brazil, Germany, India, Kuwait, Malaysia, Pakistan, South Korea and Turkey. The Sea Skua had a diameter of 9.8in (25cm), 28in (72cm) span, was 8ft 2in (2.5m) long and weighed 319lb (145kg). Range was 13.5nm (25km) and it attained a speed of Mach 0.8. The Sea Skua and Lynx combination achieved an enviable combat record with seven hits out of eight launches during the Falklands/Malvinas Conflict and sinking 10 Iraqi vessels and damaging three more during Operation GRANBY.

Sting Ray

The Marconi Sting Ray Mod.0 homing torpedo entered service in 1983 but its development began as far back as 1964 to meet Operational Requirement OR.1163 for a future homing torpedo. OR.1163 had become NASR.7511 by 1966, calling for a torpedo capable of dealing with 40kt submarine target at depths down to 2,000ft (610m). It was to enter service in 1974.

The Admiralty Underwater Weapons Establishment (AUWE) design had several novel features: frequency modulated sonar transmission with receiver signal processing for very high resolution in shallow waters; a digital computer for the search and homing logic and to provide counter-countermeasure capability; pump-jet propulsion to reduce cavitation and

Sea Skua release trials in 1980 at the Aberporth Range. The Lynx HAS.2 is XZ237. This helicopter made the first live Sea Skua firing in November 1979 and the first live warhead trial in August 1981, striking the hulked Type 15 converted frigate HMS *Rapid*. *BAE Systems via Terry Panopalis Collection*

Lynx HAS.3GMS XZ230 operating from the destroyer HMS *Cardiff* during Operation GRANBY in February 1991 achieved an impressive five hits using Sea Skua against Iraqi vessels: one FPB, one *Zhuk*-class FPB, two Lürssen TNC-45 FPBs and one T-43-class minesweeper. The kill marks can be seen on the nose. After this photograph was taken, a sixth kill, a navigation buoy mistaken for another *Zhuk* FPB was added and marked 'Oops'! *MOD via Terry Panopalis Collection*

Another Lynx 'Ace' was HAS.3GMS XZ720 'Death or Glory' of Lt Cdr David Livingstone and Lt Martin Ford aboard HMS *Gloucester*. They sank five Iraqi vessels using Sea Skuas: one assault boat, one ship, one T-43-class minesweeper and two TBC-45 FPBs. The 'kill' markings and '410' code were transferred to *Gloucester's* replacement Lynx (XZ240) in July 1991, whose cabin door this is. *Terry Panopalis Collection*

self-noise in shallow waters. A proposal to use polyethylene oxide polymer extruded from the nose cap to reduce drag was abandoned. It was an ambitious programme and serious issues were encountered during early testing with the pump-jet, instability in the water and the seawater-powered batteries were prone to catch fire. GEC-Marconi was eventually called in to replace AUWE's development team.

These problems caused the RN to consider alternatives, including buying the American NEARTIP kit for the Mk.46 torpedo used in the Ikara anti-submarine missile. Alternatively, it was thought that the technology from NASR.7511 might form the basis of Anglo-French cooperation on either a new torpedo or a retrofit kit for existing types. In the event NSR.7511 escaped cancellation and Sting Ray Mod.0 entered service nine years later than planned, the development eventually costing £920 million. The Mod.1 has an enhanced shaped-charge warhead developed by the German company TDW and improved shallow-water performance and remains in service. Sting Ray weighs 590lb (268kg) and is 12.5in (38cm) in diameter and 8ft 6in (2.6m) long. It has a 100lb (45kg) shape-charge warhead and a magnesium/silver-chloride seawater battery-powered pump-jet giving 45kt for up to 6nm (11km) and it is agile against submarines down to 2,625ft (800m).

Sting Ray had a long gestation, predating the origins of the Westland Lynx by several years, but it emerged as one of the best lightweight homing torpedoes in the world and remains in service today. Lynx HAS.2 XZ232 landing aboard the Type 42 destroyer HMS *Birmingham* is carrying two Sting Rays. *Blue Envoy Collection*

WINGS OVER THE FLEET

Replacing the Sea King

In 1968 discussions began regarding a Sea King Replacement (SKR) for the early 1980s. Naval Staff Target NST.6433 had been issued in June 1969 to replace the Wessex HU.5 in the Commando and support roles, but this was rapidly replaced by the general purpose Multi-Role Fleet Helicopter (MRFH) to replace the Sea King and Wessex. Westland began preliminary studies in March 1970, which supported the ongoing Staff discussions and drafting of the operational requirements. These studies covered both single and tandem rotor designs. At this stage the MRFH was envisioned as operating from the Command Helicopter Cruiser (soon to be ordered as the *Invincible*-class) and a Landing Platform Helicopter (LPH) ship to succeed HMS *Bulwark* and *Hermes* as commando carriers (the LPH was cancelled in the 1975 Defence Review).

By the end of 1970 Mintech had established four Working Groups covering the aircraft, armament, systems and engineering aspects. The draft requirements that emerged included a maximum speed of 180kt (dash speeds up to 250kt were also considered), an ASW mission radius of 40nm (74km) with four hours on station or 75nm (140km) radius of action in the support role. Payload in the ASW role was to be 6,000lb (2,720kg) with a cabin large enough to carry 20 troops or cargo, including a ¾ton Land Rover or the new 105mm L118 Light Gun. When folded, the airframe had to fit into a 'box' 52ft (15.8m) long, 18ft (5.4m) wide and 17ft 6in (5.3m) high.

Westland began working on the WG.24 series of studies in April 1970. These covered eight configurations, including single, tandem, compound and tilting rotor layouts. Great attention was paid to drag reduction with features such as internal weapons stowage. Westland calculated that the folded box dimensions would limit a single rotor to 67ft (20.4m) diameter and a tandem rotor to 54ft (16.4m) in order to allow them to fold within the allotted space. The ASW helicopter would need an AUW of 32–35,000lb (14,515–15,875kg) – sufficient to meet the support requirements but not cost effective for the ASW role, especially with a fuselage diameter sized for carrying a Land Rover around.

The high speed requirements led Westland to consider the F1 tiltrotor configuration based on the planned WE.01 technology demonstrator (in 1970 Westland had submitted the 24,900lb (11,295kg) WE.01 Phase III tiltrotor to the USN for the multi-purpose Sea Control role). To allow for stowage aboard ships, the wing would be rotated along the axis of the fuselage – a solution today used by the Bell-Boeing CV-22 Osprey. The F1 would be capable of reaching 290kt but lacked endurance. The D1 configuration was a 'limited-tilt' design using twin lateral rotors mounted on fixed wing tip nacelles, the rotors being able to tilt to a limited degree forwards and backwards to allow a cruising speed of over 200kt and shared the F1's rotating wing solution.

It was clear from these studies that obtaining cruising speeds of 180kt would be expensive to achieve and require a large degree of technical risk. Westland shifted to looking at conventional helicopters. The G1 tandem rotor configuration of 32,500lb (14,740kg) AUW offered the best solution, but Westland felt that if the speed, on-station hover endurance or the weapon payload requirements were relaxed, that a much smaller 24,000lb (10,885kg) AUW single rotor design would be feasible. This was configuration B1, with a 67ft diameter five-blade rotor and provision for a tail ramp. This was selected by Westland for the basis of further design work.

By the end of 1973 the refined MRFH design had become the 28,000lb (12,700 kg) WG.27. The

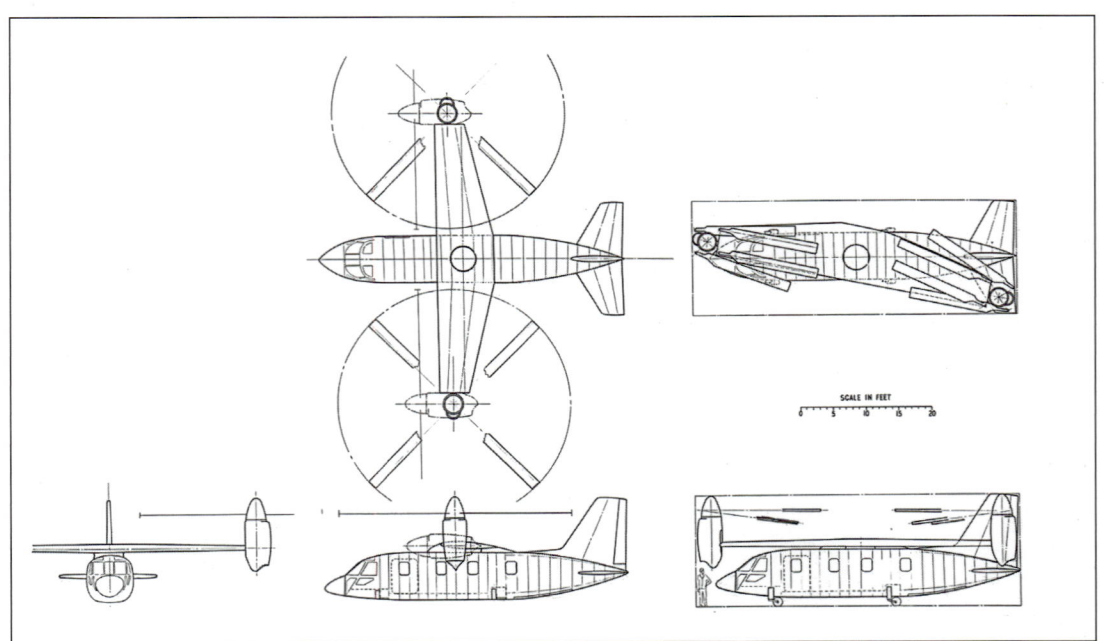

The WG.24 F1 drew on Westland's experience with the proposed WE.01 technology demonstrator and the proposed larger 70-84-seat WE.02 airliner. Ultimately Westland concluded that conventional helicopters offered the best cost-effective and low technical risk solution. *Leonardo UK via Jeremy Graham*

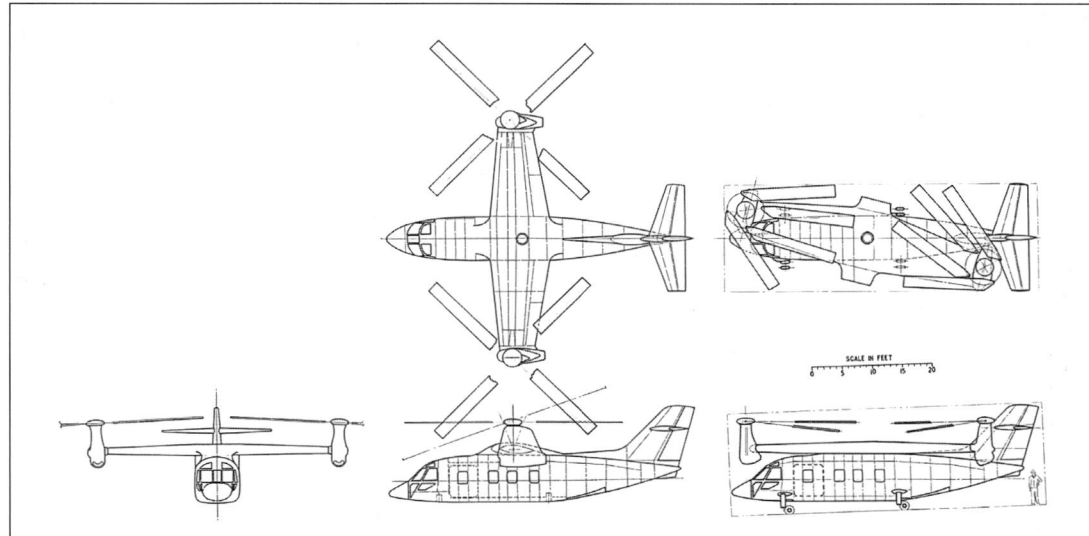

The WG.24 D1 looks like a tiltrotor but was a 'limited-tilt' aircraft with twin lateral rotors mounted on fixed nacelles. The rotors could be tilted forwards to a limited degree to give a cruising speed of over 200kt. The entire wing rotated for hangar stowage, a feature copied by the Bell Boeing V-22 Osprey a decade later. *Leonardo UK via Jeremy Graham*

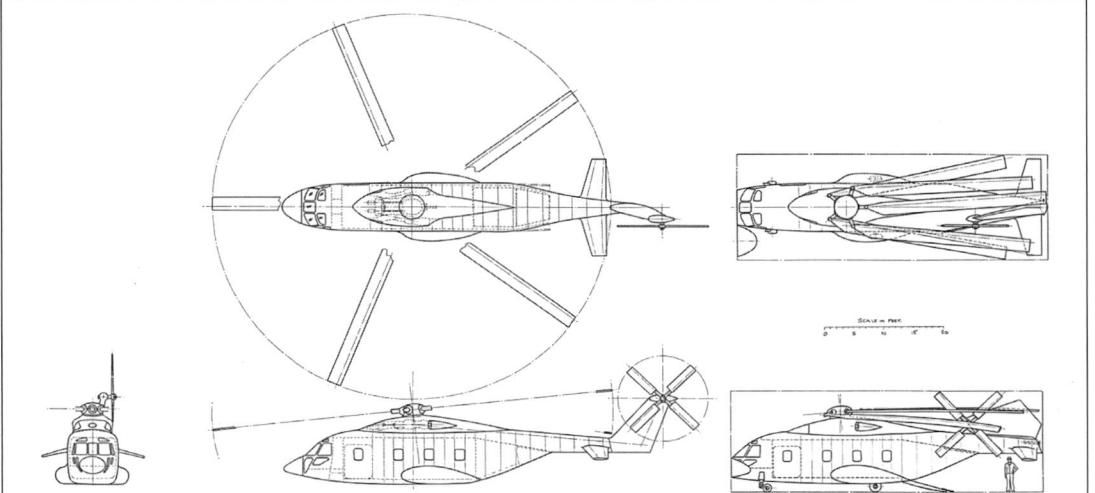

The favoured WG.24 configuration was the conventional B1 design with a five-blade main rotor. Note the folding nose cone to allow it to fit into a frigate's hangar. *Leonardo UK via Jeremy Graham*

emphasis on low drag saw the inclusion of a retractable radar radome. The cabin was to be configured to take modules to provide the equipment for various roles, including a complicated mechanism to stow the weapons internally and releasing them tail-first through the rear ramp. A novel approach of folding the main rotor and the entire rear fuselage/tail boom section allowed a larger 72ft (22m) diameter four-blade rotor to be stowed in an area significantly less than that required for a Sea King.

Westland also revisited the high speed studies with the WG.32 Supersonic Rotor Helicopter (SSRH) designs by Research Director Dr Jeff Jones. The SSRH had rotors with a supersonic tip speed which took the blades out of the stall boundary, allowing higher speeds at higher altitudes or increased payloads could be carried. The MOD was keen to let Westland examine the SSRH further, suggesting a 250kt cruise speed while lifting 44,090lb (20,000kg). Westland's study focused on the ASW screening and attack roles and Airborne Early Warning (AEW).

A pressurised cabin was provided for the crew of three; two torpedoes were carried in a ventral bay and sonobuoy launchers were fitted in the rear fuselage (more sonobouys could replace the torpedoes in the screening role.) A radar was fitted in the nose and it is possible that an aft-facing antenna would have been fitted for 360° coverage in the AEW role. The engines were two 8,079shp (6,025kW) Allison T701 turboshafts, with the

A model of the WG.32 Supersonic Rotor Helicopter. *Leonardo UK via Author's Collection*

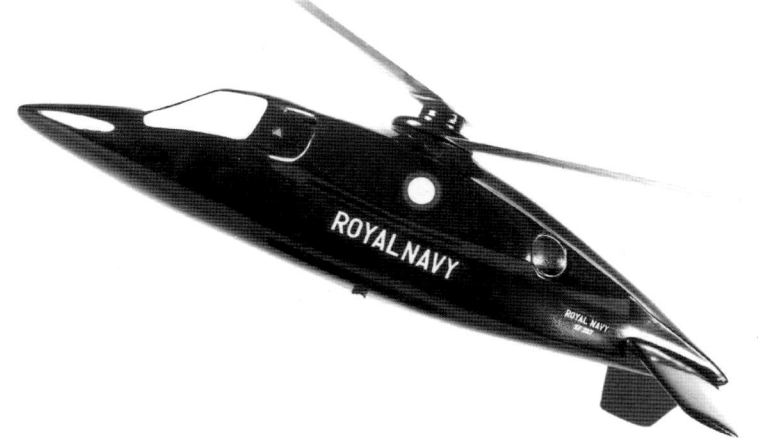

WINGS OVER THE FLEET

The Project 949 Granit-class (NATO codename *Oscar*) cruise missile submarines offered a formidable punch. The six large panels just discernible along the port side of the hull each cover two launch tubes for the P-700 Granit (SS-N-19 *Shipwreck*) long-range anti-ship/cruise missiles. With 24 such missiles, a single *Oscar* could decimate a carrier task force. Their strong double hull construction also made them difficult to sink with lightweight homing torpedoes. *US DoD*

transmission rated at 9,360shp (6,980kW). With an AUW of 25,000lb (11,340kg) and a 38ft (11.5m) diameter four-blade co-axial rotor, the WG.32 was capable of attaining 328kt at 11,000ft (3,350m) or 405kt at 15,000lb (6,800kg) AUW.

New concepts

Following the reports from the four Working Groups, the MOD conducted a series of feasibility studies between 1971 and 1975. These evaluated various detection systems including dipping sonar, towed passive sonar arrays, sonobuoys and various modes of acoustic propagation. Cost effectiveness comparisons with land-based Hawker Siddeley Nimrod MR.1 maritime patrol aircraft were also carried out. Other approaches included land-based helicopters and using datalinks to perform the information processing aboard the surface escort ships. These studies emphasised Westland's earlier conclusion that the choice of sensors was the most critical aspect. The most effective sensor was deemed to be passive and active sonobuoys.

Detection sensor technology had to keep pace with the continually evolving capabilities of Soviet submarines. Improvements in silencing machinery noise in both conventional diesel-powered and nuclear submarines and new rubberised anechoic tile coatings on the hulls were reducing passive and active sonar detection ranges, the latter by as much as 30%. Torpedo acquisition ranges also decreased by up to 40%. This raised a requirement for a secondary non-acoustic detector such as synthetic aperture radar or IR devices.

Helicopters operating in the surface surveillance role close to Soviet surface vessels were at considerable risk from the new S-300F Fort (SA-N-6 *Grumble*) and 3S90 Uragan (SA-N-7 *Gadfly*) long and medium-range SAM systems. This threat had resulted in the Lynx being equipped with Orange Crop ESM equipment, but the SKR would also require active ECM to jam Soviet search and fire-control radars.

The RN's anti-submarine concepts were changing in order to cover the GIUK Gap through which Soviet submarines would have to pass to reach their patrol areas and to attack REFORGER resupply convoys from the USA should a Third World War break out – although the RN had already concluded (correctly) that such attacks were only likely once the Soviets had protected their Arctic ballistic missile submarine 'Bastions' and secured their coastal defences. The projected Soviet threat by 1985 was 300 submarines (225 with the Arctic-based Northern Fleet alone), the majority being nuclear-powered. A new threat was the supersonic P-700 Granit (SS-N-19 *Shipwreck*) long-range anti-ship/cruise missile, capable of Mach 1.6 to 2.5 and armed with a 1,653lb (750kg) high explosive or 500kT nuclear warhead. Granits were carried aboard surface vessels (such as the large 23,400-ton nuclear-powered Project 1144 Orlan *Kirov*-class cruisers) and the 16,500-ton (submerged) nuclear-powered Project 949 Granit and Project 949A Antey (known to NATO as *Oscar-I* and *Oscar-II* respectively) cruise missile submarines. Such double-hulled submarines could dive to at least 1,970ft (600m).

In response the RN introduced the Towed Array Ship concept. These vessels would be stationed 35–52nm (64–96km) from the centre of the ASW task force, detecting and classifying submarines at ranges of up to 87nm (160km). The ASW helicopters would localise these contacts and engage them with homing torpedoes or depth charges. The increasing detection ranges meant that the helicopters also had to be upgraded with better search equipment. The Lynx – including the notional sonobuoy-equipped 'Uprated Mk.4 Lynx' studied under NST.6678 and NST.6679 – lacked the range to fully exploit the towed array's detection range. The BAe Sea Harrier FRS.1 V/STOL fighter's potential for ASW was also examined. Although useful as a fast sonobuoy layer, it lacked any sonobuoy monitoring capability and could only attack targets within a 100nm (185km) radius with its limited ASW armament of a single WE.177A nuclear depth bomb. Only the SKR was suitable for localising and attacking these sonar contacts.

The SKR affected the concepts and design of the RN's warships. Originally intended as little more than an unarmed tug for the towed array, provision for a landing pad and then a hangar for the SKR saw the Towed Array Ship grow into the larger – and much more capable – Type 23 *Duke*-class anti-submarine frigate. In 1981 the Type 23 hull had to be extended by 9ft 8in (2.94m) to accommodate the Sea King HAS.5 pending the arrival of the delayed SKR. The opportunity was also taken to modify the Type 22 Batch 2 and Batch 3 *Broadsword*-class frigates on order with a 41ft (12.5m) hull stretch for a larger flight deck and to fit the AN/SSQ-108 CLASSIC OUTBOARD (Organizational Unit Tactical Baseline Operational Area Radio Detection Countermeasures Exploitation System) passive radio direction-finding system to intercept Soviet naval and submarine communications.

The Vice Chief of the Naval Staff, Vice Admiral Sir Raymond Lygo, proposed four 'Garage Ship' vessels to accompany the Type 23 frigates to operate the SKR and possibly Sea Harriers, to increase the number of helicopters available to the task group. The main role was convoy escort in an attempt to avoid duplicating the *Invincible*-class. The ships were designed to be 21,000–25,500 tons in displacement, powered by diesel engines for 22kt and would carry 10,000 tons of fuel oil to replenish the frigates as well as nine Sea Kings operated from a large three-landing spot deck aft – although one design was a 'through-deck' mini-carrier also carrying six Sea Harriers. The cost was £50–150 million, but this escalated as capabilities increased (such as Sea Wolf SAMs) and soon 12 Sea Kings/SKRs were desired to maintain a screen of four helicopters (Sea Harrier was dropped in compensation.) These ships were never ordered, the similar 'one-stop' replenishment ship (the *Fort Victoria*-class) instead received four helicopters and was fitted for – but not with – Sea Wolf.

Design work on the Type 43 air defence destroyer began in 1976. The naval architects found it difficult to include the large flight deck required for the SKR without affecting the layout of the weapon and radar systems. The solution was to place the deck amidships, which reduced the effects of deck motion on flight operations. The pilots, however, were much less enthusiastic given the potential collision hazards posed by the forward and aft superstructure blocks. The Type 43 was cancelled by the Defence Review of 1980 and its novel layout has yet to make a reappearance. By the late 1990s the Defence Experimental Research Agency favoured using a trimaran hull to increase stability and provide ample deck space for helicopter operations. A research vessel with this layout, the MV *Triton* was completed (helicopter landing trials involved the Lynx), but the planned trimaran Future Surface Combatant to replace the Type 22 and Type 23 frigates was never built.

WG.31

Following six years of feasibility studies, NSR.6646 was issued in spring 1977 for a helicopter to enter service by 1987. The forecast need was for 74 SKRs (later reduced to 50). After some discussion by the Operational Requirements Committee and the Joint Services Helicopter Committee, a proposal to merge the RAF's Medium Lift Helicopter requirement to replace the Wessex into NSR.6646 as a common airframe later was rejected due to the incompatible requirements, which pleased the RN due to the urgency to replace the Sea King by 1990 (the RAF's needs were eventually met by an SKR variant.)

ASW was the primary role with secondary surface search and surveillance, vertical replenishment and SAR roles. The required AUW was 24,000lb (10,885kg) to meet the 27,000lb (12,245kg) ship landing deck strength limit. Cruising speed was to be 140kt with an endurance of four hours on station at a datum point 50nm (92km) away or three hours at 125nm (231km). Cruising speed and endurance took precedence over agility. Monitoring sonobuoy transmissions would require an operational altitude of 5,000ft (1,524m). The folded dimensions were not to exceed 52ft (15.8m) length, 18ft (5.4m) width and 17ft (5.1m) height. A rotor tip to vertical obstacle clearance of 17ft was required for landing on ships. Single pilot operation was desired to save an estimated £12 million in manpower and training costs over the 15-year life cycle.

WINGS OVER THE FLEET

Sea King Replacement proposals and designs

	WG.24 Design B1	WG.24 Design D1	WG.24 Design F1	WG.24 Design G1	WG.27 MRFH	WG.32 SSRH	SKR Option 1 (Sea King)
Rotor diameter	1x 67ft 0in (20.42m)	Wing span 44ft 6in (13.56m); 18ft (5.4m) folded	Wing span 51ft 0in (15.54m); 18ft (5.4m) folded	2x 54ft (16.4m)	1x 72ft 0in (21.94m)	1x 38ft (11.5m) co-axial	1x 62ft 0in (18.89m); 16ft 4in (4.97m) folded
Length	66ft 0in (20.11m) fuselage; 52ft 0in (15.84m) folded	51ft 0in (15.54m)	46ft 6in (14.17m) fuselage; 52ft 0in (15.84m) folded	48ft 8in (13.61m) fuselage; 52ft 0in (15.84m) folded	48ft 0in (14.63m) folded	?	72ft 8in (22.14m) rotors turning; 47ft 3in (14.40m) folded
All-up weight	24,000lb (10,885kg)	Up to 35,000lb (15,875kg)	Up to 35,000lb (15,875kg)	32,500lb (14,740kg)	28,000lb (12,700kg)	25,000lb (11,340kg)	24,000lb (10,885kg)
Powerplant	2x turboshafts	2x turboshafts, limited tilt rotors	2x turboprops, tilting nacelles	2x turboshafts	2x turboshafts	2x Allison T701, 8,079shp (6,025kW)	2x Turmo 1800, 1,700shp (1,267kW)
Max speed	?	200+kt (370+km/h)	290kt (537km/h)	?	?	328kt (607km/h) at 11,000ft (3,350m); 405kt (750km/h) at 15,000lb (6,800kg) AUW	?
Armament	Homing torpedoes, depth charges	Homing torpedoes, depth charges	Homing torpedoes, depth charges	Homing torpedoes, depth charges	2x homing torpedoes, depth charges	2x homing torpedoes, depth charges	4x homing torpedoes, 4x depth charges, 1x WE.177A

Associated studies under NST.6644 had concluded that modern sonobuoys were significantly more effective than dipping sonars and the Nimrod MR.2's BARRA/CAMBS acoustic processing system was selected. Stowage for 40 sonobouys was required, with 20 in automatic dispensers. The search radar and ECM were to have 360° coverage. Provision would be provided for a dipping active sonar and internally-housed MAD to aid target classification and localisation. The weapons load would be four Mk.46 or Sting Ray homing torpedoes or four Mk.11 depth bombs or one WE.177A plus two torpedoes or Mk.11 depth bombs. Two mountings in the cabin doorways for 7.62mm machine guns would also be provided.

In the Commando role the SKR had to be capable of carrying at least 20 (preferably 34) fully equipped troops in Arctic clothing or a 7,000lb (3,175kg) cargo load stowed either internally or externally over a radius of at least 100nm (185km). In the Crane role the maximum load was to be 10,000lb (4,535kg).

Five options were examined to fulfil NSR.6646. Option 2 was the cheapest minimum development; fitting Sea King with the BARRA/CAMBS sonobuoy processor, which could enter service in 1986. The estimated AUW was 21,400lb (9,705kg) but it fell short of the performance requirements and the one-hour endurance prevented its use in screening and datum investigation operations. Fitting new BERP I composite main rotor blades and 1,546shp General Electric T700 turboshafts did not offer much improvement but this concept became the basis of the interim Sea King HAS.5 with its avionics

SKR Option 2 (Sea King)	SKR Option 3 (Sea King)	SKR Option 4 (Sea King)	SKR Option 1 (WG.31)	WG.31 (final)	WG.34	WG.34A DTV	EH101/AW101 Merlin HM.1
1x 62ft 0in (18.89m); 16ft 4in (4.97m) folded	1x 62ft 0in (18.89m); 16ft 4in (4.97m) folded	1x 62ft 0in (18.89m); 16ft 4in (4.97m) folded	1x 52ft 0in (15.84m); 17ft 0in (5.18m) folded	1x 60ft 0in (18.28m), 2x engines; 58ft 0in (17.67m), 3x engines; 16ft 6in (5.02m) folded	1x 60ft 0in (18.28m)	1x 55ft 6in (16.94m)	1x 61ft 0in (18.59m); 17ft 0in (5.18m) folded
72ft 8in (22.14m) rotors turning; 47ft 3in (14.40m) folded	72ft 8in (22.14m) rotors turning; 47ft 3in (14.40m) folded	72ft 8in (22.14m) rotors turning; 47ft 3in (14.40m) folded	62ft 8in (19.10m) rotors turning; 35ft 7in (10.84m) folded	67ft 6in (20.57m) rotors turning; 56ft 9in (17.29m) fuselage	67ft 6in (20.57m) rotors turning; 56ft 9in (17.29m) fuselage	58ft 0in (17.68m) fuselage	64ft 1in (19.53m) fuselage; 51ft 6in (15.7m) folded
21,400lb (9,705kg)	24,000lb (10,885kg)	26,000lb (11,790kg)	24,000lb (10,885kg)	24,000lb (10,885kg)	27,560lb (12,500kg)	?	32,187lb (14,600kg) max take-off
2x T700, 1,546shp (1,152kW)	2x T700, 1,546shp (1,152kW); or 2x Turmo 1800, 1,700shp (1,267kW)	2x PLT 27B, 2,000shp (1,490kW)	2x PLT 27B, 2,000shp (1,490kW); or 2x Turmo 1800, 1,700shp (1,267kW)	2x PLT 27B, 2,000shp (1,490kW); or 2x PLY 27BA, 1,400shp (1,045kW); or 3x T700-GE-T401, 1,500shp (1,120kW)	3x T700-GE-T401, 1,500shp (1,120kW)	3x T700-GE-T401, 1,500shp (1,120kW)	3x RTM322-0, 2,100shp (1,566kW)
?	?	?	140kt (259km/h) max cruising	?	?	?	167kt (309km/h) never exceed; 150kt (278km/h) max cruising
4x homing torpedoes, 4x depth charges, 1x WE.177A	4x homing torpedoes, 4x depth charges, 1x WE.177A	4x homing torpedoes, 4x depth charges, 1x WE.177A	4x homing torpedoes, 4x depth charges, 1x WE.177A	4x homing torpedoes, 4x depth charges, 1x WE.177A	4x homing torpedoes, 4x depth charges, 1x WE.177A	None	4x Sting Ray homing torpedoes, 4x Mk.11 depth charges

upgrades, improved tail rotor and a strake for better crosswind handling.

The other Sea King upgrade options included new main and tail rotors, an upgraded transmission and gearboxes and new engines. Option 1 featured single pilot operation, a strengthened undercarriage and two 1,700shp (1,267kW) Turbomeca Turmo 1800 (later renamed Makila) turboshafts. The reverse direction of engine rotation compared to the Gnome required a modified power turbine or a dedicated gearbox to be fitted. Option 3 had two General Electric T700 or Turmo 1800 and retained the two-man cockpit. Option 4 – dubbed the 'Advanced Sea King' – had single pilot operation but its 26,000lb (11,790kg) AUW required radical structural redesign and a new undercarriage. Aerodynamic changes were also made and semi-conformal weapons stowage provided. The powerplant was a pair of 2,000shp (1,490kW) Avco Lycoming PLT 27B – a turboshaft version of the M-1 Abrams AGT 1500 tank engine which had been unsuccessfully submitted to several US helicopter competitions. It was estimated that all three options could receive initial service clearance during late 1986. The strengthened gearbox and mission systems later appeared on the export Sea King Mk.42B for the Indian Navy.

Westland was also working on a new design developed from the WG.27. The WG.31 was Option 5, a compact airframe with enclosed side weapon bays, widely spaced engines to minimise the height, quadricycle undercarriage for deck stability and a

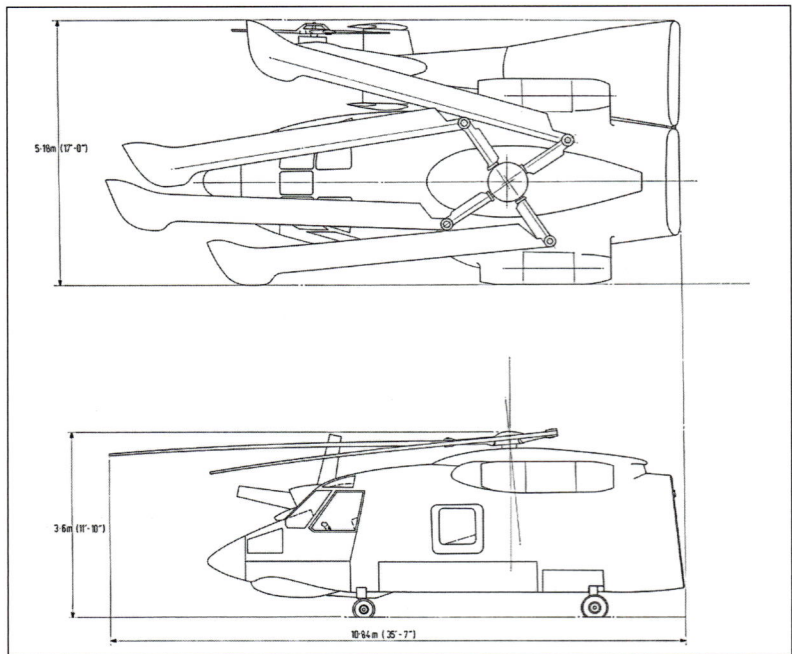

The WG.31 SKR Option 5 was a fresh sheet design, incorporating a forward-folding rear fuselage to fit into a frigate's hangar 35ft 7in (10.84m) long, 17ft (5.18m) wide and 11ft 10in (3.6m) high. The retractable search radar is located below the cockpit and the large rectangle below the cabin one of the lateral weapon bays, designed to keep the delicate homing torpedoes out of the slipstream. *Leonardo UK via Jeremy Graham*

This is the revised WG.31 which formed the baseline of the WG.34. The artwork illustrates key features of the WG.31 – 360° search radar, internal weapon stowage for NASR.7511 (Sting Ray) torpedoes and a AN/ASQ-81 towed MAD. *Leonardo UK via Jeremy Graham*

rear ramp door. The estimated AUW was 24,000lb (10,885kg). The engine choices were the Turmo 1800 or the PLT 27B, the latter offering slightly better payload capability. A three-engine version was also studied. The technical risks were judged to be acceptable with lower life cycle costs than the Sea King developments. Option 5 became the favourite and was selected in September 1978.

WG.34

The WG.31 evolved into the WG.34. The forward-folding rear fuselage, internal weapons carriage and retractable radar radome features were removed to save weight. The engine choices were two 2,000shp PLT 27B (1,490kW), or the lighter 1,400shp (1,045kW) PLY 27BA, driving a 60ft (18.2m) diameter four-blade rotor or three 1,500shp (1,120kW) T700-GE-T401 with a smaller 58ft (17.6m) diameter rotor with a bearingless hub (the third engine would be shut down during cruising flight). The rotor tip speed was restricted to 680ft/sec (207m/sec) to ensure that it could meet noise regulations in commercial service. In May 1979 Westland committed to the three-engine layout as the least risky and cheaper option.

The weight grew during the detailed design phase to 26,500lb (12,020kg). An option to radically redesign the main and tail rotors to save weight was rejected due to the technical risks and the additional weight was accepted as a justifiable compromise to meet the demanding ASW mission requirements. Weight saving measures to ensure that the maximum take-off weight remained within 27,000lb (12,245kg) included shortening the fuselage by 2ft (60cm).

Westland studied using twin tail rotors with a butterfly tail on several of its helicopter projects, including WG.34, to reduce weight, height and improve survivability. This feature was removed, however, in favour of a conventional 12ft 6in (3.81m) diameter tail rotor. The four-blade main rotor was redesigned with BERP technology using composite construction with a blade chord of 2ft 5in (73cm) and a diameter of 55ft 6in (16.9m). In early 1980 serious consideration was given to switching to a five-blade rotor to reduce vibration, especially for the planned commercial variant.

NSR.6646 required the SKR to float following a ditching for two hours at up to Sea State 3. Scale model tests in a water tank showed a tendency for the tail rotor to strike the water at speeds up to 45kt due to a tail-down pitching phenomenon caused by rotor wake impingement, which was finally cured by reshaping the contours of the rear fuselage.

Westland was responsible for the systems integration with input from GEC Marconi. The avionics fit included a 'glass cockpit' equipped with multi-function displays, Decca Doppler and Omega long-range radio navigation, Racal RIM-2 Orange Crop ESM, a variant of the Marconi AQS-901 sonobuoy acoustic processor, Ferranti Blue Kestrel radar (developed from Seaspray using Blue Fox technology), AN/ASQ-81 towed MAD and a Joint Tactical Information Distribution System (JTIDS) datalink. A MIL STD-1553B databus for weapons and systems integration was also fitted. NSR.6646 also called for an IR Passive Identification Device. Ferranti undertook technical studies but the weight of the equipment coupled with antenna siting and display requirement issues saw this requirement being dropped.

Westland aimed to reduce technical risk by building a Dynamic Test Vehicle (DTV), designated the WG.34A. The DTV would test the complete transmission (the conformal tooth spur gear split-torque Advanced Engineering Gearbox), bearingless rotor and engine systems. The main transmission was mounted on a 'raft' to minimise airframe vibration, a concept adopted from the W30 (this feature was later dropped for the production WG.34 to remove the need for – and weight and cost of – flexible shaft couplings.) The DTV would have three T700 turboshafts and the WG.34 rotor, while the fuselage made use of a W.30 cockpit section and the undercarriage came from a Sea King. The estimated first flight date was 1981 and construction was well underway when the decision to pursue a collaborative programme with Italy was taken. This would see the design of the transmission reallocated to Agusta and the redundant and incomplete WG.34A was scrapped.

A manufacturer's model of the WG.34. *Leonardo UK via Author's Collection*

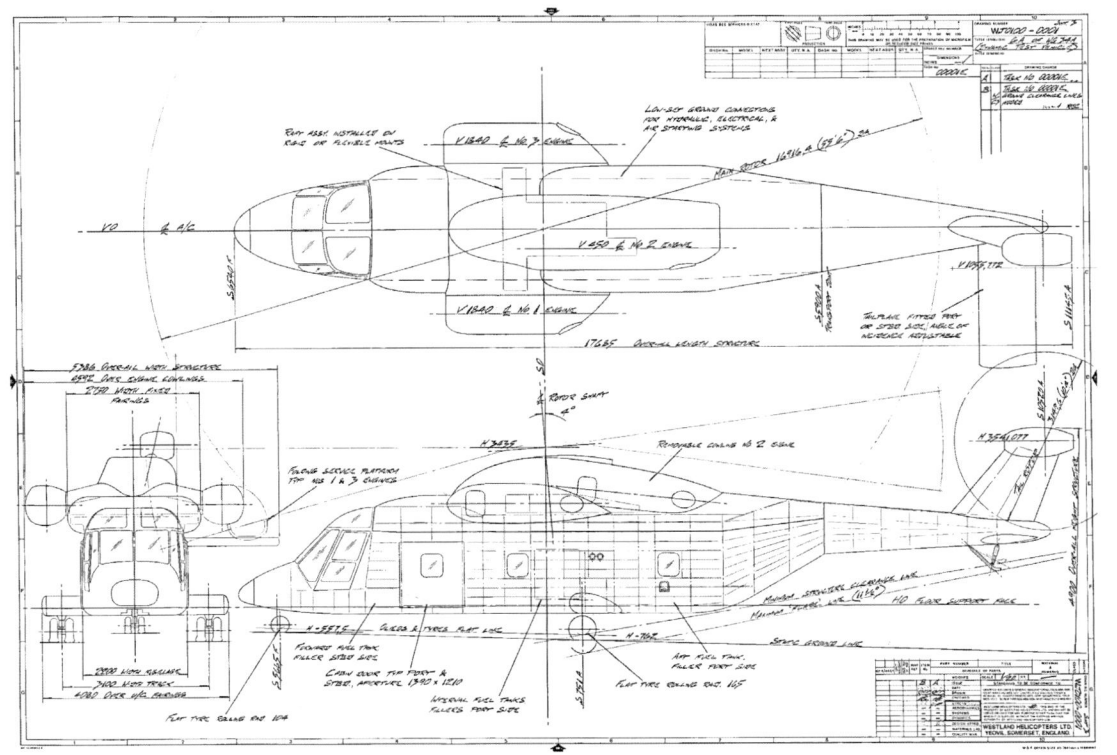

The WG.34A DTV was designed to flight test the engines and complete transmission system. The cockpit section came from the W30 transport helicopter and the undercarriage was that of the Sea King. The unfinished airframe was scrapped following the decision to proceed with a joint programme with Agusta, which secured the workshare for the transmission system. *Leonardo UK via Jeremy Graham*

Genealogy of the EH101 Merlin. Top row (from left to right): WG.31 SKR Option 5; WG.31 with weapon bays moved outboard into undercarriage sponsons; WG.34A DTV. Bottom row (from left to right): early EH101 study; Merlin HM.2; Merlin HC.4) *Chris Gibson & Author*

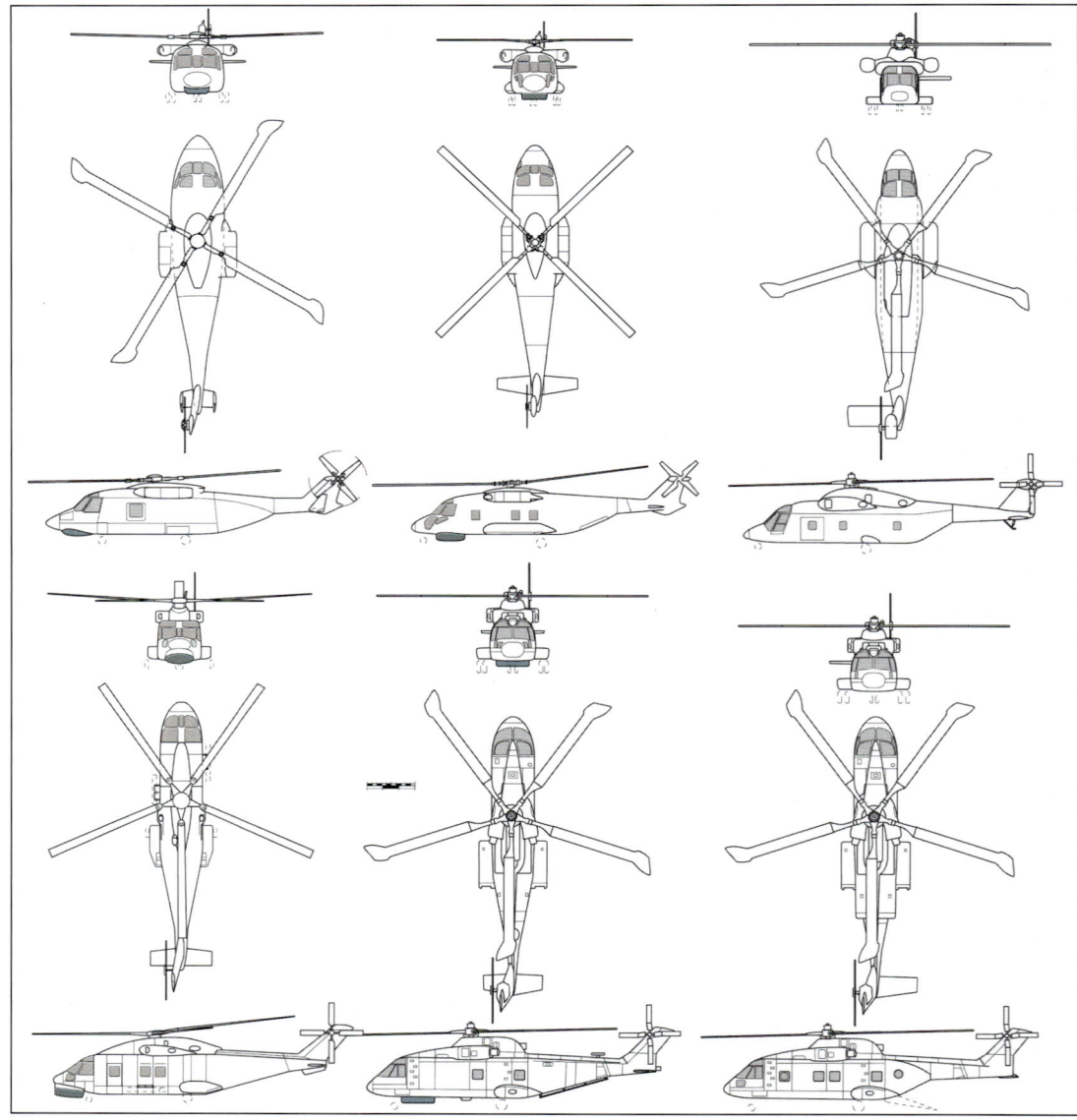

The estimated total programme cost in 1978 was £1.5 billion with the first flight of the WG.34 scheduled for May 1983. In an attempt to recoup some money, Westland envisioned a 19-seat commercial variant to serve the growing North Sea oil and gas rig transport market. During 1979–80 various cost cutting measures were investigated, including fitting the MEL Super Searcher radar. Other MOD options included Westland licence-built Sikorsky SH-60B Seahawks fitted with the Sea King's ASW system, or the USN's SH-60B Seahawk LAMPS III off-the-shelf. MOD evaluations still rated the WG.34 as the most capable and cost-effective solution and cancellation was avoided. The Secretary of State for Defence, John Nott, was keen to cancel the SKR in favour of relying on the RAF's Nimrods, but the Naval Staff fought hard to keep the SKR and offered a reduced avionics fit to save money and eventually it was reinserted into the long term costings.

Even so, the government felt that it could not afford to pay for the development costs alone and was keen to collaborate with a European partner. France, West Germany and Italy were already cooperating on the smaller NH90 tactical transport and naval ASW helicopter. Westland had been a member of the consortium, but the UK had decided not to pursue the NH90, the RN and RAF rejecting it due to its inferior endurance and payload capacity (the eventual design was reminiscent of Westland's original proposal.) Aérospatiale offered Westland some AS 332 Super Puma production in return for responsibility for the civilian WG.34 variant, but this proposal went no further.

The Italian Marina Militare Italiana (MMI) was seeking a replacement for its Sikorsky ASH-3D and ASH-3H Sea Kings and became the favoured partner. The needs of the RN and the MMI differed; the former favoured passive sonobuoys while the MMI wanted an active dipping sonar for the shallower waters of the Mediterranean. The RN required the SKR to fit aboard a 3,500-ton frigate and be capable of operating in Sea States 5 or 6 with wind speeds up to 55kt (101km/h), while the MMI favoured land-based operation. Politics and economics, however, overrode these differences.

Westland began discussions with Agusta, which proposed its 3DR9 design with a 62ft 9in (19.1m) diameter main rotor. The 3DR9 was too large to fit on the ships of either Navy, so the WG.34 became the basis of a compromise design. In November 1979 the British and Italian governments signed a Memorandum of Understanding, leading to the creation of the joint company European Helicopter Industries (EHI) in June 1980. Westland ceased work on the WG.34 and WG.34A DTV in October.

EH101 Merlin

Following the formation of EHI, design work on the EH101 began, the UK later adopting the name Merlin. (An oft-quoted tale is that the designation should have been EHI01 but that a misprinted I as 1 was never corrected.) A family of military and civil versions was planned. The project definition phase began in June 1981, entering the full development phase in 1983. Even at this early stage the MOD cut the planned production batch from 75 to 50 helicopters to reduce the estimated programme costs to £1.5 billion.

The contract for the naval EH101 was signed on 7 March 1984. Westland's design work share comprised the forward fuselage and flight deck, main cabin, undercarriage, engine installation, BERP III main rotor blades, AFCS and fuel systems. Agusta was responsible for the rear fuselage and tail unit, main rotor head, transmission (sub-contracted to Fiat Aviazione) and the electrical and hydraulic systems.

As both partners converged on a common design the gross weight was stabilised at 28,660lb (13,000kg). Some pressure from industry regarding the requirements for the civil version supported the shift to the higher gross weight. The prototypes were powered by three 1,720shp (1,282kW) GE CT7-2A turboshafts while the British and Italian production aircraft had 2,100shp (1,565kW) (take-off rating) Rolls-Royce/Turboméca RTM.322-01 and GE T700-GE-T6A1 engines respectively. Active hydraulic mounts were fitted to mitigate airframe vibrations from the rotor.

The mission avionics for the RN's Merlin version comprised Thomson Marconi AQS-903A Barra/CAMBS sonobuoy processor, Thomson Sintra Type 2089 FLASH dipping sonar, Marconi Blue Kestrel 5000 surveillance radar in a 360° radome and Racal RIM-2 Orange Reaper ESM. The inclusion of the Type 2089 sonar reflected the switch in operational emphasis to screening and littoral operations. The flight avionics consisted of the Smiths OMI 20 SEP dual-redundant digital AFCS, LINS 300 ring laser gyro and Litton Italia LISA-4000 Attitude and Heading Reference System.

The weapons payload was up to four Sting Ray Mod.1 homing torpedoes or Mk.11 depth bombs (as previously noted, the WE.177A was withdrawn

The first EH101 was PP1 ZF641 which made its maiden flight on 9 October 1987 at Yeovil before heading to Italy for basic systems development trials. *Leonardo UK via Author's Collection*

PP4 ZF644 was the common systems development aircraft. It crashed on 7 April 1995 near Yarcombe, Devon due to an uncommanded tail rotor pitch change, all four crew aboard successfully bailing out. *Leonardo UK via Author's Collection*

from service in 1992), and the installation of BAe P3T Sea Eagle ASMs was investigated during 1986. The endurance was five hours with a range of 450nm (833km) with a cruising speed of 150kt. Removing the sonar equipment allowed the carriage of up to 26 troops or four litters for casualties or 11,020lb (5,000kg) of cargo. The gross weight for the production aircraft grew to 32,190lb (15,000kg), the helicopter being qualified to operate up to a maximum weight of 34,390lb (15,600kg).

The first of nine pre-production EH101s, basic systems development aircraft PP1 ZF641 initially flew on 9 October 1987 at Yeovil before heading to Italy

PP5 ZF649 was the RN mission systems development aircraft, seen here making the first EH101 deck landing aboard the Type 23 frigate HMS *Norfolk* in November 1990. Replacing the lost PP4 on RTM.322-01 engine trials, it had ended its flying career by 2001, becoming a ground instruction airframe. *Leonardo UK via Author's Collection*

by sea for the flight test programme. ZF641 undertook rolling platform trials in 1997 at Boscombe Down following its retirement from flying. PP4 ZF644 was the naval common systems development aircraft, flying on 15 June 1989. It was lost on 7 April 1995 due to an uncommanded tail rotor pitch change at an altitude of 11,975ft (3,650m) near Yeovil, all four crew aboard successfully bailing out.

The RN mission systems development airframe was PP5 ZF649 which made its maiden on 24 October 1989 and made the first EH101 deck landing aboard the Type 23 frigate HMS *Norfolk* in November 1990. Sea trials aboard sistership *Iron Duke* in the English Channel followed during December 1992 to January 1993 and trials in the rougher waters of the North Sea aboard *Northumberland* during 27 March to 5 April 1995. In February 1999 ZF649 and the second and third production Merlin HM.1, ZH822 and ZH823, were shipped to the USA for ASW systems evaluation at the USN's Atlantic Undersea Test and Evaluation Center (AUTEC) at Andros Island in the Bahamas. The first production aircraft ZH821 flew on 6 December 1995, participating in the official roll out ceremony on 6 March 1996 before joining the development programme.

Production was delayed by serious systems development problems and in February 1990 the MOD demanded a prime contractor for mission system integration. Loral ASIC teamed with Westland and beat BAe and GEC to win the £1.5 billion contract in October 1991 (Loral was later taken over by Lockheed Martin.) The MOD committed to ordering 50 HAS.1 Merlins, along with 25 HC.2 tactical transports for the RAF to fulfil Air Staff Target 404, while the MMI committed to 42 aircraft. The HAS.1 order (soon redesignated as HM.1) was reduced to 44 due to defence cutbacks following the end of the Cold War. This was a small order given the need to equip two operational carriers plus at least 24 Merlins for the escorts. The operational emphasis switched to screening and shallow water operations, often operating autonomously and the Type 2089 FLASH dipping sonar was added to the avionics fit. The first production HM.1 was delivered on 17th May 1997. In July 2000, Westland's owners GKN and Agusta's owners Finmeccanica merged the two companies to form AgustaWestland (Finmeccanica acquired GKN's 50% share in 2004) and the EH.101 was renamed the AW101.

The first fully equipped Merlin HM.1 was the second production aircraft ZH822, which flew on 14 January 1997. The Intensive Trials Unit, 700M NAS,

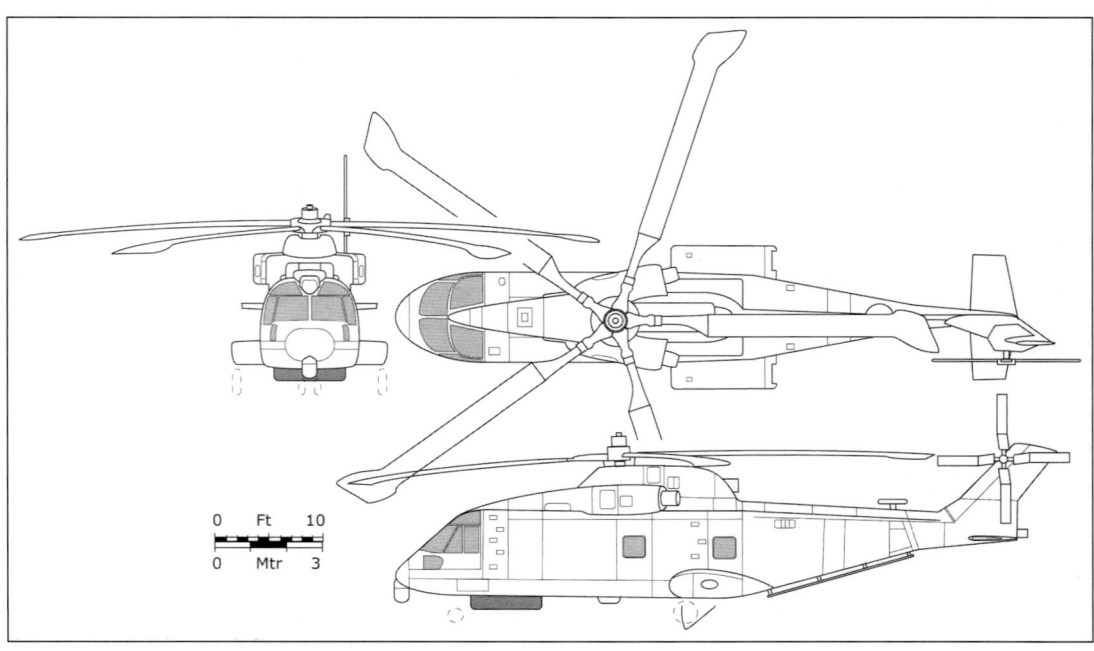

A general arrangement drawing of the Merlin HM.2. *Chris Gibson*

formed at RNAS Culdrose on 1 December 1998. In September 2001 the unit became the Merlin Operational Evaluation Unit (OEU) and in 2002 deployed to AUTEC and NATO's Fleet Operational Readiness Accuracy Check Site (FORACS) for operational trials. In 2007 the OEU deployed to the Caribbean aboard the LPH HMS *Ocean* to participate in counter narcotics operations in cooperation with the US Coastguard, helping to seize nearly half a ton of cocaine worth around £29 million. 700M NAS was disbanded on 31 March 2008, transferring its aircraft and personnel to 824 NAS, becoming 824 OEU Flight.

The Merlin HM.1 officially entered service in June 2000 with 814 NAS, 13 years later than originally specified. Three more squadrons received Merlins, all based at RNAS Culdrose; 824 NAS on 2 June 2001, 820 NAS in September 2001 and 829 NAS on 21 October 2004 (829 was merged with 814 NAS on 28 March 2018). The last Merlin HM.1 was delivered in October 2003.

824 NAS is responsible for pilot and aircrew conversion training. 814 NAS became operational in May 2002, deploying aboard HMS *Ark Royal*. The operational debut came in March 2003 during Operation T<small>ELIC</small> with four Merlin from 814 NAS embarked aboard RFA *Fort Victoria* with 12 pilots, eight observers and eight aircrewmen. The Merlins were primarily tasked as anti-surface warfare assets against small craft as well as carrying out vertical replenishment, troop transfers between task force ships and a long-range helicopter delivery service. With no submarine threat the sonar was removed to make space for eight seats or four stretchers in the cabin.

Following the crash of ZH859 on 30 March 2004 when tail rotor hub failed during a lifting operation in a hover, a redesigned tail rotor was fitted to all aircraft. Operational use has resulted in several Urgent Operational Requirements (UORs) being raised to add operational capabilities, specifically for operations in the Persian Gulf and Afghanistan. The first UOR in 2008 added AN/AAR-57 Common Missile Warning Systems, AN/ALQ-157 Matador IR Jammers and AN/ALE-47 chaff/flare dispensers. The following year a second UOR added L-3 Wescam MX-15 electro-optical/IR imaging equipment (further MX-15 mounting kits were acquired later) and other UORs have covered the installation of Bowman tactical radios, additional armour protection, a fast roping system and a 0.50in (12.7mm) M3M heavy machine gun mounted in the cabin doorway.

Merlin HM.2

The Merlin Capability Sustainment Programme to provide a mid-life avionics upgrade was contracted to Lockheed Martin UK at the cost of £750 million under Staff Requirement ST(S)6646. The programme covered 30 HM.1 airframes (an option to upgrade a further eight was not taken up). The upgrade included new mission software using open architecture for easier upgrading, new control consoles with 23.6in (60cm) widescreen colour displays, night vision goggle (NVG) compatible cockpit displays, an electro-optical camera, upgraded navigation systems with embedded GPS and a new air data computer. The Blue Kestrel radar was upgraded with digital signal processing and a new Thales acoustic processing

Merlin HM.1 ZH847 of 814 NAS deploying its Type 2089 FLASH dipping sonar. Despite the widespread use of active/passive sonobuoys the dipping sonar still remains relevant – it is not expendable and can therefore be reused for multiple contacts and its depth can be fine-tuned for local conditions of the thermal layers in the water which affect the behaviour of acoustic waves. MOD/Open Government Licence

During the interregnum between retirement of the Nimrod MR.2 in 2010 and introduction of the Boeing P-8A Poseidon MRA.1 in 2019, the Merlin was the UK's only effective ASW aircraft. This Merlin HM.1 of 829 NAS is releasing a Sting Ray Mod.1 training torpedo during an exercise off the Cornish coast. *MOD/Open Government Licence*

Merlin HM.2 ZH841 landing aboard the aircraft carrier USS *George H.W. Bush* (CVN-77) during Exercise Saxon Warrior 2017 and its assignment to the Type 23 frigate HMS *Northumberland*. ZH841 was first flown on 31 January 2000 and was used in hot weather trials until assigned to 820 NAS in October 2005. It was upgraded to HM.2 standard by 2017. *US Navy via Terry Panopalis Collection*

system with shallow-water detection and a common sonobuoy/sonar processor was fitted. Plans to replace the main and tail rotor hydraulic systems with the Helicopter Electro-mechanical Actuation Technology (HEAT) fly-by-wire system were abandoned in 2007, however, following ground rig trials.

The HM.2 performed its first shipborne test flight in September 2012 and the last conversion was delivered on 11 July 2016. The HM.2 achieved its initial operational capability (IOC) on 30 June 2014 after flying 480hr from HMS *Illustrious* during Exercise Deep Blue.

At present only 30 Merlins are in service and usually five are in maintenance at any one time, leaving 25 available aircraft, of which 14 are earmarked for deployment aboard a *Queen Elizabeth*-class aircraft carrier. In practice finding sufficient available Merlins is an issue, for example during HMS *Queen Elizabeth's* Carrier Strike Group (CSG) deployment to the Pacific in 2021 only seven Merlins were embarked within the entire CSG and only five (plus three Wildcats) during the 2023 Operation Firedrake deployment.

As related in Chapter 9, the five Crowsnest AEW conversions have had a lengthy gestation and IOC was only achieved in July 2023 with full capability likely to be attained in 2025. The Merlin HM.2 was scheduled for replacement in 2029, with the Project Proteus rotary-wing unmanned aerial system likely to complement the Merlin and Wildcat in the ASW role (and possibly the AEW role) during the late 2020s. On 11 June 2021, the MOD confirmed that the Out of Service Date had been moved back to 2040. What will ultimately replace the Merlin is open to speculation.

The MMI received 10 SH-101A for ASW/anti-ship roles, four EH-101A for AEW, 10 transport SH-101A and 12 HH-101A for combat search and rescue (CSAR). Exports have been made to several countries, mainly for SAR duties: Algeria (six Model 610); Canada (15 Model 511 CH-149 Cormorant, to be rebuilt as 16 Model 615 replacements); Denmark (eight Model 512SAR and six Model 512TTT); Norway (16 Model 612); Poland (four Model 614 for ASW and CSAR); Portugal (six Model 514 for SAR, two Model 515 fisheries patrol and four Model 516 for CSAR) and Japan (two Model 518 and 12 Kawasaki Heavy Industries-built MCH-101 for airborne mine countermeasures and transport.) EHI and Sikorsky won the Canadian New Shipborne Aircraft requirement in 1987 but a subsequent change of government saw the order for 33 (later 28) CH-148 Petrel for ASW and 15 CH-149 Chimo for SAR being cancelled in 1993. Although the civil EH101 failed to find sales success, several AW101s have been supplied for VVIP transport duties in Algeria, Indonesia, Nigeria, Saudi Arabia and Turkmenistan (orders for India and the VH-71 Kestrel Presidential Marine One programme were cancelled).

Wildcat

Following the post-Cold War drawdown, the MOD planned to operate an all-Merlin fleet for the RN but Westland (from 2000 AgustaWestland) continued private-venture development of the Super Lynx encompassing upgrades and rebuilt airframes. The Future Lynx project consisted of two studies based on the Super Lynx 300 to replace the Army Air Corps' AH.7 and the FAA's HMA.8 as the Battlefield Light Utility Helicopter (BLUH) and Surface Combatant Maritime Rotorcraft (SCMR) respectively.

A contract was awarded in July 2002 to begin the formal assessment phase and Thales was contracted to develop the avionics. The Future Lynx incorporated glass cockpit upgrades from the Merlin and the airframe used more machined components to reduce the parts count by up to 80% and attention was paid to reducing the radar cross-section. Other changes included a redesigned tail rotor, BERP IV main rotor blades and 1,362shp (1,015kW) LHTEC CTS800-4N turboshafts. The airframes and systems, even down to wiring looms, are identical to increase commonality between the two variants.

The BLUH programme faced financial problems and was recast as the Battlefield Reconnaissance Helicopter (BRH). The MOD selected the Future Lynx without an open competition, awarding a £1 billion contract on 22 June 2006 for 40 BRH and 30 SCMR helicopters with options covering an additional five of each. By July 2009 the cost had increased to £1.7 billion and the orders were reduced to 34 BRH and 28 SCMR. The Future Lynx was re-designated the AW159 Wildcat in April 2009, the first aircraft (ZZ400) flying on 12 November 2009, followed by ZZ401 on 14 October 2010 and the naval prototype ZZ402 on 19 November 2010.

The Wildcat AH.1 and the HMA.2 use the Selex Helicopter Integrated Defensive Aids System (based on that of the AgustaWestland Apache AH.1) including missile warning sensors, chaff/flare launchers and IR exhaust suppressors. The glass cockpit comprises four Smiths SDS-5000 255 x 200mm multifunction displays and a Smiths Health and Usage Monitoring System. The HMA.2's mission equipment is the SELEX Galileo Seaspray 7000E active electronically scanned array radar and an L-3 Wescam MX-15Di EO/IR sensor.

The HMA.2's missile armament comprises four MBDA Sea Venom ASMs or two multiple-tube launchers for Thales Lightweight Multirole Missile (Martlet) light ASMs, or a mix of both (see below.) The ASW weapons remain the same as the HMA.8 Lynx; two Sting Ray Mod.1 torpedoes or two Mk.11 Mod.3 depth charges. Maximum speed is 167kt and endurance is 2hr 15min or 4hr 30min with auxiliary fuel tanks. The maximum take-off weight is 13,230lb (3,300kg).

The Wildcat Fielding Squadron, 700W NAS, was formed in May 2009 to begin operational trials and by 2013 had five Wildcats. During February 2012

WINGS OVER THE FLEET

The Leonardo AW159 Wildcat's lineage from the Lynx is evident in this photograph of HMA.2 ZZ375 of 825 NAS operating over the English Channel. The facetted tail boom for reduced radar cross-section is a product of Westland's research during the 1980s. *MOD/Open Government Licence*

ZZ402 conducted deck handling trials aboard the Type 23 frigate *Iron Duke*, making 390 deck landings including 148 at night (including 76 using NVGs) over a period of 20 days. The first production HMA.2 was delivered in late 2013 and was deployed aboard HMS *Lancaster* on 23 March 2015.

700W NAS was disbanded in July 2014 and merged with 702 NAS to form 825 NAS on 10 October 2014 as the operational training unit. In September 2015 it deployed a Wildcat aboard the frigate *Duncan* for tropical temperature trials in the Persian Gulf. 815 NAS received its first four Wildcats on 19 April 2016. The final production Wildcat HMA.2 ZZ530 was delivered to 825 NAS on 25 October 2016. By 2024 the Wildcat HMA.2 had achieved a 100% availability rate achieved at sea with over 1,200 deck landings achieved. 815 NAS is the primary frontline unit with 15 Small Ship Flights as well as a Maritime Interdiction Flight to support counter-terrorism operations.

Exports so far are a 2013 South Korean order for eight to replace the Lynx Mk.99. They are equipped with the Type 2093 FLASH dipping sonar and sonobuoys and are armed with Spike NLOS missiles for an anti-boat attack capability and K745 Blue Shark homing torpedoes. The Philippine Navy ordered two Wildcats during in March 2016 for delivery during 2018. The naval Wildcat was promoted to Bangladesh and Malaysia but so far, the Wildcat has failed to match the Lynx's sales success and in early 2025 Leonardo was discussing closing the production line.

FASGW

Two separate missiles were procured to replace the Sea Skua. The Future Anti-Surface Guided Weapon (Heavy) – FASGW(H) – requirement was issued in 2001 for a more compact missile with additional targeting options for use in littoral environments.

MBDA proposed the Sea Skua IR which replaced the semi-active radar homer with a Kongsberg IR seeker. The Sea Skua 2 was proposed in 2006 with 21.5nm (40km) range, a new body and an active radar seeker for a 'fire and forget' capability. The MOD decided that collaborating on France's similar Anti-Navire Léger (Light Anti-Ship) requirement to replace the AS.15TT was the best option. The MBDA Sea Venom/ANL was selected in 2014 and initial trials began in June 2017. This high-subsonic missile has IR terminal guidance with optional semi-automatic command to line-of-sight laser guidance and can be used against land targets. It has a 66lb (30kg) blast fragmentation warhead. Propulsion is via a boost rocket motor and a sustainer motor with a ventral nozzle, the range is at least 10.4nm (20km). The Wildcat HMA.2 can carry four Sea Venoms, which have a diameter of 7.9in (20cm) diameter, are 8ft 2in (2.5m) long and weigh 240lb (110kg).

The FASGW(L) requirement for a small missile to counter fast inshore attack craft emerged in 2008. A guided 70mm rocket projectile was considered but it lacked the necessary manoeuvrability and semi-active laser guidance was problematic against dark coloured rubber boat-type targets. Thales developed the FASG(LMM) – named Martlet in British service – from the Short Brothers Starstreak SAM with laser beam-riding or semi-active laser guidance and a 6.6lb (3kg) blast HE warhead. It is launched from a tube canister-launcher, of which five or seven can be carried on each of the Wildcat's missile pylons. The Martlet is 3in (7.6cm) in diameter, 4ft 3in (1.3m) long and weighs 28.6lb (13kg). Maximum range is 5 miles (8km) and speed is Mach 1.5. An initial order covered 1,000 missiles for the Wildcat fleet.

The LMM has grown into a family of weapons with ship-launched, surface-to-surface, air-launched and FreeFall LMM glide-bomb variants. The British Army has equipped with their Starstreak-armed Stormer SAM vehicles with LMM and the Type 23 frigate *Sutherland* evaluated a modified 30 mm Automated Small Calibre Gun mounting which incorporated a five-round Martlet LMM launcher, firing four missiles at a small speedboat target at the Aberporth range in 2019. Since then, the RAF has test fired Martlet from drones and at least 650 Martlets were pledged for supply to Ukraine in late 2024.

Sea Venom and Martlet were integrated onto the Wildcat by Leonardo under a £90 million programme. The RN declared an IOC for both the Sea Venom and Martlet in May 2021 when four Wildcat HMA.2 deployed as part of CSG 21's deployment to the Pacific. The Martlet was fired operationally for the first time in October 2021 and was used during a USN SINKEX (SINK Exercise) in September 2022, hitting a retired frigate. A Wildcat HMA.2 conducted an air-to-air Martlet trial in July 2023, hitting a QinetiQ target drone. A Wildcat HMA.2 successfully fired a Sea Venom, hitting a barge target on the Aberporth Range in early October 2024 and shortly afterwards the RN announced that a Wildcat crew had successfully detected, tracked, and engaged a drone with a Martlet without any outside assistance. Both missiles should obtain their full operational capability in 2025.

A Leonardo Wildcat on display with dummy examples of the MBDA Sea Venom AML and the LMM Martlet. Both were scheduled to achieve full operational capability during 2025. *Chris Gibson*

13 Assault from the air

A stream of Westland Sea King HC.4 Commando helicopters shuttling to and from HMS *Hermes* delivering stores and supplies during Operation CORPORATE to recapture the Falklands in 1982 – the end of a long logistical trail stretching back over 7,000nm (12,965km). *MOD via Terry Panopalis Collection*

The Royal Navy has always been involved in amphibious warfare throughout its history, landing troops ashore in military operations. During the First and Second World Wars the military art of seaborne invasions was honed by the development of a multitude of specialised ships and smaller craft to get men, arms, vehicles and supplies ashore. The Admiralty had recognised the helicopter's potential use anti-submarine warfare (ASW) during the Second World War, but at that time they lacked the necessary payload capacity. The helicopter was therefore redirected to more sedate roles such as transporting naval officers ship-to-shore or ship-to-ship. By the mid-1950s larger helicopters like the Sikorsky S-55 had appeared which could carry half a dozen armed troops into combat. Early trials in cooperation with the Army and the Royal Air Force led to the adoption of the helicopter for assault, the insertion of troops from landing ships or aircraft carriers onto hostile shores. Called the 'Commando' role after the Combined Operations raiding parties of the Second World War, this concept was put into effect during the Suez Crisis of November 1956. From that moment the RN was instrumental in providing helicopter transport for the Royal Marines and Army, seeing action in Borneo and Sarawak during the 1950s and 60s.

Light fleet aircraft carriers that were too small for the latest generation of ASW aircraft were turned over for conversion into commando carriers, deploying

Commando helicopters

	Westland Whirlwind HAR.1 & HAR.3	Westland Whirlwind HAS.7 (Conversion)	Westland Wessex HU.5	Westland Sea King HC.4	Leonardo AW101 Merlin HC.4 & HC.4A
Rotor diameter	53ft 0in (16.15m)	53ft 0in (16.15m)	56ft 0in (17.07m)	62ft 0in (18.89m)	61ft 0in (18.59m)
Length	HAR.1, 41ft 8½in (12.71m); HAR.3 44ft 2in (13.46m)	41ft 8½in (12.71m)	65ft 10in (20.07m) overall; 38ft 2in (11.63m) folded	55ft 9¾in (17.01m)	64ft 1in (19.53m) fuselage; 51ft 6in (15.7m) folded
Rotor disc area	2,205ft² (204.8m²)	2,205ft² (204.8m²)	2,463ft² (228.8m²)		2,924.8ft² (271.7m²)
All-up weight	7,200lb (3,265kg)	7,800lb (3,540kg)	13,500lb (6,125kg)	21,000lb (9,525kg)	32,187lb (14,600kg) max take-off
Powerplant	HAR.1, 1x R-1340-40 Wasp, 600hp (447kW); HAR.3, 1x R-1300-3 Cyclone, 700hp (522kW)	1x Leonides Major 755/1, 750hp (559kW) Alvis	2x coupled Gnome H-1200 Mk.110/111, 1,350shp (1,006kW)	2x Gnome H-1400-1, 1,660shp (1,237kW)	3x RTM322-0, 2,100shp (1,566kW)
Max speed	86kt (159km/h) at SL	87kt (161km/h) at SL	114kt (212km/h) at SL	140kt (259km/h)	167kt (309km/h) never exceed
Service ceiling	8,600ft (2,620m)	13,000ft (3,960m)	14,100ft (4,300m)	10,000ft (3,050m)	15,000ft (4,570m)
Range	278nm (515km)	290nm (537km)	415nm (769km)	520nm (962km)	750nm (1,340km)
Capacity	5-8 troops	8 troops	16 troops; 4,000lb (1,815kg) internal payload, 3,100lb (1,405kg) external payload	27 troops; 6,000lb (2,720kg) internal payload, 8,000lb (3,630kg) external payload	30 troops; 6,725lb (3,050kg) internal payload, 12,160lb (5,520kg) external payload
Armament	Small arms	Small arms	2x 7.62mm GPMG (doorway & window hatch), 2x 7.62mm GPMG (forward firing), 2x 28-round 2in (50mm) RP pods, 4x SS.11 or AS.12	1x 7.62mm GPMG (doorway)	1x 7.62mm GPMG or 12.7mm FN-Browning MG (doorway)

Westland Whirlwind or Wessex helicopters and large numbers of troops as part of an amphibious assault group. During the Cold War the Royal Marines had a vital role as reinforcements for the northern and southern flanks of NATO in Norway and the Aegean Sea area respectively. The provision of new purpose-built Landing Platform Helicopter (LPH) ships for the task proved expensive and not until the 1990s would HMS *Ocean* be built. The supply of helicopters was another matter. The Wessex HU.5 was complemented by the larger Westland Sea King HU.4 and since 2014 has been replaced by Merlin HC.3 helicopters transferred from the RAF. Today the *Queen Elizabeth*-class carriers retain a secondary commando carrier role as part of the RN's wider amphibious assault capabilities.

Vertical transport

The 45 Sikorsky R-4B Hoverfly helicopters supplied under Lend-Lease to the Fleet Air Arm (FAA) were redirected into training and transportation roles. In September 1945 771 Naval Air Squadron (NAS) added the Hoverfly into its diverse fleet – the squadron was dedicated to the Fleet Requirements role, flying a variety of aircraft on target towing and general duties in addition to carrying out flight evaluations. Lieutenant K Reed made the first deck landing on an RN warship when he landed a Hoverfly aboard the battleship HMS *Vanguard* at anchor off Portland on 1 February 1947. Further evaluations of helicopter operations at sea in May 1947 saw the helicopter element of 771 NAS being split off to form 705 NAS at RNAS Gosport.

Westland Aircraft saw a need to diversify its products and sought a production licence for the S-51 from Sikorsky, an agreement being signed on 10 January 1947. Sikorsky provided six helicopters as patterns and assisted in production planning and Anglicisation of the technical drawings. The S-51 Dragonfly was powered by a 500hp (372kW) Alvis Leonides 521/1 radial engine; the UK prototype, registered as G-AKTW, took to the air on 5 October 1948 at Yeovil.

The RN and the RAF quickly grabbed the opportunity to buy the only helicopter then in production in the UK. In January 1949 S-51 G-AJHW was loaned to 705 NAS for two months of trials (receiving the military serial WB220). These included

A mass take-off of Fleet Air Arm Westland Dragonfly HR.3s in 1952. The type was used by 705 NAS for basic helicopter training. *Charles E. Brown via Author's Collection*

operations aboard the carrier *Vengeance*, pilot conversion, day and night search and rescue (SAR), training of winchmen and cold weather operations.

Following those successful trials an order was placed for 13 Dragonfly HR.1s with two-seats and rudimentary avionics for clear weather day flying, but useful for training, SAR and transportation. 705 NAS took delivery of its first Dragonfly on 13 January 1950, soon becoming responsible for all things rotary in the RN; including basic flying training, winchman and groundcrew training in addition to trials and communications work.

Dragonflies were used as 'plane guards' aboard aircraft carriers, loitering off the port beam of the carrier during flying operations to quickly rescue a pilot if they had to ditch into the water. The Hoverfly could hoist one person aboard via a winch, or two people could be rescued if fuel was dumped to lighten the weight. In early February 1953 five Dragonflies from 705 NAS rescued over 800 people in the Netherlands following the catastrophic North Sea Flood.

The HR.1 was followed by 71 Dragonfly HR.3s which differed in having metal rotor blades (the original wood and fabric blades suffered from poor balancing as they warped in moist conditions and the fabric covering could detach with disastrous consequences) and hydraulic powered controls. They took part in Korean War carrier deployments as plane guards and most RNAS stations acquired a pair for local SAR coverage. From 1953, 25 Dragonfly airframes were upgraded to HR.5

A pair of Douglas Skyraider AEW.1 aircraft are parked on HMS *Albion's* flight deck while the carrier's plane guard helicopter, Dragonfly HR.3 WG669, prepares to take off. The plane guard would pluck any unlucky airmen who crashed on take-off from the sea. WG669 went on to serve aboard *Eagle* and then was allocated to 705 NAS for training duties. It crashed during an autorotative landing on 9 June 1960 when one of the tail rotor blades broke off. *Blue Envoy Collection*

Westland Whirlwind HAR.1 XA868 was the seventh aircraft in the first production batch. Following tropical trials at RNAS Sembawang at Singapore in late 1954, it was allocated to the Flight servicing the Antarctic patrol ship HMS *Protector* during July 1957 to June 1966. It then became a ground instruction airframe and today is preserved at the Helicopter Museum in Weston-super-Mare. *Terry Panopalis Collection*

standard with the 540hp (402kW) Leonides 523/1, improved avionics and communications equipment. The Dragonfly laid the foundations of the helicopter in FAA service, which was able to make maximum use of helicopter technology as it then existed.

Westland secured a production licence for the larger S-55 on its own initiative in 1950. On 29 October 1952 848 NAS was formed at Gosport, receiving 10 Whirlwind HAR.1 as transports. These Sikorsky-built helicopters were powered by a 600hp (447kW) Pratt & Whitney R-1340-40 Wasp radial engine. 705 NAS used one of its Whirlwinds to experimentally tow the 450-ton minesweeper *Gavinton* at 5kt to explore a new method of minesweeping, but the Whirlwind proved to be underpowered. The 25 Whirlwind HAR.3s (37 were originally ordered) with a 700hp Wright R-1300-3 Cyclone radial replaced the Dragonfly in the plane guard role from November 1955.

In response to the growing need for more helicopters to support the Army's counter-insurgency operations against the guerillas of the Malayan Communist Party during the Malayan Emergency, 848 NAS embarked aboard the carrier maintenance tender HMS *Perseus* and arrived at RNAS Sembawang in Singapore on 8 January 1953 with its 10 Whirlwinds (four were held in reserve.) The squadron became part of No. 303 (Helicopter) Wing alongside the RAF's No. 194 Squadron. Two of the Whirlwinds were forward-based in Kuala Lumpur for troop transport and casualty evacuation in North and Central Malaya. Its first troop lift

Whirlwind HAS.1 XA870 was issued to the Antarctic patrol ship HMS *Protector* in September 1955. It received a colour scheme of Gloss Black and Gloss Light Orange (later International Orange). It rescued a Falkland Islands Dependencies Survey Unit from Roux Island off Graham Land Peninsular, Antarctica. It made its last cruise with *Protector* in 1965 and today is on display at the Aeroventure Museum, Doncaster. *Terry Panopalis Collection*

Whirlwind XL843 parked at RNAS Brawdy in July 1962 while assigned to 846 NAS, whose parent ship was HMS *Albion*. The Light Stone paintwork is indicative of the East of Suez role the Commando helicopters had at this time. In November 1962 a farmer blamed XL843 for killing 292 of his chickens following a low flight over his farm! XL843 came to grief on 6 December 1965 when the rotor blades hit the ground while landing in a snowstorm, the rotor blades severing the tail cone and the helicopter rolling onto its side. It was repaired by early 1968, flying on communications duties until it was retired in November 1970. *Terry Panopalis Collection*

mission was on 16 February during Operation Wellington II, carrying 12 soldiers of the 1st Battalion, The Worcestershire Regiment in three helicopters. Over 300 sorties followed within two months, the largest effort being Operation Commodore in May, which saw eight Whirlwinds lift 564 troops across 9 miles (14.5km) in seven hours on the first day – saving two days' marching time – and accumulating 415 sorties in 14 days, carrying 1,623 troops and 35,000lb (15,875kg) of cargo. In 1954 the squadron flew 215,000 miles, transporting over 10,000 troops.

The withdrawal of 848 NAS was postponed until April 1955 and again until 10 December 1956; HMS *Glory* delivering two Bristol Sycamores and nine Whirlwinds of No. 155 Squadron as well as five additional Whirlwinds for 848 NAS on 18 October 1954. During its time in theatre, 848 NAS evacuated 764 casualties and had carried 75% of all cargo delivered by helicopter.

The American engines proved underpowered to provide for adequate payload, especially under hot and high conditions. Westland began exploring new engine options for what it called Series II production, three HAR.3 airframes (XJ396, XJ398 and XJ445) being completed to HAR.5 standard with derated 750hp (559kW) Alvis Leonides Major 755 14-cylinder radial engines allowing fuller use of the transmission's maximum power rating. The tail boom was given 3° of droop for better rotor blade clearance along with a revised horizontal stabiliser and a sprung tail bumper. XJ396 made the first flight on 28 August 1955, appearing at the Society of British Aircraft Constructors Show at Farnborough a week later. XJ398 received an Armstrong Siddeley AS.181 turboshaft. XJ445 was meant to be completed as a HAR.6 with a Turbomeca Twin Turmo turboshaft but static trials proved unsuccessful and it was completed with the Leonides Major.

Assault from the sky

In April 1955 the Amphibious Warfare Headquarters began looking at using helicopters for amphibious assault and raiding, partly inspired by the United States Marine Corps (USMC). They examined all British helicopters then in use or in development and identified the need for two types:

- A large helicopter capable of carrying an infantry platoon (up to 33 men) or 7,000lb (3,175kg) of cargo

- A small helicopter for the raiding role capable carrying an infantry section (8 to 10 men) or 3,000lb (1,360kg) of cargo.

Both had to be capable of below-decks stowage in aircraft carriers. The Admiralty agreed to add the Raiding role to Naval Requirement NA.43 for the 'Single Package' ASW helicopter but there were doubts whether eight troops could be accommodated inside the Bristol Type 191's cabin (the Type 191 was cancelled soon after anyway.) Several RAF Whirlwind HAR.2s from the Joint Experimental Helicopter Unit (run by the RAF and the Army) carried out sorties during the Suez Crisis in November 1956 (Operation Musketeer) lifting elements of 45 Commando from the carrier HMS *Ocean* into Port Said. Before embarking aboard *Ocean,* the pilots had carried out 611 deck landings and 163 flying hours from

Ocean's sistership *Theseus*. By this time carriers did not carry AVGAS for piston engines, so some bunkers were reassigned and two Army fuel bowser lorries were parked on the edge of the flight deck to refuel six helicopters simultaneously (in the case of a fire the trucks would have simply been pushed overboard!) *Ocean* embarked six Bristol Sycamore HR.14 and six Whirlwind HAR.2 helicopters, *Theseus* carrying two Whirlwind HAR.2 and eight HAR.22 of 845 NAS. On the first day both units brought ashore 415 troops and 25 tons of stores, whilst evacuating 96 casualties for medical treatment. This was achieved with the loss of only one Whirlwind HAR.22 (due to lack of fuel) and one Sycamore put out of action by engine failure on take-off from *Ocean*.

The acquisition of two commando carriers was rapid following Suez. Two of the older *Centaur*-class light fleet carriers which could not operate the latest jet aircraft were earmarked for conversion. *Bulwark* paid off for conversion in December 1958 and recommissioned on 19 January 1960. The catapults and arrester gear were removed and the hangar modified for 16 Whirlwind helicopters and accommodation for 600 troops. Four Landing Craft Vehicle Personnel (LCVP) were carried on davits. The radar (including Type 960 air-search radar) and command spaces were modernised. *Albion* began her conversion in January 1961, her troop capacity being increased to 738 and the newer Type 965 air-search radar added; she recommissioned on 1 August 1962. Plans to refit *Centaur* were postponed and finally cancelled as part of the 1966 Defence Review, but *Bulwark* was brought up to the same standard as *Albion* in 1963–64.

In June 1964 a secondary commando carrier role was added to the planned CVA-01 fleet carrier. The ship would be capable of operating in this role for 21 days in addition to her normal carrier duties while carrying 1,125 troops, their equipment, 140 vehicles, eight 105mm guns and 14 tactical transport helicopters plus three Bell 47G unit light helicopters. The role was intended for an Internal Security deployment and not for a full amphibious assault (the CVA-01 was also cancelled as part of the 1966 Defence Review.)

From October 1959 some of the unsuccessful Whirlwind HAS.7 fleet were converted for Commando duties by stripping out the ASW gear. They were operated by 846, 847 and 848 NAS, being part of the Operation Vantage in July 1961 aboard *Bulwark* to forestall a potential invasion of Kuwait by its larger neighbour Iraq. In December 1962 the Whirlwinds of 846 NAS helped to quell an Indonesian-inspired revolt in Brunei against the Sultan's intention to join the newly formed Federation of Malaya. In 1965 17 HAS.7 were converted with a Bristol Siddeley Gnome turboshaft engine as the HAR.9 for SAR duties and for 829 NAS operating aboard the Antarctic patrol ships *Protector* and *Endurance*.

Wessex Junglies

The Wessex Commando Mk.1s served with 845 NAS, seeing action in Sarawak, Borneo alongside the older Whirlwind HAS.7 transports during 1964. These were 12 Wessex HAS.1 which had their automatic flying control system and ASW equipment removed to make way for basic seating for up to eight troops and provision to carry stretchers. Deployed by *Bulwark*, the helicopters were operated from the airport at Sibu in support of 2nd Division (West) with a forward operating base at Nanga Gaat to support the 3rd Division (East). The Wessex could carry eight troops and 11,800lb (5,330kg) of fuel from remote refuelling bases in temperatures of 30–34°C (86–93°F) with less than 5kt of wind. The flying was challenging and hazardous and included Operation CLARET missions inserting Special Air Service patrols to make limited incursions of the Indonesian border. 845 NAS was relieved by 848 NAS aboard *Albion* in 1965, the latter being equipped with new Wessex HU.5 helicopters.

Westland had begun developing the Wessex HU.5 in early 1962 based on the RAF's HC.2 tactical transport variant powered by two coupled 1,350hp (1,006kW) Bristol Siddeley Gnome H.1200 Mk.110/Mk.111 turboshafts. Specification HU.228D&P covered the development, being issued to Westland on 7 June 1962. Naval Staff Requirement AW.404 (later NSR.6404) confirmed the need for a transport helicopter and an order for 40 Wessex HU.5 was placed on 28 August 1962, followed by additional orders during 1964-65 to bring the total to 100. The prototype HU.5 XS241 first flew on 31 May 1963 with test pilot Leo De Vigne at the controls. The last production aircraft, XT774, was delivered in 1967.

The HU.5 could be armed with door-mounted and forward-firing 7.62mm GPMG machine-guns and could carry four Nord SS.11 or AS.12 wire-guided

The Westland Wessex HU.5 (like the RAF's Wessex HC.2) was powered by two coupled 1,350shp (1,006kW) Bristol Siddeley Gnome H.1200 Mk.110/Mk.111 turboshafts to provide improved performance and engine-out safety margins. *Blue Envoy Collection*

Wessex XP108 of 845 NAS, assigned to HMS *Albion* in July 1962 in the early Light Stone camouflage scheme. XP108 was brand new, having first flown on 21 February was issued to 845 NAS on 24 May. Deployed to Sarawak in October the same year, it suffered a number of mishaps, hitting bushes and tree stumps in the confined makeshift jungle clearings. An engine failure on 4 March 1965 while being flown by an RAF crew led to a crash landing on a rocky river bed. The pilot Squadron Leader MR Thompson survived despite his injuries but the co-pilot Pilot Officer AJ Williams and six Malaysian soldiers in the cabin were killed. Overnight the river rose and swept the wreckage away. *Terry Panopalis Collection*

Wessex HU.5 XP109 shows the pylon arrangement for the four Nord SS.11 guided missiles (two on each side). The plate fitted above the missiles was to deflect the heat of the exhausts away from the ordnance on the racks. *Blue Envoy Collection*

An infantry section embarks aboard HU.5 XT468 on *Albion's* flightdeck in 1968 off the coast of Borneo. From the end of 1963 the Wessex gained 'sand and spinach' camouflage of Olive Drab over Light Stone, which was retained until the early 1970s. XT468 was first flown on 29 October 1965 and was used for handling trials aboard the new Landing Platform Dock (LPD) HMS *Fearless* the following year. Deployed to Sarawak in 1968, XT468 returned from the Far East aboard *Albion* in November 1971. XT468 had a very lucky escape on 25 April 1982 when it was airborne on a test flight at the time SS *Atlantic Conveyor* was hit by an Exocet missile during the Falklands Conflict. The helicopter landed aboard *Hermes* to form part of the Commando helicopter force during the recapture of the islands. Its flying career ended in October 1987. *Terry Panopalis Collection*

anti-tank/anti-boat missiles or two 28-round 2in (50mm) rocket pods. The missiles were aimed by the co-pilot via an M.260 sight in the cockpit roof on the port side. *Albion* and *Bulwark* could carry up to 24 AS.12 missiles for their Wessex.

As noted above, 848 NAS arrived in Borneo aboard *Albion* in 1965, staying until it was relieved in 1966 by the re-equipped 845 NAS, returning home in 1968 aboard *Bulwark*. The third squadron was 846 NAS, which reformed in 1968 and undertook camouflage trials, which resulted in all the HU.5s losing their 'spinach and sand' green and stone disruptive scheme in favour of all over olive drab. 847 NAS was formed at RNAS Sembawang in March 1969, remaining based in the Far East until it was disbanded in May 1971 when the Far East Fleet in Singapore was disbanded, its Wessex going to 848 NAS.

There was involvement in the counter insurgency operations in Aden too. Operation NUTCRACKER in January 1964 pushed troops into the harsh terrain of the Radfan, supported by four Wessex of 815 NAS from *Centaur*. In May, the Bakri Ridge assault by 39 Infantry Brigade was to have involved six Wessex from *Centaur* but the situation on the ground meant that the Army could not wait another five days for *Centaur* to arrive and it went ahead without the participation of 815 NAS.

A close up of Wessex HU.5 XT464 of 847 NAS in May 1968. The external hook seen below the fuselage failed on 16 July 1968, resulting in the load being lost near East Fortune in Scotland. XT464 met its end on the Fortuna Glacier on South Georgia on 22 April 1982. *Terry Panopalis Collection*

As part of the attempts to find a new camouflage colour scheme for the Wessex HU.5, XS480 of 846 NAS received Devon Red on the upper surfaces and PRU Blue below in January 1969. *Terry Panopalis Collection*

Wessex XS480 also trialled an overall Devon Red colour scheme, while another received Olive Drab and black. Although the Devon Red seems to blend in better with the Goonhilly Down terrain, overall Olive Drab was selected as the best choice for the range of operating environments that the Wessex found itself in. *Terry Panopalis Collection*

As part of the same trials in January 1969 HU.5 XS489 received temporary Arctic camouflage with white distemper over the Olive Drab on the lower fuselage. *Terry Panopalis Collection*

Attached to Wessex HU.5 XS515 is the external beam for fitting machine guns or rocket pods. XS515 was completed in October 1964 and saw use in Northern Ireland in the late 1970s on internal security duties during Operation BANNER. Transported to the Falklands aboard MV *Atlantic Causeway* it arrived at the islands on 1 June 1982. It retired in October 1986 to become a ground instruction airframe and was scrapped in 2008. *Author's Collection*

The defence cuts of October 1970 called for *Bulwark* to decommission in 1974, in fact she was swapped with *Albion* to avoid *Albion's* forthcoming £25 million refit. *Hermes* was refitted as a dual role anti-submarine carrier (CVS) and commando carrier during October 1970 to August 1973, gaining accommodation for 803 troops and four LCVP in davits. But as Exercise SWIFT soon revealed in 1973, when used for ASW the 16 Sea King HAS.1 embarked to provide a sufficient ASW screen left no space for any Wessex HU.5 helicopters. In wartime a choice would have to be made whether to use *Hermes* for ASW or amphibious assault.

One unexpected deployment by *Hermes* was on 22 July 1974 for the evacuation of 1,630 civilians (900 by Wessex) from the northern coastal town of Kyrenia following the Turkish invasion of Cyprus. In 1977 846 NAS was disbanded and amalgamated into 845 NAS at RNAS Yeovilton. It reformed again in October 1978 for service aboard *Hermes* and *Bulwark*, replacing its Wessex with Sea King HC.4s by October 1981. 845 NAS assisted with internal security duties in Northern Ireland during the height of The Troubles.

The main wartime NATO role for the amphibious force was the reinforcement of Norway and Denmark, the northern flank of NATO's European defences, or the Aegean Islands and Greece on the southern flank. From 1969 the annual Exercise CLOCKWORK took the Wessex to the Norwegian Air Force base at Bardufoss, some 90nm (160km) inside the Arctic Circle and the barren locality around it.

Special Delivery! The Wessex HU.5 also served as a vertical replenishment – VERTREP – asset. XT480 is delivering a slung load of 4.5in gun ammunition from the replenishment ship RFA *Regent* to the Type 41 anti-aircraft frigate HMS *Jaguar*. *MOD via Terry Panopalis Collection*

WINGS OVER THE FLEET

Air-to-air refuelling was trialled using a Wessex HAS.3 as the tanker with an HU.5 as the receiver using the looped drogue system. *Blue Envoy Collection*

The HU.5's moment of glory was during the Falklands/Malvinas Conflict of 1982. Much has been written about its exploits during Operation CORPORATE, there is no room to cover this in detail, suffice to say that they were used extensively for transporting men and materiel from ship to shore and between ships, as well as their intended assault role. 845 NAS embarked 14 of its 22 Wessex among the Task Force, along with the newly reformed 848 NAS and 847 NAS using the assets of training and SAR units 707, 771 and 772 NAS. Notably *Hermes* was operated as a Sea Harrier carrier and ASW patrol asset, no use could be made of the ship's secondary Commando role. The Wessex HU.5s

The Grass Green paint finish blends into the grass well. Not an assault colour scheme, Wessex HU.5 XT772 was one of the 'Green Parrot' 'Admiral's Barges' of 781 NAS, ferrying Staff Officers and Cabinet Ministers around in their (semi) luxurious cabins. *Terry Panopalis Collection*

completed 1,841 sorties totalling 4,757 flying hours and 2,698 deck landings. Only eight were lost, six aboard the sunken container ship SS *Atlantic Conveyor* and XT473 and XT464 which crashed (without any fatalities) in white-out conditions on the Fortuna Glacier on South Georgia. Retirement finally came in March 1988.

Unbuilt Commandos

By 1962 the Admiralty was looking for a replacement for the Wessex and issued Requirement AW.165, which was merged with the Air Staff's replacement for the Bristol Belvedere HC.1 as Naval Air Staff Requirement NASR.358. This called for a general purpose helicopter to enter service by 1970 with secondary roles including logistic and tactical transport, Commando assault operations and crane lift. A fleet of 114 helicopters was desired and it was planned that each commando carrier would carry four NASR.358 helicopters in heavy lift configuration, four in ASW configuration and 14 Wessex HU.5. The radius of action would be 65nm (120km) when carrying 20 troops (15 in tropical conditions) or a Land Rover and 120mm WOMBAT recoilless gun, weighing 4,000lb (1,814kg), in the cabin. As related in Chapter 8, ultimately the Gnome-powered Boeing Vertol CH-47 Chinook was selected and NASR.358 was abandoned by the RN as it was too large for its ships.

Both the Air Staff and the Admiralty wanted a smaller medium transport helicopter to replace the Whirlwind and Wessex, their requirements being merged as NASR.365 in 1965. The aim was for the helicopter to be ready for commando carrier operations by 1975. The requirement called for a radius of action of 75nm (138km) when carrying 12–16 troops or 4,000lb (1,815kg) of cargo; or 100nm (185km) with 12 troops or 3,000lb (1,360kg.) The external payload was to be 4,000lb (1,815kg) (for example a ½ton Land Rover) carried for 50nm (92km) (the ½ ton Lightweight Land Rover Series IIA was developed in 1965 especially for carriage inside an Armstrong Whitworth Argosy C.1 transport or as a slung load under a helicopter). The Ministry of Aviation awarded Westland a feasibility study contract but, as recounted in Chapter 8, the RN abandoned NASR.365 in favour of the Sea King for the ASW role.

Westland offered the improved Wessex Mk.6 for the Commando role. The first proposal was to rebuild the HU.5 (and RAF HC.2) with wider chord rotor blades for an increased all-up weight (AUW) of 14,000lb (6,350kg) and a larger diameter five-blade tail anti-torque rotor. The cabin would receive an additional 2ft 3in (68cm)-wide door on the port side. In July 1965 the HU.5 prototype XS241 tested a five-blade tail rotor hub from the Sea King with standard Wessex tail rotor blades to determine if the increased diameter improved the yaw control and high pitch angles.

The second Mk.6 proposal had a longer cabin with a redesigned tail cone and dorsal pylon, an additional port-side door, a redesigned four-blade rotor and Sea King undercarriage including the sponsons for additional fuel capacity. Neither of the proposals went any further.

Staff Target NST.6433 was issued in June 1969 to replace the Wessex HU.5 in the Commando and support roles, but this was rapidly replaced by the general purpose Multi-Role Fleet Helicopter (MRFH) to replace the Sea King and Wessex. Westland began preliminary studies in March 1970, which covered both single and tandem rotor designs. The MRFH was envisioned as operating from the Command Helicopter Cruiser (soon to be ordered as the *Invincible*-class) and Landing Platform Helicopter (LPH) ships to succeed *Bulwark* and *Hermes* as Commando assault carriers.

The plans for new LPH ships changed frequently. In 1970 two types of LPH were under consideration. The hybrid CVS/LPH 'Military Version' was similar in arrangement to *Invincible* with a length of 639ft 9in (195m), 18,290 tons displacement and a maximum speed of 20kt. The flight deck had two deck lifts, which could be increased in size to 53ft 3in × 20ft (16.2 × 6m). The ship could accommodate 18 Wessex and 1,500 sailors and Royal Marines. The LPH 'Ferry Version' was a more basic low cost option. The intention to order two ships in 1972 was cancelled in 1971.

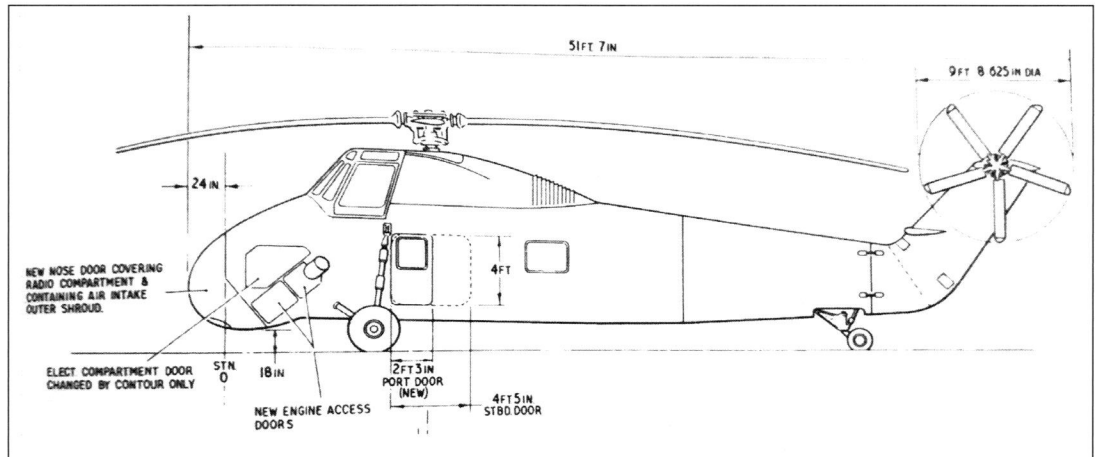

A general arrangement drawing of the proposed Wessex Mk.6 for the Commando role with an additional portside door and new five-blade tail rotor. *Leonardo UK*

The availability of the Sea King HC.4 was a welcome boost to the FAA's Commando fleet, as the helicopter could easily carry large external payloads such the Hägglunds Bv 202 articulated amphibious/snow vehicle being delivered ashore by ZA292 from HMS *Bulwark* in September 1980. The helicopter was damaged by small arms fire near Goose Green, East Falkland, during a casualty evacuation sortie on 28 May 1982. It was scrapped in 2015. *MOD via Terry Panopalis Collection*

Revised plans in 1972 foresaw ordering one LPH in 1979 to replace *Hermes* in 1983, but in 1973 this ship became a single large CVS, which in 1974 became a dual-role LPH/CVS to be built after the three *Invincible*-class ships were completed. The 1974 Defence Review then cancelled the project, along with advocating the decommissioning of *Bulwark*, assigning ASW as *Hermes*' main role, cancelling the Wessex HU.5 replacement and cutting 7,000 Royal Marines, with 41 Commando at Malta to disband by 1979, alongside abandoning the southern reinforcement mission.

Sea King Commando

The Royal Marines lacked a helicopter that could lift its heavier loads such as the new 105mm L118 Light Gun and the Bandvagn 202E articulated tracked snow vehicle. Fortuitously, four complete Sea King Commando fuselages from a cancelled Egyptian order and spare funds resulted in NSR.6101 being raised in mid-1978 and an order was quickly placed for 15 Sea King HC.4s to capitalise on both circumstances.

The Sea King HC.4 could carry up to 6,000lb (2,720kg) – 20 troops plus equipment – over a radius of 20nm (37km), or 7,420lb (3,365kg) in the crane role over the same distance. The armament was restricted to door-mounted 7.62mm GPMG machine-guns, but the standard Commando fixed undercarriage without floatation sponsons was retained to give the option of later carriage of rocket pods or missiles.

The first production aircraft ZA290 first flew on 26 September 1979 and further orders between 1982 and 1985 brought the total to 41 (another was acquired for the Empire Test Pilots School and two HC.4X were built for the Royal Aircraft Establishment for experimental work.) The additional orders provided sufficient Sea Kings to lift two companies of Royal Marines simultaneously.

The Sea King HC.4 saw extensive service worldwide and remained in frontline service until 23 March 2016. The new Sea Kings quickly saw action, being deployed during Operation CORPORATE alongside the Wessex HU.5. They were based aboard *Hermes* (although the ship did not operate in its commando carrier role). Three HC.4s were lost during the war: one on 23 April ditched while performing a nighttime transfer of supplies to another ship; another crashed into the sea on 12 May due to an altimeter failure, the crew being safely rescued; and on 19 May an HC.4 transporting SAS troops crashed into the sea while attempting to land on the amphibious assault ship HMS *Intrepid*, only nine of the 31 men aboard were rescued.

During Operation GRANBY in early 1991, following Iraq's invasion of Kuwait the previous August, 845 NAS deployed six HC.4s, being joined six from a reformed 848 NAS. They were mainly used for inter-ship transport and troop ferrying sorties ashore. In late 1992 845 NAS was deployed as part of the United Nations task force in Bosnia and Herzegovina during the violent breakup of Yugoslavia. The HC.4 again operated in the transport role, also performing

The Sea King HC.4 was still new when the Falklands conflict erupted in 1982. The helicopter proved its worth during the campaign – seen here delivering stores ashore – which later resulted in additional orders, sufficient to enable two companies of Royal Marines to be airlifted simultaneously. *MOD via Terry Panopalis Collection*

The Sea King HU.4 retained the overall Olive Drab camouflage of the Wessex HU.5. This 'Junglie' is ZA291 of 856 NAS, photographed in June 1993. *Terry Panopalis Collection*

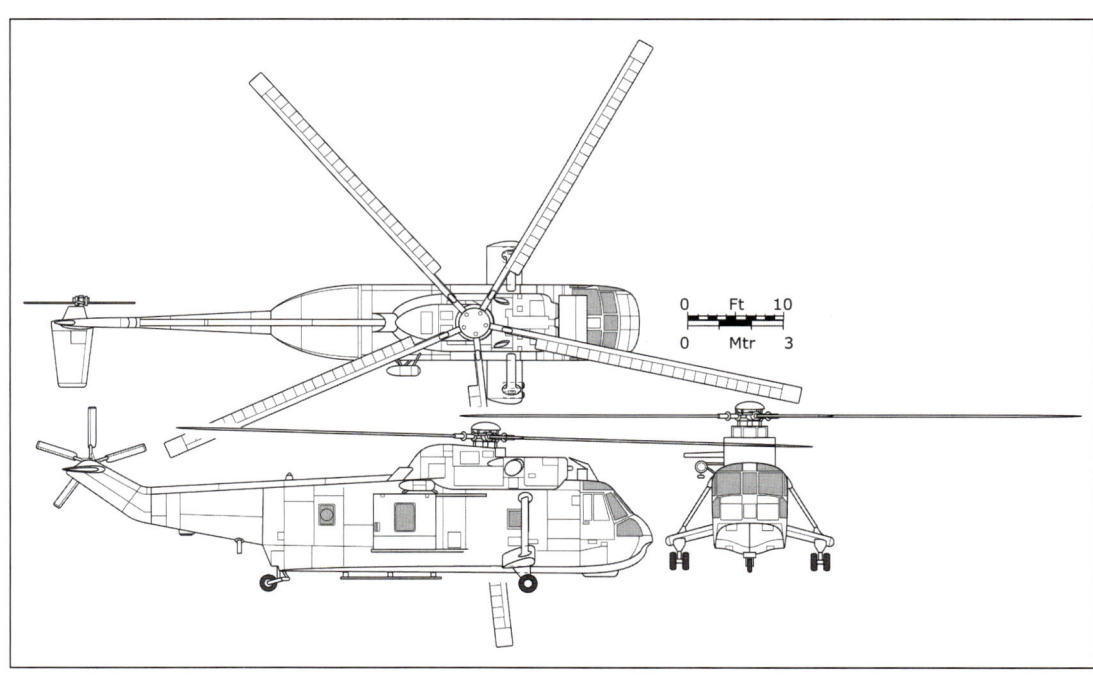

A general arrangement drawing of the Westland Sea King HC.4. *Chris Gibson*

WINGS OVER THE FLEET

The rather worn looking Sea King HC.4 ZD476 of 846 NAS shows some of the modifications fitted for Operation GRANBY: intake dust filters, M-130 chaff/flare dispensers on the rear fuselage and an FN-Herstal 0.50in machine gun in the cabin doorway. The 'Junglies' received Desert Camouflage Sand ('Desert Pink') ARTF paint and once hostilities began had most of their markings painted over. *MOD via Terry Panopalis Collection*

casualty evacuation and serving as an aerial crane role, repositioning the Royal Artillery's 105mm L118 Light Guns. The Sea Kings came under fire several times during the deployment, luckily without damage or casualties. The 'Junglie' came closer to the operating environment of its nickname in 2000 when 846 NAS participated in Operation *Palliser* in Sierra Leone from HMS *Ocean*. In July 2006 they were deployed to Cyprus to assist in Operation Highbrow, the evacuation of British citizens from Lebanon.

The HC.4 fleet was later augmented by five HAS.6(CR) utility conversions (with the ASW gear removed) used by 846 NAS until 31 March 2010. From 2007 four HC.4s were modified for use in Afghanistan in support of Operation *Herrick*. Changes to better cope with the hot, high and dusty conditions included new composite Carson main rotors, a new five blade tail rotor, a Night Vision Goggles compatible cockpit as well as decoy and defensive aids equipment. They were replaced in-theatre by the Merlin HC.3 in October 2011.

A Sea King HU.6 (a HAS.6 stripped of ASW gear for the utility role) from HMS *Invincible* lands aboard the replenishment oiler USNS *Pecos* on 23 February 2002. White ARTF disruptive camouflage has been applied over the NATO Green paintwork. *US Navy via Terry Panopalis Collection*

After much delay, budget problems and political wrangling, HMS *Ocean* finally commissioned on 30 September 1998 and served as a versatile platform for amphibious, helicopter and humanitarian operations until it was (arguably prematurely) decommissioned in March 2018 and sold to Brazil. MOD/Open Government Licence

Replacing *Hermes*

The lesson of the Falklands gave new impetus to the amphibious fleet, which the 1980 Defence Review by the Secretary of State for Defence Sir John Nott had nearly decimated. Plans in 1983 foresaw building three Landing Platform Dock (LPD) ships which would combine the roles of heavy equipment transport, helicopter assault and amphibious warfare command. This proved to be unaffordable and the plan was changed to two LPDs and one LPH. During the conversion of the purchased roll-on/roll-off ship MV *Contender Bezant* into the aviation training ship RFA *Argus* for the Royal Fleet Auxiliary, it was hoped to convert her sistership, MV *Contender Argent*, as an Aviation Support Ship (ASS, basically an LPH) but this did not happen. HMS *Bulwark* had decommissioned in 1981, followed by *Hermes* in 1984 and the three *Invincibles* were used as interim LPHs, which would not be sustainable in the long term given their vital ASW role. The ASS was not seen as just being a helicopter carrier, it would contribute to the requirement for the RN to embark two-thirds of the Commando force in specialised vessels. The Navy Department called for two LPDs and two ASS in 1986, each carrying 400 troops, 80 light vehicles, 4 LCVPs and 12 Sea King HC.4 with maintenance and support capabilities for helicopters and Sea Harriers. There were simply no funds available, however, to build even one ASS to commission in 1991 to plug the capability gap.

Not until 1988 did the Ministry of Defence (MOD) announce new amphibious warfare ships. By this time further studies had called for two ASS, each carrying 12 Medium Support Helicopters (which were envisioned to be Merlins), six Westland Lynx (on deck), 800 troops and four LCVPs. The MOD set a price tag of £110 million per ship and to save money they would be built to commercial standards; the risk of serious battle damage was accepted. Invitations to tender were sent out to industry (including Swan Hunter which had been the preferred bidder) but only two bids were received in 1989 and neither met Staff Requirement SR(S)7044. Cancellation by the government was not improbable at this stage.

In consequence, in October 1992 the Navy Department's Future Project Design Group had been asked to design an LPH conversion for the *Invincible*-class ship *Ark Royal*, allowing the ship to be returned to her original role if required. The changes included removing the GWS.30 Sea Dart missile launcher (but leaving the electronics in place, the magazine being repurposed for small arms ammunition), the Type 1022 air-search radar and the Type 2016 sonar. The aft section of the hangar would be converted for vehicle stowage, including a retractable vehicle ramp on the starboard side of the hull. Accommodation would be provided for 500 troops and four LCVP added in davits. Enough space in the hangar remained to stow seven Merlins, the remainder of the helicopters being embarked on the flight deck, which was extended forwards for sufficient helicopter parking space. The conversion cost would be £30–50 million. This fall-back plan was technically feasible but not optimal and the

WINGS OVER THE FLEET

Royal Marines aloft

The Royal Marines formed No. 3 Commando Brigade Air Squadron at Singapore in 1968, amalgamating the Brigade Flight and the Air Troops of 40 Commando, 42 Commando and 29 Commando Regiment, Royal Artillery. On returning to the UK in 1971 it also absorbed the Air Troops of 41 Commando and 45 Commando. It had one anti-tank flight, and two utility flights equipped with Westland Scout AH.1s and four reconnaissance flights with the Westland Sioux AH.1 (licence-built Agusta-Bell 47G-3B1). These helicopters officially belonged to the Army Air Corps (AAC) and maintenance was carried out by the Corps of Royal Electrical and Mechanical Engineers (REME). During 1974–75 the Sioux were replaced by 12 Westland Gazelle AH.1s.

Elements of 3 BAS were deployed in Belize, Northern Ireland and in Norway. During the Falklands/Malvinas conflict, 3 BAS deployed a squadron of six Scouts and nine Gazelles commanded by Major Peter Cameron. They were heavily involved in the ground campaign and flew 2,110 hours. Two Gazelles were shot down by ground fire on 21 May (XX411 ditching into San Carlos Bay and XX402 crashing into a hillside), three crew being killed and on 28 May Scout AH.1 XT629 was shot down by an Argentine FMA IA.58 Pucara ground-attack aircraft, killing the pilot, Lt Richard Nunn (posthumously awarded the Distinguished Flying Cross) and severely injuring the aircrewman, Sergeant Belcher.

Following the Falklands, 3 BAS received six Westland Lynx AH.1 armed with TOW anti-tank missiles to replace the aging Scouts and the unit moved to RNAS Yeovilton. On 1 September 1995 the unit was reformed as 847 Naval Air Squadron, retaining its REME engineers. Its Lynx and Gazelles were still AAC-owned but the Gazelles were modified for overwater operations. The upgraded Lynx AH.7 was operated during the late 1990s, being replaced by the Lynx AH.9A by 2012 and the Gazelles were retired in 2005.

847 NAS was deployed to Kosovo and Sierra Leone and Operation *Telic* in Iraq in March 2003 where it saw action in the Battle of Basra. Lynx AH.7 XZ614 was shot down over Basra by a shoulder-launched surface-to-air missile on 6 May 2006, killing all five aboard: 847 NAS' Officer Commanding, Lieutenant Commander Darren Chapman; Wing Commander John Coxen; Flight Lieutenant Sarah-Jayne Mulvihill (the first British servicewoman killed in action in 22 years); Marine Paul Collins; and Captain David Dobson.

From September 2008 847 NAS was deployed at Camp Bastion for seven months as part of Operation *Herrick*, followed by five-month stints in January 2011 and January 2013. During late 2013 847 NAS was assigned the new AW159 Wildcat AH.1 – of which the AAC only has 34. 847 NAS operates them in the battlefield recce role as part of Commando Helicopter Force.

Royal Marines used the SA 341 Gazelle for reconnaissance. AH.1 ZA728 seen here in August 1985 was operated by 3 Commando Air Brigade and 847 NAS until 2005. Emergency floatation bags are fitted to the skids. *Terry Panopalis Collection*

Aerial firepower for the Royal Marines took the form of the Lynx AH.1 armed with eight BGM-71 TOW anti-tank missiles. This AH.1 is XZ182 in May 1986. *Terry Panopalis Collection*

Navy Department was keen to keep the proposal 'Management in Confidence' to avoid the politicians getting their hands on it.

The Secretary of State for Defence, Malcom Rifkind, did not cancel the LPH, being convinced of its utility in the post-Cold War environment of global peacekeeping deployments. In May 1993 the MOD announced a £189 million contract for HMS Ocean with Vickers Shipbuilding & Engineering Limited (construction of the hull was sub-contracted to Kvaerner's Govan yard in Scotland.) The troop requirement had been reduced to 500, with an additional 303 in overload conditions (permanent capacity for 800 was provided via a refit later). Construction began in May 1994 and Ocean was commissioned on 30 September 1998. Within a month she was providing humanitarian aid in Nicaragua and Honduras following Hurricane Mitch; the following year Ocean provided assistance following an earthquake in Turkey and during May and June 2000 was deployed to Sierra Leone under Operation PALLISER. A refit in 2002 added the ADAWS 2000 3.1 tactical command system and during 2004-05 the ship was refitted to operate Army Air Corps (AAC) Westland WAH-64 Apache AH.1 gunship helicopters.

Joint Helicopter Command & Merlin

The 1998 Strategic Defence Review created the tri-service Joint Helicopter Command (JHC) to command all battlefield helicopters within the Army's Land Command in October 1999. The JHC included the RAF's Support Helicopter Force, 16 Air Assault Brigade and the Commando Helicopter Force (CHF). The latter at that time comprised 33 Sea King HC.4s plus six Lynx AH.7s and eight Gazelle AH.1s owned by the AAC but operated by the FAA to support the Royal Marines. Following the formation of the JHC, RAF Chinooks and AAC Lynx and Apache helicopters were regularly deployed aboard the Invincibles and Ocean. In 2024 the JHC was renamed Joint Aviation Command (JAC) to reflect the inclusion of unmanned aerial vehicles. The CHF is under the Operational Command of the Fleet Commander (formerly known as the Commander-in-Chief Fleet) and Operational Control remains with the JAC.

The EH101 Merlin was designed with a tactical utility variant in mind (acquired by the RAF to meet Air Staff Target AST.404 as the Merlin HC.2). Following the withdrawal of the Wessex HU.5 the RN wanted to maintain a simultaneous two company lift capability but there was no budget available. The smaller NH90 – then still on the drawing board – was considered but rejected because additional airframes would have been required and the planned LPH would have to be enlarged, costing more money to build.

Following several years of studies to consider a Sea King HC.4 replacement, the Future Amphibious Support Helicopter (FASH) programme was formally launched in

The solution to the need to replace the Sea King HC.4 was the transfer of the RAF's Merlin HC.3/HC.3A fleet. HC.3 ZJ118 of 846 NAS at RNAS Yeovilton retained the original Olive Drab paint. MOD/Open Government Licence

1998, aiming to enter service around 2008. FASH required the ability to carry the Royal Marines' future lightweight (5-ton) mobile artillery weapon system over a radius of 45nm (80km). AgustaWestland proposed a Merlin with upgraded 2,330shp (1,735kW) RTM322-04 turboshafts, BERP IV composite rotor blades and increased rotor RPM to raise the maximum take-off weight to 35,270lb (16,000kg).

Following the JHC's formation the RAF's Future Support Rotorcraft programme was merged with FASH to create the Support, Amphibious and Battlefield Rotorcraft (SABR) which would also replace the RAF's SA 330 Pumas and Sea King HAR.3/3As with an in-service date of 2009. Possible solutions included buying additional Chinooks (possibly navalised with folding rotors) or Merlins to upgraded HC.3+ standard or an off-the-shelf purchase of the NH90, Sikorsky S-92, CH-53E Super Stallion, Eurocopter AS 532 Cougar or the Bell-Boeing MV-22B Osprey. It was expected that two types would be procured due to the amphibious requirements with the Chinook fulfilling 'SABR-Heavy' with the Merlin for 'SABR-Light', but SABR was later cancelled and the Sea King and Puma soldiered on.

Finally, in December 2009 the MOD announced that the RAF's fleet of 19 Merlin HC.3 and six HC.3A helicopters would transfer to the FAA to replace the Sea King HC.4s. 846 NAS reformed on 30 September 2014 at RNAS Yeovilton, followed by 845 NAS on 9 July 2015.

Seven were modified to an interim iHC3 configuration with folding rotor blades, a fast roping point, modified undercarriage for deck operations and deck mooring points. The first iHC3 conversion ZJ126 flew during April 2015 and all were converted by April 2016. The fully navalised HC.4/HC.4A conversion was applied to all the HC.3/3A fleet under the Merlin Life Sustainment Programme at a cost of £399 million. Conversion included fitting the glass cockpit and avionics of the HM.2, a folding tail,

The Commando Merlins operate in various climatic conditions around the world. A Commando Mobile Air Operations Team is receiving an underslung load from an 845 NAS Merlin HC.3 during Exercise Clockwork in Norway. *MOD/Open Government Licence*

folding rotor blades, a strengthened landing gear, deck mooring points, fast-roping points and a common emergency egress system. The Merlins also lost their green camouflage, adopting the same low-visibility Medium Sea Grey as the Merlin HM.2.

The first HC.4 conversion flew on 28 October 2016 and flight trials began in September 2017, with the first delivery on 25 May 2018 and the last was delivered before the end of 2022. 'A' Flight of 845 NAS carried out the carrier qualification trials aboard HMS *Queen Elizabeth* with three HC.4s from September 2018. Operational includes Combat Search and Rescue and the FAA is keen to make use of the HC.3's built-in – but unused – in-flight refuelling probe capability in the future (this feature was flight tested and cleared for use in the Italian HH-101A for the CSAR role). The HC.4/4A fleet also provides a Carrier On-board Delivery transport capability for the *Queen Elizabeth*-class carriers alongside the RAF's Chinooks.

The 2010 Strategic Defence and Security Review led to the withdrawal of the last of the *Invincible*-class carriers, leaving *Ocean* as the RN's only 'carrier' and she took on the role of Fleet Flagship until 2011 and then again during 2015-18. Following the commissioning of *Queen Elizabeth*, *Ocean* was decommissioned on 27 March 2018 and sold to Brazil, becoming the *Atlântico*. Current plans are for the two *Queen Elizabeth*-class carriers to carry a 'Littoral Manoeuvre' package of Merlins and Wildcats for future amphibious missions and both have accommodation for 250 troops. *Queen Elizabeth* began initial amphibious assault trials during February 2018, with Royal Marines from 42 Commando embarked along with Merlin HC.3 and Chinook helicopters. During Exercise Nordic Response in May 2024, the UK Carrier Strike Group (comprising HMS *Prince of Wales*) was combined with a NATO Amphibious Task Group, reprising the Cold War reinforcement role on NATO's northern flank. In January 2025 the HC.4 and HC.4A were fully cleared to operate from the aircraft carriers, amphibious assault ships, Type 23 frigates, Type 45 destroyers and Royal Fleet Auxiliary vessels.

The Merlin HC.4/4A was originally scheduled for replacement in 2030, but on 11 June 2021 the MOD confirmed that the retirement date has been moved back to 2040. The replacement is likely to be from either NATO's Next-Generation Rotorcraft Capability programme for a new medium-lift helicopter or the Bell V-280 MV-75 Valor tiltrotor currently being developed for the US Army's Future Long-Range Assault Aircraft requirement.

The Joint Helicopter Command continues to operate aboard the RN's carriers. This No. 27 Squadron, RAF Boeing Chinook HC.6A is seen refuelling on the deck of HMS *Prince of Wales*. *MOD/Open Government Licence*

Two Leonardo AW159 Wildcat AH.1s of 847 NAS supporting Royal Marine operations aboard HMS *Prince of Wales* in 2022. *MOD/Open Government Licence*

14 Carrier Strike Group

> *"The CVF is to be a joint defence asset with the primary purpose of providing the UK with an expeditionary offensive air capability that has the flexibility to operate the largest possible range of aircraft in the widest possible range of roles."*
>
> CVF MISSION STATEMENT

This chapter takes in nearly 40 years of history, the development of new aircraft and ships taking a longer time compared with earlier generations given their technical complexity. By 1970 the Royal Navy was looking at potential replacements for the Sea Harrier for the 1990s and the early years of the 21st century. The Advanced Short Take-Off and Vertical Landing (ASTOVL) aircraft was intensely studied by aircraft designers in the United Kingdom and the United States of America during the 1980s. This effort eventually contributed to the Lockheed Martin F-35 Lightning II Joint Strike Fighter programme, which was acquired by the UK to equip the Royal Air Force for ground and sea use. The Lightnings are operated by a joint RAF/Fleet Air Arm force, the RN is back in the fixed-wing aviation world but only in partnership. The need to replace the invincible-class anti-submarine carriers in the early 2000s led to the CVF programme for two larger carriers with greater capabilities for sustaining intensive air operations in fleet defence and strike roles. The *Queen Elizabeth*-class have not been without some criticism given the demand they place on limited resources and manpower and the hollowing out of the escort fleet and amphibious warfare assets to keep them in service. But the formation of the Carrier Strike Group with regular biannual cruises to the Far East recall the days of HMS *Eagle* and *Ark Royal* a quarter of a century earlier. The

Two F-35B Lightnings of No 617 'Dambusters' Squadron embarked aboard HMS *Queen Elizabeth* during the squadron's first Carrier Sea Training deployment in June 2020. *MOD/Open Government Licence*

future points towards increasing utilisation of unmanned aerial vehicles to support the Lightnings and the Merlin and Wildcat helicopters in reconnaissance, anti-submarine warfare and airborne early warning within the next decade.

Replacing the Sea Harrier

The development of a new generation of supersonic V/STOL multirole fighters was largely tailored to the needs of the RAF but the need to replace the Sea Harrier at the end of century saw the RN's requirements being looked at. It is noteworthy that Naval Staff Requirement NSR.7097 of February 1970, which led to the *Invincible*-class, referred to a Harrier Successor that "is to be based on P.1179." The P.1179 was a set of private venture Hawker Siddeley design studies based on the technical requirements for the MRCA Multi-Role Combat Aircraft, which resulted in the Panavia Tornado. The P.1179 had a strong P.1154 lineage with single and two-seat versions and wide array of engine choices from the Turbo-Union/Rolls-Royce RB.199 to the Pegasus 9D-03 with Plenum Chamber Burning (PCB) and incorporating design lessons from the P.1154.

The Harrier was subject to joint development in collaboration with McDonnell Douglas (McDD). The HS.1184 study of 1970 led to the AV-16 Advanced Harrier in 1973 with the 24,500lbf (108.9kN) thrust Pegasus 15 (developed with input from Pratt & Whitney – P&W) in a wider fuselage with enlarged intakes, a raised cockpit and a larger wing with six hardpoints – Kingston and St. Louis designing alternative aerofoils. The US Marine Corps (USMC) planned to order 342 aircraft and a naval version with a nose radar was planned for the US Navy (USN) and the FAA – the HS.1184-3 with AN/APS-113 or a modified Ferranti Seaspray radar with capability to carry two Martel ASMs and two AIM-9 Sidewinder or six Hawker Siddeley Dynamics Taildog ASRAAM. A supersonic AV-16S was also studied. Two prototype YAV-16A aircraft were scheduled to fly in early 1977 but increasing costs forced the UK to withdraw in March 1975.

Air Staff Target AST.396 for a successor to the SEPECAT Jaguar and the Harrier had been drafted as early as 1969, being endorsed by the Operational Requirements Committee in May 1971 to enable Hawker Siddeley and the British Aircraft Corporation (BAC) to begin parametric design studies, alongside

Harrier replacements

	HS.1184/AV-16A 'Super Harrier'	BAC P.70 (EAG.8472)	BAC P.71 (EAG.8447)	BAC P.71 (EAG.8461)	BAC Jaguar M (EAG.8763)	HS.1205-5 (Naval)
Span	30ft 4in (9.24m)	29ft 6in (8.99m)	25ft 2.5in (7.68m)	22ft 11in (6.98m)	30ft 0in (9.14m); 15ft 0in (4.57m) folded	36ft 10in (11.22m)
Length	46ft 6in (14.17m)	51ft 6in (15.70m)	46ft 8.5in (14.24m)	43ft 7in (13.29m)	50ft 0in (15.25m)	54ft 0in (16.46m)
Wing area	383ft² (35.58m²)	?	?	?	430ft² (39.99m²)	380ft² (35.34m²)
t/c ratio	11.5% root, 7.5% tip	7%	7%	7%	?	?
All-up weight	28,000lb (12,700kg); 21,100lb (9,570kg) max VTO weight	34,000lb (15,422kg)	?	26,000lb (11,795kg)	?	36,525lb (16,565kg)
Powerplant	1x Pegasus 15 Mk.201/F402-RF-403, 24,500lbf (108.9kN)	1x RB.422, 25,580-26,860lbf (113.7-119.4kN) dry, 38,100-40,000lbf (169.4-177.9kN) 75% scaled PCB	1x P&W F100; 1x XJ.99 or RB.227 lift engine	1x RB.199-42R, 9,700lbf (43.1kN) dry,17,000lbf (75.6kN) reheat; 1x RB.228-02 lift engine	1x P&W F100	1x Pegasus 11D-43, 22,050lbf (98.1kN) dry, 30,850lbf (137.2kN) PCB
Max speed	625kt (1,158km/h) combat speed	Mach 1.0+	Mach 1.0+	Mach 1.0+	Mach 1.0+	Mach 1.15 at SL; March 1.71 at 36,000ft (10,975m)
Armament	1x 30mm ADEN, 7x hardpoints for missiles, bombs and other stores	2x 30mm ADEN, 6x bombs or other stores	2x 30mm ADEN, 2x AIM-9L Sidewinder, 6x bombs or other stores	2x 30mm ADEN, 2x Martel or Harpoon, 6x bombs or other stores	2x 30mm ADEN, 2x Martel or Harpoon, 6x bombs or other stores	2x 27mm Mauser BK-27, 6x AIM-9L Sidewinder, 2x Martel or Harpoon, 8,000lb (3,630kg) bomb load

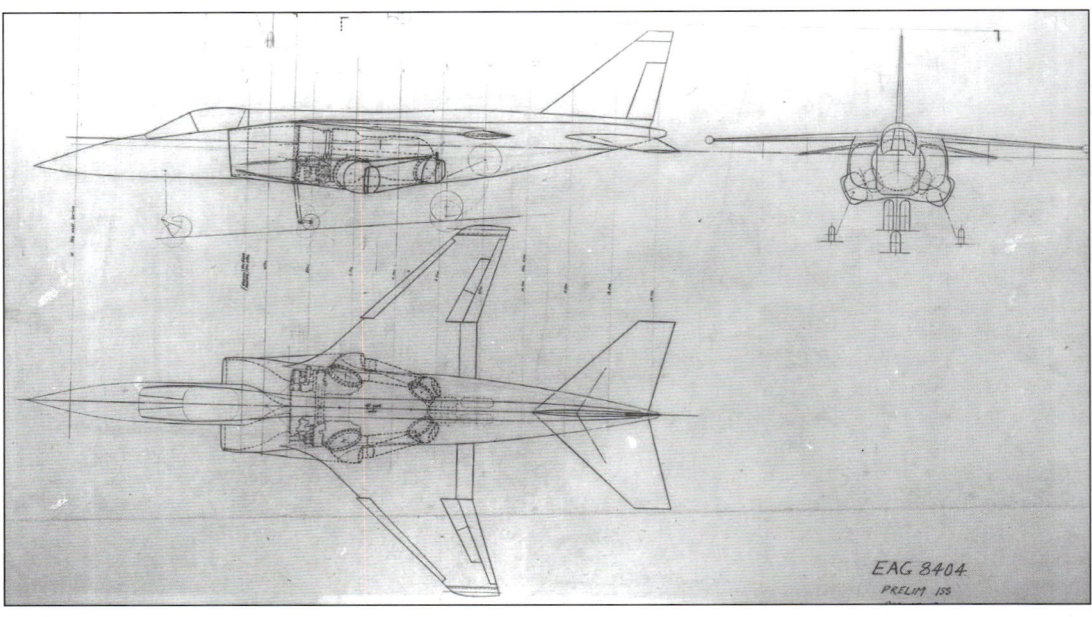

BAC Warton technical drawing EAG.8404 was the preliminary version of the P.70 with a layout similar to the Hawker Siddeley Harrier. *North West Heritage Group via Chris Gibson*

What-if? A SEPECAT Sea Jaguar FRS.3 of No. 800 Naval Air Squadron goes supersonic as it positions to make an attack on enemy ships using AJ.68 TV-guided Martel missiles. In reality, EAG.8469 was a naval study of a developed Super-STOL Jaguar with radar, two Rolls-Royce XJ.99 lift engines and two Turbo-Union/ Rolls-Royce RB.199-42R turbojets fitted with thrust-diverting cascades. *Luca Landino*

engine and avionics research contracts to Rolls-Royce and Elliott Automation. AST.396 called for a sustained speed of Mach 0.9 at low altitude with a Mach 1.1 supersonic dash, a lo-lo radius of action of 165nm (305km) or 240nm (444km) hi-lo, and high manoeuvrability, with a turning capability of 7.5g at Mach 0.8 and specific excess power (SEP) of 900–1,000ft/sec (274–305m/sec) to dogfight against modern Warsaw Pact fighters. STOL was the main aim with a vertical landing being 'desirable.'

It must be remembered that at this time the order for the *Invincible*-class and the official beginning of the Sea Harrier's development were still a year and two years away, respectively and HMS *Ark Royal* was earmarked for retirement only six years later. This made Treasury funding highly unlikely, but it shows that the RN still had options available if the political winds changed back in favour of fixed-wing aircraft and fleet carriers.

Several of BAC's P.70 and P.71 design studies based on developments of the Jaguar airframe were considered as potential naval aircraft. The first detailed P.70 design by the Warton design team, the EAG.8404 of May 1971, used the standard Jaguar S forward fuselage and empennage mated to a new centre and aft fuselage (EAG numbers are technical drawings and can refer either to a specific drawing or a block of drawings). The use of a conventional rear fuselage and the thrust-vectoring Pegasus engine required a layout like that of the Harrier. EAG.8472 was the naval version capable of carrying two Hawker Siddeley Dynamics/Matra AJ.168/AS.37 Martel air-to-surface missiles (ASMs) under the wings. The AUW was around 34,000lb (15,422kg). A 27in (69cm) diameter radar was fitted in a longer nosecone and the engine would be the Rolls-Royce RB.422 with scaled 75% PCB. The RB.422 was a development of the Pegasus with modern technology and was rated between 25,580–26,860lbf (113.7–119.4kN) dry thrust and 38,100–40,000lbf (169.4–177.9kN) reheated.

A variant of the EAG.8447 was offered with a search radar in the nose, which was 13in (34cm) longer. It was powered by a single P&W F100 turbofan with reheat and twin cascades in the lower rear fuselage to divert the thrust downwards for landing. It also had one Rolls-Royce XJ.99 or RB.227 lift engine behind the cockpit.

EAG.8469 was a navalised version of the EAG.8413 capable of carrying two AS.37 Martel ASMs with the required TV-guidance datalink pods on the outboard pylons. It was equipped with radar and had two XJ.99 lift engines along with two RB.199-42R turbojets with cascades.

The EAG.8461 was naval version of the EAG.8471 with a 24in (61cm) diameter radar in the nose. The small 22ft 11in (6.98m) span wing did not require folding and could carry two anti-ship missiles like the AGM-84A Harpoon and a pair of AIM-9 Sidewinder AAMs. It had one RB.228-02 lift engine

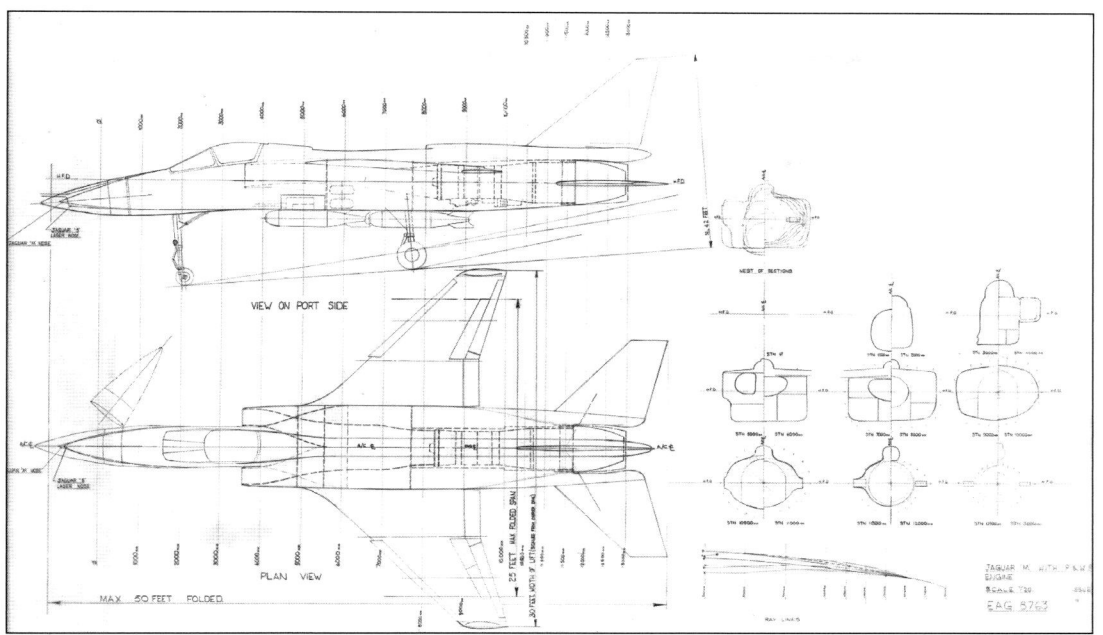

The EAG.8471 was another Jaguar development. It had a 24in (61cm) diameter radar and could carry two anti-ship missiles and a pair of AIM-9 Sidewinder AAMs. It had one RB.228-02 lift engine and a single RB.199-42R fitted with two cascades. *North West Heritage Group via Chris Gibson*

with a central blade deflector and a single RB.199-42R rated at 9,700lbf (43.1kN) dry and 17,000lbf (75.6kN) reheated and equipped with two cascades.

The report on the AST.396 pre-feasibility studies was released in September 1973 and considered that the Pegasus-powered EAG.8404C, the EAG.8413B with RB.228-02 lift engines and RB.231-02 turbofans and the EAG.8472 were all suitable.

One mystery design is the EAG.8763 of 1974 – a version of the carrier-borne Jaguar Marine with a single P&W F100 with a new rear fuselage and empennage. The drawing showed options for either the standard radar-less Jaguar M nose, or the Jaguar S 'chisel' nose for the Ferranti Laser Ranger and Marked-Target Seeker. Reference to a 33ft (10.05m) wide carrier deck lift suggests that carriage aboard *Ark Royal* was contemplated given that its lifts were 34ft (10.3m) wide. It could only have operated from a catapult and arrester gear-equipped carrier – the French Aéronavale had already cancelled its Jaguar M programme and it was too large for the *Colossus* and *Majestic*-class light fleet carriers that had been exported around the world.

AST.396 was superseded by AST.403 in July 1975, again for a Jaguar and Harrier successor but now with air superiority as the primary role. Most of

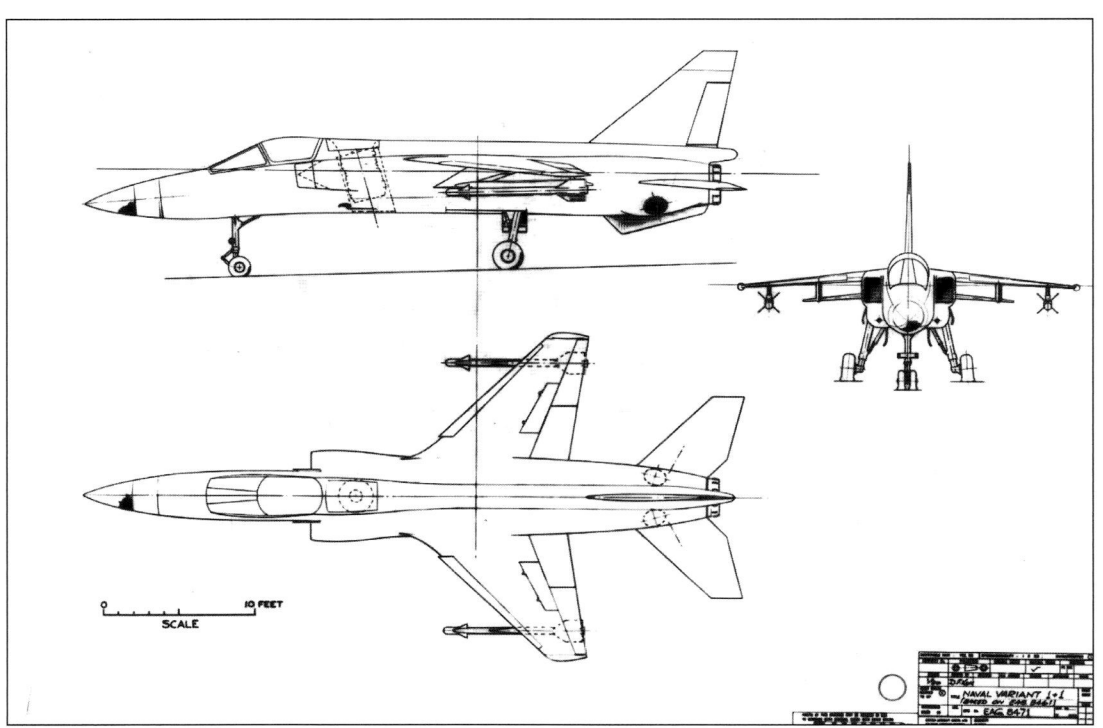

This intriguing Warton study is the French carrier-borne SEPECAT Jaguar M revised with a reheated Pratt & Whitney F100 turbofan. Presumably the EAG.8763 was offered to the Royal Navy in the early 1970s. *North West Heritage Group via Chris Gibson*

WINGS OVER THE FLEET

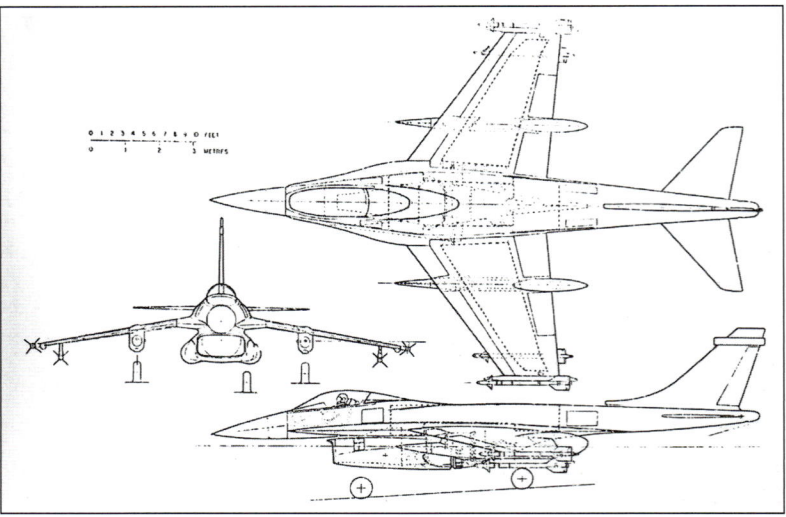

The Royal Aircraft Establishment assessed the Hawker Siddeley HS.1205-5 in the maritime intercept role in 1978. It offered a credible Sea Harrier replacement but refining the 1205's shortcomings would lead to the P.1216 series and to Naval Staff Target NST.6464. *BAE Systems via Author's Collection*

the designs studied by BAC and Hawker Siddeley were conventional aircraft, but the Kingston Project Office followed the vectored-thrust V/STOL solution with its HS.1205 series.

In September 1978 the Royal Aircraft Establishment (RAE) assessed the HS.1205-5 (which had been designed in December 1976) in the maritime intercept role. The aircraft was powered by a 30,000lbf (133.4kN) Pegasus 11D-43 with PCB, increased to 32,250lbf (143.4kN) with water injection. Removing the PCB would reduce the dry and water injected thrust to 22,050lbf (98kN) and 23,400lbf (104kN) respectively. The Pegasus was fed via a large ventral chin intake. The aircraft could be launched from 6° ski-jump at an AUW exceeding 40,000lb (18,145kg), providing a weapons and fuel load of at least 17,000lb (7,710kg). The engine lacked sufficient thrust to enable the HS.1205-5 to intercept a Mach 1.5 target at high altitude – only a Mach 1.3 target could be intercepted due to a lack of fuel or insufficient remaining intercept distance for further acceleration. PCB was required for landing, with the consequent high exhaust temperate problems of hot air reingestion and damage to deck.

The 54ft (16.5m) long fuselage and the 37ft (11.2m) span swept wing would require a folding radome and wing folding outboard of the undercarriage/cannon nacelle to achieve an 18ft (5.5m) folded span. This would allow nine HS.1205 and eight anti-submarine warfare (ASW) helicopters to be accommodated aboard an *Invincible*. The undercarriage would require modification with twin-wheels due to the deck strength limitations. The fuel load would provide a CAP endurance of 1.5-2.5hr.

The 380ft² (35.3m²) area wings carried six underwing hardpoints and two wing tip rails for AAMs. The inner hardpoints mounted on the undercarriage nacelle could carry two AAMs each; the intermediate hardpoints were stressed for a 3,000lb (1,360kg) load and the outboard hardpoints could each carry 1,000lb (454kg). Six AAMs could be carried in the intercept role and retaining the 27mm Mauser BK-27 cannon was considered

worthwhile – it might not cause catastrophic damage to a Tu-22M *Backfire* but had sufficient ammunition for 10 firing passes with 15-round bursts. The AIM-9L Sidewinder was assessed as having a 70% probability of hitting a *Backfire*. The Hawker Siddeley Dynamics Skyflash medium-range semi-active radar homing AAM was a version of the US AIM-7 Sparrow with a Marconi inverse monopulse seeker and a Thorn EMI radar fuze. The Skyflash would have a longer time interval between launches and greater launch ranges. A head-on attack at 23.8nm (44km) maximum range would see the first missile impacting the target 40sec later, the second target then being 6.5nm (12km) away, firing at 4nm (7.4km) and impacting 6.5sec later. An enemy formation would need to contain at least 11 targets to allow time for a third head-on firing. Overall, it was assessed that there was little advantage in using Skyflash over Sidewinders.

In term of avionics, a pulse-Doppler radar with a search range of at least 70nm (130km) would be required, a radar warning receiver (RWR) for passive detection and electronic countermeasures (ECM) to jam the *Backfire's* acquisition radar, delaying an ASM launch. The twin inertial platforms would be replaced by NAVHARS (Navigation Heading and Reference System), to which the autopilot would be linked to fly a CAP pattern automatically. Other requirements were secure speech communications and a secure datalink. In total the estimated naval avionics weight penalty was 270lb (122kg).

As a result of this study Kingston studied repositioning the wing to minimise interference with the jet nozzles to reduce the wave drag by 10%. The leading edge sweep was increased to 40° and area reduced to 330ft² (30.6m²) while keeping the span loading constant. The aspect ratio was increased from 3.5 to 3.28 and the weight was reduced by 300lb (136kg). Improved internal packaging aimed to reduce the fuselage length by 4ft (1.2m). The navalisation weight penalty was just under 1,000lb (454kg), a 3% increase over the baseline 36,525lb (16,565kg) AUW.

The RAE Aerodynamics Department also performed a design synthesis study on adding a second crew member to ease the pilot's high workload given the sophisticated avionics carried. It retained the original wing but was 5ft 9in (1.75m) longer and would be 2,665lb (1,210kg) heavier, reducing the CAP endurance by 3min 30sec and lowering the intercept speed to Mach 0.9–0.95.

ASTOVL: Study A

The Harrier replacement was divested from AST.403 in early 1979 into a standalone ASR.409 for the McDD/BAe Harrier II, which had emerged from McDD's ongoing wing studies following the cancellation of the AV-16 and entered service as the Harrier GR.5 in 1989. The definitive HS.1205-11 design was dropped in favour of BAe Warton's P.96F to fulfil AST.403. The 1981 Defence White Paper effectively cancelled project, however, and AST.403 was superseded by AST.414 for an Agile Combat Aircraft in May 1984. The Advanced Short Take-Off Vertical Landing (ASTOVL) Harrier replacement came under AST.410 in 1981.

Experience with the Harrier had shown that the exhaust nozzles caused thermo-vibration structural fatigue in the rear fuselage, with the vibrations affecting the reliability of any avionics housed in this area. The ultimate solution was to dispense with the rear fuselage entirely, allowing the rear nozzles to be replaced by a single rotating nozzle aft and the tail fins were moved to booms attached to the wings as an extension of the undercarriage nacelle. This led to the P.1212 and P.1216. A P.1216 flying demonstrator was suggested with a possible first flight date in 1986 and the Prime Minister Margaret Thatcher inspected the mock-up in December 1982 during a visit to Kingston. But the £3.15 billion price tag conflicted with the needs of AST.414 and the Tactical Combat Aircraft (soon to be the Agile Combat Aircraft, then the European Fighter Aircraft, finally entering service as the Eurofighter Typhoon in 2003) and work stopped in 1983.

The RAE's HS.1205 study had led to close contact between Farnborough and the Kingston design office. Chris Handsford, the head of Kingston's Future Projects Office, drafted out a set of naval requirements around the P.1212 design, which he sent to the Directorate of Naval Air Warfare. With further Staff work this formed the basis of Naval Staff Target NST.6464. After attempts to collaborate on AST.410 ended, the Assistant Chief of the Navy Staff (Operational Requirements), Rear Admiral John Kerr, redrafted NST.6464 for 60 ASTOVL aircraft to replace the Sea Harrier FRS.2 (which entered service as the F/A.2) from 1997–2000. In September 1984 the Operational Requirements Committee backed NST.6464 and approved the beginning of pre-feasibility studies. This effort was supported by the ASTOVL Steering Group which looked at several technological issues, such as hot air reingestion, thermo-vibration structural fatigue and flight control systems.

NST.6464 was more demanding than AST.410, including a Combat Air Patrol (CAP) endurance of 2.5 hours with a Mach 1.5 intercept speed, a 2.8*g* sustained turn at altitude and a SEP of 984ft/sec (300m/sec) at sea level and 328ft/sec (100m/sec) at altitude. The service ceiling would be 50,000ft (15,240m). Thrust vectoring in forward flight (VIFF) for increased agility and rapid deceleration in dogfights was still largely an unknown factor (Harrier pilots on both sides of the Atlantic had tried it, but deceleration in combat is a disadvantage in most cases because losing kinetic energy loses you the fight and so – contrary to popular myth – VIFF was not used in the Falklands nor advocated by Shar pilots except in dire straits.)

The armament in the interception role was to be six Hughes AIM-120A AMRAAM Advanced Medium Range Air-to-Air Missiles and a pair of ASRAAM

Advanced Short-Range Air-to-Air Missiles (the AIM-132 ASRAAM entered service in 1998); a single 25mm ADEN cannon would also be fitted. Four Sea Eagle ASMs would be carried in the secondary anti-ship role. Other roles included reconnaissance and land attack with weapons including the BAe ALARM anti-radar missile for air defence suppression, WE.177A tactical nuclear bomb, 'dumb' and 'smart' guided bombs as well as the planned US-UK LRSOM Long-Range Stand-Off Missile. The radar was presumed to be an improved Blue Vixen (then in development for the Sea Harrier F/A.2). The ferry range was to be at least 2,000nm (3,705km) without aerial refuelling. There was also a requirement for provision of "STEALTH", a sign that low observability was becoming important (note that this was five years before the public unveiling of the Lockheed F-117A Nighthawk).

The primary role remained the interception of Tu-22M *Backfire* bombers and their ASMs, but the Soviet Navy was now building aircraft carriers. These Heavy Aviation Cruisers carried subsonic Yakovlev Yak-38 *Forger* V/STOL fighters along with powerful batteries of anti-ship cruise missiles and surface-to-air missiles (SAMs). On 1 April 1982 the first of two 53,000-ton Project 1143.5 carriers was laid down, the *Tbilisi* being capable of operating up to 24 navalised Sukhoi Su-27 *Flanker* or Mikoyan-Gurevich MiG-29 *Fulcrum* multirole fighters and the succeeding Project 1143.7 nuclear-powered 'supercarriers' were designed to operate around 70 aircraft (*Tbilisi* was launched as the *Leonid Brezhnev* and commissioned as the *Admiral Flota Sovetskogo Soyuza Kuznetsov* in January 1991; the Project 1143.7 *Ulyanovsk* was laid down in November 1988 but was never completed; the navalised Su-33K *Flanker-D* entered service in 1995, the MiG-29K *Fulcrum-D* not until 2010). This meant that fighter versus fighter combat was now a possibility, driving the need to provide high levels of agility using fly-by-wire (FBW) flight controls and the airframe had to be stressed for 9g manoeuvres.

Analysis showed that long-range Airborne Early Warning (AEW) was required to make an ASTOVL force fully effective against *Flanker* escorted *Backfires*. The ASTOVL would form the outer layer

A Sukhoi Su-33K *Flanker-D* takes off from *Admiral Kuznetsov*'s bow ramp in the Barents Sea in 2012. In development since 1978 as the Su-27K, it caused the RN understandable worry that its Sea Harriers would be outclassed by the new Soviet carrier fleet. *Mil.ru/Wikimedia*

WINGS OVER THE FLEET

NST.6464 ASTOVL Study A proposals

	Improved Sea Harrier FRS.2	Sea Harrier 3A	Sea Harrier 3B	P.1127-2 GR.5(RN)	P.1127-3 GR.5(RN)	P.1230-1B
Design office	Kingston	Kingston	Kingston	Kingston	Kingston	Kingston
Span	26ft 2¾in (7.99m)	30ft 2in (9.2m)	37ft (11.27m); 39ft 6in (11.9m) with missiles; 23ft 3in (7.08m) folded	30ft 2in (9.2m)	37ft (11.27m); 39ft (11.9m) with missiles; 23ft 3in (7.08m) folded	41ft 6in (12.65m) with AAMs; 25ft 0in (7.62m) folded
Length	47ft 1¾in (14.37m); 43ft 1in (13.16m) folded	47ft 4in (14.43m); 43ft 6in (13.26m) folded	47ft 4in (14.43m); 43ft 6in (13.26m) folded	48ft 2in (14.7m); 45ft 1in (13.76m) folded	48ft 2in (14.7m); 45ft 1in (13.76m) folded	51ft 11in (15.83m)
Wing area	?	220.6ft² (20.5m²)	280.0ft² (26.01m²)	220.6ft² (20.5m²)	280.0ft² (26.01m²)	522.0ft² (48.54m²)
All-up weight	?	?	?	15,983lb (7,250kg) basic weight	?	38,966lb (17,675kg) maximum take-off
Powerplant	1x 24,616lbf (109.5kN) Pegasus 19-01	1x 24,616lbf (109.5kN) Pegasus 19-01	1x 24,616lbf (109.5kN) Pegasus 19-01	1x 24,616lbf (109.5kN) Pegasus 19-01	1x 27,790lbf (123.6kN) RB.532-01; later 1x 24,616lbf (109.5kN) Pegasus 19-01	1x PSE-2, 29,225lbf (130kN) dry, 40,465lbf (188kN) PCB
Max speed	Subsonic	Mach 0.93 at 36,000ft (10,970m) full external load	Mach 0.93 at 36,000ft (10,970m) full external load	Mach 0.94 at 36,000ft (10,970m)	Mach 0.91 at 36,000ft (10,970m) full external load	Mach 1.8 diving limit
Service ceiling	?	40,500ft (12,345m)	45,000ft (13,715m)	40,500ft (12,345m)	44,000ft (13,410m)	?
Radius of action/CAP endurance	?	3hr 6min CAP	?	?	2hr 48min CAP	?
Armament	1 x 25mm ADEN, 4x AIM-120A AMRAAM or AIM-9L Sidewinder, 2x Sea Eagle	1x 25mm ADEN, 6x AIM-120A AMRAAM & 2x ASRAAM, 2x Sea Eagle	1x 25mm ADEN, 6x AIM-120A AMRAAM & 2x ASRAAM, 2x Sea Eagle	1x 25mm ADEN, 6x AIM-120A AMRAAM & 2x ASRAAM, 2x Sea Eagle	1x 25mm ADEN, 6x AIM-120A AMRAAM & 2x ASRAAM, 2x Sea Eagle	1x 25mm ADEN, 6x AIM-120A AMRAAM or 4x AIM-9L Sidewinder, 2x Sea Eagle or ALARM, 1x WE.177A, 10x bombs

of a defensive shield around the fleet, allied with the future Support Defence Missile System armed Common New Generation Frigate (CNGF) (the missile emerged as the French Aster SAM but the UK, France and Italy eventually went their own ways on CNGF, resulting in the Type 45 *Daring*-class for the RN and the *Horizon*-class for other two nations), improved Sea Wolf SAMs for point defence (the planned GWS.27 Active Sea Wolf) and gun-based Close-In Weapon Systems under NSR.6650A and 6650B (for Phalanx and Goalkeeper respectively).

In November 1984 the Operational Requirements Committee allocated £500,000 for pre-feasibility studies. An ASTOVL Seminar at Farnborough in September 1983 had resulted in the collaboration with the USA, the Advanced STOL Aircraft Technology Programme looking at propulsion concepts. The hope was that a joint programme could be formed with the US Navy, increasing the production numbers above 60 to achieve a sensible price tag. The USN, however, lacked a clear requirement and therefore two studies were

P.1232	P.1216-16	P.1216-41	P.1216-45	P.1226-7	P.109N	Model 279-3
Kingston	Kingston	Kingston	Kingston	Kingston	Warton	McDonnell Douglas
25ft 3in (7.70m); 29ft 8in (9.04m) ferry tips	34ft 7in (10.54m) with AAMs; 20ft 0in (6.09m) folded	34ft 0in (10.36m); 18ft 8in (5.74m) folded	38ft 6in (11.73m); 18ft 8in (5.74m) folded	39ft (11.89m); 20ft 6in (6.3m) folded	30ft 0in (9.14m)	35ft 8in (10.90m)
47ft 2in (14.37m); 43ft 6.25in (13.25m) folded	55ft 10.5in (17.03m); 51ft 6in (15.70m) folded	55ft 10.5in (17.03m) ; 51ft 6in (15.70m) folded	51ft 10in (15.82m); 47ft 2in (14.55m) folded	48ft (14.65m); 43ft 8in (13.33m) folded	49ft 10in (15.2m)	56ft 0in (17.0m)
201.1ft² (18.68m²)	421.10ft² (39.13m²)	421.10ft² (39.13m²)	?	294.07ft² (27.32m²)	301.3ft² (28m²)	428.4ft² (39.80m²); 85.6ft² (7.95m²) canard
?	45,615lb (20,690kg) maximum take-off	46,049lb (20,844kg) fighter; 46,305lb (21,000kg) strike	24,328lb (11,035kg) basic operational weight	19,189lb (8,704kg) basic weight	38,120lb (17,290kg) maximum take-off	41,000+lb (18,600+kg); 29,840lb (13,535kg) VTO
1x 24,616lbf (109.5kN) Pegasus 19-01	1x RB.422-48, 25,500lbf (113.3kN) PCB	1x RB.532-08, 27,960lbf (124.3kN) dry, 40,350lbf (179.4kN) PCB	1x RB.532-08, 27,960lbf (124.3kN) dry, 40,350lbf (179.4kN) PCB	P.1226-7: 25,223lbf (112.2kN) Pegasus 19-01; P.1226-8: 28,236lbf (125.6kN) RB.532-07	1x Pegasus or RB.508-01 or RB.422-X Cycle 62	1x P&W STF561-C2; 34,316lbf (152.6kN) PCB
Subsonic	Mach 1.25 at SL; Mach 1.7 at 36,000ft (10,970m)	Mach 1.13 at SL; Mach 1.71 at 36,000ft (10,970m)	Mach 1.13 at SL; Mach 1.7 at 36,000ft (10,970m)	P.1226-7: Mach 0.93 at altitude P.1226-8: Mach 0.96 at altitude	Mach 1.4 at altitude	Mach 2.0 at altitude
?	?	51,200ft (15,605m)	50,000ft (15,240m)	48,000ft (14,630m)	?	62,000ft (19,050m)
?	?	630nm (1,166km) strike; 170min at 190nm (352km) CAP	120min CAP	P.1226-8: 2hr 42min CAP	?	150nm (176km) CAP; 900nm (1,535km) interdiction
1 x 25mm ADEN, 4x AIM-120A AMRAAM or AIM-9L Sidewinder, 2x Sea Eagle	1x 25mm ADEN, 6x AIM-120A AMRAAM or 4x AIM-9L Sidewinder, 2x Sea Eagle or ALARM, 1x WE.177A, 10x bombs	1x 25mm ADEN, 6x AIM-120A AMRAAM or 4x AIM-9L Sidewinder, 2x Sea Eagle or ALARM, 1x WE.177A, 10x bombs	1x 25mm ADEN, 6x AIM-120A AMRAAM or 4x AIM-9L Sidewinder, 2x Sea Eagle or ALARM, 1x WE.177A, 10x bombs	1x 25mm ADEN, 6x AIM-120A AMRAAM or 4x AIM-9L Sidewinder, 2x Sea Eagle	1x 25mm ADEN, 6x AIM-120A AMRAAM & 2x ASRAAM, 6x bombs	1x 25mm cannon; 4x AIM-120A AMRAAM or AIM-9L Sidewinder, bombs and other stores

undertaken. Study A (which received 70% of the research budget) covered aircraft available by 1997, the performance not fully meeting NST.6464, costed for only 60 aircraft. Study B was the full AST.6464 aircraft to enter service in 2000 with a proposed joint production run of 260. Compatibility with the *Invincible*-class carriers (which had a planned service life until 2005–15) meant that the aircraft had to operate safely within the deck clearance limits and fit onto the 32ft (9.75m) wide and 52ft (15.9m) long lifts, which had a weight limit of 18 tons. Up to seven ASTOVL fighters had to fit in the narrow hangar while retaining space for eight EH101 Merlin HM.1 helicopters.

Study A only covered vectored-thrust aircraft using contemporary technology given the 1997 in-service date and low production run which favoured adaptations of existing designs. BAe assigned Kingston to lead Study A (the Future Projects Office relocated to Weybridge in late 1985). Rolls-Royce had developed the Pegasus 19 using technology from the XG.15 engine core demonstrator to increase the sea level

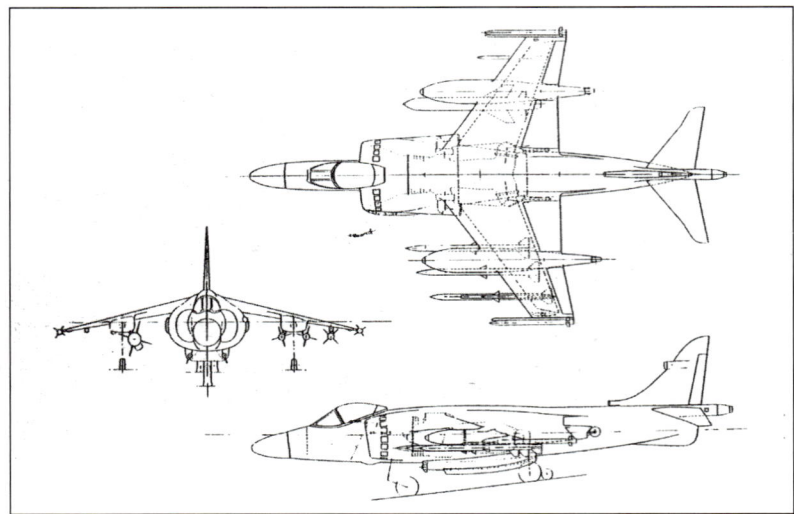

The Sea Harrier 3A was a development of the planned Sea Harrier FRS.2 with the Pegasus 19-01 engine and a new 30ft 2in (9.2m) span wing for additional fuel capacity and wing tip AAM rails. *BAE Systems via Author's Collection*

The Sea Harrier 3B had another new wing option of 39ft (11.9m) span with folding outer sections. The outrigger undercarriage pods were relocated to reduce the undercarriage track to aid deck handling. *BAE Systems via Author's Collection*

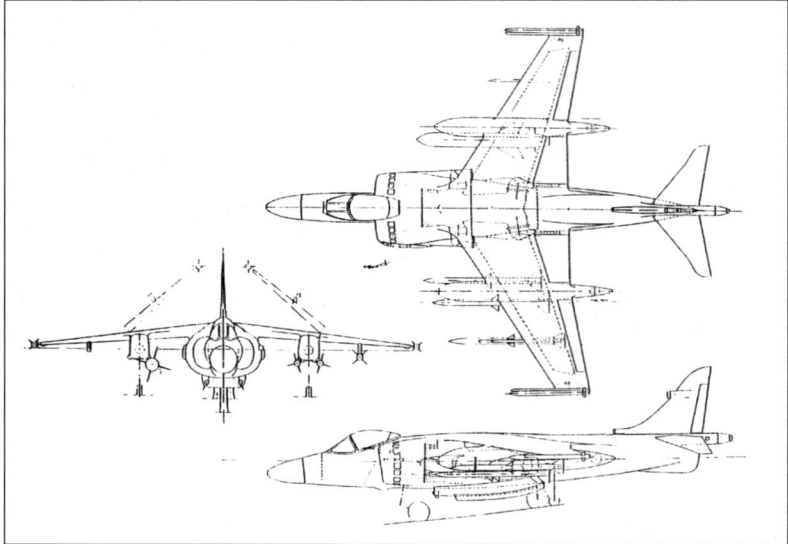

was an FRS.2 with the Pegasus 19-01 engine, 11¾in (0.3m) wing tip extensions and a 13¾in (350mm) rear fuselage plug for additional avionics space. The Sea Harrier 3A featured a new 30ft 2in (9.2m) span wing which provided additional fuel tankage (increasing CAP endurance from 1.6 to 3.1hr) and wing tip AAM rails. There were concerns about pitch instability given the similar planform to the existing Sea Harrier wing which had issues with large underwing stores.

The Sea Harrier 3B's new wing was of 39ft (11.9m) span with folding outer sections. Both wings lacked leading edge root extensions (LERX) and had repositioned outrigger undercarriage pods, reducing the track from 22ft 3in (6.8m) to 17ft (5.2m) to aid deck handling. Both the 3A and 3B had a 7.8in (200mm) fuselage extension to lengthen the intakes to improve the thrust and surge margins. Armament was four AMRAAMs mounted semi-conformally on the fuel/weapon modules attached to the front of the outrigger wheel nacelles, with another pair on underwing hardpoints and wing tip ASRAAMs. A single 25mm ADEN cannon pod would be fitted under the fuselage to starboard, balanced with a dummy pod to port. The fuel/weapon modules could carry two Sea Eagles for the anti-ship role. Both designs could attain Mach 0.93 at 36,000ft (10,970m) with full external load, the combat ceiling being 40,500ft (12,345m) for the 3A and 45,000ft (13,715m) for the 3B. The estimated development and production cost was £1.71 billion for the 3A and £1.8 billion for the 3B, plus £225 million to develop the Pegasus 19.

The P.1227 of January 1985 was a development of the Harrier II GR.5 with FRS.2 avionics – the GR.5(RN). The P.1227-1 had Sea Harrier centre and rear fuselage with an increased height fin and unkinked leading edge tailplane. The wing had LERX and the outrigger pods also held fuel and carried weapons, either a Sea Eagle or AMRAAM. ASRAAMs were carried on wing tip rails. The improved GR.5 wing reduced the early drag rise and high transonic drag by using new thinner carbon fibre composites and BAe aerofoil sections. The centre fuselage and intake ducts were extended by 8in (20cm) to reduce static pressure distortions and increase thrust for the 27,790lbf (123.6kN) RB.532-01 engine. The wingspan was 28ft 3in (8.61m) with a length of 47ft 9in (14.55m).

The P.1227-2 received a new 30ft 2in (9.2m) span wing and the 24,616lbf (109.5kN) Pegasus 19-01 while the P.1227-3 employed the 3A's larger wing, the RB.532-01 was initially used but the final submission returned to the Pegasus 19-01. The larger wing gave a CAP endurance of 2hr 48min. The -3 had a maximum speed of Mach 0.91 at 36,000ft with full external load and a 44,000ft (13,410m) combat ceiling. The -2 offered marginal improvements over the 3A and was abandoned; the estimated development and production costs for the -3 were nearly £2 billion.

The P.1227-4 had an advanced metal wing structure employing lithium alloys and titanium at a small weight

static thrust by 15% and the RB.532 using technology from the Eurofighter's XG.40 demonstrator turbofan to achieve a 30% increase. Rolls-Royce began full scale PCB recirculation tests in 1984 using a modified Pegasus 2 in a Harrier airframe which was mounted on a static rig at Shoeburyness. BAe Dynamics at Hatfield undertook studies into extending the Skyflash's range with boost rocket motors and ramjet sustainers and active-radar homing; this work became the basis of the MBDA Meteor which entered service in 2016 on the Typhoon.

Unsurprisingly Kingston began with further developments of the Sea Harrier. The Baseline Design

and cost penalty. The -6 employed digital FBW active control technology (ACT), but because the aircraft could not be drastically rebalanced it was impossible to achieve relaxed stability to make ACT worthwhile. The -7 was armed with LRAAMs (Long-Range Air-Air Missiles) but required a more powerful radar to fully utilise them. Yet another version was the -8 with a tricycle undercarriage, the main legs retracting rearwards into the wing pods to free fuselage volume for fuel and avionics and allow the carriage of longer weapons ventrally.

The P.1227-9 series were navalised GR.5s; the -9A retaining the Pegasus Mk.105 with FRS.2 avionics; the -9B had the Pegasus 19-01; the -9C was the -9A with an 8in (20cm) intake duct extension; the -9D was the -9B with the duct extension; the -9E was the -9B with a larger 100% scale LERX.

The P.1216 series was the heart of Study A. The P.1216-16 was the initial navalised proposal featuring folding outer wing sections on the 55° swept wing – which had large leading edge root extensions (LERX) to improve low speed manoeuvrability – detachable tailplanes and removable fuel/weapon modules attached to the front end of the tail booms to meet the hangar size constraints. The two-seat conversion trainer version was the P.1216-17 which had a tandem cockpit with stepped seating; this sacrificed some fuel capacity but full combat capability was retained. The P.1216-39 was a strike version of the -11 with a 30in (76cm) diameter radar and two Sea Eagle ASMs.

The P.1216-41 was the main proposal developed from the -16. Most of the airframe was built of carbon fibre composites with titanium used in high temperature areas around the nozzles. The structure was stressed for 8*g* manoeuvres rather than the specified 9*g*. In addition to the LERX the wing had leading edge vortex flaps to reduce drag, plain inboard trailing edge flaps with flaperons outboard. The two tail fins and tailplanes were all-moving surfaces. The engine was the 27,960lbf (124.3kN) RB.532-08 using the XG.40 core with a five-stage high pressure compressor and single-stage turbine driving a three-stage fan using wide-chord blades. PCB was used on the front nozzles using colander burners – boosting the thrust to 40,350lbf (179.4kN). Cushion augmentation devices (CADS) – small retractable flaps – were fitted under the fuselage to prevent hot air recirculation and make effective use of ground effect to cushion the impact of landing. The lower-powered Pegasus 19-01 was also an option. The estimated maximum speed was Mach 1.13 at sea level, rising to Mach 1.71 at 36,000ft, the combat ceiling was 51,200ft (15,605m). The strength limit of the ski-jump restricted the maximum take-off weight to 46,305lb (21,000kg).

Extended fuel/weapon modules were fitted for greater range – 2hr 50min CAP endurance at 190nm (350km) radius with 4min 30sec at Mach 1.22, or a hi-lo strike radius of 630nm (1,165km) carrying four Sea Eagles. Each module could carry a pair of AMRAAM, Sea Eagle or ALARM ASMs or four freefall bombs as well as holding 370gal (1,400L) of fuel. The

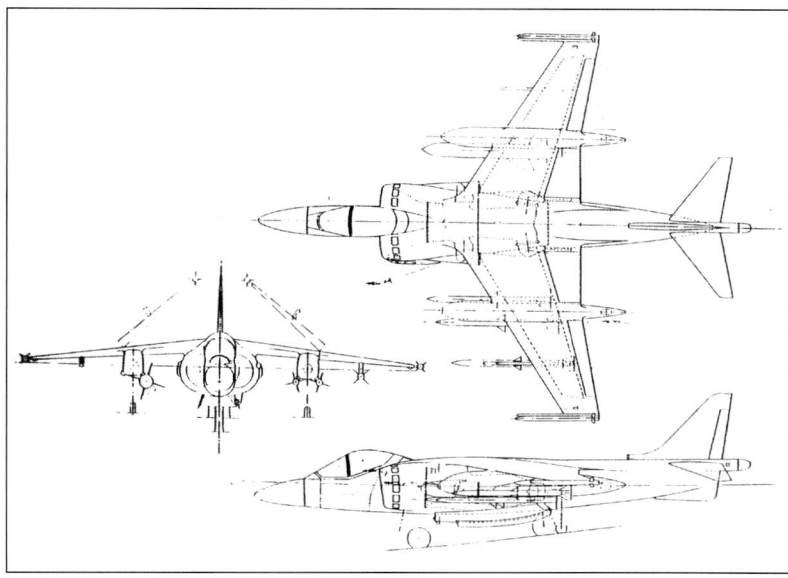

The P.1227-3 was very much like the Sea Harrier 3A design and used the same wing. The Rolls-Royce RB.532-01 was initially proposed but the final submission returned to the cheaper Pegasus 19-01. *BAE Systems via Author's Collection*

This drawing of the basic P.1216 layout reveals the twin tail booms, which also functioned as outrigger wheel nacelles and housed fuel and the weapon hardpoints. The move to a three-nozzle layout for the engine drastically reduced the thermoacoustic fatigue problems and drag, this enabled supersonic performance. *BAE Systems via Author's Collection*

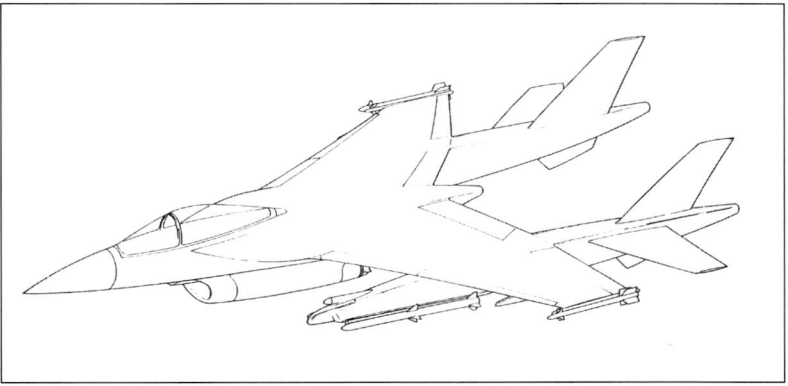

port module could carry a reconnaissance pod, while the starboard module could carry a single WE.177A nuclear bomb. Two underwing hardpoints could each carry another AMRAAM, bomb or a 270gal (1,022L) drop tank and wing tip rails could carry a pair of AMRAAM or four AIM-9L Sidewinders. A 25mm ADEN cannon was fitted in the port LERX with 150 rounds of ammunition.

The avionics were the Ferranti Blue Vixen pulse-Doppler radar, Smiths Head-Up Display/Weapon Aiming Computer (HUDWAC), Ferranti/Decca inertial navigation system, GEC Zeus RWR and Plessey Missile Warning Approach equipment from the Sea Harrier FRS.2. A forward-looking IR (FLIR) pod could be attached under the intake to port for

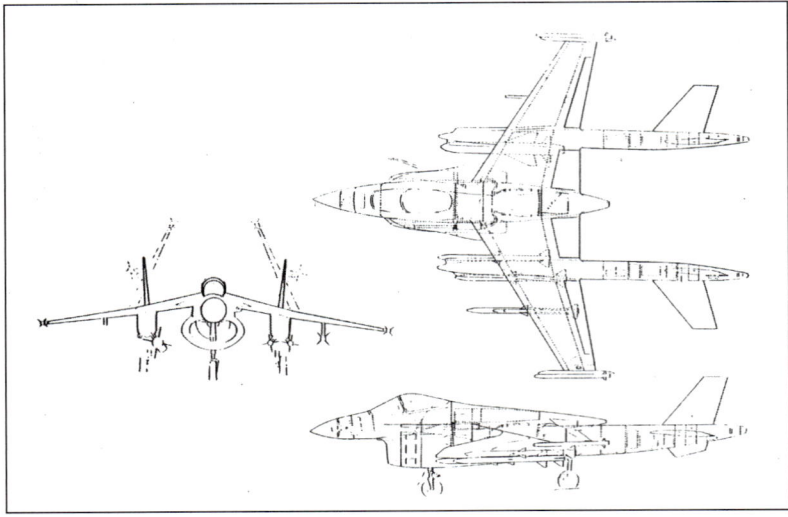

The P.1226 was a mix of the P.1216 layout with a modified version of the new Sea Harrier 3B wing to create a cheaper, subsonic alternative to the P.1216. *BAE Systems via Author's Collection*

Warton's P.109N was a navalised version of the P.109. The development cost was estimated to be the most expensive of all the Study A proposals at £2.95 billion at 1982 prices. *BAE Systems via Author's Collection*

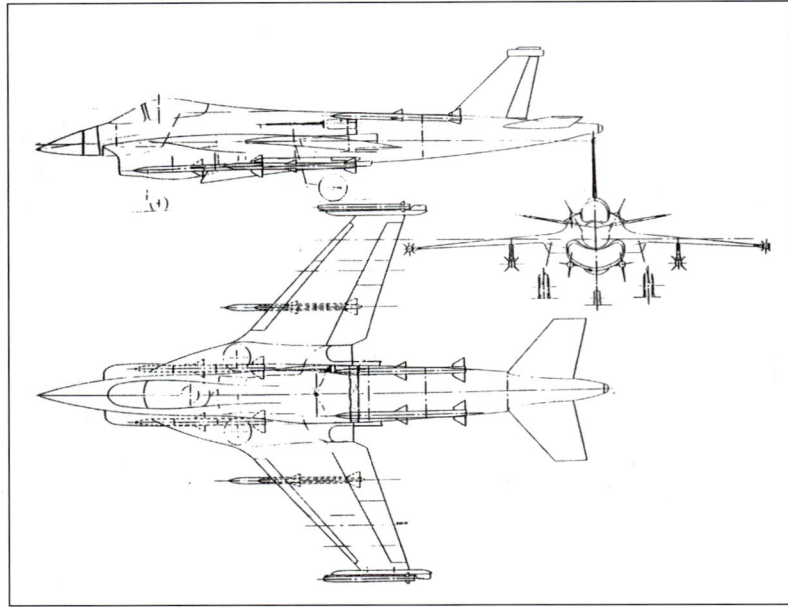

the lift/drag ratio, a shortened front fuselage and a modified empennage. The increased wing fuel capacity enabled the fuel/weapon modules to be deleted to reduce drag and improve the subsonic turning performance. CAP endurance was two hours, maximum speed was Mach 1.7 at 36,000ft with a combat ceiling of 50,000ft (15,240m). The -45 became the main P.1216 version assessed. Divisional Technical Director Ralph Hooper was not happy with the P.1216's high weight, nor the aeroelastic and drag concerns connected with the twin boom layout, especially given that Warton's more compact designs like the P.112 were offering superior performance. Chris Handsford argued that the reduced service costs and lower technical risk of the P.1216's layout gave enough advantage to offset any performance loss.

A subsonic version – the P.1226 – was also studied, with a modified folding wing based on that of the Sea Harrier 3B. The removable fuel/weapon modules would each carry four AMRAAM or one Sea Eagle each. The P.1226-7 would be powered by a Pegasus 19-01 (which was considered underpowered for the design) while the P.1226-8 had the more powerful RB.532-07. CAP endurance for the -8 was 2hr 42min, maximum speed at 36,000ft with full external load was Mach 0.93 and the combat ceiling was 48,000ft (14,630m). The estimated total programme cost was £2.56 billion.

BAe Warton's P.109N thrust-vectoring design of March 1982 was also evaluated. Based on the land-based P.109, it had a lengthened fuselage for additional fuel. The 301.3ft² (28m²) wing was modified with folding outer sections; it had LERX, variable camber leading edge flaps and plain trailing edge flaps, the thickness/chord ratio (t/c) being 7% at the root and 4.7% at the tip. The aircraft was optimised for transonic flight and was stressed for 8*g* manoeuvres, having a conventional rear fuselage and empennage. The RB.533 engine (essentially a re-fanned twin-nozzle RB.532) was fed by a chin intake and the two trapezoidal nozzles were integrated into the wing root trailing edge; this improved lift by inducing additional airflow over the inner wings. A ventral nozzle (using bypass bleed air) provided pitch control in the hover and a reaction control system (RCS) was provided for pitch, roll and yaw control. An FBW flight control system would be fitted. The estimated maximum speed was Mach 1.6, CAP endurance was 2hr 42min and the combat ceiling was 51,000ft (15,545m). Six AMRAAMs were carried – four ventrally in tandem pairs with a pair under the wings; ASRAAMs were fitted on wing tip rails. A 27mm Mauser BK-27 was installed in the starboard LERX. The estimated cost of £2.95 billion for development and production was the highest of all the Study A options.

strike missions. Communications equipment included VHF and UHF radios and the Joint Tactical Information Distribution System (JTIDS) datalink. A digital triplex FBW flight control system would be fitted, offering improved subsonic lift and manoeuvrability as well as reduced trim drag at supersonic speeds. The avionics were all linked via a MIL-STD-1553B databus. The estimated development cost was £1.5 billion.

The P.1216-42 was a two-seat strike version, the -43 being an unarmed conversion trainer and the -18 of April 1988 had side-by-side seating. The P.1216-45 had an extended span wing to improve

The McDD Model 279-3 (known within Kingston as the P.1218-1) was powered by a 34,000lbf (151.2kN) P&W STF561-C2 development of the Pegasus; PCB boosted the thrust to 36,900lbf

(164.1kN). The maximum speed was Mach 2.0, accelerating from Mach 0.8 to Mach 1.6 in 70sec. With enough fuel for a 103nm (190km) radius of action, the vertical take-off weight was 29,840lb (13,535kg), using a 12° ski-jump increased this to 48,800lb (22,135kg). The airframe had a large delta wing with an all-moving close-coupled canard forward; 41% of the airframe by weight was constructed from composites. The lateral intakes had half-cone centrebodies. A full digital FBW flight control system was to be fitted. Pitch control would be provided by the canard, roll control by the differential ailerons; the wing leading and trailing edge flaps and the canard would be deflected as a function of angle of attack and Mach number to maximise manoeuvrability. In supersonic flight the leading edge flaps were used as decamber flaps to reduce drag. The single-slot trailing edge flaps, being close to the aft nozzles helped to increase the STOL lift. A 9.2% scale model was tested in NASA Ames' wind tunnel focusing on hot gas reingestion and ground effect problems. A proposed flying demonstrator was designed to use existing components to reduce cost: the cockpit and tail fin from the F/A-18 Hornet, an AV-8A wing and a Vought A-7 Corsair II tailplane as the canard.

A navalised Model 279-3C/HS.11218-5 was developed at the request of the MOD and BAe. A Blue Vixen radar with a 26in (66cm) antenna was fitted. The -5a changed the engine to the RB532-03.

There were additional designs that were not formally submitted as part of the pre-feasibility study. The supersonic P.1228 had a swept wing canard layout and used PCB. The wing had anhedral and full-span leading edge flaps, trailing edge flaps and two-piece ailerons. The outrigger fairing was also a weapon pylon. The swept canard foreplanes had slight dihedral and were located behind the cockpit. A retractable refuelling probe was mounted above the starboard intake. The proposed armament was six AMRAAMs or two Sea Eagles with wing tip ASRAAMs.

The P.1229 used an RB.583 three-nozzle thrust-vectoring engine, without PCB. The engine was fed by a chin intake below the cockpit. The high swept anhedral wing had wing tip rails for ASRAAMs as well as the usual outrigger/weapons pylon for AMRAAMs or Sea Eagle. Wingspan was 29ft 1in (8.86m) with a length of 52ft 0in (15.84m).

A rebooted design appeared in September, the supersonic HS.1184-29/AV-16S-4 of 1974 becoming the P.1231, which combined a Sea Harrier forward fuselage and a GR.5 rear fuselage around a new centre section containing a Pegasus 19-03 for a maximum speed of Mach 1.3. Wingspan was 29ft 3in (8.91m) and length 51ft 9in (15.77m). On 10 September the P.1232 was drawn up – a Sea Harrier FRS.2 with an 8in (20.3cm) fuselage plug and intake duct extension and a GR.5 rear fuselage. The rear fuselage fatigue issue of these designs was a serious drawback compared with the P.1216.

A scale model of the McDonnell Douglas 279-3 at NASA's Lewis Research Facility in 1987 undergoing PCB flow tests. The hot air reingestion, blast, thermal and aerodynamic issues of the powerful streams of hot air created by the PCB nozzles were research topics of prime importance. *NASA/NARA*

ASTOVL: Study B

BAe Warton led Study B, which utilised the ASTOVL research undertaken for AST.410 the previous year. Avionics improvements included those for Eurofighter and other items estimated to be available by 2005, such as twin dual-redundant digital databuses, digital Active Control Technology FBW flight control, holographic HUD, laser inertial navigation with GPS input and a comprehensive suite of passive and active self-defence equipment. The future multimode radar would be able to detect a 53.8ft² (5m²) sized target at 50nm (92.6km).

The Remote-Augmented Lift System (RALS) placed the main engine in the rear fuselage, it had two vectoring nozzles at the wing trailing edge root and a normal tail jet pipe and afterburner; the two rectangular RALS nozzles beneath the forward fuselage diverted the engine bleed air 60°downwards (they closed flush in horizontal flight.) Tapped air was also used for the RCS with wing tip and tail vents. The limited thrust vectoring of the RALS nozzle and the large internal piping required were drawbacks. The engine designed for RALS was the two-spool axial-flow RB.560-01 turbofan rated at 29,925lbf (133kN) dry or 43,425lbf (193kn) when augmented (the RB.422-60 was also considered).

The delta winged P.112N carried four AMRAAM (or two Sea Eagles) under the fuselage and another four AMRAAMs or two Sea Eagles under the wings. The cannon was a 25mm General Electric Gatling gun. CAP endurance was 2hr 30min with a maximum speed of Mach 1.9 at 36,000ft and a combat ceiling of 55,500ft (16,915m). The estimated development and production cost was £8.83 billion with the UK's share being £2.04 billion.

The tandem-fan engine concept was a turbofan with two fan stages. In normal horizontal flight

WINGS OVER THE FLEET

AST.6464 ASTOVL Study B proposals

	P.112N	P.115N-1	P.103N	P.1216-43	P.1216-46	P.1230-6
Design office	Warton	Warton	Warton	Kingston	Kingston	Kingston
Span	39ft 7in (12.06m)	?	42ft 0in (12.80m); 26ft 3in (8.0m) folded	34ft 0in (10.36m); 18ft 8in (5.74m) folded	42ft 4in (13.53m); 18ft 8in (5.74m) folded	39ft 2in (11.94m); ? folded
Length	51ft 2in (15.60m)	?	?	55ft 10.5in (17.03m); 51ft 6in (15.70m) folded	55ft 10.5in (17.03m); 51ft 6in (15.70m) folded	55ft 5in (16.89m)
Wing area	536.6ft² (49.90m²)	?	?	421.10ft² (39.13m²)	?	408.06ft² (38.0m²)
All-up weight	42,110lb (19,100kg) maximum take-off	?	?	?	?	36,869lb (16,724kg)
Powerplant	1x RB.560-01, 29,925lbf (133kN) dry, 43,425lbf (193kn) augmented	2x RB.560 or RB.561	2x RB.199-62R, 20,750lbf (92.2kN) dry, 37,850lbf (168.2kN) reheat	1x PSE.2 advanced technology engine with PCB	1x RB.422-60, 40,000lbf (177.9kN) PCB	1x RB.559-01A
Max speed	Mach 1.9 at 36,000ft (10,975m)	Mach 2.0 at 36,000ft (10,975m)	Mach 1.9 at 36,000ft (10,975m)	Mach 1.7 at 36,000ft (10,970m)	Mach 1.7 at 36,000ft (10,970m)	Mach 1.8 diving limit
Service ceiling	55,500ft (16,915m)	56,000ft (17,070m)	56,000ft (17,070m)	?	54,000ft (16,460m)	?
CAP endurance	2hr 30min	2hr 26min	2hr 26min	?	2hr 24min	?
Armament	1x 25mm ADEN, 6x AIM-120A AMRAAM & 2x ASRAAM, 4x Sea Eagle	1x 25mm ADEN, 6x AIM-120A AMRAAMs & 2x ASRAAM	1x 27mm Mauser BK-27, 6x AIM-120A AMRAAM & 2x ASRAAM, 4x Sea Eagle	1x 25mm ADEN, 6x AIM-120A AMRAAM or 4x AIM-9L Sidewinder, 2x Sea Eagle or ALARM, 1x WE.177A, 10x bombs	1x 25mm ADEN, 6x AIM-120A AMRAAM or 4x AIM-9L Sidewinder, 2x Sea Eagle or ALARM, 1x WE.177A, 10x bombs	1x 25mm ADEN, 4x AIM-120A AMRAAMs & 2x ASRAAM, 6x bombs

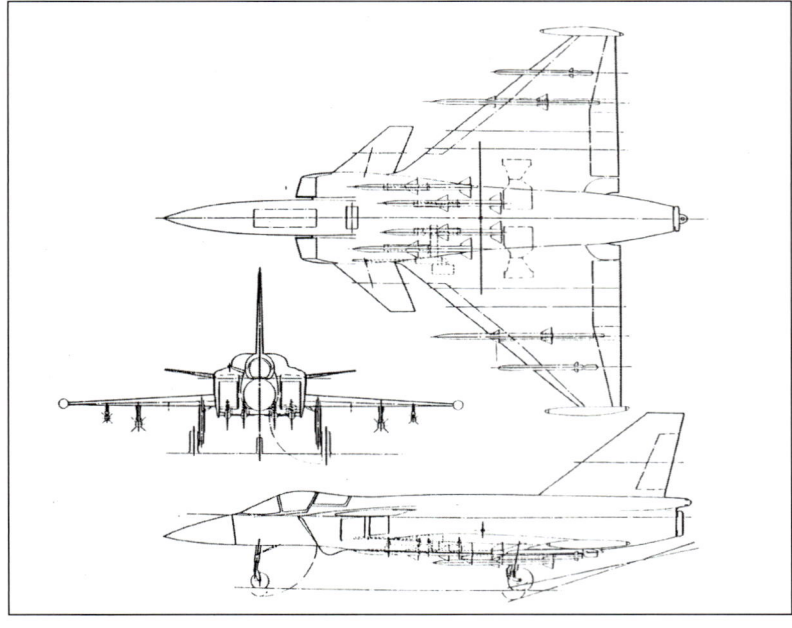

both fans worked in tandem, but for vertical flight the forward fan diverted its flow to two rectangular nozzles via diverter valves, the engine core exhausting through an aft nozzle. Warton's P.115N was a navalised version of the P.115 with folding outer wings and nose cone. It was a swept wing aircraft with a canard and a single tail fin. It was powered by two Rolls-Royce tandem-cycle fan engines in the wing roots with auxiliary intakes for the rear fan sections for vertical flight. The tandem fan gave cooler forward nozzle temperatures (reheat

The delta winged P.112N utilised the Remote-Augmented Lift System (RALS) powerplant with the rectangular RALS nozzle beneath the forward fuselage visible ahead of the four AMRAAMs on the bottom view, and the two wing root nozzles. The wing tip pods and the tail bullet carried the Reaction Control System using tapped compressor air for control at low airspeeds and in the hover. *BAE Systems via Author's Collection*

TOP RIGHT The P.115N had folding outer wings and nose cone. It was powered by two Rolls-Royce tandem-cycle fan engines, featuring auxiliary intakes for the rear fan sections for vertical flight. The tandem fan gave cooler forward nozzle temperatures and lower air pressures than RALS, an advantage for operation on carrier decks. *BAE Systems via Author's Collection*

CENTRE RIGHT The P.103N navalised version of the P.103 was a more unusual choice given that possible asymmetric thrust issues carried a high accident risk. It could carry four AMRAAMs or Sea Eagles in tandem pairs under the fuselage plus inner and outer wing hardpoints for AMRAAM and ASRAAM. *BAE Systems via Author's Collection*

BOTTOM RIGHT The P.1216-41 was the ultimate naval P.1216 version with an enlarged wing and the 40,000lbf (177.9kN) thrust RB.422-60 with PCB. *BAE Systems via Author's Collection*

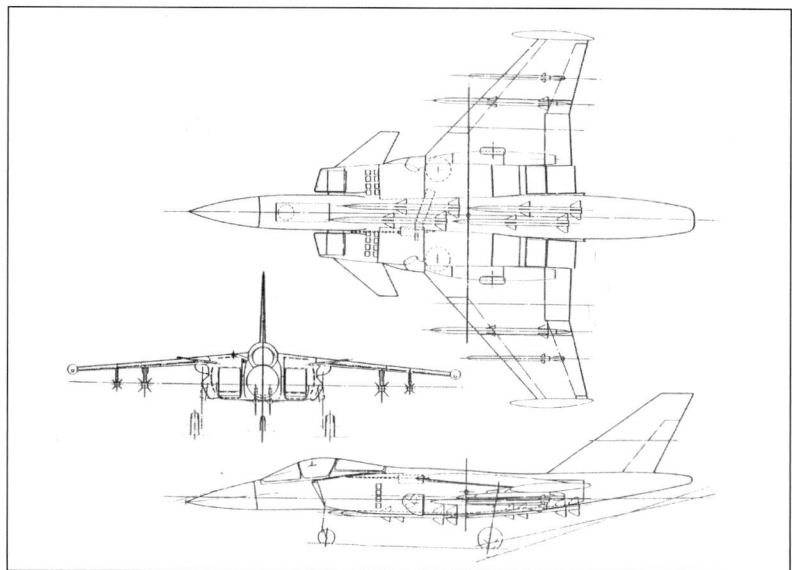

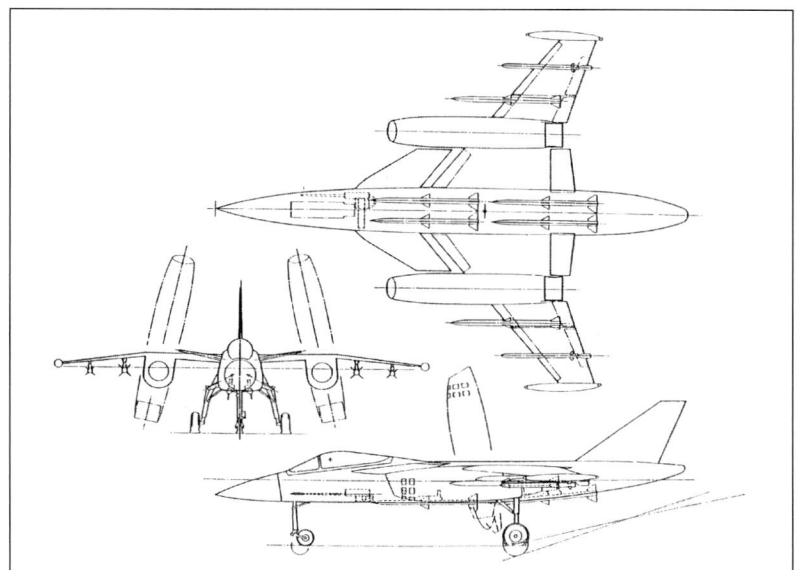

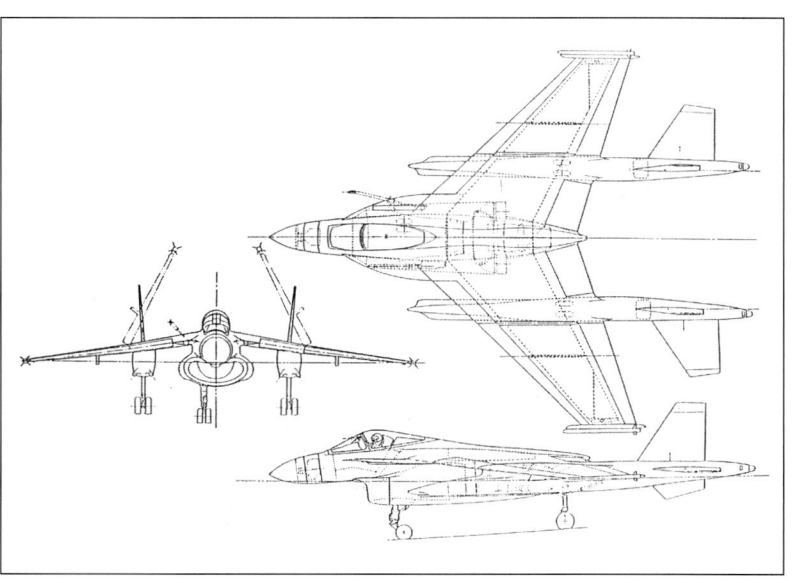

could be fitted aft) and lower air pressures than the RALS system. It could carry four AMRAAMs under the wings. CAP endurance was 2hr 36min with a maximum speed of Mach 2.0 at 36,000ft and a combat ceiling of 56,000ft. The estimated programme cost was £9.19 billion, with the UK's share being £2.21 billion.

Another Warton design was a navalised version of the P.103 twin-engin tilt-nacelle design. Ivan Yates, Warton's Divisional Managing Director, had begun developing the P.103 in 1978 for AST.403 with two tilting nacelles, each containing a reheated RB.199-62R turbojet. The P.103N had folding wing tips to reduce the span to 26ft 3in (8m) while the fuselage was fattened and lengthened for additional fuel capacity. It could carry four AMRAAM or four Sea Eagles in tandem pairs under the fuselage plus inner and outer wing hardpoints for AMRAAM and ASRAAM. Fully digital triplex Active Control Technology would provide stability with an engine control system controlling thrust in vertical flight. CAP endurance was 2hr 36min with a maximum speed of Mach 1.9 at 36,000ft and a combat ceiling of 56,000ft (17,070m). The estimated programme cost was £8.58 billion, the UK's contribution being £1.98 billion. The MoD's Directorate of Operational Requirements was not keen on the P.103's layout in comparison with the simplicity of four-poster thrust-vectoring.

Kingston offered developed P.1216 variants. The P.1216-43 featured an advanced technology engine dubbed PSE.2 based on the RB.422-60. This was quickly superseded by the P.1216-46 with a longer span wing (with increased chord compared with the -45) and the RB.422-60. This variant of the RB.422 featured the latest engine technology to develop up to 40,000lbf (177.9kN) thrust. With the PCB lit the engine provided four times more energy than the Pegasus at sea level and six times more when cruising at Mach 0.9. The forward fuselage and the

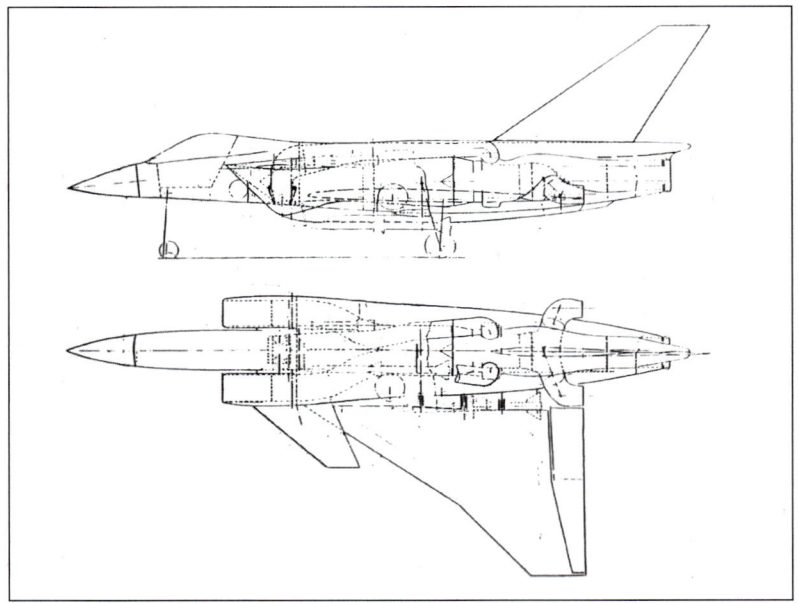

The P.112-2/5, another variant of Warton's P.112 RALS aircraft with a compound delta wing. *BAE Systems via Author's Collection*

booms were shortened to reduce length and stressed for 9g combat manoeuvres. CAP endurance was 2hr 24min with a maximum speed of Mach 1.7 at 36,000ft and a combat ceiling of 54,000ft (16,460m). The estimated development and production cost of the P.1216-46 was £8.7 billion, the UK's share of which would be £2.03 billion.

An ASTOVL Steering Group review of BAe's studies in July 1984 concluded that it was, "debatable whether the performance required by the primary CAP and Interception role of the draft NST.6464 can be achieved with an aircraft that will be compatible with the existing carrier vessels." An assessment by the MoD's Directorate of Future Systems was completed in late January 1986 (detailed technical information on the Model 279-3 had not been shared due to various political and industrial issues, so was omitted from the report.) Study A revealed that the Sea Harrier still had growth potential, especially with a larger folding wing. The GR.5 was less agile and therefore less suitable for development. The P.1226 offered little advance over the Harrier and the P.1216-45 had to keep its interception speed below Mach 1.5 to enable it to meet the CAP endurance requirements. The RAE concluded that the Sea Harrier 3 was the most cost effective solution for Study A. The assessment of Study B drew no technical conclusions on the individual designs but warned that the high jet energies on a carrier flight deck could cause serious problems that needed further investigation. The Directorate of Operational Requirements had discounted the P.103N and were not especially favourable towards the P.1216.

The obvious conclusion was that the development costs would be extremely high and the RN pushed the in-service date back to 2003-05. This allowed a focus on new technologies and greater cooperation with the USA. In January 1986 a Memorandum of Understanding (MoU) was signed by the MoD, RAE, the Department of Defense and NASA to explore ASTOVL propulsion techniques.

Several of the NST.6464 designs were re-examined. The P.112 was joined by the P.116 with an ejector-augmented lift system (basically RALS with a reheat system in the forward ejector duct). The P.115N-1 was a navalised version of the P.115C-4 with folding outer wings and nose cone, powered by one tandem fan engine with two tail fins flanking the exhaust nozzle. It could carry six AMRAAMs, two mounted conformally side by side under the fuselage, two conformally under the wing roots and two on underwing hardpoints. Kingston offered a new tandem fan design in competition with Warton's P.115, the P.1222 with an aft mounted compound delta wing with forward canards and wing tip endplate fins. It was powered by a 56,000lbf (249.1kN) Rolls-Royce Hybrid Tandem Fan engine with vectoring nozzles for the fan exhaust. Armament was four ventral and two underwing AMRAAMs and wing tip ASRAAMs.

The P.1230 revisited the HS.1205 of 1978 in terms of layout. The P.1230-1A was designed for the 1997 service entry date and had the RB.532 with PCB. The -1A could not meet all the NST.6464 requirements so was overtaken by the -1B, which aimed for the 2005 service date. It had a Rolls-Royce PSE-2 advanced engine and the wing was larger in span and chord with a thinner profile. The armament load was two semi-conformal AMRAAMs on top of the rear centre fuselage, and four AMRAAMs or Sea Eagles on the outrigger pods plus wing tip ASRAAMs. A cannon was fitted in the port LERX.

The P.1230-6 featured recontoured intakes with large boundary splitter plates and a tricycle undercarriage, the main legs retracting into large wing trailing edge fairings. Each fairing had a weapons pylon for up to three BL.755 cluster bombs. The P.1216-50 was a private venture which was not submitted under the MoU to stop its details circulating beyond McDD in the USA. It had an RB.559-03 engine and came out slightly heavier than the P.1230-6 with lower performance but its twin boom layout was the only practical solution to using PCB.

General Dynamics, Grumman, Lockheed and McDD also submitted a host of designs. Comparison became difficult with no clear winners among the numerous studies and by 1989 work on both sides of the Atlantic had stopped. BAe's internal tussles between Kingston and Warton as to the best propulsion method did not help matters either, the former having had far more experience of V/STOL technologies and robustly maintaining that thrust-vectoring was the only workable solution.

Work on NST.6464 did not stop however and further studies were conducted. In May 1989 the Future Projects Office (by now returned to Kingston) examined a new Harrier III series. The P.1244 Harrier IIIA was developed from the P.1227 with a larger carbon composite wing with leading edge vortex flaps and trailing edge flaps for combat manoeuvring and folding outer sections. It was envisioned as being ready to enter service in 1998 as an interim NST. 6464 solution. It was based on the Harrier II airframe with an 18in (45.7cm) plug ahead of the cockpit for a 30in (76cm) radar antenna and a FLIR 'ball' sensor, balanced by an 18in rear fuselage plug; the intake duct was also lengthened by 8in (20cm). An alternative new rear fuselage was also offered. The outrigger wing pods carried 1,800lb (816kg) of fuel plus two AMRAAMs; two outer wing and one ventral 1,500lb (680kg) hardpoints plus wing tip ASRAAM rails were fitted. It could also carry the tentative Modular Standoff Weapon (MSOW) (a NATO project which replaced the US/UK LRSOM). Wingspan was 35ft (10.66m), 25ft (7.62m) folded, with an area of 290.19ft² (26.96m²); the overall length was 49ft 3in (15m). By 1990 the maximum take-off weight was 33,950lb (15,400kg) and the AMRAAM outfit had grown to eight.

The P.1245 Harrier IIIB was developed from P.1231 without PCB, the P.1244 wing and the proposed Eurofighter radar, FLIR and MSOW capability. Fitting a Pegasus with PCB resulted in the P.1246 Harrier IIIC – the final design to come out of Kingston. As BAe consolidated its sites to the north (Warton, Samlesbury and Brough) during the 1990s it would be up to Warton to take the ASTOVL further – especially when the UK withdrew from the joint MoU in 1990 due to budget cutbacks. A 1992 study concluded that any Harrier developments would be ineffective against fighter escorted raids or the supersonic *Backfire* and its ASMs. ASTOVL was back on the agenda.

Towards JSF

The USA began several ASTOVL programmes during the 1990s. While McDD and BAe cooperated on yet another Harrier III (derived from the Harrier II) and the associated stealthy Harrier 21 concept, DARPA – the Defense Advanced Research Projects Agency – issued research contracts to Lockheed's Skunk Works to develop a stealthy STOVL Strike Fighter (SSF) to replace the USMC's AV-8B Harrier IIs and the US Air Force's F-16 Fighting Falcons.

In 1992 the SSF became the Common Affordable Lightweight Fighter (CALF). The following year the Department of Defense launched the Joint Advanced Strike Technology (JAST) programme to replace a wide range of attack aircraft in USAF, USN and USMC service. Following meetings in July 1994, the UK joined JAST in October, agreeing to fund 35% of the ASTOVL element and sending Commander Phil Hunt to the USA as the RN's liaison officer. During a visit to Washington DC by the First Sea Lord, Admiral Sir Jock Slater, in December 1995, the USMC's Deputy Chief of Staff for Aviation, Lieutenant General Harry Blot, advised that the RN should follow the USMC's lead; Slater later noting, "if it meets USMC requirements it will meet all of ours." JAST design studies were undertaken by McDD, Northrop, Lockheed and Boeing. McDD proposed the Gas-Driven Lift Fan (GDLF) in cooperation with General Electric using a reheated turbofan with a remote gas-driven fan for vertical lift. Northrop Grumman used Lift-Plus-Lift/Cruise (LPLC) using an auxiliary lift engine to augment the main turbofan's dry thrust with a pair of thrust-vectoring nozzles, reheat was also provided for horizontal flight. Lockheed Martin used a Shaft-Driven Lift Fan (SDLF) system in cooperation with P&W, the reheated turbofan driving a fan behind the cockpit via a powered drive shaft. Boeing decided to rely on a pair of thrust-vectoring nozzles located near the centre of gravity and a vectoring tail nozzle.

In early 1996 CALF and JAST were merged as the Joint Strike Fighter. The JSF would be built in three variants: conventional take-off and landing (CTOL), STOVL and carrier-based CTOL. A few months previously the P&W YF119 turbofan from the Lockheed Martin F-22A Raptor had been selected to power the JSF.

In mid-1996 three official tenders were submitted for the $2 billion concept demonstrator phase, with two demonstrators to be acquired. Boeing's design had a one-piece composite material delta wing, chin intake and twin tail fins. The STOVL version was originally schemed to have a tandem fan development of the YF119 but this was changed to the YF119-PW-614S with two retractable forward nozzles and a vectoring rear exhaust nozzle. A bleed air RCS for use during the transition and landing was also fitted.

McDD in partnership with Northrop Grumman and BAe made use of technology from the YF-23A Advanced Tactical Fighter demonstrator. It had a swept wing with a double cranked trailing edge with split brake/rudder/aileron surfaces outboard. The tailplane outer sections had dihedral to avoid the need for a

A relic of BAe's collaboration with McDonnell Douglas and its ASTOVL work is on display at the Newark Air Museum in Nottinghamshire, which has one of the radar cross-section (RCS) test models of a stealthy ASTOVL configuration. In the background are two RCS models of the P.1216 (one of which has been painted in RAF colours for display). *Joe Cherrie*

This design looks superficially similar to the Lockheed Martin YF-22 of the same period. McDonnell Douglas and BAe studied many configurations and the final JSF submission had a much lower angle of dihedral for the tail surfaces, becoming almost a tailless design. *Joe Cherrie*

BAE Systems test pilot Simon Hargreaves is at the controls of the Lockheed Martin X-35B over Edwards Air Force Base on 11 July 2001. This view illustrates well the Rolls-Royce LiftSystem Integrated Lift Fan Propulsion System behind the cockpit. The lift fan provides 20,000lbf (88.9kN) of vertical thrust, the Pratt & Whitney F135 provides 18,000lbf (80kN) via its Three-Bearing Swivel Duct Nozzle, with the RCS system the total lift thrust is 41,900lbf (186.3kN). *USAF*

The Boeing X-32A and Lockheed Martin X-35A JSF demonstrators at Edwards Air Force Base. *USAF*

vertical tail and to aid low speed handling. The original GDLF system was replaced by a 16,000lbf (71.1kN) General Electric/Allison/Rolls-Royce GEA-FXL lift engine and the YF-119 had retractable side nozzles for use at low speeds as well as a vectoring tail exhaust. A bleed air RCS was also fitted. The change had been largely at the instigation of the Northrop Grumman engineers who argued that the lift fan was lighter and removed the need for ducting from the engine, which was causing issues with the design for the CTOL variants. The USMC was against the change, citing additional fuel consumption and maintenance requirements as being the main drawbacks.

Lockheed Martin's STOVL version kept the SDLF concept, the YF119-PW-611 driving the lift fan behind the cockpit via a driveshaft and having a three-bearing vectoring tail exhaust nozzle. Two side nozzles would use bleed air for control at low speed.

On 16 November 1996 Boeing and Lockheed Martin were each awarded $750 million for the demonstrators. Boeing built the X-32A CTOL and X-32B STOVL prototypes while Lockheed built a X-35A CTOL prototype, which was rebuilt following just four days of flight trials into the STOVL X-35B. Following McDD's loss, BAe and Northrop Grumman joined the X-35 programme and within a year McDD was acquired by Boeing. BAe provided Lockheed with key support in STOVL, flight control systems and manufacturing processes; cooperation was close but US laws prevented access to sensitive areas such as stealth shaping and materials and software source code. Following the flight trials programme the winner was announced on 26 October 2001 as the X-35, which became the F-35 Lightning II.

FCBA

The need to replace the Sea Harrier from 2015 saw NST.6464 being recast as Staff Target (Sea/Air) 6464 (later becoming URD 6464) in 1996 for a Future Carrier Borne Aircraft (FCBA). The procurement was also tied up with the *Invincible*-class replacement, the Future Aircraft Carrier (CVF) (see below). Whether the CVF would be a catapult and arrester gear-equipped CTOL or a ski-jump STOVL carrier would influence which type of aircraft was selected. Unlike the earlier NST.6464 effort there would be no national solution, the UK's aircraft industry was no longer in the driving seat. The MOD loves acronym soup and when the RAF joined the programme in January 2001 FCBA became FJCA (Future Joint Combat Aircraft) and in January 2003 'Future' was dropped, leaving JCA.

The FCBA and the CVF overlapped with the RAF's Future Offensive Air Systems (FOAS) requirement to replace the Panavia Tornado GR.4. This led to haggling regarding how many FCBA and FOAS to buy. Inspired by the creation of Joint Force Harrier, the RN proposed creating a Joint Force 2000 – a CVF-based FAA/RAF FCBA force to replace the Sea Harrier and Harrier, with the implication that the RAF should defer FOAS until 2020. The RN wanted to ensure that command of Joint Force 2000 would be truly joint, with full operational control maintained over its own assets – interservice rivalry was still a serious issue to contend with.

The FCBA was required to operate in all weathers and by day and night in the air defence, long-range air interdiction, suppression of enemy air defences (SEAD), shore strike, close air support, anti-surface warfare and tactical reconnaissance (visual, radar and ELINT – passive electronic recce) roles, and be a 'swing role' aircraft capable of switching roles during the sortie. It had to be supersonic and have stealth features to improve survivability, including internal weapons carriage for six AMRAAM or six 1,000lb (454kg) laser-guided bombs or JDAMs (Joint Direct Attack Munition) or four ASMs. A cannon would also be fitted. The CAP radius would be 150nm (280km) with 90min on station and a 500nm (925km) radius for reconnaissance missions. The AUW would be kept below 38,000lb (17,235kg) for STOVL aircraft. The aircraft would have to be capable of flying up to five sorties daily in surge operations and up to four per day for sustained operations. The post-Cold War threat from modern fighters, strike aircraft and SAM systems was assumed to widen around the world as Russia and China began to export them in earnest.

BAe Warton had continued with its ASTOVL work. Following on from the P.140 supersonic Harrier developments around 1990, the P.145 was another supersonic design, with P.145-17 being assessed against the SSF and a navalised Eurofighter in late 1994. That assessment calculated that the SSF had a 70% kill ratio against four Sukhoi Su-24 *Fencer* strike aircraft escort by two MiG-29 *Fulcrum* fighters versus a 50% kill ratio for the P.145 and Eurofighter.

The greatest factor affecting the selection was carrier operations, especially launch and recovery. The method selected would affect the build costs, flight deck size and the aircraft's capability. The most favoured option was STOVL due to the operational knowledge amassed during two decades of Sea Harrier operations. The two STOVL JCA options were an improved Harrier or the STOVL JSF variant. The Harrier was quickly ruled out, the basic airframe and the Pegasus engine were running out of growth potential and were firmly subsonic. Since the UK and BAe were already involved in the JSF, it seemed an obvious solution. In October 1998 an MOD party visited Boeing in Seattle and Lockheed Martin at Fort Worth for briefings on the X-32 and X-35 demonstrators, accompanied by the Assistant Secretary of the Navy, John Douglass and Vice Admiral John Lockhard, the Head of Naval Air Systems Command. Douglass and Lockhard wanted the UK to remain committed to JSF (the phrase 'special relationship' was used in their discussions) and Douglass was particularly keen to widen the involvement of other NATO partners.

The CTOL options for use with catapults and arrester gear (which would have to be acquired from the USA) were the Boeing F/A-18E Super Hornet (a Boeing product since its takeover of McDD), Dassault Rafale M and the carrier-based JSF variant. JSF again topped the list. The Super Hornet was expensive, less stealthy and gave little offset return to UK industry. The Rafale had a lower weapons payload compared with the Super Hornet and the RAF was not interested given that it was committed to the Eurofighter. An offer from the French government to consider the CVF design for their second carrier in return for a Rafale purchase had little influence.

The third method was STOBAR – Short Take-Off But Arrested Recovery. The aircraft takes off using a ski-jump and uses arrester gear for landing (as used by the Su-33K *Flanker-D* aboard the *Admiral Kuznetsov*). The only option was a navalised Eurofighter. BAe had carried out pre-feasibility studies in early 1996 on a Typhoon (N) and in 1997 was awarded a 27-month contract study further CTOL and STOBAR versions. An arrester hook and a strengthened undercarriage would be fitted. Wing folding would be required and other possibilities included reprofiled wings to increase lift, three-axis thrust vectoring nozzles and increased power Eurojet EJ200 turbofans. The Eurofighter GmbH consortium also tried to interest the Italian and Indian navies.

BAE Systems (as BAe became in November 1999) suggested that using computer controlled precise landing systems and other landing aids could reduce the stresses of arrested landings to within the Typhoon's existing structural limits to avoid the need for expensive airframe and undercarriage strengthening. The MOD was disinclined to take this risk and by early 2001 the Typhoon (N) had been discounted on cost and safety grounds (the latter including low deck clearance on take-off with external stores fitted and the canards restricted the pilot's view during high angle-of-attack landings). The Typhoon (N) briefly returned as 'Plan B' in late 2005 during JSF technology transfer tussles with the Americans; receiving a periscope or a higher seat position and canopy roofline to enable the pilot to see over the canards and longer undercarriage legs with blister fairings. These studies indicated a 750lb (340kg) weight increase for STOBAR operation and 1,014lb (460kg) for catapult launching (the Naval Typhoon was also offered to India in 2011). The French renewed the offer of Rafale M's and even a joint Anglo-French Northrop Grumman E-2C Hawkeye AEW squadron.

The JSF had always been the front runner and on 17 January 2001 an MoU was signed in Washington DC to become the sole Level 1 partner. The UK

The Dassault Rafale M was offered by France; it would have required a CTOL carrier but the political offers from France acquiring a modified CVF design for their planned second carrier and a joint fleet of Grumman E-2C Hawkeye AEW aircraft. This Rafale M is taking off from the USS *Enterprise* during a cross-decking exercise in 2007. *US Navy*

The Eurofighter Typhoon takes-off at a relatively shallow angle. It was found that at the high angles of attack of carrier take-offs from ski jumps and arrested landings, the pilot's vision would be obscured by the canard foreplane, requiring a periscope to see over it. This was just one of several issues that would have had to be overcome during the navalisation process. *MOD/Open Government Licence*

Having committed to JAST in 1994, the Joint Strike Fighter was always the frontrunner to secure the FBCA and JCA requirements. The third UK F-35B Lightning, serial ZM137, is transitioning into the hover with the Integrated Lift Fan Propulsion System running and the aft Three-Bearing Swivel Duct Nozzle vectored downwards. *MOD/Open Government Licence*

agreed to fund 8% of the System Development and Demonstration phase, totalling $2 billion. In return, the UK became part of the evaluation and selection process. Through tough negotiations BAE Systems gained a 15% manufacturing workshare. Warton and Samlesbury build the aft fuselage of every F-35, plus tailplanes and vertical tails while BAE's transatlantic avionics subsidiaries are responsible for several items, including the AN/ASQ-239 Barracuda electronic warfare system, the vehicle management computer and the Active Inceptor System which provides 'feel feedback' through the pilot's controls.

The technology transfer arguments referred to earlier resulted in President George W Bush and Prime Minister Tony Blair announcing an agreement on 27 May 2006 that ensured the UK's ability to "successfully operate, upgrade, employ, and maintain the Joint Strike Fighter such that the UK retains operational sovereignty over the aircraft." This was followed in December 2006 by access to software source code and "an unbroken British chain of command" for operational use.

Despite the political developments, it was still undecided which JSF variant to acquire. The STOVL F-35B offered reduced range in comparison with the naval CTOL F-35C and an extensive analysis was conducted on both aircraft. The RN favoured the F-35B and there were rumours that the RAF also pushed for the F-35B to remove any competition with the Typhoon purchase and FOAS. The First Sea Lord and Chief of Naval Staff, Admiral Sir Alan West, announced the decision to acquire the F-35B on 30 September 2002. Even so, rumours of switching to the F-35C circulated for many years as development and production delays pushed back the in-service date.

The plan was to order 150 F-35s (costing around £7 billion), with a joint RAF/RN ownership and operational structure, to enable three 12-aircraft squadrons to be operated aboard a CVF. The production, sustainment and follow-on development phase MoU was signed on 12 December 2006, committing the UK to spending £34 million but without a formal commitment to buy any aircraft. The planned order was reduced to 138 aircraft, including 80 F-35Bs. Two CVF carriers were ordered the following year. An order for three F-35Bs for operational test and evaluation was placed on 18 March 2009. Squadron Leader Steve Long became the first British frontline pilot to fly the F-35 on 26 January 2010, following over 18 months of simulator training.

New Carriers

The NST.6464 pre-feasibility studies in 1986 had indicated that larger air groups were required. An Actual Establishment (AE) of eight ASTOVL fighters could sustain four aircraft on CAP and could destroy a third of 24 attacking subsonic bombers. A 16 aircraft AE would be required if the ASTOVL fighters were subsonic. Against supersonic bombers with fighter escorts the AE rose to 10 supersonic, 14 transonic or 16 subsonic ASTOVL fighters to destroy a third of the incoming raid, rising to 12, 19 and 22 if no AEW support was available. A larger fixed-wing AE meant building a larger carrier if AEW and ASW helicopter numbers were not to be sacrificed.

Studies for an *Invincible*-class replacement – the CVSG(R) or Aircraft Carrier, Anti-Submarine, Guided Missile (Replacement) – began in 1994 (the programme soon received the shorter CV(R) designation.) Three ships were to be commissioned in 2012, 2015 and 2019. The pre-feasibility studies identified three options:

- A ship life-extension programme (SLEP) for all three *Invincible*-class ships, including the insertion of an 80ft (24.3) hull section to increase aircraft capacity. A 1995 study by BAe-SEMA revealed that the SLEP was risky due to hull fatigue and the hull plug ahead of the island superstructure would only increase the aircraft capacity by four.

- Acquiring and converting a merchant vessel to operate 20 aircraft and helicopters. This option was quickly discarded due to high costs and low operational effectiveness.

- New-build carriers (two or three ships), the studies including STOVL, STOBAR and CTOL configurations with 15, 20, 26, 30 or 40 aircraft and helicopters, including a variant of the Landing Platform Helicopter (LPH) ship then under consideration (as discussed in Chapter 13).

The initial studies used the McDD F/A-18C Hornet, F/A-18E Super Hornet and Lockheed's SSF study as baseline aircraft, while the Lockheed S-3 Viking for AEW was soon replaced by a notional Merlin conversion (with compound wings for increased lift). The C13 steam catapults and Mk.7 arrester gear were USN items. The LPH studies were limited to 16 aircraft and 18kt unless more powerful engines were installed or a 111ft (34m) hull extension provided to boost the speed to 28kt and aircraft capacity to 22. By October 1995 a hybrid STOVL carrier (Option 26H) appeared with a ski-ramp for 20 FCBA plus a catapult for three E-2C Hawkeyes (three Merlins were also carried). The hybrid was not cost-effective compared with pure CTOL or ASTOVL carriers and was dropped. A STOBAR design had an air group of 20 navalised Eurofighters and six Merlins, but this did not save cost or size compared with a CTOL carrier due to the Eurofighter's lack of folding wings or nose cone.

By the end of 1996 the Director of Operational Requirements (Sea), Captain RJ Clapp, had concluded that the most effective new-build solution would displace 30–40,000 tons, be 984ft (300m) long and capable of operating up to 40 aircraft, including helicopters (plus surge capacity for an additional 10.) A SLEP for two of the *Invincibles* to extend their lives to 2022 was still on the cards, until another study confirmed that it was unjustified on cost and capability grounds.

By 1998 the fixed-wing squadron AE was 18 plus nine in a training squadron, which would be deployed in wartime. The proposed Joint Force 2000 would assist in filling out the Carrier Air Group. MOD studies had shown that carrier-based fighters were more cost effective than land-based fighters for fleet air defence, especially as naval task forces might move up to 580nm (1,075km) per day. The JSF's capabilities allowed the FAA to begin thinking about how it could contribute to SEAD missions.

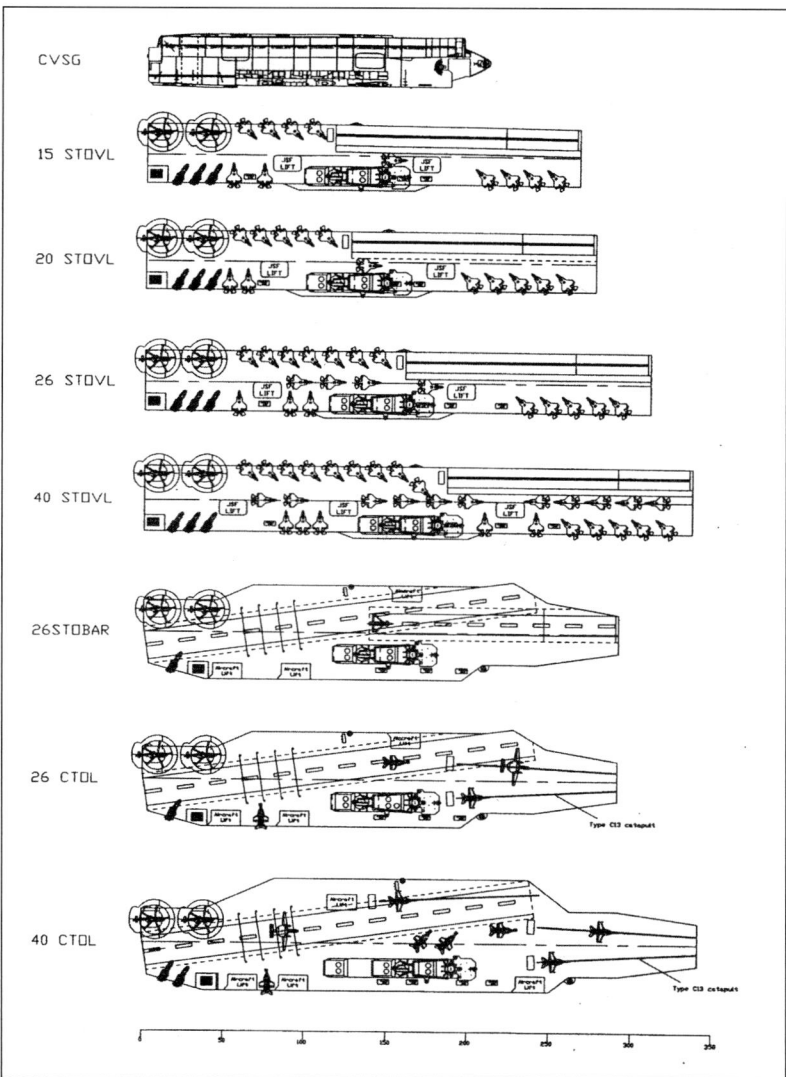

A Study Group modelled three conflict scenarios for 2020: a regional conflict in the Finnmark area of northern Norway and Finland against Russia (one CVF with 14 FCBA, four Future Organic Airborne Early Warning System (FOAEW) and six Merlin); a continental war with the Russian Federation (including Belarus and Ukraine) invading Poland (two CVF, one in the North Sea with 17 FCBA and four FOAEW, the other west of the Iceland-UK Gap with 11 FCBA, four FOAEW and six Merlin); and an Iranian-backed overthrow of the United Arab Emirates with Iranian incursions into northern Oman and Yemen threatening to invade Saudi Arabia (one CVF with 17 FCBA, four FOAEW and six Merlin). Each of the cases justified the need for the CVF for power projection and fleet defence. The Permanent Under-Secretary of State for Defence, Richard Mottram, was happy with the analysis but worried that the characteristics of the FCBA and CVF were going "back to those of the previous generation" with the implication that they were not designed for the post-Cold War world.

The programme – by now renamed CV(F) (for Future), commonly styled as CVF – was a major part

Some of the early CVF parametric studies carried out circa 1997 to decide what the optimum displacement, size and air group would be. At the top is the *Invincible*-class and there are a mix of STOVL and CTOL designs. *Crown Copyright*

Thales won the design contract for the CVF. The carriers have two islands on the starboard side, dictated by the uptakes and funnels of the Rolls-Royce MT30 gas turbines and diesel engines. The forward island is dedicated to navigation and ship operations, while the other contains the flight control position and handles aerial operations. *MOD/Open Government Licence*

HMS *Queen Elizabeth*'s flight deck is longer and wider than the last fleet carriers HMS *Eagle* and *Ark Royal*, which were laid down 50 years before the CVF programme began. Should an electromagnetic catapult be fitted to launch UAVs, its likely location will be alongside the 12° ski-jump to starboard. *MOD/Open Government Licence*

of the 1997-8 Strategic Defence Review (SDR) and a working group was established to examine the requirements against the UK's changing geopolitical and strategic policies. The SDR concluded that future force projection operations would depend on the ability to deploy offensive airpower, especially when access to suitable airbases was uncertain and CVF was seen as a 'floating airbase'. Experiences during the Gulf War, Bosnia and Kosovo demonstrated problems with airbase availability and congestion; the carriers provided flexibility and a measure of deterrence – as demonstrated by *Ark Royal's* Buccaneers over British Honduras (Belize) in 1971.

The SDR cleared the way for Staff Target ST(S) 7068 for the CVF to be approved in late 1998. Nine Key User Requirements were laid down covering interoperability for joint and combined operations; integration into the joint battlespace with command, control, communications, computers and intelligence (C4I) capabilities; availability; deployability for global operations; sustainability; aircraft operation to deploy offensive air power; survivability; flexibility to operate the largest possible range of aircraft; and versatility to operate in the widest range of roles. Despite increasing criticisms of cost the Secretary of State for Defence, Geoff Hoon, in June 2001 reaffirmed the commitment to build two ships and acquire the JSF for a total cost of around £10 billion. The War on Terror and operations in Afghanistan and Iraq during the 2000s and 2010s affirmed the need for a mobile airbase able to project airpower.

As noted above, the air group requirement was for 40 aircraft, including helicopters, with the ability to support 50 in surge conditions. The CVF was originally required to be able to sustain up to 150 sorties per day – 12 sorties every two hours – but this was reduced to 130 daily sorties. In peacetime the carriers would carry a Tailored Air Group (TAG), with the types and numbers of aircraft embarked being adjusted to meet operational needs. The basic TAG would consist of two JCA squadrons (24 aircraft), six Merlin HM.1 helicopters and four (FOAEW) Maritime Airborne Surveillance and Control (MASC) aircraft (see Chapter 9.) The carriers would also embark Joint Helicopter Command's (JHC) Westland Sea King HC.4s, CH-47 Chinooks, Westland Lynx AH.7, AH.9 and Apache AH.1 helicopters as well as Unmanned Aerial Vehicles (UAVs).

Two industrial consortiums were formed to compete for the CVF contract. The BAE Systems team included Lockheed Martin, Northrop Grumman, Vosper Thornycroft, AMS, Rolls-Royce, Swan Hunter, Babcock BES, Fleet Support Limited and Strachan & Henshaw. The Thales team included Lockheed Martin as well as Raytheon, BMT Defence Services, DML, Halliburton KBR, Alstom and CAE Electronics.

Assessment Phase 1 studies during 2000 by the two industrial teams were followed by 12-month Assessment Phase 2 study contracts worth £25 million each. Displacement and size increased – the

Defence Procurement Agency's estimates were around 46,000 tons, but BAE Systems was looking at designs between 30–50,000 tons (by 2002 up to 60,000 tons). The First Sea Lord, Admiral Sir Michael Boyce, was keen to acquire a larger carrier, which would be more cost effective and easier to upgrade over the planned 30–50 year service life.

By May 2002 BAE Systems was proposing a CTOL carrier 985ft (300m) long, displacing 64,000 tons at full load, capable of carrying an air group of 24–36 F-35C, four E-2C Hawkeyes and six Merlin HM.1. It had two steam catapults (supplied via steam generators) and two deck edge lifts. The alternative STOVL design displaced 58,000 tons fully loaded. The Thales design of April 2002 was 950ft (290m) long, displacing around 50,000 tons with a 230ft (70m) wide flight deck with two deck lifts. BAE Systems and Thales developed flexible designs which could be adapted from CTOL to STOVL with minimal changes, essentially building a CTOL carrier initially fitted for STOVL operations.

The Thales consortium won the contract, which was announced in July 2007 and issued on 3 July 2008. The consortium became the Aircraft Carrier Alliance, which included Thales Group, Babcock International, A&P Group and BAE Systems. The second carrier was confirmed in 2014 to ensure that at least one carrier would be operational at all times. The cost for both ships was £7.6 billion (at 2019 prices).

The first steel was cut for HMS *Queen Elizabeth* on 7 July 2009, the hull being floated out of BAE's shipyard in Portsmouth on 17 July 2014 and was formally commissioned on 7 December 2017. *Prince of Wales* began construction on 26 May 2011, being floated out on 21 December 2017 and commissioned on 10 December 2019. Displacing 79,300 tons at full load, the flight deck is 918ft (280m) long and 229ft 6in (70m) wide with a 12° ski-jump at the bows. The hangar is 509ft (155m) long, 110ft (33.5m) wide and 22–33ft (6.7–10m) high, sufficient to accommodate up to 20 fixed- and rotary-wing aircraft – the remainder of the theoretical capacity of 72 aircraft (typically 40) would be parked on the deck. The two 88ft 6in × 49ft 3in (27 × 15m) lifts can fit two F-35Bs or one Chinook with a maximum load capacity of 120,150lb (54,500kg). Between 250 and 900 troops can be carried in the commando role.

SDSR

The Conservative-Liberal Democrat coalition government in 2010 conducted a Strategic Defence and Security Review (SDSR) with major implications for the RN. The carrier fleet had already been reduced when *Invincible* was decommissioned on 3 August 2005 and placed on the Naval Reserve List (only 20 months after extensive refit to extend her service life by 10 years). Under the SDSR *Ark Royal* was decommissioned on 11 March 2011 rather than 2016 as scheduled. *Illustrious* was decommissioned on 28 August 2014 and *Invincible* was scrapped in 2011. The UK Carrier Strike Group that was formed in 2006 was no more. The Joint Force Harrier was disbanded in December 2010 and the Harrier GR.7 and GR.9s sold to the USMC as spares (the reason given was to release funds for CVF.)

In addition the RAF's BAE Systems Nimrod MRA.4 programme was cancelled, leaving the UK without a dedicated maritime patrol aircraft for a decade until the first of nine Boeing P-8A Poseidon MRA.1 entered service in 2019. This removed the RN's access to a long-range ASW and intelligence gathering asset.

The F-35 and CVF were not immune to turmoil. The SDSR closed RAF Lossiemouth, the planned F-35 base and suggested that only one carrier would be commissioned, with an AE of 12 F-35s. The SDSR also called for the F-35C to be procured and for *Queen Elizabeth* to be completed with catapults and arrester gear. In May 2012 this was reversed when it became clear that the conversion costs were too great and the F-35C's unit cost was also higher. Two months later the Secretary of State for Defence, Philip Hammond, announced that 48 F-35B Lightnings would be ordered (note the MOD dropped the 'II' from the name and no role designation has been applied). In May 2014 *Prince of Wales* was reprieved.

Lightning

By October 2024 the UK had taken delivery of 35 of the first tranche of 48 F-35Bs Lightnings, with the remainder due for delivery in 2025 (there will only be 47 as ZM152 was lost on 16 November 2021 in circumstances described below.) The Defence Command Paper *Defence in a Competitive Age* of 22 March 2021 removed the commitment to procure 138 F-35s, instead providing an open ended intention to increase the fleet beyond the 48 already ordered; the First Sea Lord Admiral

Sir Tony Radakin estimated that the final fleet would be 60 to 80 aircraft.

A number of UK weapons are to be integrated under the Block 4 software package: a pair of ASRAAM, the MBDA Meteor long-range AAM –

The CVF carriers offer the most optimised facilities for air operations of any carrier that the RN has operated. Each of the deck lifts can accommodate two Lightnings, or in this case one Lightning and one Merlin HM.2 Crowsnest. *MOD/ Open Government Licence*

The ethos of the Joint Harrier Force lives on. The first carrier-qualified squadron was the RAF's No. 617. The Lightning squadrons have pilots from all three Services and at the time of writing 'The Dambusters' were commanded by a Royal Marine pilot. The two Lightnings are ZM144 and ZM146. The Hawk T.1A in the background is XX261 of No.100 Squadron, used for dissimilar 'aggressor' air combat training until 31 March 2022. *MOD/Open Government Licence*

four internally and possibly with another four externally under the wings in the less-stealthy 'Beast Mode'. Strike weapons include up to six 500lb (227kg) Paveway IV guided bombs (two mounted internally) or up to eight MBDA SPEAR 3 cruise missiles internally. SPEAR 3 has a range of 75nm (140km) and the multimode seeker head uses millimetric wave radar, IR-homing and semi-active laser modes for precision strike.

The RAF established No. 17 Test and Evaluation Squadron on 12 April 2013 at Edwards Air Force Base in California as the Lightning's Operational Evaluation Unit, it also forming part of the Joint Operational Test Team at Edwards AFB, being embedded with the USAF's 461st Flight Test Squadron. No. 17 embarked its three F-35Bs aboard *Queen Elizabeth* for the first time on 13 October 2019.

The initial frontline squadron was No. 617, the famous 'Dambusters.' Training began in 2017 at Marine Corps Air Station Beaufort, South Carolina, before the squadron was reformed on 18 April 2018, flying four F-35Bs (ZM145, ZM146, ZM147 and ZM148) across the Atlantic to their new home at RAF Marham in Norfolk on 6 June. No. 617 Squadron achieved combat capability on 10 January 2019, embarking aboard *Queen Elizabeth* alongside No. 17 Squadron on 13 October. The first combat mission had occurred on 16 June when two F-35s conducted a patrol over Syria as part of Operation SHADER.

The Operational Conversion Unit at Marham is No. 207 Squadron (its numberplate was selected due to its heritage as a Royal Naval Air Service and RAF squadron). Six F-35Bs (ZM137, ZM139, ZM149, ZM150, ZM151 and ZM152) were ferried from MCAS Beaufort to Marham on 16 July 2019, the unit formally being re-formed on 1 August.

The second frontline squadron is 809 NAS, which formed at Marham on 8 December 2023. The squadron embarked its aircraft aboard *Prince of Wales* on 1 October 2024 for a month's intensive training in the North Sea; the first carrier-borne FAA squadron for almost fifteen years.

There have been challenges in providing enough pilots. In late 2022 there were only 30 qualified RAF and FAA pilots because of backlogs in the training system (plus three USMC and Australian exchange pilots). Air Chief Marshal Sir Mike Wigston, the Chief of the Air Staff, reported in February 2023 that there were 34 F-35 pilots, with a further seven due to complete their training by August. A full fleet of 80 Lightnings would see four squadrons being formed (two RAF, two FAA), but until that happens – if ever – it leaves the 'Dambusters' and 'The Immortals' as the only deployable squadrons. The MOD has assigned an out of service date of 2069 for the F-35B.

Carrier Strike Group

The UK Carrier Strike Group was reformed in 2020 when *Queen Elizabeth* became operational. It includes escort and auxiliary support ship contributions from the Netherlands and Norway as a NATO force. The *Queen Elizabeth*-class carriers took part in trials and training to relearn the ropes of operating carriers. *Queen Elizabeth's* first major deployment was WESTLANT 18 during autumn 2018 for F-35B and helicopter amphibious assault trials off the Western Coast of the USA. A pair of USMC F-35Bs from development squadron VX-23 based at Naval Air Station Patuxent River were used. These tests included the first demonstration of the rolling vertical landing technique, which is the primary method of recovery aboard the two ships. WESTLANT 19 took place during the following autumn with No. 617 Squadron embarked alongside No. 17 Squadron. Flight trials with No. 207 Squadron followed and in June 2020 No. 617 Squadron began preparing for initial operating capability, which was formally granted on 4 January 2021; *Queen Elizabeth* became the Fleet Flagship on the 27th.

The first deployment to the Far East, Carrier Strike Group 21, departed on 24 May 2021, taking part in a NATO exercise in the Eastern Atlantic before heading to the Mediterranean, transiting Suez Canal to conduct joint exercises with the Indian Navy. *Queen Elizabeth* had her combat debut with 15 F-35Bs – five of No. 617 Squadron and 10 from USMC Fighter Attack Squadron 211 (VMFA-211) – launching attacks against ISIS, supporting Operation Inherent Resolve on 18 June. The CSG then proceed to enter the South China Sea, before visiting South Korea and Japan. During the return to the UK, F-35B ZM152 of No. 207 Squadron crashed into Mediterranean following take-off on 16 November 2021 due to the left intake blank having been inadvertently not removed; the pilot ejected safely.

Carrier Strike Deployment 23 in September 2023 saw *Queen Elizabeth* embarking eight F-35Bs of No. 617 Squadron, five Merlin HM.2 of 820 NAS (including two in Crowsnest AEW configuration) and three 847 NAS Wildcat HMA.2 for Operation Firedrake in northern European waters.

The ships have been dogged by flooding and propeller shaft coupling issues which have been highlighted in the media, becoming the focus of despair and mockery (as has the 'carriers without aircraft' jibe). Declared fully operational in October 2021, *Prince of Wales* took over as Flagship of NATO's maritime high readiness force on 1 January 2022, spending the year on a series of exercises in the

Return of the Sea Vixen?

Project Vixen was revealed on 24 March 2021 to evaluate the use of fixed-wing, maritime, uncrewed air systems (MUAS) (the MoD's latest parlance for naval UAVs) for persistent wide area surveillance, air-to-air refuelling, electronic warfare and strike. The MUAS will be capable of carrying two 1,100lb (500kg) modular payloads.

A Request For Information was issued the same month for the supply and fitting of electromagnetic catapults (EMALS) and arrester gear within five years, capable of launching and recovering MUAS up to maximum weights of 55,000lb (24,950kg) and 47,000lb (21,320kg) respectively. It is a remarkable sign of progress when you consider that this system is intended as a secondary installation for UAVs when the Mk.10 arrester gear of 1946 was rated at 20,000lb (9,070kg) for frontline fighters and strike aircraft.

The first fixed-wing UAV take-off was by a QinetiQ Banshee Jet 80+ (a modified target drone) from Prince of Wales in September 2021 as part of Project Vampire, an evaluation of how lightweight fixed-wing MUAS can be integrated onto the carriers. The Banshee can carry a sensor or weapon payload and is recovered by parachute. It has a maximum speed of 388kt, over 45 minutes endurance and an altitude range of 16–30,000ft (5–9,144m). The MoD opened a tender process in January 2022 to acquire four fixed-wing MUAS, a launcher and a control station with future options for up to 10 more MUAS and two launchers.

Project Vixen became entwined with the RAF's Lightweight Affordable Novel Combat Aircraft (LANCA) programme and its Spirit Mosquito technology demonstrator (the RAF envisioned operating Project Mosquito from the *Queen Elizabeth*-class). Hopes for a common solution were dashed when the MoD cancelled Project Mosquito on 24 June 2022 in favour of more cost-effective solutions, although what these were was not stated by the MoD.

Project Ark Royal was announced on 24 May 2023 during the Combined Naval Event 2023 conference at Farnborough. The project aims to explore the widespread operation of MUAS from the RN's warships. The objective is to enable the operation of high-performance strike and support MUAS – termed the Future Maritime Aviation Force (FMAF) – with a phased introduction of launching and recovery equipment, progressing from STOVL to STOL, STOBAR and finally CTOL operations using EMALS and arrester gear. The FMAF will use open data architectures with a Naval Strike Network to provide common communication and data-sharing infrastructure across the fleet.

Proteus is rotary-winged MUAS, being funded under the Spearhead programme for ASW capable of carrying two 1,100lb (500kg) modular payloads. It is intended to evolve

The General Atomics Mojave during its trial off the US East Coast on 15 November 2023 aboard HMS *Prince of Wales*. The Mojave was the largest UAV to have been operated from an RN carrier to date. *MOD/Open Government Licence*

from the Maritime Intra-Theatre Lift logistics role to submarine detection, reconnaissance and armed roles including dropping lightweight homing torpedoes. It may even provide a replacement for Crowsnest. Leonardo was awarded a 4-year, £60 million contract to build a demonstrator, first flight of which was scheduled in 2025.

Other FMAF assets include Peregrine, the Schiebel S-100 Camcopter for warships operating in the Persian Gulf under the Future Tactical Uncrewed Air System (FUTAS) programme, and Panther – the Uncrewed Aerial System Heavy Lift Challenge (UASHLC) – for a ship-to-ship and ship-to-shore logistics MUAS. Tests were carried out on seven contenders at Predannack airfield in March 2023 and aboard the replenishment tanker RFA Tideforce.

Prince of Wales began a series of trials in September 2023, beginning with the British-built W Autonomous Systems WAS, a twin-engine, twin-boom aircraft capable of carrying 200lb (100kg) of cargo over 540nm (1,000km) for Carrier Onboard Delivery (COD). Off the US East Coast on 15 November 2023, *Prince of Wales* performed a take-off and landing of a General Atomics Mojave – at that time the largest and heaviest UAV to be operated from a non-USN carrier. The Mojave has been developed from the MQ-1C Gray Eagle. It has an endurance of over 25 hours and is capable of carrying reconnaissance equipment or up to 3,600lb (1,600kg) of weapons on its seven hardpoints, including up to 16 AGM-114 Hellfire or AGM-179 Joint Air-to-Ground Missile (JAGM) ASMs. It can take off and land within 300ft (90m) and does not need carrier arrester gear in calm conditions.

Project Vixen seems to be continuing at a slow pace; recent MoD presentations have used the Boeing Australia MQ-28 Ghost Bat UCAV with an arrester hook as a placeholder image. The plan is for Vixen to carry two 1,100lb (500kg) modular payloads. The requirements may be fulfilled by an existing design or a new development. Whatever the case, it will be the 2030s before Vixen reaches service.

The future of naval airpower? This QinetiQ Banshee Jet 80+ target drone was launched and recovered aboard HMS *Prince of Wales* in September 2021 as part of Project Vampire to investigate the operation of unmanned aerial vehicles from the aircraft carriers. *MOD/Open Government Licence*

The F-35B requires the piloting skill of vertical landing, just like the Sea Harrier did. The advanced of cockpit controls give a true 'throttle and stick' intuitive control system that does not require a third control input to reduce cockpit workload and potential handling errors. This F-35B Lightning of No. 617 Squadron is landing aboard HMS *Queen Elizabeth* during the WESTLANT 19 deployment. *MOD/Open Government Licence*

Arctic, Baltic, Mediterranean and western Atlantic. On 12 February 2024, *Prince of Wales* sailed to Norwegian waters for Exercise Steadfast Defender, replacing *Queen Elizabeth* which was suffering from propeller shaft problems. Carrier Strike Group 25 saw *Prince of Wales* embarking 24 F-35Bs (the largest deployment of the Lightning so far) leaving Portsmouth on 22 April 2025 for another Far East cruise, including visits to India and Japan.

As impressive as these deployments have been, there are still issues with the air wing. The Crowsnest AEW upgrade is yet to be declared fully operational, so too has the Wildcat's anti-ship capability with Sea Venom and Martlet ASMs. These are likely be attained during 2025, and demonstrated during the 2025 deployment. Full 'Carrier Enabled Power Projection' capability with two squadrons of F-35Bs is expected during 2026, nearly 30 years after the original CVF and Joint Force 2000 plans.

The F-35B Lightning is a controversial aircraft for many reasons, but there is no denying that it is the most advanced military aircraft to operate aboard an RN carrier and will serve until 2069 at least, if not beyond. This Lightning is ZM159, which was delivered to the UK in October 2021. *MOD/Open Government Licence*

Lightning ZM156 starts its take-off run with the lift fan running during Exercise ACHILLEAN aboard HMS *Queen Elizabeth* in 2023. *MOD/Open Government Licence*

By 2060 its likely that replacement studies for the Lightning and the carriers will be underway and the Merlin will have been retired in the 2040s. Crystal ball gazing is perhaps fruitless given the advent of unmanned combat aircraft and the threats from hypersonic anti-ship missiles, but it is a fair bet that the RN will operate an aircraft carrier of some form. *MOD/Open Government Licence*

WINGS OVER THE FLEET

Appendix One

Royal Navy Aircraft Carriers & Helicopter Ships

This appendix outlines the careers of the Royal Navy's aircraft carriers, helicopter carriers, dedicated helicopter training vessels and maintenance carriers from 1946 to the present day.

Illustrious Class

HMS *Illustrious*
Pennant: R87
Deck Identification Letter: D
Builder: Vickers-Armstrong, Barrow-in-Furness; laid down 27.04.1937, launched 05.04.1939, commissioned 25.05.1940.
History: assigned as trials carrier from 24.06.1946; refit and modernisation 01-08.1948; troop transport to Cyrus 11.1951; mirror landing sight trials 1953; entered reserve 12.1954, decommissioned 28.02.1955; sold for scrapping 03.11.1956.
Squadrons: A&AEE 'C' Squadron 08.1948-54; 1830 NAS (Firefly) 27.08-10.09.1949; 802 (Sea Fury) & 814 (Firefly) 07.1951; 814 (Firefly) 10.1951; 824, No. 4 & No. 860 Sqn Royal Netherlands Naval Aviation Service (RNNAS) (Sea Fury & Firefly) 01-25.09.1952; 824 & No. 4 Sqn RNNAS (Firefly) 16.06.1953; 801 (Sea Fury) 1953; 751 (Avenger ECM) 08-10.1953.

HMS *Victorious*
Pennant: R38
Deck Identification Letter: S (1946-47), Y (1947-48), V (1948-68)
Builder: Vickers-Armstrong, Newcastle upon Tyne; laid down 04.05.1937, launched 14.09.1939, commissioned 15.05.1941.
History: returned to UK 27.10.45, repatriation trooping duties, into reserve at Devonport 15.01.1947; refitted as training ship, joined Home Fleet Training Squadron 01.10.1947, refit at Rosyth 1949; reconstruction with 8° angled deck and 2× BS.4 steam catapults at Portsmouth Dockyard 1950-58, recommissioned 14.01.1958; Operation Vantage to support Kuwait 07.1961; to Far East Fleet 1961, Sunda Strait Crisis caused by the ship sailing through the Sunda Strait 27.08.1964 sparking diplomatic protest from Indonesia; second Far East deployment 04.1966-06.1967; minor fire following refit on 11.11.1967, recommissioning cancelled and instead decommissioned 13.03.1968; sold for scrapping, towed to Faslane 13.07.1969.
Squadrons: 701C NAS (Dragonfly) 11.1957-07.1958; 803 (Scimitar), 824 (Whirlwind HAS.7), 849B (Skyraider AEW), 893 (Sea Venom) & Ship's Flt (Whirlwind) 26.09.1958-13.01.1959 & 21.02-23.03.1959; 831B (Sea Venom ECM.22) 11.1958-12.1958; 803, 824, 849B & Ship's Flt 04.05-22.07.1959; 894 Detachment 6 (Sea Venom) 09-22.06 & 30.06-09.08.1959; 803, 824, 831B, 849B, 894 & Ship's Flt 15.09-14.12.1959; 893 15.09-01.10 & 30.10-14.12.1959; 892B (Sea Vixen) 13-23.10.1959; 803, 805 (Sea Venom), 825 (Whirlwind), 831A (Gannet ECM), 849B, 893 & Ship's Flt 25.01-22.02.1960; 803, 825, 849B (Gannet AEW), 892 (Sea Vixen) & Ship's Flt 21.10-18.12.1960, 30.01-11.12.1961 (892 left 08.12) & 30.01-30.03.1962 (892 rejoined 09.02); 801 (Buccaneer), 814 (Wessex), 849A (Gannet AEW), 893 (Sea Vixen) & Ship's Flt 14.08.1963-22.07.1965, 14.05-08.06.1966 & 08.07.1966-13.06.1967.

HMS *Formidable*
Pennant: 67
Deck Identification Letter: R (1946-47)
Builder: Harland & Wolff, Belfast; laid down 17.06.1937, launched 17.08.1939, commissioned 24.11.1940.
History: repatriation trooping duties 1946; into reserve 1947, survey reveals poor material condition, decommissioned 12.08.1949; sold for scrapping 01.1953.

HMS *Indomitable*
Pennant: 92
Deck Identification Letter: A
Builder: Vickers-Armstrong, Barrow-in-Furness; laid down 10.11.1937, launched 26.03.1940, commissioned 10.10.1941.
History: returned to UK 11.1945; into reserve 1947, refit 1947-50; becomes Home Fleet Flagship 1951; damaged by internal fire and explosion 03.02.1953; prototype mirror landing sight trials 06.1953; modernisation rebuild cancelled, to unmaintained reserve 10.1953; sold for scrapping, arrived Faslane 30.09.1955.
Squadrons: 11th CAG: 857 NAS (Avenger), 1839 & 1844 (Hellcat) 25.07.1944-11.1945; 801 (Sea Fury) 1951-52; 802 (Sea Fury) 1952; 809 (Sea Hornet NF.21) 1952.

Implacable Class

HMS *Implacable*
Pennant: 86
Deck Identification Letter: C
Builder: Fairfield, Govan, Clydebank; laid down 21.03.1939, launched 10.12.1941, commissioned 28.08.1944.
History: repatriation trooping duties in Far East, returned to UK 03.06.1946; deck landing training carrier for Home Fleet 08.1946; refit 04 to 10.1947; to reserve 09.1950; refitted as training ship, recommissioned as Flagship of Home Fleet Training Squadron 16.01.1952; modernisation rebuild cancelled 06.1952; troopship to British Guiana 10.1953; relieved as Flagship by HMS Theseus 19.08.1954, decommissioned 01.09.1954; sold for scrapping 10.1955, scrapping begun 03.11.1955.
Squadrons: 8th CAG: 801 & 800 NAS (Seafire), 828 (Avenger) & 1771 (Firefly) 30.06.1945-04.1946; 719 (Barracuda) 24-31.10.1946; 794 (Seafire) 13.08-01.10, 22-31.10 & 7-15.11.1946; 795 (Firefly) 13.08-05.11.1946 & 14.01-24.03.1947; 813 (Firebrand) 10.1947-07.1950; 801 (Sea Hornet) 03.1948-07.1950; 733 (Seafire) 18-25.03.1949 & 26-31.03.1950; 702 (Sea Vampire) 09-11.1949; 815 (Barracuda) 05-06.1950.

HMS *Indefatigable*
Pennant: 10
Deck Identification Letter: none
Builder: John Brown, Govan, Clydebank; laid down 03.11.1939, launched 08.12.1942, commissioned 03.05.1944.
History: returned to UK 16.03.1946, used as transport to Australia and Far East, decommissioned 12.1946; refit as training ship, recommissioned 28.05.1950; decommissioned 10.1954; sold for scrapping 09.1956.
Squadrons: 7th CAG: 894 NAS (Seafire) 27.02.1945-15.03.1946.

APPENDIX ONE

Unicorn Class

HMS *Unicorn*
Pennant: I72
Deck Identification Letter: U
Builder: Harland & Wolff, Belfast; laid down 29.06.1939, launched 20.11.1941, commissioned 12.03.1943.
History: maintenance aircraft carrier, returned to UK 01.1946, into reserve; recommissioned 1949 to support HMS *Triumph* 1949, replenishment carrier for Korean operations 07-1950-15.10.1953, including only carrier to carry out a shore bombardment with guns; arrived in UK 17.11.1953, into reserve; rebuilding with single-level hangar and steam catapult cancelled 11.1952, redesignated as ferry carrier 06.1953; reduced to extended reserve 03.1957; sold for scrapping 06.1959.

Ark Royal Class

HMS *Eagle* (ex-*Audacious*)
Pennant: R05
Deck Identification Letter: J (1951-58), E (1958-72)
Builder: Harland & Wolff, Belfast; laid down 24.10.1942 (as *Audacious*), launched 19.03.1946 (as *Eagle*), commissioned 01.10.1951.
History: sea trials begun 31.10.1951, initial flying trials begun 14.02.1952, accepted into service 01.03.1952, assigned to Home Fleet; to Mediterranean Fleet 02-05.1954; refit with 5.5° angled deck 06.1954-02.1955; to Mediterranean Fleet 05.1956, Operation MUSKETEER deployment to Suez 11.1956; refit with 8.5° angled deck and 2x BS.4 steam catapults at Devenport Dockyard 1959-05.1964; to Far East Fleet, Beria Patrol 02-05.1966; refit including DAX.1 prototype arrester gear 1966-67; refit to fully operate Phantoms cancelled 1970, decommissioned 26.01.1972; into reserve, moored in Rover Tamar (later Devonport) and stripped for parts to keep HMS *Ark Royal* operational; sold for scrapping, towed to Cairnryan 14.10.1978.
Squadrons: 890 NAS (Attacker) 10-12.1952; 800 (Attacker) 01.1953-05.1954; 809 (Sea Hornet NF.21) 01.1953-01.1954; 812 & 814 (Firefly) 01-10.1953; 827 NAS (Firebrand) 01-10.1953; 849A (Skyraider AEW) 01.1953-03.1959; 849C (Skyraider AEW) 06-10.1953; 815 (Avenger) 01.1954-05.1954; 825 (Firefly) 01.1954-05.1954; 849B (Skyraider AEW) 01-05.1954; 803 (Attacker) 02-04.1954; 806 NAS (Sea Hawk) 02.1954-05.1954; 802 (Sea Hawk) 05.1955; 804 (Sea Hawk) 05-11.1955; 813 & 827 (Wyvern) 05-11.1955; 826 (Gannet) 05-11.1955; 897 & 899 (Sea Hawk) 04.1956-01.1957; 812 (Gannet) 04.1956-01.1957; 830 (Wyvern) 04.1956-01.1957; 892 & 893 (Sea Venom) 08-12.1956; 803 & 806 (Sea Hawk) 08-11.1957; 813 (Wyvern) 08.1957-03.1958; 814 (Gannet) 08.1957-04.1959; 894 (Sea Venom) 08.1957-04.1959; 898 (Sea Hawk) 05.1958-04.1959; 701A (Whirlwind) 05-12.1958; 800 (Buccaneer) 12.1964-01.1972; 800B (Scimitar) 12.1964-08.1965; 820 (Wessex) 12.1964-12.1970; 849A (Gannet AEW & COD) 08.1965-08.1966; 899 (Sea Vixen) 08.1965-04.1969; 849D (Gannet AEW & COD) 06.1967-01.1972; 826 (Sea King) 01.1972-01.1972.

HMS *Ark Royal*
Pennant: R09
Deck Identification Letter: O (1955-59), R (1959-78)
Builder: Cammell Laird, Birkenhead; laid down 03.05.1943, launched 03.05.1950, commissioned 25.02.1955.
History: assigned to Mediterranean 05.1955; refit at Portsmouth 30.04.1956-01.11.956; repairs due to engine problems 02-

HMS *Eagle* at Cape Town in South Africa on 13 September 1969. *Terry Panopalis Collection*

HMS *Ark Royal* during its final refit in September 1977. *Terry Panopalis Collection*

04.1957; refit at Devonport 21.07.1958-28.12.1959; P.1127 trials 1963; refit at Devonport to remove guns and engine repairs 02-11.1964; Beria Patrol 03.1965 to 02.1966; refit to operate Phantoms 1967-02.1970; collision with Soviet destroyer *Bravyy* in the Mediterranean 09.11.1970; show of force over British Honduras (Belize) 01.1972; documentary series Sailor filmed aboard ship 02 to 07.1976, United States Bicentennial at Fort Lauderdale, Florida 04.1976; laid up at Devonport 04.12.1978, decommissioned 14.02.1979; sold for scrapping, towed to Cairnryan 22.09.1980.
Squadrons: 800 NAS (Sea Hawk) 27.09-24.10.1955 & 17.02-26.03.1956; 898 (Sea Hawk) 28.09.1955-06.03.1956; 824 (Gannet), 849B (Skyraider AEW) & Ship's Flt (Whirlwind) 05.10.1955-05.04.1956; 891 (Sea Venom) 07.01-26.03.1956; 815 (Gannet), 831 (Wyvern), 849B & Ship's Flt 09.01-25.02.1957; 804 (Sea Hawk) 04-28.02.1957; 893 (Sea Venom) 05-25.02.1957; 898 (Sea Hawk) 09.01-25.02.1957; 802, 804 & 898 (Sea Hawk), 815, 849B, 893 & Ship's Flt 06.05-18.07-1957 (898 left 28.06), 30.08-28.11.1957; 800, 802, 804, 815, 849B, 893 & Ship's Flt (Dragonfly) 27.01-25.06.1958; 831 (Sea Venom ECM.22) 1958; 800 & 807 (Scimitar), 820 (Whirlwind), 849A (Gannet AEW), 892A (Sea Vixen) & Ship's Flt (Whirlwind) 03.03-30.09.1960; 800, 807, 824 (Whirlwind), 849A, 893 & Ship's Flt 26.10.1960-27.02.1961;

371

WINGS OVER THE FLEET

800, 815 (Wessex), 849C (Gannet AEW), 890 (Sea Vixen) & Ship's Flt 13.11.1961-10.01.1962, 10.03-14.12.1962, 19-28.02.1963 & 04.05-31.12.1963; A&AEE 'C' Squadron (Buccaneer) 02.1963; 801 (Buccaneer) 07-19.03.1963; 803 (Scimitar), 819 (Wessex), 849C (Gannet AEW & COD), 890 & Ship's Flt 23.01-16.03.1965; 803, 815 (Wessex), 849C, 890 & Ship's Flt 17.06.1965-13.06.1966, 02-25.08.1966 & 20.09-01.10.1966; 809 (Buccaneer), 824 (Sea King), 849B (Gannet AEW & COD), 892 NAS (Phantom) & Ship's Flt (Wessex) 14.06-09.07.1970, 09-26.09.1970, 15.04-14.08 1971, 15.09-08.10.1971, 29.10-06.12.1971, 19.01-08.03.1972, 12.06-17.07.1972, 04.09-18.10.1972, 07.11-11.12.1972, 09.02-14.03.1973, 02.05-24.07.1973, 06-17.06.1974, 03-25.07.1974, 05.09-03.11.1974, 08.01-09.06.1975, 06.10-20.11.1975, 06.02-14.07.1976, 04.09.18.10.1976, 05.09-12.12.1977, 23.02-05.03.1978 & 06.04-15.12.1978.

Colossus Class

HMS Colossus
Pennant: 15
Deck Identification Letter: none
Builder: Vickers-Armstrong, Newcastle upon Tyne; laid down 01.06.1942, launched 30.09.1943, commissioned 16.11.1944.
History: refitted at Simonstown, South Africa 17.01 to 26.03.1946; loaned to France as Arromanches 1946, purchased in 1951; decommissioned 22.01.1974, scrapped 1978.

HMS Glory
Pennant: R62
Deck Identification Letter: R
Builder: Harland & Wolff, Belfast; laid down 27.08.1942, launched 27.11.1943, commissioned 02.04.1945.
History: repatriation trooping duties in Far East and to Canada, returned to UK 1947, into reserve; recommissioned 12.1950; Korea deployments 23.04-30.09.1951, 27.01-05.05.1952 & 08.11.1952-19.05.1953; redesignated as ferry carrier and troop transport 1954; decommissioned 06.1956; sold for scrapping 1961.
Squadrons: 16th CAG: 837 NAS (Firefly NF.1) & 1831 (Corsair) 1945-1946; 801 (Sea Fury) & 812 (Firefly) 1951; 898 (Sea Fury) 21.07-15.08.1952; 804 (Sea Fury) & 812 01.1952-12.1953; 849C (Skyraider AEW) 30.11-16.12.1953.

HMS Ocean
Pennant: R68
Deck Identification Letter: O
Builder: Stephen & Sons, Glasgow; laid down 08.11.1942, launched 08.07.1943, commissioned 08.08.1945.
History: refit to operate night fighters 11.1945; first carrier jet landing by Vampire 03.12.1945; to Mediterranean Fleet 12.1945; troopship to Singapore 06.1946, part of task force for withdrawal from Palestine 05.1948; Korea deployments 05.05-08.11.1952 and 17.05-31.10.1953; to Home Fleet Training Squadron 08.1954; Operation Musketeer deployment to Suez 11.1956 as commando carrier; into extended reserve 1958; sold for scrapping 1960.
Squadrons: 805 NAS (Seafire), 892 (Hellcat) & 816 (Firefly NF.1) 22-29.11.1945, 07-.12.1945-04.01.1946 & 18.02-16.04.1946; 1702 Detachment 3 (Sea Otter) 25.07-12.09.1946; 898 (Sea Fury) 24.07-03.08.1951, 12.09-12.10.1951, 12.11.1951-26.02.1952 & 09.12.1952-01.01.1953; 802 (Sea Fury) & 825 (Firefly) 1952; 807 (Sea Fury) & 810 (Firefly) 1953; 845 (Whirlwind) 06-10.1956 & 01.1957; JEHU (Whirlwind & Sycamore) 19.10-31.12.1956.

HMS Venerable
Pennant: R63
Deck Identification Letter: none
Builder: Cammell Laird, Birkenhead; laid down 03.12.1942, launched 30.12.1943, commissioned 17.01.1945.
History: repatriation trooping duties in Far East; refit at Garden Island, Sydney 01-02.1946; returned to UK 26.03.1947, decommissioned 01.04.1947; acquired by the Netherlands 01.04.1948, commissioned as HNLMS Karel Doorman 28.05.1948; acquired by Argentina 15.10.1968, commissioned as ARA Veinticinco de Mayo 12.03.1969, Harrier demonstration 09.1969; scrapped in India in 2000.
Squadrons: 15th CAG: 814 NAS (Barracuda) & 1851 (Corsair) 06.03.1945-07.06.1946.

HMS Vengeance
Pennant: R71
Deck Identification Letter: Q
Builder: Swan Hunter, Tyne and Wear; laid down 16.11.1942, launched 23.02.1944, commissioned 15.01.1945.
History: returned to UK 13.08.1946; assigned as training carrier; to 3rd Aircraft Carrier Squadron, Home Fleet in early 1948; Operation Rusty Arctic operational trial 05.02-08.03.1949; loaned to Australia as HMS Vengeance 01.1952, commissioned 13.11.1952; returned to UK 13.08.1955, not reactivated; acquired by Brazil 14.12.1956, reconstruction in the Netherlands with 8.5° angled deck and 1× BS.4 steam catapult 1957-60, commissioned as Minas Gerais 06.12.1960; decommissioned 16.10.2001; scrapped in India from 07.2004.
Squadrons: 13th CAG: 1850 NAS (Corsair) 25.02.1945-12.08.1946; 1851 (Corsair) 11.06-13.08.1946; 802 (Seafire) 09.1946-03.1947; 733 (Seafire) 26-30.03.1950; 801 (Sea Fury) 05.1951; 809 (Sea Hornet NF.21) 05-08.1951 & 1952; 1830 (Firefly) 02-13.07.1951.

HMS Warrior
Pennant: R31
Deck Identification Letter: J (1948-49)
Builder: Harland & Wolff, Belfast; laid down 12.12.1942, launched 20.05.1944, commissioned 02.04.1945.
History: loaned to Canada as HMCS Warrior, commissioned 24.01.1946, returned to UK 20.02.1948; recommissioned 23.03.1948; refit for Flexible Deck at Devonport Dockyard, trials 11.1948-03.1949; into reserve 03.1949; reactivated as ferry carrier and troop transport 06.1950, deployment to Korea 08.1950, deployment to Cyprus 06.1951; refit at Devonport Dockyard 1952-53; to Far East Fleet for Korea armistice patrols 1954; refit at Devonport Dockyard with 5° angled deck for trials 1955, redesignated as training and trials ship; headquarters ship for Operation Grapple H-Bomb tests at Christmas Island 1956-57; decommissioned 02.1958; acquired by Argentina, renamed ARA Independencia 06.08.1958, commissioned 08.06.1959; into reserve 1970; sold for scrapping 1971.
Squadrons: A&AEE 'C' Squadron 1948-49; 811 NAS (Sea Fury) 1953-54; 825 (Firefly) 1953.

HMS Theseus
Pennant: R64
Deck Identification Letter: T
Builder: Fairfield, Govan, Glasgow; laid down 06.01.1943, launched 06.07.1944, commissioned 09.02.1946.
History: commissioned as a trials carrier; assigned as Flagship for

the Flag Officer Air, Far East, became Flagship of the 1st Aircraft Carrier Squadron, British Pacific Fleet in 1947; returned to UK, to 3rd Aircraft Carrier Squadron Home Fleet; Korea deployment 07.1950-01.1952; return to UK, becomes Flagship 2nd Aircraft Carrier Squadron, Home Fleet, becomes Flagship of Home Fleet in 1952, deployed to Mediterranean to relieve HMS Glory 1952; Operation MUSKETEER deployment to Suez 11.1956 as commando carrier; into reserve 1957; sold for scrapping 1960.
Squadrons: 794 NAS (Seafire) 21-31.05.1946; 804 (Seafire), 812 (Firefly) & Ship's Flt (Sea Otter) 21.02-14.12.1947; 733 (Seafire) 21.01-05.02.1949; 807 NAS (Sea Fury) & 810 (Firefly) 14.08.1950-27.05.1951; 807, 814 (Firefly) & Ship's Flt (Hoverfly) 14.10-06.12.1951; 898 (Sea Fury) 26.02-09.04 1952, 21.04-15.05.1952 & 15.10-28.11.1952; JEHU (Whirlwind & Sycamore) 30.09-14.10.1956; 845 (Whirlwind) 14.10-21.12.1956.

HMS Triumph
Pennant: R16
Deck Identification Letter: P
Builder: Hawthorne Leslie, Hebburn; laid down 27.01.1943, launched 01.10.1944, commissioned 09.05.1946.
History: visit to Kronstadt, USSR 26.07.1946; to 2nd Aircraft Carrier Squadron, Mediterranean Fleet 02.1947, return to UK 08.1948; to Far East Fleet and cruise to Japan 06.1950, Korea deployment 25.06.1950-29.09.1950; return to UK, assigned as cadet training ship 1951, has 3× Boulton Paul Sea Balliol trainers aboard for air-mindedness training; angled deck trials with repainted deck markings 1952; reconstruction to heavy repair ship 1956-65, recommissioned with pennant A108; to Far East Fleet; into reserve at Chatham 1975; stricken 1981, sold for scrapping in Spain 12.1981.
Squadrons: 800 NAS (Seafire) & 827 (Firefly) 05-09.1950.

HMS Pioneer (ex-Mars)
Pennant: R76
Deck Identification Letter: none
Builder: Vickers-Armstrong, Barrow-in-Furness; laid down 02.12.1942 (as Mars), launched 20.05,1944, commissioned 08.02.1945 (as Pioneer).
History: completed as maintenance aircraft carrier; returned to UK 17.02.1946, into reserve; sold for scrapping 09.1954.

HMS Perseus (ex-Edgar)
Pennant: R51
Deck Identification Letter: none
Builder: Vickers-Armstrong, Newcastle upon Tyne; laid down 12.12.1942 (as Edgar), launched 20.05.1944, commissioned 02.04.1945 (as Perseus).
History: completed as maintenance aircraft carrier; arrived in Australia 21.12.1945, returned to UK 17.05.1946, placed in reserve; refitted with prototype BXS.1 steam catapult, trials 1950-52; refit to ferry carrier 1952, delivered 848 NAS Whirlwind HAR.1 to Singapore 08.01.1953, delivered MDAP order of Avengers from USA to UK; Whirlwind HAS.7 trials 20.01.1954, ferried unit to Malta 04.1954; into reserve 13.07.1954; towed to Belfast for submarine depot ship conversion in 1955, conversion cancelled 04.1957; sold for scrapping 05.1958.
Squadron: A&AEE 'C' Squadron 1950; 848 NAS (Whirlwind) 12.12.1952-08.01.1953; 706 NAS (later renumbered 845) (Whirlwind) 20.01 & 21.04-07.1954.

Majestic Class

HMS Majestic/HMAS Melbourne
Pennant: R77 (as Majestic), R21 (as Melbourne)
Deck Identification Letter: Y
Builder: Vickers-Armstrong, Barrow-in-Furness; laid down 15.04.1943, launched 28.02.1945, commissioned 28.10.1955 (as Melbourne)
History: acquired by Australia in 06.1947, completed to a modified design with 5.5° angled deck and 1× BS.1 steam catapult (3rd carrier in the world built with these features); decommissioned 30.06.1982, towed to China for scrapping 27.05.1985.

HMS Terrible/HMAS Sydney
Pennant: 93 (as Terrible), R17 (as Sydney)
Deck Identification Letter: K (as Sydney)
Builder: HM Dockyard Devonport; laid down 19.08.1943, launched 30.09.1944, commissioned 16.12.1948 (as HMAS Sydney)
History: acquired by Australia in 06.1947; entered operational service 05.02.1949; converted as Fast Troop Transport (A214) 1961-62; decommissioned 12.11.1973, towed to China for scrapping 23.12.1975 (was studied by the People's Liberation Army Navy, possibly not fully scrapped until the 2000s).

HMS Magnificent/HMCS Magnificent
Pennant: CVL 21 (as HMCS Magnificent)
Deck Identification Letter: CVL 21
Builder: Harland & Wolff, Belfast; laid down 29.07.1943, launched 16.11.1944, commissioned 21.03.1948 (as HMCS Magnificent).
History: loaned to Canada as HMCS Magnificent, completed with modifications for cold climate operations; decommissioned at Plymouth 14.06.1957, returned to RN, into reserve; placed on disposal list in 1961, sold for scrapping in 1965.

HMS Hercules/INS Vikrant
Pennant: R49 (planned)
Deck Identification Letter: none
Builder: Vickers-Armstrong, Newcastle upon Tyne; laid down 14.10.1943, launched 22.09.1945.
History: construction suspended 05.1946, 75% complete, preserved and laid up in Gareloch; acquired by India 01.1957, completed to modified design by Harland & Wolff with angled deck and steam catapult, commissioned as INS Vikrant 04.03.1961; decommissioned 31.01.1997; sold for scrapping in 2014.

HMS Powerful/HMCS Bonaventure
Pennant:
Deck Identification Letter:
Builder: Harland & Wolff, Belfast; laid down 27.11.1943, launched 27.02.1945.
History: construction suspended 05.1946, acquired by Canada 23.04.1952; completed to modified design by Harland & Wolff with angled deck and steam catapult, commissioned as HMCS Bonaventure 17.01.1957; decommissioned 03.07.1970; sold for scrapping in Taiwan in 1971.

WINGS OVER THE FLEET

HMS *Hermes* in 1983 with its 12° ski-jump and with Sea Kings and Sea Harriers on the flight deck. *MOD/Open Government Licence*

HMS *Tiger* in July 1977. The two helicopter cruisers of this class sacrificed their aft 6in (152mm) Mk.26 gun turret (which had automatic loading for a rate of fire of 15–20 rounds per minute) for the hangar and helicopter deck. Two of the three 3in (76mm) L70 Mk.6 gun mounts were replaced by Sea Cat SAMs. *Terry Panopalis Collection*

Centaur Class

HMS *Centaur*
Pennant: R06
Deck Identification Letter: L (1953), C (1954-65)
Builder: Harland & Wolff, Belfast; laid down 30.05.1944, launched 22.04.1947, commissioned 01.09.1953.
History: assigned to Mediterranean Fleet 07.1954; Far East tour 10.01-15.05.1956; partial modernisation with 6° angled deck and 2× BS.4 steam catapults 06.1956-08.1958; recommissioned 03.09.1958; Far East tour 05.1959-06.1960; refit 09.1960-03.1961; Operation Vantage to support Kuwait 07.1961; Far East tour 10.1961-05.1962; refit 06-11.1963; Far East tour 12.1963-12.1964, deployed off Tanganyika coast in response to mutiny there 01.1964; decommissioned 27.09.1965; assigned as accommodation ship 1966-1970; sold for scrapping 11.08.1972.
Squadrons: 806 NAS (Sea Hawk), 810 (Sea Fury), 820 (Avenger) & Ship's Flt (Dragonfly) 20.07.1954-23.02.1955; 803 (Sea Hawk), 814 (Avenger); 751 (Avenger ECM) & Ship's Flt 15.03.-06.06.1955; 806 (Sea Hawk) 26.04-27.05.1955; 803, 806, 814 & Ship's Flt 31.08-04.11.1955; 801 & 811 (Sea Hawk), 820 (Gannet) & Ship's Flt 10.01-16.05.1956; 800 (Sea Hawk) & Ship's Flt 29.11-02.12.1958; 801 (Sea Hawk), 845 (Whirlwind), 849D (Skyraider AEW), 891 (Sea Venom) & Ship's Flt 23.01-23.03.1959, 29.04.1959-25.04.1960 & 14.06-22.07.1960; 807 (Scimitar), 824 (Whirlwind), 849A (Gannet AEW), 893 (Sea Vixen) & Ship's Flt 10.04-01.09.1961 & 20.10.1961-14.05.1962; 824, 849A, 893 & Ship's Flt (Whirlwind) 12.07-25.10.1962, 22.01-14.02.1963; 21.02-22.05.1963 & 25.05-06.06.1963; 815 (Wessex), 849B (Gannet AEW), 892 (Sea Vixen) & Ship's Flt 22.12.1963-20.12.1964 & 08.04-27.07.1965; No. 26 Sqn RAF (Belvedere) 21.01-02.1964.

HMS *Albion*
Pennant: R07
Deck Identification Letter: Z (1954-61), A (1962-71)
Builder: Swan Hunter, Tyne and Wear; laid down 23.03.1944, launched 06.05.1947, commissioned 26.05.1954.
History: assigned to Mediterranean Fleet 09.1954, assigned as Flagship Flag Officer Aircraft Carriers 10.1954; Operation Musketeer deployment to Suez 11.1956; refit as commando carrier 1961; deployed to Borneo 1962-65, earning nickname 'The Old Grey Ghost of the Borneo Coast'; deployed for withdrawal from Aden 1968; deployed for withdrawal from Singapore 03.1971-24.01.1972; decommissioned 02.03.1973; sold, heavy lift vessel conversion for North Sea oil exploration cancelled and scrapped instead at Faslane.
Squadrons: 803 NAS (Sea Hawk), 813 (Wyvern), 815 (Avenger), 849C (Skyraider AEW), 890 (Sea Venom) & Ship's Flt (Dragonfly) 17.09.1954-31.03.1955 (890 left 03.12.54, returned 22.03.55); 807 (Sea Hawk), 815, 849C, 890 & Ship's Flt 19.07-02.11.1955 (890 left 12.09, 815 left 13.10); 810 (Sea Hawk) & Ship's Flt (Whirlwind) 06.01-14.05.1956; 800 & 802 (Sea Hawk), 809 (Sea Venom), 849C (Skyraider AEW) & Ship's Flt 15.09.1956-05.03.1957 (800 left 28.10.56, returned 25.01.57); 800, 845 (Whirlwind), 809, 849C & Ship's Flt 16.04-01.06.1957; 800, 809, 849C & Ship's Flt 18.06-10.07.1957; 800, 802, 809, 849C & Ship's Flt 03.09-31.10.1957; 804 (Sea Hawk), 809, 824 (Gannet), 849C & Ship's Flt 07.07-15.09.1958 & 20.10.1958-17.08.1959; 820 (Whirlwind) 20.10.1958-17.08.1959; 806 (Sea Hawk), 815 (Whirlwind), 849D (Skyraider AEW), 894 (Sea Venom) & Ship's Flt 05.02-19,12.1960; 845 (Wessex) & 846 (Whirlwind) 02.11-14.12.1962 & ?.02-15.04.1964; 848 (Wessex HU.5) 12.03.1965-09.1966, 20.09-13.10.1968, 03.1970, 03-05.1971, 14.11.1971-20.01.1972 & 15.06-05.07.1972; 815 (Whirlwind) 05-07.1965; 845 (Wessex HU.5) 02.1971 & 07.1972-1973; 826 (Sea King) 23.11-12.1971.

HMS *Bulwark*
Pennant: R08
Deck Identification Letter: B
Builder: Harland & Wolff, Belfast; laid down 10.05,1945, launched 22.06,1948, commissioned 04.11.1954.
History: Operation Musketeer deployment to Suez 11.1956; refit as commando carrier 1958-1960; Operation Vantage to support Kuwait 07.1961; deployed to Borneo 1964-65; Kestrel V/STOL trials 1966; refit 1968; Far East tour 1970; deployed for withdrawal from Malta 1972; into reserve 03.1976, offered for sale to Peru; ASW carrier refit 1978, recommissioned 23.02.1979; boiler fire 15.03.1980; decommissioned 27.03.1981; surveyed during Falklands Conflict but could not be reactivated quickly enough; sold for scrapping 04.1983.

Squadrons: 751 NAS (Avenger), 807 & 811 (Sea Hawk) & Ship's Flt (Dragonfly & Avenger) 19.02-03.03.1955; 751, 811, 898 (Sea Hawk) & Ship's Flt 23.05-04.06.1955; 893 (Sea Venom) & Ship's Flt (Dragonfly) 08.01-20.06.1956; 899 (Sea Hawk) 31.01-10.02.1956; 804 (Sea Hawk) 23.06-01.07.1956 & 06.06-01.12.1956; 895 (Sea Hawk) 25.06-02.07.1956 & 03.08-17.12.1956; 810 (Sea Hawk) & Ship's Flt 06.08-17.12.1956; 801 (Sea Hawk), 820 (Gannet), 845 (Whirlwind), 849D (Skyraider AEW), 891 (Sea Venom) & Ship's Flt 25.06-05.08.1957 & 28.08-27.11.1957; 898 (Sea Hawk) 28.06-05.08.1957 & 01-25.11.1957; 801, 845, 849D, 891, 898 & Ship's Flt 12.01-11.1958 (894D left 27.10); 845 (Whirlwind) 28.08-21.10.1957 & 17.01-28.04.1958; 848 (Whirlwind) 14.03-30.05.1960 ; 825 (Whirlwind) 19.04.1961; 815 (Wessex) 04.1962; 845 (Wessex) & 846 (Whirlwind) 11-12.1962; 706B (Wessex) 01.1964; 845 (Wessex) 01.1964-08.65; 40 Commando Air Troop (Sioux) 02.03-04.1965; 845 (Wessex HU.5) 1966-70, 05-11.1971 & 19.05-07.1972; 848 (Wessex HU.5) 01-07.1970, 19.04.1974-1976; 3 CBAS (Sioux) 04-05.1973; 826 (Sea King HAS) 03.1979-1980; 846 (Sea King HU.4) 20.03.1979-02.1981; 820 (Sea King HAS) 03.1979-02.1981; 846 (Wessex HU.5) 01-04.1980.

HMS *Hermes* (ex-*Elephant*)
Pennant: R12
Deck Identification Letter: H
Builder: Vickers-Armstrong, Barrow-in-Furness; laid down 21.06.1944, launched 16.02.1953, commissioned 18.11.1959.
History: construction suspended in 1945, resumed in 1952 to clear the slipway, preserved and laid up; construction resumed to modified design 1957; Phantom trials 1969-70; offered to Australia in 1968 but rejected; refit as commando carrier 1971-73; refit to ASW carrier 1976; refit for Sea Harrier with 12° ski-jump 1980-06.1981; 12.04.1981; Operation CORPORATE deployment to Falklands as Task Force Flagship 05.04-21.07.1982; another offer to Australia declined in 1983; into reserve 11.1983; decommissioned 12.04.1984; acquired by India 04.1986, refitted and commissioned as INS *Viraat* 12.05.1987; decommissioned 06.03.2017; scrapped 2021.
Squadrons: 804 NAS (Scimitar), 814 (Whirlwind), 849C (Gannet AEW), 890 (Sea Vixen) & Ship's Flt (Dragonfly) 06.07.1960-05.09.1960 (890 left 24.08) & 15-29.09.1960; 719 (Whirlwind) 04-14.10.1960; 804, 814 (Whirlwind), 849C & Ship's Flt 07.11.1960-19.04.1961; 890 (Sea Venom) 11.11.1960-08.05.1961; 804, 849C, 890 & Ship's Flt 29.05-22.06.1961; 804, 814 (Whirlwind), 849C, 890 & Ship's Flt 30.06-24.07.1961 & 30.07-25.08.1961; 831 (Sea Venom ECM.22); 803 NAS (Scimitar), 814 (Wessex), 849B (Gannet AEW), 892 (Sea Vixen) & Ship's Flt (Whirlwind) 25.05.1962-01.10.1962, 12.11.1962-29.07.1963; 803, 819 (Wessex), 849B, 892 & Ship's Flt 26.09-22.10.1963; 803, 819 & Ship's Flt 27.12-02.1964; 809 (Buccaneer), 826 (Wessex), 849B, 892 & Ship's Flt (Wessex) 24.09-20.10.1966, 08-30.11.1966, 18.01-29.09.1967 & 01.11.1967-18.02.1968; 801 (Buccaneer), 814 (Wessex), 849A (Gannet AEW & COD), 893 (Sea Vixen) & Ship's Flt 31.05-20.06.1968, 09.07.1968-30.03.1969, 25.09-27.10.1969, 14.11-04.12.1969, 19.01-17.06.1970; 814 (Sea King) 08.1973-12.1979; 845 (Wessex HU.5) 08.1973-1977; 824 (Sea King) 22.09.1973-04.1974; 846 (Wessex HU.5) 06-07.1977; 820 (Sea King) 01-03.1980; 700A (Sea Harrier) 10-11.1979; 800 (Sea Harrier) 09.1981-11.83; 826 (Sea King) 09.1981-03.84; 845 (Wessex HU.5) 1981-84; 846 (Sea King HC.4) 1981-83; 899 detachment (Sea Harrier) & No.1 Sqn RAF (Harrier) 05.04-21.07.1982; 814 (Sea King HAS.2) 01-06.1983; 845 (Wessex HU.5) & 846 (Sea King HC.4) 09-11.1983.

Lofoten Class

HMS *Lofoten* (ex-L 3027)
Pennant: K07
Deck Identification Letter: LT
Builder: Blyth Drydock & Shipbuilding, Blyth; laid down 30.05.1944, launched 21.01.1945, commissioned 24.10.1945 (as L 3027).
History: completed as LST(3) Landing Ship Tank; into reserve; renamed HMS *Lofoten* 1947; Operation MUSKETEER deployment to Suez 11.1956; trials with landing Wessex 1963; refit as helicopter support and training ship 1964 with landing deck for 4-6× Wessex, recommissioned 23.06.1964; replaced by RFA *Engadine*, laid up 1969, assigned as accommodation ship for nuclear submarine crews at Rosyth; stricken 1991, sold for scrapping in Belgium 1993.

Engadine Class

RFA *Engadine*
Pennant: K08
Deck Identification Letter: EN
Builder: Henry Robb, Leith; laid down 09.08.1965, launched 16.09.1966, commissioned 15.12.1967.
History: helicopter support and training ship; designated as one of the PYTHON continuity of government vessels in the event of nuclear war; Sea King HAS.1 deck trials 02.07.1969; Lynx HAS.2 deck trials 29.06.1973; Falklands Conflict deployment 10.05-30.07.1982; refit to lengthen deck for 2nd Sea King landing spot; decommissioned 03.1989; sold to Greek owners but never entered service; scrapped in India 09.1996.
Squadrons: 706 NAS (Sea King) 02.1979-82; 847 (Wessex HU.5) 10.05-30.07.1982; 810 (Sea King) 02.1983-01.1989; 702 (Lynx) 11.1986 & 03.1988.

Tiger Class

HMS *Blake* (ex-*Tiger*, ex-*Blake*)
Pennant: C99
Deck Identification Letters: BL
Builder: Fairfield, Govan, Clydebank; laid down 17.08.1942, launched 20.12.1945, commissioned 08.03.1961
History: construction halted 07.1946 and restart announced 15.10.1954; laid up 1963. Conversion as helicopter cruiser began 1965, recommissioned 23.04.1969; decommissioned 06.12.1979; to Chatham following Rosyth refit for Reserve Fleet, surveyed during Falklands Conflict but could not be reactivated quickly enough; scrapping begun 29.10.1982.
Squadrons: 820 NAS (Wessex, Sea King from 1973) 05.1969-12.12.1979.

HMS *Tiger* (ex-*Bellerophon*)
Pennant: C24
Deck Identification Letters: TG
Builder: John Brown, Govan, Clydebank; laid down 01.10.1941, launched 25.10.1945, commissioned 18.03.1959
History: conversion as helicopter cruiser began 1968, recommissioned 02.07.1972. Decommissioned 20.04.1978, surveyed during Falklands Conflict but could not be reactivated quickly enough; towed for scrapping 23.09.1986.
Squadrons: 826 NAS (Sea King) 08.1972-20.04.1978; 820 (Sea King) 12.1974.

WINGS OVER THE FLEET

Royal Navy Fleet Carriers 1946-2025

Class	Illustrious Class			Implacable Class
Ship	HMS *Illustrious*	HMS *Victorious* (as reconstructed)	HMS *Indomitable*	HMS *Implacable* & *Indefatigable*
Displacement	29,110 tons deep load, 1945	35,500 tons deep load	29,730 tons deep load, 1945; 32,100 tons deep load, 1951	32,110 tons deep load, 1945; 32,820 tons deep load, 1951
Length	740ft (225.6m) overall; 710ft (216.4m) waterline	778ft 3in (237.2m) overall; 710ft (216.4m) waterline	753ft 11in (229.8m) overall; 710ft (216.4m) waterline	766ft 6in (233.6m) overall; 730ft (222.5m) waterline
Beam	95ft 9in (29.2m) hull; 106ft 9in (32.5m) overall	103ft (31.4m) over hull bulges	95ft 9in (29.2m) hull; 116ft 3in (35.4m) overall	95ft 9in (29.2m) hull, 114ft 5in (34.8m) overall
Draught	28ft 10in (8.8m) deep load	31ft 7in (9.6m)	28ft 10in (8.8m) deep load	29ft 4in (8.9m) deep load
Flight deck length/width	753 x 95ft (229.5 x 29m); 740ft (225.6m) usable length, 1944	775 x 145ft 9in (236.2 x 44.42m)	750 x 95ft (228.6 x 29m) overall; 745ft (227m) usable length, 1943	760 x 102ft (231.6 x 31.1m)
Flight deck type	Axial	8° angled	Axial	Axial
Catapults	1x BH.3 hydraulic, 20,000lb (9,070kg) at 56kt	2x BS.4 steam, 145ft (44m) bow & waist, 50,000lb (22,780kg) at 97kt	1x BH.3 hydraulic, 20,000lb (9,070kg) at 56kt	1x BH.3 hydraulic, 20,000lb (9,070kg) at 56kt
Arrester gear	Mk.4, 9x wires, 20,000lb (9,070kg) at 60kt, 1946; Mk.6*, 20,000lb at 62kt, 1950; Mk.6**, 20,000lb at 68kt, 1950	Mk.13, 4x wires, 30,000lb (16,605kg) at 112kt	Mk.4, 9x wires, 20,000lb (9,070kg) at 60kt, 1946	Mk.4, 9x wires, 20,000lb (9,070kg) at 60kt, 1946; Mk.6*, 20,000lb at 62kt, 1950; Mk.6**, 20,000lb at 68kt, Implacable 1950
Lifts	1946 refit: 2x 48ft 9in x 22ft 9in (14.8 x 6.9m); 24,000lb (10,885kg) capacity	1x 58 x 40ft (17.6 x 12.1m); 1x 54ft x 34ft (16.4 x 10.3m); 40,000lb (18,140kg) capacity	2x 45ft x 22ft (13.7 x 6.7m); 14,000lb (6,350kg) capacity	45ft x 33ft (13.7 x 10.1m) for upper hangar, 45ft x 22ft (13.7 x 6.7m) for lower hangar; 20,000lb (9,070kg) capacity
Hangar length/width/height	456 x 62 x 16ft (139 x 18.9m x 4.9m)	360 x 65ft 6in x 17ft 6in (109.7 x 19.9 x 5.3m)	456 x 62 x 14ft (139 x 18.9 x 4.3m) upper; 168 x 62 x 16ft (51.2 x 18.9 x 4.9m) lower	458 x 62 x 14ft (139.6 x 18.9 x 4.3m) upper; 208 x 62 x 16ft (63.4 x 18.9 x 4.9m) lower
Engines	6x Admiralty 3-drum boilers, 3x geared steam turbines, 111,000shp (82,770kW), 3x shafts	6x Foster-Wheeler boilers, 3x geared steam turbines, 111,000shp (82,770kW), 3x shafts	6x Admiralty 3-drum boilers, 3x geared steam turbines, 111,000shp (82,770kW), 3x shafts	8x Admiralty 3-drum boilers, 4x geared steam turbines, 148,000shp (110,360kW), 4x shafts
Max speed	29kt, by 1946	31kt	30.5kt	31.5kt
Range	10,700nm (19,815km) at 10kt	11,000nm (20,370km) at 14kt	10,000nm (18,520km) at 10kt	12,000nm (22,220km) at 10kt
Armour	4.5in (114mm) belt; 4.5in (114mm) hangar sides and ends; 3in (76mm) flight deck	4in (102mm) belt; 4in (102mm) hangar sides and ends; 3in (76mm) flight deck, 2in (51mm) hangar deck	4.5in (114mm) belt; 4.5in (114mm) hangar sides and ends; 3in (76mm) flight deck	4.5in (114mm) belt; 2in (51mm) hangar sides & ends and bulkheads; 3in (76mm) flight deck; 3-4.5in (76-114mm) magazines

APPENDIX ONE

1952 Design	Ark Royal Class		CVA-01	CVF/Queen Elizabeth Class
Project	HMS *Eagle*	HMS *Ark Royal*	Project	HMS *Queen Elizabeth* & *Prince of Wales*
53,150 tons deep load	36,880 tons standard, 1951; 43,060 tons standard, 1957; 54,100 tons standard, 1964	49,950 tons deep load, 1955; 53,340 tons deep load, 1966; 50,786 tons deep load, 1978	54,500 tons deep load	79,300 tons deep load
815ft (248.4m) overall	803ft 9in (244.9m) overall; 750ft (228.6m) waterline	803ft 9in (244.9m) overall; 845ft (257.5m) overall, including catapult bridle, 1970; 750ft (228.6m) waterline	963ft 3in (292.6m) overall, including catapult bridle; 925ft (281.9m) overall hull; 890ft (271.2m) waterline	932ft (284m)
116ft (35.3m) hull	112ft 9in (34.3m) hull, 135ft (41.1m) overall 1951; 171ft (52m) overall 1964	112ft 9in (34.3m) hull; 158ft (48.1m) overall 1955; 164ft 6in (50.1m) overall, 1966; 166ft (50.6m) overall, 1970	122ft (37.2m) hull; 231ft 4in (70.5m) overall	128ft (39m) hull; 240ft (73m) overall
33ft 6in deep load	33ft 1in (10.1m) 1951; 36ft (11m) 1964	34ft 8in (10.5m) deep load, 1955; 37ft (11.2m) deep load, 1970	32ft 2in (9.8m) mean	36ft (10m)
1,000 x 160ft (304.8 x 48.7m)	795 x 115ft (242.3 x 35m), 1951	800 x 112ft (243.8m x 34.1m), 1955; 171ft (52m), 1978	890ft (271.2m) x 189ft (57.6m)	918ft 6in (280m) x 229ft 6in (70m)
8.5° angled	Axial, 1951; 5.5° angled, 1954; 8.5° angled, 1964	5.5° angled; 8.5° angled, 1970	3° parallel deck	Axial, 12° ski-jump
2x BS.4 steam, 200ft (61m) & 150ft (46m), 60,000lb (27,200kg) capacity	2x BH.5 hydraulic, 30,000lb (16,605kg) at 82.5kt, 1951; 2x BS.4 steam, 151ft (46m) bow & waist, 50,000lb (22,780kg) at 91kt, 1954; 2x BS.4 steam, 151ft bow & 199ft (61m) waist, 50,000lb at 94-105kt, 1964	2x BS.4 steam, 151ft (46m) bow & waist, 50,000lb (22,780kg) at 91kt, 1955; 2x BS.5 steam, 151ft bow & 199ft (61m) waist, 50,000lb at 94-105kt, 1970	2x BS.6 steam, 250ft (76.2m), 60,000lb (27,200kg) at 150kt	N/A; electromagnetic catapult may be retrofitted for UAVs
45,000lb (20,410kg) capacity	Mk.10, 30,000lb (16,605kg) at 75kt, 8x wires, 1951; Mk.10*, 30,000lb at 75kt, 1955; Mk.13, 30,000lb at 120kt; Mk.14, 4x wires, 40,000lb (18,140kg) at 125kt	Mk.13, 6-4x wires, 30,000lb (16,605kg) at 120kt; 1967; DA.2, 4x wires, 40,000lb 18,140kg) at 125kt, 1970	DAG.1, 4x wires, 40,000lb (18,100kg) at 125kt	N/A; may be retrofitted for UAVs
2x deck edge lifts & 1x inboard; 60,000lb (27,215kg) capacity	1x 54 x 44ft (16.4 x 13.4m); 1x 54 x 33ft (16.4 x 10.1m); 40,000lb (18,140kg) capacity	1x 54 x 44ft (16.4 x 13.4m); 1x 54 x 33ft (16.4 x 10.1m); 1x 57ft 6in x 35ft (17.5 x 10.6m) deck edge (1955-58 only)	1x 70 x 35ft (21.3m x 10.7m) centreline; 1x 70 x 32ft (21.3 x 9.8m) deck edge; 70,000lb (31,750kg) capacity	2x 88ft 6in x 49ft 2in (27 x 15m) x 49ft 2in (15m) deck edge; 119,930lb (54,400kg) capacity
? x ? x 17ft 6in (5.3m)	364 x 67 x 17ft 6in (110.9 x 20.4 x 5.3m) upper; 364 x 54 x 17ft 6in (110.9 x 16.4 x 5.3m) lower, 1951; 172ft (52.4m) lower length, 1964	364 x 67 x 17ft 6in (110.9 x 20.4 x 5.3m) upper; 364 x 54 x 17ft 6in (110.9 x 16.4 x 5.3m) lower, 1955; 295ft (89.9m) lower length, 1958; 217ft (66.1m) lower length, 1970	670ft (204.2m) x 80ft (24.3m) x 18ft (5.49m)	508ft 6in (155m) x 111ft 6in (34m) x 22ft 11in to 33ft (7-10m)
4x YEAD.1 boiler and geared steam turbine units, 180,000shp (134,225kW), 4x shafts	8x Admiralty 3-drum boilers, 4x geared steam turbines, 152,000shp (113,340kW), 4x shafts	8x Admiralty 3-drum boilers, 4x geared steam turbines, 152,000shp (113,340kW), 4x shafts	6x high-pressure boilers, 3x geared steam turbines, 135,000shp (100,670kW), 3x shafts	2x Rolls-Royce Trent MT30 gas turbines, 48,000hp (36MW); 2x Wärtsilä 16V38 & 2x 12V38 diesel engines, 54,000hp (40MW); 4x GE Advanced Induction Motors, 27,000hp (20MW), 2x shafts
30kt	31.5kt	30.5kt	30kt	25+kt
5,215nm (9,655km) at 22kt	7,000nm (12,965km) at 18kt	7,000nm (12,965km) at 14kt, 5,000nm (9,260km) at 24kt	5,215nm (9,655km) at 20kt, 6 months out of dock	10,000nm (18,520km)
2in (51mm) belt; 2in (51mm) hangar sides; 2in (51mm) flight deck; 3.5in (89mm) magazines & steering compartment	4in (102mm) belt; 1in (25mm) hangar sides & deck; 1-4in (25-102mm) flight deck, 2.5in (63.5mm) from 1964	4in (102mm) belt; 1in (25mm) hangar sides & deck; 2.5in (63.5mm) flight deck	Use of structural steel for splinter protection: 1.25in (32mm) flight deck; 1.5in (38mm) over machinery; 1.5-2.5in (38-64mm) magazines & 2in (51mm) Sea Dart magazine; 1.5in (38mm) operations spaces	Classified, likely to be Kevlar or composite armour around command & engineering spaces and magazines

continued overleaf...

Royal Navy Fleet Carriers 1946-2025 (continued)

Class	Illustrious Class			Implacable Class
Ship	HMS *Illustrious*	HMS *Victorious* (as reconstructed)	HMS *Indomitable*	HMS *Implacable* & *Indefatigable*
Armament	8x2 4.5in (114mm) L/45 QF Mk.III dual-purpose guns; 6x8 2-pdr (40mm) 'Pom-Pom' AA guns (1947 5x8); 17x1 & 2x2 40mm Bofors (1947 17x1, 1948 19x1 & 2x2); 18x1 20mm Oerlikon (1947 16x1, 1948 6x1)	6x2 3in (76mm) L/50 Mk.33; 6x1 40mm Bofors	8x2 4.5in (114mm) L/45 QF Mk.III dual-purpose guns; 6x8 2-pdr (40mm) 'Pom-Pom' AA guns; 40mm Bofors; 20mm Oerlikon	1946: 8x2 4.5in (114mm) L/45 QF Mk.III dual-purpose guns; 5x8 & 1x4 2-pdr (40mm) 'Pom-Pom' AA guns; 40mm Bofors, 12x1 Implacable, 11x1 Indefatigable; 20mm Oerlikon; 8x2 & 14x1 Implacable, 6x2 & 7x1 Indefatigable
Search radars	Type 960	Type 984	1952: Type 960	Type 281
Fighter direction radars	SM-1 (CXBL) & Type 293M	Type 293Q	Type 293 & 2x Type 277 height finding	Type 293 & Type 277 height finding
Command and Control	Action Information Office (AIO)	Comprehensive Display System (CDS)	Action Information Office (AIO)	Action Information Office (AIO)
Landing aids	Type 72 & YE radio homing	Mirror landing sight; Type 961 CCA radar	YE radio homing	YE radio homing
Aircraft capacity	36 in hangar, 21 in deck park	28-36 total	48 in hangars, 7 in deck park	48 in hangars, 33 in deck park
Aviation fuel capacity	50,650gal (230,300L)	425,000gal (1,932,090L)	75,400gal (342,775L)	94,650gal (430,290L)
Complement	1,090, as training carrier	1,1785-2,200	2,100 max	2,300 max

Invincible Class

HMS *Invincible*
Pennant: R05
Deck Identification Letter: N
Builder: Vickers Shipbuilding, Barrow-in-Furness; laid down 20.07.1973, launched 03.05.1977, commissioned 11.07.1980.
History: sold to Australia 25.02.1982, sale cancelled due to Falklands Conflict; Operation Corporate deployment to Falklands 04.04-17.09.1982; refit for CIWS 18.09.1982-02.1983; refit for 12° ski-jump and enlarged hangar 04.1986-05.1989; deployment to Adriatic to support UN operations in Bosnia 22.07.1993-01.1994, 24.08.1994-02.1995 07.1995-09.12.1995; deployed to Persian Gulf for Operation Bolton 11.1997-02.1998; deployed to Adriatic to support NATO operations in Kosovo 21.05-01.06.1999; refit for Harrier GR.9, Sea Dart SAM removed 1999-2000; decommissioned 03.08.2005 into low readiness reserve, stricken 10.09.2010; towed for scrapping in Turkey 24.04.2011.
Squadrons: 819 NAS (Sea King) 05.1979; 801 (Sea Harrier) & 820 (Sea King) 1980-12.1985; 899 NAS (Sea Harrier) 04.04-17.09.1982; 845 (Wessex HU.5) 1988; 814 (Sea King HAS) & 849A (Sea King AEW) 1989-1993; 845 & 846 (Sea King HC.4) spring 1990; 800 (Sea Harrier), 814, 849A & 845 (Sea King HC.4) 12.05-11.1992; 800, 814 & 849A 22.07.1993-01.1994, 24.08.1994-02.1995, 07-12.1995, 08.12.1996 & 21.05-01.06.1999; 800, 814 & No. 1(F) Sqn RAF (Harrier GR.7) 11.1997-01.1998; 800 & 899 (Sea Harrier) 09-12.1999.

HMS *Illustrious*
Pennant: R06
Deck Identification Letter: L
Builder: Swan Hunter, Tyne and Wear; laid down 07.10.1976, launched 01.12.1978, commissioned 20.06.1982.
History: sailed to the Falklands following completion of trials, commissioned at sea, on station until 09.1982; formally commissioned 20.03.1983; refit and gearbox repairs 18.12.1986-27.04.1987; deployment to Adriatic to support UN operations in Bosnia 02-05.1995 & 09.12.1995-02.1996; deployed to Persian Gulf 1998; Flagship for Operation Palliser deployment to Sierra Leone 05.2000; refit and modernisation 2003-12.2004; last Harriers flown off 24.11.2010; refit as interim LPH 2011; decommissioned 28.08.2014; towed for scrapping in Turkey 07.12.2016.
Squadrons: 809 NAS (Sea Harrier), 814 (Sea King HAS) & 824D (Sea King AEW) 08-12.1982; 800 (Sea Harrier) & 820 (Sea King) 09.1983-87; 814 (Sea King) 14.07-08.1984 & 1989; 846 (Sea King HC.4) 11.1984; 849A (Sea King AEW) 21.07.1986-1989; 845 & 846 (Sea King HC.4) 11.1987; 814 (Sea King) 1988; 849B (Sea King AEW) 1992; 801 (Sea Harrier), 820 (Sea King) & 849B 02-07.1995, 09.12.1995-02.1996; 1996, 1997 & 28.09-01.10.1999; 814 (Merlin) & 849A (Sea King AEW 29.03-07.2006; No. 4 Sqn RAF (Harrier GR.9) 03.2007; 857 (Sea King AEW) 05.2007 & 01.04.2008; Naval Strike Wing (Harrier GR.9), 814 & 849A 02-31.05.2008; 815 (Lynx) & 849A 10-11.2009; 814 (Merlin) 05.2012; 814, 845 & 846 (Sea King HC.4), 854 (Sea King AEW) & No. 656 Sqn AAC (Apache) 01.10-12.2012; 829 (Merlin), 845 (Sea King HC.4) & No. 659 Sqn AAC (Lynx) 12.08.2013-01.2014; 820 (Merlin) 16.06-22.07.2014.

APPENDIX ONE

1952 Design	Ark Royal Class		CVA-01	CVF/ Queen Elizabeth Class
Project	HMS *Eagle*	HMS *Ark Royal*	*Project*	HMS *Queen Elizabeth* & *Prince of Wales*
8x2 3in (76mm) L/70 dual-purpose guns	8x2 4.5in (114mm) L/45 QF Mk.III dual-purpose guns (1964 4x2); 8x6, 2x2 & 9x1 40mm Bofors (1955 7x6, 2x2 & 6x1; 1964 none); fitted for but not with 6x4 Sea Cat SAM launchers in 1964	8x2 4.5in (114mm) L/45 QF Mk.III dual-purpose guns (1956 6x2, 1959 6x2, 1964 2x2, 1970 none); 6x6, 2x2 & 12x1 40mm Bofors (1955 7x6, 2x2 & 6x1; 1970 none); fitted for but not with 4x4 Sea Cat SAM launchers in 1970	1x2 GWS.30 Sea Dart SAM launcher (38x missiles)	3x Phalanx CIWS; 4x1 30mm DS30M Mk.2 (fitted for but not with); 6x1 7.62mm Miniguns, replaced in 2023 by 6x1 0.5in (12.7mm) Browning MGs
1x or 2x Type 984	Type 960; 1964: Type 984 3-D air search & Type 965	Type 960M air search (Type 965 from 1962); 2x Type 965, 1970	Type 988	S1850M & Type 997 Artisan
	1951: 2x Type 982 & 2x Type 983 height finding	1955: 2x Type 982, 2x Type 983 height finding & Type 293 (Type 993 from 1970)	Type 992Q	
Comprehensive Display System (CDS)	Action Data Automation (ADA), 1964	Action Information Office (AIO)	Action Data Automation Weapons System 3 (ADAWS 3)	Combat Management System (CMS)
Mirror landing sight	Mirror landing sight; Type 961 CCA radar (Type 963 from 1964)	Mirror landing sight; AN/SPN-35 CCA radar	2x deck landing projector sights; Type 963 or AN/SPA-35 CCA	Type 1008 radar, Ultra Series 2500 Electro Optical System, Glide Path Camera
53 normal, 82 maximum	60 total, 1951; 45 total, 1964; 39x total, 1971	50 total, 1955; 38 total, 1970	47 normal; plus 17 helicopters in Commando role	40 typical (20 in hangar), 72 max in wartime
500,000gal (2,273,045L)	448,000gal (2,036,650L), 1951; 487,480gal (2,216,130L), 1965	384,000gal (1,745,700L), 1955; 541,000gal (2,459,435L), 1957	600,000gal (2,727,654L)	659,905gal (3,000,000L)
?	2,500-2750	2,250-2,640	2,980 normal, 3,230 max; 1,125 troops in commando role	1,600 max, 250-900 troops

HMS *Ark Royal*
Pennant: R07
Deck Identification Letter: R
Builder: Swan Hunter, Tyne and Wear; laid down 14.12.1978, launched 02.06.1981, commissioned 01.11.985; towed for scrapping in Turkey 20.05.2013.
History: deployment to Adriatic to support UN operations in Bosnia 1993; refit, Sea Dart SAM removed 05.1999-11.2001, recommissioned 22.12.2001; Operation TELIC deployment 01-05.2003; refit 04.2004-10.2006; assigned as temporary LPH , first WAH-64 Apache landing 16.11.2006; assigned Fleet Flagship 05.2007; decommissioned 11.03.2011; towed for scrapping in Turkey 10.06.2013.
Squadrons: 801 NAS (Sea Harrier), 820 (Sea King) & 849B (Sea King AEW) 17.06-05.11.1986, 12.01-03.1987, 03.1988, 13.06-15.12.1988, 18.04-05.07.1990, 10.01-04.1990; 845 (Sea King HC.4) 05.11.1986; 801, 820 & 846 (Sea King HC.4) 14.01-08.1993; 801, 820 & 849B 11.01-17.05.2003; Naval Strike Wing (Harrier GR.9), 815 (Lynx) & 814 NAS (Merlin) 04.2010; No. 656 Sqn AAC (Apache) 10-11.2010; Naval Strike Wing (800 NAS & No. 1(F) Sqn RAF) (Harrier GR.9), 814 (Merlin), 854 (Sea King AEW) 10-11.2010; 771 (Sea King HAS.5) & 854 30.11-03.12.2010.

Reliant Class
RFA *Reliant* (ex-MV *Astronomer*)
Pennant: A131
Deck Identification Letter:
Builder: Gdansk Shipyard, Poland; completed 20.01.1977; converted by Cammell Laird, Birkenhead; commissioned 13.11.1983.
History: Ship Taken-Up From Trade (STUFT) vessel acquired from Harrison Line for Falklands Conflict 31.05.1982, basic conversion to operate 13× helicopters, arrived Falklands 27.06.1982; charter extended and refit for Arapaho containerized aircraft handling system 12.1982-83; deployed to Lebanon 02.1984; Falklands deployment 1984-85; decommissioned 25.07.1986 and sold as merchant ship, Admiralty Island; scrapped in India 1998.
Squadrons: 846 NAS (Sea King HC.4) 11.01-02.1984; 826 (Sea King HAS.2) 11.1984-1985.

Argus Class
RFA *Argus* (ex- MV *Contender Bezant*)
Pennant: A135
Deck Identification Letter: AS
Builder: C.N. Breda, Venezia; completed 31.07.1981; converted by Harland & Wolff, Belfast 1984-88, commissioned 01.06.1988.
History: Ship Taken-Up From Trade (STUFT) vessel acquired from Contender 2 Ltd. for Falklands Conflict 05.1982, basic conversion to operate helicopters and Harriers, arrived Falklands 19.06.1982, returned to UK 08.1982; acquired 14.03.1984 for conversion as an Air Training Ship; Operation GRANBY deployment 10.1990-

379

WINGS OVER THE FLEET

Royal Navy Light Carriers and Landing Platform helicopter ships 1946-2025

Class	Colossus Class	Centaur Class		
Ship	Typical RN 1946	HMS *Centaur*	HMS *Albion*	HMS *Bulwark*
Displacement	18,040 tons deep load; 19,540 tons deep load, Warrior 1955	26,118 tons deep load	27,000 tons design full load	27,800 tons deep load
Length	693ft 1in (211.3m) overall; 650ft (198.2m) waterline	736ft (224.3m) overall; 686ft 9in (209.3m) waterline	737ft 9in (224.8m) overall; 686ft 9in (209.3m) waterline	737ft 9in (224.8m) overall; 686ft 9in (209.3m) waterline
Beam	80ft (24.3) hull; 112ft 6in (34.3m) overall	90ft (27.4m) hull; 120ft 6in (36.8m) overall, later 123ft 6ft (37.6m) overall	90ft (27.4m) hull; 123ft 6ft (37.6m) overall	90ft (27.4m) hull; 123ft 6ft (37.6m) overall
Draught	23ft 3in (7.09m) deep load	27ft 2in (8.3m)	27ft 8in (8.4m)	28ft 2in deep load
Flight deck length/width	690ft (210m)	732ft 9in (223.3m)		
Flight deck type	Axial; 5° angled Warrior 1955	Axial; 5.5° angled 1954	5.5° angled	5.5° angled
Catapults	1x BH.III hydraulic, 20,000lb (9,070kg) at 56kt; 1x BXS.1 prototype steam, 200ft (61m), Perseus 1950	2x BH.5 hydraulic, 30,000lb (13,605kg) at 56kt; 2x BS.4 steam, 139ft (42m), 40,000lb (18,140kg) at 94kt, 1958	2x BH.5 hydraulic, 30,000lb (13,605kg) at 56kt	2x BH.5 hydraulic, 30,000lb (13,605kg) at 56kt
Arrester gear	Mk.8, 10x wires, 15,000lb (6,800kg) at 60kt or Mk.8*, 16,000lb (7,255kg) at 61kt; Mk.12, 20,000lb (9,070kg) at 85+kt, Warrior 1955	Mk.11, 6x wires, 30,000lb (16,605kg) at 75kt; Mk.11*, 30,000lb at 75kt, 1956; Mk.13, 30,000lb (16,605kg) at 112kt, 1958	Mk.11, 6x wires, 30,000lb (16,605kg) at 75kt; Mk.11*, 30,000lb at 75kt, 1956	Mk.11, 6x wires, 30,000lb (16,605kg) at 88kt; Mk.11*, 30,000lb at 100kt, 1956
Lifts	2x 34 x 45ft (10.3 x 13.7m); 15,000lb (6,800kg) capacity; 20,000lb (9,070kg) capacity, Warrior 1955	2x 54 x 44ft (16.4 x 13.4m); 35,000lb (15,875kg) capacity	2x 54 x 44ft (16.4 x 13.4m); 35,000lb (15,875kg) capacity	2x 54 x 44ft (16.4 x 13.4m); 35,000lb (15,875kg) capacity
Hangar length/width/height	445 x 52ft x 17ft 6in (135.6 x 15.8 x 5.3m)	329 x 62 x 17ft 6in (100.2 x 18.9 x 5.3m)	329 x 62 x 17ft 6in (100.2 x 18.9 x 5.3m)	329 x 62 x 17ft 6in (100.2 x 18.9 x 5.3m)
Engines	4x Admiralty 3-drum boilers, 2x geared steam turbines, 40,000shp (29,830kW), 2x shafts	4x Admiralty 3-drum boilers, 2x geared steam turbines, 76,000shp (56,670kW), 2x shafts	4x Admiralty 3-drum boilers, 2x geared steam turbines, 76,000shp (56,670kW), 2x shafts	4x Admiralty 3-drum boilers, 2x geared steam turbines, 76,000shp (56,670kW), 2x shafts
Max speed	25kt	29kt		28kt
Range	12,000nm (22,225km) at 14kt	6,000nm (11,110km) at 20kt	6,000nm (11,110km) at 20kt	6,000nm (11,110km) at 20kt
Armour	None	1-2in (25-51mm) flight deck	1-2in (25-51mm) flight deck	1-2in (25-51mm) flight deck
Armament	6x4 2-pdr (40mm) 'pom-pom' anti-aircraft guns, 7x1 2-pdr Ocean 1946; 40mm Bofors, 12x1 Ocean 1946, 4x2 & 3x1 Warrior 1955	2x6, 8x2 & 4x1 40mm Bofors	2x6, 8x2 & 4x1 40mm Bofors	2x6, 5x2 & 4x1 40mm Bofors
Search radars	Warrior 1956: Type 281Q	Type 960 (Type 965 from 1963)	Type 960 (Type 965 from 1964)	Type 960
Fighter direction radars	Warrior 1956: Type 277Q height finder	Type 293, 2x Type 982 & Type 983 height finder	Type 293, 2x Type 982 & Type 983 height finder	Type 293, 2x Type 982 & Type 983 height finder
Command and Control	Action Information Office (AIO)	Action Information Office (AIO)	Action Information Office (AIO)	Action Information Office (AIO)
Landing aids	Warrior 1956: Mirror landing sight; Type 961 CCA radar	Mirror landing sight	Mirror landing sight	Mirror landing sight
Aircraft capacity	52 max	42 normal, 26 by 1963	42; 16 helicopters as Commando Carrier	42; 16 helicopters as Commando Carrier
Aviation fuel capacity	80,000gal; 179,000gal, Warrior 1955	351,700gal (1,598,860L)	351,700gal (1,598,860L)	351,700gal (1,598,860L)
Complement	1,050 typical	1,390	1,596; 900 troops as Commando Carrier	1,037; 950 plus 800 troops as Commando Carrier

APPENDIX ONE

	Invincible Class				**Ocean Class**
HMS *Hermes*	HMS *Invincible*	HMS *Illustrious*	HMS *Ark Royal*		HMS *Ocean*
27,800 tons deep load	22,000 tons	22,000 tons	22,000 tons		20,500 tons standard
744ft 3in (226.8m) overall; 744ft 5in (226.9m) overall, 1981	677ft (206.3m) overall; 633ft (192.9m) waterline	677ft (206.3m) overall; 633ft (192.9m) waterline	677ft (206.3m) overall; 633ft (192.9m) waterline		667ft 3in (203.4m) overall; 652ft 2in (198.8m) waterline
90ft hull; 144ft (43.8m) overall	90ft 2in (27.4m) hull; 118ft (36m) overall	90ft 2in (27.4m) hull; 118ft (36m) overall	90ft 2in (27.4m) hull; 118ft (36m) overall		94ft 3in (28.5m) hull; 118ft 3in (36.1m) overall
27ft 11in (8.5m)	28ft 9in (8.8m)	28ft 9in (8.8m)	28ft 9in (8.8m)		21ft (6.5m)
738ft 10in (225.2m)	550 x 55ft (167.6 x 16.7m)	550 x 55ft (167.6 x 16.7m)	550 x 55ft (167.6 x 16.7m)		557ft 6in x 106ft 11in (170 x 32.6m)
8° angled; 12° ski-jump, 1981	Axial, 6.5° ski-jump; 12° ski-jump, 1989	Axial, 6.5° ski-jump; 12° ski-jump, 1987	Axial, 12° ski-jump		Axial
2x BS.4 steam, 151ft (46m) bow & 175ft (53m) waist, 50,000lb (22,780kg) at 105kt	N/A	N/A	N/A		N/A
Mk.13, 30,000lb (16,605kg) at 112kt	N/A	N/A	N/A		N/A
1x 54 x 44ft; 1x 54ft 3in x 35ft deck edge; 40,000lb (18,140kg) capacity	2x 31ft 8in x 54ft 8in (9.6 x 16.6m); 35,000lb (15,875kg) capacity	2x 31ft 8in x 54ft 8in (9.6 x 16.6m); 35,000lb (15,875kg) capacity	2x 31ft 8in x 54ft 8in (9.6 x 16.6m); 35,000lb (15,875kg) capacity		2x lifts
329 x 62 x 17ft 6in (100.2 x 18.9 x 5.3m)	500 x 74-40 x 20ft (152.4 x 22.5-12.1 x 6.1m)	500 x 74-40 x 20ft (152.4 x 22.5-12.1 x 6.1m)	500 x 74-40 x 20ft (152.4 x 22.5-12.1 x 6.1m)		?
4x Admiralty 3-drum boilers, 2x geared steam turbines, 76,000shp (56,670kW), 2x shafts	4x Rolls-Royce Olympus TM3B gas turbines, 97,000shp (72,333kW); 8x Paxman Valenta diesel engines; 2x shafts	4x Rolls-Royce Olympus TM3B gas turbines, 97,000shp (72,333kW); 8x Paxman Valenta diesel engines; 2x shafts	4x Rolls-Royce Olympus TM3B gas turbines, 97,000shp (72,333kW); 8x Paxman Valenta diesel engines; 2x shafts		2x Crossley Pielstick 16 PC2.6 V 200 diesel engines, 23,904hp (17,825kW)
28.6kt	28kt	28kt	28kt		18kt
7,000nm (12,965km) at 18kt	7,000nm (12,965km) at 18kt	7,000nm (12,965km) at 18kt	7,000nm (12,965km) at 18kt		8,000nm (14,800km) at 15kt
1-2in (25-51mm) flight deck	None	None	None		None
7x2 40mm Bofors; 2x4 Sea Cat SAM launchers, 1970	1x2 GWS.30 Sea Dart SAM launcher (22x missiles) (removed 1999); 2x1 20mm GAM-BO1, 1982; 2x 20mm Phalanx Mk 15 CIWS, 1982 (replaced in 1989 with 3x 30mm Goalkeeper CIWS)	1x2 GWS.30 Sea Dart SAM launcher (22x missiles) (removed 2003); 2x1 20mm GAM-BO1, 1982; 3x 30mm Goalkeeper CIWS, 1990	1x2 GWS.30 Sea Dart SAM launcher (22x missiles) (removed 1999); 2x1 20mm GAM-BO1; 3x 20mm Phalanx Mk 15 CIWS		4x1 30mm DS30M Mk.2; 3x 20mm Phalanx Mk 15 CIWS; 4x1 7.62mm Miniguns; 8x1 7.62mm GPMGs
Type 984 (Type 965 from 1973)	Type 1022 & Type 1006 navigation	Type 1022 & Type 1006 navigation	Type 1022 & Type 1006 navigation		Type 997
Type 293Q (Type 993 from 1966)	Type 992 (Type 996 from 1999)	Type 992 (Type 996 from 2003)	Type 992 (Type 996 from 1999)		
Comprehensive Display System (CDS)	Action Data Automation Weapons System 6 (ADAWS 6)	Action Data Automation Weapons System 6 (ADAWS 6)	Action Data Automation Weapons System 10 (ADAWS 10)		ADAWS 2000
Mirror landing sight; from 1981 3x Harrier Approach Path Indicators	2x Harrier Approach Path Indicator, Close Approach Indicators; later Deck Approach Projector Sight	2x Harrier Approach Path Indicator, Close Approach Indicators; later Deck Approach Projector Sight	2x Harrier Approach Path Indicator, Close Approach Indicators; later Deck Approach Projector Sight		Type 1008 radar
40 max, 1964; 37 max, 17 typical, 1981	18 typical, 22 max	18 typical, 22 max	18 typical, 22 max		12 max in hangar, 6 in deck park
370,500gal (1,684,325L)	305,955gal (1,390,900L) (estimated)	305,955gal (1,390,900L) (estimated)	305,955gal (1,390,900L) (estimated)		305,955gal (1,390,900L) (estimated)
2,100	1,051-1,318	1,051; up to 500 troops as LPH	1,051; up to 500 troops as LPH		465; up to 830 troops max

RFA *Argus* was a thorough conversion of a Roll-On Roll-Off container ship and had a large landing deck aft, offset to port. Helicopters and Sea Harriers could operate from the deck (the latter in VTOL mode only.) A Merlin HM.2 of 845 NAS is landing aboard during the disaster relief efforts off the coast of Honduras in November 2020. A Wildcat HMA.1 of 815 NAS was also aboard. By this time the vessel had extensive medical facilities aboard as a hospital ship. *MOD/Open Government Licence*

04.1991; refitted with full hospital facilities 1991; deployed to Adriatic to support UN operations in Bosnia 1993; deployed to Adriatic to support NATO operations in Kosovo 1999; deployed as hospital ship to Sierra Leone 2000-01; Operation TELIC deployment 03-05.2003; refit 2007; deployed to Persian Gulf with Sea King ASaC.7s 2008; assigned principal Primary Casualty Receiving Ship role 2009; Wildcat training 2013; deployed as hospital ship to Sierra Leone 11.10.2014-07.04.2015 due to Ebola outbreak; scheduled 2024 retirement postponed; refit for littoral strike role 2023; deployed to Indian Ocean 10.2023-10.2024; refit 10.2024-03.2025; scheduled for CSG 25 Pacific deployment in 2025.

Squadrons: 846 NAS (Sea King HC.4) 10.1990-04.1991; 848 (Sea King HC.4) 01-04.1991; 845 & 846 (Sea King HC.4) 04-06.1991; 3 CBAS (Lynx & Gazelle) 04-06.1991; 845B (Sea King HC.4) 11.1992; 820 (Sea King HAS) 01-05.2003; 849 (Sea King AEW) 2008; 700W (Wildcat) 11-12.2011; Argus Flight (Lynx HMA.8) 04-11.2012; 820 (Merlin HM.2) 10.2014-04.2015; 825 (Wildcat) 06.2017; 847 (Wildcat) 06.2018; 845B (Merlin HC.4) 06.2018; 845 (Merlin HC.4) & 847 (Wildcat) 06.2019; 845 (Merlin HC.4) 04-06.2020; 845B (Merlin HC.4) & 847 (Wildcat) 09-12.2022; 845 (Merlin HC.4) 10.2023-03.2024.

Ocean Class

HMS *Ocean*
Pennant: L12
Deck Identification Letter: O
Builder: VSEL, Barrow-in-Furness, hull built by Kvaerner, Govan; laid down 30.05.1994, launched 11.10.1995, commissioned 30.09.1998.
History: deployed to Honduras and Nicaragua for humanitarian assistance following Hurricane Mitch 11.1998; Operation PALLISER deployment to Sierra Leone 05.2000; Operation Telic deployment 01-05.2003, awarded Battle Honour Al Faw 2003; Maritime Interim Operational Capability with WAH-64 Apache 09.2006; refit 2007-08; deployment to Libya 05.2011; logistics support ship anchored in River Thames for London 2012 Olympics; refit 2013-14; assigned Fleet Flagship 06.2015; humanitarian assistance following Hurricane Irma and Hurricane Maria 2017; decommissioned 27.03.2018; acquired by Brazil 19.02.2018, commissioned as *Atlântico* 29.06.2018.

Squadrons: 845 NAS (Sea King HC.4) & 847 (Lynx) 10-11.1998; 846 (Sea King HC.4), 847 (Lynx & Gazelle) & No. 7 Sqn RAF (Chinook) 05.2000; 845 (Sea King HC.4) & 847 (Lynx & Gazelle) 01-05.2003; No. 656 Sqn AAC (Apache) 09-10.2005; 854 (Sea King AEW) 03-07.2007; 847 (Lynx) 10.2011; 700(M) (Merlin HM.1) 05.2007; 854 (Sea King AEW) 05.2007; 702 (Lynx) & No. 656 Sqn AAC (Apache) 09.2009; 857 (Sea King AEW) 05-11.2011; No. 656 Sqn AAC (Apache) 04-12.2011; 845 (Sea King HC.4), No. 656 Sqn AAC (Apache) & No. 27 Sqn RAF (Chinook) 04.2015; 820 (Merlin HM.1) & No. 7 Sqn RAF (Chinook) 09.2016-03.2017.

Queen Elizabeth Class

HMS *Queen Elizabeth*
Pennant: R08
Deck Identification Letter: Q
Builder: Aircraft Carrier Alliance, Rosyth; laid down 07.07.2009, launched 17.07.2014, commissioned 07.12.2017.
History: began sea trials 26.06.2017; initial Operational Sea Training 02.2018; WESTLANT 18 deployment to the USA for F-35B training 18.08-11.2018; WESTLANT 19 deployment 30.08-04.12.2019; initial operating capability declared 04.01.2021; CSG 21 Pacific deployment 24.05-12.2021; CSG 23 deployment
Squadrons: 820 NAS (Merlin HM.2) 03.07.2017 & 18.08-12.2018 & 26.09-04.12.2019; 845 (Merlin HC.4) 20.08.2018; No. 17 Sqn RAF & No. 617 Sqn RAF (F-35B) 10.2019; VFMAT 501 USMC (F-35B) 09-12.2019; No. 617 Sqn RAF (F-35B) & 820 (Merlin HM.2 & Crowsnest) 27.04-08.12.2021; VMFA-211 USMC (F-35B) 05-11.2021; 847 (Wildcat) 2023, 846 (Merlin HC.4) 09.2024.

HMS *Prince of Wales*
Pennant: R09
Deck Identification Letter: P
Builder: Aircraft Carrier Alliance, Rosyth; laid down 26.05.2011, launched 21.12.2017, commissioned 10.12.2019
History: began sea trials 09.2019; repairs due to flooding 05.2020 & 10.2020; declared fully operational 10.2021; assigned as NATO maritime high readiness force command ship 01.2022; propeller shaft damage 29.08.2022, returned to sea 21.07.2023; MUAS trials 09.2023; 12.02.24 Exercise STEADFAST DEFENDER; scheduled for CSG 25 Pacific deployment in 2025.
Squadrons: 820 NAS (Merlin HM.2) 23.09.2019; No. 617 Sqn RAF (F-35B) 02-03.2024; No. 656 Sqn AAC (Apache) 06.2021; 820 (Merlin HM.2 & Crowsnest) & 847 NAS (Wildcat) 12.02-03.2024; 809 (F-35B) & 846 (Merlin HC.3) 30.09-10.2024.

Appendix Two

Production lists

This appendix lists the production numbers and serial numbers assigned to the Fleet Air Arm's combat aircraft and helicopters since 1946. Aircraft ordered for the RAF and for export nations are not shown, unless otherwise indicated or if serial numbers were applied. Numbers in paratheses are totals per sub-variant/mark.

Blackburn B.48/Y.A.1 Firecrest
Prototypes: RT651 & VF172; RT656 was not built, VF254, VF257 & VF262 were cancelled.

Blackburn B.54/Y.A.5
Prototypes: WB781, WB788 & WB797.

Blackburn Buccaneer
Development Batch: XK486-491 & XK523-536 (20).

S.1: XN922-935 & XN948-983 (XN974-983 were reordered as S.2) (40).

S.2: XN974-983, XT269-XT288, XV152-168, XV332-361 & XV863-877 (XV780-877 cancelled 21.11.1967) (84).

Bristol Type 191
Type 191: XG354-398 & XG419-441 (68); only XG354-356 built before cancellation, used as ground test rigs.

British Aerospace Sea Harrier
Development Batch: XZ438-440.

FRS.1: XZ450-460, XZ491-500, ZA174-177, ZA190-195, ZD578-582, ZD607-615 & ZE690-698 (54).

F/A.2: ZH796-813 (18).

FRS.1 conversions to F/A.2: XZ439-440, XZ455, XZ457, XZ459, XZ492, XZ494-495, XZ497, XZ499, ZA175, ZA176, ZA195 (DB1), ZD578-582, ZD607-608, ZD610-615, ZE690-698 (35).

T.4: ZB600-603.

T.2 conversions to T.8: ZD990-993.

de Havilland Sea Hornet
Hornet conversions as Sea Hornet prototypes: PX211-214, PX219, PX222, PX230 & PX239 (8).

F.20: TT186-213, T247-248, VR837-864, VR891-892, VZ707-715 & WE235-242 (77); TT249-295, TT310-332 & VR611-620 & VR893-912 cancelled (100).

NF.21: VV430-441, VW945-980, VX245-252, VZ671-682 & VZ690-699 (78).

PR.22: VW930-939, VZ655-664 & WE245-247 (23).

de Havilland Vampire & Sea Vampire
Second DH.100 Vampire prototype transferred to RN: LZ551.

Vampire F.1 transferred to RN: TG285-286, TG314, TG328, TG426 & VF268-269 (7).

Buccaneer S.2 XT273 of 809 NAS flying over HMS *Ark Royal* in 1970. A Mk.20 aerial refuelling pod is fitted under the wing. First flown on 28 June 1965, the aircraft was transferred to the RAF in October 1973 and converted to S.2A standard. *Blue Envoy Collection*

BAe Sea Harrier FRS.1 XZ454 of 800 NAS in flight over the southern coast of England in 1980. *Terry Panopalis Collection*

Vampire F.3 aircraft transferred as Sea Vampire prototypes: VF315 as F.20, VG701 as F.21.

Vampire F.3 conversions as Sea Vampire F.21: VT795 & VT802-805 (5).

Vampire FB.5 conversions as Sea Vampire F.20: VV136-165 (19) (VV154-165 cancelled).

de Havilland Sea Venom
NF.20 prototypes: WK376, WK379 & WK385.

FAW.20: WM500-523 & WM542-567 (50).

FAW.21 prototype: XA539.

FAW.21: WM568-577, WW137-154, WW186-225, WW261-298, XG606-638 & XG653-680 (167); WZ893-911 & WZ927-946 (37) completed as FAW.53 for Royal Australian Navy, WZ947-956 (9) cancelled.

FAW.22: XG681-702 & XG721-737 (37).

The fourth Sea Venom FAW.21 completed was WM571, which was taken on charge with the FAA on 17 December 1954. It was later converted to FAW.22 and ECM.22 standards. Retired in May 1969, it survived in preservation and today is with the Classic British Jet Collection at Bruntingthorpe. *Blue Envoy Collection*

Sea Vixen FAW.2 XS577 of 899 NAS and a Scimitar S.1 of 800B NAS on the deck of HMS *Eagle* during the Beira oil blockade in the Mozambique Strait during April 1966. XS577 was the second production FAW.2 and first flew on 5 November 1964. Converted as a D.3 target drone in 1976 for the Royal Aircraft Establishment, it was not retired until 1980, passing to Flight Refuelling Ltd. for radar trials until 1985. It was scrapped in 1996 but the cockpit section survives in Switzerland. *Terry Panopalis Collection*

de Havilland Sea Vixen
Mk.20X prototype: XF828.

FAW.1: XJ474-494, XJ513-528, XJ556-586, XJ602-611, XN647-658, XN683-710 & XP918 (119).

FAW.2: XP919-925 & XP953-959 & XS576-590 (29).

FAW.1 conversions to FAW.2: XJ483, XJ489-491, XJ494, ZJ516-518, XJ521, XJ524, XJ526, XJ558-561, XJ564-565, XJ570-572, XJ574-576, XJ578-582, XJ584, XJ602, XJ604, XJ606-610, XN647, XN649-658, XN683-694, XN696-697, XN699-700, XN702, XN705-707, XP918 (67).

Douglas Skyraider
AEW.1, Mutual Defense Assistance Programme transfer: WT097, WT112, WT121, WT761, WT849, WT944-969, WT984-987, WV102-107 & WV177-185 (50); WT970-981, WV110-121 & WV157-176 (44) not taken up.

Fairey Firefly
Note that only Marks 5 to 7 are shown.

Mark 5: FR.5 & AS.5, VT362-381, VT392-441, VT458-504, VX371-396 (originally ordered as FR.IV), VX413-438 (originally ordered as FR.IV), WB243-272, WB281-316, WB330-382, WB391-421, WD824-872 (FR.5) & WD878-923 (FR.5) (413); VT505-507, VT520-569 & WD924-925 cancelled (54).

Mark 6: WB422-440 (AS.6, originally ordered as AS.5), WB505-510, WB516-523, WH627-632 (FR.6) & WJ104-121 (AS.6) (57).

AS.7 prototypes: WJ215-216.

AS.7: WJ146-174, WJ187-209, WK348-373, WM761-779, WM796-809, WM811-822, WM824-832 & WM855 (all except WJ146-153 completed as T.7) (133); WM810, WM823, WM856-863, WM880-899 & WP351-354 (34) completed as U.8; WP355-400, WP421-453, WP469-490, WV967-991 & WW103-128 cancelled (152).

Fairey Gannet
Prototypes: VR546, VR557 & WE488.

AS.1: WN339-378, WN390-429, WN445-464, XA319-364 & XA387-411 (171); WN365 was later converted by Fairey as a T.2 then to T.5.

AS.1 for Royal Australian Navy: XA434, XA436, XG784-785, XG787, XG789, XG791-792, XG795-796 & XG825-826 (12).

T.2: XG869-881 (13).

AEW.3 Prototype: XJ440.

AEW.3: XL449-456, XL471-482, XL493-503, XP197-199, XP224-229 & XR431-433 (43).

AS.4: XA412-433, XA435, XA454-473, XA508-530, XD898, XG783, XG786, XG788, XG790, XG793-794, XG797-798 & XG827-832 (81) (XA531 cancelled and replaced by XD898); XG833-836, XG839-840, XG843-844, XG846, XG849-850, XG852-853 (13) cancelled and completed for West German Marineflieger; XG837-838, XG841-842, XG845, XG847-848, XG851 & XG854-855 (10) cancelled.

T.5: XG882-890 (XG888 completed as a T.2 for the Royal Australian Navy).

Grumman Avenger
Mutual Defense Assistance Program transfer: XB296-332, XB355-404 & XB437-479 (100).

Hawker Sea Hawk
P.1040 prototypes: VP401 (converted to P.1072 in 1950), VP413 & VP422.

F.1: WF143-192, WF196-235 & WM901-095 (195).

F.2: WF240-279 (40).

F.3: WF280-289, WF293-303, WM906-945, WM960-999 & WN105-119 (116).

FGA.4: WV792-807, WV824-871, WV902-922 & XE327-338 (97); XG934-947 & XG961-992 cancelled (47).

FGA.6: XE339-344, XE362-411, XE435-463 & XE489-498 (XE491-498 cancelled) (95); were originally ordered as FGA.4.

FB.50 for Royal Netherlands Navy: were issued serials XL237-241, XL269-275 & XL305-314 (22).

Leonardo AW101 Merlin
EH101 naval prototypes: ZF641, ZF644 & ZF649.

HM.1: ZH821-864 (44).

HC.3 transferred from RAF: ZJ117-138 (22).

HC.3A transferred from RAF: ZJ990, ZJ992, ZJ994-995, ZJ998 & ZK001 (6).

Leonardo AW159 Wildcat
HMA.2: ZZ375-381, ZZ396-397, ZZ412-415, ZZ513-519, ZZ522 & ZZ528-535 (29).

Lockheed Martin Lightning
F-35B: ZM135-182 (48) (ZM183-200 reserved for future orders).

McDonnell Douglas Phantom
YF-4K: XT595 & XT596.

F-4K FG.1: XT597-598, XT857-876 & XV565-592 (XV751, XV573-578 & XV580-585 delivered to RAF; XV604-610 cancelled 26.10.1966) (37 received by FAA).

Short SB.3
Prototypes: WF632 & WF636 (WF636 not completed).

Short Seamew
Prototypes: XA209, XA213 & XA216 (XA216 completed as static structural test rig).

AS.1: XE169-172, XE221-231 & XE263-277 (30); only XE169-172 & XE205-210 completed and flown, XE211 never flown and XE212-217 incomplete on cancellation.

MR.2 (for RAF): XE173-186 & XE205-220 (30); only XE173-186 completed, XE175 onwards being transferred to FAA for conversion to AS.1, XE205-220 batch re-assigned to FAA.

Supermarine Attacker
Type 392 prototype: TS409.

Type 398 prototype: TS413.

Type 513 prototype: TS416.

The third production Sea Hawk F.1 WF145 during landing and catapult take-off trials aboard HMS *Eagle* in June 1952. Retired from trials work in 1955, it became a ground instruction airframe. The cockpit section survives in private ownership. *Tony Buttler Collection*

Phantom FG.1 XT864 was delivered to RNAS Yeovilton on 19 July 1968, where it is seen two months later on the strength of 700P NAS. It was transferred to the RAF in November 1978. It is preserved on display at the Ulster Aviation Society, Long Kesh, Lisburn. *Terry Panopalis Collection*

E.1/45: VH987-990 (non-folding wings), VH995-999 & VJ110-118 (folding wings) (24), all cancelled.

Type 398 F.1: WA469-498, WA505-537 (WA525-537 completed as FB.1) (63).

FB.1: WT851.

FB.2: WK319-342, WP275-304 & WZ273-302 (84).

Supermarine Type 508
Prototypes: VX133, VX136 (completed as Type 529) & VX138 (completed as Type 525).

Supermarine Scimitar
Type 544 prototypes: WT854, WT859 & WW134.

F.1: XD212-250, XD264-282 & XD316-333 (76); XD334-357 cancelled (24).

Type 556 prototype: XH451 (cancelled).

WINGS OVER THE FLEET

An unidentified Wyvern S.4, but presumably one of the early production aircraft given the aerodynamic dummy drop tanks under the wings. *Blue Envoy Collection*

Westland Wyvern
W.34 prototypes: TS371, TS375, TS378, TS380, TS384 & TS387.

W.34 TF.1 pre-production: VR131-150 (only VR131-134 delivered, VR141-50 cancelled).

W.35 TF.2 prototypes: VP109, VP113 & VP120.

W.35 TF.2: VR159 (cancelled), VW867-886 (VW880-886 completed as S.4).
W.38 T.3 prototype: VZ379.

W.35 S.4: VW880-886, VZ745-766, VZ772-799, WL876-888, WN324-336 & WP336-346 (94).

Westland Dragonfly
HR.1: VX595-600 & VZ960-966 (13)

HR.3: WG661-672, WG705-709, WG714, WG718-726, WG748-754, WH989-992, WN492-500 & WP493-504 (59); WP505-510 & WV933-944 cancelled (18).

Westland Whirlwind
Sikorsky S-55 HAR.21, Mutual Defense Assistance Program transfer: WV189-198 (10).

Sikorsky S-55 HAS.22, Mutual Defense Assistance Program transfer: WV199-205 & WV218-225 (15); WV226-250 cancelled (25).

HAR.1: XA862-871 (10).

HAR.3: XG572-XG588, XD763-772 (serials already allotted to RAF Canadair Sabre F.4s, reassigned XJ393-402, XJ396 & 398 converted as HAR.5/turboshaft testbeds, XJ402 completed as HAR.5) (24)

HAR.6 prototype: XJ445.

HAS.7: XG589-597, XK906-912, XK933-945, XL833-854, XL867-884, XL896-900, XM660-669, XM683-687, XN258-264, XN297-314, XN357-362 & XN379-387 (129).

Westland Wessex
Sikorsky S-58: XL722.

HAS.1 pre-production: XL727-729, XM299-301 & XM326-331 (12).

HAS.1: XM832-845, XM868-876, XM915-931, XP103-118, XP137-160, XS115-128, XS149-154 & XS862-889 (128).

HAS.3 prototypes: XT255-257.

HU.5 prototype: XS241.

HU.5: XS479-500, XS506-523, XT448-487 & XT755-774 (100).

Westland Wasp
Saro P.531-0: XN332-334.

HAS.1 prototypes: XS463 & XS476.

HAS.1: XS527-545, XS562-572, XT414-443, XT778-795 & XV622-639 (96); XS802-812 & XS834-852 cancelled (30).

Westland Sea King
Sikorsky S-61 SH-3D: XV370-373.

HAS.1: XV642-677 & XV695-714 (56).

HAS.1 conversions to HAS.2: XV642-643, XV647-649, XV651-661, XV663-666, XV668, XV670-677, XV696-701, XV703-714 (47).

Wessex HU.5 XT451 aboard HMS *Bulwark* in 1973. Emblazoned on the rotor gearbox fairing is the squadron badge of 845 NAS. The helicopter took part in the Falklands Conflict, arriving at Port San Carlos on 30 May 1982. On return to the UK it was retired from flying and scrapped in 1994. *Phil Butler Collection via Author*

Lynx HMA.8 XZ236 was built as a HAS.2 and first flown on 26 May 1977. It was used by Westland and A&AEE for trials work. Converted to HAS.3 standard during 1987–89, it continued as a trials aircraft. Converted to HMA.8 in 1995, it flew development trials for that variant, as well as the SRU and SATURN upgrades. It was retired from flying in 2006 and used as a ground instruction airframe. *MOD/Open Government Licence*

HAS.2: XZ570-582, XV915-922 (21).

HAS.2 conversions to HAS.5: XV643, XV647-648, XV651-655, XV657, XV659-661, XV663, XV665-666, XV668, XV670, XV673-677, XV696, XV699-701, XV703, XV705-706, XV708-713, XZ570-571, XZ573-582, XZ915, XZ916 (HAS.5 prototype), XZ917-918 & XZ920-922 (54).

AEW.2 conversions: XV649-650, XV656, XV664, XV671, XV697, XV704, XV707, XV714, ZD636, ZE418, ZE420 (12).

HC.4: ZA290-314, ZD476-480, ZD625-627, ZE425-428, ZF115-124 & ZG820-822 (40).

HC.4X testbeds: ZB506-507 & ZG829.

HAS.5: ZA166-170, ZD630-637 & ZE418-422 (18).

HAS.5 conversions to HU.5: XV647, XV661, XV699, XZ920, ZA130 & ZA137.

HAS.5 conversions to HAS.6: XV643, XV653-655, XV659-660, XV663, XV665, XV674-677, XV696, XV700-701, XV703, XV706, XV708-713, XZ574, XZ579-581, XZ921-922, ZA126-129, ZA131, ZA133, ZA135-136, ZA168-169, ZD630-631, ZD633-634, ZD637, ZE419 & ZE422 (46).

Mk.5X conversion (Carson composite blade testbed): XZ575.

HAS.6: ZG816-819 & ZG875 (5).

HAS.6 conversions to HAS.6(CR): XV703, XZ580 & XZ922.

HAS.6 conversions to HU.6: ZA133.

ASaC.7 conversions: XV649-650, XV656, XV664, XV671, XV697, XV704, XV707, XV714, XZ570 (development), ZA126, ZD636, ZE418 ('AEW.7' prototype), ZE420 & ZE422 (15).

Westland Lynx

WG.13 naval development batch aircraft: XX469, XX510, XX910, XX911 (French Mk.2 prototype) & XZ166.

HAS.2: XZ227-252, XZ254-257, XZ689-700 & XZ719-736 (60).

HAS.3: ZD249-268, ZD565-567, ZF557-563 (ZF558 & 561 completed as Mk.95 for Portuguese Navy) (28).

HMA.8 conversions: XZ236 (prototype), XZ255-256, XZ689-692, XZ695, XZ697-698, XZ719, XZ721-723, XZ725-726, XZ728-729, XZ731-732, XZ736, ZD252, ZD257-262, ZD265-268, ZD565-566, ZF557-558, ZF560, ZF562-563 (39).

WINGS OVER THE FLEET

Appendix Three

Requirements & Specifications

The Admiralty, the War Office and the Air Ministry – from 1964 combined as the Ministry of Defence MOD – would both issue operational requirements (ORs) for new equipment, whether it be for an aircraft, a radar or a tank. Initially a Staff Target would be drawn up, listing the ideal technical characteristics and specifications that would be subject to Staff and industry feasibility studies. Once the need for a particular aircraft or weapon was approved, it was formalised as a Requirement.

Admiralty Staff Targets for aircraft were prefixed AW, with weapon systems coming under the GD series, underwater weapons being USW and the naval aircraft requirements were prefixed NR/A (but often styled as NA.). Following the formation of the MoD, this system was formalised with the prefixes 'A' for Air, 'N' for Naval and 'G' for General Staff (e.g. ASR, GST, NASR etc.) and when targets became requirements they kept the same identification number. Today the system is simplified with ST and SR prefixes. The date given is that of initial approval. The associated projects and acquired aircraft are listed for reference.

Requirements (pre-1960)

AW.59 For the *Pentane* anti-submarine homing torpedo, 1954.
AW.110 For a stand-off anti-submarine weapon, 1960. Ikara.
AW.111 For a stand-off anti-submarine weapon, 1960.
AW.121 For the *Red Hawk* all-aspect all-weather air-to-air missile, also for RAF under AST.1056, 1950.
AW.162 For the Hawker Siddeley Buccaneer S.3 with an improved blind bombing system, 1962.
AW.165 For a general purpose helicopter for the RN, 1962 (became NASR.358).
AW.166 For an Airborne Early Warning Aircraft for RN (led to NSAR.6166), 1962.
AW.168 For a general purpose helicopter for the RN, 1963 (became NASR.365).
AW.261 For a napalm bomb for fighter bombers.
AW.319 For an anti-ship guided bomb, 1954. Fairey *Green Cheese*.
AW.389 For an airborne aerial interception radar noise jammer, also for the RAF under OR.3521, 1960.
AW.391 For a surface-search radar and display unit for the Westland Wessex HAS.1.
AW.393 For the Westland Wasp HAS.1, led to Spec. 216D&P, 1961.
AW.396 For the Hawker Siddeley Buccaneer S.2, led to Spec. M.232D&P, 1963.
AW.404 For the Westland Wessex HU.5 (superseded by NSR.6404).
AW.406 For a two-seat naval all-weather interceptor, led to OR.356/NASR.356 and Spec. F.242D, 1960. Hawker Siddeley P.1154B.
AW.408 For the Westland Wessex HAS.3 (superseded by NSR.6408).
AW.418 For the Hawker Siddeley Buccaneer S.2*, led to meet NSR.6148 and Spec. M.258D&P, 1963.
GD 81/48 For an anti-ship missile defensive system for warships, 1948. Popsy A surface-to-air missile & DACR gun system.
GD 165/55 For the Mopsy surface-to-air missile.
GD.302 For a self-defence surface-to-air missile system, 1967. Confessor and Sea Wolf.
GDA.101 For an air-to-surface missile, linked to OR.1168 for the RAF (became NASR.1168), 1962. AJ.168 Martel.
GDA.103 For an all-aspect all-weather air-to-air missile to replace *Red Top* for the AW.406/OR.356 interceptor, also linked to AST.1193, 1960. CW *Red Top/Blue Dolphin*, air-to-air CF.299, Hawker Siddeley Dynamics Family & BAC Weybridge design.
NR/A.7 For a turboprop-powered version of the Westland W.34, also linked to OR.213 and Spec. N.12/45. W.35 Wyvern TF.2 & S.4.
NR/A.9 For a turboprop-powered naval anti-submarine aircraft, also linked to OR.275, led to Spec. GR.17/45 and GR.117P.
NR/A.14 For a two-seat naval night fighter, led to Spec. N.14/49 and N.114T.
NR/A.17 For a single-seat naval fighter, led to Spec. N.9/47, 1947. Later re-issued as NR/A.17/2 for a swept wing variant (Spec. N.113). Supermarine Type 508; N.113: Type 525 & Type 544 Scimitar F.1.
NR/A.18 For a two-seat naval strike variant of the Spec. N.40/46 aircraft, led to N.8/49, 1949. de Havilland DH.110 variant.
NR/A.19 For a naval strike variant of the Supermarine Type 508, 1947. Supermarine Type 522 & 537.
NR/A.27 For a single-seat naval fighter. Supermarine Type 398 Attacker.
NR/A.28 For a three-seat development of the Fairey Firefly AS.5, led to Spec. M.101, 1950. Fairey Firefly AS.7.
NR/A.30 For a naval night fighter development of the de Havilland Venom NF.3 as an interim solution for NR/A.14, led to Spec. N.107, 1951. Sea Venom FAW.20.
NR/A.32 For a light naval anti-submarine aircraft, led to Spec. M.123D, 1952. Short SB.6 Seamew.
NR/A.34 For an interim swept wing single-seat naval day fighter, led to Spec N.105D&P, 1952. Hawker P.1083 Hunter & P.1087 and Supermarine Type 548 Hooked Swift.
NR/A.37 For the Sikorsky S-55 Whirlwind for air-sea rescue and transport, led to Spec. HR.127P, 1952.
NR/A.38 For the de Havilland Sea Vixen FAW.1, led to Spec. N.139D&P, 1954.
NR/A.39 For a two-seat naval strike aircraft, led to Spec. M.148T, 1954; re-issued as NR/A.39/2 for the Blackburn Buccaneer S.1, 1960.
NR/A.43 For a 'single package' search and attack anti-submarine helicopter, later led to Spec. HR.146, 1952. Bristol 191, Fairey/Piasecki H-21 Workhorse; revised with Spec. 170D&P in 1956 for Westland Wessex HAS.1.
NR/A.47 For a mixed jet/rocket-powered single-seat interceptor for the RAF to meet OR.337 and the RN, led to Spec. F.177D, 1956. Saro P.177N.
NR/A.64 For a naval Airborne Early Warning aircraft to replace the Douglas Skyraider AEW.1, led to Spec. AEW.154D, 1955. Fairey Gannet AEW.3.

NR/A.107 For a naval Airborne Early Warning aircraft, 1957. Avro Type 768, Blackburn design; then Blackburn P.119 & P.139, Vickers Type 582 & 583 and Hawker Siddeley HS.125 AEW.

OR.174 For a single-seat long-range naval fighter, led to N.11/44. Westland W.34 TF.1.

OR.195 For a naval version of the Supermarine Type 392 Attacker, led to Spec. E.1/45.

OR.218 For a jet-powered single-seat naval fighter, led to Spec. N.7/46. Hawker P.1040.

OR.226 For a naval two-seat night fighter, led to Spec. N.21/45.

OR.246 For a jet-powered two-seat naval night fighter, led to Spec. N.40/46.

OR.319 For an ultralight reconnaissance helicopter for the RAF/Army, led to Spec. HR.144. 1952. Fairey Ultra-Light.

OR.325 For a general purpose helicopter for the RAF, led to Spec. HR.150D&P, 1952. Bristol Type 192 Belvedere.

OR.326 A variant of the NR/A.43 'single package' anti-submarine helicopter for the RAF, led to Spec. HR.149D&P, 1952. Bristol Type 191.

GOR.339 For a supersonic tactical bomber and reconnaissance aircraft for the RAF (superseded by OR.343), led to TSR.2.

OR.346 For a two-seat naval strike/interceptor aircraft and research aircraft, led to Spec. ER.206, 1960.

OR.356 For a naval interceptor/strike aircraft (merged with AW.406 to form NASR.356). BAC VG Lightning, Hawker Siddeley P.1154, BAC Type 583 & 583V.

OR.1058 For the *Pentane* anti-submarine homing torpedo, for RAF use, 1954.

OR.1059 For a television camera-guided bomb, 1947. Vickers *Blue Boar*.

OR.1094 For the Mk.30 *Dealer-B* anti-submarine homing torpedo, for RAF use.

OR.1123 For the *Green Cheese* anti-ship missile, 1953.

USW.158/62 For a stand-off anti-submarine weapon, 1960. Led to Ikara.

USW.368 For the Ikara stand-off anti-submarine weapon, 1963 (became NSR.7668).

Requirements (post-1960)

NASR.356 For a supersonic V/STOL single-seat ground attack fighter for the RAF and two-seat all-weather interceptor for the RN, merger of AW.406 OR.356, 1961. Hawker Siddeley P.1154.

OR.358 For a large general purpose helicopter for the RAF, 1962 (became NASR.358).

NASR.358 For a large general purpose helicopter for the RAF and RN, 1962.

ASR.365 For a medium general purpose helicopter for the RAF, 1963 (became NASR.365).

NASR.365 For a medium general purpose helicopter for the RAF and RN, 1965.

ASR.387 For an Airborne Early Warning Aircraft for the RAF (with possible AEW helicopter for RN), 1966.

ASR.394 For the Avro Shackleton AEW.2 for the RAF, led to Spec. 274D&P, 1970.

AST.396 For a SEPECAT Jaguar GR.1 and Hawker Siddeley Harrier GR.1 replacement for the RAF (superseded by AST.403), 1970.

ASR.400 For an Airborne Early Warning Aircraft for the RAF, 1972. BAe Nimrod AEW.3 then Boeing E-3D Sentry.

AST.403 For a SEPECAT Jaguar GR.1 and Hawker Siddeley Harrier GR.1 replacement for the RAF (superseded by AST.414), 1975.

AST.404 For a support helicopter to replace the RAF's Westland Wessex and Aérospatiale Puma. EH101 Merlin HC.3.

ASR.409 For the BAe Harrier II GR.5.

AST.410 For an ASTOVL multi-role fighter to replace the Harrier for the RAF, 1981. BAe P.1216.

AST.414 For a multi-role agile fighter for the RAF (replaced AST.403), 1984. Eurofighter Typhoon.

NAST.517 For an all-weather flight control and navigation system for naval helicopters, 1965.

ASR.1012 For an upgrade of the Buccaneer S.2 with BAe Sea Eagle anti-ship missiles.

NASR.853 For active ECM for fighters and strike aircraft (became ASR.853), 1968.

NASR.1024 For Mk.31 lightweight anti-submarine homing torpedo, 1965 (superseded by NASR.7709)

NASR.1168 For an air-to-surface missile, linked to GDA.101 and superseded OR.1168), 1963. AJ.168 Martel.

AST.1193 For an all-aspect all-weather air-to-air missile to replace *Red Top* for the AW.406/OR.356 interceptor, also linked to GDA.103, 1960. CW *Red Top/Blue Dolphin*, air-to-air CF.299, Hawker Siddeley Dynamics Family & BAC Weybridge design.

AST.1197 For a bomblet dispenser.

NASR.1226 For an air-launched anti-ship missile (later became ASR.1226). BAe Sea Eagle.

NASR.1354 For a low-altitude day camera for tactical reconnaissance aircraft (superseded NASR.8024), 1972.

NASR.1356 For in-flight film processing equipment for the F.95 day camera.

NSR.1894 For an improved AN/ART-28 *Bellhop* AEW data transmission system, 1964.

NGASR.3335 For the Westland WG.13 Lynx programme for the Army Air Corps, RN and RAF, led to Spec. 268D, 1965, the naval version led to Spec. 273D&P.

NSR.6101 For the Westland Sea King HC.4 Commando, 1978.

NSR.6118 For the Blue Vixen multimode radar for the BAe Sea Harrier F/A.2.

NSR.6119 For the Westland Sea King AEW.2, 1982.

NSR.6124 For a long-range Beyond Visual Range air-to-air missile for the BAe Sea Harrier F/A.2. AIM-120 AMRAAM.

NSR.6148 For the Blackburn Buccaneer S.2*, led to Spec. M258.D&P, 1965.

NASR.6166 For an Airborne Early Warning Aircraft for the RAF and RN, 1962. BAC A-F series, BAC Gannet 'AEW.7' & Hawker Siddeley P.139.

NASR.6167 For a Carrier On-Board Delivery aircraft for the RAF and assault transport for the RAF, variant of NASR.6166 airframe, 1962.

NST.6169 For a stand-off anti-submarine weapon for helicopters, 1965.

NSR.6393 For a higher all-up weight for the Westland Wasp HAS.1, led to Spec. HAS.216D&P Issue 2, 1964.

NSR.6404 For the Westland Wessex HU.5, superseded AW.404 and led to Spec. HU.228D&P, 1962.

NSR.6408 For the Westland Wessex HAS.3, superseded AW.408 and led to Spec. HAS.227D&P, 1963.

NSR.6425 For the EMI/Hawker Siddeley Dynamics Type 401 infrared linescanner for the Hawker Siddeley Buccaneer S.2, 1966.

NSR.6429 For the Westland Sea King HAS.1, led to Spec. HAS.261D&P, 1966.

Every piece of military equipment has an operational requirement and a technical specification attached to it. Staff Target SR(S)7068 covered the CVF/*Queen Elizabeth*-class aircraft carrier programme while the F-35B began life as Naval Staff Target NST.6464 in 1985, which by the late 1990s had become SR(S)6464. *MOD/Open Government Licence*

NST.6433 For a Wessex HU.5 replacement, Multi-Role Fleet Helicopter, 1969.
NSR.6434 For a passive acoustic submarine detection system for the Westland Lynx, 1967.
NSR.6435 For a Tail Warning radar for the Hawker Siddeley Buccaneer S.2, 1966.
NSR.6449 For the Ferranti ARI.5759 Seaspray search radar for the Westland Lynx, 1967.
NSR.6451 For Hawker Hunter T.8 conversions as Sea Harrier/Blue Fox radar testbeds, led to Spec 288D&P, 1976.
SR(S)6453 For the BAe Harrier T.8N conversion trainer for the RN.
NST.6455 For the BAe Sea Harrier mid-life upgrade. BAe Sea Harrier F/A.2.
NST.6464 For an ASTOVL Sea Harrier replacement, 1985.
NSR.6473 For the Hawker Siddeley Sea Harrier FRS.1, led to Spec. 287D&P, 1975.
NGAST.6643 For a Passive Identification Device (infrared) for the Sea King Replacement.
NST.6644 For a submarine localisation and attack system for the Sea King Replacement.
NST.6678 For an improved Westland Lynx with dipping sonar, 1977.
NST.6679 For a submarine localisation and attack system for the Westland Lynx, 1977.
NSR.6473 For the Hawker Siddeley Sea Harrier FRS.1, led to Spec. 287D&P, 1972.
NSR.6623 For an interim air-to-surface missile for helicopters, 1967. Nord AS.12.
NSR.6624 For an all-weather air-to-surface missile for the Westland Lynx, 1967. Sea Skua.
NSR.6634 For a passive acoustic submarine detection system for helicopters, 1967.
NSR.6646 For a Sea King Replacement helicopter, 1977. Westland WG.34; later became ST(S)6646 for EH101 Merlin.
NSR.6649 For a search and targeting radar for the Lynx, 1967. Ferranti Seaspray.

NSR.6666 For the Westland Sea King HAS.5, 1977.
ST(S)6849 For the Future Organic Airborne Early Warning programme, 1997. Conversions of EH101 Merlin, Bell/Boeing V-22 Osprey, Lockheed S-3A Viking & Grumman Turbo-Tracker; BAe Sea Harrier F/A.2 Sidetrack; led to Crowsnest.
SR(S)7044 For a Landing Platform Helicopter ship, 1988. *Ocean*-class.
SR(S)7068 For the CVF aircraft carrier programme. *Queen Elizabeth*-class.
NSR.7097 For the Escort Cruiser, then the Command Cruiser, 1964. *Invincible*-class.
NSR.7110 For the JTIDS datalink system (later became SR(S)7110).
NSR.7276 For a helicopter-to-ship datalink system, 1963.
NASR.7511 For a lightweight anti-submarine homing torpedo (superseded NASR.7709). Sting Ray.
NSR.7668 For the Ikara stand-off anti-submarine missile, 1968 (previously USW.368).
NASR.7709 For Mk.31 lightweight anti-submarine homing torpedo (replaced NASR.1024).

Specifications

Specifications were issued by the Ministry of Supply and its successors – the Ministry of Aviation, Ministry of Technology and the Ministry of Defence (Procurement Executive). They were based on the formal requirements but were more detailed and formed the basis of the invitation to tender sent to industry. From the tenders a winning design would be selected and contracted for. Until 1949 a sequential system was used with a role prefix/number/year arrangement. For example N.7/46 indicated Naval, seventh specification issued in 1946. Production specifications lacked the role prefix but gained a 'P' suffix.

From 1950 a new sequential system starting from 100 was used with a role prefix, running until at least 1976 in this format. A suffix indicated 'T' for tender, 'D' for development and 'P' for production as the specification progressed alongside

APPENDIX ONE

development of the aircraft. Subsequent issues of the specification (e.g. if major changes were incorporated for a new Mark of aircraft) were signified by either Issue 2 etc. or just the numeral after the suffix. By the 1990s the numbers had adopted an SR/A prefix.

S.22/38 For a rotary-wing (gyroplane or helicopter) for naval reconnaissance. Hafner AR.V Gyroplane and Weir W.7.
O.5/43 For a naval dive bomber/torpedo bomber to meet OR.144. Fairey Spearfish.
N.22/43 For Hawker Sea Fury.
E.6/44 For a single-seat jet-powered flying boat fighter to meet OR.170. Saunders Roe SR.A/1.
E.10/44 For a jet-powered development of the Supermarine Spiteful to meet OR.182. Type 392 Attacker.
N.11/44 For a single-seat long-range naval fighter to meet OR.174. Westland W.34 Wyvern TF.1.
O.21/44 For a twin-engine naval dive bomber/torpedo bomber, issued to Fairey.
E.1/45 For a naval version of the Supermarine Type 392 Attacker to meet OR.195. Type 398 Attacker F.1.
N.5/45 For a naval version of the Supermarine Spiteful. Supermarine Sea Fang.
S.10/45 For the Blackburn B.48 Firecrest.
F.11/45 For a jet-powered single-seat naval fighter. de Havilland Sea Vampire & Westland design.
N.12/45 For a turboprop-powered version of the Westland W.34 to meet OR.213 and NR/A.7. W.35 Wyvern TF.2 & S.4.
N.16/45 For a twin-turboprop-powered naval strike, reconnaissance aircraft, issued to Fairey.
GR.17/45 For a turboprop-powered naval anti-submarine aircraft to meet OR.220 (production under Spec GR.117P). Blackburn B.54/Y.A.5, Fairey Q/Project 17 & Westland GR.17/45.
N.21/45 For a naval two-seat night fighter to meet OR.226. de Havilland Sea Hornet F.21.
N.7/46 For a jet-powered single-seat naval fighter to meet OR.218. Hawker P.1040.
N.40/46 For a jet-powered two-seat naval night fighter to meet OR.246. Blackburn B.67, Gloster P.231, Westland N.40/46; then B.67, de Havilland DH.110, Fairey N.40/46 & Westland N.40/46.
E.41/46 For a swept wing version of the E.10/44 (Attacker). Supermarine Type 510.
F.43/46 For a jet-powered single-seat day fighter for the RAF to meet OR.228.
F.44/46 For a jet-powered two-seat night fighter for the RAF to meet OR.227.
45/46/P For production of the de Havilland Sea Vampire F.20 and F.21 prototypes.
46/46/P For production of the de Havilland Sea Vampire F.20.
N.9/47 For a single-seat naval fighter to meet NR/A.17 and OR.254. Supermarine Type 508.
T.12/48 For a two-seat conversion trainer variant of the Westland W.35 Wyvern. W.38 Wyvern T.3.
25/48/P For production of the Hawker Sea Hawk F.1.
M.6/49 For the Short S.B.3 to meet NR/A.9 and OR.275.
N.7/49 For a two-seat naval all-weather fighter to meet NR/A.14, superseded by N.14/49.
N.8/49 For a naval strike variant of the N.40/46 aircraft to meet NR/A.18. de Havilland DH.110 variant.
N.14/49 For a two-seat naval night fighter to meet NR/A.14 (superseded by N.114T).

M.101D For a three-seat development of the Fairey Firefly AS.5 to meet NR/A.28, 1950. Fairey Firefly AS.7.
M.101P For Fairey Firefly AS.7 & T.7 production, 1952.
N.105D&P For an interim swept wing single-seat naval day fighter to meet NR/A.34, 1952. Supermarine Type 548 Hooked Swift.
N.107D For a naval night fighter development of the de Havilland Venom NF.3 to meet NR/A.30, 1951. Sea Venom NF.20.
N.107P For production of the Sea Venom FAW.20, 1951.
ER.110T For a supersonic fighter with variable-geometry wings, 1951. Armstrong Whitworth AW.59, Blackburn B.90, Boulton Paul P.121, Bristol Type 183 & Saro P.149.
N.113D For a swept wing single-seat naval day fighter based on the Supermarine Type 508 to meet NR/A.17, 1951. Supermarine Type 525.
N.113P For production of the Supermarine Type 544 Scimitar F.1, 1953.
N.114T For a two-seat naval all-weather fighter, to meet NR/A.14, superseded Spec. N.14/49. Armstrong Whitworth AW.165, Blackburn B.89, Fairey N.114T, Saro P.148, Short PD.4 & Westland N.114T.
GR.117P For production of the Fairey Gannet AS.1, 1951.
M.123D For a light naval anti-submarine aircraft to meet NR/A.32, 1952. Blackburn B.81 & B.91, Short PD.4 & S.B.6 and Westland M.123.
M.123P For production of the Short Seamew AS.1; M.123P2 for the RAF's MR.2, 1954.
HR.127P For the Sikorsky S-55 Whirlwind HAR.1 to meet NR/A.37, 1952.
N.131T For the de Havilland DH.116 Developed Venom two-seat naval all-weather fighter, 1952.
N.139D&P For the de Havilland DH.110 Sea Vixen FAW.1 to meet NR/A.38/3 and NR./A.38/4, 1954. Sea Vixen FAW.1 & Supermarine Type 556.
HR.144T For an ultralight reconnaissance helicopter for the RAF/Army to meet OR.319, 1953. Fairey Ultra-Light.
HR.146D&P For the Bristol 191 'single package' search and attack anti-submarine helicopter to meet NR/A.43, 1953 (the RAF's Type 191s were under Spec. HR.149D&P).
M.148T For a two-seat naval strike aircraft to meet NR/A.39, 1954. Armstrong Whitworth AW.168, Blackburn B.103, Fairey M.148, Short PD.13 & Westland M.148 (Hawker P.1108 and Saro P.178 not formally submitted).
M.148D&P For the production of the Blackburn Buccaneer S.1 to meet NR/A.39/2, 1960.
HR.149D&P For the Bristol 191 'single package' search and attack anti-submarine helicopter to meet OR.326 for the RAF, 1955.
AEW.154D For a naval Airborne Early Warning aircraft to replace the Douglas Skyraider AEW.1 to meet NR/A.64, 1955. Blackburn B.88 & Fairey Gannet AEW.3.
HAS.170D&P For the Westland Wessex HAS.1 to meet NR/A.43, 1956.
F.177D For a mixed jet/rocket-powered single-seat interceptor for the RAF and RN to meet OR.337 and NR/A.47, 1956. Saro P.177N.
HAS.191D For the evaluation of the Fairey Ultra-Light for the light anti-submarine role, 1958.
HAS.194D For the evaluation of the Saro P.531-0 for the light anti-submarine role, 1959.
ER.206D For a variable-geometry wing naval interceptor/strike aircraft and research aircraft to meet OR.346, 1960. Blackburn B.123, Hawker P.1151, 1152 & P.1153, Vickers Type 581, 582, 583, 589 & 590.

WINGS OVER THE FLEET

Supermarine 508 VX133 was developed to meet Naval Requirement NR/A.17 and Specification N.9/47. Following its retirement from flying, VX133 ended up at RNAS Culdrose in 1964 as a training aid for aircraft tug drivers, the outer wings being removed. It is seen here in 1966 in a rather dented condition. Worse was to follow: in 1970 it went to Predannack to train firefighters and was totally destroyed by 1984. *Terry Panopalis Collection*

HAS.211T For a Westland design study to develop an improved variant of the Wessex HAS.1, 1960 (superseded by HAS.227D&P).

HAS.216D&P For the Westland Wasp HAS.1 to meet AW.393, 1961. HAS.216D&P Issue 2 for a higher all-up weight to meet NSR.6393, 1964.

HAS.227D&P For the Westland Wessex HAS.3 to meet AW.408 and NSR.6408, 1963.

HU.228D&P For the Westland Wessex HU.5 to meet AW.404 and NSR.6404, 1962.

M.232D&P For the Hawker Siddeley Buccaneer S.2 to meet AW.396, 1963.

F.242D For the Hawker Siddeley P.1154B V/STOL all-weather interceptor to meet AW.406 and NASR.356, 1961.

M.258D&P For the Hawker Siddeley Buccaneer S.2* to meet NSR.6148, 1965.

HAS.261D&P For the Westland Sea King HAS.1 to meet NSR.6429, 1966.

268D For the Westland WG.13 Lynx prototypes, 1969.

273D&P For the Westland Lynx HAS.1 to meet NGSR.3335, 1970.

274D&P For the Avro Shackleton AEW.2 for the RAF to meet ASR.394, 1970.

287D&P For the Hawker Siddeley Sea Harrier FRS.1 to meet NSR.6473, 1976.

288D&P For Hawker Hunter T.8 conversions as Sea Harrier/Blue Fox radar testbeds, to meet NSR.6451, 1976.

Glossary

A&AEE Aeroplane & Armament Experimental Establishment (1918–1992). Aircraft & Armament Evaluation Establishment (1992–date)
AAC Army Air Corps
AAM Air-to-Air Missile
ADDL Airfield Dummy Deck Landing
AEW Airborne Early Warning
AFCS Automatic Flight Control System
ARTF Alkali-Removable Temporary Finish
ASM Air-to-Surface Missile
ASR Air-Sea Rescue
ASW Anti-Submarine Warfare
AVMF Soviet Naval Aviation (Aviatsiya voyenno-morskogo flota)
AUW All-Up Weight
AUWE Admiralty Underwater Weapons Establishment
BAC British Aircraft Corporation
COD Carrier Onboard Delivery
CNR Chief Naval Representative
CVA Aircraft Carrier Attack
CVS Aircraft Carrier Anti-Submarine
DLCO Deck Landing Control Officer
DMARD Director of Military Aircraft Research and Development
DNAD Director Naval Air Division
DNAW Director Naval Air Warfare
DNC Director of Naval Construction
DOR Director of Operational Requirements
DTD Director of Technical Development
E-in-C Engineer-in-Chief
FAA Fleet Air Arm
FAW Fighter, All-Weather
FOAC Flag Officer Aircraft Carriers
FPB Fast Patrol Boat
HMA His Majesty's Airship
HSA Hawker Siddeley Aviation
IFTU Intensive Flying Trials Unit
ITP Instruction to Proceed
JTIDS Joint Tactical Information Distribution System
LPH Landing Platform, Helicopter
MAD Magnetic Anomaly Detector
MAP Ministry of Aircraft Production
McDD McDonnell Douglas Corporation
MDAP Mutual Defense Assistance Program
MoA Ministry of Aviation
MOD Ministry of Defence
MoS Ministry of Supply
MUAS Maritime Uncrewed Air Systems
MWDP Mutual Weapons Development Program
NAD Naval Aviation Department
NAS Naval Air Squadron
NASR Naval Air Staff Requirement
NAST Naval Air Staff Target
NAWDU Naval Air Warfare Development Unit
NIGS New Naval Guided Weapons System
NGTE National Gas Turbine Establishment
NSR Naval Staff Requirement
NST Naval Staff Target
OEU Operational Evaluation Unit
OR Operational Requirement
PDTD(A) Principal Director of Technical Development (Air)
RAE Royal Aircraft Establishment
RAF Royal Air Force
RFA Royal Fleet Auxiliary
RNAS Royal Naval Air Station
RNVR Royal Navy Volunteer Reserve
RP Rocket Projectile
SAR Search and Rescue
SBAC Society of British Aircraft Constructors
SIGS Small Ship Integrated Guided Weapon System
SLAR Sideways Looking Airborne Radar
TACAN Tactical Air Navigation
t/c Thickness-to-Chord Ratio
TFR Terrain-Following Radar
USN United States Navy
WDC Weapons Development Committee

Seven Wessex HU.5 of 707 NAS wait to land aboard HMS *Hermes* in 1977. *Hermes* was a dual-role anti-submarine and Commando carrier, with the later role becoming secondary as countering the Soviet submarine threat was seen as one of the top priorities within NATO. *MOD via Terry Panopalis Collection*

Bibliography and sources

A mixed formation of five DH Sea Vixen FAW.1s and four Scimitar F.1s during an aerial display. *Blue Envoy Collection*

During the research for this book a great deal of primary source material was consulted, including documents held by The National Archives at Kew and individuals as noted in the acknowledgments. There is not space here to list every file but the following File Divisions were consulted at Kew:

ADM 1, 201, 219, 249, 264, 302, 327
AIR 2, 10, 19, 65
AVIA 6, 13, 15, 18, 53, 54, 55, 65
DEFE 7, 13, 58, 67, 69, 71, 72
DSIR 23, 24, 69
FCO 179
T 225

Good secondary sources are important starting points for further research and for cross-checking other sources. Listed here are the most important ones that were consulted:

Buttler, Tony, *British Secret Projects: Volume 1, Jet Fighters since 1950*, 2nd Ed., Crécy Publishing, 2017
Buttler, Tony, *British Secret Projects: Volume 2, Jet Bombers since 1949*, 2nd Ed., Crécy Publishing, 2018
Buttler, Tony, *British Secret Projects: Volume 4, Bombers 1935 to 1950*, Crécy Publishing, 2020
Buttler, Tony, Collins, David & Derry, Martin, *DH Hornet & Sea Hornet: de Havilland's Ultimate Piston-Engined Fighter*, Dalrymple & Verdun Publishing, 2010

Carbonel, Jean-Christophe, *French Secret Projects, Vol.2: Cold War Bombers, Patrol and Assault Aircraft*, Crécy Publishing, 2017
Flintham, Vic, *Aircraft in British Military Service*, Airlife Publishing, 1998
Franks, Richard A, *Scimitar: Supermarine's Last Fighter*, Dalrymple & Verdun Publishing, 2009
Friedman, Norman, *British Carrier Aviation: The Evolution of the Ships and their Aircraft*, Conway Maritime Press, 1988
Friedman, Norman, *British Destroyers & Frigates: The Second World War and After*, Chatham Publishing, 2006
Gardner, Charles, *British Aircraft Corporation: A History*, Anchor Press, 1981
Gibson, Chris, *The Admiralty and AEW: Royal Navy Airborne Early Warning Projects*, Blue Envoy Press, 2011
Graham, Jeremy & Smith, Ron, *Westland Aircraft & Rotorcraft*, Tempest Books, 2024
Hampshire, Edward, *The Royal Navy in the Cold War Years 1966-1990: Retreat and Revival*, Seaforth Publishing, 2024
Howard, Lee, Burrow, Mick & Myall, Eric, *Fleet Air Arm Helicopters since 1943*, Air-Britain, 2011
Jackson, James, *The Admiralty and the Helicopter: Royal Navy Helicopter Projects*, Blue Envoy Press, 2018
James, Derek N, *Westland Aircraft since 1915*, Putnam, 2001
Jones, Barry, *British Experimental Turbojet Aircraft*, Crowood Press, 2003
Meekcoms, Ken & Morgan, Eric, *The British Aircraft Specifications File*, Air-Britain, 1994
Meekcoms, Ken & Morgan, Eric, Ed. Butler, Phil & Gibson, Chris, *British Aircraft Specifications 1950-1976*, Air-Britain, 2024
Morgan, Eric & Stevens, John, *The Scimitar File*, Air-Britain, 2000
Petit, Martin H. et al, *British Military Aircraft Serials and Markings*, British Aviation Research Group, 1980
Pryce, Michael, *BAe P.1216 Supersonic ASTOVL Aircraft*, 2nd Ed., Blue Envoy Press, 2015
Taylor, Michael (Ed.), *Brassey's World Aircraft & Systems Directory 1996/97 (1st Ed.)*, Brassey's Publishing, 1996
Sturtivant, Ray, Burrow, Mick & Howard, Lee, *Fleet Air Arm Fixed-Wing Aircraft since 1946*, Air-Britain, 2004
Taylor, HA, *Fairey Aircraft since 1915*, Putnam, 1974
Thetford, Owen, *British Naval Aircraft since 1912*, Putnam, 6th Ed., 1991

Various issues of the following journals, periodicals and magazines were also consulted:
Aeroplane Monthly
Air-Britain publications *Aeromilitaria* and *Aviation World*
Aviation Historian
Flight/ Flight International
Jane's International Defence Review
Royal Air Force Historical Society Journal

Index

AIRCRAFT & PROJECTS

Aérospatiale
 AS 332 Super Puma 316
Agusta
 3DR9 317
 101G 211
Armstrong Whitworth
 AW.168 113, 114, 115, 122, 123, 124, 391
Avro
 Shackleton 166, 232, 233, 280, 389, 392
 Type 720 47
 Type 728 147, 148
 Type 748 220, 221
 Type 768 220, 222, 389
Bell
 Airacobra, P-39 37
 HSL-1 182, 184, 185
 Model 212 299
Bell-Boeing Vertol
 Osprey, V-22 236, 237, 308, 309, 341, 390
Blackburn
 B.46 Firebrand 51, 52, 56, 61
 B.48/Y.B.1 Firecrest 51, 60, 61, 170, 171, 383, 391
 B.50 61
 B.54/Y.A.5 170, 171, 217, 383, 391
 B.62/Y.A.6 61
 B.67 86, 87, 88, 89, 391
 B.83 174, 175
 B.88/Y.B.1 61, 165, 170, 171, 172, 217, 391
 B.89 96, 97, 100, 101, 102, 116, 391
 B.95 102
 B.101 Beverley 101, 120
 B.102 102
 B.103 Buccaneer 102, 110, 111, 115, 116, 117, 122, 123, 124, 125, 126, 127, 128, 129, 130, 132, 133, 134, 135, 136, 137, 138, 139, 140, 141, 152, 208, 223, 224, 241, 251, 257, 260, 266, 268, 269, 270, 273, 383, 388, 390, 391, 392
 B.108 130, 131
 B.112 139, 251
 B.117 251
 B.123 250, 251, 391
 NA.107 222, 223
 P.39 222, 223, 253, 255
 P.119 222, 223, 224, 389
 P.135 250, 251, 252
 P.139 222, 223, 224, 226, 227, 230, 231, 232, 389
 Y.A.7 170
Boeing
 Ghost Bat, MQ-28 238, 367
 Poseidon, P-8A 320, 365
 Super Hornet, F/A-18E/F 361, 363
 X-32 236, 360, 361
Boeing Vertol
 Chinook, CH-47 203, 205, 206, 208, 211, 232, 335, 341, 342, 365

 KV-107 301
 Sea Knight, CH-46 202
Boulton Paul
 P.130 273, 274
 P.133B 273, 274, 275
 P.137 274, 275
Breguet
 Br. 123A & B 227, 231
Bristol
 Type 171 Sycamore 182, 329
 Type 173 180, 181, 184, 185, 186
 Type 188N 148, 149
 Type 191 184, 185, 186, 187, 188, 206, 328, 383, 389, 391
 Type 192 Belvedere 184, 186, 187, 188, 298, 389
 Type 193 184, 186, 187
British Aerospace (BAe)/BAE Systems
 125-600 288, 289
 EAG.8404 346, 347
 EAG.8413 346, 347
 EAG.8447 345, 346
 EAG.8461 345, 346
 EAG.8471 347
 EAG.8472 345, 346, 347
 EAG.8763 345, 347
 Harrier II, GR.5, GR.7 & GR.9 9, 271, 289, 292, 293, 294, 295, 296, 396, 348, 350, 352, 353, 355, 358, 359, 365, 378, 389
 P.70 345, 346
 P.71 345, 346
 P.103N 356, 357, 358
 P.109N 351, 354
 P.112N 354, 355, 356, 358
 P.115N 356, 357, 358
 P.116 358
 P.140 361
 P.145 361
 HS.1184 345, 355
 P.1216 348, 349, 351, 353, 354, 355, 356, 357, 358, 359, 389
 P.1216-6 AEW 235
 P.1218 354, 355
 P.1222 358
 P.1226 351, 354, 358
 P.1227 352, 353, 358
 P.1230 350, 356, 358
 P.1231 355, 359
 P.1232 351, 355
 P.1244 Harrier IIIA, B & C 358, 359
 P.1246 359
 Sea Harrier, FRS.1 9, 233, 271, 281, 282, 283, 284, 285, 286, 287, 289, 290, 291, 292, 293, 311, 383, 390, 392
 Sea Harrier, FA.2 9, 236, 271, 287, 288, 289, 290, 291, 292, 293, 294, 349, 350, 352, 353, 383
 Sea Harrier 3 352, 353, 354, 358
British Aircraft Corporation (BAC)
 Anglo-French Variable Geometry (AFVG) 270
 Lightning Phase III 253, 254

 NASR.6166 226, 227, 228, 230
 TSR.2 130, 132, 136, 140, 141, 243, 255, 257, 263, 268, 389
Dassault
 Mirage IIIV 223, 255, 257
 Rafale M 361
 Spirale, MD.410 225, 232
de Havilland
 DH.98 Sea Mosquito 51
 DH.103 Sea Hornet 13, 15, 51, 52, 84, 85, 86, 383, 391
 DH.100 Sea Vampire 9, 12, 14, 15, 15, 17, 37, 38, 39, 42, 47, 49, 383, 391
 DH.110 Sea Vixen 9, 50, 81, 83, 92, 104, 105, 106, 107, 108, 109, 130, 135, 137, 142, 143, 147, 151, 152, 153,154, 155, 156, 157, 161, 208, 220, 241, 258, 260, 270, 385, 388, 391
 DH.112 Sea Venom 8, 19, 47, 49, 91, 92, 93, 102, 383, 388, 391
 DH.116 Developed Venom 102, 103, 391
 DH.127 & 128 249, 250
 GOR.339 131, 242
Douglas
 Skyraider 8, 10, 30, 50, 214, 215, 216, 217, 326, 388, 391
English Electric
 Canberra 40, 41, 95, 96, 101, 113, 130, 284, 286
Eurocopter
 AS 532 Cougar 341
 NH90 237, 316, 341
Eurofighter
 Typhoon 349, 352, 362, 389
 Typhoon (N) 361
Fairey
 Barracuda 61, 158,
 FD.2 91, 120
 Firefly 52, 53, 84, 85, 86, 159, 160, 161, 173, 183, 383, 388, 391
 Gannet, Type Q/Project 17 9, 10, 49, 50, 58, 101,111, 112, 120, 158, 160, 161, 162, 163, 164, 165, 166, 167, 168, 169, 170, 171, 174, 176, 180, 184, 217, 224, 384, 391
 Gannet, AEW 10, 153, 214, 216, 217, 218, 219, 220, 225, 226, 228, 232, 233, 260, 384, 388, 389, 391
 N.14/49 89, 90, 91, 97, 388, 391
 N.40/46 88, 89, 90, 391
 N.114T 97, 100, 101, 102, 391
 M.148T 117, 122, 123, 391
 Project 45 174, 175
 Rotodyne 120, 162, 193
 Spearfish 51, 52, 215, 391
 Type K 272
 Type R/FD.1 272
 Ultra-Light 120, 192, 193, 194, 195, 196, 389, 391
Folland
 Gnat 94, 95, 96
 Midge 95

General Atomics
 Mojave 238, 367
General Dynamics
 F-111 138, 241, 268, 269
Gloster
 E.1/44 (Ace) 22, 24
 Meteor 12, 14, 15, 23, 28, 38, 86, 119
 P.231 86, 87, 391
Grumman
 Avenger, TBF/TBM 158, 161, 162, 166, 169, 173, 174, 214, 384
 F-111B 241
 Hawkeye, E-2 220, 221, 222, 227, 232, 236, 361, 363, 365
 Panther, F9F 41
 Tracer, E-1 220
 Tracker, S-2 91, 169, 236, 390
Hawker/Hawker Siddeley
 APD.1017 255, 256, 257
 APD.1022 256, 257
 HS.125 222, 224, 225
 HS.1205 345, 348, 349, 358
 Hunter 26, 27, 90, 93, 94, 283, 285, 388, 390, 392
 Kestrel 276
 Nimrod 212, 234, 280, 310, 312, 316, 365, 389
 P.1040 17, 22, 23, 24, 26, 27, 30, 34, 40, 63, 384, 389, 391
 P.1052 23, 26, 34, 35, 36,
 P.1063 63
 P.1072 27, 384
 P.1081 26, 27, 31, 93, 94
 P.1087 93, 94, 388
 P.1108 120, 121, 123, 391
 P.1121 130, 131
 P.1127 230, 257, 270, 275, 276
 P.1138 275
 P.1147 252
 P.1148 252
 P.1151 252, 391
 P.1152 250, 252, 391
 P.1153 252, 253, 391
 P.1154 9, 140, 141, 240, 253, 257, 258, 259, 260, 261, 262, 263, 268, 276, 388, 389, 392
 P.1179 345
 Sea Fury 12, 15, 22, 23, 24, 391
 Sea Hawk 9, 12, 17, 19, 22, 23, 24, 25, 26, 27, 28, 29, 30, 31, 32, 35, 36, 42, 50, 52, 73, 92, 93, 137, 216, 287, 384, 385, 391
 SP.113 260, 261
Ilyushin
 Il-28 *Beagle* 90, 96, 143
Leonardo
 AW101 Merlin 10, 11, 213, 214, 235, 236, 237, 238, 297, 313, 316, 320, 321, 325, 338, 339, 341, 342, 345, 351, 363, 364, 365, 366, 385, 389, 390
 AW159 Wildcat 10, 302, 304, 321, 322, 323, 340, 342, 343, 345, 366, 368, 385
 Proteus 238, 321, 367

395

Lockheed/Lockheed Martin
  Lightning II, F-35 11, 344, 360, 362, 365, 366, 368, 385
  Neptune, P-3 166
  SSF 359, 361, 363
  Viking, S-3 236, 363, 390
  X-35 236, 360, 361

McDonnell/McDonnell Douglas
  Advanced Harrier, AV-16 345, 348, 355
  Harrier 21 359
  Model 279-3 351, 354, 355, 358
  Phantom, F-4 9, 50, 138, 239, 240, 241, 261, 262, 263, 264, 265, 266, 267, 268, 269, 270, 280, 281, 285, 385

Mikoyan-Gurevich
  MiG-15 *Fagot* 51, 82, 143
  MiG-17 *Fresco* 90
  MiG-29 *Fulcrum* 288, 349, 361

Percival
  P.66 Pembroke 226

Piasecki
  Workhorse, H-21 184, 185, 388

QinetiQ
  Banshee Jet 80+ 367

Saunders-Roe
  P.121/1 43, 45
  P.121/2 43, 45, 46
  P.121/3 46
  P.148 97, 98, 100, 101, 391
  P.177 6, 9. 142, 144, 146, 147, 148, 149, 150, 151, 152, 388, 391
  P.178 120, 122, 123, 391
  P.531 194, 195, 196, 386, 391
  SR/A.1 45
  SR.53 147, 150, 151, 152

Schiebel
  S-100 Camcopter 367

SEPECAT
  Jaguar M 270, 345, 347

Short Brothers
  PD.4 174, 391
  PD.5 43, 98, 99, 100, 101
  PD.13 117, 118, 121, 122, 123, 124, 391
  PD.23 274
  S.A.1 Sturgeon 51, 61, 84, 171, 173
  S.A.3 Jet Sturgeon 84
  S.B.3 170, 171, 173, 385, 391
  S.B.6 Seamew 10, 120, 168, 174, 175, 176, 177, 178, 385, 388, 391
  S.C.1 120, 274

Sikorsky
  S-55, HO4S 182, 184, 327, 386,
  S-61 Sea King, SH-3 202, 207, 208, 211, 316, 386
  S-61R Pelican, CH-3B 202
  S-65 Sea Stallion, CH-53A 202, 211,
  S-70 Seahawk, SH-60B 299, 303, 316
  S-80 Super Stallion, CH-53E 341
  S-92 341

Sud Aviation
  SA 321 Super Frelon 202, 211

SA 330 Puma 206, 207, 297, 341, 389
SA341 Gazelle 297, 340, 341

Sud-Est
  Aquilon 92
  SE 319B Alouette III Astazou 298

Sukhoi
  Su-24 *Fencer* 361
  Su-27 *Flanker* 349, 361
  Su-33 *Flanker*-D 349, 361

Tupolev
  Tu-4 *Bull* 90, 144
  Tu-14 *Bosun* 90
  Tu-16 *Badger* 144, 154, 259
  Tu-22 *Blinder* 259, 280
  Tu-22M *Backfire* 280, 281, 348, 349
  Tu-95 *Bear* 144, 280

Vickers-Armstrongs
  Type 571 131, 243
  Type 581/ER.206 243, 244, 245, 246, 391
  Type 582 222, 223, 245, 246, 248, 249, 389
  Type 583 253, 254, 257, 260, 262, 389
  Type 583V 253, 255, 259, 389
  Type 588 254
  Type 589 249, 255
  Valiant 111

Vickers-Armstrongs (Supermarine)
  Seafire 12, 15, 33, 52, 181
  Type 398 Attacker 9, 12, 15, 16, 17, 18, 19, 20, 21, 33, 34, 36, 42, 47, 52, 93, 385, 388, 389, 391
  Type 505 41, 42, 43, 63
  Type 508 42, 63, 64, 67, 70, 71, 385, 388, 391
  Type 510 Swift 16, 21, 34, 35, 26, 67, 93, 391
  Type 522 64, 65, 66, 67, 70, 388
  Type 525 67, 68, 69, 70, 93, 95, 385, 388, 391
  Type 526 67
  Type 527 Attacker Mk.2 18, 20, 21
  Type 529 64, 65, 66, 70, 305
  Type 539 76
  Type 541 Swift 71, 254
  Type 543 42, 43, 44, 45
  Type 544 Scimitar 8, 9, 42, 51, 69, 70, 71, 72, 73, 74, 75, 76, 77, 78, 81, 94, 109, 110, 112, 129, 130, 151, 254, 272, 385, 388, 391
  Type 548 Naval Swift 93, 94, 388, 391
  Type 556 77, 104, 108, 109, 385, 391
  Type 558 Scimitar Mk.2 77, 78
  Type 561 77, 78
  Type 562 77, 78, 81
  Type 563 76, 78
  Type 564 79, 81
  Type 565 79, 130
  Type 575 79, 81
  Type 576 79, 80, 81

W Autonomous Systems
  WAS 367

Westland/AgustaWestland
  Apache, WAH-64 321, 341, 364
  Dragonfly 180, 325, 326, 327, 386
  Lynx 10, 201, 282, 293, 297, 298, 299, 300, 301, 303, 304, 305, 306, 307, 310, 311, 321, 322, 339, 340, 341, 364, 387, 389, 390, 392
  Lynx 3 301, 302, 303
  M.148T 119, 120, 121, 123, 391
  N.40/46 86, 87, 88, 391
  N.114T 99, 100, 101, 391
  Sea King 180, 191, 198, 208, 209, 210, 211, 212, 213, 214, 232, 233, 234, 235, 236, 237, 266, 279, 280, 293, 311, 312, 313, 314, 324, 325, 333, 335, 336, 337, 338, 339, 341, 364, 386, 389, 390, 392
  Sioux 340
  W.36 58, 59
  W.37 61, 62, 63
  W.81 181
  Wasp 195, 196, 197, 198, 199, 201, 211, 297, 298, 300, 301, 386, 388, 389, 392
  Wessex 10, 180, 185, 188, 189, 190, 191, 199, 201, 205, 206, 208, 210, 211, 212, 241, 277, 308, 311, 325, 329, 330, 331, 332, 333, 334, 335, 336, 341, 386, 388, 389, 390, 391, 392
  WG.1 202, 203, 204
  WG.2 203, 204
  WG.3 297, 298
  WG.7 206, 207
  WG.9 203, 204, 206
  WG.11 204, 205, 206
  WG.24 308, 309, 312,
  WG.27 308, 309, 312, 313
  WG.31 311, 312, 313, 314, 316
  WG.32 309, 310, 312
  WG.34 313, 314, 315, 316, 317, 390
  WG.34A 313, 315, 317
  Whirlwind 10, 169, 182, 183, 184, 193, 206, 241, 298, 325, 327, 328, 329, 386, 388, 391
  Wyvern 49, 52, 53, 54, 55, 56, 57, 58, 59, 61, 64, 90, 111, 386, 388, 391

Yakovlev
  Yak-38 *Forger* 349

AVIONICS
Datalinks
  AN/ART-28 *Bellhop* 215, 218, 220, 221, 389
  Joint Tactical Information Distribution System (JTIDS) 235, 289, 291, 315, 354, 390

Electronic Warfare
  ABC/Airborne Cigar 162
  AN/APR-9 93, 162
  AN/APT-1 162
  AN/APT-4 162

ARI.18144 Orange Harvest 162, 169,
Orange Crop, MIR-2 212, 301, 303, 310, 315
Orange Reaper 213, 317

Navigational Equipment
  ARI.5880 *Blue Jacket* 125, 127, 128, 139
  ARI.X5880 *Yellow Lemon* 78, 81, 113, 125
  ARI.5885 *Blue Silk* 72, 77, 78, 81, 167, 169, 218
  ARI.18048 & ARI.18107/1 *Green Salad* 30, 72, 218
  ARI.18120 *Violet Picture* 169
  Blue Orchid 188, 202

Radars
  AI.9 87, 88
  AI.10 (SCR-720) 87, 91
  AI.16 88, 90, 97, 98
  AI.18 96, 99, 104, 105, 108, 109, 143, 153, 154, 155
  AI.20 *Green Willow* 148, 149
  AI.21 (AN/APS-57) 92
  AI.23 AIRPASS 77, 78, 81, 95, 125, 130, 149, 150, 251, 254
  AN/APS-4 ASH 52, 84, 159
  AN/APS-20 214, 215, 216, 217, 218, 219, 220, 232
  AN/APS-96 220, 221, 222
  ARI.23129 Ferranti FLR 140, 141,
  ARI.5930 Blue Parrot 81, 125, 126, 127, 128, 130, 137, 139, 140, 141, 223
  ARI.5595 AW.391 188, 210, 388
  ARI.5979 Seaspray 10, 282, 298, 301, 303, 304, 305, 315, 321, 345, 390
  ARI.5982 Blue Fox 281, 282, 283, 285, 288, 315, 390, 392
  ASV.15 162
  ASV.19A 161
  ASV.19B 165, 174, 175, 181
  ASV.20 112, 167
  ASV.21 112, 113, 125,
  Blue Kestrel 315, 317, 319
  Blue Vixen 288, 289, 290, 291, 349, 353, 355, 389
  Sea Searcher 212, 213, 301
  Seaspray 7000E 321
  Searchwater 11, 233, 234, 236, 238

Self-Defence Systems
  AN/ALE-40 286, 289, 292
  AN/ALE-47 319
  AN/ALQ-157 Matador 213, 319
  ARI.18105 *Blue Saga* 125

Sonars and sonobuoys
  AN/AQS-4 182, 183, 184
  AN/AQS-81 212
  AQS-901 315
  AQS-902G-DS 213
  AQS-903A 317
  ARI.181008 Sonobuoy Mk.1C 169
  SSQ-801 Barra 212, 301, 312, 317
  SSQ-963A CAMBS III 301, 312, 317
  T.1945 NDRSB 167, 174, 182

INDEX

T.1946 DRSB1 167
Type 194 182, 184,
Type 194B 182, 188, 189
Type 195 182, 188, 190, 199, 202, 203, 205, 206, 207
Type 195M 209, 210, 211, 212
Type 2069 213
Type 2089 FLASH 317, 318

ENGINES
Alvis
　Leonides 180, 226, 325, 327
　Leonides Major 184, 186, 328
Armstrong Siddeley
　ASDM Double Mamba 58, 163, 165, 166, 168, 169, 171, 217, 219, 220
　ASM Mamba 163, 173, 174, 175, 181, 184
　ASP Python 54, 55, 56 58, 61, 170
　Cobra 58
　P.156 167, 168, 169
Avco Lycoming
　PLF1 226, 227
　PLT 27B 313, 314
Bristol/Bristol Siddeley
　BE.15 43
　BE.33 116, 119, 129
　BE.52 275
　BE.53 275
　BE.55 132
　BE.61 243, 244
　BS.100 114, 253, 255, 257, 258, 259, 260,
　BS.360 Gem 298, 299, 301, 302, 304
　BS.605 133, 137
　Centaurus 60, 61
　Gnome 203, 204, 05, 206, 207, 211, 213, 226, 230, 313, 325, 329, 335
　Nimbus 195, 197, 198
　Olympus 95, 97, 101, 130, 249, 252, 253, 256, 257, 275, 381
　Orpheus 94, 95, 102, 132, 249, 273, 274, 275
　Pegasus 255, 261, 275, 276, 282, 286, 289, 292, 294, 296, 345, 346, 347, 348, 350, 351, 352, 353, 354, 355, 357, 359, 361
　Proteus 58, 60, 61
　Sapphire 43, 45, 46, 61, 67, 78, 79, 86, 96, 97, 98, 99, 100, 101, 102, 116
de Havilland
　Ghost 18, 91, 92, 103
　Goblin 14
　Gyron Junior 78, 81, 113, 114, 116, 117, 119, 120, 123, 125, 129, 130, 131, 132, 147, 148, 150, 152, 223, 273, 274
　Spectre 79, 80, 81, 102, 108, 148, 150
General Electric
　CT7 301, 302, 317
　T64 203, 204, 225, 226, 227, 228, 230, 231
　T700 312, 313, 314, 315, 317

LHTEC
　CTS800 302, 304, 321
Metrovick
　F.9 58, 86, 87
Napier
　E.131 87, 88
　E.141 Double Eland 58, 59
　E.145 Nomad 58
　Eland 58, 168
　Gazelle 185, 186, 187, 188, 193
　Naiad 170
　Sabre 54
Pratt & Whitney
　F100 345, 346, 347
　F119 359, 360
　PT6A 298, 299
Rolls-Royce
　AJ.65 (Avon) 22, 23, 24, 26, 34, 41, 43, 58, 86, 87, 88, 90, 272
　AP.25 Coupled Tweed 162, 163, 167, 170, 171
　Avon 18, 20, 21, 43, 55, 59, 61, 63, 64, 67, 68, 69, 70, 71, 72, 77, 78, 87, 88, 89, 90, 94, 96, 97, 98, 99, 100, 101, 102, 103, 104, 108, 109, 113, 115, 117, 118, 123, 124, 154, 274, 275
　Conway 78, 79
　Eagle 53, 54, 58
　Griffon 52, 53, 61, 85, 159, 160, 161, 166, 170, 172, 217
　Merlin 12, 85, 162, 173, 174, 175,
　RB.39 Clyde 54, 55, 58, 60, 61
　RB.41 Nene 16, 18, 19, 20, 22, 23, 24, 25, 26, 27, 28, 30, 34, 35, 61, 94
　RB.53 Dart 174, 175, 188, 221, 222, 226, 227 228, 230, 231
　RB.106 Thames 108, 113
　RB.109 Tyne 168, 221, 222
　RB.115 120, 121, 123
　RB.141 Medway 153, 251, 255,
　RB.142 Medway 131, 244, 245
　RB.146 Avon 300 Series 79, 80, 81
　RB.153 222, 223, 225, 226, 227, 242, 243, 244, 245, 246, 252, 253, 254, 255, 274, 275
　RB.156 249, 250
　RB.162 222, 223, 226, 230, 249, 250, 251, 252, 253, 255
　RB.163 Spey 132,153, 222, 223, 245, 246, 258,
　RB.165 245, 246
　RB.168 Spey 108, 132, 139, 153, 222, 224, 239, 250, 251, 253, 254, 255, 259, 261, 262, 263, 265, 266
　RB.172 222, 224, 226, 227, 230, 231
　RB.173 252
　RB.177 250, 252
　RB.199, Turbo-Union 345, 346, 347, 356, 357
　RB.227 345, 346
　RB.228 345, 346, 347

　RB.231 347
　RB.422 345, 346, 351, 355, 356, 357
　RB.532 350, 351, 352, 353, 354, 358
　RB.533 354
　RB.559 356, 358
　RB.560 355, 356
　RB.583 355
　XJ.99 345, 346
Rolls-Royce/Turbomeca
　RTM.322 301, 317
　SNECMA
　M45 222, 224, 227, 230, 231
　M46 227, 231
Turbomeca/Blackburn
　Palouste 192, 195
　Turmo 195, 207, 232, 312, 313, 314, 328

GENERAL
Beira Patrol 75, 157, 384
Falklands/Malvinas Conflict (Operation CORPORATE) 8, 9, 10, 84, 146, 201, 212, 235, 279, 282, 283, 284, 285, 286, 288, 300, 301, 306, 324, 331, 333, 334, 336, 337, 340, 349, 374, 375, 378, 379
Korean War 52, 53, 71, 141, 215, 326,
Malayan Emergency 53, 327, 328
Mutual Defence Aid Programme (MDAP) 27, 30, 31, 161, 162, 166, 182, 184, 215
Mutual Weapons Development Programme (MWDP) 137, 151, 152, 258, 275
Operation BOLTON 293, 294, 378,
Operation DENY FLIGHT 291
Operation GRANBY 10, 139, 212, 301, 306, 336, 338, 379
Operation MUSKETEER 30, 58, 92, 216, 324, 328, 329, 371, 372, 374, 375
Operation ALLIED FORCE 292

ORGANISATIONS
Admiralty Underwater Weapons Establishment (AUWE) 182, 306, 307
Aéronavale 31, 92, 298, 304, 347
Aeroplane and Armament Experimental Establishment (A&AEE) 15, 16, 17, 18, 19, 24, 26, 27, 28, 34, 56, 69, 71, 72, 108, 151, 154, 165, 176, 265, 277, 285, 286, 299, 301, 370, 372, 373
Atlantic Undersea Test and Evaluation Center (AUTEC) 199, 318, 319
Coastal Command, RAF 158, 159, 166, 182, 184
Commando Helicopter Force (CHF) 340, 341, 342
Indian Navy 32, 278, 287, 313, 366
Joint Helicopter Command (JHC) 341, 342, 364,

Marina Militare Italiana (MMI) 236, 316
Marineflieger 32, 76, 137, 151, 169, 384
National Aeronautics and Space Administration (NASA) 244, 246, 275, 355, 358
National Gas Turbine Establishment (NGTE) 16, 119, 273, 274
Royal Aircraft Establishment (RAE) 14, 15, 16, 17, 18, 22, 24, 27, 28, 34, 36, 37, 40, 41, 42, 48, 49, 54, 64, 67, 68, 72, 85, 87, 89, 94, 100, 101, 122, 124, 126, 127, 138, 139, 141, 144, 258, 259, 261, 273, 276, 277, 279, 283, 288, 304, 348, 349, 358
Royal Australian Navy (RAN) 52, 91, 167, 188, 280, 298, 383, 384
Royal Canadian Air Force (RCAF) 81, 137
Royal Canadian Navy (RCN) 52, 152, 169, 183, 184, 187, 192, 193
Royal Naval Volunteer Reserve (RNVR) 19, 30, 162, 174, 177
South African Air Force (SAAF) 137, 138
United States Air Force (USAF) 41, 202, 292, 359, 366
United States Navy (USN) 14, 18, 36, 37, 41, 47, 49, 83, 109, 130, 137, 182, 183, 184, 214, 215, 216, 220, 237, 241, 261, 272, 276, 278, 298, 308, 323, 350, 359
United States Marine Corps (USMC) 41, 276, 277, 278, 296, 328, 345, 359, 360, 365, 366

PEOPLE
Amery, Julian 262
Anson, Lt Cdr Edward Rosebury 126
Ashmore, Admiral Sir Edward 233, 281
Balmford, David 298
Batt, Lt Cdr Gordon Walter James 286
Bayldon, Captain Edward 192
Bedford, Bill 275, 276
Bingley, Rear Admiral Sir Alexander 215, 221
Bishop, Ronald Eric 89, 102, 103, 104
Blot, Lt General Harry 359
Bolt, Captain Arthur 272
Boddington, Lewis 46, 47
Boot, Roy 115, 133, 141
Boyce, Admiral Sir Michael 365
Brennan, Maurice 149
Brie, Wing Commander Reginald 179
Bristow, Lt Alan 179, 180, 213
Brown, Lt Cdr Eric 8, 12, 14, 16, 26, 37, 38, 39, 201, 258, 259, 260, 261, 262

397

WINGS OVER THE FLEET

Burns, John Goodwin 126
Cambell, Captain Dennis RF 47, 49
Camm, Sir Sydney 22, 23, 24, 25, 26, 113, 130, 258, 259, 275
Carrington, Lord 260
Case, Richard 301
Chaplin, Herbert Eugene 52, 163, 217, 272
Chichester Smith, Charles Henry 89
Chilton, Lt Cdr (Cdr) Patrick CS 30, 71, 72
Ciastula, Tadeusz 298
Clark, Lt ABB 15
Clapp, Captain RJ 363
Clemow, Brigadier John 111
Clifton, Alan 69, 79
Cohen, J 46, 101
Copeman, Gordon 128
Curtis, Lt Al 286
Davenport, Arthur 32, 54
Davies, Brian Lt Cdr 265, 266
Davies, Handel 22, 146
Davies, Stuart 249
De Vigne, Leo 329
Digby, FJW 54, 97
Douglas-Hamilton, Earl of Selkirk George 152
Douglass, John 361
Dunning, Squadron Commander Edwin 277
Edwards, Admiral Sir Ralph 113
Ermen, Captain ACG 23
Essex-Crosby, Ken 141
Evans, Captain Charles LG 47, 93
Eyton-Jones, Lt Cdr John 286
Facer, Lt AE 91
Farley, John 277, 278, 283
Folland, Henry 95
Forbat, John 242, 245
Forsyth, Captain A Graham 162
Fozzard, John 252, 259
Frewen, Admiral Sir John 260
Frick, Heinz 287, 289
Gardner, Henry 111
Gardner, GWH 121, 149
Garner, Peter 54, 55
Gellatly, Ron 198, 299
Gibbings, David 299
Graves, Squadron Leader Mike 55
Green, Major Fred M 37
Hafner, Raoul 179, 180, 181, 182, 184
Hammond, Philip 365
Handsford, Chris 349, 354
Hawkins, Roy 144
Healey, Denis 224, 263, 268, 269, 279, 281
Henson, George 69, 79
Hickson, Cdr Ken 85
Higgs, Lt Cdr Geoff 72, 134
Hives, Ernest 54
Hollis Williams, DL 89, 90, 164
Hooker, Stanley 275
Hoon, Geoff 364
Hooper, Ralph 258, 275, 354
Hopkins, Captain (Vice Admiral) Frank HE 183, 192, 241, 260
Humble, William 26

Hull, General Richard 268
Hunt, Cdr Phil 359
John, Admiral Sir Caspar 257
Jones, Aubrey 152
Jones, Dr Jeff 309
Julian, Lt Cdr HG 72
Keith-Lucas, David 174
Kerr, John 349
King-Joyce, Lt. Tobias 18
Küchemann, Diettrich 144
Laight, Barry 115, 124, 223
Law-Chapman, Air Marshal Iver 19
Leahy, Cdr Alan John 126
Lecky, Squadron Leader Tom 277
Lewin, Captain Duncan 109, 141
Lewis, Gordon 275
Liptrot, Captain 24
Lithgow, Lt Cdr Mike 16, 34, 64, 68, 69, 71, 72
Little, Lt Cdr Colin 69
Lockhard, Vice Admiral John 361
Long, Squadron Leader Steve 362
Luce, Admiral Sir David 268, 269, 270
Lygo, Captain (Vice Admiral) Raymond 141, 233, 311
McGrigor, Admiral Sir Rhoderick 71
McMullan, Derek 301
MacNamara, Robert 262
Macfadyen, Air Vice-Marshal Douglas 94, 97
Macfarlane, Lt BO 56
Mackintosh of Mackintosh, Rear Admiral LD 26
Macmillan, Harold 132, 142
Mason, Roy 281
Mayhew, Christopher 270
Merewether, Hugh 276, 277
Messmer, Pierre 224
Middleton, Captain Linley 233
Mitchell, Colin 48
Moaxam, Roy 299
Mottram, Dennis 287
Mottram, Richard 363
Mortimer, Flt Lt Ian 286
Morton, John GP 192, 299
Mountbatten, Admiral Lord Louis 141, 268
Noble, Lt WH 40
Norman, Lt Cdr Danny 72
Nott, John 279, 316, 339
O'Brien, Captain WD 155, 157
Orr, Cdr Stan 69
Parker, Lt Cdr DG 16, 34
Parker, Gartrell Richard Ian 126, 128
Parker, Sir Harold 109
Pedder, Rear Admiral AR 188, 278
Perrett, Lt Peter 15
Petter, William Edward Willoughby 32, 53, 54, 95
Petty, George Edward 101, 102, 115
Poole, Lt Cdr David 286
Quill, Jeffery 16
Quintin Hogg, 2nd Viscount Hailsham 147
Radakin, Admiral Sir Tony 365
Richardson, Lt Nick 292

Rickell, Lt Cdr Tony 68
Rifkind, Malcolm 341
Roberts, Chris 285
Rogers, Vic 298
Rowe, NE 22, 23, 37, 41, 42, 61, 102
Runciman, Squadron Leader Walter J 175, 176, 177
Russell, Cdr JD 73
Rydill, Professor Louis 270
Sandys, Ducan 50, 130, 142, 144, 151, 152, 153
Scott Hall, Stuart 42, 89, 102
Sear, William H 'Slim' 188
Serby, JE 24, 35, 89, 90
Shattock, Captain Ernest 28, 64
Shaw, RA 273
Slade, Group Captain Richard Gordon 164, 165
Slater, Admiral Sir Jock 293, 359
Slattery, MS 42
Smeeton, Captain RM 102
Smith, Joe 12, 16, 17, 18, 34, 37, 41, 42, 63, 64, 69, 94, 109
Snelling, Mike 283, 285
Stanbury, JV 22, 25
Sterne, LHG 141
Swallow, Captain RG 218
Taylor, Lt Cdr Douglas 279
Taylor, Lt Nick 286
Taylor-Scott, Humphrey 285, 286
Thatcher, Margaret 279, 349
Thorneycroft, Peter 257, 260, 262
Trend, Burke 268, 269
Tuttle, Air Vice-Marshall Geoffrey 40
Vincent-Jones, Captain Desmond 239, 257, 258
Wallis, Barnes 244
Ward, Lt Cdr Nigel 285
Wardle, Air Commodore AR 23
Watson, BJ 126
Watson, HR 'Hal' 113, 124
Watkinson, Harold 242, 257
Webber, JR 120
West, Admiral Sir Alan 362
Whitehead, Lt Cdr Derek 69, 71, 72, 126
Wibault, Michel 275
Wigston, Air Chief Marshal Sir Mike 366
Williams, Ralph 148, 260
Wilson, Harold 268
Woodward Nutt, AE 26, 102, 103, 122
Yates, Ivan 357
Yorke, Captain Philip 215

PLACES
Beaufort, Marine Corps Air Station 366
Bedford (Thurleigh) 40, 64, 71, 72, 93, 126, 127, 197, 273, 279, 299
Boscombe Down 15, 16, 18, 26, 34, 38, 55, 64, 68, 69, 71, 154, 165, 176, 190, 299, 318
Brawdy, RNAS 30, 31, 134, 328
Belize (British Honduras) 48, 135, 340, 341, 364, 371

Brough 101, 115, 128, 133, 223, 224, 225, 230, 231, 249, 251, 359
Chilbolton 35, 65, 68
Cochin, India 278
Culdrose, RNAS 15, 85, 167, 169, 191, 213, 215, 218, 234, 319, 392
Dunsfold 275, 283, 287, 289, 293
Eastleigh 71, 151
Edwards Air Force Base, California 360, 366
Eglinton, RNAS 161
Farnborough 6, 14, 16, 21, 32, 35, 37, 40, 46, 48, 49, 57, 64, 65, 67, 68, 74, 91, 104, 106, 132, 160, 165, 170, 172, 173, 175, 177, 178, 192, 199, 208, 219, 276, 283, 302, 303, 328, 349, 350, 367
Fleetlands, RNAS 30
Ford, RNAS 14, 19, 28, 37, 56, 64, 72
Goa, India 278, 287
Gosport, RNAS 325, 327
Hal Far, RNAS 57, 183
Hatfield 91, 155, 249, 352
Holme-on-Spalding Moor 126, 128
Khormaksar, RAF 198
Kingston upon Thames 24, 27, 130, 148, 235, 249, 252, 255, 258, 259, 260, 275, 281, 345, 348, 349, 351, 352, 354, 357, 358, 359
Kinloss, RAF 232
Langley 26, 27
Lee-on-Solent, RNAS 37, 93, 167, 169, 190
Leuchars, RAF 74, 267
Lossiemouth, RNAS 74, 75, 126, 128, 129, 133, 134, 138, 177, 220, 365
Marham, RAF 366
Marignane, France 299
Norfolk, Virginia 277
Patuxent River, Maryland 41, 366
Portland, RNAS 300, 304, 325
Prestwick 161, 213
St Athan, RAF 138, 267
St Mawgan, RAF 182
St Merryn, RNAS 161
Sembawang, RNAS 327, 331
Shoeburyness 48, 56, 64, 65, 69, 352
South Marston 17, 34, 71
Sydenham 101, 177
Warton 236, 249, 254, 346, 348, 354, 355, 356, 357, 358, 359, 361, 362
Weybridge 225, 226, 244, 254, 255, 289, 351
Watton, RAF 93, 162
West Raynham, RAF 15
Yeovil 53, 55, 120, 184, 188, 191, 211, 299, 317, 318, 325
Yeovilton, RNAS 58, 92, 108, 157, 265, 279, 284, 285, 286, 290, 291, 293, 294, 299, 333, 340, 341

INDEX

SHIPS
Abdiel, HMS 84
Admiral Flota Sovetskogo Soyuza Kuznetsov 349, 361
Albion, HMS 13, 29, 30, 47, 48, 50, 56, 92, 93,176, 208, 216, 326, 329, 331, 333, 374, 380
Alférez Sobral, ARA 300
Andrea Doria 276, 278
Antietam, USS 30, 41, 47
Antrim, HMS 201
Ardent, HMS 301
Argus, RFA 339, 379, 382
Ark Royal, HMS (1950-79) 9, 13, 17, 30, 46, 48, 49, 50, 56, 71, 72, 74, 75, 93, 128, 133,134, 135, 136, 138, 157, 208, 210, 214, 218, 220, 239, 241, 261, 262, 266, 267, 269, 270, 276, 277, 278, 344, 346, 347, 371, 377, 383
Ark Royal, HMS (1981-2011) 235, 279, 280, 289, 293, 295, 319, 339, 365, 379, 381
Atlantic Conveyor, SS 284, 301, 331, 335
Bahía Buen Suceso, ARA 286
Bennington, USS 49
Birmingham, HMS 299, 307
Blake, HMS 212, 276, 277, 278, 375
Bonaventure, HMCS 152, 373
Brilliant, HMS 201, 300
Bulwark, HMS 13, 28, 30, 48, 49, 50, 92, 93, 162, 175, 176, 208, 276, 308, 329, 331, 333, 335, 336, 339, 374, 380, 386
Centaur, HMS 13, 46, 48, 50, 64, 74, 90, 107, 129, 154, 157, 162, 218, 241, 329, 331, 374, 380
Charles de Gaulle 236
Chichester, HMS 84
Coral Sea, USS 264, 265
Contender Argent, MV 339
Contender Bezant, MV 339, 379
Coventry, HMS 301
Daghestan, SS 179
Eilat 304
Empire Jersey 179
Endurance, HMS 201, 301, 329
Engadine, RFA 191, 201, 211, 299, 375
Fleetwood, HMS 193
Fort Victoria, RFA 319
Furious, HMS 179, 277
Gavinton, HMS 183, 327
Giuseppe Garibaldi 276
Glorious, HMS 48
Glory, HMS 16, 53, 141, 328, 372, 373
Grenville, HMS 192
Hampshire, HMS 220
Helmsdale, HMS 180
Hermes, HMS 13, 17, 28, 36, 48, 49, 50, 73, 75, 82, 83, 127, 129, 134, 137, 155, 157, 233, 241, 262, 263, 268, 269, 270, 283, 285, 287, 308, 324, 333, 334, 336, 339, 374, 375, 381, 393
Illustrious, HMS (1940-54) 13,14, 15, 16, 18, 19, 27, 28, 34, 47, 48, 49, 50, 56, 85, 61, 162, 165, 170, 370, 376
Illustrious, HMS (1982-2014) 234, 237, 271, 279, 285, 286, 290, 293, 295, 321, 365, 378, 381
Implacable, HMS 13, 14, 15, 16, 49, 55, 56, 370, 376, 378
Indefatigable, HMS 49, 370, 376, 378
Independence, USS 276
Indomitable, HMS 49, 50, 370, 376, 378
Invincible, HMS 13, 233, 279, 280, 285, 290, 291, 292, 293, 294, 338, 365, 378, 381
Iron Duke, HMS 318, 322
John F. Kennedy, USS 265
Juno, HMS 199
Karel Doorman, HNLMS 32, 278, 372
Labrador, HMCS 192
Lancaster, HMS 322
La Salle, USS 277
Lincoln, HMS 84
Llandaff, HMS 84
Magnificent, HMCS 15, 373
Majestic, HMS 32, 373
Minas Gerais 278, 372
Mohawk, HMS 198
Montrose, HMS 304
Narwal 286
Norfolk, HMS 318
Northumberland, HMS 318, 320
Nubian, HMS 198
Ocean, HMS (carrier) 8, 12, 13, 14, 53, 328, 329, 372, 380
Ocean, HMS (LPH) 10, 319, 325, 338, 339, 341, 342, 381, 382
Perseus, HMS 48, 161, 327, 373, 380
Phoebe, HMS 300
Plymouth, HMS 201
Pretoria Castle, HMS 15, 37
Prince of Wales, HMS 238, 342, 343, 365, 366, 367, 368, 377, 379, 382
Protector, HMS 327, 329
Queen Elizabeth, HMS 11, 238, 297, 342, 344, 365, 366, 368, 377, 379, 382, 390
Raleigh, USS 276, 277
Ranger, USS 262
Río Carcarañá 286
Rio Iguazu 286
Rothesay, HMS 180
Salisbury, HMS 84
Saratoga, USS 265, 266
Scylla, HMS 84
Sirius, HMS 199
Sutherland, HMS 323
Sydney, HMAS 53, 167, 373
Theseus, HMS 12, 15, 53, 329, 370, 372, 373
Tideforce, RFA 367
Tiger, HMS 278, 374, 375
Torrey Canyon 134
Tourville 299
Triton, MV 311
Triumph, HMS 14,16, 47, 52, 53, 371, 373
Undaunted, HMS 193, 196
Vanguard, HMS 111, 325
Venerable, HMS 32, 278, 372
Vengeance, HMS 49, 278, 326, 372
Veinticinco de Mayo, ARA 278, 372
Victorious, HMS 8, 48, 49, 50, 73, 83, 93, 126, 129, 133, 134, 157, 241, 262, 370, 376, 378
Vikrant, INS 32, 278, 287, 373
Viraat, INS 287, 288, 375
Vittorio Veneto 276, 278
Warrior, HMS 38, 39, 40, 41, 47, 49, 50, 53, 177, 372, 380
Whirlwind, HMS 183

SUBMARINES
Ambush, HMS 182
Churchill, HMS 211
Santa Fe, ARA 201
Tiptoe, HMS 199
Tireless, HMS 196
Valiant, HMS 199, 201

UNITS
Anti-Submarine Warfare Development Unit (ASWDU) 15, 182
Joint Experimental Helicopter Unit (JEHU) 328, 372, 373
Naval Air Radio Installation Unit 93, 162, 169
Naval Air Squadrons
700A NAS 285, 375
700H NAS 184, 188, 191
700L NAS 299, 304
700M NAS 318, 319
700P NAS 263, 265, 385
700S NAS 211
700W NAS 321, 322, 382
700X NAS 72, 73
700Z NAS 126, 128
700 NAS 30, 177, 196, 284
702 NAS 15, 299, 300, 322
703 NAS 15, 28, 37, 166, 198, 199
706 NAS 182, 189, 373, 375
719 NAS 161
737 NAS 181, 191
750 NAS 160, 161
751 NAS 162, 370, 374, 375
767 NAS 263, 265, 266, 267, 400
771 NAS 182, 196, 213, 325, 334, 370, 379
778 NAS14, 37, 52, 215
782 NAS 52
787 NAS 15
796 NAS 161
800 NAS 19, 74, 75, 93, 129, 134, 271, 285, 286, 291, 294, 295, 296, 370, 371, 373, 379
800B 75, 129, 371, 384
801 NAS 28, 31, 46, 133, 285, 290, 291, 293, 294, 296, 379
802 NAS 30, 53, 285, 370, 371, 372, 374
803 NAS 8, 73, 74, 129, 133, 134, 370, 371, 372, 374, 375
804 NAS 30, 53, 75, 371, 372, 373, 374, 375
807 NAS 74, 75, 371, 372, 373, 374, 375
809 NAS 6, 11, 85, 91, 92, 110, 127, 128, 134, 138, 141, 284, 285, 286, 293, 366, 370, 371, 372, 374, 375, 378, 382, 383
810 NAS 30, 53, 372, 374, 375
812 NAS 52, 53, 371, 372, 373
813 NAS 56, 58, 370, 371, 374
814 NAS 160, 161, 191, 213, 319, 370, 371, 372, 373, 374, 375, 378, 379
815 NAS 161, 188, 300, 304, 322, 331, 370, 371, 372, 375, 378, 379, 382
820 NAS 161, 184, 212, 238, 297, 319, 366, 371, 374, 375, 378, 379, 382
821 NAS 53
824 NAS 161, 167, 169, 211, 234, 319, 370, 371, 372, 374, 375, 378
825 NAS 53, 167, 322, 370, 371, 372, 375, 382
826 NAS 167, 189, 212, 371, 374, 375, 379
827 NAS 53, 56, 371, 373
829 NAS 197, 319, 320, 329, 378
830 NAS 56, 57, 58, 371
831 NAS 56, 58, 93, 162, 169, 370, 371, 375
845 NAS 183, 329, 330, 331, 333, 334, 336, 341, 342, 372, 373, 374, 375, 378, 379, 382
846 NAS 328, 329, 331, 332, 333, 338, 341, 374, 375, 378, 379, 382
847 NAS 279, 329, 331, 334, 340, 343, 366, 375, 382
848 NAS 327, 328, 329, 331, 334, 336, 373, 374, 375, 382
849 NAS 8, 169, 214, 215, 219, 220, 221, 234, 235, 293, 370, 371, 372, 374, 375, 378, 379, 382
890 NAS 92, 108, 371, 372, 374, 375
891 NAS 92, 93, 371, 374, 375
892 NAS 9, 108, 155, 266, 267, 370, 371, 372, 374, 375
893 NAS 8, 92, 93, 107, 108, 370, 371, 374, 375
895 NAS 30, 375
897 NAS 30, 371
899 NAS 30, 108, 156, 157, 283, 285, 290, 293, 294, 370, 375, 378
Naval Air Squadron Flights
700B 133
700G 218, 219
703W 56
703X 166, 167

399

WINGS OVER THE FLEET

Phantom FG.1 XT865 in service with 767 NAS in 1971 with two Matra pods for 2.75in (68mm) SNEB rockets. Between September 1968 and October 1970 it had been used for carrier suitability and clearance trials by the A&AEE's 'C' Squadron. Issued to 892 NAS in January 1973 it again carried out trials work in 1975, before transfer to the RAF in November 1978. *Terry Panopalis Collection*

Royal Air Force Squadrons
No. 17 366, 382
No. 155 328
No. 194 327
No. 207 366
No. 210 159
No. 617 11, 366, 382
Royal Australian Navy Squadrons
816 NAS 167
817 NAS 53, 167
Squadrons
No. 24, South African Air Force 138
No.300, Indian Navy 287

WEAPONS
AAM-N-3 Sparrow II 79
AAM-N-6 Sparrow III 79, 153, 242
AGM-12 Bullpup 51, 75, 76, 106, 108, 125, 126, 132, 141, 154, 156, 245, 246, 251, 254, 258, 260, 263
AIM-7 Sparrow 262, 265, 305, 348
AIM-9 Sidewinder 74, 75, 76, 95, 236, 254, 263, 282, 283, 286, 287, 288, 289, 293, 296, 345, 346, 348, 353

AIM-120 AMRAAM 288, 289, 290, 291, 294, 349, 352, 353, 354, 355, 356, 357, 358, 259, 361, 389
AIM-132 ASRAAM 296, 345, 349, 357, 358, 359, 365
Blue Boar 111
Blue Envoy 142, 144, 152
Blue Dolphin/Blue Jay Mk.5 78, 153, 242, 388, 389
Blue Jay/Firestreak 77, 78, 81, 92, 94, 95, 105, 154, 161, 251, 254
Blue Sky/Fireflash 67, 96, 97, 98, 99, 100
Blue Slug 111
Blue Vesta/Blue Jay Mk.4 79, 251, 268
Brimstone 294, 296
CRV-7 288
Exocet 300, 305
Green Cheese 111, 112, 113, 116, 117, 119, 120, 121, 122, 125, 167, 168, 169, 388, 389
Ikara 163, 200, 208, 211, 241, 307, 388, 389, 390
Kh-22 (AS-4 *Kitchen*) 143, 281
KS-1 Kometa (AS-1 *Kennel*) 143
Lightweight Multirole Missile/ Martlet 321, 323, 368
LRSOM 349, 359

Mk.30 Dealer-B 163, 167, 169, 174, 181, 184, 186, 188, 389
Martel 133, 135, 136, 137, 138, 139, 140, 141, 258, 263, 270, 278, 345, 346, 388, 389
Meteor 352, 365
Mopsy 145, 388
NIGS (New Naval Guided Weapons System) 144, 145, 259
Orange Nell 145
Paveway 288, 296, 366
Pentane 163, 165, 167, 174, 181, 184, 185, 187, 188, 193, 388, 389
Popsy A & B 145, 388
Red Angel 58, 61, 64, 65, 111, 113
Red Beard/TMB 71, 74, 77, 78, 80, 81, 108, 112, 113, 117, 118, 120, 124, 125, 126, 128, 130, 136, 249, 273,
Sea Cat 146, 198, 266, 305
Red Dean 67, 96, 98, 99, 100, 109, 111
Red Hawk 88, 388
Red Top 78, 81, 142, 150, 153, 154, 155, 242, 251, 253, 254, 255, 257, 258, 260, 262, 263, 388, 389
RG.10 249, 251

Sea Dart 208, 240, 241, 242, 259, 260, 278, 279, 281, 339, 378, 379,
Sea Eagle, P3T 139, 283, 285, 286, 287, 289, 317, 349, 352, 353, 354, 355, 357, 358, 389
Sea Skua 10, 298, 299, 300, 301, 304, 305, 306, 307, 322, 323, 390
Sea Slug 83, 111, 143, 144, 147, 151, 153, 161, 208, 220, 259, 278
Sea Venom 321, 323, 368
Sea Wolf 146, 305, 311, 350, 388
Skyflash 348, 352
Sting Ray 200, 298, 300, 304, 306, 307, 312, 317, 320, 321, 390
UK Mk.44 163, 184, 195, 197, 200, 202, 209, 210, 211, 218, 298
US Mk.43 163, 166, 184, 186, 188, 192, 194, 195, 196, 199, 213
US Mk.46 163, 200, 202, 210, 307, 312
WE.177 136, 138, 141, 188, 190, 197, 198, 200, 202, 210, 253, 258, 263, 279, 283, 289, 298, 304, 311, 312, 317, 349, 353

400